HISTORY

OF THE

STATE OF RHODE ISLAND

AND

PROVIDENCE PLANTATIONS.

FROM THE SETTLEMENT OF THE STATE, 1636, TO THE ADOPTION OF THE FEDERAL CONSTITUTION, 1790.

BY

SAMUEL GREENE ARNOLD.

IN TWO VOLUMES.

VOL. II.

1700—1790.

NEW YORK:
D. APPLETON & COMPANY, 443 & 445 BROADWAY.
LONDON: 16 LITTLE BRITAIN.
1860.

CONTENTS.

THE

HISTORY OF RHODE ISLAND.

CHAPTER XIII.

1701—1713.

FROM THE DEATH OF LORD BELLEMONT, MARCH 1701, TO THE CLOSE OF QUEEN ANNE'S WAR, APRIL 1713.

CHAP. XIII. 1701. March

Although the death of the Earl of Bellemont occurred at a fortunate moment for Rhode Island, we shall soon see that it did not restore peace to the colony. His successor pursued the same line of policy with even greater pertinacity but with less ability, and met with a defeat the more humiliating as his measures were more personal and direct. A special session of the General Assembly was 29.
held shortly after this event, to lay a tax of four hundred pounds for the public service. The apportionment indicates that Providence had recovered its relative prosperity, lost during Philip's war. The duties which in our day are performed by the State Auditor, were formerly assigned to committees, the members of which were usually selected, one from each town, by the Assembly. This "general audit," as it was termed, was appointed as often

CHAP. XIII. as the accounts of the colony required examination, or a new tax was to be laid.

1701. The right of the Assembly to expel any of its members, was never exercised except in extreme cases. At this session, an assistant who had illegally united a couple in marriage, through misapprehension of his power to perform that ceremony, refusing to admit his error, was suspended from office until the next election.

April 18. Soon after the Assembly rose, Gov. Cranston wrote to the Board of Trade, and, by their order, sent a full statement of the modes of proceeding in the various Courts of Rhode Island. This paper gives a clear view of the structure of the Courts, and of the legal forms in use at that day in the colony.[1]

An act which would have proved fatal to the liberties of Rhode Island and Connecticut, had it passed, was now prepared in parliament by the enemies of these charter Governments, chief of whom was Col. Joseph Dudley, Governor of Massachusetts. This man had been Governor of Massachusetts prior to the accession of Sir Edmund Andros, by whom he was made Chief Justice of New England. After the fall of Andros, he attempted to regain his former position with the intention of including all New England, but was forestalled by Bellemont. The new act proposed a direct reunion to the crown of all the American Governments, whether chartered, proprietary, or provincial, including the Bahama Islands. Its intended effect was to erect a great vice-royalty in America, more comprehensive than the government of Andros had been, while the local affairs of each Government were to be administered by its own Colonial Assembly. The irregularities in respect to trade and piracy, with the consequent injury to the revenue of the kingdom, were the reasons assigned for the movement. The bill was prepared near the close of the reign of William III. It was

[1] Original in Br. S. P. O. Proprieties, vol. 6.

stoutly opposed by Sir Henry Ashurst, agent of Connecticut, who obtained a hearing at the bar of the House of Commons against it. So cogent were the arguments of its opponents, and so successful the efforts of the friends of the colonists, that when the bill was afterward brought up early in the reign of Queen Anne, it was defeated, and this scheme, begotten by the ability of Bellemont and the ambition of Dudley, fell to the ground.[1] CHAP. XIII. 1701. May 3.

At the general election, Governor Cranston, and Deputy-Governor Clarke, were re-elected. Thirteen justices of the peace were chosen. This is the first time that the names of these officers are reported in connection with the other general officers of the colony. The salary of the Governor was raised to forty pounds a year, besides which, almost every year considerable additional gratuities were voted for his benefit. Measures were taken for a thorough reorganization of the militia. The law of marriage was revised. Notice of the intention was to be set up in some public place for fourteen days, by consent of a magistrate. Persons coming from other colonies were required to produce a certificate that they had there conformed to the publication laws. Fine and suspension from office were the penalties for any violation of this law by a magistrate, and fine, imprisonment, or whipping were the punishments for the principals who should disregard it. A bill to sustain the governor in enforcing the navigation act was passed. It required all ship-masters to enter at the collector's office before breaking bulk; to report their passengers, and to obtain permits for shipping seamen belonging to the colony; that none but the regular boarding officers should approach any vessel off the port without leave from the governor, or two assistants; that the governor should establish a naval office, the fees of which were to be stated by the general council; that 7.

[1] The act is found in Antiquities of Connt., pp. 299—304; see Trumbull's Hist. ch. xvii.

CHAP. XIII. 1701. May 7. foreign traders, residing for one month in the colony, should be subject to taxation as other inhabitants; that the commander of the fort, to be appointed by the governor, should have power to bring to any inward bound vessel by the usual modes; and that the tonnage law, enacted ten years before, should remain in force. This was the most complete act which had ever been passed upon the subject. It was one that was fraught with infinite peril to the inward peace, and the outward welfare of the colony. The dangers that threatened from the home government, led the people to acquiesce in a measure to which they were naturally averse.

The stanch loyalty of the Westerly men, continued to subject them to annoyances from their neighbors. Two of their officers were taken prisoners, and carried to Connecticut. Their cause was assumed by the Assembly, who voted to defray their expenses and to send them requisite aid.

June 28. Additional powers were now conferred upon Dudley, already appointed Governor of Massachusetts and New Hampshire. He was made Vice-Admiral of those places, and also of Rhode Island, and King's Province, and orders were issued to hasten his departure for America. This enlargement of his powers soon caused much trouble to Rhode Island, and great annoyance to himself.[1]

Sept. 18. The hostile acts of Connecticut in seizing the people of Westerly, led Mr. Brenton to memorialize the Board of Trade on the subject, asking an adjudication of the controversy.[2]
Oct. 9. The General Assembly appointed a committee to treat with Rhode Island. These attempts, although often renewed, had thus far proved abortive for want of a common ground upon which the disputants could agree as a starting point for negotiation.

1701-2 March 24. On the last day of the year, at a special session of the Assembly, a tax of two hundred pounds was laid, and the

[1] Br. S. P. O. New England, vol. xi. [2] Br. S. P. O. Proprieties, vol. vi.

sedition act was repealed. The population of the whole colony at this time, was estimated at ten thousand souls, exclusive of Indians. The apportionment of the new tax among the towns, was not made till after the election of another Assembly, when a further tax of three hundred pounds was made.

CHAP. XIII.

1702. May 6.

The Westquanoid purchase had been made from the Indians forty years before, by some Providence men. It embraced the lands south of the north branch of the Pawtuxet River. The proprietors petitioned to be erected into a township, but although leave was granted them provisionally, the plan was never carried out.

The Recorder of the colony was forbidden to practise as an attorney, except in his own case or that of the town or colony. A vagrant act was passed at this session, forbidding the harboring of strangers coming from other colonies; deserters from the King's service; or passengers brought by sea and landed without consent of the authorities. Heavy penalties were imposed for any violation of this law. A jail was ordered to be built at Newport. Much attention was bestowed upon fortifications. The King's fort was inadequate to the defence of the harbor. A new fort, afterwards called Queen Anne's, to mount twelve guns, was ordered to be built. The governor and council were authorized to purchase the battery and stores necessary to complete it. The proceeds of all forfeitures, belonging to the general treasury, especially the gold plate and money taken from convicted pirates, were appropriated to this purpose. The fort was built upon Goat Island, upon the same place where fort Woolcot now stands. The first battery erected at Newport was close to the water, in front of Governor Arnold's house, near the spot now occupied by the Union Bank.[1] These were timely preparations, for in Europe the alarm of war had already broken the peace of Ryswick. That short-lived

[1] Bull's Memoirs.

CHAP. XIII. treaty of only four years, was ended by the war of the Spanish succession, which gave rise to the national debt
1702. of England. While the Assembly were arming the colony,
May 7. letters announcing the Queen's declaration of war against France and Spain were issued.[1] Upon their reception,
June 25. hostilities were proclaimed, according to custom, in each town of the colony, and active measures were taken.
July 6. The brigantine Greyhound, of one hundred tons, mounting twelve guns, and manned with one hundred men and boys, was fitted for sea and placed in command of Capt. William Wanton, a shipwright of Portsmouth, with a privateer commission to cruise for five months. His instructions limited his operations within the Banks of Newfoundland on the east, and the thirtieth parallel of north latitude on the south, and were directed against French and Spanish vessels or piratical craft. He gave bonds in the sum of one thousand pounds for the faithful discharge of his trust, and to return to port within two months.[2]

The usual delay in collecting the tax, caused the General Assembly to adopt stringent measures to enforce its
Aug. 25. payment. Mr. Brenton returned home at this time, leaving the colony without an agent in England.

Governor Dudley, soon after his arrival, visited the eastern portions of his government as far as Pemaquid during the summer, and then turned his attention to Rhode Island, as being included in his Vice-Admiralty jurisdiction. Accompanied by Lieutenant-Governor Povey, with six of his council and an escort of troops, he came to Newport and had an interview with Governor Cranston
Sept. 3. and his council, at which Dudley's commissions as commander of the militia during war, and as Vice-Admiral of Rhode Island were read, and the oaths therein required

[1] May 4, 1702, the war was declared.

[2] The commission, instructions and bond are found in Br. S. P. O. Proprieties, vol. vii.

were, at his request, administered to him. The next day CHAP.
Dudley demanded, by virtue of his military commission, XIII.
that the troops of the colony, estimated at two thousand Sept.
men, should be placed under his orders. The militia 4.
clause of the charter was read to him, and it was urged that the power therein conferred upon the civil authorities of the colony, was paramount to that conveyed in Dudley's commission. Governor Cranston held that he could not comply with the demand until the matter was laid before the General Assembly. Dudley replied that he had nothing to do with any assembly but only with the governor and council, and directed Major Martindale, of the Island regiment, to order out his troops the next morning. At Cranston's request copies of Dudley's commissions were entered upon the book of records. The
companies did not appear under arms as required, but the 5.
Major informed Dudley that he could not call out his men without orders from the Assembly or from the governor. Disgusted at this repulse, Dudley left the island at noon, and went to Bristol. On Monday he, with his suite, crossed over to Narragansett, where he was respectfully received. Capt. Eldredge's company appeared un- 7.
der arms. The commissions were read, and the oaths taken as at Newport, after which the oath of allegiance was administered by Dudley to the soldiers, and cheerfully taken.

In consequence of these proceedings, a special session 17.
of the Assembly was called, at which the firm stand taken by the governor was approved, a committee to memorialize the home government in defence of the militia powers conferred by the charter was appointed, an answer to this effect was sent to Dudley, and measures were taken to send an agent to England upon this vital subject. Dudley's letter to the Board of Trade, enclosing the journal of his visit to Rhode Island, denounces the government of the colony in bitter terms, which the reply he received from the General Assembly was not calculated to soften.

CHAP. XIII. They urged the militia clause of the charter and the confirmation thereof by William and Mary, after the fruitless
Sept. attempt of Sir Willliam Phipps, ten years before, to assume the command of the Rhode Island troops, and notified him of their intention to appeal to the Queen.[1]

Some time during this year, the Puritan Church, following the Baptist, Quaker, and Episcopal Churches, obtained a permanent foothold in the colony. A Congregational Society already existed in Newport, and six years prior to this had erected a meeting house, where the Rev. Nathaniel Clapp officiated; but it was not till 1720 that a church was gathered, and Mr. Clapp was ordained as the pastor.[2] Another Congregational Society was now formed in Kingston, who obtained the Rev. Samuel Niles to preach for them, which he did for eight years.[3] These were the earliest churches of this order in Rhode Island, except that which the founders of Aquedneck brought with them, and which appears to have survived but a few years.[4]

The death of William III., and the accession of Queen Ann, gave occasion for a formal address on that subject, in which condolence and congratulation are curiously
29. mingled. A few days later, another address upon the all-important subject of their chartered powers was sent to

[1] Br. S. P. O. New England, vol. xi.; R. I. Col. Rec. iii., 459—63.

[2] Elton's Callender, 119.

[3] Niles' deposition in the suit about the Church lands in Narragansett. Mr. Niles was born at Block Island, 1674, and graduated at Harvard, 1699, being the first student from Rhode Island who ever entered that college. In 1702, before he had been ordained, he was called to the pastoral charge of the Congregational "or Presbyterian" Society at Kingstown, where he remained till 1710, and soon after, in May, 1711, was ordained and settled over the church at Braintree. He afterwards returned to Rhode Island and became pastor of a church in Charlestown, composed chiefly of Indians. He died in 1762. He was the author of several published works mentioned by Mr. Updike in Hist. of the Narrt. Church, p. 36. That by which he is best known is a History of the French and Indian wars, written in 1760, and partly published from the original MS. long after his death, by the Mass. Hist. Society in 3 M. H. C., vol. vi.

[4] See Vol. I., chap. v., pp. 139, 140.

CHAP. XIII. 1702. Sept.

the Queen. Capt. Wanton had returned, after a two months' cruise in the Gulf of St. Lawrence, crowned with brilliant success. He captured and brought into port three French ships, one of them a privateer of two hundred and sixty tons, carrying twenty guns and forty-eight men, another was a vessel of three hundred tons, with sixteen guns, and the third was of one hundred and sixty tons, mounting eight guns. They were loaded with dried fish. Dudley attempted to interfere with the proceedings of the Admiralty Court, long since established at Newport, in the condemnation of the prizes, threatening to confiscate the property and to treat the captors as pirates, if they did not accede to the demands which he, as Vice-Admiral, sought to impose upon them. He attempted to supplant the existing Court of Admiralty by one of his own creation, and to deny the validity of the commission issued to Wanton. The effect of this conduct was favorable to Rhode Island, for it was a wrong so great that it served to cover the many cases of previous irregularity wherein she was actually culpable. Dudley overshot his mark by this impolitic procedure, and by excess of zeal cancelled the injury he sought to produce. The address to the Queen recited in full the militia clause of the charter, stated the proceedings in regard to the Greyhound, and the conduct of Dudley in both of these matters, set forth the exposed condition of the colony, and humbly solicited a confirmation of the patent. It was one of the eras, perhaps the turning point, in the history of Rhode Island, when after so many attacks upon her, and so much foundation in her own conduct for the charges of her enemies, the current began to change in her favor through the increased rashness of her accusers, and the greater caution of her rulers. Just at this critical moment, when her agent, Mr. Brenton, had returned home, and a new one had not yet been sent out, William Penn, then high in favor at the Court of Queen Anne, was charged with the interests of the infant State, where many of his own principles were

CHAP. XIII. 1702. Sept. 29. so deservedly popular. The two addresses to the throne were enclosed to the Earl of Nottingham, asking his intercession with her Majesty in behalf of the colony, and his advice and assistance for Penn as the temporary agent of Rhode Island.[1]

Oct. 8. A more successful effort was now made to adjust the long-pending dispute on the western border. The General Assembly of Connecticut appointed a committee of five, any three of whom were authorized to settle the difficulty with Rhode Island, with no other limitation of their powers than that the fourth article of the agreement between Clark and Winthrop, which secured the right of property to the owners, should be respected. This was a great concession compared with the instructions to previous committees who had always been forbidden to surrender any territory claimed by Connecticut, and were thus cut off from the possibility of adjustment or of compromise. A sincere desire to terminate this unhappy quarrel now actuated the government of Connecticut, and was met with a similar feeling on the part of Rhode
28. Island. The Assembly at Providence appointed five commissioners[2] to meet with those named by Connecticut, and instructed the governor to commission them accordingly.[3]

Nov. 24. The ambitious designs of Dudley were so far successful, that the Board of Trade recommended him to be appointed Governor of Rhode Island, citing in justification the report of the law officers of the crown, eight years before, that in case of emergency the royal authority

[1] The originals of these three papers are in Br. S. P. O. Proprieties, vol. 7.

[2] Capt. Joseph Sheffield, Major Henry Tew, Major John Dexter, Randal Holden, and Weston Clarke.

[3] The records of the Oct. session, 1702, held at Providence have disappeared from the files of the Secretary's office, and do not appear in the printed Colonial Records. Certified copies of the act appointing the commissioners, and of the commissions and instructions issued to them by the governor on the 6th of April following, are found in the Br. S. P. O. Proprieties, vol. xi.

might be exercised for the repeal of proprietary or chartered privileges.[1] Fortunately for the colony, the advice was not adopted by the Queen's council. The indiscretions of Dudley, and the powerful influence of Penn, no doubt combined to avert so grave a disaster, and to preserve the charter of Rhode Island intact. It was deemed important that a special agent should be sent to defend the colony at the English Court, and Capt. Joseph Sheffield, who had before been selected for that trust, was again appointed by the Assembly A tax of six hundred pounds was ordered to defray the expenses of the mission, but several deputies protested against it, so that it was never collected; and the agency itself was abandoned upon further news from England seeming to render it unnecessary. At the same session a further tax of five hundred pounds was assessed to pay for the fort and jail previously ordered. The commutation rate allowed two and threepence a bushel for corn, two shillings for barley, four for wheat, two and fourpence for rye, fourteen pence for oats, ninepence a pound for wool.

CHAP. XIII. 1702.

1702-3 Feb. 2.

Lord Cornberry, Governor of New York, demanded aid from Rhode Island for the war against the French and Indians. The usual excuse, a most valid one, was given for refusing it; the exposed condition of this colony made the utmost efforts of the people inadequate even for their own protection. Upon hearing of the first victories of the Duke of Marlborough against the French in Holland, Governor Cranston, by the Queen's order, issued a proclamation for a day of thanksgiving to be kept on the fifteenth of April, which was duly observed with salutes and illuminations throughout the colony.

1703. April 1.

Wolves were not yet exterminated. The Assembly at an adjourned session offered a premium of twenty shillings a head for every wolf that should be killed. 6.

The Assembly, as usual, convened the day previous to May 3.

[1] Br. S. P. O. Proprieties, vol. 28, p. 244.

CHAP. XIII. 1703. May 12. election, for organization and for the admission of freemen. There was no change in general officers. The commissioners of Rhode Island and Connecticut met at Stonington, and agreed upon a line between the two colonies, which twenty-three years later was confirmed by the King. It varied but little from that claimed by Rhode Island under the charter, and remains to this day the boundary line between the two States. Thus, after forty years of strife, this useless and costly controversy was in effect determined by mutual agreement, and the long-disputed jurisdiction of Narraganset was conceded to Rhode Island by her opponents as it had been by Winthrop in the arbitration with Clarke. It is to the firmness of the men of Westerly, in every stage of this protracted conflict, that the State owes this favorable result, for had they succumbed to their more powerful neighbors, the feeble government of Rhode Island could never have compelled their allegiance against the superior strength of Connecticut. This amicable adjustment was virtually a final one, although so long a period elapsed before its confirmation. It removed the most serious source of domestic difficulty, and enabled the colony to develop its real strength more rapidly than it had hitherto done. Except the obtaining of the two charters, it was the most important event in the history of the State up to that time.[1] On account of this meeting of commissioners, the Assembly adjourned till June, when the proceedings were approved, and the commissions and agreement were entered upon the records. Surveyors[2] were appointed to run the line in accordance with the report. A division of the colony into two counties was made. The islands formed Rhode Island county with Newport as the shire town. The

June 22.

[1] The agreement is printed in Potter's Narraganset R. I. H. C., iii. 204, and R. I. Col. Rec., iii. 474, from the original A certified copy in Br. S. P. O. Proprieties, vol. xi., gives the date as May 20, a difference of eight days. The true date is probably the 12th as above given.

[2] James Carder, of Warwick, and John Mumford, of Newport.

mainland formed the county of Providence Plantations, CHAP.
of which Providence was the shire town. Two Courts of XIII.
Common Pleas were appointed to be held yearly in each 1703.
county; the first year at Providence and Warwick, the June
next at Kingstown and Westerly, for Providence county; those for Rhode Island county were held at Newport.

The exposed condition of New York and Massachusetts from the French and Indians, led the Board of Trade to require that aid should be furnished them by Rhode Island and Connecticut. The perils of an extended seaboard required all the efforts of these colonies to repel invasion by the enemies' ships, and were not properly considered by the home government; while their failure to comply with the demand of Dudley on one side, and of Cornberry on the other, gave these enemies of all chartered rights constant occasion to renew their attacks.
This led the Assembly to apply to the Board of Trade, for 30.
a copy of the charges against Rhode Island, and for an opportunity to defend their conduct.

At the autumn session, held in Warwick, the highways Oct. 27.
in Kingstown, recently laid out, were received and confirmed. The power of each house to decide upon the right of a member to his seat was not then recognized. A doubt existing as to the qualifications of one of the deputies, the two houses met in grand committee to debate the question, and it was decided in favor of the claimant by a majority vote.

The boldness of Rhode Island in assuming admiralty jurisdiction was one of the chief points upon which her enemies relied to accomplish their designs. The Board
of Trade, at the instigation of Dudley, applied to the at- Dec. 2.
torney-general for his opinion whether her conduct in exercising that power, by the act of 1694, did not furnish sufficient cause for a repeal of the charter. The attorney
replied that the act in question was certainly a stretch of 24.
power, but as it was limited in its terms, "until his Majesty's pleasure be further known," it did not warrant

CHAP. XIII. 1703-4 a forfeiture of the charter, but he advised that notice should be sent to the colony to repeal the act forthwith, upon penalty of prosecution.[1]

Jan. 13. The Board of Trade addressed the Queen in accordance with this advice, and urged that Dudley's authority should be extended over Rhode Island. This most indefatigable enemy was absorbed in the desire to extend his government over all New England in utter disregard to chartered rights, or to any other consideration beyond his own selfish ends. Jan. 28. An order was issued by the royal council, annulling the admiralty act, and directing notice thereof to be sent to Rhode Island. The Queen's letter was prepared accordingly, Feb. 16. to be sent to the governor and council, placing all admiralty matters in charge of Governor Dudley, Mar. 17. as Vice-Admiral of New England.[2] This was forwarded to Governor Dudley with a letter from the Board to Rhode Island, and soon after another royal letter was 23. written, censuring the colony for not furnishing the required aid to Massachusetts.[3]

Jan. 4. Meanwhile, the General Assembly held a special session at Newport. Captive Indians taken at the eastward, where Col. Church was prosecuting the war with vigor, were brought into the colony for sale. This was forbidden under a heavy penalty, and those already brought in were required to be sent out. A tax of five hundred pounds was laid for the support of government. An act was passed for raising twelve scouts to be employed on military service during the war, under orders from the two Majors. The tenths of the prizes taken by Capt. Wanton,

[1] Br. S. P. O. Proprieties, vol. xxviii., p. 387, and vol. vii. of the same.

[2] Br. S. P. O. Proprieties, vol. xxviii., p. 439. The admiralty act about which so much clamor was made was framed by the governor and council of R. I. and confirmed by the General Assembly, January 7, 1694–5. The records of that period are lost, but a copy of the obnoxious statute is found in the British State Paper Office enclosed with the opinion, above referred to, of the attorney-general thereupon. See App. H.

[3] Br. S. P. O. Proprieties, vol. xxviii., pp. 471, 480.

due to the crown, were appropriated to arm the forts, CHAP.
pending the result of a petition for that purpose already XIII.
sent to the Queen. All Indians and negroes were forbidden 1704. to walk the streets of Newport after nine o'clock at night without a pass, and no housekeeper was allowed to entertain them after that hour. The laws had often been revised but never yet printed. A committee was appointed to put them to press as soon as a new revision could be completed, but many years elapsed before this vote was carried into effect.

Many Rhode Island troops volunteered under Col. May 3. Church for the war against the French and the Indians. To defray their expenses another tax of seven hundred pounds was made by the new General Assembly, and the assessors were empowered to administer an engagement, or oath, to every tax-payer, that the list he presented of his ratable estate was correct. The island of Conanicut was surveyed at this time, the highways laid out, and farms platted, and the surveyors' report placed upon record. The pay of the soldiers at the fort was fixed at twelve pounds a year, with rations, and that of the scouts at three shillings a day while on duty.

The great battle of Blenheim gave occasion for another Aug. day of thanksgiving, which was ordered by a circular 2. letter to all the colonies from the Board of Trade. 25.

The serious charges in respect to the admiralty act, Sept. which led to its being annulled, were answered at great 25. length by Rhode Island. The act seemed to be one of necessity when it was passed; a valuable French prize having been brought into Newport and no power there existing by which it could be legally condemned. Copies of the captain's petition upon the subject, and of all the papers pertaining thereto, were sent to England. The excuse for resisting the demands of the governors of Massachusetts on this subject was a valid one, Rhode Island not being named in their commissions, and the conduct of that colony in times past having been such that any

CHAP. XIII. 1704. claim from that source to power over Rhode Island was, to say the least, suspicious, and aroused a well-grounded feeling of jealousy.[1]

Oct. 25. The October session of the Assembly was held at Providence, at which appeal cases were heard. When sitting as a Court of Appeals the two branches of the Assembly united in grand committee. The propriety of this measure will not be questioned when it is remembered that the governor and council, or upper house, at this time composed the Supreme Court, or General Court of Trials, as it was termed, and continued so to do till the creation of a judicial branch of the government forty-three years later.

The opinion of the law officers of the crown, given upon a representation of the Board of Trade, instigated by Dudley and Lord Cornberry, that a governor might be appointed over the chartered colonies of Connecticut and Rhode Island, was sent to the Queen; whereupon an
Nov. 16. order was issued for the agents of these colonies to appear within two weeks and show cause, if they had any, why this course should not be adopted. On the appointed
30. day, Sir Henry Ashurst petitioned for a postponement, which was granted for two weeks longer. Meanwhile,
Dec. 11. another delay of three weeks was obtained, and almost immediately after this a month more was given to pre-
14. pare the defence.[2]

That there was a concerted plan between Dudley and Cornberry to break up the chartered colonies adjoining their governments, their well-timed measures proved. Dudley sent a requisition to Governor Cranston for troops to defend Massachusetts against the Indians, while Cornberry called on Connecticut for pecuniary aid in behalf
Dec. 27. of New York. A special session of the Assembly was convened at Newport. A quorum of both houses were present, but the attendance was not full. Col. Dudley's de-

[1] Br. S. P. O. Proprieties, vol. viii.; R. I. Col. Rec. iii., 508—510.
[2] Do. do. vol. vii.

mands were presented, and the next day an answer was made to him that the required aid should be sent, if practicable, when the Assembly again met at its adjourned session. CHAP. XIII. 1704. Dec. 28.

The Rev. James Honeyman was this year sent over, by the society for the propagation of the gospel in foreign parts, as a missionary to Rhode Island, in compliance with petitions from Newport, the eastern shore, and Narraganset, sent to them and the bishop of London two years before, for ministers of the Church of England. He became the rector of Trinity Church, and also visited the three towns on the main, Freetown, Tiverton, and Little Compton by turns, on week days, for eight years, until a missionary was sent to them. He then had more leisure, established a lecture, and preached once a fortnight at Portsmouth. His Christian deportment gained him many friends, and ensured him a full audience wherever he preached. His memory is perpetuated in the name of the highest hill on the southern extremity of the island, the eastern slope of which Bishop Berkely afterwards selected for his home.

The hearing of the cases of Rhode Island and Connecticut having been postponed from time to time for nearly three months, could no longer be deferred. Her Majesty and a full council were present. Sir Henry Ashurst had used every means in his power to avert the threatened repeal of the Connecticut charter. He had high connections, and great parliamentary influence enlisted on his side, and employed two of the ablest lawyers in Parliament to argue the cause against the law officers of the crown. The defence occupied but an hour and a half, and was so far successful as to obtain the chief point desired, that time should be allowed for the colonies to reply to the accusations before final proceedings were taken against them.[1] 1704 5 Feb. 12.

[1] A full account of this hearing, derived from the correspondence of Sir Henry Ashurst, is given in Trumbull's Hist. of Conn., chap. xvii., pp. 414—

CHAP. XIII. 1704-5 An order was issued for the Board to prepare charges against the two colonies to be given to their agents to answer within six months, and copies of the same were to be sent to Governor Dudley and Lord Cornberry, to collect evidence in their support, and to furnish other copies to the governors of Rhode Island and Connecticut to prepare their defence.[1]

Feb. 14. The General Assembly denied the truth of Dudley's complaints of their not furnishing aid to Massachusetts. They had sent one company of volunteers, under Church, the preceding summer, notwithstanding the heavy taxes assessed for strengthening their own defences, and they now took measures to enlist the quota of forty-eight men assigned to them. A tax of five hundred pounds was levied for this purpose upon the already overburdened colony.

28. Governor Cranston then informed Dudley of what had been done, and requested him to appoint commissioners, to meet with the same number selected by the Assembly, to agree upon the mode of disposal and of support for the soldiers.[2]

1705. May 7. Most of the towns had charters granted them by the General Assembly, by which they were empowered to regulate their local affairs. A similar power was conferred upon Newport by special statute. The Indians at Block Island were ordered to be trained for military service, and the quota of troops that were to be sent to Col. Dudley was withdrawn. The first movement towards settling the north line of the colony, was made at this session upon petition from Providence. The line was described as running north from Pawtucket falls till it meets the south boundary of Massachusetts, and thence west to the Connecticut line. Gov. Dudley was requested to lay

418. No mention of the Rhode Island agent is therein made, but we know that Penn had been requested to take the agency after the return of Brenton, and no successor had yet been appointed. The orders in council mention the presence of agents of both colonies.

[1] Br. S. P. O. Proprieties, vol. viii.; R. I. Col. Rec., iii. 496.

[2] Br. S. P. O. Proprieties, vol. viii.; R. I. Col. Rec., iii. 496, 497.

the matter before his provincial Assembly for them to select commissioners to unite with the three appointed by Rhode Island[1] to run the line. This appeared to be a very plain case, but was destined, like the other boundary questions, to be a source of protracted contest. As Plymouth had been absorbed by Massachusetts, there were now two territorial disputes to be settled between Rhode Island and her powerful antagonist. 1705.

Captain John Halsey, of the brigantine Charles, to whom Governor Cranston had granted a privateer commission in November, arrived at this time, with a valuable Spanish prize taken in the West Indies. He applied to Nathaniel Byfield, Judge of Admiralty, to condemn her as a lawful prize. Byfield gave a warrant to discharge the cargo, and held a court on the question of condemnation. It appeared that the commission was granted after the receipt of her Majesty's orders annulling the admiralty act of 1694, and hence it was declared void, and condemnation was refused. This caused so much excitement, that Byfield adjourned the court in order to consult the Vice-Admiral. Gov. Cranston addressed a letter to the judge, requiring him to condemn the prize, or to give reasons for his refusal, claiming that the commission was valid under the declaration of war upon which it was granted. John Coleman, one of the owners of the Charles, and as commissioner of prizes, agent for the Lord High Admiral, complained to Dudley of the conduct of Byfield in refusing to condemn the prize. Capt. Halsey was ready for another cruise but could not sail until this matter was adjusted. The General Assembly was convened upon this subject, and also to lay a tax of five hundred pounds, a portion of which was to pay the tenths of prize money due to the Lord High Admiral. An act was passed, in reference to the conduct of Byfield, which forcibly displays the boldness of the people in claiming ad-

June 6. 16. 19.

[1] Major William Hopkins, Joseph Jenckes, and Thomas Olney.

CHAP. XIII. miralty jurisdiction, in the face of the recent decree, annulling their former action upon this point. It declared
1705. that the governors of the colony, with permission of the
June Assembly, "have had and still have full power and authority to grant commissions to private men-of-war against her Majesty's public enemies; and that the said governors have been and still are justified therein, provided they have and do take bond and do all other things as the law directs relating to private men of war;" and in answer to the claim of the Judge of Admiralty that the Marshal of his court held the power of water bailiff within the colony, the Assembly declared that that power vested in this government alone, by the charter, and by the laws of Eng-
23. land. The owners of the Charles petitioned Dudley to legalize the commission under which they had acted;
25. whereupon he ordered Byfield to condemn the prize to the captors on the ground that the government of Rhode Island would not do justice to her Majesty, and that the cargo would be lost if speedy action was not taken. The Court of Admiralty was immediately convened, and the
27. prize was condemned, although in the opinion of the Judge, the commission under which the capture was made was illegal. During the proceedings a paper was handed to the register of the court containing a justification of the governor's conduct in granting the commission. Byfield would not permit it to be read and adjourned the court. A mob followed and insulted him in the streets, but no violence was offered to him. This conduct, and also the passage of the admiralty act, were attributed by
July 19. Byfield, in his account of the affair sent to the British ministry, with all the documents pertaining thereto, to the influence of Coleman, the commissioner of prizes and agent of the Lord High Admiral, who was also an owner in the Charles.

Scarcely was this matter disposed of, when Gov.
25. Cranston received from Dudley a copy of the charges prepared by the Board of Trade against Rhode Island. Dud-

ley proceeded at once to collect evidence to sustain them. All persons who had any cause of discontent with the colony were sought out, and their affidavits obtained, to swell the mass of proofs with which her ambitious foe expected to crush the charter government of Rhode Island. The outrage upon the French settlers some years before, was represented with great minuteness by Pierre Ayrault in a remonstrance sent to Gov. Dudley. It was the most flagrant case that could be brought against the people, but it was one of those acts of border violence with which the history of all new countries abound, for which the government could not fairly be held responsible.

CHAP. XIII. 1705

Aug. 20.

A special session of the Assembly was held to reply to the charges. The governor and Joseph Sheffield were appointed a committee for this purpose, and a tax of one thousand pounds was laid to raise funds for the agent in England. The charges were contained in thirteen articles, relating to violations of the acts of trade; to harboring deserters; refusing the quota; to irregularities in judicial proceedings; to exercising military and admiralty powers; and to a few more trivial matters.[1] The answers were firm and well drawn, giving a categorical denial to the greater portion, and in some cases defending their conduct as being warranted by the charter, or by the exigencies of the times. Dudley was not so prompt in forwarding his side of the question to the ministry. It required time to collect all the evidence he desired. He sought for it even in New York, where depositions were taken concerning piracies that occurred several years before, and which inculpated the other colonies as much as they did Rhode Island.

28.

Sept. 5 & 8.

The subject of a Court of Chancery was discussed in the General Assembly, but as it was one of great importance, and could not be fully settled at once, it was voted

[1] They were prepared March 26, 1705, and are found in Br. S. P. O. Proprieties, vol. xxix. pp. 133—138. See R. I. Col. Rec., iii. 543, and Ibid, 546—9 for the answers.

CHAP. XIII. that the Assembly itself should continue to act, as it had hitherto done, as a Chancery Court until one could be 1705. properly constituted. The line between Greenwich and Oct. 31. Kingstown was established. The office of Public Notary was erected, and the Recorder was appointed to fill it till the next election.

Nov. 2. At length Dudley, having collected an immense amount of evidence to sustain the charges against Rhode Island, dispatched it to England. It was a truly formidably array of testimony, well calculated to accomplish the selfish purpose of extending his own authority over a neighboring colony upon the ruins of her chartered rights. More than forty documents, being affidavits, copies of records and transcripts of laws, certified by himself, some of them of great length and covering a period of many years, were arranged under the thirteen articles of impeachment which they were intended to sustain. Scarcely had this mass of evidence been sent away, before still more 9. was accumulated. Nathaniel Coddington wrote to Dudley in regard to the Narragansett disputes, and also presented a gloomy picture of the partisan spirit that animated the government of the colony, of whom he was himself one, being the first assistant from Newport. It was an unfortunate thing for Rhode Island that the ambition of her neighbors often gave opportunity for any who were discontented to pour their grievances into the willing ears of her enemies. Such *ex parte* statements lost nothing by the transfer, and frequently involved the colony in further and unnecessary difficulties. The purpose of Coddington in this communication to Dudley is not apparent, but it served to stimulate the Narragansett proprietors, the remnants of the old Atherton company, residing in Boston, and always the bitter foes of Rhode Island, to 14. address Dudley upon their own affairs. This they did in a very long document, reciting the history of Narragansett from the beginning, and referring, in flattering terms, to the prior administration of Dudley, when they had their own way and their own members in the council, but avoiding any reference to the succeeding government of Andros, who had revoked the unjust acts of Dudley, and had restored to Rhode Island her rights. This paper was the last effort of the claimants for "the mortgaged lands," a claim founded in fraud, and maintained by force until exposed by the luminous Report of Sir Edmund Andros. It was forwarded by Dudley to the Board of Trade, with the intimation that if Rhode Island was placed under him the petitioners should have justice. 1705. Nov. 15.

But Dudley was not working alone in these assaults upon the colony. Lord Cornberry desired to add Connecticut to New York, and each aided the other to accomplish the repeal of the charters. Both had been furnished with copies of the charges, and ordered to collect evidence upon them. 26. Cornberry's letter is to the same effect as Dudley's, but relates more particularly to Connecticut. Each was indefatigable in pursuit of a common end, and both alike suffered a humiliating defeat; for the proofs, although very voluminous, did not sustain the charges, and the replies of the accused exposed the falsity or the frivolity of them all. Rhode Island proved that within seven years she had expended more than six thousand pounds in forts and military operations, and Connecticut showed that although, like Rhode Island, she had sometimes refused her quota to New York, she had over five hundred men in the field the past year, most of them aiding the complaining colonies. Equally convincing was the refutation upon other important points, and triumphant was the appeal of the agents when they again appeared in presence of the Board of Trade with all the evidence on either side before them.[1]

Ex-Governor John Easton, died at the close of this Dec. 12.

[1] The originals of nearly all the documents referred to in 1705, are in the Br. S. P. O. Proprieties, vol. viii., filling almost the entire bundle. A few are in New England Papers, vol. xiii., and the most important ones are given in R. I. Col. Rec., iii. pp. 537, 543—9.

CHAP. XIII. year. He was the son of Gov. Nicholas Easton, and was for two years deputy-governor, during Philip's war, of 1705. which he wrote a brief account recently published in Dec. Albany. He was afterwards, for five years, governor of the colony.[1]

The Pawtuxet men revived their old complaint against 18. the government of Rhode Island in the Harris case, and obtained an order from the Queen summoning the colony 20. to answer the petitioners before the council. Two days later another order was issued to the Board of Trade requiring them to report upon the illegal proceedings of the charter and proprietary governments in America, and upon the expediency of reducing them to more imme- 1705-6 diate subjection to the crown. This renewed action was Jan. 10. taken at the instigation of Dudley, whose charges formed the basis of the report which was rendered within three weeks. It was aimed chiefly at Massachusetts, Rhode Island and Connecticut, the three governments sought by him to be united under his jurisdiction. The attempt, like the preceding ones, proved abortive, no further action being had upon the report; but it was not yet abandoned, as we shall presently see. It is worthy of note that one of the charges is, "that these colonies promote and encourage woollen and other manufactures proper to England, instead of applying their thoughts to the production of such commodities as are fit to be encouraged in these parts." The same spirit which, seventy years later, denied that "even a hob nail should be manufactured in America," here finds its first official expression.[2]

1706. The General Assembly ordered an investigation into May 1. the long suspended controversy with Pawtuxet, that an account of it might be sent to their solicitor, William Wharton. Two taxes amounting to seven hundred pounds were voted, of which five hundred pounds were for finish-

[1] 1690–95.

[2] The report is in Br. S. P. O. Proprieties, vol. xxix. p. 238, and is printed in R. I. Col. Rec., iv. 12—15.

ing Fort Ann. Every inhabitant was required to bring in a true statement of his taxable property within four months. The exigencies of the war demanded vigorous efforts. Every thing in the colony was placed upon a war footing, and almost every man became a soldier, or in some way assisted in the common defence. The coast line was covered with scouts, a permanent garrison was maintained on Block Island, and extraordinary preparations were made on every side to resist an expected invasion. A powerful French fleet was harassing the British West Indies, and might at any day appear off the seaboard. An event soon occurred to show the advantage of this martial activity. A sloop loaded with provisions was taken by a French privateer near Block Island. The news reached the governor the next day. Proclamation for volunteers was forthwith issued, two sloops were taken up for the expedition, and within two hours' time were manned by a hundred and twenty men, under command of Capt. John Wanton, and in less than three hours afterward captured the privateer, retook her prize, and brought them into Newport. The promptness and success of this gallant adventure astonished and delighted the country, and added fresh laurels to the naval glory of Rhode Island. The General Assembly was convened at Newport and voted a gratuity to the governor for his trouble in fitting out the sloops. They also empowered him, in case of invasion, to press any vessels into the colony service, and provided for their proper appraisal by two men, one to be selected by the governor, the other by the owners, the charges to be paid from the treasury. Another tax of three hundred pounds was voted, two hundred of which were on account of the recent expedition.

CHAP. XIII. 1706. May 1. June July 3.

The papers in the Pawtuxet case having been prepared, were sent to Wharton, the agent, with a letter to the Board of Trade, giving an account of the defences of the colony, and of the late victory by Capt. Wanton. The number of prisoners of war brought into Rhode Island,

Sept. 14.

CHAP. XIII. had become a heavy charge upon the treasury, and relief from that burden was asked.[1]

1706. Oct. 4. Byfield, Judge of Admiralty, soon after wrote to the ministry, defending his conduct in the case of Halsey's privateer, Charles, the last year, and relating the exploit of Wanton, whose prize he condemned without exacting the legal fees, "in order to encourage so brisk an action."[2]

31. The Assembly appointed two annual fairs to be held at Portsmouth, in May and November, each to continue for three days. It is said that this plan was suggested by George Fox when visiting his co-religionists in that town. The following year the act was repealed upon petition of the people of Portsmouth.

The second Episcopal Society in the colony was formed this year at Kingstown, under the Rev. Christopher Bridge, and a church erected the following year. Ninety-three years afterwards this building was removed to Wickford, where it is still used for divine service as St. Paul's Church.[3]

The northern boundary began to be a source of dispute. It appears by a petition from the people of Mendon to their general court, that they understood the claim of Rhode Island to be based upon the indefinite grant of the Sachems in 1639, which had caused so much trouble among the grantees themselves. The expression "up the streams of Pawtucket and Pawtuxet without limits," was construed literally by the petitioners, if not by the Providence committee, and covered half the township of Mendon, with much more besides, within the limits of Massachusetts. After a delay of more than a year, the general court appointed five commissioners to run out the line as it had been done in 1642, and instructed the governor to
Nov. 6. request Rhode Island also to appoint a committee to join

[1] Original in Br. S. P. O. Proprieties, vol. viii.; R. I. Col. Rec., iii. 559–61.
[2] Original in Br. S. P. O. Proprieties, vol. viii.
[3] Updike's Narragansett Church, p. 39.

them in the survey.[1] Gov. Dudley wrote accordingly to Gov. Cranston, and named Colonel Byfield as chairman of the committee on the part of Massachusetts. The subject was presented at a special session of the Assembly, called at Newport on account of a threatened invasion of New England by the French and Indians. Six commissioners[2] were selected to unite in the survey, provided the starting point was right, or to forbid it if otherwise, and especially if the line should cross Pawtucket River into the township of Providence. They were also to run the line north from Pawtucket Falls to the south line of Massachusetts. The governor was requested to notify the Connecticut government to be present to secure the rights of that colony in establishing the point of departure. It does not appear that any action was taken by these committees.

CHAP. XIII. 1706-7 Feb. 25.

At the request of Col. Dudley it was voted to equip the Rhode Island quota of troops under command of Major William or Capt. John Wanton, and to fit out a cruiser, at the expense of the colony, whose operations should be confined between the thirtieth and forty-fifth degrees of latitude. A tax of five hundred pounds was

[1] The R. I. Assembly in May, 1705, had appointed commissioners to run the north line, and requested Gov. Dudley to present the subject to his Provincial Assembly that they might also appoint a committee for the same purpose. Nothing was done by Dudley. The R. I. men proceeded to act alone. The people of Mendon appointed a committee to meet with those from Providence to learn from them the basis of their claim. This done, the above petition was sent September 5, 1705. An order from the council of Mass. was issued on the 15th to the select men of Mendon to forbid the survey by R. I., to deface the marks set up, and to arrest the trespassers. On the 8th of August following, the House of Representatives named a committee of five men to run the line in connection with a R. I. committee, and the governor was requested to write to Gov. Cranston to that effect. The subject was not acted upon by the Council or upper House till again brought to their notice, November 5, 1706. The measure was concurred in by both houses the next day, and the letter written as above.—From MS. files of General Court of Mass.

[2] Thomas Olney, Joseph Jenckes, Richard Arnold, Jonathan Sprague, Randal Holden, and James Carder.

CHAP. XIII. levied for the purposes of the war. This was for the unfortunate expedition against Acadie, conceived by Col.
1706-7 Feb. 25. Dudley, and undertaken without assistance from England, which returned during the summer, having been repulsed before the strong fortress of Port Royal. In his speech to the Assembly, Dudley acknowledges that "he had received a very honorable assistance from Rhode Island, and a proper force from New Hampshire."[1]

In those days the sale of bread was regulated by law. An act was passed requiring every baker to have a distinct mark, and to make his loaves of a certain weight according to the price of wheat, on penalty of forfeiting his bread to the use of the poor of the town.

1707. May 7. The Board of Trade addressed a circular to the Governors of Rhode Island, Connecticut, and Pennsylvania, requiring annual returns to be made of the acts of their Assemblies, and making inquiries as to the population and commerce of those colonies. It also announced the union of the crowns of England and Scotland, which was ordered to be published in a solemn manner, and decreed that henceforth Scotchmen should everywhere be considered as Englishmen.[2]

April 19. The town of Portsmouth voted to petition the Assem-

[1] Hutchinson's Mass. ii. 165. The expedition consisted of about 1150 men, in two regiments, the red and the blue, the latter led by Col. Hilton, of New Hampshire, and Lieutenant-Colonel Wanton, of R. I. In the fleet was the sloop Bathsheba, Captain Cranston, of 8 guns and 26 men from R. I. The fleet sailed on the 13th May, landed the troops at Port Royal on the 26th, and they re-embarked on 5th June. Jealousy among the officers, and a mutinous spirit fostered thereby among the men, rather than French prowess, caused the failure of the attempt. Cols. Hilton and Wanton are expressly named as having had no part in the disagreements which produced this result. Autobiography of Rev. John Barnard. See 3 Mass. His. Colls. vol. v. pp. 190–5. Colonel Wanton arrived at Newport the 15th June, and on the 18th visited Boston with Capt. Sheffield, the treasurer of the colony, to advise with Dudley in regard to the war. MS. letters of Cranston to Dudley on Court Files of Mass.

[2] Br. S. P. O. Proprieties, B. T. vol. xxix. p. 466, printed in R. I. Col. Rec., iv. 22.

bly concerning "several grievances and oppressions" CHAP. XIII.
under which they suffered.[1] In consequence of this, a
town charter was granted to them, as had been done for 1707.
Newport two years before. The war with France caused May 10.
renewed efforts on the part of the colony. A special session of the Assembly was called by the governor, at which 28.
a tax of fifteen hundred pounds was voted, a far heavier tax than any that had ever before been assessed. The colony yielded all control over the shores of rivers, coves, and other waters, to the respective towns in which they were included, the better to promote trade and navigation by building wharves and warehouses thereupon. A new ferry was established between Kingstown and Conanicut. The dwelling house and its appurtenances belonging to the governor of the colony was exempted from taxation during his term of office. A singular case of posthumous punishment, intended as a terror to malefactors, occurred at this time. A slave in Kingstown had committed a murder, under circumstances of peculiar barbarity, upon the wife of his master, and had drowned himself, as was supposed, to avoid being taken alive. His body was found on the shore at Little Compton about two weeks afterward. The Assembly ordered that his head, legs, and arms should be hung up in some public place near Newport, and his body be burnt to ashes.

The dispute on the northern frontier now assumed a Oct.
serious aspect. An armed force from Mendon invaded Rhode Island, and seizing two of the inhabitants of Providence, carried them as prisoners to Boston. An express 14.
was sent to Gov. Cranston, who wrote to Col. Dudley,
warning him of danger from the outraged citizens of 18.
Providence, and urging a joint commission to settle the
line. The General Assembly met at Warwick, and again 29.
appointed commissioners[2] to treat with any who might be

[1] See Portsmouth Records, April 19, 1707.

[2] Randal Holden, James Carder, John Eldridge, Thomas Fry, and Weston Clarke.

CHAP. XIII. 1707. Oct. 29. named by Massachusetts upon this question, but should she refuse to act, then the matter was to be referred to the agent in England to procure a royal order for settling the line. A letter to this effect was sent to Dudley, recommending also the mutual discharge of prisoners, by which it appears that retaliatory measures had been promptly taken by the people of Providence. A committee was also appointed to survey and plat the vacant lands in Narragansett, in order to their better settlement. Massachusetts acted at once upon the communication from Nov. 5. Rhode Island, and discharged the prisoners.

The hostility to the charter governments still continued, fermented by the desire of Col. Dudley to annex Rhode Island to his jurisdiction, and of Lord Cornberry to unite Connecticut with New York. The Board of Trade presented a report to Parliament, with charges prepared by order of the Queen, against these two colonies, 28. and supported by the opinion of the law officers of the crown that a royal governor might legally be placed over 1707-8 Jan. 6. them. The report was referred to a committee of the House of Lords, who called for the papers from the Board 7. of Trade. The opinion of the Attorney and Solicitor General, rendered the next day, while professing to concur with that given thirteen years before by the crown officers of the preceding reign,[1] actually goes much further and declares that there is nothing in the charters to preclude the appointment of a royal governor.[2] Fortunately for the colonies, no action was taken upon this report. The master-spirit of Bellemont had passed away, and the present agitators were too powerless, or too distant from the court to pursue their advantage.

It appears by a later record that a special session of the Assembly was held in February, at which an act was

[1] See Chap. XII. Vol. I. p. 528 of this work.

[2] The original order for the papers, and a copy of the opinion, are in Br. S. P. O. Proprieties, vol. ix. pp. 16, 17. The latter is printed in R. I. Col. Rec., iv. 15.

passed laying a duty of three pounds upon every negro imported into the colony. No record of this session remains; but the subject of this act was one that had begun to excite much attention with the home government, as well as in the colonies. The African Slave Trade, previously a monopoly of the Royal African Company, but which had been opened to all British merchants six years before, by act of Parliament, "for the well supplying of the plantations and colonies with sufficient numbers of negroes at reasonable prices," formed the subject of a circular, addressed by the Board of Trade to all the American colonies, to ascertain the exact condition of that trade, and how far the business of the company was affected by the operations of separate traders.[1] The first replies were to embrace the nine and a half years from the opening of the trade to the past Christmas, after which, semi-annual reports on the subject were required, and so important was it considered, that no other matter was to be included in these official records of the slave trade. By the reply of Rhode Island we learn that but one vessel had ever arrived direct from the coast, and that was two years pre-

CHAP. XIII. 1708.

April 15.

1696.

[1] The earliest English trade with Guinea commenced in the reign of Edward VI. The English having no colonies at that time, the trade was chiefly confined to gold and ivory. The first organized trading company to Africa was incorporated in 30th Elizabeth. This was succeeded by the "Company of Royal Adventurers," chartered in 1662, which was so unsuccessful that in ten years it sold out to a new company called the Royal African Company, chartered September 27, 1672. The expense of maintaining forts upon the coast, and the losses sustained through wars with the rival Dutch and French companies, led Parliament to open the trade to all merchants on the 24th June, 1698, for a term of 14 years, and to impose an export duty of 10 per cent. on all goods sent to Africa, to defray the expense to the company of keeping up the forts. The revenue thus derived was insufficient for the purpose. Upon the expiration of the act in 1712, the people required that the trade should continue open. Compensation was long afterward made to the company for their military outlay, a new "company of merchants trading to Africa" was formed, and on the 10th April, 1752, the Royal African Company ceased to exist.

The circular is in Br. S. P. O. Plantations General, vol. xxxvii. p. 165. Printed in R. I. Col. Rec., iv. 53

CHAP. XIII. vious to the act of Parliament referred to. She brought forty-seven slaves, fourteen of whom were sold in the colony at thirty to thirty-five pounds each, and the remainder were sent by land to Boston, where the vessel
1700. was owned. Four years later, three slavers, owned in Barbadoes, sailed from Newport for the coast of Africa. Barbadoes was the source whence Rhode Island received most of her slaves. From twenty to thirty was the average annual supply, and from thirty to forty pounds each the usual price. No more than these could be disposed of, owing "to the general dislike our planters have for them, by reason of their turbulent and unruly tempers," to the natural increase of those already here, and "to the inclination of our people in general, to employ white servants before negroes."[1]

1708. April 28. The Assembly met by adjournment at Newport, and, in conformity with the letter from the Board of Trade of the previous May, ordered a census of the whole colony to be taken. This was the first general census ever made in Rhode Island. The number of inhabitants was found to be 7,181, of whom 1,015 were freemen, fifty-six white, and four hundred and twenty-six black servants, and the militia force, which included all males between the ages of sixteen and sixty years, was reported at 1362. Each of these was required to provide himself with a musket,

[1] Original in Br. S. P. O. Proprieties, vol. ix., p. 86. Printed in R. I. Col. Rec., iv., 54. By a singular coincidence, while the author was writing this earliest official record of slavery in Rhode Island, "the last of the R. I. slaves" expired. The subjoined newspaper paragraph commemorates the event. "LAST OF THE RHODE ISLAND SLAVES. James Howland, the last of the Rhode Island *slaves*, died at the residence of John Howland, Jamestown, R. I., on the 3d inst., at the ripe old age of one hundred years. He had always been a faithful servant in the Howland family. Up to the hour of his death he retained all his faculties unimpaired, and on the night of January 2d, attended to his usual duties about the house. On the morning of the 3d he arose, dressed himself, and was about to descend the stairs from his chamber, when he fainted, and expired in a few moments. He was the last of the Rhode Island slaves."—*Providence Daily Tribune, Monday, January* 10, 1859.

a sword or bayonet, a cartridge box, one pound of powder, and four pounds of bullets, and upon any alarm to repair at once to their places of rendezvous, subject to the orders of their officers.[1] A tax of eight hundred pounds was laid, in payment of which Indian corn was to be taken at two shillings a bushel, barley at one and eight pence, rye at two and six pence, oats at fourteen pence, wheat at three shillings, and wool at nine pence a pound. The registry act had fallen into disuse from the want of a penalty attached to its violation. It was therefore re-enacted, with a suitable fine to enforce its execution. Power was given to the governor and council, to press vessels, or any other property, into the public service, should an emergency require.

CHAP. XIII. 1708.

The general election made no important changes in the list of officers. The session was chiefly occupied in hearing cases of appeal from the court of trials. The exposed condition of Block Island, constantly in danger of being again attacked by the French, as it had so often been during the previous war, caused the Assembly to pass an act for its defence. A quota of fifteen men was voted, to form the nucleus of a garrison upon the island. To establish a uniform value for foreign coins in the colonies, and to encourage trade to America, engaged the attention of Parliament, and formed the subject of another circular from the Board of Trade.[2] Additional instructions to the several colonial governments were submitted to the Queen. These related to the Acts of Trade, one clause of which, requiring plantation produce to be imported into the United Kingdom before being sent to foreign countries, had been constantly violated by the colonies. Rice and molasses are specially named as having been thus illegally exported. The instructions were approved by her Majesty, and brought out by Lord Lovelace, the newly appointed

May 5.

14.

June 29.

July 3.

[1] The original census roll is in Br. S. P. O. Proprieties, vol. ix., p. 89. Printed in R. I. Col. Rec., iv., 59.

[2] Br. S. P. O. Plantations General, vol. xxxvii., p. 184.

CHAP. XIII. successor to Lord Cornberry as Governor of New York.[1]

1708. Aug. 25. The object of a summer session of the Assembly, held this year, is not apparent. The record of its proceedings, so far as they are preserved, is an exact transcript of what was done in April.[2]

The appearance of French privateers on the coast, again called forth the energy and naval spirit of Rhode Island. Intelligence that two vessels had been taken at Martha's
Sept. 8. Vineyard was received at Newport, and within three hours two sloops, commanded by Major William Wanton, and Capt. John Cranston, were despatched against the enemy. The French destroyed their prizes, and putting to sea, escaped after a twenty-four hours' chase.[3] Public auctions were established in Newport by the next General
Oct. 27. Assembly held at Providence, and the townsmen were empowered to select a "vendue master" to conduct them. A committee was appointed to agree with Ninigret, Sachem of the Niantics, as to the amount and location of the land required by his tribe, and also to examine into the condition of Narragansett, with a view to the settlement of a new town. The business of the Assembly as a Court of Equity and Appeals, had so greatly increased, that a tax of three pounds was henceforth required to be paid by every appellant before his case should be heard, but if judgment was rendered in his favor, this tax was to be allowed in his bill of costs. No war measures were proposed at this session, probably because sufficient power had already been vested in the council, for defence against the enemy. The neighboring colonies were active in this

[1] Ibid, p. 211. Printed in R. I. Col. Rec., iv., 91.

[2] Both sessions are reported as being held on "the last Tuesday" of the month, so that we are inclined to think that this report of an August session may be a clerical error of the Recorder, who has inserted a portion of the April proceedings twice, and headed them "the last Tuesday of *August*" instead of April.

[3] Letters of Gov. Cranston to the Board of Trade, Dec. 5, 1708, in Br. S. P. O. Proprieties, vol. ix., p. 88.

CHAP. XIII. 1708.

respect, and the Connecticut Assembly appropriated fifty pounds "for the bringing up and maintaining of dogs in the northern frontier towns in that colony, to hunt after the Indian enemy."[1]

Dec. 5. To the several letters and circulars of the Board of Trade, received in the past year, Gov. Cranston wrote minute replies, and forwarded the census roll and commercial statistics as required. From these we learn that the amount of annual exports to England, sent by way of Boston, was estimated at twenty thousand pounds. The principal direct trade was to the West Indies. Within the past twenty years the amount of shipping had increased six fold, owing "to the inclination the youth on Rhode Island have for the sea," because the whole island was already taken up in small farms. The fact that but two or three of our vessels had ever been taken by the enemy, by reason of their superior sailing qualities, is also assigned as a cause for this predilection; "they being light and sharp for runners, so that very few of the enemy's privateers, in a gale of wind, will run or outsail one of our loaded vessels." Within eleven years, eighty-four vessels of all sizes, from ships to sloops, had been built in the colony,[2] twenty-nine were then owned here, all but two or three of them in Newport, and the number of native seamen was one hundred and forty.[3]

We have before seen that Sabbatarian views prevailed to such an extent in Newport, that two weekly market

[1] At a General Assembly held at New Haven, Oct. 14, 1708. Antiquities of Conn., 338. This is the only instance we know of in New England history where it was proposed to use dogs to hunt down the Indians—a measure for which the United States government was so severely and justly condemned during the Seminole war.

[2] The classes of vessels built were ships, brigantines and sloops. The schooner, now the favorite rig for coasters, was as yet unknown. It is a purely American invention of later date. The first schooner was launched at Gloucester, Mass., in 1714. See 1 M. H. C., ix. 234, and x. 195.

[3] Br. S. P. O. Proprieties, vol. ix., pp. 87—90. R. I. Col. Rec., iv., 55—60.

CHAP. XIII. 1708. days were appointed to accommodate those who kept Saturday as the proper Sabbath.[1] A distinct church had been formed by some members of the Baptist Church under Dr. Clarke, and others who held these sentiments, over which the Rev. William Hiscox was pastor.[2] Previous to this a number of the members of Clarke's church had emigrated to Westerly,[3] where they afterwards embraced the Sabbatarian doctrine, and this year organized the second church of that order in the colony, in what is now Hopkinton, under the care of John Maxson, jr., as elder.[4] A year of warlike preparation now opened upon
1708-9 Feb. 28. the colonies. A royal order was issued announcing the intended invasion of Canada, and requiring aid to be furnished in accordance with a plan submitted by Col. Vetch, who was clothed with full powers to arrange the cam-
1709. Mar. 22. paign. Wharton, a London Solicitor, whom William Penn had employed in the interest of Rhode Island, during his agency, at forty pounds a year, had given such satisfaction, that the General Assembly increased his annual salary thirty pounds for his past services, and appointed him the colony agent hereafter, at a salary of eighty pounds. This arrangement closed the official connection between Rhode Island and the celebrated Penn. A tax of five hundred pounds was voted. A printing press was to be set up at Newport, and a public printer was appointed, for the first time, at this session. One Bradford, whose father was a printer in New York, proposed "to find paper and print all things that may relate to the colony and government, for fifty pounds per annum, if it be but for one year or two." The proposal was accepted for one year. The new Assembly were fully occupied in preparing for the Canada expedition, as required by the Queen's letter. A war tax of one thousand pounds was

[1] In May, 1677. See vol. i., chap. x., p. 427.

[2] In 1671. Elton's Callender, 119.

[3] In 1665. Ibid.

[4] Seventh Day Baptist Memorial, vol. i., p. 52.

levied, and a special council of war was appointed to aid the governor.[1] Capt. Edward Thurston was chosen commissary, to provide all military stores for the colony. May 4. Provision was made to entertain the Queen's messenger, Col. Vetch, and the commander-in-chief, Gen. Nicholson, former Lieutenant-Governor of New York, under Andros, at the public charge. Two vessels for war purposes were purchased by the colony, and several transports provided to carry the troops to Boston. Two hundred effective men were equipped and drilled for the service in little more than one month, and sailed for Nantasket, the rendezvous of the fleet, where they arrived in three days. June 19. There they were destined to remain for five months, under pay by the colony, but inactive owing to the non-arrival of the British fleet with which they were to co-operate. The colony sent a congratulatory address to Nicholson, 27. who was to command the land forces, fifteen hundred strong, raised in the provinces west and south of Rhode Island, and Gov. Cranston wrote him a private letter at the same time, in which he refers to his generosity in aiding the churches; Nicholson having been a liberal patron of Trinity church at its foundation.[2] Another tax of one thousand pounds was voted at the next session, and the proceeds of the sale of public lands in Narragansett were Aug. 31. also appropriated to the Canada expedition.[3] The unaccountable delay in the arrival of the promised fleet from England, without which the great efforts of the colonies must prove fruitless, caused a meeting of all the governors to consult with Vetch and Nicholson. This occasioned Sept. 30. a special session of the Assembly to be convened at Kingstown, at which a committee of eleven persons, five from

[1] It consisted of Major William Wanton, Major Henry Tew, Col. John Wanton, Job Almy, and Capt. John Brown.

[2] New York Colonial MSS. liii., 104. R. I. Col. Rec., iv. 73.

[3] The report of the committee on these lands subsequently made, shows the amount of £3,795 15*s* 10*d*, received for them, at the rate of about 1*s* 6*d* per acre, or 18¾ cents.

CHAP. XIII. 1709. Oct. 11. each house, with the deputy governor, was appointed to assist the governor at the meeting, and the full powers of the Assembly were delegated to them. As this congress was about to meet, news arrived from England of the defeat of the allies in Spain, and the consequent withdrawal of the fleet designed against Canada. An address to the Queen was adopted, urging the importance of reducing the French in North America, and praying assistance for that purpose.[1] A few days later the Rhode Island As-
26. sembly met at Warwick, and disbanded the troops and transports which all this time had been idly waiting near Boston. The expenses of this fruitless effort had fallen heavily upon all the colonies. Connecticut, New York, and New Jersey, following the example of Massachusetts, twenty years before, during the first expedition against Canada, of issuing bills of credit, now put out their first paper money. Rhode Island was soon to commit the
1709-10 Feb. 28. same serious error. Her expenses had exhausted the heavy tax already voted for the year, and at an adjourned session of the Assembly, a further tax of twelve hundred pounds was made. The price of all produce had risen, from the increased demand for military purposes.

1710. May 3. The same officers were re-chosen at the general election. Although so great efforts had been made the past year against the French, and without success, yet the war spirit remained undiminished. Massachusetts urged Connecticut and Rhode Island to unite in fitting out an armed
June 30. vessel to cruise for the protection of trade south of Cape Cod. A second attempt against Port Royal, destined to be more successful than that of three years before, was pro-

[1] This meeting of the governors was called by Col. Vetch to assemble at New London, but Newport was thought to be more convenient, so the members met there, but for some cause adjourned to Rehoboth. It was called for the 4th of Oct., but did not meet till the 12th or later; and was over before the 19th. The delay was for the sake of hearing from England, and the news received deprived the congress of the opportunity of doing any thing of importance except adopting the Address to the Queen. Historical Magazine, vol. iii., p. 123.

posed. Gov. Cranston convened the Assembly by special warrant. A recess of five days was taken, after which they voted to equip one hundred and fifty-five men, with stores for three months, and the necessary transports for the expedition.[1] To meet the extraordinary expenses thus incurred, Rhode Island adopted the plan pursued by her neighbors. An act for issuing bills of credit was passed. Five thousand pounds, in denominations from five pound to two shilling bills were issued, signed the sixteenth of August, and to be equal in value to current silver of New England, which was eight shillings to the ounce. The body of the bills recited that they should be received for all payments due to the treasury. A committee was appointed to sign them. They were to be redeemed in specie at the end of five years, and were secured by an annual tax of one thousand pounds, levied solely for this purpose. It was declared felony to counterfeit or deface them. Thus commenced in Rhode Island a system of paper money issues fraught with disaster to the commercial interests of the colony, whose baleful influence was to extend over nearly a century, distracting alike the political, financial, and even the social condition of the people, and which was to be the occasion of most bitter partisan strife long after the revolutionary war had left us an independent State. If we except the principles upon which the colony was founded, and which, from their intrinsic truth, have since become universal, this adoption of the paper money system is perhaps the first act of our colonial legislation, whose influence extends beyond the period of independence.

CHAP. XIII. 1710. July 25. 30.

The council of war called upon Rhode Island for more troops, and urged that two hundred men be sent from this colony. This was much more than her proportion, but was promptly allowed by the General Assembly at a

Aug. 14.

[1] The apportionment of this force among the towns, their rates of pay, and the list of stores provided, are detailed in the several acts of this session. See R. I. Col. Rec., iv. 93—96, 98.

CHAP. XIII. 1710. special session held for this purpose, and the draft for the additional forty-five men was appointed among the towns. Lest this voluntary increase of the quota should be taken as a precedent in future, it was resolved to address the Queen upon the subject. Lieutenant-Colonel John Cranston was appointed to command the Rhode Island forces, and another transport was taken up to convey the new levies. The fleet, consisting of twelve ships of war, and twenty-four transports, of which fourteen were in the pay of Massachusetts, two of New Hampshire, three of Rhode Island, and five of Connecticut, with five regiments, the
Sept. 18. whole under command of Gen. Nicholson, sailed from
24. Nantasket for Port Royal, where they arrived in six days. One of the Connecticut transports, the Mary, was wrecked
Oct. 2. and twenty-six men were drowned. The fort surrendered after a short siege, in which the English loss was only fourteen or fifteen men. The name of the port was changed to Annapolis Royal. Col. Vetch was left in command of the garrison, and the fleet returned in triumph to Boston.[1] Great was the joy throughout New England at this important success, and a gratuity was voted to Major George Lee, who brought the news to Rhode Island.

25. To give greater value to the bills of credit, the Assembly voted to receive them in payment of taxes, at five per cent. premium. A further issue of one thousand pounds in these bills was ordered. The pressure of business at the Court of Trials had become so great, and the causes often so trifling, that the plan, which for two years had been pursued by the Court of Appeals, was adopted, requiring a fee before entering any case upon the docket. Five shillings were hereafter to be paid by the plaintiff, upon commencing an action, to be returned to him if he recovered his suit. Much difficulty was caused by the arbitrary conduct of the revenue officers in exacting unu-

[1] Hutchinson's Mass., ii., 181.

sual fees, and in allowing but one port of entry for each colony, thus subjecting shipmasters to needless trouble, often injurious to their small trade, in obtaining their papers. Rhode Island established a table of fees, and enforced the statute with severe penalties. The subject was communicated to the Board of Trade by Gov. Cranston, enclosing a copy of the act, asking its confirmation by the Board, and also that the collectors be required to appoint deputies at each trading port.[1]

CHAP. XIII.

Nov. 15.

Again the Assembly was convened by the governor's warrant, it being the sixth session held during the year. The law against counterfeiting bills of credit did not embrace those issued by the other New England governments. These were now included in a new act of the same nature, and provision for the extradition of counterfeiters was made. Another issue of one thousand pounds was ordered, and a tax to redeem that amount of bills was levied. Two hundred and fifty pounds were sent to England to protect the interests of the colony.

27.

The subject of education, and other domestic regulations pertained to the towns. In Newport schools and highways received much attention. The public school was placed in charge of the town council, and a place was provided for Mr. Galloway to open a Latin school. The first town crier was appointed this year. A survey and plat of the town were made, and the council was required to give names to the streets and alleys. Liberty was granted to take limestone from the rocks in the harbor, to be made into lime.[2] In Providence the bridges were the chief object of attention, and often required the action of the legislature.[3]

1710--11. Jan. 31.

The Board of Trade favorably received the letter of Gov. Cranston, and in their reply required a copy of the

Feb, 19.

[1] Original, with attested copy of the Act and Table of Fees, in Br. S. P. O. Proprieties, vol. ix., pp. 7, 8. R. I. Col. Rec., iv. 108.

[2] Bull's Memoir of R. I., 1710—11.

[3] Staple's Annals, 186.

CHAP. XIII. 1711. March 27. laws of the colony to be sent to them, with the reasons for any that might be of a special character.[1] The Assembly accordingly ordered the laws to be prepared for the press. They also relieved all river craft, trading as far as Connecticut, from paying custom dues, and enacted that for free goods the officers should receive no fees. The northern boundary, after much negotiation, had been, as was supposed, satisfactorily adjusted.[2] The two commissioners were paid for their services, and surveyors were appointed to run out the line in accordance with the articles of agreement which had been prepared. But this arrangement proved not to be final or satisfactory. Massachusetts still claimed the land lying north of Pawtucket
May 2. River; so that several of the inhabitants of that tract petitioned the Assembly to sustain them in their rights as citizens of Rhode Island, and the governor was directed to prohibit the exercise of any other authority than that of this colony within the line recently established. The disputed territory was placed under the jurisdiction of Providence, and the officers of that town were required

[1] Br. S. P. O. Proprieties, vol. xxx., p. 262. R. I. Col. Rec., iv. 109.

[2] The R. I. Committee reported, Feb. 28, 1709—10, that when they met the Mass. men, it was found that these had not sufficient power to complete the business. They had therefore run the line by themselves. The Assembly, at that session, desiring a mutual agreement, requested Mass. to fully empower their committee. This was not done, but Col. Dudley intimated that if Major Joseph Jenckes was commissioned for the purpose, they two could agree upon a settlement. Jenckes was accordingly invested with full power for six months to treat with Dudley, July 30, 1710, upon the line from Pawtucket Falls north to Mass. south line, and thence west to Conn. At the October session, Jenckes was authorized to settle with Dudley on any other terms that he might think proper. R. I. was anxious for an adjustment. In November, Capt. Samuel Wilkinson was joined with Jenckes in the commission, and on 19th January, articles of settlement between the two colonies were drawn up, which being reported at this session, March 27, 1711, were accepted, and Major Jenckes and John Mumford were appointed to run the line in accordance therewith. For some reason this was not done at that time. May 25, 1715, the Mass. Assy. appointed a committee to carry out the agreement, and the next year, May, 1716, R. I. named commissioners to act with them.

to prevent any encroachment upon its limits. Westerly was entitled to only two deputies, but for some cause certificates were given by the town clerk to four. The return was declared void, and a new election ordered to be held forthwith. The three bridges on the high road laid out through the colony from Pawtucket River to Pawcatuck, over which the travel from Boston to New York chiefly passed, one at Pawtucket, one at Weybosset, now Market square in Providence, and one at Pawtuxet, had been built and kept in repair by private contribution in the several colonies interested in their maintenance. They required rebuilding, and an appropriation of two hundred pounds was made for this purpose, to be added to the sum raised by subscription. An act passed at this time for raising a troop of horse in the mainland towns. This was the third cavalry corps organized in the colony, and the second in this portion of it.[1] 1711. May 2.

Gov. Cranston informed Dudley of the Assembly's action in regard to the disputed territory, whereupon the legislature of Massachusetts voted to refer the matter to the Queen, and meanwhile to resist the authority of Rhode Island, forbidding the inhabitants from submitting thereto.[2] 28. June 14.

After the capture of Port Royal, General Nicholson, who, in the preceding autumn, had gone to England to secure aid for that expedition, encouraged by his former success, made a second voyage to urge the ministry to send out a still larger force this year for the conquest of Canada. To the surprise and delight of the colonies, this mission was also successful. Nicholson himself brought the news to Boston, and a few days later, while a convention of governors was held at New London to plan the campaign, the fleet arrived. The exertions of the colonists surpassed all they had hitherto made. A great deal was to be done in a short time, for the fleet had come without 21. 24.

[1] The first was on the island, Aug., 1667, prior to which the mounted men were not organized; the second was on the mainland, Oct., 1682.

[2] Mass. Files, vol. iii., p. 36, in R. I. H. S.

CHAP. XIII. provisions, and two armies were to be equipped at once.
All the legislatures were convened, and the most energetic
1711. measures adopted. Letters of thanks were everywhere
voted to the Queen and to Gen. Nicholson for their zeal in
defence of the colonies. Still there was a suspicion that
the Tory ministry of Ann intended some injury to New
England, where the people were all Whigs; and the
June 28. result tended to confirm this opinion. Rhode Island
raised a hundred and seventy-nine men, and furnished
vessels and stores for the expedition. The one thousand
pounds provided to meet the bills of credit, were diverted
to defray the expenses of the war, and an additional issue
of bills to the amount of six thousand pounds was
made.[1] By unparalleled exertions, in little more than a
month, every thing was ready, and the fleet, consisting of
fifteen ships of war, and forty transports under command
July 30. of Sir Hovendon Walker, with an army of five British
and two colonial regiments, amounting to nearly seven
thousand men, under Brigadier Hill, sailed from Boston.
On the same day Nicholson began his journey for Albany,
to take command of the colonial army that was to march
Aug. 14. against Montreal.[2] The fleet entered the St. Lawrence
safely, and there waited six days for the arrival of the
22. transports. Two days afterwards a violent storm caused
the loss of so many vessels, with nearly a thousand men,
that the expedition was abandoned. The time lost in
Gaspee Bay would have sufficed to reach Quebec. Nicholson
received news of the disaster before reaching Lake
Champlain, and immediately returned with his army. It
was attempted to throw the blame of this failure upon the
colonies, who were the severest sufferers by it, not only on
account of their efforts in fitting the expedition, but also

[1] The apportionment of this force, the prices and amount of provisions, and the pay of troops for the Canada expedition, are detailed in the several acts of this session. R. I. Col. Rec., iv., 120—4.

[2] The strength of this force is variously stated. Trumbull mentions it as 4,000 men. Hildreth says 2,300, of whom 800 were Indians.

from the exposure to French and Indian invasion with which they were now threatened. CHAP. XIII.

An adjourned session of the Assembly was held at Newport. Wharton, the Solicitor of Sir William Penn had died, and Penn, as agent of the colony, was requested to make out the account with the widow. A Massachusetts officer attempting to exercise authority in that part of Attleboro' claimed by Rhode Island, was seized, and required to give bonds to appear at the Court of Trials in Warwick. The legislature of that province appointed counsel to conduct the defence, and to assert their claim to the whole of Attleboro' as a part of the ancient domain of Plymouth.[1] 1711. Aug. 28. Oct. 26.

All the colonies adopted addresses to the Queen, setting forth their exertions, and desiring another expedition to be sent the next year against Canada. That of Rhode Island was prepared by the governor and council. The Assembly met at Warwick, to consider propositions for retaining the alliance of the Five Nations, who were suspected of a design to join the French. It was decided that Rhode Island should bear her part with the rest in this object, and a committee of two from each house[2] was chosen to assist the governor in the matter. A loan of three hundred pounds in bills of credit, for four years, without interest, was voted to James Green for services rendered twenty-five years before, and an issue of new bills to that amount was ordered. At the subsequent session, more important measures were adopted. The navigation act, that constant source of annoyance to Rhode Island, had been practically annulled by clandestine traders in several important particulars. To secure its better enforcement and to protect the interests of the people, a law was passed requiring all persons resident for three months in the colony and intending to leave, to advertise their in- 24. 1711-12. Feb. 27.

[1] Mass. Files, MS. vol. ii., fol. 116. R. I. H. S.

[2] Joseph Jenckes and Randall Holden of the Council. Nathaniel Sheffield and Benjamin Ellery of the Assembly.

CHAP. XIII. 1711-12. tention ten days beforehand, so that their creditors might have due notice.[1] A certificate that this had been done was to be presented to some officer in Newport before a permit to embark could be obtained. Shipmasters importing slaves into the colony, were required to furnish a sworn manifest, with full details, and to pay three pounds for each negro, and two pounds for an Indian, before being allowed to land. These acts were enforced with severe penalties, and all shipmasters were required to give bonds in the sum of fifty pounds at the naval office, for their proper observance of them. The earliest Quarantine act in Rhode Island was passed at this time, to prevent the introduction of small-pox, which had several times broken out in Newport. The statute of limitations, quieting land titles after twenty years' possession, the basis of the present State law upon the subject, was also enacted. The Chancery powers of the Assembly, which had been questioned seven years before in that body, were reconsidered at this session, owing to the reversal in England of a decision made by them upon appeal from the Court of Trials, in a question of land title, which was afterward heard before the Royal Council. The act constituting the Assembly a Court of Chancery was repealed, and the intention of erecting a proper Chancery Court was declared; but appeals "by way of petition," for relief in matters cognizable by the Assembly, were still to be allowed. The sealer of weights and measures, complained that they varied from those of the adjacent colonies, and proposed the introduction of metallic in place of wooden standards of measure, as being more exact. He was em-
1712. powered to obtain such, and to adjust them with those of
May 7. Massachusetts. The present year was one of very little historical importance, and we may therefore feel less regret at the loss of the colony records, of which only those of the spring session are preserved. No warlike en-

[1] A similar law exists at this day in Russia.

terprise being contemplated, the ship belonging to the colony was sold. The request for a bridge near Pawcatuck River, to be built by contribution, was allowed. Bridges and ferries were frequent subjects of legislation.[1] The latter was the only matter of public interest acted upon at the adjourned session, when the conditions and rates of ferriage were prescribed by statute, and the whole care of the ferries was placed in charge of a committee.

CHAP. XIII. 1712. June 30.

The war of the Spanish succession, known also as Queen Anne's war, which had lasted for eleven years, was drawing to a close. The prestige of British arms had been secured by the genius of Marlborough. The balance of power, that old idea of transatlantic diplomacy, so rashly attempted only a few years ago by European statesmen to be applied to the Western Continent, was satisfactorily adjusted, on what appeared to be a permanent basis, by the treaty of Utrecht. The ratifications were promptly exchanged by the belligerent parties a few days later, and peace once more smiled upon an exhausted world. The last war of religious and political principle was ended. A new era had commenced. Commercial privilege henceforth usurped the throne of priestly and kingly prerogative. Trade was to be the battle cry in future contests. Mercantile adventure and territorial aggrandizement were soon to become the occasion and the object of further strife, and colonial affairs, the conflict for the possession of the Western world, were ere long to assume an importance hitherto unknown. By the peace of Utrecht the

1713. April 11. NS 28.

[1] Gov. Cranston communicated to the Assembly, Feb. 27, 1711—12, a letter from Joseph Jenckes, stating that parties in Mass. would aid in erecting the bridge at Pawtucket, whereupon a letter was written to Mass. on the subject. On the 20th March, that colony appointed a committee to select a location for the bridge. The next year this committee reported, May 29, 1713, the best site to be at the Falls. The bridge was there built at a cost of £223 14*s.* 11*d.*, of which sum Mass. paid out of the public treasury £111 17*s.* 5½*d.*, as appears by a later record of her General Court, and afterwards, June 14, 1716, resolved to lay out a highway within that province, leading to the said bridge.

CHAP. XIII. 1713. crowns of France and Spain were forever disunited. Protestant ascendency and the peaceful accession of the House of Hanover were secured to England. Acadia, henceforth known as Nova Scotia, Newfoundland, and Hudson's Bay were given up to the British crown, and continental boundaries were defined very nearly as they exist at the present time. But two evils, destined to swell to colossal magnitude, grew out of this brilliant and decisive war; the national debt of England, and the increased stimulus given to the slave trade. A debt of fifty millions sterling was the burden entailed upon the British nation to this day, in return for the glory that their fathers won in this memorable struggle. Spain, stripped of her continental provinces, and losing upon her own soil the stronghold of Gibraltar, retained her colonial possessions under circumstances disastrous alike to herself and to her conquerors. The assiento, a contract with the old French Guinea company for furnishing Spanish America with negro slaves, which had been in operation for eleven years, was conveyed to the English by the treaty of Utrecht, and consigned to the South Sea Company, who thereby agreed to land forty-eight hundred slaves annually for thirty years, or 144,000 Africans, in the New World. By this treaty England became the great slave trader of Christendom, and from the spoils of African humanity, perpetuated the system of bondage over both Americas.

APPENDIX H.

ADMIRALTY ACT OF RHODE ISLAND, PASSED JANUARY 7, 1694 '5.

(FROM BRITISH STATE PAPER OFFICE. PROPRIETIES, VOL. 7.)

APP. H. Whereas Captain John Hore commander of the Dublin frigate of Jamaica hath by virtue of his commission granted by the Right honored Sir W^{m}. Beestow, Knt. their Maj^{ts}. Lieut-Govr., Commander in chief in and over their Island of Jamaica, and other the territories depending thereon in America, and Vice Admiral of the same, bearing date the 21st day of January, 1694, hath taken a Prize from the French, his Maj[ty]. publick Enemies, subjects to the French King, as appears by evidence of the Boatswain, Quarter-Master of the said Prize, and prays condemnation of said Prize and goods unto her belonging, of the honored Gov[r]. of their Maj[ts]. Colony of Rhode Island and Providence Plantations, and the Gov[r]. Dep. Gov[r]. and Generall Councill takeing the presentation and request of Capt[n]. John Hore and Comp[y]. into their serious consideration, having not, since the grant of our gratious Charter from King Charles the second of Blessed memory, had the like occasion for precedent, and seeing a necessity in these times of War to encourage those who serve his Maj[ty]. against his publick Enemies, doe conceive that by virtue of our Charter giveing full power to act in all things for the preservation of his Maj[ty's]. subjects and the Honor of the Crown of England, doe judge although in express words in our Charter we are not called nor mentioned an Admiralty, conceive we are in like manner authorized, and finding a necessity to encourage as aforesaid doe deem the General Council of this Colony to have the power of Admiralty of this Colony, that there may be a foundation laid to assist his Maj[ts]. subjects in these times of Warr until his Maj[ty's]. pleasure be further known.

These above written is voted an Act of the Generall Councill and is allowed and approved of by the General Assembly of the Colony, sitting the 7th day of Jan[r]. 1694, that the Generall Councill in such cases shall be deemed an Admiralty Court for the condemning of prizes, and other seafaring actions as occasion shall require.

The above writen is a true copy, as attested,

Weston Clarke, Secretary.

CHAPTER XIV.

1713—1727.

FROM THE PEACE OF UTRECHT APRIL 1713, TO THE DEATH OF GOVERNOR SAMUEL CRANSTON, APRIL 1727.

CHAP. XIV. 1713. April. THE treaty of Utrecht restored peace to the world. The colonies, relieved from the perils and the excitement of war, found leisure to devote to their internal condition. Political discussions arose, and parties were formed upon questions of domestic policy, that hitherto had been overlooked amid more exciting topics of thought. The paper-money system in various forms was soon to agitate society, commencing in Massachusetts, where the bills of credit originated.

May 5. The General Assembly met as usual, at Newport, the day previous to the election, for the purposes of organization and of admission of freemen.[1] This meeting, composed of the deputies and of all the freemen in person or by proxy, was commonly called the Court of Election, and upon it devolved the choice of the upper house, or court of assistants, ten in number, and of the general officers, who were the governor, deputy-governor, recorder, sheriff, general treasurer, general attorney, and two majors, one for the main, and one for the island towns. It was common for the Assembly to fill vacancies in the list of assist-

[1] This had long been an invariable custom. See Chap. xi., vol. i. p. 453.

ants from among those returned to the court of election as deputies, and then to elect new deputies to the places thus vacated. At this session the practice of electing a clerk of the Assembly, to serve in the house and not to be a member thereof, was introduced, and his salary fixed at six shillings a day.[1] A tax of five thousand pounds, payable in annual instalments for five years had been assessed, when the first bills of credit were issued, to secure their redemption, since which further issues of eight thousand pounds in bills had been made. To redeem these a tax for this amount was voted to take effect as soon as the former tax was paid in, and in the same manner. The military stores belonging to the colony were given up by the commissary; those of a perishable nature were sold, and the rest properly cared for. The cannon were tarred, and laid upon logs on the governor's wharf. It was ordered that the great highway from Pawtucket to Pawcatuck should be repaired, and a new one opened from Providence to Plainfield, through Warwick and West Greenwich.[2] Sometimes it happened, in cases of emergency, that special courts were convened to try cases at the request of parties interested. It was ordered, that in such cases the party who was cast in the suit should pay the entire costs of these special courts. This was the third act of this nature, in restraint of litigation, that had been passed with-

[1] John Hammett was the first clerk chosen by the Assembly under this law. The next year he was elected by the town of Newport to be the schoolmaster at the public school for three years. At the October session the above act was repealed, so far as required the clerk to be elected by the whole Assembly, and the deputies were left to choose a clerk or not as they saw fit, which had been the case ever since they were made a distinct branch of the Assembly in 1696.

[2] Another road to Plainfield from Providence had before been laid out by a different route, and both roads were received by the Assembly, October, 1714. But the next year the old road was closed by order of the Assembly, July, 1715, as it intersected the new one in many places, and both could not well be sustained.

CHAP. XIV. 1713. in five years.[1] For thirty-six years the commissioned officers of militia had been chosen by the towns, contrary to a provision of the charter requiring their election by the Assembly. The reason of this deviation was, that at that time the inhabitants were few, and for the most part
June 16. freemen. Of late some disturbances had occurred at these military elections. The act of 1677 was therefore repealed, and the ordinances of the charter upon this
Oct. 28. point were re-enacted. The autumn session at Warwick was occupied in hearing cases of appeal from the Court of Trials, and then adjourned to meet at Newport. Grain had become scarce, owing to the extent of its exportation
Nov. 25. to foreign countries. A law was passed to prohibit this, and the prices at which imported produce should be sold were fixed at ten shillings and sixpence a bushel for wheat, five shillings for rye, four shillings for corn and barley, and thirty shillings a hundred for flour and biscuit. The act was to be in force for one year. An account of the stock of provisions in Newport was taken, and a committee was appointed to register imports of
1713-14. these articles. Pedlars were forbidden, by a stringent statute, to sell dry goods anywhere in the colony. Two
Feb. 14. thousand pounds in bills of credit were ordered to be burnt. This order was not obeyed, and the neglect of it served to increase the excitement fast rising in the colony upon the money question.[2]

The paper-money system had become a political question of absorbing interest. Massachusetts was divided by it into three distinct parties. The smallest was the specie party, who desired to withdraw the bills of credit, and depend solely on a gold and silver currency. The other two were in favor of banks, based on radically different principles; one advocating a private bank system,

[1] The first was in October, 1708, for the Court of Appeals; the second in October, 1710, for the Court of Trials.

[2] Sir Edmund Andros died at this time, about February 20th, 1714, in London.

which was the issuing of bills of credit, secured upon real estate, to be received as money by all the members of the banking company, but at no fixed relative value as to gold and silver. This party was composed of persons whose affairs were more or less involved, or who owned real estate but had little ready money. The other party favored a public bank on the loan of bills from the government to any who would give mortgage security on their estates, with interest annually, to be applied to the support of government. This latter scheme had the most influential supporters, and being considered less objectionable than the private bank by the specie party, ultimately received their support, and after a struggle of more than a year, obtained the ascendency, and a public bank, or loan of fifty thousand pounds, for five years was created.[1] In Rhode Island the contest was narrowed to two parties, the specie or "hard money" party, and the paper money party; the latter favoring the further issue of bills of credit, and subsequently adopting the public bank system of Massachusetts. The controversy was conducted with great bitterness in both these colonies, distracting whole communities, and even dividing families. In Providence a town meeting had been held the past year, and a protest sent to the Assembly against the bills of credit. In the other towns the subject was no less earnestly discussed. We are, therefore, prepared to find a greater interest in the elections, and more complete changes in the members of the Assembly than had occurred since the old struggle between the Quakers, and the war party, forty years before. At this election the specie party triumphed. Of the twenty-eight deputies, composing the lower house, but six of the old members were returned. The former treasurer had neglected to comply with the act requiring

CHAP. XIV. 1714.

May 5.

[1] Hutchinson's Mass., ii. 207—9.*

* This form of banking originated in South Carolina, where, in 1712, a "bank" or stock of £48,000 was created, and the bills loaned to individuals to be repaid in annual instalments. Massachusetts followed two years later, as above related. Hildreth. His. of U. S., ii. 285.

CHAP. XIV. 1714. two thousand pounds of the bills to be burnt. A new treasurer was therefore chosen, and a new recorder was also elected. The treaty of peace enabled the colony to reduce its military expenses, and to discharge the garrison at Fort Ann.

May 22. The death of the deputy-governor, Walter Clarke, took place at this time. He had been in public life ever since Philip's war, during which he was first chosen deputy-governor. He had been four times elected governor,[1] and twenty-three times deputy-governor;[2] for the last fifteen years he had been successively chosen to that office. June 15. The Assembly elected Henry Tew to fill the vacancy. They also repealed all the existing militia laws, including the recent act vesting in the Assembly the choice of officers. Against this latter proceeding, as being a violation of the charter, the governor and four others,[3] entered a protest upon the records. The first burning of bills, to the amount of £1102, 8*s* 6*d*, all that could be collected for the purpose, was held in presence of both houses.

Aug. 1. Upon the death of Queen Anne, a regency was immediately appointed, and George I. was proclaimed the same day. Sept. 15. The news was brought to America by a merchant ship. No orders respecting the proclamation were received, but the several colonies acted upon the news 29. without awaiting official instructions. In Rhode Island the King was proclaimed by order of the governor and Oct. 27. council, and the Assembly afterward assumed the expenses of the ceremony. They also voted to raise three troops of horse, one on the island and two on the mainland, who were to choose their own officers, and to parade twice a 1714–15. year. The three bridges, ordered three years before, were

[1] 1676, '86, '96, and '97.

[2] In 1675. 1679 to 1685. 1700 to 1714 inclusive.

[3] Job Greene, assistant; William Wanton, William Coddington, and Simon Ray, jr., representatives.

at length completed.[1] The Assembly were convened to examine the accounts of the overseers, which were cut down, and the contractors were authorized to sue those delinquents who had not paid their subscriptions. CHAP. XIV. 1714-15. Feb. 23.

The most complete change occurred at the spring election; unparalleled, indeed, in the history of the State, so that it became known as "the great revolution." Deputy-governor Tew was dropped, and Joseph Jenckes elected in his place. Only five out of the twenty-eight former members were returned, and every assistant, save one, was removed. Yet, amid this storm of popular denunciation, Gov. Cranston retained his popularity, and kept his place. Both parties esteemed him too highly to remove so energetic and long tried an executive. The Yemassee war, now desolating South Carolina, caused many of the planters to remove. Several females, whose names indicate their Huguenot origin, fled to Rhode Island, bringing with them a few Indian slaves. These ladies petitioned the Assembly for relief from the import duty upon their slaves, which was granted. Since the death of Wharton the interest of the colony had suffered for want of an agent in England, and Richard Partridge was now appointed to that duty with a salary of forty pounds a year. The annual salary of the deputy-governor, which had long been but six pounds, was raised to twenty pounds. 1715. May 5. June 13.

Wolves were still so numerous that the old bounty of one pound a head was raised to thirty shillings.[2] Besides the public bounties that were paid for wolves and foxes, the towns often offered rewards for the destruction of vermin of various sorts within their precincts. Portsmouth paid one penny each for crows and blackbirds. Providence paid threepence each for gray squirrels, and afterwards offered the same price for rats. Wildcats, at

[1] See May, 1711 and 1712, and note on p. 47 ante.

[2] Two years later, October, 1717, this bounty was raised to £5, "the wolves yet abounding, to the unspeakable damage of the inhabitants," and in October, 1732, the bounty was doubled.

CHAP. XIV. 1715. a later period became so destructive, that a bounty of five shillings was offered for them by the Assembly, which was afterwards doubled.[1]

The statute premium upon bills of credit paid into the treasury for taxes was repealed, and the bills were required to be received at their par value hereafter. This was preparatory to the creation of a "bank," or loan, on

July 5. the principle before described. The Assembly deemed it necessary to recite in a preamble their reasons for this act, which were, the scarcity of specie or other mediums of exchange, consequent upon a decay of trade, the prostration of the agricultural interests, and the general distress among all classes, while the recent war expenses, and the present demands for money for works of public necessity could only be met, or remedied, by the measures proposed. Thirty thousand pounds in bills from five pounds to one shilling, were issued, and proportioned among the towns to be loaned to the people for ten years, at five per cent. interest, on mortgage security of double the value. The payment of interest was unfortunately secured by bonds instead of being included in the mortgages, by reason of which a large part of the interest was afterward lost to the colony. One thousand pounds of this interest money were to be annually applied to redeem the bills, and the rest to be used for the support of government. At a later session another issue of ten thou-

Oct. 26. sand pounds was voted, making forty thousand this year, known as the "first bank."

July. Newport, "as the metropolitan town in this colony," received a grant of funds derived from duties upon imported slaves, for the purpose of paving the street leading up to the colony house, and the duties accruing from the same source for seven years, were appropriated to pave other streets in the town, and to building a bridge across

[1] In February, 1733—4, a bounty of one pound was offered for bears, and the same sum for wild cats; and in October, 1736, the bounty on bears was raised to three pounds.

Potowomut River.[1] So many crimes had of late been perpetrated by Indian slaves, that it was forbidden to import them. To prevent fraudulent voting, every freeman was required to endorse his name at full length upon his ballot. This was the first passage of a law which, although it was repealed the next year,[2] was afterwards re-enacted, and continued in force until a very recent period. The punishment prescribed for illegal voting, was a fine of five pounds, or whipping, not to exceed twenty-one stripes, or imprisonment for one month, for each offence. More fugitives from South Carolina arrived, bringing nine Indian slaves into the colony. The Assembly remitted the duties, and permitted them to remain.

CHAP. XIV. 1715. Aug. 31.

The house of deputies was constantly changing its members, for they were elected semi-annually, and the service was not so much coveted as it has been in later times. The returns of this branch of the Assembly, would indicate as great a revulsion in public sentiment as that of the past year, only five of the old members retaining their seats; but the assistants and general officers remained nearly the same, and as these were elected annually, the day after the organization of the house, it is to them that we look with greater certainty for the proof of a political revolution. The influence of Governor Cranston is seen in the returns from Newport, where his son and his nephew both appear among the new deputies. The latter, Col. John Cranston, already distinguished for his naval exploits in the late war, was chosen Speaker of the House.

1716. May 1.

The most important act of this Assembly, one which illustrates the principles of the founders of the colony, shows that the spirit of religious freedom, in its original brightness, survived the trials to which it had been sub-

2.

[1] Called also "Reynolds' alias Hunt's River," in a later act. The bridge was completed the next year, at a cost of £49 5*s*. 6*d*., being nearly £11 less than the appropriation for it allowed.

[2] May 2, 1716.

CHAP. XIV. 1716. jected, and presents a striking contrast to the legislation upon the same subject that was passing at this very time in a neighboring colony, was an act "for the timely preventing" the various churches from "making use of the civil power for the enforcing of a maintenance for their respective ministers." To secure this object it was enacted "that what maintenance or salary may be thought needful or necessary by any of the churches, congregations, or societies of people now inhabiting, or that hereafter may inhabit within any part of this government, for the support of their, or either of their minister or ministers, may be raised by a free contribution, and no other ways."[1]

June 19. Starve Goat Island was granted, upon petition of three fishermen of Providence, for the purpose of curing and drying fish.

July 26. The small pox had again appeared in the colony. In Providence it is mentioned in the records, and at Newport a town meeting was held to order the immediate erection of a hospital on Coaster's Harbor Island, to be finished within one month.

Aug. 31. We have before seen that ample provision for education had early been made in Newport and Providence.

[1] The preamble to this act refers to that portion of the charter of Charles II., granting liberty of conscience, and adds, "it being a moral privilege due to every Christian, *as by His said Majesty is observed*, that true piety rightly grounded upon gospel principles, will give the best and greatest security to sovereignty," &c. The custom of holding the signer of a document, or, as in this case, the grantor of a charter, responsible for the language or the ideas it contains, is sometimes suggestive of strange incongruities. To those who are familiar with the private life of "the merry monarch," or know the character of his chief favorites and counsellors, Rochester, Buckingham, and the like, the terms of the declaration of Breda, and the above cited clause of the Rhode Island Charter, must appear as the "beautiful sentiments" of a veritable and royal Joseph Surface. The impression of the absurdity of such language from such lips is only removed when we remember its official nature, and that the draft of the charter was made by John Clarke—but who penned the declaration of Breda, therein partly embodied, is unknown.

Portsmouth now moved in the matter. By the recommendation of a committee to dispose of vacant lands on the south side of the town, "having considered how excellent an ornament learning is to mankind, and the great necessity there is in building of a public school house on said south side," the town made an appropriation for this object, and appointed a committee to build the school house, and to obtain contributions to finish it. The terms of the record would imply that a school already existed in the north, the old part of the town, but no trace of it remains. Six years later two other school houses were built.[1] CHAP. XIV. 1716. Sept. 10.

At the fall session in Providence, Gabriel Bernon presented a petition against one of the assistants, that caused some excitement. The charges were investigated, and being found to be false and slanderous, Bernon was required to send a written acknowledgment to the offended party, and his own conduct at the examination being indecorous to the Assembly, he was also compelled to ask pardon in writing, of that body.[2] Oct. 11. Nov. 2. 3.

At the annual election, the same general officers were continued. The accession of the House of Hanover caused many changes in colonial administration. In Massachusetts, Gov. Dudley was succeeded by Col. Shute, who, soon after his arrival, proposed to visit Rhode Island, and a public reception was voted to him by the Assembly. The care of the Indian lands was assumed by the colony upon petition of Ninigret, and overseers were appointed to lease the same for the benefit of the tribe, and to dispossess all trespassers. There was so little public business at this time, that a quorum at the adjourned session could not be convened. The attendance at Warwick was unusually small. Little was done beside the hearing of appeals and the passing of another act in restraint of litigation, 1717. May 1. June 18. Sept. 10. Oct. 30.

[1] March 18, 1723—they were ordered, one to be 16 feet square and the other 30x25 feet. Ports. Records.

[2] Both of these papers are printed in R. I. Col. Rec., iv., 215.

CHAP. XIV. 1717. whereby rehearings in causes settled by default, or by judgment obtained upon a bond were denied, except in special cases, and then additional costs were to be taxed.[1] Many attempts had been made to collect and arrange the laws upon demand of the home government, that copies of them should be sent to England. This had been partially accomplished by the perseverance of Lord Bellemont seventeen years before; but repeated efforts to put them in a form to print for the convenience of the people had failed. Of the many committees appointed for this duty, none had yet proved efficient. Another trial was now made, which was destined to terminate successfully in the publication of the earliest edition of the Laws of Rhode Island. The deputy-governor and two others, with the recorder[2] were elected for this difficult task, and it was afterwards[3] ordered that a copy of the charter should be printed with the laws.

A memorial was presented in behalf of Asquasuthuks, granddaughter of Miantinomi, setting forth her claim as
1718. heir to the Narraganset lands. A long reply was made
May 2. to it at the next session, disproving her claim, and curiously enough tracing the title through old Ninigret, as the survivor of, and joint tenant of the sachemdom with Casuckqunce, who was the brother and successor of Miantinomi, after the murder of the latter, to his son the present Niantic sachem.[4] The frauds practised upon Indians occasioned the passage of an act to permit their being sued for debt,[5] and forbidding their being held to service without
June 17. a valid consideration. It was ordered that a real estate of

[1] Public Laws, edit. 1719, p. 84.

[2] Joseph Jenckes, Thomas Fry, Nathaniel Nudigate and Richard Ward.

[3] Sept. 18, 1718.

[4] This curious document is printed in full in R. I. Col. Rec., iv., 229—33.

[5] This act was chiefly intended to prevent drunkenness, by depriving the Indians of credit at the taverns. It was construed to apply to all Indians, in all cases, so that in June, 1724, an explanatory act was passed, limiting its application to the descendants of old Ninigret, and subjecting all other Indians to action for debt, except for liquors.

CHAP. XIV.

the value of fifty pounds should entitle its possessor to be an inhabitant in the town where it was located if he chose to settle there.[1] A new and very complete militia law was enacted, reorganizing the whole system. It is in this act that the title of "Captain, General, and Commander-in-chief" was given to the governor, and that of Lieutenant-general to the deputy-governor. All the commissioned officers were to be chosen by the General Assembly, as required by charter. Every company was to parade twice a year, and a "general muster" or regimental training was to be held once in five years. The power of the governor to equip a force against privateers or pirates was confirmed, and the prizes taken were to enure to the captors. Whoever was disabled upon such a service was to be pensioned for life. The English law of primogeniture, whereby the whole real estate of an intestate descended to his eldest son, was modified by the statute of distributions giving to the widow one-third of the property, the remainder to be equally divided among the children, except that the eldest son should receive a double share. This law, with the exception of the latter clause, although repealed ten years later, was subsequently re-enacted, and remains the same in substance at the present time. To discourage vexatious suits, two and sixpence for every ten miles of travel, and two shillings a day for attendance, were allowed to the party obtaining judgment and to the witnesses in the case, to be taxed in the bill of costs.[2] At the adjourned session, a few old bills of credit were burnt, and some pirates at Newport jail were held for trial till the King's will could be known whether they should be tried here or sent to England The governor and nearly one-half of the members were absent from the meeting of the Assembly at Providence.

1718. June 17.

Sept. 9.

Oct. 29.

[1] The distinction between a resident and an inhabitant, should here be borne in mind. See chap. viii., vol. i., p. 256.

[2] This was the fifth act in restraint of litigation that had been passed within ten years.

CHAP. XIV. 1718. To facilitate business at the Court of Trials, it was forbidden that more than two attorneys should plead on the same side in any cause, one of whom must be a freeholder of the colony. Connecticut had passed laws regulating trade with the other colonies, and levying duties upon them, which were injurious to her neighbors, and in violation of the acts of trade and navigation. A recent order had been made by the Board of Trade, requiring all acts upon this subject to be sent to them for approval before being executed, but it had never been received in the colonies. In consequence of this, Kay, the collector of
Nov. 24. Newport, wrote to the Board, requesting that the order should be sent without delay.[1]

1719. The first edition of the Laws of Rhode Island was printed in Boston early in the year. The Assembly took
May 6. eighty copies, of which one was given to each member, and the remainder distributed among the towns.[2] Since the report of the commissioners on the Massachusetts line was made to the Assembly,[3] much negotiation had been
June 16. had on the subject, many obstacles to a settlement had been surmounted, and the line had finally been run.[4] A

[1] Br. S. P. O., Proprieties, vol. x., p. 175. See R. I. Col. Rec., iv. 244.

[2] Copies of this edition are now very rare. It has two title-pages, the first prefacing the charter, which occupies 8 pages, and then comes the title-page to the laws, which fill 102 pages. The imprint is on each title-page, and reads "Boston, in New England. Printed by John Allen, for Nicholas Boone, at the sign of the Bible, in Cornhill, 1719." On the second title-page the date, by error of type, is 1179.

[3] March 27, 1711. See p. 42, and note 2, ante.

[4] May 25, 1715, Mass. appointed a committee to run the line according to the agreement made at Roxbury 17th Jan., 1710–11, and the next year, May, 1716, R. I. named commissioners to act with them. Nothing more was done till, upon petition of the people of Mendon, a new committee was appointed Nov. 21, 1716. The season was too far advanced to proceed that winter. At the May session, 1717, the R. I. Committee was continued, with more ample powers. June 18, 1717, the Mass. Committee was directed to perform the work within four months. On 22d Nov., they were vested with equal powers with the R. I. men, but both committees felt bound by the Roxbury agreement of seven years before. To remove this obstacle the R. I. Assy. in June, 1718, vested their committee with plenary powers

joint report of the commissioners of both colonies was made, establishing the line, and approved by the Assembly. This settlement embraced only the northern line of the colony, and time has proved that even that adjustment was not to remain undisturbed. The whole eastern line between the old colony of Plymouth and Rhode Island was still open, and remained for years the subject of frequent and bitter contention. CHAP. XIV. 1719.

John Clarke had devised certain real estate in Newport for the relief of the poor, and the education of youth. The bequest having been diverted from its object, a statute to punish breaches of trust in such cases was enacted. The town councils were constituted a court of inquiry to compel trustees to a proper discharge of their trusts, with power to issue execution upon the estates of delinquents. An appeal from their judgment might be taken to the governor and council.

Parliament had lately passed an act to prevent frauds in the customs, wherein the quality of pitch and tar imported from the plantations was directed to be examined. The act was transmitted by William Popple, Secretary of the Board of Trade, to this colony, together with a statement of the Russian methods of making tar and raising hemp.[1] The independence of English restraint, assumed by the charter governments, was a source of great annoyance to the crown officers in those colonies, and Aug. 26.

to settle by compromise. The two committees met at Rehoboth, Oct. 22, 1718, and agreed upon preliminaries, and on the 29th, the R. I. men reported to the Assy. This report and the acts of Mass. on the subject, were ordered to be entered on the records, which was done Dec. 9th. On 12th May, 1719, the two committees again met on Wrentham Plain, and run the line to a point two miles west of Alum Pond, finishing it in two days. The report was signed at Five Mile River, May 14, 1719, presented, approved, and entered upon the records of both colonies in June.

[1] The autograph letter of Popple, with the method of preparing tar in Russia, is preserved in the Foster Papers, Miscellaneous, vol. 3. The revenue act, and the Russian mode of raising hemp, accompanying it, have disappeared.

CHAP. XIV. many and bitter were the complaints made by them to the Board of Trade. Caleb Heathcote, in a very long letter
1719. from Newport, mentioned the acts of Rhode Island that
Sept. 7. conflicted with the authority of the crown, the chief of which were those for issuing bills of credit, and for regulating custom fees; the latter being specially grievous to the writer. He relates the seizure of some smuggled claret wine that was rescued by a mob, and how immediately afterward, John Wanton, to please the people, had issued a warrant against the collector upon a charge of extortion in clearing vessels. Kay was acquitted by the governor, and at once arrested a second time by Wanton on a similar charge, and committed without bail. These proceedings occasioned the letter in which Heathcote complains of the charter, and urges that all laws should be approved in England before being operative in Rhode Island.[1]

8. At the September session, nothing of interest occurred. At Warwick the Assembly empowered the town councils
Oct. 28. to preserve and improve the fishing in their rivers, forbidding the setting of weirs, dams, or nets, and also established vendue masters in every town, to be chosen at the annual election, whose fees were to be two and a half per cent. on the amount of sales, and who were to settle with the owners of the goods within five days. An order having been received to send home a map of the colony, a committee was appointed to run the lines and make a chart.[2] This revived the question of the Western boundary line, which had been agreed upon seventeen years before, but had not yet been run by a joint commission of the two colonies, although there had of late been some negotiation to that end, and committees had already been

[1] Original in Br. S. P. O., Proprieties, vol. xi., R. 15. See R. I. Col. Rec., iv. 258.

[2] Joseph Jenckes, Randal Holden, Wm. Wanton, and Thomas Fry, were the committee, with John Mumford as surveyor.

CHAP. XIV.

appointed for the purpose.[1] Prompt action was now required, but when the committees met at Warwick, they could not agree as to their powers. Those of Connecticut were authorized only to run the twenty-mile line west from Warwick Neck, while the Rhode Island men were required to run all the lines, and would not permit the others to join with them in any part of the survey unless they would unite in the whole. It was, however, agreed that they should accompany the Rhode Island men while they run the twenty-mile line, which was completed the next day, and a report was drawn by the surveyor of the Connecticut commission, to be presented to his government.[2] The Rhode Island survey was completed, and the map presented at the next session. The Connecticut Assembly mildly resented the treatment their commissioners had received, and directed a letter to be sent to Rhode Island, expressing their surprise, which was done.[3] The Rhode Island Assembly at once sent a commission to take depositions at Westerly, respecting the acts of the royal commissioners of 1664, preparatory to presenting the case to the King, and also despatched a messenger to Connecticut to learn whether that colony would abide by the agreement formerly made as to the boundary.

1720. April 12. 13. 18. May 4. 12. June 1. 14.

[1] June 22, 1703, R. I. appointed surveyors to run the line according to the agreement made at Stonington, May 12. Connecticut neglected the matter, and thus it rested till June 15, 1714, when the R. I. Assy. empowered the governor to appoint a joint committee with Conn. to run the lines. In Nov., 1716, the R. I. Committee was appointed. In May, 1719, the Conn. Assy. ordered a survey, in connection with a R. I. Commission, to ascertain the terminus of a twenty-mile line west from Warwick Neck, and thus to establish the Eastern line of that colony, and notified R. I. accordingly. On 16th June, the R. I. Assy. named commissioners to unite with them to run the whole division line, and on 8th Sept., ordered them to meet on 6th Oct., which the Conn. men failed to do, so that on 28th Oct. the Assy. instructed their men to run the line alone, unless Conn. would join. Both commissioners met, as above, April 12, 1720, at Warwick.

[2] This Report, from Conn. Records, Colonial Boundaries, vol. i., Doc. 208, is in R. I. Col. Rec., iv. 273.

[3] R. I. Col. Rec., iv. 275.

CHAP. XIV. 1720. Another proof of the respect for the rights of conscience, entertained in Rhode Island, was given by this Assembly. The words "as in the presence of God," in the engagement given to the deputies, being objected to by many persons, whose service was thus lost to the colony, they were ordered in future to be stricken from the form. The population of Providence, then including the entire county, had increased so much that great inconvenience was felt in the more remote portions of the township at attending the military parades. The north-west part was therefore made a separate military district, having its own trainband.

The letter of Gov. Cranston, explaining the map, briefly stated the disputes between this colony and her neighbors. The territory claimed by Rhode Island, was bounded by red lines, within which were green lines to show what she actually possessed, the disputed tracts being between the two lines. As these disputes were soon to be referred to the King in council, this call for the map was timely.[1]

July 7. Connecticut having refused to abide by the agreement of the commissioners of 1703, the Assembly met at Newport and appointed the deputy-governor, Joseph Jenckes, its joint agent with Partridge, to bring both boundary disputes before the King. Three hundred pounds were voted for this purpose, and Jenckes was empowered to draw for seven hundred pounds besides; sixty pounds were given him for an outfit, and the same sum annually was allowed for his salary, together with his expenses. Connecticut was duly notified of this action, that she might be prepared to meet it. The letter written on this occasion, charges that "through the private and clandestine deception of your agent, Col. Winthrop, you got your charter to be bounded upon the Narraganset River, contrary to

[1] The original letter, but without the map, is in Br. S. P. O., Proprieties, vol. x., Q. 206, and is printed in R. I. C. R., iv. 279.

his solemn promise and engagement to our agent, Mr. CHAP.
John Clarke."[1] Rarely, indeed, in the course of this pro- XIV.
tracted and angry controversy, had Rhode Island retorted 1720.
upon Winthrop the abuse so freely heaped by her enemies July
upon Clarke, and which was equally unjust to both, although she had better reason for doing so, than they had
to assail her agent. But the secret history of that transaction had not then been divulged. Rhode Island only
knew the deep wrong she was suffering, and which she
had reason to suppose was due to the duplicity of Winthrop. That the Atherton company had a secret agent in
London, capable of any infamy, was known in that day
only to the parties interested, and they were her bitterest
enemies.[2]

The Assembly met again at Newport, to commission 27.
Doctor John Jenckes to attend upon his father, and appropriated thirty pounds for his outfit, and the same sum for
his salary. Testimony was taken concerning the source Aug. 16.
of Pawcatuck River. Every thing being ready, Rhode
Island again notified Connecticut to prepare for the trial, 18.
informing her of the day on which Jenckes was to sail.
Gov. Saltonstall replied in a very courteous letter to Gov.
Cranston, full of kind expressions of personal regard for 22.
himself and for Col. Jenckes. The next day he sent to
Mr. Dummer, agent of Connecticut, a brief of the con- 23.
troversy, stating that Rhode Island claimed ten miles west
of Pawcatuck River, but for which enhanced claim the
dispute would not have been revived. The old claim over
the whole of Narraganset to the bay, was thus virtually
waived, as by the agreement of 1703, and the difference
rested upon what was the real source or head of Pawcatuck River.[3] This varies from the official letter of Con- Sept. 14.

[1] R. I. Hist. Soc., Conn. MSS., vol. ii., p. 56. R. I. Col. Rec., iv. 276.

[2] This subject is fully discussed in chap. ix., and its appendices C. & E., vol. i., pp. 298–301, 371–6, 383–6.

[3] The above letters are printed in R. I. Col. Rec., iv. 280–3. John Jenckes died shortly after reaching England.

CHAP. XIV. necticut, to the Board of Trade, accompanying a map of that colony, wherein the old claim to Narraganset is earnestly urged.[1] 1720. Oct. 26. Nothing remained to be done by the Assembly at Providence. Jenckes had already arrived in England, and in connection with Partridge, presented a 1720-1 Jan. 3. petition to the King for redress,[2] which was referred to the committee on appeals, who, after hearing both parties, Feb. 20. ordered Dummer to return an answer in writing, within one week, and postponed a rehearing till the next summer. Dummer's answer rested upon the old plea that Nar- 25. raganset and Pawcatuck Rivers were different streams, and denied that Connecticut claimed any thing beyond what her charter included.[3]

A singular tradition relating to Block Island had its origin about this time, in the loss, near that place, of the emigrant ship Palatine from Holland, bound to Pennsylvania. Most of the passengers had died from disease and hardship, caused, as they supposed, by a design of the captain to get possession of their effects. Some seventeen of the survivors were landed on the island, all but three of whom died. One lady who had much gold and silver plate on board, refused to land. The ship floated off the rocks and soon after disappeared, never to be heard from again. One year later, a curious irradiation, like a blaze of fire, emitting luminous rays, was seen to rise from the ocean near the north end of the island. This appearance was considered supernatural, and from its supposed connection with the mysterious crime that involved the ill-fated ship, was known as the Palatine light. It appeared at irregular intervals down to 1832, since which it has not been seen. This light has been the theme of much learned discussion within the present century, and while the superstition connected with it is of course rejected, science

[1] Br. S. P. O., Proprieties, vol. xi., R. 2.

[2] Br. S. P. O., Proprieties, vol. xi., R. 8. R. I. Col. Rec., iv. 283.

[3] Br. S. P. O., Proprieties, vol. xi., R. 8.

has failed thus far in giving to it a satisfactory explanation.[1] CHAP. XIV.

At the spring election, John Wanton was chosen deputy-governor. Samuel Bissell of Newport, a blacksmith, petitioned the Assembly for encouragement to carry on the manufacture of nails, and received a loan of two hundred pounds from the treasury for that purpose.[2] The salary of the assistants, paid by the colony, was fixed at ten pounds, and that of the deputies at six shillings a day, instead of three shillings as formerly, to be paid by the towns. A second bank, or public loan of forty thousand pounds in bills of credit was made for similar reasons, and on the same terms as the former loan. Hemp or flax was to be received in payment of the interest, the former at eightpence, the latter at tenpence a pound, one-half of which was to be divided ratably among the towns, and the other half was appropriated to repairing Fort Ann. So scarce had specie become, that an English halfpenny was received at three halfpence. Col. Jenckes had returned from England to collect further evidence in the western boundary suit. Connecticut, equally alive to her interest, sent to her agent a very long and elaborate argument with voluminous testimony in defence of her claim.[3]

1721. May 3.

June 13.

20.

The small-pox was raging with great violence in Boston, where it had been introduced from the West Indies in the spring.[4] In Newport a quarantine building had been erected by order of the town[5] on Coasters' Harbor,

[1] See Appendix I., for further information about the Palatine light.

[2] The manufacture of iron, in various forms, has always been a prominent branch of industry in this vicinity. It is said, that the first cold cut nail in the world was made in 1777, by Jeremiah Wilkinson, of Cumberland, R. I., who died in 1832, at the advanced age of 90 years.

[3] The letter of Gov. Saltonstall to Mr. Dummer, sent at this time, occupies forty pages of manuscript, exclusive of the testimony, and is in Conn. documents, vol. ii., pp. 73–113, in R. I. Hist. Soc.

[4] In Boston there were 5,889 cases, of whom 844 died. Hutchison's Mass., ii. 273–6.

[5] April 26.

CHAP. XIV. at some distance from the hospital. The Turkish discovery of inoculation had just been made known in England,[1]
1721. but was violently opposed in Massachusetts by the medical profession, only one of whom, Dr. Boyleston, dared to practise it in opposition to popular prejudice. Even a bill to prohibit it passed the House of Representatives, but was stopped in the council. The General Assembly
Aug. passed an act in order to prevent the disease from spread-
10. ing to this colony, requiring all goods brought from Massachusetts, by land or sea, to be aired and cleansed, all vessels from infected ports to be quarantined, and travellers from that colony to be detained five days on the frontier, under heavy penalties.

New York and Massachusetts both presented claims
Oct. upon this colony for expenses in the late war, which the
25. Assembly rejected as Rhode Island had paid her full proportion. The committee to whom the boundary petitions had been referred a year ago, desired to have the opinion
1721-2 of the Board of Trade on the subject before rendering a
Jan. decision. They therefore referred it to that Board to as-
19. certain the boundaries of the two colonies, and a few days later the Duke of Hamilton, whose ancient claim included the disputed lands, sought to revive that long-slumbering
24. question by asking for a copy of the report made upon the petition of his grandmother, the late duchess, twenty-five years before.[2]

Feb. Collector Kay wrote to Secretary Popple against the
27. late issue of bills of credit, the effect of which had been to raise the value of all produce, and to encourage speculation in lands to the exclusion of new settlers.[3] These colonial banks were in some sense a violation of the acts of trade, the renewal of which was from time to time
1722. required from the colonies, with bonds for their proper

[1] See chap. xii., vol. i., p. 523, note 1.

[2] Br. S. P. O., Proprieties, vol. xi., R. 8 and 9. R. I. Col. Rec., iv. 291. See chap. xii., vol. i., pp. 537, 538.

[3] Br. S. P. O., Proprieties, vol. xi., R. 12.

observance. The Board of Trade applied to the Attorney- CHAP.
General to furnish the form of a bond, to be sent out with XIV.
fresh instructions to the colonies. The desired draft not 1722.
being sent, the request was renewed.[1] The form of the April 16.
bond was sent, to be entered into by the governor of 24.
Rhode Island, the location of which colony was therein 27.
described as being "in the West Indies in America."

At the election, Joseph Jenckes was re-elected deputy- May 2.
governor in place of John Wanton, and the salary of that
office was raised to thirty pounds. Additional depositions
were taken upon the western boundary, and sent home,
with the agreement of 1703, certified by the governor. June
At the same time Dummer presented to the Board his 7.
very long and elaborate argument in behalf of Connecticut.

The town of Kingstown had become sufficiently populous to form two towns, and a committee was appointed 19.
to make the division. Each was to have one assistant, which was an apparent violation of the charter prescription that there should be ten assistants, to be chosen by general ticket. Hence arose the custom of choosing the assistants, one from each town, which is continued at the present day in the constitution of the State Senate, composed of one member from every town in the State. Several subdivisions of military districts, similar to those already made in Providence, were accorded to other towns.

Questions of admiralty jurisdiction had risen between
Rhode Island and Massachusetts, which were referred to
the Lords of Admiralty, who applied to the Board of Trade 28.
for a copy of the charter and of the order in council, issued nineteen years before, restraining Rhode Island from
exercising that power. The charter was furnished, but July 7.
the order was not, and that with the other papers relating
to the quarrel with Dudley upon this subject, were again
applied for, but the matter proceeded no further.[2] 10.

[1] Br. S. P. O., Proprieties, vol. xxxi., pp. 243, 245.

[2] See chap. xiii., pp. 17, 18, ante.

CHAP. XIV. 1722. Aug. 28. An exclusive bounty for ten years, of one pound for each bolt of hemp duck made in Rhode Island, that should be equal to Holland duck, was granted to William Borden.[1] The argument of Rhode Island in reply to Connecticut was sent to the Secretary of the Board of Trade, by Oct. 8. Mr. Partridge, with a letter asking a speedy hearing "in case they should not think fit to report in our favor without, which its not improbable they may, the manifest plainness and justice of our case considered." An Indian war, that was to last three years, had broken out at the eastward, instigated by the French. Gov. Shute applied 31. to Rhode Island for aid. A messenger was sent by the Assembly to arrange with him for the quota of men or money to be furnished by this colony, but we can find no record of what was done in the matter.

1722-3 Feb. 15. At the hearing before the Board of Trade in the case of Connecticut and Rhode Island, a vast mass of testimony with all the original evidence from the time of the charter, a period of sixty years, was presented by the March 22. rival parties.[2] The Board rendered a very full report to the Privy Council, condensing the arguments on either side, deciding that Rhode Island, if not technically right, was clearly so morally, and concluding with the wish that both colonies might voluntarily surrender their charters and be annexed to New Hampshire![3]

Feb. 26. The Kingstown committee reported to the Assembly at Providence, a line of division between North and South Kingstown, which was accepted, and the townsmen were ordered to proceed with their elections as other towns.

[1] A loan of £500 for three years, on mortgage security, was afterward, May, 1725, made to him for assistance in the manufacture of duck, and in June, 1728, another loan of £3,000 for ten years was made, he to manufacture 150 bolts of duck annually.

[2] Nearly all the documents referred to in this year, except the final Report of the Board of Trade, are found in Br. S. P. O., Proprieties, vol. xi., filling almost the whole volume.

[3] Br. S. P. O., Proprieties, vol. xxxi., pp. 280–96. R. I. Col. Rec., iv. 303–8.

Charters were prepared for both towns, the old one being void by the act of division. North Kingstown retained the records and was declared to be the older town. CHAP. XIV. 1723.

A great storm that occurred this winter, carried away the pier at Block Island. To construct a new one the people of New Shoreham were authorized by the Assembly May 3. to collect subscriptions in the colony, and to levy a tax upon the town; and afterward received an appropriation June 18. of a hundred and twenty-three pounds for that object.

Extensive piracies had been recently committed in the West Indies and along the American coast by two sloops, which, sailing northward, at length attacked the British sloop of war Greyhound, of twenty guns, off Long Island, 10. mistaking her for a merchant ship. On discovering their error, one of the piratical vessels escaped, the other was captured and taken to Newport with her crew of thirty-six men. The Assembly ordered a military force to guard 18. the prison. An admiralty court was summoned to try July the prisoners. William Dummer, Lieutenant-governor 10. of Massachusetts, president; Richard Ward, register; Jahleel Brenton, jr., provost marshal; with the governor and collector of Rhode Island, four of the Massachusetts council, and some other officers formed the court. The trial occupied two days, resulting in the conviction of twenty-six of the pirates, who were sentenced to be hanged. 11–12. It was a great event in the history of those times.[1] The execution took place on Gravelly Point, called also Bull's 19. Point in the printed account, and the bodies were buried on Goat Island shore, between high and low-water mark.

The Privy Council, to whom the report of the Board of Trade upon the boundary dispute with Connecticut, was made in March, referred it back to the Board to inquire 17. of the agents whether their principals would agree to the recommendations therein contained, and if the agents were

[1] The trial was published in pamphlet form in Boston, and is reprinted in full in Bull's Memoirs of R. I., which appeared in the R. I. Republican, 1832–6, and are now being republished in the Newport Mercury

CHAP. XIV. 1723. July 17. not empowered to treat on that subject, then to direct them to apply to their respective colonies for instructions thereupon. Nor was this dispute the only matter that gave trouble to the home government. The order in council, requiring a bond in the sum of two thousand pounds for the taking the oath and for the due observance of the acts of trade and navigation, was considered a great hardship by this colony. For twenty-five years Gov. Cranston had taken the required oath and faithfully kept it, so that this new movement was felt to be oppressive and in violation of the chartered rights of Rhode Island. Partridge, the agent, had protested against it in a petition to the King at the time the order and instructions to the Governor of Massachusetts were sent over, fifteen months before, and had asked for its repeal. The council to whom his petition was referred, now in turn referred it to the
26. Board of Trade to inquire what powers were reserved to the King in the Rhode Island charter, and how far the oaths had been taken, and the acts of trade observed in the colony.

31. The first alms house in Rhode Island was erected at this time in Newport, by a vote of the town.

The northern boundary line had been run according to the terms of the compromise agreement at Rehoboth, whereby a tract one mile in width, belonging to Rhode Island by the former agreement made at Roxbury, was conceded to Massachusetts, upon which, it proved, that some farms had already been laid out by Providence men. The understanding was, that such farms should be confirmed to their owners in consideration of this concession, and that Mr. Belling should have a tract of seven hundred acres which he had improved within the line of Providence. Local geography was but little understood in those days, as we have before seen in the case of Narraganset,[1] so that to carry out the Rehoboth agreement, this

[1] See chap. ix., vol. i., pp. 298, 382.

further explanation was necessary. The Massachusetts council voted to confirm the Providence titles, but the representatives refused to concur. The government of Rhode Island therefore wrote to Gov. Shute, that if the House should non-concur, upon a reconsideration of the matter, they would expect Massachusetts to appoint a committee, in connection with Rhode Island, to measure off the said mile of land to the town of Providence, according to the Roxbury agreement.[1] Thus this dispute, settled at Five Mile River, was renewed by the failure of Massachusetts to confirm the promise of their commissioners. The General Assembly took no action upon the subject at present.

CHAP. XIV. 1723. Aug. 6.

Sept. 10.

The government of Connecticut, having received from their agent the proposal to surrender the charter, addressed a brief reply to the Board of Trade, declining to do so; and recognizing the boundary question as the occasion of this startling proposition, they avowed their readiness to abide forever by the King's decision upon it.

Oct. 28.

Although Bristol county was still under the jurisdiction of Massachusetts, and was destined to remain so for many years, whatever of interest occurred there at this period, may properly be included in the history of the State. By the letters of Rev. N. Cotton, of the Congregational Church at Bristol, we learn that two great calamities at this time visited the town. The first was a destructive fire, whereby two valuable buildings, with "sundry English goods," were consumed, and two nights later a violent storm broke up all the wharves, destroyed the bridges and drove several vessels on shore, doing damage to the extent of two thousand pounds.[2]

30.

At the autumn session of the Assembly, the letter of Richard Partridge containing the proposal for a surrender

Nov. 26.

[1] See pp. 42, 62, and notes, ante. MS. Letters and Papers of Mass., 1st series, vol. ii., p. 124, in R. I. Hist. Soc. R. I. Col. Rec., iv. 335.

[2] MS. Letters and Papers of Mass., 1st series, vol. i., p. 130, in R. I. Hist. Soc.

CHAP. XIV. 1723. of the charter was presented, and an answer returned at great length. In this reply the colony rehearsed their early history, and then proceeded to answer the four points upon which the proposition was based, arguing that such a course would neither be for the interest of Great Britain, nor tend to quiet the dispute, nor aid the defence of the country, nor promote trade. In the course of the argument, they took occasion to read a lesson in geography to the Lords of Trade for proposing annexation to New Hampshire. This lesson was further en-
1723-4 Feb. 10. forced by Partridge in his letter to the Board, inclosing that from Rhode Island, wherein he presents an abstract of the inclosure, and asks that a hearing upon the original question of boundary may be speedily granted.[1]

An Episcopal Church had already been formed, three years before in Bristol, under the care of Mr. Orem, who was succeeded by Rev. John Usher, the past year, both having been sent out by the Society for propagating the Gospel. The first Episcopal Church in Providence, and the third in the colony, as it then existed, owed its origin to the persevering piety of Gabriel Bernon, the first signer of the petition for Trinity Church in Newport, twenty-five years before. Rev. James McSparran, who for two years past had been settled over St. Paul's Church in Kingstown, as a missionary from the English Society, was the first to conduct public service according to the forms of the church of England in this town.[2] A sufficient sum was raised by subscription to erect a church, which was built this year upon the spot now occupied by St. John's Church, and after standing eighty-seven years, gave place to the present beautiful structure.[3] Rev. George Pigot

[1] R. I. Col. Rec., iv. 334. All the documents above referred to in this year, are in Br. S. P. O., Proprieties, vol. xi.

[2] Dr. Humfries assigns that honor to Honeyman, and McSparran claims it for himself in "America Dissected," written in 1752. The Bernon Papers settle the question in favor of the latter, Updike's Narrt. Church, p. 46.

[3] Humfries says, the frame was raised on St. Barnabas' day, 1722. Pres.

was the first settled missionary over this church. The Puritan Church, already introduced in the southern portions of the colony, which, for the past four years, had existed as a distinct society in Providence, also erected their first house of worship here during this year. This building, known at present as "the Old Town House," after being occupied as a church for seventy-one years, was sold to the town, and the following year the new church, standing on the spot now occupied by the First Congregational Society, was dedicated to religious service.[1]

CHAP. XIV. 1723 4

This winter the Assembly passed the celebrated act requiring a freehold qualification of the value of one hundred pounds, or an annual income of two pounds derived from real estate, to entitle any man to become a freeman. The eldest son of a freeman might vote in right of his father's freehold. Those who had before been admitted freemen, although possessing no freehold, retained their franchise. This law, requiring a permanent interest in the soil as a prerequisite to electoral privilege, had become necessary from the influx of new settlers in the colony, large numbers of whom were admitted as freemen at every session of the Assembly. The spirit of English law was thereby preserved, an essential point to be cared for by a colony whose institutions were so frequently a subject of inquiry by the home government, while the peculiar principles of the people were thus protected by excluding from a voice in legislation all transient residents, from the neighboring colonies, who had not a vested interest in the welfare of the State. For one hundred and twenty years

Feb. 18.

Styles says, it was built (by which he probably meant completed) in 1723, which was the time when Pigot the missionary at Stratford, Conn., left his charge to come to Providence.

[1] This edifice was destroyed by fire in 1814. The next year, the present substantial and elegant stone church was erected. This church and society, generally known as the Benevolent Congregational Society, by which name it was incorporated in Oct., 1770, is now under the pastoral charge of Rev. E. B. Hall, D.D., and formed the first Unitarian Church in Rhode Island.

CHAP. XIV. 1723-4 this law remained unchanged, save in the value of the required freehold, and the same instinct of self-preservation, the same determination of the people to keep in their own hands the framing of their own laws, dictated the provision in the present constitution of the State requiring all men of foreign birth to hold a small amount of real estate before being entitled to vote. Another act that has had less of historic celebrity, but of which the principle has been adopted extensively in the western States, and has caused much discussion in its application by them to the Federal Congress, was one allowing freemen of the towns, who were not freemen of the colony, to vote for deputies. A law forbidding this had been recently passed, and was now repealed, "it being found inconvenient." It was, however, a matter of less importance in Rhode Island, where those who were freemen of the towns were always made free of the colony upon request to the Assembly, than it is in its later application by some of the New States, to their members of Congress, where it becomes a grave question of international law, whether those whom the constitution of the United States excludes from a voice in the general government, should be permitted to use that power because conferred upon them by State law. But this is not the place to discuss such a point; suffice it to say, that good or bad, the principle had its origin in this State, and is found, with the reasons for it, in the above-mentioned repeal of a statute.

1724. May 6. The same general officers were re-elected for the ensuing year. For nearly sixty years the deputies had been exempt from arrest or attachment during their term of office. This exemption was now limited to the period of the sessions and for three days before and after each session. June 23. A new ferry was established to run from Warwick Neck to the north end of Prudence Island.

Oct. 8. The Connecticut Assembly once more appointed commissioners with full powers to arrange the boundary line, and Rhode Island did the same. The scarcity of small silver and copper money had led to a practice of tearing the bills of credit into fractional portions for the purpose of making change.[1] An act was passed to prevent their mutilation. Gov. Talcott gave commissions to the men appointed by Connecticut to settle the boundary. The Rhode Island Assembly struck from the act appointing the boundary commissioners the words "to our bounds given us by our charter," to enable them to make a final adjustment by compromise. A messenger was sent to Connecticut to exchange copies of the acts, and commissions upon this subject. The war with the eastern Indians still continuing after the destruction of Norridgewock, Massachusetts again applied to Rhode Island to furnish her quota of troops, and to unite in sending messengers to Canada. The request for aid was declined in a letter, stating the reasons for refusal, but offering to send a remonstrance jointly with Massachusetts, to Vaudreil, governor of Canada, against the encouragement offered by the French to the Indian enemy.[2] Owing to a failure of the crops, the exportation of grain was forbidden. The treasurer was directed to buy two thousand bushels of Indian corn to be sold at cost to the people, no person in Newport to have over four bushels at a time, nor more than eight bushels in the other towns.

CHAP. XIV. 1724. Oct. Dec, 25. 29.

Gov. Cranston's commission to the boundary committee, contained full instructions and advice how they should proceed, and clothed them with ample powers according to the act of Assembly.[3] The next day Gov. Talcott instructed the Connecticut commissioners in a similar manner, and authorized them to recede from the bounds set in their charter. Both parties thus met at Westerly, prepared to compromise, but no report of their proceedings can be found. It is probable that advices from England

1724-5 Feb. 12. 13. 17.

[1] It will be remembered that a little more than twenty years ago, after the commercial revulsion of 1837, a similar difficulty was met by the issuing of fractional bank bills of the denominations of $1 25, $1 50, and $1 75.

[2] R. I. Col. Rec., iv. 351–353.

[3] R. I. Col. Rec., iv. 354–348.

CHAP. XIV. as to the progress of the suit led them to postpone any action, yet we find that Connecticut appointed another
1725. committee for the same purpose in the spring.

May Very little of interest occurred during the year. The Sabbatarians of Westerly were complained of, for working on Sunday, to the annoyance of their neighbors, and the
5. scandal of the colony abroad. The Assembly advised and cautioned them "that, although the ordinances of men may not square with their private principle, yet they must be subject to them, for the Lord's sake." Collector Kay kept the Board of Trade advised of all laws respecting bills of credit and other matters, supposed to conflict with the royal authority. A recent act continuing the two issues of these bills in Rhode Island, was sent home
10. by him at this time.[1] The mode of laying out highways in the towns was prescribed. An act for docking and
June 15. cutting off estates' tail, pursuant to the laws of England, was passed, creating the proper offices for that purpose. The mainland towns were empowered to build a house of correction for vagrants, and "to keep mad persons in." This is the earliest law in which mention is made of insanity in Rhode Island, as well as the first approach to the disciplinary and reformatory institutions so numerous and well conducted at the present day in this State.

The regular meetings of the Quakers, or Society of Friends, had long been organized, and their principles had rapidly extended in this and the neighboring colonies. Besides their meetings on the island, before noticed, the Greenwich monthly meeting, embracing members living west of Narragánset Bay, had been in existence twenty-six years, and two meeting-houses were already erected
July 9. in Providence county.[2] It was now proposed to build a

[1] Br. S. P. O., vol. xi., R. 31.

[2] The first of these, called after the division of the county into townships, "Lower Smithfield," was built in 1704, the next, or "Upper Smithfield," at Woonsocket, in 1719. For more minute details of the Quakers and other religious societies, than the limits of this work will permit, see Staples' Annals of Providence, chapter vii.

CHAP. XIV. 1725.

third meeting-house in the town of Providence, and five years later the fourth in the county was erected in what is now Cranston. The military spirit of Rhode Island, ever ready to enlist in warlike enterprise, placed no restraint upon the peaceful followers of Fox. The law sustained them in the indefeasible rights of conscience, while it equally maintained the prowess of the colony amid the continual conflicts of a martial age.

Oct. 27. By a law that had been in operation four years, common drunkards were to be posted by town councils, and dealers were forbidden to sell spirits to such persons. It was found that they would get supplied in neighboring towns, to prevent which it was ordered that drunkards should be posted in the adjoining towns as well as in their own. A second ferry from Newport, to run from Easton's point to Jamestown, was established.

1725-6 Jan. 10. To meet the action of the Connecticut Assembly in May, the Rhode Island Assembly, at a special session, again appointed commissioners on the boundary; but the matter had progressed too far in England to render their proceedings important. The Board of Trade, whose report, made three years before, had been referred back to them by the Privy Council, made a second report,[1] upon 25. the map and new evidence since presented, still more favorable to Rhode Island, recommending that the boundary be fixed at the green lines on the map, in accordance with the agreement of 1703. This was a final triumph for Rhode Island, although another year was to elapse, in the slow routine of official business, before the royal decree confirming the report should issue.

1726. May 4. Still less of any historical importance, was done in the colony during the ensuing year. The Assembly adopted an address, congratulating his Majesty on his escape from shipwreck in crossing from Holland in January, during a violent storm.[2] The rate of millers' toll was fixed at

[1] Br. S. P. O., Proprieties, vol. xxxi., pp. 346–51.

[2] Br. S. P. O., America and West Indies, vol. 379.

CHAP. XIV. 1726. May two quarts of grain for each bushel ground. In a private case, judgment on appeal was awarded for one hundred pounds in silver money, or one hundred and eighty-one pounds ten shillings in bills of credit, which determines the rate of depreciation of paper money at that time. The frame of the second church, built by the First Baptist
30. Society, was raised, and the building was completed during the year.[1] The present Trinity Church in Newport was also completed this year. The old building having become too small for the society, was removed, and the new one erected on its site. The prospect of war with
June 14. Spain, caused a new militia act to be passed, authorizing the soldiers to elect their own officers, to be confirmed by the governor and council, and to hold their commissions for three years.[2] Neglect of military duty was heavily fined, but the rights of conscience were guarded by a provision, releasing from the penalty any one known to be averse to war upon religious grounds, who should present a certificate to that effect from the meeting with

[1] Their first meeting-house was on the west side of North Main, nearly opposite Star Street, and was built about 1700, prior to which the church met in a grove, or in stormy weather, at private houses. The second house, built in 1726, was occupied until 1775, when the present church was completed, and opened for divine service on the 28th of May.—See Benedict's Hist. of the Baptists, and Staples' Annals of Providence. The superb spire of this church stands unrivalled for its beauty of proportion and its architectural elegance, among all the subsequent creations of ecclesiastical art, and until a very recent period, was also the loftiest spire in the United States. This church and society were incorporated 4th May, 1774, as The Charitable Baptist Society. It was the fifth chartered church in the colony. The preamble to the charter describes it as "being the oldest Christian church in this colony, and professing to believe that Water Baptism ought to be administered by Immersion only, and that professed Believers in Jesus Christ, and no others, are proper subjects of the same." What was the opinion of those who lived almost a century nearer to the time of its origin than we do, upon the question of priority, recently contested, may be gathered from this extract. See chaps. iv., v., vol. i., pp. 107, 8, 139, 40, notes.

[2] This law was repealed four years later, as the election of officers by the soldiers "was found to be of ill-consequence."

CHAP. XIV. 1726.

which he was connected. Such persons, however, were required to aid in the common defence in every way except by actual fighting. The English statute of limitation of personal actions enacted in twenty-first James I. was adopted. It often happened in cases of appeal to the King in council from the decisions of the Assembly, as a Court of Errors, that these decisions were reversed; meanwhile execution had been granted by the Assembly, and no security given by the appellee to make restitution in case of such reversal. The subject was acted upon by the July 5. Privy Council,[1] 28. and instructions were sent to all the colonies to suspend execution in such cases until the final issue, unless adequate security was given by the appellee.[2]

Trouble had recently been caused by persons from Connecticut running lines within the border towns of Rhode Island, to prevent which the Assembly ordered the Oct. 26. arrest and committal to Newport jail of any such intruders. The occasion for this was soon removed by the action of the home government. The committee of the Privy Council adopted the report of the Board of Trade, 1726-7 Jan. 20. and made their final report to the King in conformity thereto, whereupon a decree was issued which settled forever the western line of the colony, in accordance with the Feb. 8. agreement at Stonington twenty-four years before.[3] There remained only for the two colonies to run out the lines agreeably with the decree.

The death of Governor Samuel Cranston, was no or- 1727. April 26. dinary event in the history of the colony. In the strength of his intellect, the courage and firmness of his administration, and the skill with which he conducted public affairs in every crisis, he resembles the early race of Rhode Islanders. Thirty times successively chosen to the highest office, he preserved his popularity amidst political convulsions that had swept away every other official in

[1] Br. S. P. O., Plantations General, vol. xxxix., p. 32.

[2] Br. S. P. O., Proprieties, vol. xxxi., p. 401.

[3] Br. S. P. O., Proprieties, vol. xi., R. 80. R. I. Col. Rec., iv., 370-3.

CHAP. XIV. 1727.

the colony. He was the connecting link between two centuries of its history, and seemed, as it were, the bridge over which it passed in safety, from the long struggle for existence with the royal governors of Massachusetts, to the peaceful possession of its chartered rights under the House of Hanover. The piratical period, the strife about the acts of trade, the desperate efforts of Bellemont and his successors, a long and exhausting foreign war, and two bitter boundary disputes involving the largest portion of the colony, one of which he lived to see favorably and finally settled, were some of the perplexing questions of his administration. The romance of history illustrates every period of his public career, and forms a fitting complement to that singular romance of private life which pertained to his early manhood.[1]

[1] Although the limits of this work permit no biographical sketches, the story here referred to is so remarkable that the reader will pardon its insertion in a note. The facts are taken from a notice of Gov. Cranston in Bull's Memoir of R. I. In early life, soon after his marriage with Mary, a grand-daughter of Roger Williams, he went to sea, and was not heard from for many years. It proved that he had been captured by pirates, and perhaps, like Wm. Harris, had been taken to Algiers. At any rate, he was unable to communicate with his family, who had long given him up for dead. Here we take up the narrative as related by Mr. Bull. "His wife, having an offer of marriage, accepted it, and was on the eve of solemnizing the marriage ceremony; but Cranston, having arrived in Boston, hastened homeward, and at Howland's Ferry, just before night, was informed that his wife was to be married that evening. With increased speed he flew to Newport, but not until the wedding guests had begun to assemble! She was called by a servant into the kitchen—'a person being there who wished to speak with her.' A man in sailor's habit advanced and informed her that 'her husband had arrived in Boston, and requested him to inform her that he was on his way to Newport.' This information induced her to question the man very closely; he then told her that what he had said was the truth, for he had seen her husband at Howland's Ferry that very afternoon, and that he was on his way to Newport; he then, stepping towards her, raised his cap, and pointed to a scar on his head, or forehead, and said, 'do you recollect that scar?' from which she at once recognized her husband actually in her presence! He then entertained the wedding guests with a story of his adventures and sufferings, having been taken by pirates, and not having had the opportunity or means of communicating the fact to

CHAP. XIV. 1727.

A brief and general notice of the religious condition of the colony, will conclude this chapter. The number of new churches springing up in the first quarter of the eighteenth century in Rhode Island, and the steady and rapid increase, during the same period, of those already occupying the ground,—the Baptists, and Quakers,—furnish evidence of a degree of religious interest pervading the colony, that is both gratifying in itself, and conclusive in refutation of sectarian slanders. We should receive with caution the statements of writers, zealous in their own faith, but sceptical as to all others, whose free denunciations of "the heretical colony," upon this point, would be more safely interpreted to imply that their peculiar tenets were not so prevalent in Rhode Island, as were those of the early settlers of the State. There is no one point upon which intelligent and educated men are so prone to err, as in supposing that the highest type of Christian character is rarely to be found without the sphere of their particular church; and there is no subject upon which a more general ignorance exists, among the same class of men, than that of the theological views, or distinctive dogmas of other churches than their own. The history of Rhode Island furnishes, perhaps, the best illustration of these truths, because here was the only ground upon which all sects stood equal before the laws, and where the champions of each could display their real characters, and show the influence of their respective theologies. Cotton Mather, writing at the close of the past century, describes Rhode Island as "a colluvies of Antinomians, Familists, Anabaptists, Antisabbatarians, Arminians, Socinians, Quakers, Ranters, every thing in the world but Roman Catholics and true Christians."[1] Humfries, the historian of the society under whose auspi-

her; having at last escaped out of their hands, on his way home he arrived at Boston, and from thence to Howland's Ferry, and from thence with increased anxiety and speed to the arms of his wife."

[1] Magnalia, b. vii., chap. iii., sec. 12, written in 1695.

CHAP. XIV. 1727. ces the Church of England was introduced, deriving his information from the missionaries in Rhode Island, says: "The people were negligent of all religion till about the year 1722; the very best were such as called themselves Baptists, or Quakers, but it was feared many were Gortonians or Deists."[1] The Rev. N. Prince, missionary at Westerly, expresses his astonishment at the kind treatment he received, so unlike that which everywhere else was accorded to those who differed from the prevailing religious sentiment. He says: "The sectaries here are chiefly Baptists, that keep the Saturday as a sabbath, and are more numerous than all the other persuasions throughout the town put together;" and then proceeds to express his wonder: "that those Baptists who I imagined would oppose me, and all of the same interest with me, should be so far from it, that they have expressed a gladness of a minister's coming to those of a different persuasion from them; that instead of separating and keeping at a distance, they should many of them come with my own hearers, and be as constant as most of them, and but few that would not occasionally do it, and manifest their liking; that when I supposed that if they did come, it would be to pick, and carp, and find fault, and then go away and make the worst of it, that they should come after a sermon and thank me for it; that instead of shunning me and keeping off from an acquaintance with me, they should invite me to their houses, and be sorry if I would pass by without calling; that their two ministers in the town, who I expected would be virulent and fierce against me, and stir up their people to stand to their arms, should not only hear me, thank me, visit me, but take my part against some few of their own persuasion that showed a narrow spirit towards us, and be the most charitable

[1] See Staples' Annals, p. 444; also McSparran's "America Dissected," in Updike's Narrt. Church, Appendix, to the same effect.

and catholic, whom I thought to have found the most stiff and prejudiced."[1] CHAP. XIV.

The fact is, that the operation of the voluntary principle was unknown beyond the limits of Rhode Island. 1727. The ministers of the various sects, brought hither the peculiar spirit of their own churches, and reflected that spirit in their reports, while expressing surprise at the kindness of their reception, or attributing the absence of fanaticism to a negligence of all religion. They were, by this time, nearly all represented in the Rhode Island "colluvies;" and we have yet to discover any evidence, other than that furnished by the sectarian bias proceeding from their ignorance of the distinctive principles of the founders of the State, that this harmonious union was not more conducive to the spiritual welfare of the people, than was the predominance of any one of the new-coming sects, with its resulting union of church and State, which everywhere else prevailed.

The liberal Baptist, denying any mortal power over the immortal mind; the benign Quaker, seeking only to be guided by "the inner light;" the mystical Gortonist, merging his humanity in the Divine essence,—these had framed and founded the institutions of a State, upon principles broad enough to embrace the whole human family as the children of One common Father. The polished Episcopalian and the zealous Puritan, each claiming in his despatches to be "the true church," speedily followed to occupy a field at once so novel and so inviting. Each learned something he had never known before, and all were improved by the mutual contact; so that even Mather, a quarter of a century later than the denunciation above given, after having himself assisted at the ordination of a Baptist clergyman in Boston,[2] writes in a letter to

[1] This letter was written in 1721–2, and is found in Mass. Hist. Soc. Letters and Papers, 1721–1760, p. 7, No. 1, and in MS. Letters and Papers, 1 Series, vol. ii., pp. 102–7, in R. I. Hist. Soc.

[1] Rev. Elisha Callender, settled over the Boston Baptist Church in 1718.

CHAP. XIV. 1727. Lord Barrington, describing, although not acknowledging, the progress of Rhode Island principles, that "Calvinists with Lutherans, Presbyterians with Episcopalians, Pedobaptists with Anabaptists, beholding one another to fear God and work righteousness, do with delight sit down together at the same table of the Lord."[1]

The triumph of liberal sentiments, achieved through the spirit of Williams, the sufferings of Gorton, the trials of Clarke, and the persecution of the Quakers, is here confessed, in a single passage, by the high priest of the Puritans.

The reign of bigotry had ceased.

APP. I.

APPENDIX I.

THE PALATINE LIGHT.

FROM BULL'S MEMOIRS OF RHODE ISLAND. R. I. REPUBLICAN OF MARCH 16, 1836.

The following account of the Palatine light, is taken from a publication called the Parthenon. It was written by Dr. Aaron C. Willey, a resident physician of the island, to Dr. Samuel L. Mitchell, of New York :—

Block Island, *December* 10, 1811.

Dear Sir :—In a former letter I promised to give you an account of the singular light which is sometimes seen from this place; I now hasten to fulfil my engagement. I should long since have communicated the fact to the literary world, but was unwilling to depend wholly upon the information of others, when by a little delay, there was probability of my receiving occular demonstration. I have not,

Both the Mathers assisted at the ceremony, and Cotton Mather preached the ordination sermon, which was printed under the title "Good Men United." Hildreth's U. S., ii., 306.

[1] Mass. Hist. Coll., vol. i., p. 105.

however, been so fortunate in this respect as I could wish, having had only two opportunities of viewing this phenomenon. My residing nearly six miles from the shore which lies next to the region of its exhibition, and behind elevated ground, has prevented me from seeing it so frequently, perhaps, as I might otherwise have done. The people who have always lived here, are so familiarized to the sight, that they never think of giving notice to those who do not happen to be present, or even of mentioning it afterwards, unless they hear some particular inquiries made.

This curious irradiation rises from the ocean near the northern part of the island. Its appearance is nothing different from a blaze of fire; whether it actually touches the water, or merely hovers over it, is uncertain, for I am informed that no person has been near enough to decide accurately. It beams with various magnitudes, and appears to bear no more analogy to the ignis fatuus than it does to the aurora borealis. Sometimes it is small, resembling the light through a distant window; at others expanding to the highness of a ship with all her canvas spread. When large it displays either a pyramidical form, or three constant streams. In the latter case the streams are somewhat blended together at the bottom, but separate and distinct at the top, while the middle one rises rather higher than the other two. It may have the same appearance when small, but owing to the distance and surrounding vapors, cannot be clearly perceived. This light often seems to be in a constant state of mutation; decreasing by degrees it becomes invisible, or resembles a lucid point, then shining anew sometimes with a sudden flare, at others by a gradual increasement, to its former size. Often the mutability regards the lustre only, becoming less and less bright until it disappears, or nothing but a pale outline can be discerned of its full size; then resuming its former splendor in the manner before related. The duration of its greatest and least state of illumination is not commonly more than two or three minutes; this inconstancy, however, does not appear in every instance.

After the radiance seems to be wholly extinct, it does not always return in the same place, but is not unfrequently seen shining at some inconsiderable distance from which it disappeared. In this transfer of locality it seems to have no certain line of direction.

When most expanded, this blaze is generally wavering, like the flame of a torch. At one time it appears stationary, at another progressive. It is seen at all seasons of the year, and for the most part in the calm weather which precedes an easterly or southerly storm. It has, however, been noticed during a severe northwestern gale, and when no storm immediately followed. Its continuance is sometimes but transient, and others throughout the night, and it has been known to appear several nights in succession.

CHAP. XIV. APP. I.

This blaze actually emits luminous rays. A gentleman whose house is situated near the sea, informs me that he has known it to illuminate considerably the walls of his room through the windows. This happens only when the light is within half a mile of the shore, for it is often seen blazing at six or seven miles distance, and strangers suppose it to be a vessel on fire.

Having given a concise, but general description of this unusual radiance, in which I have been aided by the concurrent testimony of divers veritable characters, I will now offer you those observations afforded me by the opportunities I have had for visiting it myself. The first time I beheld it, was at evening twilight, in February, 1810. It was large, and gently lambent, very bright, broad at the bottom, and terminating acutely upward. From each side seemed to issue rays of faint light, similar to those perceptible in any blaze placed in the open air at night. It continued about fifteen minutes from the time I first observed it, then gradually became smaller until more dim, and it was entirely extinguished.

I saw it again on the evening of December 20. It was then small, and I supposed it to be a light on board of some vessel, but I was soon undeceived. It moved along, apparently parallel to the shore, for about two miles, in the time that I was riding one at a moderate pace. An ascent of ground then hid it for a few minutes from my view. Passing this, I observed it about half way back to the place where it had commenced its vagrant career. I then stopped to observe it more attentively. The light then remained still for some time, then moved off quickly for several rods, and made a halt; thus being in a state of alternate motion and rest. Its magnitude and lustre were subject to the same unsteadiness described above.

This lucid meteor has long been known by the name of the Palatine light. By the ignorant and superstitious it is thought to be supernatural. Its appellation originated from that of a ship called the Palatine, which was designedly cast away at this place, in the beginning of the last century, in order to conceal, as tradition reports, the inhuman treatment and murder of some of its unfortunate passengers. From this time, it is said, the Palatine light appeared, and there are many who believe it to be a ship of fire, to which their fantastic and distempered imaginations figure masts, ropes, and flowing sails.

The cause of this "roving brightness" is a curious subject for philosophical investigation. Some, perhaps, will suppose it will depend upon a peculiar modification of electricity; others upon the inflammation of phlogogistous (hydrogenous) gas. But there are possibly many other means, unknown to us, by which light may be evolved from those materials with which it is latently associated, by the power of chemical affinities.

I have stated to you facts, but feel a reluctance to hazard any speculations. These I leave to you and to other acute researchers of created things. Your opinion I would be much pleased with.

With the highest feeling of respect,

I remain yours, &c.,

AARON C. WILLEY.

Hon. S. L. Mitchell.

We regret that the reply of the learned and eccentric doctor to this admirable description of a most singular phenomenon cannot be found.

CHAPTER XV.

1727—1739.

FROM THE ACCESSION OF GEORGE II., 1727, TO THE CLOSE OF THE PEACEFUL PERIOD IN 1739.

CHAP. XV. 1727. May 3. Almost a whole generation had passed away since any change was made in the office of governor, and we have nearly lost sight of the fact, that the charter was always placed in his custody, and the duplicate copy of it in that of the deputy-governor. Joseph Jenckes was chosen to succeed Gov. Cranston, and Jonathan Nichols was elected in his place, as deputy-governor. Gov. Jenckes resided at Pawtucket. It was deemed "highly necessary for the governor of this colony to live at Newport, the metropolis of the government," and an appropriation of one hundred pounds was therefore made to defray the expenses of his removal.

June 10. The death of George I. occurred very suddenly at Osnaburg, while on the way to visit his hereditary dominion of Hanover. His son, the Prince of Wales, succeeded to the throne as George II., but no change in the policy of the empire resulted.

13. The Assembly sent notice to Connecticut of the settlement of the boundary line by the King. Another ferry was established between Portsmouth and Bristol. The old one, which for over forty years had been run from Tripp's landing, had lately been removed to a new spot, and was now restored; so that two ferries now connected the north

end of the island with the opposite shore of Bristol. An CHAP.
assault with intent to kill had recently been committed XV.
by an Indian lad in Portsmouth, upon his master. There 1727.
was no law adequate to such cases. The culprit was June 17.
branded with a hot iron on the forehead with the letter R,
and whipped at the cart's tail at all the corners in Newport, ten lashes at each place, and his master was required to sell him out of the colony, for his unexpired time, and so much longer as was necessary to pay the charges, never to return here again.

By the death of deputy-governor Nichols, who had Aug. 2.
held the office but three months, the election of his successor devolved upon the General Assembly in grand com- 22.
mittee. They chose Thomas Fry, the Speaker of the House, to fill that place. One Hardman, having published a pamphlet wherein sundry "vile and mutinous expressions" were contained, was ordered to make acknowledgment of his fault, in writing, and the books were publicly burnt, in front of the colony house, by the town sergeant. News of the death of George I. having been received, the acts of the last session, and legal processes, since issued in his name, were declared to be of equal force, as if bearing the name of the present King. An address to his Majesty was voted, wherein it is stated that "a regular and beautiful fortification of stone, with a battery" capable of mounting fifty cannon, had been built at Newport. This address was afterwards presented by Partridge, enclosing a petition for forty cannon, thirty of eighteen-pound calibre, and ten of twelve-pounds, to arm the fort; the ammunition to be furnished at the expense of the colony.[1] An appropriation was made for the formal proclamation of George II., which took place at New- 24.
port with military honors, and at Providence the next
day. Orders for the proclamation were not received from 25.
England till later in the season, so that the Assembly,

[1] Br. S. P. O., America and West Indies, vol. 379. The address is in R. I. Col. Rec., iv., 393.

CHAP. XV. 1727. Oct. 25. sitting at Warwick, again proclaimed the King at that place; and also that all crown officers should be continued for six months from the death of his late Majesty. All commissions, civil and military, were renewed in the name of George II. Upon request of Charles Augustus Ninigret, son of the late sachem, certain lands of his in Westerly, were granted as a site for a house of worship, to be laid out by his trustees.[1] The law for registering births, marriages, and deaths, had become so neglected, that increased penalties were affixed to its violation, and power was given to the town clerks to sue for the same.

29. The great earthquake in New England occurred at this time, causing much alarm throughout the country, but producing no serious accident. For several months afterward more gentle shocks were occasionally felt.

The progress of the Press in America was slow. Five years before this, James Franklin had commenced the New England Courant at Boston, in connection with his younger brother Benjamin. The paper suffered from the censorship, and finally expired for want of support. James came to Newport, and set up a printing establishment. A pamphlet printed by him this year is still in existence, and the press with which he worked yet remains.

1728. Feb. 27. The Assembly, at its winter session, offered a premium of sixpence a pound on hemp, raised and well cured in the colony. Governor Burnet of New York, was transferred by George II. to Massachusetts, in place of Col. Shute. As he was to pass through Rhode Island, on the way to his new government, the Assembly voted him a public reception.

The policy of public loans, which was truly enough described as "the art of enriching themselves by running in debt,"[2] had become established in New England. As each "bank" expired by limitation, it was renewed by

[1] At Feb. session, 1734–5, twenty acres of this land were laid out and deeded for the use of the Church of England in Westerly.

[2] "America Dissected," in Updike's Narrt. Church, 516.

statute, and further issues on new banks were created, CHAP. XV. until, as we shall see hereafter, the rapid depreciation of the bills of credit was so accelerated, that utter bankruptcy 1728. ensued. May 1. The first bank, originally limited to five years, had been continued to ten, and payment was now further postponed for three years, after which the redemption of the bills was to be effected in ten annual instalments without interest. The same course was adopted in June with the second bank, and at this session a new loan, the third, of forty thousand pounds, was issued for thirteen years, for the same specious but delusive reasons—the decay of trade and scarcity of bullion.

Repeated efforts were made by Rhode Island to run the western boundary jointly with Connecticut, but that colony, for various assigned causes, failed to unite in the survey. A new commission was now appointed for the purpose, with orders to proceed at once, *ex parte*, unless Connecticut would join, and notice of this action was sent to Hartford. That Assembly accordingly appointed commissioners to meet with those of Rhode Island. A misunderstanding between the parties prevented their concurrence. 21. The Connecticut men refused to proceed unless the twenty-mile line, west from Warwick Neck, was again run. The Rhode Island men therefore surveyed the western line *ex parte*, and both commissions reported to their respective legislatures. This difference was fortunate for Rhode Island, as in the final survey it was found that the twenty-mile line, as formerly run by Rhode Island, fell considerably short of its proper terminus. The Rhode Island committee[1] was continued, June 18. and negotiations for another survey were opened with Connecticut. To preserve deer in the colony, it was forbidden to kill them from January to July. A general law against pedlars, more comprehensive than the last, which related only to

[1] William Wanton, Francis Willett, John Waterman, William Jenckes, and Benjamin Ellery, with John Mumford and William Green as surveyors.

CHAP. XV. dry-goods, was passed, forbidding every sort of merchandise to be sold by them on penalty of forfeiture.

1728. July 12. A ship of war from England brought Burnet, the new Governor of Massachusetts, to Newport. Salutes were exchanged at the fort, a public reception was given him, 13. and the next day he proceeded to Boston.

Sept. 18. The joint commission having agreed upon preliminaries, met at Warwick, and completed the survey of the twenty-mile line, and then of the whole western line, setting up bounds at short intervals along its entire length. The business occupied nine days, when the final agreement 27. was signed at Westerly, which settled forever this vexed question after a controversy of sixty-five years.

Oct. 30. When the report was presented to the Assembly, the account of the commissioners, amounting to one hundred and sixteen pounds, was allowed, and copies of the Connecticut commissions were ordered to be entered upon the records. Pawtucket Bridge required rebuilding, and one half the expense was voted by this colony, provided Massachusetts would pay the remainder. The death of John Menzies, Judge of Admiralty, left a vacancy in that court. The Assembly commissioned William Whiting to fill the place till his Majesty should appoint another.

1728-9 Feb. 19. At the winter session, the Assembly prohibited the manumission of any slaves, without sufficient bonds first given to the town for their maintenance by the owner, in case of their becoming disabled. The whole criminal code was revised at this session, in a single act enumerating the various crimes with their statute penalties,[1] and a new license law, forbidding the sale of liquors in less quantities than one gallon without special license, and giving town councils the power of granting such, was passed.

1729. May 7. At the spring election, John Wanton was chosen deputy-governor in the place of Thomas Fry. The oath

[1] Public Laws, edit. 1730, pp. 169–176.

CHAP. XV. 1729.

to support the acts of trade and navigation, was taken by the governor in the presence of the Assembly, and also of the collector and the Judge of Admiralty, Nathaniel Byfield, who had been appointed by the King. This is the first time in which the presence of any of the crown officers at this ceremony is mentioned, and they also were duly sworn. Edward Greenman, who, ten years before, upon conviction of counterfeiting bills of credit, had been fined six hundred pounds and compelled to deposit fifteen hundred pounds in the treasury, to redeem the counterfeits, was allowed, upon petition, to withdraw what portion of the deposit remained, as all the forged bills had been exchanged for the genuine. The revenue derived from the duty of three pounds a head upon all imported slaves was appropriated, one half to paving the streets of Newport, and the other half to repairing bridges on the main. Disturbances having occurred at town meetings, from the refusal of moderators to put questions to vote when desired to do so, it was ordered that every question should be put to vote upon request of seven freemen, but no law or money question should be decided at town-meetings, unless it was mentioned in the clerk's warrant calling the meeting. Indian dances were another source of annoyance. The town councils were empowered to regulate them, and to fine persons who should sell or give any strong liquors at such dances. Military stores, to equip a colony vessel against pirates and privateers, being needed, a hundred pistols and cutlasses, forty boarding pikes, a hundred and fifty muskets, and twelve mounted guns, were ordered to be bought.

June 16.

The increase of population required a re-organization of the colony into three counties. The islands formed Newport county, including the towns of Portsmouth, Newport, Jamestown, and New Shoreham, with Newport as the shire town. The mainland was divided into two counties; King's province was called King's county, and embraced Westerly and North and South Kingstown.

CHAP. XV. 1729. with the latter as the shire town. All North of this, containing the towns of East Greenwich, Warwick, and Providence, with the latter as the shire town, was called Providence county. The judicial system was revised to meet this change. The justices of the peace in each county, or any five of them, were made a court of criminal jurisdiction, except in capital cases. This was called the "Court of General Sessions of the Peace." The Inferior Court of Common Pleas, for the trial of civil causes, was composed of four judges for each county, any three of whom, with a clerk, might hold the court. The judges and clerk for every county were appointed by the General Assembly. The jurors for both these courts were elected at the town meeting preceding the sittings of court. Both courts were to sit twice a year in each county, and an appeal from either of them might be taken to the Superior Court. This was composed of the upper house of Assembly, any five of whom were to sit at Newport in March and September for the trial of all causes, civil or criminal. Each county was to have its court-house and jail.

Oct. 29. At the meeting of the Assembly in Warwick, the general treasurer was required to give bonds to the amount of twenty thousand pounds, and his annual salary was fixed at one hundred pounds, which was doubled two years later. Practising lawyers were forbidden to be deputies. The act was repealed at the next session, but has since been at various times introduced. This distrust of the legal profession has so often been shown in the world's history, that it cannot be without some foundation.[1] The

[1] The memorable capitulation between Charles V. and Pizarro, which defined the powers of the conqueror and first Captain-General of Peru, and arranged the basis of his government, "strictly prohibited lawyers and attorneys, whose presence was considered as boding ill to the harmony of the new settlements, from setting foot in them." This capitulation was signed July 26, 1529. Prescott's Peru, i., 307. The same dread of the legal profession inspired the people of R. I., two centuries later, and was occasionally manifested, as we shall see, at subsequent periods. In 1848, while the writer was in South America, a similar controversy was going on in the

reason assigned for it in this case, was that their presence in the Assembly, when sitting as a Court of Appeals, was "found to be of ill consequence." CHAP. XV. 1729.

A petition from Attleboro' for annexation to Rhode Island again brought up the boundary dispute. A committee was appointed to run the line north from Pawtucket falls to Massachusetts south line, and notice thereof was sent to that province. The council of Massachusetts appointed commissioners for this purpose, but for some reason the House refused to concur.[1] Dec. 29.

The arrival of George Berkely, Dean of Derry, and afterward bishop of Cloyne, was a joyful event in the history of Newport, and important in its results to the other colonies. A corps of literary men and artists accompanied him, among whom was Smibert, to whose advent is due the earliest impulse given to American art. From the collection of pictures that he brought, Copley first drew his inspiration, and West was taught to breathe his spirit upon the undying canvass. The benevolent design of Berkely to found a college in the Bermudas, was abandoned from necessity, but his liberal benefactions to Harvard and Yale still exist, as proofs of his zeal in the cause of classical learning. To combat the progress of materialism, and subvert the Epicurian theories of Hobbes, Berkely had become the champion of the immaterial system of philosophy, and argued the non-existence of matter, or rather its entire subjection to the ideal. The purity of his character was the delight of his friends, and the admiration of his opponents. In a single line Pope has accorded 1729–30. Jan. 23.

"To Berkely, every virtue under Heaven."

British colony of Honduras. A great opposition to lawyers' taking part in legislative proceedings was manifested, a strong party in that colony desiring to exclude them entirely. A few years since, the only members in the United States Senate who were not lawyers were the two Senators from Rhode Island. The opinion of the highest authority, eighteen centuries ago, upon this subject, may be found in Luke xi., 46, 52!

[1] Mass. Court Files, iii., 53, in R. I. Hist. Soc.

CHAP. XV. 1729-30. The arrival of such a man could not fail to be attended with good results. He purchased a farm in Middletown, about three miles from Newport, and called it after the residence of the early archbishops of England, Whitehall, a name which it still retains, and was soon admitted a freeman of the colony. Here he resided for more than two years, and wrote his Alciphron or Minute Philosopher, an ingenious defence of the Christian religion. Soon after his arrival, he formed a society for the purpose of discussing philosophical questions and of collecting books. This was the origin of the Redwood library, organized some years later. One of the members of this society was Edward Scott, the grand uncle of Sir Walter Scott, who, for nearly twenty years, had been master of the grammar school at Newport, the first classical school established in Rhode Island. Berkely's Theory of Vision is the first satisfactory account we have of the phenomena of sight; his Alciphron was printed in Newport by James Franklin; but the most enduring monument of his genius is the ode "On the Prospect of the Arts and Sciences in America," of which the concluding stanza "will live immortal as the verse of Gray."[1]

There was a small strip of land on the south-west corner of Warwick, of which the ownership was claimed by the proprietors of the "great purchase" of vacant lands. Feb. 25. The Assembly voted to refer the question to disinterested persons in Massachusetts, and directed the attorney-general in case it was not speedily decided, to bring writs of ejectment against the occupants. The dispute was afterwards settled by the courts. More than a year had passed since the Assembly had voted to rebuild Pawtucket bridge jointly with Massachusetts, but that colony had taken no action in the matter. A letter was now sent to Massachu-

[1] Westward the course of empire takes its way;
The four first acts already past,
A fifth shall close the drama with the day,
Time's noblest offspring is the last."

setts to remind them of this vote, and to advise, in case of their refusal to rebuild, that the bridge be "demolished, that it may not remain as a trap to endanger men's lives." CHAP. XV. 1730.

May 6. Sheriffs for the three counties were chosen for the first time at the general election.[1] This Assembly passed an act for the relief of poor sailors, which is perhaps the origin of the present hospital money system in the United States. Sixpence a month was to be deducted, by the naval officer, from the wages of every Rhode Island seaman, and paid to the town where he belonged, to create a fund for the support of disabled mariners and their families.

The committee to run the line from Pawtucket falls, reported that they had performed their duty, as instructed, without the concurrence of Massachusetts. The Attleboro' petitioners falling within the line, the Assembly asserted the claim of Rhode Island to all that territory now comprised in the town of Cumberland. Massachusetts was willing to adopt the suggestion of Rhode Island with regard to Pawtucket bridge, and appointed men to join 30.
with some from this colony in its destruction.

The repeal of the late militia act, exposed the Quakers to do military service. As this was considered a violation June 15.
of the rights of conscience, the Assembly re-enacted the clauses of that law which were for their benefit. To protect the rights of the Indians, it was required that the assent of two justices should be obtained, to any bond of apprenticeship to which they were parties. By direction of the Board of Trade, a census was ordered. The result showed the population of the colony to be about eighteen thousand, an increase of six thousand within ten years, of whom were fifteen thousand three hundred whites, sixteen hundred and fifty blacks, and nine hundred and eighty-five Indians, nearly equally divided among the three counties, and the militia force numbered nearly nineteen hundred men.

[1] Jahleel Brenton, Esq., for Newport, Capt. Daniel Abbot for Providence, and Immanuel Northup, Esq., for Kings County.

CHAP. In Massachusetts the lower house concurred with the
XV. council in reference to Pawtucket bridge. The commit-
1730. tees of both colonies met accordingly, and the bridge was
July 21. demolished.[1] The cost of its destruction, as appears by
Sept. the report submitted to the Massachusetts legislature, was
16. about four pounds. The iron was divided between the
two colonies, and sold.[2] This removal of the only convenient means of connection at the point of disputed jurisdiction, tended to increase the difficulties arising from that
source. The tax collector of Attleboro' with his aid, were
Oct. arrested by a Rhode Island officer, and convicted at a jus-
22. tice's court in Providence. Complaint was made to Gov.
25. Jenckes, who, by order of the Assembly, sent a proposi-
Dec. tion that commissioners be appointed by both colonies, to
10. settle the line. This was acceded to by the council, who
19. appointed a committee on their part, and concurred in by
1730-1 the house, who added four members. The Assembly ap-
Jan. 1. Feb. pointed a like committee of seven to meet them. Both
17. parties, by the terms of their commissions, were empowered
to settle the whole eastern line, and pending the adjustment, the inhabitants of the disputed territory were released from all taxes by both governments.

The town of Providence was divided into four towns. The outlands, as they were termed, had become populous. The old seven-mile line was made the western limit of Providence, and a point half a mile north of Pawtucket falls was fixed upon as its northern boundary. All north of that limit and east of the seven-mile line was called Smithfield. Of all west of the seven-mile line and north of Warwick, two towns were made. The division between them was a line from the northwest corner of Providence, westward to Connecticut, south of which was called Scituate, and all north of it Gloucester. Each of the new towns was to send two deputies to the next General Assembly.

[1] William Jenckes was the committee on the part of R. I.

[2] Mass. Court Files, ii., 119–121.

At the election, the same general officers were continued. A memorial against further issues of bills of credit was presented, which became the basis of important proceedings. Many laws to encourage and regulate trade were enacted this year. Surveyors of lumber, in all its forms, and viewers of packed meats and fish were appointed. The gauge of casks was established. The manufacture of duck received further aid. Insolvents were allowed to compound with their creditors, and obtain a discharge upon consent of two-thirds, in number and value, of the latter. The premium upon hemp was raised to ninepence a pound, and on flax to fourpence. To encourage the whale[1] and cod fisheries, a bounty of five shillings for every barrel of whale oil, one penny a pound for bone, and five shillings a quintal for codfish, caught by Rhode Island vessels, and brought into this colony, was offered, to be paid from the interest accruing upon a new bank, or issue of bills of credit to the amount of sixty thousand pounds, which was made at this session.

CHAP. XV. 1731. May 5. June 14.

Prohibitions were set up in Attleboro', forbidding any one to levy taxes or exercise jurisdiction there, until the boundary was settled. Commissioners were appointed to meet any who might be named by Massachusetts upon this question, and in case of their non-agreement, preparations were made to carry the matter to England; provided the inhabitants of the tract in dispute would advance two hundred pounds towards the expenses, and other parties would guarantee four thousand pounds to the colony for this purpose, but this proviso was repealed in October. The Massachusetts council had already

March 29.

[1] It is said that the first person who killed a whale upon this coast was a Scotchman, named William Hamilton, who "in early life settled on Cape Cod, whence he removed to Rhode Island, he being persecuted for killing the whale, by the inhabitants of the Cape, as one who dealt with evil spirits." Hamilton died in Connecticut in 1746, aged 103 years. This must have occurred some time prior to 1690, when the art of taking whales with boats from the shore was introduced at Nantucket by Ichabod Paddock from Cape Cod.

CHAP. XV. ordered that a majority of their commissioners should bind
the whole, and then instructed them to consider what
1731. should be done in respect to the residents of Attleboro'.
June 18. The committee reported that the act releasing them from
taxes ought to be repealed, and that the right of the province to all the lands east of Pawtucket River should be maintained.[1]

Gov. Jenckes was opposed to the paper-money system,
and the day after the Assembly rose, he entered his dis-
25. sent upon the records, under the act creating the new
loan. This caused great dissatisfaction. Party spirit ran high. The opponents of paper currency applied to the secretary for copies of the act, to which the governor appended the requisite certificate of that officer's official character, and affixed the colony seal thereto, as usual in such cases. This was seized upon by the opposition to misrepresent Jenckes, as having endangered the existence
of the charter by affixing the seal to a complaint against
Aug. 3. the government. Deputy-governor Wanton convened the
Assembly, the governor refusing to do so. They declared the entry to be null, and censured the governor. His dissent not having been expressed during the session, the act had already taken effect. The subsequent entry was deemed to be irregular in its nature, and since other votes preceded the bank act, it was also uncertain in its application, and finally "the post-entry of said dissent deprived the General Assembly of the benefit of considering the consequence thereof." These were the reasons embodied in the resolution, but there were others not less important or exciting. The question of the veto power of the executive, was also involved in the controversy. The Assembly took away the attested papers intended for England, and dismissed the memorial presented by the opponents of the
20. measure. Jenckes wrote directly to the King, stating the
facts, and asking his Majesty's decision upon the veto

[1] Mass. Court Files, iii., 59–63.

question, and also whether the governor could refuse to affix the seal of attestation to the secretary's copies of acts to be sent home, or should be required to read all such acts before sealing them; the secretary being a sworn officer. The specie party also petitioned the King against the further issue of bills, and the conduct of the dominant faction in the Assembly, enclosing copies of their rejected memorial, and of the bank acts for the past twenty-one years. At the same time they addressed the Board of Trade, complaining of the conduct of the Assembly in seizing the attested papers. Collector Kay also wrote to the Board of Trade on the subject, and all the papers were sent to Thomas Sandford, a London merchant doing business for the colony. These four[1] documents were formidable checks upon the headlong policy of the Assembly; but the mischief was already done. Besides the regular loans, four of which had now been issued, there had been at various times, smaller amounts put out for the temporary supply of the treasury, or to meet present emergencies; so that, exclusive of the new bank of sixty thousand pounds, there had been emitted, up to this time, one hundred and ninety-five thousand three hundred pounds in bills of public credit of this colony, of which over one hundred and twenty thousand pounds were still outstanding! The value of silver, formerly eight shillings an ounce, had risen to twenty shillings, showing the rapid depreciation of this baseless paper.

CHAP. XV. 1731. Aug. 30. Sept. 2.

Massachusetts demanded satisfaction for violence done to her people by the Rhode Island officers, and took measures to represent the matter to their agent in England. Seizure, and imprisonment of officers had occurred on both sides. Two Massachusetts men were released by the Assembly, and that province was desired to reciprocate. It was resolved to propose a reference of the dispute to gentlemen in other colonies, and three were named

22. 30.

[1] Br. S. P. O., Proprieties, vol. xiii., s. 9, 10, 29. R. I. Col. Rec., iv. 457–461.

CHAP. XV. 1731. Oct. 27. to act in behalf of Rhode Island.[1] If this overture should be declined, then a committee was to draw up a statement of the case, to present to the next General Assembly for transmission to England.

One hundred pounds was voted to William Jenckes towards the Rhode Island half of the expense of rebuilding Pawtucket bridge, which was completed the next year, when the balance was paid. A new edition of the laws was called for, and partly printed this year at Newport by James Franklin.[2]

The trade of the colony was increasing. Ten years before, the shipping, consisting of some sixty small vessels, amounted to thirty-five hundred tons. It now counted five thousand tons, and embraced two ships, besides a few brigs, with many sloops, and was manned by four hundred sailors. Most of the supplies were received from Boston, but two vessels annually arrived from England, as many from Holland and the Mediterranean, and ten or twelve from the West Indies. The articles of export comprised horses, live-stock, logwood, lumber, fish, and the produce of the field and the dairy, and amounted to ten thousand pounds sterling annually. In reply to inquiries of the Board of Trade as to the condition of the Nov. 9. colony, these facts were stated, and the ordinary expenses of government were estimated at two thousand pounds a year, and the extraordinary at twenty-five hundred pounds, colonial currency. Partridge, the colonial agent, of course represented the dominant party in the paper-money controversy, and hence the memorials of the minority had been sent to another person. He petitioned for copies of these papers in order to prepare a reply.[3] Dec. 20. The request was granted.

[1] Col. Willett of West Chester, Col. Isaac Hicks, and Mr. James Jackson of Flushing, all of New York.

[2] Both title-pages of this edition are dated 1730, but the volume, containing 243 pages besides the Charter and Index, includes the entire proceedings of 1731.

[3] Br. S. P. O., Proprieties, vol. xiii., s. 14, 16.

The proposal of Rhode Island to refer the boundary CHAP. XV.
question, was communicated to Massachusetts by Gov.
Jenckes, and met a favorable reception. The provincial 1731.
Assembly ordered a bill to be prepared for that purpose, Dec. 28.
and four weeks later appointed three commissioners to 1731-2
meet with those of Rhode Island.[1] Jan. 26.

Partridge was absent from London when Sandford received the memorials against bills of credit. On his return, he wrote to Sandford, urging him not to deliver Feb. 2.
them till he could again hear from Rhode Island. Meanwhile Gov. Jenckes had written to Sandford, to withhold his petition to the King on account of the clause contained in it, relating to the veto power; so a letter from the Assembly to Partridge stated, but Sandford denied having received any such communication from Jenckes. At any rate they were both too late. All the papers had already been delivered, and orders of reference had upon them. Partridge also wrote to deputy-governor Wanton, depre- 4.
cating this dispute as being disastrous to the interests of Rhode Island, and exerted his influence, although vainly, as the sequel proves, to prevent the prosecution.[2] A reply to this letter, and an answer to the memorials were prepared 1732. May 3.
by the Assembly, to be used in defence of the colony.

Gov. Jenckes had given notice when last elected, that he should not again be a candidate. William Wanton was chosen governor, and his brother John was re-elected deputy-governor. This continued for two years, and is the only case in which two brothers held the two executive offices at the same time. The proxies from New Shoreham were thrown out, not being returned by a person duly appointed at the town meeting. The import duty on negro slaves was repealed by order of the King.

[1] Mass. Court Files, iii. 64, 5. Roger Walcot of Windsor, Osias Pitkin of Hartford, and Joseph Fowler of Lebanon, all of Connecticut, were the commissioners selected by the Mass. Committee, and approved by the R. I. Ass'y. in May following.

[2] These two letters from Partridge are in Foster Papers, bound vol. ii. pp. 146–150.

CHAP. XV. 1732. More care in the wording of statutes had become necessary. The old custom was for the Assembly to pass an act in substance, leaving it for the clerk or recorder to put it in proper form. The inconvenience of such a loose mode of proceeding, had more than once been felt, and there is reason to believe that the intention of the Assembly had sometimes been misrepresented, through carelessness or design, from this cause. In one matter, at least, which has become of historical importance, although of no practical moment at the time, the State has suffered to the present day from this inadvertence. We refer to the interpolated phrases in the law regulating the admission of freemen.[1] The recently adopted plan of printing the laws, and the frequent requisitions from England for copies of them, compelled greater care in their composi-
June 12. tion. An engrossing committee was therefore appointed at this session. Franklin petitioned to be employed as public printer, which was allowed for one year, at a salary of twenty pounds. Tavern-keepers were barred the right of action in cases where they trusted any one for liquor beyond the amount of twenty shillings.

The petition of Gov. Jenckes, having passed the usual routine through the Privy Council to the Board of Trade, was referred by them to the law officers of the crown, whose
Aug. 5. opinion was rendered clearly and decisively that, by the charter of Rhode Island, the governor had no veto power; that it was his duty to seal attested copies of public acts, but not necessary that he should examine them before sealing; and more than all, that the King himself had no power reserved in the charter, either to sanction or to veto any act of the Assembly that was not inconsistent with the laws of England; but if any act conflicted with these, then it was in itself void by the terms of the charter.[2]

Sept. 27. The first newspaper published in Rhode Island, and

[1] See chaps. IX. XI. Vol. i. pp. 311, 479, n.

[2] Br. S. P. O., Proprieties, vol. xiii. s. 29.

the fourth in New England, was commenced by James Franklin. It was called the Rhode Island Gazette, and appeared on Thursday of each week.[1] It was a single sheet only eight inches by twelve. But a very few numbers of it are now in existence. It lasted only six months, and was then discontinued for want of patronage. CHAP. XV. 1732.

For purposes of defence, a duty of sixpence a ton was levied on all vessels entering the colony, except fishermen. The governor received a fee of five shillings from the treasury for every commission to colonial officers signed by him. Two constables of Attleboro' having exercised jurisdiction within the "gore" claimed by Rhode Island, were committed for examination by the justices of Providence county. The Massachusetts Assembly proposed to re-survey the northern line of Rhode Island, in order to renew the stakes and bounds set up thirteen years before.[2] Oct. 25. Dec. 8.

The lottery system, soon destined to make an important figure in the history of the State, and to receive the sanction of the legislature, was first introduced by private persons, and suppressed by statute. The reason assigned for the act was, that by these "unlawful games, called lotteries, many people have been led into a foolish expense of money." They were forbidden to be drawn under a penalty of five hundred pounds, with a fine of ten pounds for any one who should take a ticket. 1732-3 Jan. 23.

It was a work of time to arrange the preliminaries for a reference of the boundary question to gentlemen residing at a great distance. Both here and in Massachusetts the subject came up at almost every session of the legislature. A messenger was sent to the New York commissioners, to inquire if they would meet those named by Massachusetts at the appointed time in New London. Committees were selected by both colonies to present 1733. May 2.

[1] Mr. Thomas, in his History of Printing, says the first number appeared Sept. 27, 1732, which was on Wednesday.

[2] Mass. Court Files, iii. 67.

CHAP. XV. 1733. June 11.

their case at the meeting. Judge Byfield of the Admiralty Court having died, the Assembly appointed his deputy, George Dunbar, of Newport to fill the place till the King's will could be known. The whale fishery had long been conducted on a small scale within the colony. Whales frequented the quiet waters of the Narraganset, and were often taken with boats. A stimulus had been given to this enterprise by the recent premium placed upon it, so that vessels began to be fitted out for the purpose. The first regularly equipped whaleman from Rhode Island, of which we have any knowledge, arrived in Newport at this time with one hundred and fourteen barrels of oil, and two hundred pounds of bone, upon which the bounty was paid. It was the sloop Pelican, of Newport, owned by Benjamin Thurston. About fifteen years before, small sloops had begun to be used at Nantucket for taking whales, and at this time some twenty-five sail, all under fifty tons burden, were there employed, obtaining about thirty-seven hundred barrels of oil annually. This was the commencement of that career of "victorious industry," which was long afterward illustrated in the British House of Commons by the splendid rhetoric of Burke.[1]

[1] "Look at the manner in which the people of New England have of late carried on the whale fishery. Whilst we follow them among the tumbling mountains of ice, and behold them penetrating into the deepest frozen recesses of Hudson's Bay and Davis' Straits, whilst we are looking for them beneath the Arctic circle, we hear that they have pierced into the opposite region of polar cold, that they are at the antipodes, and engaged under the frozen serpent of the south. Falkland Island, which seemed too remote and romantic an object for the grasp of national ambition, is but a stage and resting-place in the progress of their victorious industry. Nor is the equinoctial heat more discouraging to them, than the accumulated winter of both the poles. We know that whilst some of them draw the line and strike the harpoon on the coast of Africa, others run the longitude, and pursue their gigantic game along the coast of Brazil. No sea but what is vexed by their fisheries. No climate that is not witness to their toils. Neither the perseverance of Holland, nor the activity of France, nor the dexterous and firm sagacity of English enterprise, ever carried this most perilous mode of hardy industry to the extent to which it has been pushed by this recent people; a

CHAP. XV. 1733.

One hundred pounds were voted to assist the towns in rebuilding Pawtucket bridge. The statute revising the judiciary system, prescribed that the judges and clerks of Common Pleas should hold their places during good behavior. This tenure was now abolished, and the system of annual election by the Assembly was adopted. The deputies had always been chosen semi-annually. It was ordered that in future they be elected to serve the whole year, but this alteration was so repulsive to public sentiment, that the act was repealed before the year expired.

July 2.

The schedules of the General Assembly, printed by Franklin, were first distributed to the towns during this summer, and the October sessions were appointed to be held at Providence and South Kingstown alternately.

General Oglethorpe, having just established his colony in Georgia, and founded the city of Savannah, was invited by Massachusetts to visit that province on his return to England. The Rhode Island Assembly voted him a public reception, but the pressure of business compelled him to decline these merited courtesies.

A fifth bank, amounting to one hundred thousand pounds, was created, on similar terms with the former issues, besides an emission of four thousand pounds to be used for arming Fort George. The interest for the first year, on this new loan at five per cent, was appropriated for a pier or harbor at Block Island to benefit the fisheries. Of the remaining interest, one half was to go to the treasury, and the other to be divided rateably among the towns. Collector Kay sent a copy of this act to the Board of Trade, with a letter complaining also of the tonnage duty laid by the Assembly for purposes of defence, as violations of the acts of trade.[1]

Sept. 4.

The joint committee from New York and Connecticut

people who are still, as it were, in the gristle, and not yet hardened into the bone of manhood." Speech on moving resolutions for conciliation with the Colonies, March 22, 1775.

[1] Br. S. P. O., Proprieties, vol. xiii. s. 55.

CHAP. XV. 1733. met in New London this summer to decide the controversy between Massachusetts and Rhode Island. They were unable to agree upon a settlement of the boundaries, or the choice of an umpire, which was allowed them in case of a tie. The Assembly at Kingstown, convened for the
Oct. 31. first time in the new colony house in that town, voted three silver tankards of the value of fifty pounds each, with the arms of Rhode Island handsomely engraved on them, to be sent to the gentlemen who had acted in behalf of the colony, "with the acknowledgment of this General Assembly, for their assistance in endeavoring to reconcile and put an end to the dispute between the two governments."[1]

Massachusetts, prevented by royal instructions from issuing any more bills of credit, was alarmed at the great loan in Rhode Island, and endeavored to prevent its circu-
Nov. 6. lation in that province. The legislature published a proclamation, warning the people against receiving Rhode Island bills, and the council proposed a law to prohibit
7. their circulation.[2] The House non-concurred, but advised the merchants to combine in a refusal to take them in payment for goods. This was done for a while, but soon gave way. A private bank of one hundred and ten thousand pounds was created, to provide a substitute, redeemable in ten years in silver at nineteen shillings an ounce. But the flood of paper from other colonies, and the advantage of the Rhode Island trade to the merchants of Boston, were irresistible. The combination gave way. Silver rose to twenty-seven shillings an ounce, and foreign exchange in proportion. The private bank bills at nineteen shillings were withdrawn from circulation. Debts

[1] Col. Willett of Westchester did not attend. Col. Lewis Morris, jr., of the same place, Col. Isaac Hicks of Hempstead, and Mr. James Jackson of Flushing, were the Commissioners to whom these pieces of plate were voted. It would be curious to know what has become of these tankards, or whether any of them are still owned by the heirs of those gentlemen.

[2] Mass. Court Files, iii. 69–72.

were paid at a loss of some thirty-three per cent. to the creditor, and a fearful stride towards the impending bankruptcy was made. CHAP. XV. 1733.

Except the clergy of the Church of England, the Quakers were the only religious society whose preachers were, as yet, authorized to perform the marriage ceremony. This privilege had been accorded by the King. The Assembly now empowered the ministers of all denominations to unite persons in marriage, and established the legal fee on such occasions at three shillings. The free passage of Pawtucket bridge had been obstructed by adjacent landowners and toll demanded. This was deemed a nuisance, which the authorities of Providence county were directed to abate. The appeal to the King upon the eastern boundary dispute was sent to England. Dec. 3.

Soon after the Assembly rose, Gov. Wanton died. His long career of public service had endeared him to the colonists, and his daring naval exploits had won for him the regard of his sovereign. In consequence of these, when the two brothers afterwards visited England, they were received at court, and presented by Queen Anne with a silver punch bowl and salver. They were further honored by the addition to their family coat of arms of the device of a gamecock alighting on a hawk. For the past two years they had enjoyed the unequalled honor, as brothers, of being associated in the highest offices of the colony.[1]

There was a session of the Assembly at Warwick during the winter, at which only private business was transacted. 1733-4 Feb. 4.

[1] A good story is told of Wm. Wanton in Deane's Scituate. Before his removal from that place to Newport, prior to 1700, he had married Ruth Bryant, daughter of a Congregational deacon. Wanton's family were Quakers. "Religious objections were made to the match on both sides. He said, 'Friend Ruth, let us break from this unreasonable bondage—*I* will give up *my* religion, and *thou* shalt *thine*, and we will go over to the Church of England, *and go to the devil together*.' They fulfilled this resolution so far," says our author, "as to go to the Church of England, and marrying, and adhering to the Church of England during life."

CHAP. XV. The petition of Rhode Island upon the eastern boundary dispute, was presented to the King. It set forth the
1734. April 19. charter limits of the colony, and that Massachusetts claimed about twenty thousand acres east of Pawtucket River, besides the three miles east of Narraganset bay, that were clearly granted to Rhode Island.

May 1. John Wanton was chosen governor, and George Hassard deputy-governor at the spring election. This continued for five years. The House now comprised thirty-six deputies, who with the ten assistants and three general officers, secretary, attorney, and treasurer, made the number of a full Assembly forty-nine. The sheriffs, formerly general, had now become county officers.

June 13. Massachusetts wrote to request an exchange of prisoners, promising fair trials in their own courts of any complaints against them. Agreeably to this request, the Assembly returned a prisoner to the custody of that province
17. for trial. Some damage had resulted from backwater at
Oct. various mill dams in the colony. The Assembly at Provi-
30. dence passed their first law on the subject of flowage, requiring mill owners to make ponds, and regulating the modes of assessing damages by a jury, in such cases, and of settling controversies among the owners of mills. Bridges over the south branch of Pawtuxet River, and at the point in Newport, were ordered.

Dec. 19. The Rhode Island boundary petition was referred by the Privy Council to the Plantations' Committee, and by
1734-5 Jan. 13. them to the Board of Trade, in the usual course. The agent of Massachusetts was notified in due form, and thus the matter rested for two years, while the replies were preparing.

Feb. 18. The winter session of the Assembly was the first ever held at Greenwich. Attention was directed to the preservation of oysters in the bay, large quantities of them having been taken to burn for lime. The town councils were empowered to prevent this wasteful destruction. The attempt to cut through the beach at Block Island was reported by the committee to be a failure. They were therefore ordered to repair and enlarge the old pier. Fort George had been completed at a cost of ten thousand pounds, but was not fully armed. The colony again petitioned for cannon and round shot to mount the battery, which was referred, as usual, to the Board of Trade.[1] CHAP. XV. 1735. May 1.

At the general election no change was made. The Block Island pier was the only matter of interest at the adjourned session. Too much timber had been purchased for it; the contractor was sued by the dealers, and the Assembly ordered it to be sold, except enough to finish the pier. The harbor at Westerly being closed by the filling of the outlet from the salt pond, it was proposed to divert the course of Pawcatuck River into the pond, so as to secure a good harbor, by keeping this outlet always open, and deepening the water on the bar. The Assembly agreed to pay three-fourths of the expense of this work, if Westerly would keep up the bridges, and pay the remainder. To protect the river fisheries it was forbidden to erect dams or weirs on any stream to hinder the passage of fish, or to catch them, for three days in the week, except by hook and line. Leave was granted to George Taylor to teach a school in a chamber of the county house in Providence, on certain conditions.[2] Aid was given to build bridges over both branches of the Pawtuxet River on the Plainfield Road in Scituate. The Court of Vice-Admiralty sometimes exceeded their proper jurisdiction in trying causes, not of a maritime nature, that were brought before them. The judges of the Superior Court were empowered to issue injunctions upon such proceedings in future. This was a bold measure, for the Admiralty Court, being of royal appointment, would be likely to 7. June 16. Aug. 18.

[1] Br. S. P. O., Proprieties, vol. xiii. s. 48.

[2] He is the second schoolmaster of whom there is any record in Providence. The first was Wm. Turpin, more than fifty years before a teacher in Providence, and now the town treasurer.

CHAP. XV. assert jurisdiction paramount to the colonial tribunals, and to claim the exclusive construction of its own powers.

1735. Oct. 29. Nothing was done at the session in South Kingstown.

Dec. 1. In reply to a letter from the Board of Trade, inquiring what revenue duties were laid upon British commerce in this colony, Gov. Wanton wrote, that the impost on slaves brought from the West Indies, having been removed, there were now no duties levied here affecting the direct trade with England.[1]

A fearful epidemic, known as the "throat distemper," which appeared in the spring in New Hampshire, continued through the year and till the following summer, extending as far as Carolina. It is described as a "swelled throat, with white or ash-colored specks, an efflorescence on the skin, great debility of the whole system, and a strong tendency to putridity."[2] It was the greatest scourge ever known in New England, and especially fatal to children. Among the losses sustained by this colony, but whether from the prevailing epidemic or not is unknown,
1735-6 Feb. 1. was that of Gabriel Bernon, the distinguished Huguenot, who for nearly forty years had been a resident of Rhode Island. The first three Episcopal churches in the colony owed their origin to his untiring zeal. He died at the advanced age of ninety-one years and ten months, and was buried beneath St. John's Church, with unusual marks of respect.

18. The Assembly, at its winter session gave their principal attention to bridges. No less than six, three on the Plainfield Road, one at Woonsocket, at Newport, and at Queen's River in South Kingstown, were ordered to be built or repaired.

1736. May 4 & 5. The May session had of late been devoted exclusively to the admission of freemen to the general election; putting all other business over to the adjournment. The

[1] Br. S. P. O., Proprieties, vol. xiii., s. 70.

[2] Belknap's N. Hamp., ii. 118.

town councils had long possessed full power to open highways, and to assess damages connected therewith, which was again confirmed. A line of stages between Boston and Newport was established, and exclusive privileges for seven years, were granted by the Assembly to encourage the enterprise. A law was passed to prevent bribery at elections. Both offenders were to forfeit double the sum offered or received, and to be debarred the right of voting for three years.

1736. June 14. Oct. 27.

The reply of Massachusetts to the Rhode Island appeal, was presented to the Board of Trade, claiming the whole tract east of Narraganset Bay and Pawtucket River under the Plymouth colony patent, confirmed, as was contended, by the royal commissioners in 1664.[1] That adjustment was not considered by the commissioners themselves to be final, but only temporary, till the King's will could be known; but the tacit consent of both colonies since that time had given a color of right to the Massachusetts claim.

1736-7 Jan. 9.

The winter session, held for the second time at Greenwich, was occupied with private business. His Majesty's ship Tartar, of twenty guns, being in the harbor of Newport, the Assembly ordered that "a score of the best sheep that may be got be presented" to her commander, Matthew Norris, for the use of the crew. Heretofore the expenses of jurors were paid out of the treasury, but this being found inconvenient, the Assembly fixed the fees at six shillings a day, they to defray their own expenses. To preserve the perch in Easton's pond, it was forbidden to draw seines or nets either in the pond or creek. The earliest law exempting active firemen from military or jury duty, was enacted in favor of the two engine companies recently organized in Newport.[2]

1737. Feb. 15. May 4. June 13.

New Hampshire was involved in a dispute with Mas-

[1] See chap. ix., Vol. i., p. 315.

[2] In Feb., 1763, this exemption was extended to the firemen in Providence.

CHAP. XV. 1737. sachusetts respecting her eastern and southern boundaries. It was referred to a board of twenty commissioners, five each from the councils of New York, New Jersey, Rhode Island, and Nova Scotia, of whom five should form a quorum. Aug. 1. Eight of these, three from Nova Scotia and the five from Rhode Island,[1] met at Hampton, and were afterward joined by Philip Livingston from New York, who Sept. 2. was made president. The decree of the commissioners as to the eastern line was definite, and was confirmed by the King; that upon the southern line was contingent upon the construction of the Massachusetts charter. Both parties appealed, and New Hampshire ultimately gained on the south more than she had claimed before the commissioners. Meanwhile, the dispute between Massachusetts and Rhode Island was progressing in England. Mr. Partridge presented to the Board of Trade his answer to Oct. 27. the memorial of the Massachusetts agent,[2] in reply to the Rhode Island petition. It is a document of great length, combatting the position of Wilkes in twenty sections, seventeen of which relate to the Attleboro' gore, and the remainder to the eastern shore, where the towns of Tiverton and Seconnet, with the greater part of Bristol, and Freetown are claimed under the charter of King Charles.[3]

26. Nothing of public interest was done by the Assembly at South Kingstown. Nov. 22. There was an adjourned session at Newport, at which a fifth judge of Common Pleas for each county was appointed, to avoid the inconvenience of a tie in the decisions of the bench. Power was given to town councils to remove any person who, by vote of the 1737-8 town, might be rejected as an inhabitant. At the next Feb. 14. adjourned session, an act was passed to secure the interest on the bills of credit loaned to individuals, much of which had been lost by their removal from the colony. The principal was secured by mortgage, but the interest was

[1] Samuel Vernon, John Gardner, John Potter, Ezekiel Warner, and George Cornell. Belknap's N. Hamp., ii. 134.

[2] Francis Wilkes.

[3] Br. S. P. O., Proprieties, vol. 14.

not. A purchaser who bought lands under mortgage, CHAP.
became responsible for the principal, but not for the in- XV.
terest. It was now enacted that no transfer to such pur- 1737-8
chaser should be valid, without a proper bond given by
him for the payment of interest also.

At the spring election, the same officers were chosen. 1738.
Nothing was done at the adjourned session. The death May 3. June
of the deputy-governor, Hon. George Hassard, who, for 13.
five successive years had been elected to that office, occasioned a special meeting of the Assembly, at which Daniel
Abbott was chosen as his successor. The Assembly then July 5.
adjourned till the next month, when the town of Westerly Aug.
was divided, and Charlestown set off from it; each town 22.
to send two deputies to the legislature. A new bank, the
sixth, of one hundred thousand pounds was created, on
the same terms as the former loans, except that the interest, as well as the principal, was secured by mortgage
on real estate. At the autumn session in Providence, Oct.
nothing was done. 25.

The papers relating to the eastern boundary having all
been presented, and several hearings had by the agents May
before the Board of Trade, they reported to the Planta- 10.
tions' Committee, recommending that commissioners
from the neighboring provinces be appointed by the King
to determine the line. Against this recommendation,
Wilkes petitioned the King, reciting the substance of his June
memorial to the Board of Trade in reply to Rhode Island, 19.
and praying that no new commissions should be granted.
His petition took the usual course of reference to the July
Plantations' Committee, before whom the cause was again 20.
argued by the agents, and the petition was rejected as Nov.
being frivolous and vexatious. This second report being 1.
made to the Privy Council, an order was given directing 30.
commissions to be issued for settling the line; but nearly
two years elapsed before this was done. Four pirates,
tried at the October term, were executed this month at
Newport.

CHAP. XV. The Assembly were in the habit of adjourning the regular May and October sessions, often to different
1738. counties. At an adjourned session in Providence, it was
Dec. 19. decided that the adjournments in future should be to some town in the same county where the regular session for that season was held. Another law to prevent illegal voting was passed; whoever should put in two votes was to be deprived of his franchise for three years, and to forfeit two pounds, and any unqualified person voting
1738-9 Feb. 20. was to be fined the same amount. A further adjournment was made to Warwick. A new colony house was ordered for Newport. The bridges at Woonsocket, Pawtucket, and Chepachet received additional aid from the treasury. The towns were empowered to assess traders from abroad for a fair proportion of the expenses of the local governments.

1739. May 2. At the annual election, Daniel Abbott was chosen deputy-governor, thus confirming the act of the Assembly, and John Wanton was re-elected governor. A commit-
June 6. tee, instructed by this Assembly, wrote to Massachusetts concerning the eastern boundary, proposing another effort to settle the dispute by a joint commission, and thus save the heavy expense of further litigation in England. The
9. General Court referred the letter to a committee of both houses to report thereon. They recommended the ap-
11. pointment of commissioners, with full powers to arrange the whole controversy with those equally empowered by Rhode Island, and in case of disagreement, then this joint commission should select seven men to determine the
July 7. matter. The report was adopted, and commissioners were appointed at the next meeting of the General Court.
10. The Assembly promptly seconded this conciliatory measure, by appointing commissioners to meet them, and requiring that the business should be adjusted within three
Aug. 21. months. At a special session soon afterward, they authorized the commissioners in case of disagreement, to remit to England the necessary funds to defray the charges

of taking out the commission recommended by the Board of Trade. CHAP. XV.

The publication of Callender's Century Sermon, the only authentic account of early Rhode Island, embracing the first century of the history of Aquedneck, was the great literary event of this year. In a tone of candor, and with a freedom from sectarian bias, the more remarkable from his nearness to the exciting period he describes, the reverend author narrates the sufferings of the first colonists in a spirit that illustrates the religion he professed. The accuracy of his narrative, so far as he descends to details, leaves little for the later historian to correct, and awakens regret that the plan of his Discourse, did not permit him to enlarge his work to the scope and dimensions of a civil history. From him we learn that at this time there were thirty-three churches of the several denominations in the colony, of which twelve were Baptist, ten Quakers, six Congregational or Presbyterian, and five Episcopalian, besides other religious assemblies, not yet organized into churches, and having no regular houses of worship. Mr. Callender's own church, the Baptist, outnumbered any other, and, excluding the Quakers, all others in the colony, and was represented in every town. A degree of harmony in Christian intercourse prevailed among the several churches, which might be vainly sought elsewhere until a very recent period. The voluntary principle had achieved its own triumph, and was exerting upon the neighboring colonies the powerful though silent influence, of successful example. 1739.

NOTE.—The following note should be appended to line 23 on page 114.—The earliest mill grant in R. I. was made in 1646, to John Smith to establish a grist-mill. He was to pay the cost of "the stampers" that had been imported from England by the colonists, amounting to about £100. These wooden stampers were used to pulverize corn. The mill was located just above Mill Bridge, in Providence. The street leading up the hill from the mill was called Stampers street, probably from these works rather than from the tradition cited in note 3, p. 258, vol. i. In excavating for the Blackstone Canal, many years ago, some of the old timbers forming the bottom of the dam were discovered. This was no doubt the first hydraulic work in this State, if not in New England.

CHAPTER XVI.

1739—1746.

FROM THE COMMENCEMENT OF THE SECOND SPANISH WAR, OCTOBER, 1739, TO THE FINAL ADJUSTMENT OF THE EASTERN BOUNDARY, FEBRUARY, 1746-7.

CHAP. XVI. 1739. THE alarm of war again roused the martial spirit of the colony. The affairs of Spain were hurrying that power into a conflict with Great Britain, which the genius of Walpole and the peaceful policy of the British ministry could no longer avert. Rumors of a ministerial crisis, involving the peace of Europe, had reached the colonies, Aug. 21. and Rhode Island prepared for a fight upon her favorite element, the sea. The governor was instructed to grant all privateer commissions that he should deem needful, pursuant to the King's warrant. Three of the principal merchants of Newport[1] fitted out a ship immediately, receiving her armament from the public stores. The action was none too rapid. Already had the Right of Search been exercised by the Spaniards, under their treaty with England, in a manner to give offence to the latter power. Spain had not yet lost the supremacy of the sea which, before the age of Elizabeth, she had held undisputed. She was still a first-rate maritime power, and defended her privilege with equal firmness, but with far less insolence than was shown at a later day, upon the same ques-

[1] Godfrey Malbone, John Brown, and George Wanton.

tion, by her great rival. The violation of treaty stipulations regulating trade between England and the Spanish American colonies was incessant. The shrewdness of British merchants, overleaping all the bounds of law, compelled Spain to a rigid exercise of her right, under the treaty, to search vessels suspected of contraband trading. All experience has shown that this right of search, however limited, can have no vital existence without imperiling the peace of nations. And here it may be added, that history has equally proved that successive maritime States have resisted this right while exerted against themselves, and in turn asserted it when they had won the dominion of the seas. May it never prove that the United States, after their glorious vindication of the freedom of the seas in the last war with Great Britain, shall follow the historic example, by claiming exclusive rights hereafter, and sacrifice their noblest principle to gratify the cravings of national ambition! The war about commencing, was ostensibly a struggle for the freedom of the British flag against what were termed the arrogant pretensions of Spain. It was, in fact, a war of commercial rivalry, in which the trade of Spanish America was to be the prize. The undefined limits of Georgia, and the payment of the Spanish debt, were insignificant causes by the side of this brilliant guerdon.

The Whig ministry were finally overborne by the popular clamor, and Walpole committed the great error of his political life in retaining his place at the expense of his principles and convictions. War was declared amidst extravagant demonstrations of joy; but the remark of the Premier was verified within ten years, when the ringing of bells gave place to the wringing of hands. Oct. 19.

There was another point, directly affecting British interests, connected with the trade between the colonies and the West Indies, upon which this war was to exert a material influence. The "molasses act," as it was termed, had been passed six years before, imposing a heavy tax

CHAP. XVI. 1739. upon West India products imported from foreign islands, especially the French, into the northern colonies. Rhode Island protested against this act, on the ground that it was only by this produce that she could be paid for her exports thither, and thereby be enabled to purchase English manufactures. Newport was largely engaged in distilling rum, which interfered in some measure with the trade of the English sugar islands. The other colonies equally opposed the act, and Partridge, the Rhode Island agent, conducted the affair for them also. In his letter to the Board of Trade, enclosing the petition, he claimed that the bill divested the colonists of their rights as Englishmen, in laying taxes against their consent, and without their being represented on the floor of Parliament.

The war-cry of revolution, which was ere long to rally the American colonies in the struggle for independence, was here first sounded by the Quaker agent of Rhode Island, to cease only with the dismemberment of the British empire. Further restrictions were proposed to be placed Oct. 31. upon the West India trade. The Assembly therefore requested the governor to "write to our agent, strenuously to oppose at home the making any addition to the sugar act, that so much affects the northern plantations; and that his Honor also write to the neighboring governments, requesting them to join with us in opposing the same."

Notice was sent to Massachusetts, that Rhode Island would proceed no farther in the attempt to obtain an amicable adjustment of the eastern boundary, but would await the royal commission. The marks and bounds set up on the western line, requiring renewal, a joint committee of the two colonies had been appointed for the purpose three years before. The Connecticut men had failed to attend upon several appointments, and the Rhode Island committee therefore proceeded alone to renew the Nov. 15–20. stone heaps and tree marks along the whole line, occupying six days in the work. Their report was made at an adjourned session of the Assembly in South Kingstown, and entered in full upon the records. CHAP. XVI.

The news of the declaration of war with Spain, occasioned a special session of the Assembly at the same place. The small pox had again broken out in the colony. A quarantine house was built on Dutch Island, and relief extended to the towns of Portsmouth and Jamestown, for their care of the sick. But the chief purpose of this extra session was to place the colony upon a war establishment. A garrison of fifty-two men, under command of Col. John Cranston, was thrown into Fort George, and the works were put in fighting order. Military stores were provided. Troops were sent to New Shoreham, and a mounted battery of six heavy guns was furnished for the defence of Block Island. Seven watchtowers were erected along the coast and on the shores of the bay, in which the towns where they were located were to keep a constant guard under direction of the council of war. Five beacons were established upon commanding heights, the outermost at Block Island, and the northernmost at Portsmouth, to convey intelligence of any hostile demonstration. Thus much being done for internal defence, the colony ordered the sloop Tartar, of one hundred and fifteen tons, to be built for war purposes, and during the coming year five privateers, manned by four hundred men, were fitted out by the merchants of Newport, to cruise against the Spaniards. 1739–40. Feb. 26.

At the spring election, John Wanton was again chosen governor, and Richard Ward, who some years before had been secretary of the colony, was elected deputy-governor. Advices of the intended expedition under Admiral Vernon against the Spanish West Indies, with orders to raise troops to join the royal squadron at Jamaica, having been received in the colonies, the Assembly at once enlisted soldiers and provided two transports to convey them. The colony sloop Tartar, being completed, was armed by order of the Assembly, with twelve carriage 1740. May 7. June 17.

CHAP. XVI. and as many swivel guns, and fitted for sea under command of Captain Cranston. She was a spacious vessel
1740. of her class, having deck-room sufficient for a hundred men
June 30. to engage in battle. Gov. Belcher of Massachusetts informed Gov. Wanton that a suspicious looking ship had appeared off the coast. The Tartar immediately sailed in pursuit, captured the vessel, which proved to be a French contraband schooner, and brought her into Newport, where she was condemned by the Vice Admiralty Court.

July 5. It was at this exciting juncture, when the deeds in which the old governor had won so much distinction in his youth were being re-enacted, that John Wanton died. For the past twelve years, the first five as deputy-governor and the last seven as chief magistrate, he had held the highest offices of the State—a merited return for the higher honor that his personal qualities had long before conferred upon the colony. The Assembly convened to fill the vacancy, promoted Richard Ward to the position
15. of governor, and elected William Greene in his place as deputy-governor.

Orders were received from the head-quarters at New York for only two companies, of one hundred men each, to be drafted in Rhode Island, and two English lieutenants came on to collect them. This caused the discharge of a large number of soldiers enlisted in May, who were now paid off. Captain Joseph Sheffield had command of the first company that was equipped at Newport in the spring. The Providence company was commanded by Capt. Wil-
Aug. 18. liam Hopkins. When all was prepared for sailing, the Assembly invited the commissioned officers to dine with the court, and entertained the soldiers at public expense.
Sept. The transports sailed for New York with the two companies, to join the grand squadron at Jamaica, soon afterward destined to a fatal repulse before the stupendous fortress of Carthagena.

The arrival of George Whitefield, who, for some time had been preaching in the southern and middle colonies,

formed an era in the religious history of New England. CHAP. XVI.
The "great revival" had already commenced, under the
lead of Jonathan Edwards, when Whitefield's thrilling 1740.
eloquence carried the excitement to its height. Commencing at Newport, whither great crowds resorted to hear him from all parts of the colony, he travelled through other portions of New England for six months before his return to London. The extravagancies of the new converts, roused the opposition of many in the established church, especially in Connecticut, but a large portion of the ministers, among whom was Edwards, looked with favor upon his work, and recognised in it a divine influence.

In contrast with the demonstrative character of the great revivalist, came the calm Quaker, Samuel Fothergill, an eminent preacher among the Friends. He remained for some months in Newport at the house of his brother-in-law, John Proud. The influence of both these celebrated preachers, was long felt throughout the colony, in the rapid increase of the Quaker and Baptist societies, most of Whitefield's converts uniting with the latter church.

The emission of paper money by the colonies, had April
already occupied the attention of Parliament. The 25.
House of Commons addressed the King, urging that a full account of all these issues should be obtained, to lay
before the House. An order in council was passed, calling 30.
on the Board of Trade to furnish the facts. The Board
required every colony to send a statement of the amount, May
tenor, and sterling value of the bills of credit issued by 20.
each, with a plan for their redemption in the most easy and
effectual manner. The address of the Commons, com- Aug.
plaining of the injuries to British commerce caused by 19.
these bills, was soon afterward sent to Rhode Island by the Board, with information that circulars had been sent to all the royal governments in America, suspending the

CHAP. XVI. 1740. further issue of paper money.[1] This was a significant warning to the charter and proprietary governments, but unfortunately it was not regarded by Rhode Island. The expenses of the war demanded another loan of public credit. The Assembly therefore created a new bank of Sept. 23. twenty thousand pounds for ten years, at four per cent. The former bills had merely expressed on the face their nominal value in pounds, shillings, and pence, but in these it was attempted to fix the value by further stating the exact amount of gold or silver that they should represent. Hence they were termed New Tenor bills. The rate established estimated silver at nine shillings an ounce, and gold at £6, 13*s* 4*d*. an ounce. Besides this new bank, an issue of ten thousand pounds of the old tenor bills was made to supply the treasury. The value of silver in the old bills was twenty-seven shillings an ounce. Against these proceedings, two assistants[2] and five deputies[3] entered a protest upon the records, giving as their reasons for disapproval, that the new act would depreciate the outstanding bills, injure trade, and oppress those whose estates were in money, and was impolitic in view of the Oct. 29. late action in Parliament. At the next session a representation of the whole paper money system was ordered to be drawn up, in reply to the enquiries of the Board of Trade. The last communication from that source, made it expedient to amend the bank act so far as to make the value of silver conform to the English standard, which Dec. 2. was done at an adjourned session held in Warwick. In-

[1] These letters from the Board of Trade on the paper currency are printed in R. I. Col. Rec., vol. v., p. 7.

[2] Benjamin Ellery and Peter Bours.

[3] William Ellery, William Anthony, Ezbon Sandford, George Goulding, George Lawton. The last clause of the protest is worthy of record. "Because the ruin of this flourishing colony will probably in a great measure be owing to this fatal act; we would have the whole colony and posterity know we have not deserved their imprecations on this occasion, but have endeavored to preserve and deliver down to posterity the privileges and the property which our ancestors earned with so much hazard, toil, and expense."

stead of nine shillings an ounce, the new bills stated silver at six shillings and ninepence sterling, and gold at five pounds an ounce, so that a new tenor bill was four times the value of an old bill, and was soon afterward required to be taken at that rate in business exchanges. CHAP. XVI. 1740.

The notice sent by Rhode Island that the boundary question must be determined by a royal commission, left nothing further to be done than for these commissions to be sued out in England. The Board of Trade therefore wrote to the governor, requiring the appointment of two officers in Rhode Island upon whom all processes in the case might be served, and also that a full statement of the boundaries claimed should be furnished. The royal letters patent were issued to five gentlemen from each of the provinces of New York, New Jersey, and Nova Scotia, any five of whom were to be a quorum, to settle the eastern line of Rhode Island. The commissioners were to meet at Providence on the first Tuesday in April ensuing, and to annex to their final report a map or draught of the boundaries agreed upon. Either colony might appeal within three months after the decision had been rendered, and if no such appeal was then taken, the decision was to be final upon confirmation by the King. All expenses were to be equally divided between the litigants.[1] The Assembly ordered copies of the commission to be sent to each of the gentlemen therein named, with letters to those at Annapolis Royal, informing them that a vessel would be sent from Rhode Island to bring them hither at the appointed time. A committee was appointed to prepare the case, and to conduct it before the commissioners, and also to provide accommodations for them during their stay in Providence. Massachusetts also appointed a committee to prepare her case, and named the two officers required in the commission. Aug. 1. Sept. 4. Dec. 2. 31.

The representation concerning paper currency, was at

[1] The letter and commission, containing the names of the 15 commissioners, are printed in R. I. Col. Rec., iv. 586–90.

CHAP. XVI. 1740-1 Jan. 9. last sent to the Board of Trade, signed by Gov. Ward. It is a very long and interesting document, reciting the objects and the history of these issues, with a sketch of the condition of the colony. From this we learn that the commerce of Rhode Island had greatly increased within ten years, since the last returns, and now numbered a hundred and twenty vessels engaged in the West Indian, African, European, and Coasting trade, of which seven or eight were employed in direct trade with England, heretofore chiefly conducted by Boston merchants.[1]

The exigencies of war demanded a revision of the militia system. France was about to ally with Spain, so that further measures were required to defend the colony. The Assembly repealed the act empowering the soldiers
27. to choose their own officers, and vested that right where the charter placed it, in the legislature. A permanent council of war, to consist of the governor and council, with the field-officers and captains, was established. A more thorough drill-system was adopted. Two additional companies were raised in Newport. Fort George was enlarged so as to mount ten more cannon. A powder magazine of brick was constructed, and the military stores were increased in every county. Ten new field-pieces were ordered. Those whose consciences forbade their fighting, were required to act as scouts or guards, to furnish their horses for service in case of alarm, and to do any other duty not repulsive to their religious views. The war sloop Tartar was fitted to be ready for sea in the spring. These preparations occupied the entire session.

The governor was requested to despatch a suitable vessel to Nova Scotia to bring the boundary commissioners
1741. Mar. to Providence. Massachusetts added two members to
27. the committee appointed to prepare her case, one of whom was William Shirley, who, a few months later, succeeded
31. Belcher as governor of the province. A brief statement

[1] Printed in R. I. Col. Rec., vol. v., p. 8–14.

of the claim to be submitted to the commissioners was reported, asserting the middle of the east passage of Narraganset Bay, and so up the Pawtucket River to the starting point of the northern line of Rhode Island, as run in 1719, to be the proper boundary of the two colonies. The General Assembly empowered their committee to employ counsel, and named the two officers[1] required by the commission, upon whom process might be served. On the appointed day, only two of the commissioners[2] appeared. The commission was read, clerks were chosen, and the claims were presented and filed. Rhode Island claimed, under the royal charter, from a point three miles east-north-east of Assonet, due south to the ocean, and westerly to Fox Point; thence by the east bank of the river to Pawtucket falls, and thence due north to the Massachusetts line. The court met and adjourned every week, awaiting the arrival of more members, until the end of the month, when three others[3] having arrived, a quorum was made. Two surveyors[4] were appointed to prepare plans for the use of the court. The next day the clerks were ordered to issue summonses for witnesses, and two officers were named[5] to serve them. The surveyors were required to prepare a plat of the whole of Rhode Island, as well as of the territory in dispute. The court adjourned from time to time through the month, awaiting their report. The General Assembly voted a salary of six shillings sterling, per diem, to each of the commissioners in attendance, besides one half of their expenses. Three other members

CHAP. XVI. 1741. April 1. 7. 30. May 1. 2. 6.

[1] Ezekiel Warner and George Brown.

[2] Archibald Kennedy and James Delancey, of New York.

[3] William Skene, William Shireff, and Erasmus James Phillips, of Nova Scotia.

[4] James Helme of South Kingstown, and William Chandler of Thompson, Conn.

[5] Nathaniel Church of Bristol for Mass., and Thomas Rice of Warwick for R. I.

CHAP. XVI. of the court arrived early in the month,[1] one of whom,
Cadwallader Colden, was made president. Several ad-
1741. journments were had until the witnesses could be collect-
June 3. ed, when the examination was commenced, and continued
from day to day through the month. A vast amount of
record evidence was presented, and a great number of tes-
timonies taken, the whole occupying a large volume.[2]
When this was concluded, and the surveyors had made
24. their report, the pleading commenced. The two attorneys
25–6. for Rhode Island[3] opened the case. The two following days
27. were occupied by the three attorneys for Massachusetts,[4]
and then the Rhode Island counsel made the closing argument. The charter of Connecticut was offered as evi-
29. dence on the part of Massachusetts, and received. The
judgment of the court was made up and filed the next
30. day. Defining Narraganset bay to end at Bullock's Point,
it gave to Rhode Island all the land within three miles
of the shore, south and east of a line measured three miles
north-east from the end of Bullock's Neck, and designated
five places, to the south and east, whence the three-mile
lines were to be run, to define this eastern boundary.
From the south-west corner of Bullock's Neck to Pawtucket falls, high water mark was to be the dividing line,
and thence, a due north line to the established southern
line of Massachusetts was to complete the boundary. An
attested copy of the judgment, with the accompanying map,
July was given to the agents of each party, and the court adjourned to the fourth of September.

Aug. Massachusetts decided to appeal from every part of
27. the judgment as being grievous and injurious. Rhode
Island objecting to the limits given to Narraganset Bay,
that Bullock's Neck, instead of Fox Point, was taken as

[1] Cadwallader Colden and Philip Livingstone of New York, and Otho Hamilton of New Jersey.

[2] Br. S. P. O., America, No. 378.

[3] Daniel Updike and William Bollam.

[4] John Read, Samuel Welles, and William Shirley.

PLAN OF THE DISPUTED TERRITORY

Reduced from a Map, prepared for the

COMMISSION

in 1741

Original in the British State Paper Off.

America No. 378

Massachusetts Bay South Line

Woodward's & Saffery's Stake

GLOCESTER

SENECHATACONET

Abbots Run

ATTLEBOROUGH

Pawtucket Falls

Providence

SEACONK

REHOBOTHE

PROVIDENCE TOWNSHIP

SCITUATE

Keute Point

Patuxet River

Bullock's Neck

Palmer River

SWANSEY

BARRINGTON

Towoset Neck

Mattapoiset

Shawamet

Taunton River

Assonet Neck

Assonet Bridge

E.N.E. 3 miles

FREETON

WARWICK

Bullock's Point

WARREN

BRISTOL

Kenemicut Point

Slade's Ferry

Fall River

Nassauket

Warwick Neck

Bristol

Mt. Hope

EAST GREENWICH

Potowoome

Patience

Hogs Island

TIVERTON

Pocasset

Howland's Ferry

Prudence

Portsmouth

Hope

Nanequaket

DARTMOUTH

Updikes Harbor

Secoquonset

NORTH KINGSTOWN

Plumb Beach Pt.

Rhode Island

Puncatest

LITTLE COMPTON

Conaicut

Dutch Island

Newport

Sekonet

Petaquamscut Ponds

Boston Neck

SOUTH KINGSTOWN

Bonnett

Beaver Tail

Whale Rock

Brenton's Reef

Seaconet Point

Point Pirrill

Point Judith Ponds

Point Judith

M.M.M. Line claimed by Massachusetts,

R.R.R. " " " Rhode Island.

The line marked thus:------ indicates the line ascertained in 1845 by Mr. Borden, under the direction of the Commrs. of Massachusetts.

The lines ABCDEFG I were drawn by order of Court, June 30. 1741

Jas. Helme, Wm. Chandler, Surveyors

the mouth of Providence River, and that Assonet was not CHAP. XVI.
considered as the north-east point of the bay, whereby a
smaller territory, and a more complicated line, than she 1741.
claimed, were assigned to her, appealed from that portion Aug. 18.
of the judgment, but accepted the remainder. Both ap- Sept. 4.
peals were entered at the meeting of the court, held for
that purpose. Two subsequent meetings were held, at
which costs were taxed, the records of the court were
ordered to be deposited with the secretary of New York, 8.
and three copies to be made, one to be sent to England,
and one for each of the litigating parties, after which the
court finally adjourned. The General Assembly resolved Oct. 28.
to appeal to the King and voted two hundred pounds sterling for this purpose.

In order to embrace at a single glance the whole of
this controversy, to its ultimate adjudication by the King,
we must anticipate the current of events in the colony, 1741-2
and transfer our attention for awhile to England. Massachusetts appointed two agents[1] to conduct the appeal in Jan. 6.
her behalf, prepared duplicate instructions and statements 8.
of the case for their use, and appropriated five hundred 13.
pounds sterling to defray the expenses. The appeal was 1742.
presented in the name of the agents. The Rhode Island July
petition arrived first, and was referred to the Plantation 29. Sept.
Committee. The same course was taken with that of 15.
Massachusetts. More than two years elapsed before the 1744.
case was fully argued by counsel, in several hearings, Nov.
after the last of which the committee reported to the 6, 13,
King, dismissing both appeals, and confirming the deci- 26. Dec.
sion of the commissioners. Kilby afterward petitioned, 11.
in behalf of Massachusetts, for a rehearing of the case, and 1745-6
Partridge, the Rhode Island agent, filed a counter peti- Feb.
tion remonstrating against it. Both of these new peti- 27.
tions were referred again to the Plantation Committee. 1746. April
Their report condemned the application of Kilby, and 21.

[1] Robert Auchmuty and Christopher Kilby.

CHAP. XVI. 1746. May 28. reaffirmed their former decision in favor of the judgment of the commissioners; whereupon an order in council was issued, confirming by royal decree the decision of the court, and finally settling the eastern boundary of Rhode Island in accordance therewith. This closed, at least during the colonial period, a controversy which was coeval with the charter of King Charles, and had virtually commenced soon after the settlement of Aquedneck. A century later was to witness the revival of this territorial dispute before another tribunal, upon grounds equally untenable with those that were thus summarily dismissed by the Privy Council.

Nov. 11. Soon after the royal decree was received in Rhode Island, the Assembly appointed a committee[1] to run the line, and notified Massachusetts to unite in the survey. Gov. Shirley refused to appoint a committee, or to convene the legislature for that purpose—a course which Rhode Island justly considered as but a part of the long series of neglects, intended to delay a settlement of the Dec. 2. boundary. The committee therefore proceeded, ex parte, 1746-7 Jan. 6. to run the line according to the royal decree, and their report was accepted by the Assembly. Gov. Shirley referred to the subject in his speech to the General Court, but the committee to whom the matter was referred, re- 14. ported that it was inexpedient to proceed further. Thus the affair remained till after the adoption of the constitution of the United States.

1741. April 1. We will now return to the period when the boundary dispute was settled by the commissioners at Providence, and trace the progress of the colony since that time. The war sloop Tartar was armed and officered for instant service, and the governor was empowered to enlist one hundred men beside the regular crew, and to order them to sea whenever an enemy should appear on the coast. The governor and council were further authorized to lay an

[1] James Honeyman, jr., Gideon Cornel, George Brown, George Wanton, and Walter Chaloner.

embargo upon any or all outward bound vessels whenever CHAP. XVI.
they might see fit. This was the first instance of the grant
of these extraordinary powers, which we shall see at a 1741. April. 1.
later period were frequently exercised.

James Greene and others petitioned for the right to place a dam across the south branch of Pawtuxet River, in the town of Warwick, and to erect works thereupon for the refining of iron. By the law for protecting fisheries, no permanent dam could be built across any stream; hence this petition, which was granted, and the "old ore bed," afterwards so famous for the anchors and cannon cast there, began to be worked. Pawtucket bridge was again rebuilt, and William Jenckes received sixty pounds from the treasury for the cost of the Rhode Island half of the work. East Greenwich had become so populous, that the inhabitants petitioned for a division of the town, which was made, and West Greenwich was incorporated with the same rights as the other towns. The first election of town officers and of deputies to the Assembly was 21.
held three weeks later.

At the general election, the choice of the Assembly May 6.
made in July previous, was confirmed by the people. The office of attorney-general was abolished, and a King's attorney for each county was appointed in lieu thereof. Twenty men were sent from Providence and Kings counties to reinforce the garrison at Block Island for six months. Their pay was fixed at three pounds a month. Two thousand pounds in bills of credit of the new tenor were issued
to supply the treasury. A form of prayer for the royal June 22.
family having been received, with an order in council for its use in all places of public worship, a copy of the order was sent to the minister or elder, of every society in the colony. The trial of causes taken by appeal from the Superior Court to the General Assembly having "by long experience been found prejudicial," a court of equity to determine such appeals was appointed. It consisted of five judges, elected annually by the Assembly, who were

CHAP. XVI. 1741. to decide all appeals in personal actions, "agreeably to law and equity," as fully as the Assembly had hitherto done.

Two years before this time, the monuments on the western boundary had been renewed by Rhode Island, after repeated but vain efforts to obtain the concurrence of Connecticut in the renewal. Soon after this was done, Connecticut appointed a committee[1] to do the work, and it was reported that this committee had displaced the old bound at the south-west corner of Warwick. The Assem-
July 7. bly now sent surveyors to examine into the facts. They visited the spot and found that the great stone heap set up at that point had been moved about two and a half rods eastward from its proper place, and the tree marks altered to correspond; but by whom the fraud was attempted was unknown. The same outrage had been perpetrated once before, and was detected and rectified at the last renewal of the bounds. The report of this committee, like the former one, was entered in full upon the records.

The same reasons that led to the incorporation of
Aug. 18. West Greenwich, required a division of Warwick. The western portion of it was therefore set off to form a new town called Coventry, and a warrant was issued for the first town meeting, at which the requisite officers were
31. chosen.

The British forces having been repulsed at Carthagena, in March, and lost more than one half their number in less than two days by yellow fever, designed another expedition to retrieve their fortunes. Santiago de Cuba was the destined point of attack. Gen. Wentworth, commanding the land forces, now reduced by sickness to three
12. thousand men, sent Capt. William Hopkins home to Rhode Island, to muster recruits for this new enterprise.[2] Gov.
Oct. 6. Ward, by order of the Assembly, issued a proclamation

[1] In May, 1740.

[2] Wentworth's letter to Gov. Ward is printed in R. I. Col. Rec. vol. v., p. 30.

offering a bounty of five pounds currency, and a watch coat in addition to the royal bounty of two pounds sterling, to all who would enlist for the invasion of Cuba. The Tartar was equipped to convey the recruits, and being filled with all the men the vessel could carry, sailed for Cuba. But even before the colonial recruits had sailed, the attempt upon Santiago was abandoned, after a reconnoisance of the works, to the great disgrace of the British commanders. The evils of a divided authority were never more clearly illustrated than in the first attempt of the English ministry against the Spanish West Indies. To defray the charges which this effort cost to Rhode Island, two thousand pounds in new tenor bills were issued. At the session in South Kingstown, reports were made on the removal of the monuments at the south-west corner of Warwick,[1] and on the division lines between Warwick and Coventry,[2] but no new business of any interest was transacted. Oct. 28.

In Providence the religious proprieties of the place were startled by a bugle note of doctrinal war, sounded by one Moses Bartlett. Dissent from the Puritan establishment had obtained a firm position in the stronghold of Presbyterian theology. Baptists had churches in Boston, Quakers held meetings in Massachusetts, and neither found "aught to molest or make them afraid." Antinomian liberality had supplanted Legalist proscription in the home of the Puritans, but the change was offensive to this zealous champion of "real Christianity." In a spirit of Quixotic piety, that would have done credit to the preceding century, he hurled a formal challenge at both divisions of the heretic camp whence the invasion of his cherished principles had proceeded; and, not satisfied with this display of religious chivalry, or displeased, it may be, that his enthusiasm met no response from those whom it was intended to arouse, he published the challenge, a few days later, in the Boston Gazette. Perhaps Nov. 9. 24.

[1] See R. I. Col. Rec., v. 34. [2] Ibid. 36.

CHAP. XVI. 1741. no little sting was added to this display of bitterness by the fact that the great revival, which the preaching of Whitefield was now producing in New England, resulted, especially in Connecticut to which he refers, in larger accessions of new converts to the Baptist churches than to those of the dominant sect; while the presence of Fothergill, the eminent Quaker preacher at Newport, was giving a fresh stimulus to the society of Friends. But whether these results were yet apparent, or Bartlett foresaw them with prophetic dread, his hostile missives are worth preserving as the latest curiosity of their kind.[1]

1741-2 Feb. 1. At an adjourned meeting of the Assembly, the Newport Artillery were incorporated. This ancient corps is therefore the oldest chartered company in the State, and preserves to this day the character for efficient discipline which the circumstances of its origin produced.

[1] PROVIDENCE, *November* 9, 1741.—You Baptist Elders and Teachers in this town and Colony: There is a wonderful Reformation among the Presbyterians in Connecticut government; and the true everlasting gospel is preached among them; but I apprehend you preach the Doctrine of Devils: Therefore in order to vindicate yourselves, come on, and have a public Dispute with me, in order to clear yourselves, or else lie under the charge; which you please: You shall have as many able men as you will, if there be as many as there was Prophets of *Baal;* and we will have it all writ, only I will have as much time as you. It may be you will desire to know what People I am of; You may call me a Presbyterian if you please; but I call myself a real Christian; *Moses Bartlett* is my name, who wrote an answer to a letter which gave an account of a tumultuous confusion at Min. Noyce's house at New Haven at the time of the Commencement.

PROVIDENCE, *November* 9, 1741.

To the Quaker Ministers in this town and Colony: There is a wonderful Reformation in Connecticut Colony among the Presbyterians, where the everlasting gospel is preached; but I have heard some of you blaspheme against it abominably; but I desire you to Dispute me in order to vindicate your Orders; which you call Friends Orders, for they are antiscriptural, and so consequently of the Devil; You shall have the liberty to pick out as many able men as you please, if it be as many as there was Prophets of Baal; only I will have the same measure of time as you; and we will have it all written. It may be you will ask what People I am of? To which I answer, you may call me a Presbyterian if you please, but I call myself a real Christian.

MOSES BARTLETT.

Gov. Ward and deputy-governor Greene, were again chosen at the spring election. The year 1742 is made memorable in the history of the colony and the country, by the birth of General Nathaniel Greene. He was born at Potowomut, in the township of Warwick, which for a century had been the home of his ancestors, and where the family still retain the ancient homestead, soon afterward rendered illustrious by his martial deeds. 1742. May 22.

The accounts relating to the expedition against the Spaniards were examined, and allowed by the Assembly to the amount of more than sixty-four hundred pounds. The great annoyance resulting from counterfeiting the bills of credit has already been mentioned. Scarcely a session of the Assembly had occurred since the issue of the first bank, without the subject being presented in some form, and the courts were repeatedly occupied in the trial of counterfeiters. The same difficulty harassed the neighboring colonies. The new tenor bills, from their greater value, were soon subjected to the same process, so that the first issue was called in, to be redeemed by other bills printed upon a new plate. A large amount of these bills were burnt by the Assembly. But a yet greater trouble arose from the non-payment of the interest bonds. These were a constant source of litigation. To facilitate their collection by legal process, the plan of having a King's attorney for each county had been adopted, and the bonds distributed among them to be sued in the respective counties where the defendants resided. The experiment having failed, the new office was abolished, and that of attorney-general was restored. The general treasurer, as in former times, was charged with the collection of debts due to the colony, and ordered to sue the bonds. Seven bridges in different parts of the colony received appropriations for building and repairs. All public bridges, and most of the great highways, as we have seen, were built and maintained at the common expense, June 21. Sept. 14.

CHAP. XVI. and as they continued to be so for a long period, we shall not refer to them again.

1742. Oct. 27. A Newport privateer, having brought in as prisoners four Spanish officers, the Assembly ordered that they should be entertained, and their passages paid from the treasury as soon as they could be sent away. The care of insane and imbecile persons, was given to the town councils, with power to appoint guardians for their estates. Jurors had hitherto been chosen by the people at town meetings. The custom of drawing the names from a box
Nov. 22. was now adopted, and the mode of doing so was regulated by law. Uniform days for election of deputies and general officers in all the towns, were fixed by statute. The first Tuesday of March, afterward changed to the third Wednesday in April, and the last Tuesday in August were the appointed times. On the former day, the deputies for the May session were chosen, and proxies for general officers were deposited; on the latter, deputies for the October session were elected. Two new ferries were established to facilitate access to Newport from Providence county; one from Warwick Neck to the north end of Prudence Island, the other from the south end of Prudence to Lawton's valley.

The dispute with Connecticut about the monument at
25. the old south-west corner of Warwick, now the corner of West Greenwich and Coventry, was settled by a joint commission of the two colonies, who set up a permanent and massive stone pillar with suitable inscriptions thereupon. Their report was entered upon the records of the
1742-3 March 8. next Assembly.[1] The Judge of Admiralty having gone to England, John Gidley, of Newport, was appointed to that place till the King's will could be known. North Kingstown was divided, and the western portion incorporated as the town of Exeter. A town meeting was
22. called forthwith, and the requisite officers were elected.

[1] R. I. Col. Rec., v. 59.

CHAP. XVI.

1743. May 4.

Governor Ward declined a re-election, and deputy-governor William Greene was chosen in his place. Joseph Whipple was elected deputy-governor. The amount of labor devolving upon the court of election, had become so great, that for many years past all other business had been deferred till June. Besides the governor and council, attorney, secretary, and treasurer, fifteen State officers elected by the people, there were the three field officers of each county regiment, five judges of the colony, and five of each county court, with the clerks of each court, and sheriffs of counties, a list of justices of the peace in every town, varying from fifty to a hundred in the whole, the three commissioned officers of every regimental company in the colony, of which there were now eight in Newport, fifteen in Providence, and fourteen in King's county, and sometimes six or eight trustees, and a committee of two from each town, called the grand committee, to supervise the issue and loan of bills of credit, making between two and three hundred officials, about two-fifths of whom were military officers, to be elected by the Assembly every May; and this number was increased with the admission of each new town.

The country portion of Newport, in the north-east part of the township, at that time a thickly wooded district, wished to be separated from the town, and had petitioned during the past year for that purpose. The Assembly now took action in the matter, divided the town, and at an adjourned session incorporated the new township by the name of Middletown. The first meeting to organize under the act was held the following week. June 20. Aug. 23. 30.

The jealousy of royal interference with any privileges claimed, or heretofore exercised, under the charter or by act of Parliament, was illustrated by this Assembly in the case of one Leonard Lockman, who produced a commission as clerk of the naval office in Newport. A committee of inquiry reported "that his Majesty was mistaken in said grant," for that the naval officer was, and always

CHAP. XVI. had been, in the appointment of the governor, who was alone responsible for the conduct of such officer. The

1743. Sept. 27. report was adopted. An adjourned session was held at Newport for private business only. The affair of Lock-

Oct. 26. man stimulated the legislature to a more definite and tangible assertion of their rights, at the regular meeting in South Kingstown. The custom fees to be charged by the collector and naval officer, were revised, and severe penalties for any violation of the tariff thus established were enacted. A table of fees for the court of Vice Admiralty, which had never before been framed, was also adopted, with similar penalties for its violation. This law was in part induced by the conduct of the court in a recent case, condemning the Dutch bark Gertrude, of which act complaints were made by the minister of the States General.[1] A committee was appointed to inquire into the facts, that the whole proceedings might be sent to England. The preambles of both these acts assert "the undoubted right of the General Assembly of this colony" to state the fees of all officers and courts within the same. The rate of damage upon protested bills of foreign exchange was fixed at ten per cent.

1743-4 Feb. 14. Another issue of new tenor bills to the amount of forty thousand pounds was made, to be loaned for ten years at four per cent., and at the expiration of that time, to be paid, like the former banks, in ten annual instalments. One quarter of the interest money was to be divided yearly among the towns, the remainder to be for the use of the colony. An earnest protest against this measure, similar to the one entered three years before, appears upon the records.[2] All the quarantine laws were repealed, and a new one, more complete in its terms, but similar in substance to those before noticed, was enacted. The Equity Court was abolished, and in its place the Superior Court

[1] Letters, 1742–1745, R. I. Sec. of State's Office, No. 44. R. I. Col. Rec., v. 80.

[2] R. I. Col. Rec., v. 75.

was empowered to grant rehearings upon writs of review. CHAP. XVI.
So many Spanish prisoners were brought into Newport
by the privateers, that an act to regulate their mainte- 1743-4
nance was passed, allowing to each one fifteen shillings a week, and providing for their liberation and return as soon as possible.

But the Spanish war was soon to be lost in the greater 1744.
complications of European politics. The whole continent was in arms, and battles by sea and land, as fruitless as they were ceaseless, presented a scene of blood that had never been equalled in modern times. The Jacobites availed themselves of this dire confusion to press the
claims of the Pretender. France espoused the cause of Mar.
Charles Edward, and declared war against England. A 15.
proclamation of war against France was forthwith issued.[1] 31.
A more brilliant period of colonial history was commencing, that called for yet greater efforts and led to more decisive results.

The Assembly adopted measures to strengthen the May
defences of the colony. Military stores were procured, and 22.
the garrisons at Fort George and Block Island were augmented. The people of Gloucester petitioned that an artillery company might be incorporated in that town. It was granted on condition that the members should all be from Providence county, and the corps should be called the "Artillery company of the county of Providence." This was the second chartered company in the State, and the origin of the flourishing corps known at this day as the Cadet company.[2] The news of war
reached the French colonies before it was received in New 24.
England, and an expedition was sent at once from Cape

[1] The letter of the Duke of Newcastle to Gov. Greene, announcing the war, is printed in R. I. Col. Rec., v., p. 80.

[2] At the June session, 1774, this act was amended by a change of name to "The Cadet Company of the County of Providence," the corps was officered upon a regimental basis, and the position of the company on all field days was assigned "on the right wing of the regiment in whose district the said company is included."

CHAP. XVI. Breton to break up the fishing establishments, and to
capture Fort Canso. French privateers harassed the
1744. coast of New England, destroying commerce, and almost
annihilating the fisheries. The Indians were enlisted un-
June der the French banner, causing great alarm on the frontiers. It was even feared that our old allies the Six Nations might join the league. A meeting of commissioners
12. was held at Albany, to devise measures for the common
5. defence, and Gov. Shirley wrote to Rhode Island to take
part in the deliberations. At the announcement of war,
the Assembly was convened by warrant of the governor.
19. Eighty barrels of powder, and fifteen hundred pounds of
musket balls were ordered. Fort George was still further enlarged. The Tartar, in command of Capt. Daniel Fones, with John Stafford as lieutenant, was sent to sea with a force of ninety men, to cruise in company with the Connecticut armed sloop, between Martha's Vineyard and the Jersey coast. Twenty-five hundred pounds in bills of credit were issued to meet these expenses, and a tax of ten thousand pounds was laid upon the colony to provide for their redemption. A commissary general was appointed, to be elected annually, to have charge of all munitions of war, and to superintend all military expeditions. John Gardner was chosen to that office. The old tonnage duty upon all vessels entering the colony, which more than fifty years before had been levied to provide powder for the common defence, and was soon afterward repealed by order from England, was revived, to continue through the war. Sixpence a ton was laid upon every vessel that should arrive, except coasters, which paid threepence; the proceeds to be applied to the use of Fort George. A petition to the King was prepared, asking for cannon and military stores. John Cranston was commander of Fort George, and Robert Carr was made lieutenant. The old watch-tower and beacon at Point Judith, and Beaver Tail were renewed. A number of French prisoners in Newport jail were allowed to reside in Provi-

dence upon parole, there to support themselves until further orders, if they so desired. CHAP. XVI.

Upon the approach of war, the Assembly had always revived the act for the relief of tender consciences. This delicate regard for the principles of the Quakers, was again exhibited by exempting them from bearing arms, although requiring them to render all other aid not inconsistent with their religious views. An extra session was held, to determine the value of rateable property, and to apportion the war-tax among the towns. Leonard Lockman, whose crown-commission as clerk in the naval office had the year before been disregarded by the Assembly, had received the appointment of Judge of Admiralty in this colony; and having complained to the Lords of Admiralty against the independent legislation of Rhode Island upon these subjects, a letter in reply to his representations was prepared, vindicating the conduct of the colony. These complaints were considered as a direct attack upon the charter, and a recent movement in the House of Commons against bills of credit, supposed to be specially aimed at Rhode Island, still further alarmed the colony. The Assembly voted five hundred and fifty pounds sterling, in addition to one hundred and fifty recently sent to their agent in England, to be expended in repelling these assaults. 1744. Aug. 21. Sept. 18. Oct. 31.

The bounties upon hemp, oil, and other articles, were repealed. The lottery system, which eleven years before had been denounced by the Assembly, was now legalized by this legislature. A scheme of fifteen thousand pounds was allowed for building Weybosset bridge in Providence. There were five thousand tickets at three pounds each, and a thousand prizes, amounting to twelve thousand pounds. Samuel Chace was appointed clerk to draw the lottery. The act was slightly amended at the next session, bringing it to the form here stated. Nov. 28.

An expedition against Cape Breton was designed by Gov. Shirley, and a special messenger was sent to Rhode 1744-5 Jan. 29.

CHAP. XVI. 1744-5 Feb. 5. Island to obtain aid.[1] A detailed plan for the reduction of Louisburg, the strongest fortress north of the Gulf of Mexico, was presented to the Assembly, convened at Providence for the purpose.[2] The war sloop Tartar, Capt. Daniel Fones, was equipped for a four months' cruise, manned with a hundred and thirty men, placed at the disposal of the commodore for the attack on Louisburg. The charges were defrayed by an issue of twenty-five hundred pounds in new tenor bills, to be sunk by taxation at the end of four years. The governor was again empowered to lay an embargo on all outward bound vessels. One hundred and fifty men were voted as a land force for the expedition, to be divided into three companies, and a transport was hired to convey them. John Cahoone was chosen lieutenant of the Tartar. Besides this force, amounting in all to about three hundred men, Godfrey Malbone, at the request of Gov. Shirley, was commissioned to raise a regiment of three hundred and fifty men in Rhode Island, to be received in the pay of Massachusetts, and a bounty of two pounds was paid by this colony to every man thus enlisted. The Rhode Island troops were to be attached to the Connecticut regiment under Col. Burro.[3] The command of the expedition was given to William Pepperrell, of Maine, afterward knighted for his successful exploit. The greatest effort was made by Massachusetts. More than thirty-two hundred men, and ten armed vessels, two of them privateer ships belonging to Newport, were got ready within two months by that province. Each of the other New England colonies sent

[1] Shirley's letter to Greene is printed in R. I. Col. Rec., v. 74.

[2] See letters, 1742–1745, in the office of the R. I. Secretary of State, Nos. 88, 89, 90. The care bestowed by the Hon. John R. Bartlett in arranging these documents, and placing them in a permanent and convenient form for reference, is deserving of all commendation. The accomplished editor of the R. I. Colonial Records has thus added another claim to the gratitude of his native State and of every student of American history.

[3] Letter No. 108.

one armed vessel. New York, New Jersey, and Pennsyl- CHAP.
vania, voted small supplies of money, but sent no men. XVI.
Connecticut furnished five hundred troops under Roger 1745.
Walcott, the second in command of the expedition. New
Hampshire and Rhode Island sent three hundred each. March
The former were first at Canso, the rendezvous, arriving 31. April
there two days before the main army from Boston.[1] One 2.
half of the Rhode Island troops arrived too late to share
the glory of the enterprise; but the Tartar, which, with
the Connecticut sloop of war, was convoying the transports of the latter colony, fell in with the French frigate
Renommée, of thirty-six guns, and sustained some damage in an engagement which, fortunately for the colonies,
the frigate, bearing despatches to France, did not delay
to finish.[2] While the fleet were detained at Canso by the
ice, Commodore Warren, with a part of the West India 23.
squadron arrived, and in the next two days, the Tartar,
with the Connecticut transports, appeared. As soon as 25.
the ice permitted, the siege of Louisburg commenced. 30.

At the spring election, Gideon Wanton was chosen May 1.
governor, and William Robinson deputy-governor.

During the progress of the siege, earnest calls for recruits were made by the commanders, who lost many of
their men by sickness and by the casualties of war. Gov.
Shirley wrote to Rhode Island for further aid.[3] The cap- 18.
ture of the French ship Vigilant, of sixty-four guns, soon
occasioned another draft for seamen to man the prize. 20.
The Assembly ordered forward the three companies voted 28.
in March, which for some reason had not yet sailed.[4] The

[1] Belknap's N. Hamp., ii. 212.

[2] Hutchinson, ii. 415. Letter No. 139.

[3] Letter No. 115, R. I. Col. Rec., v. 134.

[4] The officers of these three companies were—of the 1st, Richard Mumford, Captain; Edward Cole, 1st Lieut.; Samuel Hall, 2d Lieut., or Ensign. Of the 2d, Benjamin Potter, Capt.; Richard Smith, 1st Lieut.; Richard Hoyle, 2d Lieut. Of the 3d, Joshua Champlin, Capt.; Samuel Eldred, 1st Lieut.; Jeoffroy Champlin, 2d Lieut. Some other officers were afterwards sent with recruits in July.

CHAP. XVI. transport brig Success was hired to convey them, but
arrived too late. The troops remained to garrison the
1745. captured fortress. When the news of the capture of the
June 1. Vigilant reached Boston, the council ordered three hun-
5. dred men to be sent as a prize crew. Gov. Shirley wrote
to Gov. Wanton to impress foreign sailors, a large number of whom had fled to Newport to avoid the impress-
18. ment at Boston.[1] The Assembly immediately ordered
two hundred sailors to be raised, offering a large bounty
to those who would enlist, and giving the sheriff ample
power to impress men for the service. Within six days
seventy-four seamen were sent to Boston. Meanwhile all
the ferries were closed against sailors for eight days, and
the commander of Fort George was ordered to prevent all
boats or vessels from leaving the harbor of Newport during that time. This course proved as effectual as it was
20. energetic. Gov. Shirley issued a proclamation, placing
these levies upon the same footing with other seamen in
the fleet, and afterward requested Gov. Wanton to pro-
24. hibit the export of gunpowder, which was done.

Meanwhile, the Tartar and two other war sloops, under
7. command of Capt. Fones, were sent to the Bay of Verte,
to intercept a large force of French and Indians, some
twelve hundred strong, who were advancing from the
15. siege of Annapolis, to the relief of Louisburg. Fones met
them at Famme Goose Bay, and after a sharp action, dispersed their fleet, consisting of two sloops, two schooners,
a shallop, and fifty canoes.[2] Two days later, Louisburg
17. surrendered to the New England forces, after a siege of
seven weeks. The ships of Commodore Warren had
served to blockade the port and cut off supplies, but the
plan and conduct of the siege were entirely in the hands
of the Americans. Great was the joy in the colonies, and
the astonishment in Europe at this brilliant achievement,
by far the most important one of the war. Pepperrell

[1] Letters No. 112, 113, R. I. Col. Rec., v. 135, 136. [2] Letters No. 133.

was created a baronet, the only American colonist upon whom this honor was ever conferred; Warren was made admiral, and Gov. Shirley, for planning the expedition, was made a colonel.[1] CHAP. XVI. 1745.

The people of Rhode Island went into this war with great spirit, although Gov. Shirley complained of the delay in sending forward the land forces. The large draft for volunteers in Col. Malbone's regiment, counted as Massachusetts troops, doubtless impeded the enlistment of those in the pay of Rhode Island, while the latter were incorporated in a Connecticut regiment, and hence appear officially as being from that colony. But the sea was the favorite element of Rhode Island warfare. The Tartar did efficient service throughout the siege, yet the battle at Famme Goose Bay is not mentioned in the official reports, overshadowed as it was by the great event which so soon followed it. From ten to fifteen privateers, some of large size and heavy force, were fitted out, and sent more than twenty prizes into Newport during the year. Besides the transports furnished by the colony, the merchants contributed eight thousand pounds, and placed a twenty-gun ship at the disposal of the commodore. The home government afterwards acknowledged these services, by a grant to the colony of six thousand three hundred and twenty-two pounds sterling.

To hold the fortress against a re-capture, and to provide for the French prisoners, required great preparations. A garrison of four thousand men, besides a fleet of ten large, and many smaller ships of war, were to be sustained July
at Louisburg. Gov. Shirley wrote to Gov. Wanton for 3.
aid, especially in provisions. A few days later, seven
hundred prisoners reached Boston, and more than two 12.
thousand remained on board the fleet to be sent back to
France. Pepperrell also wrote to Wanton, announcing 25.
the arrival of the Rhode Island troops, and the necessity

[1] Parsons's Life of Sir Wm. Pepperrell, p. 109.

CHAP. XVI. of their remaining, and asking for supplies for the garrison. Earnest letters to the same effect were sent by the
1745. Massachusetts council, and by Capt. Fones, whose sloop
Aug. 14. Tartar was too well liked by the commodore to be dis-
20. charged.[1] In reply to these solicitations, the Assembly
sent orders to Fones to draw for supplies, to the land
forces to await orders from England, and to the transport
Success to return immediately. Commodore Warren
Sept. 13. wrote to Gov. Wanton a long letter, thanking the colony
for its services, and urging the importance of retaining
Louisburg. Gen. Pepperrell also wrote, asking that
Rhode Island would send twenty-eight more men to supply the losses by sickness of the three companies in the
garrison, and also bedding, provisions, and clothing for
24. the troops.[2] The Assembly at once enlisted the men,
purchased eight months' provisions, with bedding and
blankets for the three companies, hired a transport to take
them to Louisburg, and sent three thousand pounds to pay
the troops. To meet these expenses, five thousand pounds
in bills of credit were issued, and a tax was levied to redeem them within four years. A force of some four hundred men was sent from Louisburg, under convoy of the
26. Tartar, against St. Johns, on Prince Edwards Island,
which immediately surrendered.

The third edition of the colony laws was printed this
year at Newport, by Anne Franklin, widow of James,
including the revised statutes down to the month of June.
The death of Col. John, eldest son of the late Gov. Cran-
Oct. ston, and leader of the Rhode Island force at the capture
15. of Port Royal, took place at this time. The Assembly
30. appointed James Angell commissary to the troops at
Cape Breton, and made Edward Cole captain, in place
of Mumford, deceased, Joseph Weeden, first lieutenant,

[1] Letters Nos. 135, 138, 157, 158, 159. These and many other letters relating to the Louisberg expedition are printed in R. I. Col. Rec., v. 132–151.

[2] Letters Nos. 165, 167, 168.

CHAP. XVI.

in place of Cole, and Benjamin Allen, second lieutenant. They also wrote to Captain Fones to return home with the Tartar. The Indians in New York having attacked Saratoga, Gov. Clinton wrote to all the colonies for aid. Massachusetts declared war, and urged Rhode Island to do the same.[1] 1745. Nov. 25. Dec. 2.

A great calamity occurred at Newport near the close of the year. Two large privateers, chiefly owned by Col. Malbone, each mounting twenty-two guns, and manned by over two hundred men, sailed the day before Christmas, at the commencement of a violent north-east snowstorm, bound for the Spanish main. 24. The gale increased to a hurricane, and lasted for two days. The ships were never heard from, and both probably went down in the storm with all on board. By this fearful disaster, more than four hundred lives were lost, and nearly two hundred women in Newport were made widows. The ships were just built, and of great value.

The Six Nations refused to join the English in war 1745-6 Jan. 27. against the French Indians. It was proposed to have a meeting of commissioners from the several colonies, to consider what could be done, and Gov. Clinton wrote to Rhode Island to lay the matter before the Assembly, but Feb. 10. no action upon it is recorded.

A statement and account of the services and expenses of Rhode Island were prepared to send to England, in case the claims of the other colonies should be assumed by the home government. These were accompanied with orignal letters from the several commanders, in support of the justice of the claim. The mortality at Louisburg 1746. during the winter, was frightful. The three Rhode Island companies had been consolidated into two, and one of these, as appears by a list of deaths sent home by Lieut. Hoyle, had already lost its captain and more than one half the men.[2] The condition of the country, an unexpected invasion

[1] Letters, 1742–5, Nos. 176, 179.

[2] Letters, 1746–50, No. 5, Feb. 2, 1745–6.

CHAP. XVI. 1746. Mar. 31. from France, and the activity of the colonial French and Indians, again suggested a meeting of commissioners from the several colonies to devise means of security, and Gov. Clinton once more wrote to Rhode Island to send men to the conference. The capture of Cape Breton renewed the desire to attempt, for the fourth time, the conquest of Canada. The ministry favored the design, but feared to intrust it to the colonies, lest another success, like that they had already achieved, should teach them too plainly their power. Eight regiments were therefore sent from April 9. England under General St. Clair, and orders were issued for raising an army in North America.[1] The New England forces were to unite with the British at Louisburg, while those of the other colonies were to invade Canada by land—the same plan that had twice before failed.

May 6. At the spring election, William Greene and Joseph Whipple, who, for two successive years previous to the last, had been governor and deputy-governor, were re-elected; superseding Wanton and Robinson, to be in turn, again supplanted by them the following year. The Tartar, with ninety men and eight officers, was ordered to cruise along the coast till October. Fort George was garrisoned with thirty men. Stephen Hopkins, and William Ellery were appointed commissioners, to meet with those from the other colonies to consult for the defence of the country. These were the two patriots who, thirty years later, signed in behalf of Rhode Island, the declaration of independence.

Letters were sent to Gen. Pepperrell and Admiral Warren, requesting the return of the soldiers and sailors of Rhode Island, and on the same day a joint letter from them was written at Louisburg, announcing the arrival of a British garrison, and the consequent discharge of such of the colonial forces as might wish to return home.[2]

29. The arrival of the orders from England to raise an

[1] R. I. Col. Rec., v. 162. [2] Ibid., 171.

army for the invasion of Canada, caused great activity. CHAP.
French prisoners were placed in confinement, and other XVI.
measures taken to prevent a knowledge of the design 1746.
from reaching the enemy.[1] Gov. Greene at once con- May 30.
vened the Assembly. Three companies of one hundred June
men each were raised, military stores and provisions for 2.
six months were provided, and transports hired to convey them to Louisburg, and thence to Quebec.[2] Large bounties were offered for pilots of the river St. Lawrence to enter the colony's service. The Tartar was withdrawn from her cruise for coast defence, to accompany the expedition, and an issue of eleven thousand two hundred and fifty pounds in bills of credit was made to meet these expenses, redeemable in eight years by taxes duly apportioned among the towns. The soldiers were to receive a new suit of clothes, or an equivalent of twenty-six pounds. The ferries were closed against all enlisted men.

Much correspondence had been held with the governor of Havana on account of a seizure of twenty-two Spaniards, by two Rhode Island privateers during the past winter, who had been sold as slaves in the northern colonies. The Defiance, Capt. John Dennis, and the Duke of Marlboro', Capt. Robert Morris, were the offending vessels, and nineteen of Dennis's crew had been captured, and were imprisoned in Havana, till the Spaniards should be returned. One of these prisoners, Daniel Denton, was sent home from Havana, on parole, to procure the release of the Spaniards. The fact of their freedom being established, which rendered the seizure unlawful, the Assembly ordered the slaves to be sought out and returned by a 12.
flag of truce, and their purchasers to be indemnified. Den-

[1] Letters, No. 24.

[2] The officers of these companies were as follows. Captains—Joshua Sawyer, William Rice, Edward Cole. First Lieutenants—Nathan Carpenter, Thomas Streight, Samuel Eldred. Second Lieuts.—Philip Wilkinson, jr., Robert Sterry, Silas Helme. Ensigns—Samuel Nichols, Stephen Colegrove, Jeoffroy Champlin. Edward Kinnicut, of Providence, was afterwards appointed Lieut. Col. in command of the three companies.

CHAP. XVI. ton accompanied them to Havana to effect an exchange for his shipmates. A vessel was procured by order of the
1746. Assembly for this purpose. Recruiting for service in
June 24. Canada continued. Meanwhile measures were in progress which were to render abortive this long cherished plan, and to spread terror throughout the colonies. That an attempt would be made to recover Louisburg had been anticipated, but the tremendous preparations which contemplated, not merely a restoration of lost possessions, but the conquest of all British North America, were well calculated to alarm the exhausted colonists. A fleet of sixty-six sail, including twenty-five ships of war, carrying nearly twelve hundred guns, and fifteen thousand men,
22. with a land army eight thousand strong, sailed from Rochelle under the Duke d'Anville. So quietly had this formidable armament been prepared, that nothing was known of it by the colonists for nearly three months, so that their military plans remained as yet unchanged.[1] Admiral Warren came from Louisburg to Boston, to
29. hasten the movement against Canada. He wrote to Gov. Greene to obtain all the sailors possible, especially pilots, and suggested the capture of Crown Point.[2] At Boston
July 7. an embargo was laid upon all vessels, in order to secure sailors for the fleet, and Rhode Island was urged to do
8. the same. The Assembly hired three transports for Canada, directed that the companies should be filled by impressment, except from Kings county, unless the complement was made up before orders were received to embark, and quartered the troops on Goat Island to await these orders from the admiral.

The depreciation of the currency had become so great,
Aug. 19. that the property qualification for freemen, hitherto two hundred pounds, was doubled, and a stringent law was passed against fraudulent voting and bribery at elections.

[1] A list of the French fleet is contained in Letters, 1746–50. Nos. 21, 39.

[2] R. I. Col. Rec., v. 183

An oath was prepared to be administered to every voter, and another to be taken by every officer, not to receive or offer bribes in any manner. A single vote cast for any officer under such inducements should invalidate his election, and in all trials under the act, the evidence of the person offering a bribe might be taken against the accused. The law was to be read in town meeting, at each semi-annual election for five years, and the name of any violator of it was to be struck from the roll of freemen. CHAP. XVI. 1746.

The troops were sent on board the transports, which were anchored close under Goat Island, daily expecting the order to sail; but the vacillating ministry had already changed their plans. The fleet destined for America was withheld, and its non-arrival caused the invasion of Canada to be abandoned. Attention was now directed to the capture of Crown Point, which, in the hands of the French was a constant annoyance, and if taken, would facilitate the operations against Canada another year. These views were expressed by Shirley and Warren to Gov. Greene, desiring that the Rhode Island troops might be sent to Albany.[1] Aug. 25.

But the public mind was soon to be diverted from schemes of conquest to the more imminent necessity of defence. Rumors of the great armada of France were brought to Louisburg by a captured merchantman,[2] and soon afterwards the fleet was seen off Nova Scotia. Governor Shirley sent orders to Rhode Island to hold the troops in readiness to march, but whither, was yet uncertain. The greatest alarm pervaded the colonies. The Assembly was convened by warrant from the governor. Ammunition for Fort George was procured, and new batteries were ordered to be built adjoining it, upon Goat Island. This act was protested against by a few members, on the ground that the works were already strong enough to resist privateers, and no new ones would Sept. 11. 16. 22. 29.

[1] Letters, No. 43.

[2] Letters, Nos. 39, 52, 57.

CHAP. XVI. 1746. suffice for defence against a hostile fleet.[1] It was conjectured that Nova Scotia was the destined point of attack. Troops were hurried off to the defence of Annapolis Roy-
Oct. 14. al. Shirley and Warren wrote for the Rhode Island com-
21. panies to be sent thither. The Assembly was again convened. The transports were ordered to sail under convoy of the Tartar, as soon as it could be ascertained what direction they should take, and all further matters connected with their departure were intrusted to the council of
23. war. Shirley advised that they touch at Passamaquoddy, for orders from Gov. Mascarene of Annapolis, for the movements of the French were quite inexplicable.[2] It was not yet known that pestilence and storm had so weakened and shattered the great armada, causing the death of d'Anville, and the suicide of his successor, that the expedition was abandoned, and the ships had returned singly to France.

Nov. 2. Soon after the Rhode Island troops sailed, great disasters overtook them, and a company of Massachusetts troops, on their voyage to Annapolis. Some of the transports were cast away at Mt. Desert, and more than one half of their men perished by drowning and exposure. A severe sickness wasted the others. Some were left at Martha's Vineyard, others found their way to Boston, and were sent home by Gov. Shirley.[3] The weather was severe, and the sufferings of the soldiers were extreme, so that no further attempt to reach Annapolis was made by this colony during the winter; but the companies were retained in service, a part on furlough and others at Fort George.

Oct. 29. The Assembly had held repeated extra sessions during the year, at which the engrossing topics of the war occu-

[1] Fort George was armed with 37 heavy cannon, 25 24-pounders and 12 18's.

[2] Letters, Nos. 61, 62.

[3] Letters, Nos. 1, 4.

Most of these letters are printed in R. I. Col. Rec., v. 183–7, 191–3, 195–6.

pied their attention. The regular autumn session was CHAP. XVI.
devoted to private business, and a special one was called
soon after, upon reception of the royal decree settling the 1746.
eastern boundary, and requiring the lines to be forthwith Nov. 11.
run in accordance therewith; for which purpose a committee was appointed.

They proceeded, in the absence of commissioners from Dec. 2.
Massachusetts, to run the lines, ex parte, and reported at 1746-7 Jan.
an adjourned session.[1] A special session was called to 6.
organize this large accession of territory, which was finally 27.
made a part of Rhode Island. The five towns of Bristol, Tiverton, Little Compton, Warren and Cumberland were incorporated, the laws of the colony extended over them, and a justice appointed for each town. Land titles were confirmed, and the Massachusetts statute of distributions
upon estates yet unsettled was legalized. The elections Feb.
necessary to perfect the organization of the towns were 10.
soon after held, and then an extra session of the Assembly was called, at which the ten new deputies were present, 17.
to arrange the county jurisdiction. The two southern towns were annexed to Newport county, Cumberland to Providence, and the intervening district was separately organized as Bristol county with Bristol as the shire town. This act made a revision of the judicial and military systems of the colony necessary, which occupied the session. The Superior Court of Judicature, Court of Assize, and General Jail Delivery, was established, consisting of a chief justice, and four associate justices, to be annually chosen by the General Assembly. Henceforth the assistants, or upper house of Assembly, ceased to exercise high judicial powers, although they continued to be a court of probate until 1802. The Judiciary now assumed its proper rank as a co-ordinate branch of the government. The Superior Court was to sit twice a year in each county. An Inferior Court of Common Pleas, and a Justices'

[1] R. I. Col. Rec., v. 199.

CHAP. XVI. 1746-7 Court, such as existed in each of the other counties, were established in Bristol county. In Tiverton, two companies of militia, and one in each of the other new towns, were organized. The Warren and Cumberland soldiers were attached to the Providence regiment, and those of the other three towns to Newport.

Thus was completed the annexation of territory, originally granted to Rhode Island by the charter of Charles II., but which had been held in abeyance, under the jurisdiction of Plymouth and Massachusetts, ever since the decision of the royal commissioners. The colony was now complete in all its parts, and being freed from the incessant conflict for existence, which for a century had distracted its councils, and weakened its power, was better prepared for those trying scenes in which it was ere long to bear a leading part.

The earlier history of these five new towns, is identified with that of Plymouth and Massachusetts. Cumberland formed a small section on the western border of the town of Attleboro', bounded on the Blackstone River. The
1694. Oct. 19. country between Taunton and Rehoboth, called the North Purchase, and previously attached to Rehoboth, was incorporated under the name of Attleboro', two years after the union of Plymouth with Massachusetts was completed. The portion now assigned to Rhode Island, was known as the Attleboro' Gore, and was described as embracing about twenty thousand acres of land. Its inhabitants were imbued with the sentiments of their nearer neighbors of Rhode Island, rather than with those of Massachusetts. That they desired a union with this colony, is evident from their petitions to the General Assembly before referred to, and by their conduct towards the various boundary commissions in whose decisions they were so deeply interested.

Warren, including the present town of Barrington, formed a part of Swanzea, till the annexation. Swanzea was settled by men whose views on the question of reli-

gious freedom were too liberal even for the tolerant spirit CHAP. XVI.
of the Pilgrims. Rev. John Miles, a Baptist minister
from Wales, with his friends had settled in Plymouth, 1667.
where their dissent from the prevailing creed, soon placed
them under the ban of the authorities. They were re- July 2.
quired to remove from the immediate neighborhood, but
were permitted to settle within the limits claimed by
Plymouth. Soon afterward the court granted to Capt. Oct. 30.
Thomas Willet, Mr. Miles and others, all the land west of
Taunton and Rehoboth as far as the bay, which included
also the present towns of Swanzea and Somerset. The act
of incorporation secured freedom of conscience to the settlers, who were thus left in the unmolested enjoyment of
their religion. Capt. Willet, who afterward became the
first English mayor of New York, was not himself a Baptist, but sympathized with Miles on the point of religious
freedom. The place was named Swanzea from the Welch
town whence Miles and most of his church had emigrated.

The assumption of jurisdiction by Plymouth over this 1621.
territory, was an act of usurpation. The original grant
of the council of Plymouth to John Pierce and his associates, conveyed title to the soil, but did not and could June 1.
not invest them with jurisdiction over it. It was a patent,
not a charter. Four years before the incorporation of
Swanzea, the charter of Rhode Island had expressly con- 1663.
veyed jurisdiction over the country extending for three
miles east of Narraganset Bay. This charter did not
affect the title, but its conveyance of the jurisdiction was
absolute. The ownership remained the same, but the
political supremacy was conceded to Rhode Island, and
when the great charter uniting Plymouth and Massachu- 1691.
setts under one royal governor, was issued twenty-eight Oct. 7.
years later, it defined the western boundary of the late
Plymouth colony, to be at the eastern bound of Rhode
Island, thus leaving the charter of Charles II. as the authority that was to define where Massachusetts should
terminate. The legal claim of Rhode Island to this ter-

CHAP. XVI. ritory, was unquestionable, and we can only wonder that for more than eighty years it was held in abeyance.

1675. We have already seen how severe were the sufferings of the people of Swanzea during Philip's war. The centre of population in this extensive township changed soon after the war, so that it became necessary to erect a new
1680. meeting-house near Kelly's bridge, which was done partly by aid from the town, and a parsonage was built for Mr. Miles, to indemnify him for money advanced towards the expenses of the war.[1] In the course of twenty years, the growth of the town required another change in the loca-
1700. tion of the church, which was accordingly removed to North Swanzea. This left the people in what is now Barrington without suitable accommodations. A congregational church was therefore erected in that part of the town, as many of the inhabitants were of that denomination.

So long as the more liberal colony of Plymouth held jurisdiction over this territory, the rights of conscience, agreeably to the terms of the act of incorporation, were strictly maintained. The majority of the people were Baptists, but there were many Congregationalists also, and all coincided in the essential doctrine established by their neighbors in Rhode Island. But the Massachusetts
1691. charter was destined to institute a new order of things. Upon the arrival of Sir William Phipps, the policy of Massachusetts was extended over the Plymouth territory. It
1692. soon interfered with the most cherished idea of the people of Swanzea. A warrant from the court of quarter ses-
1693. Aug. 28. sions was read in town meeting, "requiring the town to choose a minister according to law." The church replied "that they had a minister that they apprehended was according to law, viz., Elder Samuel Luther, and desired the vote of the town to see their assent and approbation."[2]

[1] Tustin's Historical Discourse, p. 98.

[2] Upon the death of Mr. Miles, in 1683, the church remained for two years without a pastor, when Rev. Samuel Luther was ordained and settled

The purpose of this warrant could not be mistaken. It CHAP.
caused much debate in the town and anxiety in the minds XVI.
of the people. At an adjourned meeting, the town voted 1693.
upon the question, and "chose elder Samuel Luther min- Oct. 17.
ister in the town of Swanzea."[1] But the Puritan system
required also the election of tithing men. This collection 1694.
of tithes for the support of the church was another infringement upon the chartered rights of the people. In
this case, too, they conformed to the letter of the law by
choosing four men who were Baptists, representing the July 30.
feeling of the town upon this question, and would not
enforce the odious statute. This mode of evading the law
in maintenance of their vested rights, was continued for
several years. Nor were these officers always chosen at
the annual election; their numbers varied from four down
to one; the same men were never re-chosen; the office
was merely nominal; the voluntary system was sustained
by the sturdy townsmen, and no tithes were ever collected. At length some of the inhabitants in the west part
of the town, where a Congregational church had already 1700.
been erected, petitioned the general court to have the 1711.
town divided. The petition was referred to a meeting of July 7.
the town, and was rejected. The selectmen were appointed to answer the petition, and to defend the rights of the
town, with power to levy a tax for their expenses in the
affair.[2] The next year the same petitioners again appear- 1712.
ed before the general court, praying for a division of the May 28.
town, or that one hundred pounds should be collected
therein for the support of the ministry. This referred to
the minister of the established church that had been or-

over them in 1685, and continued there till his death in 1716. Tustin's Historical Discourse, p. 103.

[1] Swanzea Records, p. 93. The design of Massachusetts to have a clergyman of the established Puritan church settled over the Baptists in Swanzea, was frustrated by this act of the people, who by their votes conformed to the letter of the law, while they violated its spirit and intent.

[2] Swanzea Records, p. 162.

CHAP. XVI. 1712. Oct. 24. ganized twelve years before. The town again voted not to comply with the conditions of the petition, but "that all the inhabitants of this town shall enjoy their conscience liberty agreeably to the foundation settlement of said town, and are obliged to uphold and maintain the worship of God where they respectively belong or assemble, and not obliged to do it elsewhere." Five men were chosen to maintain the rights of the town to freedom of conscience, and to petition her Majesty's council in case that justice should be denied them by the court, and five hundred pounds were voted for this purpose.[1] 1717. May 14. Five years later the subject was revived by another petition from the same source, to raise one hundred and twenty pounds to support a minister, or to divide the town. The record states, that "after a considerable fair and loving conference with said petitioners upon the premises, it was agreed, voted, and concluded, that all the inhabitants of the town of Swanzea should enjoy their conscience liberty according to said foundation settlement of said town," and then proceeded in the same terms as the previous vote.[2] But this arrangement did not satisfy the petitioners. They renewed their efforts with the general court, for a division of the town, which, notwithstanding the opposition of the 1718. others, was granted the next year, and the territory west of Warren River was incorporated under the name of Barrington. It remained a distinct town until the annexation to Rhode Island, when it became a part of Warren. The sympathy of the people of Swanzea with those of Rhode Island, was still further shown as the time approached when the long controversy for jurisdiction was 1741. Feb. 24. to be settled. At a town meeting a vote was passed, expressing their "unanimous wish to come under the Rhode Island government, as we apprehend we do belong there."[3]

[1] Swanzea Records, p. 166. [2] Ibid., p. 181.

[3] A more minute account of the local history of Warren and Barrington, prior to the annexation, than the limits of this work will permit, may be found in the Historical Discourse of Rev. J. P. Tustin, and in the History of

Bristol was an Indian township long before it was CHAP.
settled by the whites. Among the old Indian grants con- XVI.
veying lands to the English, is one relating to Warren, 1653.
wherein Massasoit and his son agree to remove from the March
within granted premises in favor of the Plymouth pur- 29.
chasers. Soon after the death of Massasoit and his elder
son, the remnant of the Wampanoags under Philip,
gathered about Mount Hope. A fence was built across
the neck from Warren to Kickemuet rivers, to mark the
line between the Indians and the English, at the present
boundary between Warren and Bristol. At the close of
Philip's war, these Indian lands were claimed by Plym- 1680.
outh by right of conquest, and after a struggle with other Jan.
claimants, were confirmed to that colony by royal decree. 12.
They were soon after conveyed by deed, for eleven hun- Sept.
dred pounds,[1] to four Boston merchants, one of whom was 14.
Nathaniel Byfield, and the settlement was immediately
commenced. By the terms of the deed, the town was to
be exempt from taxation by the colony for seven years.
Col. Benjamin Church was one of the first settlers, and
became their first representative at the general court.
The following year the name of Bristol was given to the 1681. Sept.
town by the proprietors, and at the next session of the 1.
court they were incorporated. The next year efficient Oct.
provision was made for education. The people, who were 28. 1682.
Congregationalists, erected a spacious church edifice on 1684.

Warren by Gen. G. M. Fessenden. The two works were published in one volume, Providence, 1845. Mr. Fessenden there shows very clearly the location of Sowams, the residence of Massasoit, to be that of the present town of Warren. The uncertainties of Indian geography have extended the name to the adjacent region, but the spot of the Sachem's residence, the proper village of Sowams, is well established in the work referred to. An ingenious and well-sustained theory of Mr. Fessenden's in regard to Roger Williams, that he came by water with his companions, from Salem to Seekonk, a copy of which, in MS., is in the archives of the R. I. Hist. Soc., has never been published. It ought to be printed, for it reconciles many points in regard to the fourteen weeks of Williams's wanderings, that cannot otherwise be explained.

[1] About $3,666.

CHAP. XVI. the spot where the court-house now stands, but the
society was not organized till three years later, when Mr.
1687. Woodbridge, their first minister, was succeeded by Mr.
May 8. Lee. The town increased rapidly in wealth and population, and soon became the most flourishing in the colony.
1685. Upon the division of the colony into three counties, Bristol was made the shire town of the county that received
its name. The annals of Bristol present no striking points
1693. of history prior to the annexation. The custom of open-
Mar. 23. ing and closing the town meetings with prayer, which
was established by vote, and enforced by a fine of one
shilling upon whoever should leave before the meeting
was thus dismissed, attests the attachment of the people
to their Puritan ideas, wherein they differed from most
of their neighbors. The established church continued to
be the only one in the town, until the Episcopal society,
1721. already referred to, was gathered. Appropriations for
the support of the ministry in both churches were made
1744. by the town; but shortly before the annexation, the town
Oct. 7. voted to apply to the general court for a law enabling
each society to tax its own congregation for the support
of their respective ministers.. This was an approach to
Rhode Island customs, that showed a preparation in the
popular mind, for the change that was soon to occur in
their political relations.[1]

The Indian name of Tiverton was Pocasset. It was
1680. originally purchased from the Sachems by the Plymouth
Mar. 5. colonists, and by them was sold for eleven hundred pounds
to Edward Gray and seven others. Col. Church, then
living at Punkateest at the south end of the town, with
Christopher and Job Almy of Portsmouth, were among
the purchasers. The settlers were mostly of Pilgrim ex-
traction, with a strong infusion of the Rhode Island element. They were but few in number, and were closely

[1] The Annals of Bristol, from its foundation to A. D. 1800, were published, from the town records, in the Bristol Phenix, 1845, in a series of articles that deserve to be placed in a more permanent form.

identified with the older and larger town of Freetown, which included Fall River, and upon which Pocasset was bounded on the north. It was not till two years after the union of Plymouth with Massachusetts, that the town was incorporated and received the name of Tiverton. There was no settled minister either there or at Freetown, and presentments against the towns were frequently made to the court for this cause, but with little effect. The Society for Propagating the Gospel, sent out a missionary to the three towns of Freetown, Tiverton, and Little Compton, but his efforts to gather an Episcopal church, were unsuccessful. The neglect of religious and educational duties in Freetown and Tiverton, formed quite a contrast in these respects to most of their neighbors. It was not till five months prior to the annexation, that the first Congregational church was organized in the south part of Tiverton. It was composed of eleven members from the church of Little Compton, who settled the Rev. Othniel Campbell as their pastor.[1]

CHAP. XVI.

1694.

1712.

1746. Aug. 20.

The original purchasers of Little Compton, were residents of Duxbury and Marshfield. A large tract of land on what was then called Taunton River, embracing a portion of Seaconnet, was sold by the Sachems to William Paybody, Josiah Winslow, and others.[2] A son of Paybody settled on a part of this tract, and afterward sold another portion of it to Benjamin Church, who became the first English settler in what is now Little Compton, having moved there, as is said, by the advice of Samuel Gorton. Scarcely had he commenced his plantation, when Philip's war broke out, and obliged him to abandon the attempt. Shortly after the close of the war, the settlement of the place was renewed. It increased so rapidly that in a few years, upon petition of Joseph Church and

1659.

1674.

1682. June 6.

[1] The reader is referred to the Historical Sketch of Fall River by Rev. Orin Fowler, Fall River, 1841, for a succinct account of the local history of Tiverton.

[2] 2 Mass. Hist. Col., x. 66.

CHAP. XVI. other inhabitants, it was incorporated by the court of
New Plymouth, and called Little Compton. The author-
1683. ity of the magistrates of the town was extended over
July Punkateest and Pocasset the next year. The same disre-
1685. gard to the law requiring the support of a minister, that
June existed at a later period in Tiverton, was displayed by the
2. people of Little Compton. They were required to raise
July 27. fifteen pounds for this object. The town refused to do so,
and notified the court that they would consider the subject, and answer at the next court, whereupon a warrant
Oct. 27. was issued against them for neglect and contempt. The
1685-6 town appointed two agents to appear in their behalf.
Feb. These agents offered an excuse under the hand of the
town clerk, but took exception to the process as illegal.
The court maintained its own authority, and fined the
Mar. 2. town twenty pounds for their neglect of its orders and
contempt of its dignity.

1690. Although the population of Bristol was larger, as is
June 5. shown by the military levy in the colony for the expedition against Canada, in which the former is required to
furnish six and the latter four of the fifty-one men to be
raised from the county, yet the list of rateable estates,
Nov. made the same year as the basis of a war tax, shows the
4. wealth of Little Compton to be nearly double that of
Bristol.[1] The people refused to be taxed for the support
of a minister, but they were not without an organized
church of the established order, from which, as we have
seen, the church in Tiverton was subsequently formed.

The increase of population by the addition of these five towns to Rhode Island, was about forty-eight hundred,[2] nearly all of whom seem to have been not only willing, but desirous to come under a jurisdiction where the power of the magistrate over men's consciences was

[1] Little Compton was rated at £2,000, and Bristol at £1,049. Plym. Col. Rec., vi. 252.

[2] Their aggregate population was 4,767—of whom 4,196 were whites, 343 blacks, and 228 Indians.

denied, and where the union of church and State, so obnoxious to the larger portion of them, was unknown. They readily acquiesced in what was to them a new, but congenial method of government; and no portion of the State was ever more loyal to its institutions, or more spirited in their support, than were these people who had so long felt the injustice of the Puritan system.

CHAPTER XVII.

1747—1762.

FROM THE ANNEXATION OF THE EASTERN TOWNS, FEBRUARY, 1747, TO THE CLOSE OF THE "OLD FRENCH," OR FOURTH INTERCOLONIAL WAR, FEBRUARY, 1763.

CHAP. XVII. 1747. THE war with France and Spain was drawing to a close. A powerful French fleet renewed the attempt upon British North America, but were defeated by Lord Anson and Admiral Warren early in the year. Both parties were wearied of a contest in which neither was likely to gain much advantage, so that the coming year is mainly devoid of stirring incident. The Rhode Island privateers were so successful against the enemy in the West Indies, that the French at Martinique sent out a vessel of fourteen guns and a hundred and forty men, especially to capture Capt. Dennis, who was the most famous for his daring exploits. The fortunes of war were illustrated in this attempt. After an action of four hours, in which Dennis was slightly wounded, the Frenchman struck his flag, and was taken, as a prize, to the English island of St. Kitts.

May 6. Gideon Wanton and William Robinson were again elected governor and deputy-governor, in place of Greene and Whipple. The Tartar was sent out on a summer cruise, with the Connecticut war sloop, to guard the coast. The garrison of Fort George was renewed, with Walter Chaloner as captain, and Robert Carr as lieutenant. To retain the friendship of the Six Nations, all the colonies

were requested to contribute to their supplies. Gov. CHAP.
Shirley presented the subject to Rhode Island,[1] and again XVII.
urged its importance in a pressing letter. But this colony 1747.
being in no condition to contribute funds, the Assembly June 9.
declined to do so. A meeting of commissioners from all
the colonies was proposed, to be held at New York in 29.
September, to consult in regard to the French and Indians, and particularly to secure the fidelity of the Six
Nations.[2] An exchange of prisoners having been ar- July
ranged between Beauharnois, governor of Canada, and 26.
Gov. Shirley, a flag of truce arrived at Boston, with one Aug.
hundred and seventy-one prisoners, six of whom belonged 16.
to Rhode Island. The inactivity of the contending powers foreshadowed the peace that was concluded the
following year. The Assembly ordered an account of the 18.
expenses incurred for the expedition against Canada, to be prepared for the home government.

The Redwood library, at Newport, having been endowed by Abraham Redwood with five hundred pounds sterling for the purchase of books, was incorporated at this session.[3] It had grown out of the literary society formed by Bishop Berkeley seventeen years before. Charlestown was divided into two towns. That part lying north of Pawcatuck River, was incorporated under the name of Richmond, and an election of deputies and
local officers for the new town was held. There were at 28.
this time nineteen ferries within the colony, thirteen of which connected with different parts of the island of
Rhode Island. The whole were regulated by a special 31.
statute, revising all the old laws upon this subject. The proceedings of every session of the Assembly had hitherto been copied by the Secretary, and sent to every town in the colony. The increased number of towns caused great delay, as well as much useless labor, in carrying out

[1] R. I. Col. Rec., v. 216. [2] Ibid., 219.

[3] Mr. Redwood died at Newport, March 8, 1788, in the 80th year of his age.

CHAP. XVII. this system. It was therefore enacted by the Assembly, that hereafter the public laws and orders passed at each
1747. session, should be printed and distributed, as heretofore,
Oct. 28. among the towns.

Orders were received from England to abandon the invasion of Canada, and discharge all the colonial forces.
31. Gov. Shirley's proclamation was issued accordingly, disbanding the troops. Parliament resolved to reimburse the colonies for their heavy expenditures during the war.
Dec. For this purpose eight hundred thousand pounds were
4. appropriated.[1] Mr. Hutchinson, afterwards governor of the province of Massachusetts, presented a plan for sinking the paper money of the colonies, and substituting a
1747-8 specie currency with the funds thus provided. Massachu-
Feb. setts wisely adopted the plan after much discussion, but
25. Rhode Island and Connecticut, to whom it was earnestly
29. recommended by Shirley,[2] refused to embrace it. The effect of this refusal was felt almost immediately in the loss of their trade, and in a severe commercial revulsion from which Massachusetts was exempt. Rhode Island had heretofore imported largely from the West Indies for that province. This trade at once ceased, and great distress followed. At the winter session the Assembly
28. granted a second lottery. This was for paving the streets of Newport. The system having thus become legalized, continued till within a very recent period. A new ferry between South Kingstown and Jamestown was established, to accommodate the increasing travel. A tax of five thousand pounds was laid upon the colony, to redeem a portion of the bills of credit before issued, to meet the expenses of the war. The towns were impowered to make

[1] Letter 73. The expenses of R. I. for the campaign 1746–7, keeping 300 men in the service, were £7,507–4, which were paid. Her whole expenses for the expedition against Canada were £12,338, and the balance was paid in 1750 from the above appropriation. Trumbull Papers, vol. i., p. 30.

[2] Letter 66.

their own local regulations, and to levy taxes for municipal purposes. CHAP. XVII.

Preliminaries of a treaty being agreed upon at Aix, a cessation of hostilities ensued. An armistice of four months was promulgated. Notice of it was sent to the colonies, and the war was in fact ended. At the spring election, Wanton[1] gave place to William Greene as governor, who continued in that office for seven successive years. William Ellery was chosen deputy governor. The war sloop Tartar, Capt. James Holmes, was sent to sea on her last cruise to guard the coast. The day after he sailed, Holmes captured a schooner off Point Judith, claiming to be a flag of truce, but fully loaded with sugar, from Hispaniola bound to a northern colony. The prize was sent into Newport, under charge of Lieut. Daniel Vaughan. A committee of inquiry was appointed by the next Assembly, upon the conduct of these officers in capturing what claimed to be a flag of truce; but later proceedings of the Admiralty would seem to justify the act. The expenses of the colony for the Canada expedition, amounted to ten thousand one hundred and forty-four pounds sterling. The account had been sent to Partridge the agent, who petitioned that it might be allowed. This was granted, and the bills drawn for the amount were accepted at the Treasury, long before the Cape Breton money was paid.[2] Shirley opposed the Rhode Island ac-

1748. April 19. May 4. 22. June 13. 8. 17.

[1] Gov. Gideon Wanton died Sept. 12, 1767, in his 74th year. He was for 12 years, from 1732 to 1744, General Treasurer, and in 1745 and 1747 was Governor of the Colony.

[2] The exact amounts allowed to Rhode Island for these two expeditions were £6,322 12*s.* 10*d.* for Cape Breton, and £10,144 9*s.* 6*d.* for Canada, being the exact amount of the accounts rendered, reduced to sterling money at the then current rate of exchange, which was 570 per cent. The sums first allowed to all the colonies were afterwards reduced. R. I. received but £7,507 4*s.* 4*d.* for the Canada expedition. The surplus of £2,637 5*s.* 2*d.* already paid, was deducted from the allowance due on the Cape Breton expedition, which was not adjusted till 1750. Partridge labored in vain to prevent this injustice. See his letter of March 17th, 1749–50, and August 10th, 1750, in Letters 1745–1750, R. I. Record Office.

CHAP. XVII. 1748. count, but his objections were met by Partridge, and the amount was allowed and paid at the maturity of the bills. The Cape Breton money was not remitted till long afterward.

June 13. The Assembly revised the laws relating to legal residence in the towns, and to the removal of paupers. New comers were required to give a month's notice of intention to become residents, after which, if they remained one year without being warned to leave, they were admitted as lawful inhabitants of the town. The purchase of a freehold estate, of the value of thirty pounds sterling, also gave a legal residence. Apprentices having served their time in any town, might elect their residence there, or return to the place of their birth. Paupers not having acquired a legal settlement, might be removed by the councils on complaint of the overseer of the poor, to the place of their last legal residence, or to that of their birth. The manner in which this should be done, and the remedies to prevent injustice in such cases, were fully prescribed in the statute.

Complaints were made to the Lords of Admiralty, that illicit trade had been carried on at Rhode Island, during the past year, under cover of flags of truce, to the West Indies, in vessels hired to convey prisoners to the enemies' ports, and in contravention to the laws of war, but few prisoners, in fact, being conveyed in any of these
July 8. vessels. The Admiralty addressed a letter to Gov. Greene, to prevent such violations of law in future.[1]

Aug. 22. News of the armistice having been received, the garrison at Fort George was disbanded, and the Tartar dismantled and laid up. All the ferries had hitherto been private property, but the two on the west side of Jamestown were now ordered to be purchased by the colony.[2] The act against swearing was revised. The penalty was a fine of five shillings, or confinement for three hours in

[1] R. I. Col. Rec., v. 258.

[2] The colony kept them but a short time. In August, 1750, they were ordered to be sold at public auction.

the stocks. To insure a full attendance, the Assembly imposed a fine of two pounds for the first day's absence of any member, without good cause, and one pound for each subsequent day. CHAP. XVII. 1748.

A memorial from merchants in Massachusetts was presented to the Lords of the Treasury, against bills of credit in New England, asking that the war indemnity should not be paid to the colonies till they adopted some plan for their redemption. The treaty of peace was definitely signed at Aix-la-Chapelle. All conquests were mutually restored, so that Cape Breton, that glory of New England prowess, reverted to the French. This was a sore disappointment to the colonists, but not more disgraceful to the British ministry than the fact that the Right of Search, the prime cause of the war, was not even mentioned in the treaty. The Spanish American trade remained as before, in the hands of its rightful owners. Sept. 24. Oct. 7.

The old sloop of war Tartar was ordered to be sold at auction, with all her stores and equipments. This vessel had done efficient service throughout the war, and had fought in some severe engagements, of which mention has already been made.[1] In order to reply to inquiries from the Board of Trade, a census of the colony was taken this autumn. The population was found to be thirty-four thousand one hundred and twenty-eight, of whom twenty-nine thousand seven hundred and fifty were whites, and the remainder blacks and Indians. Newport contained forty-six hundred and forty, and Providence thirty-four hundred and fifty-two inhabitants.[2] 26.

The Assembly granted a lottery for the relief of Joseph Fox, a prisoner for debt in Newport jail. The case was peculiar, and his petition was urged by the 1748-9 Jan. 3.

[1] Two of her guns now stand by the fountain in Washington square, Newport. Bull's Memoirs of R. I.

[2] These Queries from the Board of Trade are printed in the R. I. Col. Rec., v. 257. A copy of the census, taken from Douglas's Summary, and printed on p. 270, differs somewhat from the statement given in the text.

CHAP. XVII. 1748-9 principal merchants of the town. This was the third lottery granted by statute. The system had now become established.

Jan. 26. The death of Rev. John Callender, pastor of the first Baptist church in Newport, and author of the discourse upon the early history of Rhode Island, known as the Century Sermon, was a source of deep grief to the colony. He died at the age of forty-two, while in the full career of usefulness.

Feb. 27. The committee to whom the sale of bills of exchange on England was intrusted, reported the sale of seventy-eight hundred pounds sterling at an exchange of ten hundred and fifty pounds currency, for one hundred pounds sterling, showing the great and rapid depreciation in the paper money of the colony. The exchange, only a few months before, when the account was rendered to the agent, as above mentioned, was five hundred and seventy per cent. So rapid a fall betokened the crash that was soon to overtake the commercial interests of the colony. The highway across Easton's Point in Middletown, was laid out. Hogs were prevented from running at large in the compact parts of Newport and Providence. A
1749. light-house was ordered to be built at Beaver Tail, the south end of Conanicut, for the safety of commerce, which was accomplished during the next year.

The movement in opposition to bills of credit, caused
May 3. much alarm in Rhode Island. The Assembly appointed a committee to prepare instructions upon the subject. In
30. the House of Commons an inquiry was made as to the tenor and amount of this paper money, and orders were sent to every colony to prepare an accurate statement upon these points. The instructions for Partridge[1] being
June 12. approved, were signed by the governor, and sent to England together with a copy of the record of the last lot of
July 19. bills burnt in presence of the Assembly. A copy of the

[1] R. I. Col. Rec., v. 270.

vote in the House of Commons was sent to Rhode Island, with orders from Whitehall to furnish the required information.[1] Every year the tenth bonds given for the payment of the earlier bank issues were becoming due, and as fast as they were received into the treasury, the bills with which they were paid were burnt, and at nearly every session, reports of the trustees, or "grand committee," as they were called, were made concerning these bonds. Those that were not paid, were issued by the treasurer, but the interest on a large portion of the earlier issues was lost, because it was not secured, as was the principal, and at a later date, the interest bonds also, by mortgage on real estate. The committee's report at this time, shows over half a million of pounds in bills of the several banks received by them.[2]

CHAP. XVII. 1749.

Aug. 21.

An act of Parliament, passed in favor of the Moravian society, Unitas Fratrum, was sent to all the colonies, commending that noble band of missionaries to special regard. Two preachers of the order, stopping at Newport on their way to Surinam this year, organized a church in that place. Richard Haywood was their first convert, and one of them, Matthew Reutz, remained at Newport for many years as a schoolmaster.

James Muzzey, of Mendon, believing his land to be within the limits of this colony, petitioned that the north line should again be run, and surveyors were chosen for that purpose. But the time appointed by Rhode Island had passed before the Massachusetts Assembly met.

Oct. 9.

Several criminal statutes were enacted, and the first case that we have noticed, where a divorce was granted by the Assembly, occurred at this time. The Rhode Island commissioners having adjourned for three weeks, and then not meeting with any from Massachusetts, ran the line ex parte. The Massachusetts legislature, as soon as it met, appointed commissioners to unite with those of Rhode Island in renewing the line whenever this colony

25.

30.

Dec. 14.

[1] R. I. Col. Rec., v. 278. [2] Ibid., 273.

CHAP. XVII. was ready to do so. Accordingly, at the winter session, after hearing the report of their committee upon the line, 1749–50. Feb. 27. the Assembly re-appointed them, and fixed a day for the line again to be run.[1]

The committee to prepare the statistics for the House of Commons, made a full report, showing the sum of three hundred and twelve thousand three hundred pounds in bills of credit, emitted to supply the treasury since May 1710, of which one hundred and seventy-seven thousand had been burned at various times, and one hundred and thirty-five thousand pounds were now outstanding. This was doubtless the most favorable report that could be made. The bills are represented at their legislative, not their nominal value, and those only are considered as outstanding which had not yet become due. The whole amount here represented as having been issued, was worth in sterling money, about thirty-six thousand pounds. A large number of English statutes were adopted as laws of the colony.[2]
1750. April 10. The governor notified Massachusetts of the action in regard to the boundary line. The two committees met in Wrentham, and spent two days in a vain attempt to agree upon a starting point. The Rhode Island men then measured off a line from the southernmost part of Charles River, three miles south, and thence west to the Connecticut frontier—the same line they had run in October, and which conformed to the terms of the charter. The Massachusetts men claimed to start from a point fixed in 1642, four or five miles further south. No trace of this old starting point could be found, but the testimony of aged persons was taken as to its location. Both parties agreed to meet again at a future time, if authorized by their legislatures, and the Massachusetts men rendered their
12. report the next day.[3] The General Assembly continued their commissioners, desired Massachusetts to refrain from

[1] The report, dated 22 Jan. 1749–50, is printed in R. I. Col. Rec., v. 280.

[2] R. I. Col. Rec., v. 285.

[3] Mass. Court files, iii. 85.

taxing the inhabitants within the disputed lines, ordered a map of the tract to be prepared, and requested Connecticut to assist at the next meeting of the commissioners.

1750. May 2.

Robert Hazard was chosen deputy-governor in place of Ellery. The fire department in Newport was more thoroughly organized, by the appointment of fire wards, and the town ordered a fire engine to be procured in England.[1]

June 11.

The towns of East and West Greenwich, Warwick and Coventry, were taken off from Providence county, and erected into a separate jurisdiction as the county of Kent, with East Greenwich as its capital, and the people were required at their own expense to build a court-house. The act against pedlars had been avoided by these persons hiring shops, in which to carry on their trade for a short time, and not being inhabitants of the towns, they escaped taxation. To remedy this evil, the assessors were required to tax such persons at their discretion, in proportion to the amount of their business.

July 6.

The long-deferred Cape Breton accounts, were at last settled, and the money paid to Mr. Partridge, deducting the balance overpaid on the Canada expedition ; that account having been cut down after the appropriation for it had once been made and paid over.[2] All the colonies were alike subjected to this reduction.

The attempt of Massachusetts to levy taxes within the disputed territory, led to a riot, in which certain Rhode Island officers were implicated. Some of the rioters were arrested and taken to Worcester for trial. The Assembly interceded for their discharge, and again urged a cessation of taxes until the line could be arranged. The Jews were becoming important merchants in the colony, and we find that Moses Lopez of Newport was excused, at his own request, from all other civil duties, on account of his gratuitous services to the government in translating Spanish documents.

Aug. 20.

[1] R. Partridge's letter, June 9, 1750. [2] See note on page 171 ante.

CHAP. XVII. 1750. A singular affair, of which the explanation must ever remain a mystery, occurred at this time. A vessel coming from the westward with all sail set, and altering her course when close in so as to avoid the reef, came ashore on the north-west corner of Easton's Beach. Upon being boarded by some fishermen who had watched her approach, they found the breakfast table set, the kettle boiling on the fire, a dog and cat in the cabin, and every thing undisturbed, except that the long boat was missing, as if the crew had just left her. Not a soul was on board, nor was any thing ever heard of from any of the crew, nor any trace of them or of their boat ever discovered. She was a brig from Honduras, belonging to Isaac Stelle, a merchant of Newport, and had been hourly expected, as she was spoken but a day or two before by a vessel since arrived. The captain's name was John Huxham. He, with all hands, had evidently deserted her but a very short time before she stranded, although from what motive is not apparent, and what had become of them was equally inexplicable. It was surmised that the men, alarmed at the roar of the breakers, had taken to the boat and been swamped in the surf, but no bodies or pieces of the boat ever floated on shore. The brig was got off and sold to Henry Collins, then an extensive merchant in Newport, who changed her name to the Beach Bird. She made several voyages afterward, and her hulk was still lying in the harbor of Newport, at the time of the British occupation, when it was raised, and converted into an armed galley by the enemy.[1]

The commissioners of the two colonies having agreed to meet in October to settle the boundary, the Rhode Island men[2] repaired to the appointed place in Wrentham, where after waiting two days without seeing the others, they
Oct. 12. proceeded to survey for a point three miles south of

[1] Bull's Memoirs of R. I.

[2] Jonathan Randal, Richard Steere, Thomas Lapham, Joseph Harrison, and Matthew Robinson. Their report is in R. I. Col. Rec., v. 322–5.

Charles River, which proved to vary somewhat from that CHAP.
determined by the former commissioners the year before. XVII.
They adjourned from time to time, notifying the govern- 1750.
ment of Massachusetts of each adjournment, hoping to be joined by the commissioners from that province. Finally they completed the survey ex parte, and their report was entered in full upon the Assembly records in the following March. The Assembly passed a law prohibiting ap- Oct.
peals to England from judgment rendered upon bonds for 31.
the payment of money. The paper-money party had obtained a majority in the lower house, but the assistants were opposed to the system. A joint committee was ap- Dec.
pointed to take the subject into consideration, and report 3.
by bill at the next session. No separate report was made, 1750-1
but a bill was introduced, which complicated still further Mar.
the existing monetary system, and soon rendered all cal- 18.
culations almost impossible from the accumulated varieties of worthless currency with which the colony was flooded. A ninth bank was issued, upon new plates, to the amount of twenty-five thousand pounds. By the act, as amended at the next session, the bills were to be let for ten years at five per cent. interest, and at the end of that time to be paid in five equal instalments. The bills were to be equal to silver at six shillings nine pence an ounce, and six shillings nine pence in these bills were made equivalent to sixteen shillings of new tenor, or sixty-four shillings of old tenor bills. The scale of values was established at £137 10*s*. of the new bills, or £275 of new tenor, or £1,100 of old tenor for one hundred pounds sterling. The ostensible purpose of the act was to afford a bounty upon manufactured wool, flax, and the fisheries; but these bounties were repealed at the next session, the former as being offensive to England, and the others as useless, and the interest money was devoted to the redemption of bills issued to supply the treasury. Heavy penalties were laid to prevent depreciation below the established scale, and "death to counterfeit this bill" was

CHAP. XVII. 1750. Mar. 18. inscribed on the new plate. The effect of this wretched system of finance was daily becoming manifest in the changing conditions of Massachusetts and Rhode Island. In April, we are told by Douglas in his Summary of the condition of the colonies, the bills of the two colonies were of equal value. In September, Rhode Island bills were twenty per cent. below those of her neighbor. Sterling exchange, which in the spring had been at eleven and a half for one, in the autumn stood at nine and a half for one, under the operation of the Massachusetts system; while in Rhode Island no such advance was realized, but on the contrary, bills on London now sold for eleven hundred per cent. premium in Rhode Island currency, as appears by the report of a committee entered on the records at this session; and the new tenor bills had already sunk to less than half their stated value. Many old laws had to be revised to make them efficient by increasing the penalties attached to their violation, so great was the depreciation in values. Among these was the Sunday law, passed seventy-two years before, and also that forbidding the entertainment of servants, with certain modifications. An excise upon liquors sold at retail in Newport was established, to be paid by all inn-keepers and dealers. Street lamps were set up in Newport by private enterprise. To prevent them from being broken, a law was passed punishing such wilful offence by public whipping, not to exceed twenty lashes, or by a fine of twenty pounds, old tenor. A law was also enacted to prevent setting fire to the woods in any part of the colony.

Massachusetts, after having repeatedly failed to unite with Rhode Island in adjusting the northern boundary, even when her own men had appointed the time of meeting, complained to Gov. Greene that this colony exercised jurisdiction within the disputed lines, and withheld the taxes due to her from the people there residing. No Mar. 28. reply being made to the letter, a committee was appointed to consider what course to adopt. Their report advises that the whole subject be referred to the agent in England to represent the case to the King.[1] CHAP. XVII.

Joseph Whipple, who had several times been deputy-governor, was again chosen to that office. The new bank act excited some misgivings in the minds of its friends, and great hostility in its foes. This was natural, but a more formidable opposition was soon to be developed. The motion in Parliament, already mentioned, had secured the data upon which direct action could be taken, and already an act was introduced "to regulate and restrain paper bills of credit" in the New England colonies. Violent opposition to the system was made in Newport. An ably drawn petition[2] to the King, from the merchants of that place, was received while the bill was under debate in the House of Commons. Partridge opposed its passage, by counsel, as being unjust towards Rhode Island. This very long and plausible argument, resulted in securing certain amendments which, to use his own expression, "took the sting out of it." The ministry were determined on its passage, so that Partridge, having secured the desired ameliorations in the Commons, withdrew his opposition in the Lords, and the bill passed.[3] 1751. May 1. Mar. 27. May 8. 20.

Meanwhile, Gov. Greene had replied to the letter from Massachusetts, which announced their determination to refer the dispute to England. The provincial council resolved to continue to exercise jurisdiction over the territory.[4] The General Assembly ordered a full statement of the case to be prepared, and presented at the next session. The Newport petition against paper money, caused much excitement. A hostile committee, appointed to examine the facts therein stated, and to ascertain the June 5. 10.

[1] Mass. Court Files, iii. 88–90.

[2] A copy of this petition, dated Newport, Sept. 4, 1750, and signed by 72 persons, is preserved in the State Record Office.

[3] See R. Partridge's letter of May 17, 1751, in Letters 1750–56 R. I. Record Office.

[4] Mass. Court Files, iii. 91.

CHAP. XVII. 1751. characters of the signers, were compelled to report that the allegations were substantially correct. The names of the signers sufficiently attested their respectability. July 9. Official notice of the law restraining paper issues was sent from Whitehall. Aug. 19. A vain effort was made to arrest the depreciation of the bills by statutes, prescribing that judgments of court should be made up upon the basis of the new scale of values, and binding parties, before granting executions upon such judgments, by an oath that they had not varied from that scale in their dealings.

Hitherto there had been but one notary public for the whole colony, residing in Newport. The increasing business of Providence required greater facilities, so that one Oct. 30. was appointed in that town. An appropriation was made for a quarantine house at Providence. The small-pox had been brought there from sea, and there was no hospital in the colony except at Newport.

1752. Jan. 1. By a late act of Parliament, the calendar year, heretofore begun on the twenty-fifth of March, commenced on the first of January, so that we are henceforth freed from the confusion arising from the double date of the year between those days, and the consequent uncertainty attending the precise date of many important events, arising from a diversity in the custom of counting the twenty-fifth or the first days of March as in the new year. The entire month of March had hitherto been called the first month, although five-sixths of it belonged in the old year. It now became the third month.[1]

Since the establishment of the lottery system, it had been employed to raise funds for many and various objects, for public works and private charities. The streets of Newport were originally paved, and some bridges in

[1] The act to correct the calendar was introduced Feb. 25, 1751, by the Earl of Chesterfield, and passed without debate, upon the second reading, on the 18th March. The new year was to begin on the 1st January—but the correction of 11 days in the day of the month was not to take effect till Sept. 1752.

the colony constructed, from the proceeds of duties on CHAP.
imported slaves. This source of revenue having been cut XVII.
off by act of Parliament as before stated, a lottery was now 1752.
granted for paving the streets; the parade, then called Feb. 24.
Queen street, and Thames street, were to be finished first.

The Lords Justices called for a copy of the laws of the April 28.
colony to be sent to them.

The north-line committee visited Hartford, and there,
in connection with Connecticut government, drew up a 4.
statement of the case, which was presented to the General May 6.
Assembly, showing that the corner stake set by Massachusetts in 1642, and agreed to by Connecticut and Rhode Island in their subsequent settlements of the line with that province, was four miles and fifty-six poles too far south, and that the latter agreements had been made without a survey by the adverse parties—they not suspecting any error or fraud on the part of Massachusetts, nor detecting any till the recent surveys were made by Rhode Island. The report concludes by advising that both parties unite in prosecuting the claim against Massachusetts in England.[1] The blind confidence shown by Rhode Island in the settlement of 1719, after the experience she had had of the spirit of her neighbors in matters of jurisdiction, has been, perhaps deservedly, punished by the ultimate loss of the valuable tract in dispute, after another century of contest. But this result does not justify the false measurement by Massachusetts of the three miles from the southernmost part of Charles River, to which the terms of both charters confined her; nor does it make a compromise agreement, the basis of which was, to use the mildest terms, a gross error, any more binding in equity
that it has been decided to be valid in law. The accounts June 1.
of the parties concerned in this affair, were presented at
the next session and allowed. Private business, the usual
objects of which were the granting of new trials, the Aug. 17.

[1] See R. I. Col. Rec. v. 346.

CHAP. XVII. naturalization of foreigners, and the examination of accounts chiefly occupied the Assembly.

1752. May 7. The great law-suit for the possession of the glebe lands in Narraganset, was decided by the King in council after a litigation of nearly thirty years. It arose from a grant
1668. of three hundred acres of land, made eighty-four years before, by the Pettaquamscot purchasers, for the support of an Orthodox minister. The grantors at that time were mostly of the Church of England but no occupation of
1702. the lands for the purpose designated was had, and thirty-four years after the grant, the lands were entered upon and improved by two private parties. The grantors had meanwhile left the Church of England, and attached themselves to other religious societies, chiefly Congregational, and had then, by a later deed, confirmed the original grant. Niles, the Congregational minister, not then ordained, began to preach in that vicinity the same year that possession was taken of the land, but never claimed it for his church.
1719. The principal trespasser afterward sold his assumed rights to another occupant. The other, who had but twenty acres,
1721. surrendered possession to McSparran upon his arrival.
1723. He brought a writ of ejectment to recover the other portion of the tract, but was cast in the suit. The original deed could not be found. Torrey, the Presbyterian minister, duly ordained, also brought an action for the same land,
1734. in behalf of his church, which on appeal to England, was decided in his favor. Afterward, the original deed hav-
1737. ing been found, McSparran brought a new action. The case was contested between the Episcopal and Presbyte-
1739. rian churches for many years, and decided by the Superior Court of Rhode Island in favor of the latter; which ver-
1752. dict was this year finally confirmed by the King, upon the ground that by the Rhode Island charter all denominations were Orthodox, and that a majority of the grantors, when the deed took effect, were Presbyterians or Congregationalists. The case excited great interest in

CHAP. XVII.

the colony, and the papers relating to it are very voluminous.[1]

1752. Sept. 3. / 14.

The law adopting the Gregorian or New Style, now took effect by adding eleven days to the current day of the month. The day following the second of September was counted as the fourteenth.

Oct. 28.

No public business was done at the next session. The fourth edition of printed laws was published this summer by Ann and James Franklin at Newport, and copies were sent to England as required.[2]

1753.

At the winter session, the people of Kent county, having built the court-house at Greenwich at their own expense, petitioned for a lottery grant to enable them to finish and furnish it, which was allowed. The towns in Providence county were impowered to build a work-house, to be paid for by proportionate taxation, and each town was to support its own paupers therein. A similar measure had been proposed fifteen years before, and had failed. How long this continued as a joint concern, is unknown. The poor-house in Providence resulted from this movement at a somewhat later day.

Stephen Decatur, said to have been a native of Genoa, who for seven years past had been an officer of one of the Newport privateers, and had married in that town, took the requisite oaths, and was naturalized at this session. His son, the celebrated Commodore Decatur, was born in Newport the April previous.

May 2. June 11. Aug. 20.

At the general election, the same officers were chosen. The adjourned session was occupied with private business. Beaver Tail lighthouse having been burnt down, the Assembly ordered a new one to be forthwith constructed of brick or stone, with a house adjoining for the use of the

[1] A more full account of this famous lawsuit than our limits will permit is given in Updike's Nart. Church, pp. 70–82.

[2] No copy of this edition exists in the Secretary's office. The allowance of £355 for printing and stitching it was made to the Franklins by the Assembly in August, 1753. The number of laws in this edition is stated at 471.

CHAP. XVII. 1753. keeper. It was difficult to find men willing to be overseers of the poor. To remedy this, a refusal to accept the office was punished by fine, and power was given to overseers to bind out idle or indigent persons to service. One John Martin, having been convicted of abusing the General Assembly, was sentenced to close confinement in Newport jail, without the use of writing materials, or having communication with any one but the sheriff. This summary treatment soon brought him to repentance, and Aug. 23. three days after sentence he acknowledged his offence, asked pardon of the Assembly, and was accordingly discharged, on payment of costs.

The calendar of private petitions shows how severe was the financial revulsion which now came upon the colony. The ruinous system of paper money was working its legitimate result; yet, worthless as it was, and severe as were the penalties for counterfeiting it, already had the depreciation of the latest issue commenced, hastened by the boldness of forgers. But this last blow was not needed to condemn a system whose intrinsic falsity could not fail in time to become apparent. Among the victims of the crash that had now come upon the colony, was Joseph Whipple, the deputy-governor, whose extensive mercantile operations could no longer be sustained under a disordered and factitious currency He surrendered all his property to the use of his creditors, and received the benefit of a special act of insolvency. The terms of his petition are truly pathetic, such as, under the circumstances, and in an age when failures were almost unknown, an honest and honorable man in his position might well employ.

Oct. 31. Nov. 2. When the next Assembly met at South Kingstown, Mr. Whipple resigned his place as deputy-governor, and Jonathan Nichols was elected to that office. A new courthouse was built at South Kingstown, and new jails for Kings and Providence counties. Parliament had passed an act to encourage the making of potash in the colonies.

Moses Lopez obtained from the Assembly a patent for ten years upon an improved method of making it, known only to himself. CHAP. XVII. 1753.

The cloud of war was once more gathering. The attempt made during the past year, by the commissioners at Paris, to define the boundaries of the French and English possessions in North America, had failed. The colonies of the rival nations pushed their advanced posts nearer to each other. Orders were sent from Whitehall[1] to all the colonies, first to remonstrate and then to repel force by force if necessary. It was in consequence of this that the name of George Washington first appears in history, as Nov. the bearer of a letter of remonstrance from Gov. Dinwiddie to the French commander at Fort Le Bœuf. The Board of Trade having proposed a meeting of commissioners from all the colonies, at Albany, to treat with the Six 1754. Mar. 29. Nations, Gov. Delancey, of New York wrote to Rhode Island naming the fourteenth of June for this purpose. Active measures were taken by both parties to fortify their frontiers, and to occupy the intervening region of the Ohio valley. While on his mission to the French, Washington observed the commanding position for a fort at the head of the Ohio River, and a few soldiers were soon sent there by Gov. Dinwiddie to construct one. The French drove them off, and commenced building Fort Duquesne, named for their governor-general, on the spot April 17. where Pittsburg now stands. To counteract these movements, Gov. Delancey proposed erecting forts in northern New York, and wrote to this colony stating his plans.[2] 22. Affairs were hastening to a crisis. A regiment of six hundred Virginians were already on their march to the frontier, when the news of the occupation of Fort Duquesne reached them. Lieutenant-colonel Washington, with a small detachment, pushed forward to reconnoitre. Near the Great Meadows they surprised, by night, an ad-

[1] Dated 28th August, 1753. See Letters 1750–6.

[2] R. I. Col. Rec. v. 383.

CHAP. XVII. 1754. May 27. vanced party of French troops under Jumonville. It was then that Washington himself fired the first musket of the war. A short, sharp action ensued. The French commander and ten of his men were slain. This was the first blood shed in the fourth intercolonial war, generally known at this day as "the old French war." Its momentous results no human eye could foresee!

Feb. 25. The General Assembly at the winter session chartered the Providence library association, and gave them the use of the council chamber for depositing their books. This was the second incorporated library in the State. A patent for making pearl ashes was issued to James Rodgers of Newport, on similar terms with that to Lopez for potash.

May 1. John Gardner was chosen deputy-governor at the spring election. James Sheffield was made captain of Fort George. The penalty of death was denounced against June 10. counterfeiters. The Fellowship Club, a benevolent association of sea-captains, for mutual assistance, which afterward became the Newport Marine Society, was incorporated.[1] Providence now contained over six hundred freemen, and covered so large a territory, that the southern portion of it was set off as a new township, and incorporated with the name of Cranston. The first charter election 25. in the new town was held without delay. Stephen Hopkins and Martin Howard, jr., were appointed commissioners to attend the convention at Albany, and aid, to the amount of one hundred pounds sterling, was voted to further 19. the objects of the conference. At this congress of delegates, the affair with the Six Nations having been satisfactorily arranged, a plan of union of all the colonies for common defence, submitted by Benjamin Franklin, was debated, and by a singular coincidence, was adopted July 4. by the delegates on the fourth day of July,[2] but it did not meet the approval of either the colonial or home gov-

[1] In June, 1785, the charter was amended, and the name "Marine Society" adopted.

[2] Belknap's New Hampshire, ii. 286.

ernments, and was subsequently abandoned. The Rhode Island delegates reported to the Assembly, the proceedings of the Congress.[1] The warlike aspect of affairs, called for efficient action, and the bills of credit were falling due. To meet these demands, taxes to the amount of thirty thousand pounds were levied on the colony, five thousand of which were for repairing Fort George. The tonnage dues were increased to defray the expenses of keeping up the lighthouse at Beaver Tail, the rebuilding of which had just been completed. An additional tax of five thousand pounds was levied by the next Assembly for the repairs of Fort George. The entire tax of thirty-five thousand pounds was apportioned among the towns, one-fifth of it to Newport. A fire-engine was ordered for Providence, to be paid for by taxing the houses in the compact part of the town, and every housekeeper was required to keep two leather fire buckets ready for service. 1754. Aug. 20. Oct. 30.

Orders were sent from Whitehall to raise two thousand men in New England, under command of Shirley and Pepperell, and two regiments of regulars were detailed for Virginia, there to be reinforced by troops raised in that province. Provisions and money were to be furnished by the colonies. Upon receipt of this order, Gov. Greene convened the Assembly. A fund of four thousand pounds, old tenor, at ten per cent. interest was provided, and one hundred men were enlisted. A commissary-general was appointed, and, upon petition from Westerly and Charlestown, an artillery company of a hundred men was chartered, on the same terms with those of Newport and Providence. They adjourned for one month, and then revised the militia law, increasing the fines for neglect of duty, replenished the military stores in each county, constructed a powder magazine in Newport, and organized a troop of horse in Newport, under Benjamin Sherburne. They also drew up a petition, to be sent with a plan of 26. 1755. Jan. 1. Feb. 3.

[1] R. I. Col. Rec. v. 393.

CHAP. XVII. 1755. Fort George, asking for additional cannon, and empowered the captain of the fort to enlist fifty men to exercise at the guns, and garrison the works. A committee of war was chosen to have the general direction of military affairs. While the Assembly was in session, a letter was sent from Gov. Shirley, highly complimenting the promptness of their action, and desiring that ten men be added to the one hundred already ordered.[1] The Assembly complied by increasing the number to a hundred and thirteen. All French subjects found in Massachusetts were placed in confinement, to prevent their sending aid or advices to the enemy, and Shirley urged Rhode Island to adopt the same summary measures, and also to prohibit the exportation of provisions.[2] Shirley had conceived the plan of attacking the French in Nova Scotia, and thus, by dividing the enemy's forces, to assist Gov. Dinwiddie's operations on the Ohio, and at the same time to attack Crown Point, and erect a fort near that strong position. For this latter purpose he appointed Col. William Johnson, of the Mohawk country, to the chief command, whose influence with the Six Nations was unbounded. These plans were communicated to Gov. Greene, with a request that he would at once convene the Assembly to act upon them, and Thomas Hutchinson, afterward governor of Massachusetts, and historian of that province, was sent to Rhode Island to urge their co-operation.[3] The Assembly was called by special warrant. Four hundred men were voted for the Crown Point expedition, to be under command of Col. Christopher Harris, and the former acts for a hundred and thirteen men were repealed.[4] Provisions

Feb. 5.

17.

24.

March 3.

6.

[1] Shirley's MS. letters. R. I. Col. Rec. v. 412.

[2] R. I. Col. Rec. v. 413.

[3] Shirley's MS. letters. R. I. Col. Rec. v. 414–17.

[4] This force was divided into four companies, officered as follows: Christopher Harris, Colonel. Captains—Edward Cole, Robert Sterry, Henry Babcock, Abraham Francis. Lieutenants—Samuel Nichols, David Dexter, Edward Gray, John Wardwell. Ensigns—Joshua Bill, Thomas Burket, Ichabod Babcock, Joseph Potter.

for two months, with ammunition and warlike stores were ordered to be sent forward to Albany. Sixty thousand pounds in old tenor bills were issued to meet the expenses, redeemable by taxation within two years, and the words "Crown Point" were to be stamped on the back of these notes. Christopher Champlin was appointed commissary to the troops. An annual pension of fifty pounds was pledged to any one who should lose a limb or be disabled in the expedition. Acts were passed to prevent the shipment of provisions to French ports, and empowering the magistrates to arrest all French subjects within the colony.

1755.

The jealousy of Rhode Island at any movement that might affect her charter privileges has often been noticed in these pages. The projected union of the colonies at the late convention in Albany, and a contemplated plan to the same effect by the British ministry, were calculated to arouse this feeling in full vigor. Hitherto the agressions of unsympathizing neighbors, the ambition of royal governors, or the opposition of ministers to the democratic element embodied in the charter, had been the sources of peril which, for more than a century, quickened the spirit of eternal vigilance. A new direction was given to it by these proposals. A union, for whatever purpose, that might compromise the chartered liberties of the State, was not to be considered without long and serious debate. The spirit which thirty-five years later gave rise to the fiercest struggle ever known in Rhode Island, was now first manifested in a vote of the Assembly upon a letter to be sent to the agent, wherein he was "directed to be upon his watch, and if any thing shall be moved in Parliament, respecting the plan for a union of his Majesty's northern colonies, projected at Albany, which may have a tendency to infringe on our chartered privileges, that he use his utmost endeavors to get it put off, until such time as the government is furnished with a copy, and have opportunity of making answer thereunto." At a later

CHAP. XVII. date we shall have occasion to revert to this significant resolution.

1755. A stormy period in Rhode Island annals, both civic and martial, had commenced. Since the political excitement ceased, on the election of Gov. Arnold, at the close of Philip's war, there had been but very few occasions for the display of party spirit. The paper-money system had elicited a strong opposition, and presented the only important question for many years, to distract the colony. But a new issue was about to offer, that was destined to divide the people down to the period when all minor matters were absorbed in the momentous measures of independence. This was, to a great extent, a merely personal issue between rival candidates; but it also combined, in various modes and degrees, at different times, most of the great topics that had ever before divided the popular mind. Questions of peace or war, of hard money or paper, were blended with personal preferences for the prominent candidates, while the growth of the centres of population now added another element of contention, which seems for a time to have overshadowed all the rest in a struggle between town and country. The bitterness of party strife is often developed in an inverse ratio to the intrinsic merits of the controversy. No hostility is so keen, as that which has for its basis persons, rather than principles, or more unrelenting than one that, without just foundation, arrays men against each other, in something like a war of classes, upon local divisions or differences of position, whether geographical or social. When position becomes the criterion of party, principles soon perish in the conflict.

What is known as the Ward and Hopkins controversy, commenced at this time with Gov. Greene. He was on terms of most intimate friendship with Samuel Ward, whose name will presently appear in the struggle.[1]

[1] His son, the second Governor William Greene, married Catherine Ray of New Shoreham, a sister of the wife of Gov. Samuel Ward.

Family pride and local interests combined to embitter the CHAP.
protracted feud. The contest at this election was very XVII.
severe, resulting in a change of one half the upper house. 1755.
Stephen Hopkins was chosen governor, and Jonathan May 7.
Nichols deputy-governor for two successive years.

The Assembly placed the four companies for Crown
Point upon a regimental footing. The officers were to be
commissioned by the council of war, and were authorized
to recruit their ranks from the other colonies, or from the
Six Nations if necessary. Transports were hired at five
hundred pounds each to convey the troops, each company June
with its arms and stores in a separate vessel. A further 4.
issue of forty thousand pounds was made, on the same 9.
conditions with the emission in March.

The defeat and death of Gen. Braddock, near Fort July
Duquesne, spread consternation throughout the colonies. 9.
It was in that action that the provincial troops, led by
Washington, showed their superiority over regulars in the
conduct of Indian warfare, and were enabled to cover the
retreat of the routed English. To strike a counter blow
that should save the whole continent from falling into the
hands of the French, was now imperative. Additional
forces must be sent against the enemy at Crown Point,
and great efforts were made by all the colonies. Gov.
Hopkins convened the Assembly by special warrant. Aug.
Three new companies of fifty men each, were raised, and 11.
hurried forward by land to Albany, in order to reach the
army before an action should take place. They were
joined to Col. Harris's command, and thus increased the
Rhode Island regiment to five hundred and fifty men.[1]
Seven members of the Assembly protested against this
levy, on the ground that the colony having already sent
its full quota, they were unwilling to burden their con-

[1] The officers of these three companies were as follows: Captains—John Whiting, Amos Hammond, William Bradford. Lieutenants—Benjamin Hall, Stephen Arnold (of Smithfield), Robert Hopkins (of Exeter). Ensigns—Benjamin Bosworth, Joseph Davis of (Cumberland), Jonathan Andrew.

CHAP. XVII. 1755. stituents further. Twenty thousand pounds of Crown Point bills of credit were issued to meet the expenses, on the same terms with the one hundred thousand already emitted this year. Another appropriation of five thousand pounds was made to enlarge Fort George, and two thousand more were conditionally allowed, provided Newport would contribute five thousand for the same object. Six vessels that had cleared for the West Indies and Africa were embargoed, and a part of their cargo of provisions was taken from them to supply the troops. Complaints having been made by Shirley, who, by the death of Braddock became commander-in-chief, that Cape Breton and other French colonies received supplies from Rhode Island, a committee was appointed to examine into the facts. They reported that no such act had been committed, and explained clearly the circumstances that had given rise to the charge. Certain French subjects, who for some months had been confined to their houses under surveillance of the committee of war, were ordered to leave the colony within twenty days. A law for the relief of poor and disabled persons was enacted, requiring that they should be supported by their relatives, if able to do so, under direction of the justices of the peace.

Gov. Hopkins was elected chief justice of the Superior Court; a union of the highest executive and judicial powers in the colony, as rare as it would, at this day, be thought dangerous. It attests the confidence of the people in his integrity and uncommon mental endowments.

Meanwhile, the colonial army, six thousand strong, under Gen. Lyman of Connecticut, had taken post at the head of Hudson River, and built Fort Lyman, afterward called Fort Edward. There they were joined by Gen. Johnson, with some artillery, who assumed the command, and advanced to Lake George. Baron Dieskau, with three thousand men, marched from Montreal to besiege Fort Lyman, but, suddenly changing his plan, turned to attack Johnson. In a narrow defile near Johnson's camp,

CHAP. XVII. 1755. Sept. 8.

he encountered a detachment of Massachusetts troops and Indians, led by Col. Williams, and Hendrick, the Mohawk chief, and defeated them with the loss of both their commanders. Within three miles of this fatal ravine, was the main camp, on the margin of Lake George. Dieskau pressed forward to the attack. The intrenchments were incomplete, but a few heavy guns brought up from the lake opened an unexpected fire, which disordered the advancing columns and terrified their Indian allies. It was near noon when the battle began. Johnson received a ball in the thigh early in the fight, and retired from the ground, leaving Gen. Lyman in command. Dieskau fought most gallantly, and although three times severely wounded, refused to be borne off the field. For five hours the battle raged, sustained by the courage of the New England troops, who poured upon the enemy a continual fire, "the most violent that had yet been known in America."[1] The loss of the Americans was about three hundred; that of the French more than three times that number. The remnants of Dieskau's army retreated to Crown Point, leaving their leader a prisoner and mortally wounded. Later in the day, the enemy's baggage was captured by some New Hampshire troops, after a short struggle with the guard. For this action, Johnson was knighted, and received five thousand pounds from Parliament; but the honor of the victory belongs to Lyman. He alone conducted the battle from the commencement, but history has yet to accord to him the glory which is his due.

Col. Harris had returned to Rhode Island, to obtain clothing for his regiment, leaving Lieutenant-colonel Cole, of whom Johnson speaks highly as an active officer, in command.[2] Shirley was at Oswego designing to attack Niagara. An army from Massachusetts under Winslow, had gone to expel the French from the Bay of Fundy.

[1] Bancroft, iv. 211. [2] Johnson's MS. letter, Aug. 20, 1755.

CHAP. XVII. 1755. Sept. 8.

The extent of the military operations in hand, required new levies of troops to be made in all the colonies, and on the same day with the battle of Lake George, Gov. Hopkins had called an extra session of the Assembly for this purpose. Of the three companies raised in August, two had already marched by land to Albany, and Capt. Whiting's company, having been hitherto delayed, was now ordered to embark in a sloop to join the army. Four additional companies of fifty men each were raised, and sent forward in all haste to join Col. Harris's command, making the Rhode Island regiment seven hundred and fifty men, divided into eleven companies.[1] The expenses of so large a force fell heavily upon the feeble colony, weakened as it was by the financial derangement which every new emission of paper bills served to increase. But there was now no remedy for this; the troops must be sustained, and another issue of Crown Point bills to the amount of sixty thousand pounds was made.

Under Monckton and Winslow, the French forts in the Bay of Fundy had been broken up, but the people of Nova Scotia, who, by the terms of their surrender forty years before, were excused from bearing arms against their kindred, and hence were known as "the neutral French," were suspected of aiding the enemy. It was decreed that they should be driven from their native soil, and distributed among the other American colonies. This was done under circumstances so atrocious, that history affords no parallel, since the expulsion of the Jews from Spain, to the violence of the sufferings inflicted upon these unhappy Acadians.

Although the war was so fiercely waged on the western continent, no formal declaration had yet been made,

[1] These four companies were officered as follows: Captains—Daniel Bosworth, John Potter, jr., Robert Hopkins, Barzillai Richmond. Lieutenants—Christopher Hargil, William Richmond, jr., Ebenezer Cahoone, Ebenezer Jenckes. Ensigns—William Nichols, James Tew, jr., Giles Russell, Nathaniel Peck.

CHAP. XVII. 1755.

but depredations upon French commerce had commenced, and the channel ports were thronged with French prizes.[1] This system of reprisals had begun somewhat earlier in the colonies. A vessel belonging to the Marquis of Lambertie, which had put in to Newport in June, was there seized and condemned by the Court of Admiralty, and the marquis imprisoned, under the act for that purpose, until sent to England, where he complained of his treatment in Rhode Island, but obtained no redress.

Shirley desired a conference with the several governors, to be held at New York, to arrange a plan of campaign for the next year. The General Assembly appointed Gov. Hopkins and Daniel Updike as delegates to this convention. (Oct. 29.) One hundred and eighty thousand pounds in old tenor bills had been issued the present year, to defray the expenses of the war. To redeem a portion of this Crown Point paper, as it was called, a tax of seventy thousand pounds was levied upon the colony, one-fifth of which, as in the last tax, was assessed on Newport.

(Nov.) The progress of the war in America led to the establishment, by the post-office department, of a monthly line of packets between Falmouth and New York. Letters of thanks were sent to all the colonies for their zeal in the common cause.[2] (11.)

The Board of Trade forwarded a series of inquiries into the condition of the colony, similar to those before emanating from that source. Upon its reception, the Assembly was again called together, and adopted measures to furnish the required information. (Dec. 22.) A census was taken. The population of the colony was found to be but little short of forty thousand, of whom about thirty-six thousand were whites, and the number of men capable of bearing arms was eight thousand two hundred and sixty-two, of whom about fifteen hundred were soon after engaged in manning privateers. Shirley having disbanded

[1] Partridge's MS. letter, September 13.

[2] That to this colony is in R. I. Col. Rec. v. 467.

CHAP. XVII. 1756. the greater portion of the army for the winter, the Assembly voted to retain a hundred and eighty-five men in military service, one hundred of them at home, and the others in the garrisons of Fort Edward and Fort William Henry, near Lake George. The Rhode Island troops
Jan. were at the latter fort, and formed nearly one-third of the garrison. Capt. Whiting, of the fifth Rhode Island company, was made fort-major and adjutant of the garrison, and his conduct is highly commended in the official reports.[1]

Feb. The reduction of Crown Point was definitely abandoned for the winter by Shirley. In fact, some of the colonial Assemblies were dissatisfied with the results of the past year, and had lost confidence in the commander-in-chief. Rhode Island did not share in this distrust, but continued her preparations to take the field in the coming spring. A regiment of five hundred men, including the
23. company at Fort William Henry, was voted, divided into ten companies, and officered.[2] A vote of thanks to Major-General Johnson and to Capt. William Eyre, engineer-in-chief, for their services in the late campaign, was adopted. The militia act was amended. Five thousand pounds, in addition to the previous sums, were appropriated to rebuild Fort George. John Rodgers, and others of Newport, formerly commissioned officers, but now exempt

[1] Commander Glasier's MS. letter of January 12. R. I. Col. Rec. v. 472.

[2] The officers of this regiment were as follows: Christopher Harris, Colonel; Christopher Champlin, jr., Lieut. Col.; Samuel Angel, Major; Thomas Burket, 1st Lieut., and Elkanah Spear, 2d Lieut. of Col. H.'s company. William Richmond, jr., 1st, and Benjamin Bosworth, 2d Lieut. of Lieut. Col. C.'s company. Silas Cook, 1st Lieut., and Mark Noble 2d Lieut. of Major A.'s company. Of the other six companies now raised the officers were: Captains—George Gardner, jr., Henry Babcock, Barzillai Richmond, John Potter, jr., Daniel Bosworth, Amos Hammond. 1st Lieutenants—John Linscomb, Giles Russel, Joseph Davis, Grindal Reynolds, Christopher Hargil, Samuel Champlin. 2d Lieutenants—James Tew, jr., Samuel Hearne, Nathaniel Peck, George Shearman, Edward Talby, Samuel Rose. Joshua Brown was made 2d lieutenant of Capt. John Whiting's company at Fort William Henry. Rufus Hopkins, commissary. In May, Giles Russel was made adjutant of the regiment, and Ephraim Starkweather, chaplain.

from military duty, petitioned for a charter, and were incorporated as an independent company. The martial spirit of the people was thoroughly roused, and no efforts were spared to render efficient service to the common cause. To meet the expense, an issue of eight thousand pounds in bills of credit of a new form, called "lawful money," was made. These bills were printed in type; they were to pass at the rate of those in the neighboring colonies; their value was stated in silver at six and eightpence an ounce, and they were dated from the passage of the act. Any money that might be received from England for war expenses, was to be used in redeeming the Crown Point bills. The balance of them was to be sunk by taxation; and finally, the value of old or new tenor paper was not to be effected by these lawful money bills. Spanish dollars had begun to appear in circulation, and the genius of counterfeiters, hitherto exercised on the paper money, was now directed to this more reliable currency.

CHAP. XVII. 1756. Feb. 27.

Shirley was superseded as commander-in-chief in America, by Lord Loudoun, who was to bring out with him a large force of regular troops to prosecute the war with vigor. To encourage the colonists to renewed exertions, a grant of one hundred and fifteen thousand pounds sterling was made towards their expenses during the past year.[1]

Mar. 13.

The General Assembly ordered the regiment to be completed by impressment if necessary. A large quantity of military stores to arm the troops were received from Shirley. John Wanton and others petitioned that sea captains be drafted to exercise at the guns on Fort George, in lieu of other military duty, and the captain of the fort was empowered to enlist fifty men for that purpose. William Mumford was chosen to command the

May 5.

[1] The amount assigned to R. I. from this grant was £6,684 12*s.* 3*d.*, which was received in gold and silver, in September. See Apthorpe & Sons' letter and order of 31st August, 1756. R. I. Col. Rec. v. 533.

CHAP. XVII. fort. The Assembly appointed the twentieth of May as
a day of fasting and prayer, and the governor issued his
1756. proclamation accordingly. This is the earliest record we
find of a public fast day in this colony, appointed by the
Assembly. The British fleet at Halifax required seamen,
May 12. and Shirley wrote to Gov. Hopkins to ship as many sailors
as possible for that service, and also to hasten forward the
land forces to Albany.

At length, after two years of active war on the Western continent, and several months of actual hostilities in
18. Europe, war was formally proclaimed by Great Britain,
and shortly afterward declared by France.

The "seven years war," so called, dates from this
period, but to America it was, in fact, a nine years conflict.

The derangement of the currency, and the expenses of
the war, bore heavily on the commercial prosperity of the
colony. Failures in business became so frequent, that a
June 8. general act for the relief of insolvent debtors was passed.
The debtor, upon surrendering all his property for the
satisfaction of his creditors, was thereby released from
further liability for debts contracted prior to his taking
the benefit of the act. The preparations for war were
stimulated by the appointment of the Earl of Loudoun,
and were nowhere more actively pursued than in this
14. colony. Gen. Winslow asserts in a letter to the governor,
that Rhode Island "comes nearest up to their quota."
22. The Assembly was convened, by special warrant, to prevent the exportation of provisions, and military stores, and
to provide for maintaining the troops expected from England. It was voted to enlist one hundred additional men,
exclusive of officers, to be sent in two companies on the
expedition against Crown Point. A deputy-commissary[1]
for the forces was appointed to assist Mr. Hopkins. Upon
July 23. the day of his arrival at New York, Lord Loudoun wrote

[1] William Thurston Gardner. This is the earliest case of the use of a middle name noticed on the records.

to Gov. Hopkins for copies of the votes of the Assembly for raising troops, and of the instructions given to them. The activity of the French, and a difficulty in arranging the terms upon which the provincial troops would serve with the regulars under Loudoun, required his immediate presence with the army at Albany. The capture of Oswego, with a large quantity of military stores by Montcalm, the successor of Dieskau, caused an urgent letter from Loudoun to Gov. Hopkins, asking for more troops, and a supply of teams for transport purposes to be sent from Rhode Island.[1] These incessant drains upon the resources of the colony for the war upon land, did not subdue the spirit of naval enterprise. Privateers were fitted out, as in the former war, and one of them, the Foy, of eighteen guns and a hundred and eighty men, was placed in command of Capt. Dennis, the hero of Martinique, who sailed for the Spanish main, his old cruising ground, but was never heard from again.[2]

Aug. 14.

20.

22.

23.

The letter of the Earl of Loudoun was communicated to the Assembly with a message from the governor, indicating the important subjects that required their deliberation. These were: in what manner the bills of credit should be called in and sunk with the money lately received from England; how the remaining bills should be redeemed or made available to preserve the credit of the colony; and how the treasury could be supplied, as the Crown Point appropriations were exhausted, while the exigencies of the war were imperative[3]. These were matters of vast importance, but of which the solution was most difficult. The Crown Point bills were ordered to be called in, and two-thirds of them to be redeemed at the rate of four pounds for a Spanish dollar, and the other

[1] R. I. Col. Rec. v. 510.

[2] He was the father of Capt. William Dennis, who, during the revolutionary war, in which he commanded thirteen privateers, fully sustained the fame of his gallant sire. Bull's Memoir of Rhode Island.

[3] R. I. Col. Rec. v. 502.

CHAP. XVII. 1756. one-third by promissory notes of the treasurer, payable at the same rate, on or before the close of the next year. The war committee was authorized to contract a loan of fifty thousand pounds, old tenor, at six per cent., to meet which a tax of fifty-three thousand pounds was assessed upon the colony. The circulation of the bills of other colonies was prohibited. Messengers were dispatched to confer with Connecticut and Massachusetts upon the threatened advance of the victorious French, and measures were taken to provide arms, provisions, and stores for five hundred men. A garrison of twenty men, under Lieut. Caleb Carr, was placed at Fort George, and a lottery of ten thousand pounds was granted, the proceeds to be used in repairing the fort.

Sept. 8. While the Assembly was holding an adjourned session, the deputy-governor, Jonathan Nichols, died.[1] During the funeral, minute guns were fired from the fort. John Gardner, who had held the office two years before, was elected to fill the vacancy, and retained the post through all the changes of party, for eight successive years until his death. News of the advance of the French army upon Lake George, occasioned a special session of the Assembly. Oct. 14. It was voted to raise four hundred men, and send them forward with all haste to Albany. The list, from which drafts were to be made, included every man between sixteen and sixty years of age, except public officers, ministers, and those who made oath or affirmation that it was against their conscience to bear arms. The governor was chosen colonel of the regiment.[2] Six thousand pounds in "lawful money" bills of credit were issued to meet the expenses of this new levy. A special 20. Court of Admiralty, composed of seven commissioners

[1] He was the son of Dep. Gov. Jonathan Nichols, who also died while in that office, in 1727.

[2] The list of officers for these eight companies is not given, because in a few days an order came from the Earl of Loudoun to countermand their marching, and they were disbanded.

from Boston, was convened at Providence for the trial of Capt. Joseph Hughes, for the murder of Michael Clarke. He was convicted, and sentenced to death. The small-pox having broken out among the army at Albany, the Assembly voted to delay the marching of the new regiment, till an express could be sent to Lord Loudoun for orders. These orders, to withhold the troops, as the season was too far advanced for further operations, were already on the way, and, upon their reception, the soldiers were discharged by vote of the Assembly. A large amount of Crown Point bills were burnt at this session.

CHAP. XVII. 1756. Oct. 27. Nov. 15.

The firmness with which the General Assembly asserted its authority, has before been exemplified in these pages. Another case occurred at this time. One Samuel Thayer, being accused of applying abusive language to that body, was brought before them by warrant, and having confessed the act, was committed to jail in Providence.

The ill success of this campaign in America, led to a change in the British ministry, by which William Pitt took the place lately held by Fox as an under Secretary of State, of which the usual notice was sent to all the colonies. The Earl of Loudoun proposed a council of governors and commissioners to be held at Boston in January, to arrange the next campaign, and in his letter to Gov. Hopkins, desired that the several legislatures might be convened at the same time.[1] In consequence of this, the Assembly met at Providence to appoint and instruct their commissioners. The governor, with James Honyman and George Brown were chosen to attend the council. They were instructed to report to Lord Loudoun the exact condition of the colony, to request him to represent it to the King, and to ask a suitable allowance for the military stores furnished in the past year. They were also to recommend to his lordship Capt. Walter Chaloner, who had held a commission in the expedition against Carthagena, as a person deserving of his favor.

Dec. 7. 22. 1757. Jan. 10.

[1] R. I. Col. Rec. v. 570.

CHAP. XVII. 1757. Jan. 13. Loudoun's plan of operations for the coming season, submitted to the Congress at Boston, was chiefly defensive. An attempt to recover Louisburg was the only aggressive measure proposed. While the council were 26. deliberating, a special session of the Assembly was called by the deputy-governor, to act upon a letter from Gov. Hopkins, relating to the part which Rhode Island was to take in the next campaign. This being done, the Assembly adjourned for a few days to await further action of Feb. 1. the council. Private business occupied the week, until the Congress broke up, when Gov. Hopkins and the other 7. commissioners resumed their seats in the Assembly. The mode of ascertaining the value of rateable estates was revised, with a view to the proper apportionment of taxes among the towns. It was resolved to build a sloop of war of a hundred and twenty tons to guard the coast,[1] and to raise a force of four hundred and fifty men, in five companies, to serve for one year under command of the Earl of Loudoun.[2] The treasurer was empowered to hire sixty thousand pounds, old tenor, for six months, and a tax of one hundred thousand pounds was assessed to redeem the loan. The plans of the commander-in-chief required that an embargo should be laid on all the north- Mar. 2. ern ports. He therefore wrote to Rhode Island, recom-

[1] Obadiah and George Brown, and Joseph Sheldon, were the committee to build the vessel, charging nothing for their services. She never went to sea, but was ordered to be sold for the benefit of the colony by the Assembly, in December, 1758.

[2] Col. Samuel Angel was chosen to command the regiment, and Dr. William Hunter served as surgeon. "Dr. Hunter gave the first course of medical lectures ever delivered in America." They were given in 1754, 1755, and 1756, and drew many pupils from abroad. *Dr. Usher Parsons' speech at the Re-union at Newport, Aug.* 23, 1859. The other officers were: Captains—George Gardner, John Potter, John Whiting, Jeremiah Greene, Daniel Wall. 1st Lieutenants—Christopher Hargil, Elkanah Spear, James Tew, jr., Giles Russel, Nathaniel Peck. 2d Do.—Isaac Wilbore, Mark Noble, George Shearman, Samuel Hearn, Edward Tallbee. Ensigns—Israel Peck, Samuel Saunders, Amos Whiting, Geoffrey Wilcox, jr., Abel Gibbs. Christopher Nichols was chosen surgeon's mate.

mending that course, which was adopted. The Assembly CHAP.
renewed the garrison at Fort George. The demands of XVII.
the war caused so great a scarcity of military stores, that 1757.
the lead roofing of the court-house at Newport was order- Mar. 14.
ed to be removed and placed in charge of the sheriff for
the use of the colony. The governor was empowered to
send out a vessel to defend the coast, in case the enemy
should appear. The privateer Abercrombie, Capt. Joseph
Rivers, was hired by the government for this purpose.
The people in the north part of Westerly, petitioned for
a division of the town. This was granted, and that portion of Westerly north of Pawcatuck River was incorporated, with the name of Hopkinton.

At the annual election, the Ward party triumphed in May 4.
the choice of Gov. William Greene, and seven of the ten
assistants. But the policy of the government in regard to
the war, was not affected by the change of officers. The
new Assembly, in consequence of an appeal from Lord
Loudoun, voted to raise an additional force of a hundred
and fifty men to be ready in case of requisition from Major-
Gen. Webb, then in command at Fort Edward. The attack on Louisburg was prevented by the activity of the
French. A powerful fleet, including seventeen ships of
the line, sailed from Brest for North America, five days 3.
before Admiral Holburne, with twenty ships, carrying ten
hundred and forty guns, and six thousand troops, left 8.
Cork for Halifax.[1] Meanwhile, great preparations were
made by Loudoun to co-operate with Holburne, and it
was to prevent the enemy from receiving intelligence of
the proposed expedition that the embargo had been laid.
This useless annoyance vexed the colonists. Violations June
of the embargo were frequent, and are complained of by 5.
Loudoun in a letter to Rhode Island. The Assembly 13.
took up the subject, and passed a stringent act, punishing

[1] R. Partridge's letter to R. I. of May 19, 1757, contains a list of Admiral Holburne's fleet.

CHAP. XVII. with imprisonment and forfeiture of the vessel, any who should carry on trade with the French West Indies.

1757. June 13. Augustus Johnston was elected attorney-general in place of Daniel Updike deceased.[1] The population of Prudence Island, an appendage of the town of Portsmouth, had become so large, that in consequence of the inconvenience of attending the militia trainings in that town, a separate military company for the island was organized by the Assembly. Many slaves had been carried to sea on privateers and merchant vessels, without consent of their owners. To prevent this, a fine of five hundred pounds was imposed upon any captain who should thus abduct a slave, and a right of action against the captain or owners of the vessel to recover double damages, was allowed. Liberty to search any vessel suspected of concealing slaves was granted by the act. The war vessel built for the colony was ordered to be rigged as a brigantine.

The controversy between Samuel Ward and Stephen Hopkins, had now progressed beyond the limits of political difference, and become a bitter personal contest, in which the interference of the legislature was invoked. Gov. Hopkins brought a suit against Ward for slander, laying his damages at twenty thousand pounds. The trial was to come on the next week in Providence, where Hopkins resided. Ward had petitioned the Assembly in May for a change of venue, alleging that the plaintiff's influence in the county of Providence would preclude an impartial trial, and also that his own life had been threatened by the excited partisans of his opponent. Hopkins was served with a copy of the petition, and cited to appear at this session, and was required, meanwhile, to stay proceedings. He evaded the order by withdrawing his suit, and commencing a new one for the same cause. Both

[1] Mr. Updike had served for twenty-four years as Attorney-General of the colony—from 1722 to 1732, and from 1743 till his death, May 15, 1757. He was a fine scholar and a distinguished advocate.

parties now appeared before the Assembly, and agreed in writing that the plaintiff would withdraw his action in Providence, provided the defendant would meet him at Rehoboth, on or before the twenty-third instant, there to be arrested, and the action to be tried under the Massachusetts laws; the defendant waiving the plea of want of jurisdiction. This agreement was allowed, and approved by the Assembly.[1] 1757.

June 20. After much delay, the Earl of Loudoun sailed from New York with six thousand troops to join the British fleet at Halifax; but the arrival of the French squadron in the harbor of Louisburg, frustrated the plan. Loudoun returned to New York too late to prevent the effect of his folly; for no sooner had the expedition sailed, than a grand demonstration was planned and executed by the energy of Montcalm. This was an attack on the posts near Lake George. The advance of the French army led Major-Gen. Webb to call on the colonies for their reserve forces, and a pressing letter was sent to Rhode Island for the hundred and fifty men to march at once to the scene of conflict. Fort William Henry was garrisoned by two thousand men under Col. Monroe, when Montcalm commenced the siege with an army of eleven thousand French and Indians.[2] No assistance was sent by Webb, who was at Fort Edward, only fourteen miles distant, with four thousand men. After a gallant but hopeless defence for six days, Monroe surrendered with the honors of war. The alarm occasioned by this disaster, July 30. Aug. 3. 9.

[1] Hopkins commenced his action on June 20, 1757, at the Common Pleas in Worcester, Mass. The writ was served at Rehoboth in August, and a bond for £5,000, the amount of damages laid in the writ, was taken of Ward. The case was tried in September, and verdict given for the defendant. Hopkins appealed to the Superior Court, to meet at Worcester the same month. The case was continued, and meanwhile submitted to a reference, and at the end of two years, in September, 1759, was finally withdrawn, Hopkins paying the costs of suit, taxed at £22 13*s.* 9*d.*, for which sum execution was issued September 13, 1760. A report of this case is given in the Monthly Law Reporter for October, 1859, vol. 22, pp. 327–39.

[2] Capt. Christie's letter of August 5, 1757.

CHAP. XVII. 1757. was intense throughout the colonies. Before the result was known in Rhode Island, the Assembly had been convened in consequence of advices from the seat of war. One-sixth part of the entire militia of the colony were ordered to be drafted for the service, and to rendezvous at Providence and Kingstown within one week, thence to proceed on horseback to Albany. They were to form one regiment, for which officers were appointed.[1] The treasurer was authorized to make a loan for this object, and the governor and council were empowered to raise yet more troops in case they should be called for by Major-Gen. Webb, during the recess of the Assembly. But Montcalm, instead of following up his success as was expected, withdrew with his army into Canada. The colonial forces were placed on the winter establishment. The larger number were dismissed, and a corps of rangers was
Sept. organized for winter service. The quota assigned to
7. Rhode Island, by order of the Earl of Loudoun, was
19. ninety men. The Assembly voted to retain seventy men in the service, and to send transports to Albany to bring back the remainder of the soldiers. Flags of truce were equipped to convey away the French prisoners, and the masters of such vessels were required to give bonds to the amount of a thousand pounds sterling, not to take any merchandise under cover of their flags. A tax of a hundred and fifty thousand pounds, old tenor, was assessed, one-fifth of which was appointed to Newport.

Oct. 9. Lord Loudoun was incensed that the Assembly had voted to retain but seventy rangers instead of ninety, as he had demanded, and wrote a sharp letter on the subject, wherein he forgot his own proposition, and states the required quota to be one hundred men. The letter, although unjust in its charges, and insulting in its tone, had the desired effect upon the Assembly, who, at their next ses-
26. sion, voted thirty additional men for the ranger's corps,

[1] These were, John Andrews, Colonel; Joseph Wanton, jr., Lieut.-Col.; Henry Babcock, 2d Lieut.-Col., and Stephen Potter, Major.

CHAP. XVII. 1757.

and also resolved to re-enlist two hundred and fifty of the returning troops, to be billeted on the colony ready for any emergency. The regiment so expeditiously raised in August, had proceeded some distance into Connecticut when it was recalled, and provision for the payment of the men was now made. A tax of four thousand pounds in "lawful money" bills, emitted early in the previous year, was assessed in order to call in those bills. An idea of the value of the old tenor bills may be formed from a scale adopted at this session in the payment for provisions furnished to the troops. Pork was valued at six shillings and sixpence a pound, dried beef and cheese at six shillings, and hams at eight shillings. A memorial was presented from merchants in Providence, setting forth that a large number of private men-of-war were owned in the colony, and that there were no adequate means of condemning prizes, no judge of Vice-Admiralty residing in the colony, but only a deputy, whose acts were controlled by his superior who lived elsewhere, and praying, as a remedy for the inconveniences and expenses thereby resulting, that application be made to the colony's agent in England, for some suitable person to be appointed Judge of the Court of Vice-Admiralty, within and for this colony. The governor was requested to prepare the letter, and to recommend Col. John Andrews for the place,[1] and also to inform the Earl of Loudoun of the action of the Assembly in regard to the quota of rangers, and the additional two hundred and fifty men retained in the service.

Oct. 29. Nov. 20.

The letter of Gov. Greene to Lord Loudoun, changed the tone of the Earl's communications. In his reply he compliments the colony more highly for its public spirit, than he had before abused it for the partial neglect of his commands, and promises to represent its zeal and loyalty

[1] John Andrews, Esq., received the appointment of Judge of the Admiralty Court of the colony of Rhode Island, by order of the Admiralty Commissioners, May 12, 1758.

CHAP. XVII. 1757. in the highest terms to the King. He retained but ninety Rhode Island troops, who were quartered at Saratoga, and sent the remainder home.

The ill-success of the war up to this time, exasperated the English people, and compelled a change in the ministry. Pitt, who early in the year had lost his place in the cabinet, was recalled and given a higher position as Secretary of State, where, under the nominal leadership of Newcastle, he soon became the virtual premier, and assumed the whole conduct of the war. More vigorous
Dec. 30. measures were now taken against the French. A circular was sent to all the colonies, calling on them to raise twenty thousand men, who should be equipped by the home government, and promising assistance from Parliament towards their payment. The Earl of Loudoun was superseded by Major-Gen. Abercrombie in the chief command.

1758. Feb. 7. Another annual council of war was called by Lord Loudoun to meet at Hartford. The Assembly appointed the governor, with Col. John Andrews, and Samuel Ward
14. to attend it, and added to the instructions of the previous year the request that the Rhode Island levies might be under the command of their own officers, subject only to the general-in-chief. The value of the Spanish milled dollar was fixed at six shillings, lawful money,—the rate at which the latter description of bills were issued, and which was the standard value in other New England colonies. The New England currency of six shillings to a dollar, that has ever since prevailed, may be dated from this period. The daily royal allowance for the support of recruits was fourpence sterling, an insufficient amount. To oblige the inhabitants to entertain recruits, the Assembly added a weekly stipend of three pounds four shillings, old tenor, to be paid from the treasury, and empowered the civil officers to billet the troops upon innkeepers and others at their discretion.

20. The results of the council at Hartford were of no im-

portance, for Loudoun's recall was already on its way, and the conduct of the war had passed into more vigorous hands at home. The severe illness of Gov. Greene, which had prevented his attendance upon the Assembly, terminated in death. Only eighteen years had passed since a governor had died in office, and he was now the eighth who had thus fallen at his post since the settlement of the colony. His career had been long and active, embracing some of the most stormy periods in Rhode Island annals.[1] He left a son named for him, who, twenty years later, was to occupy his father's place, and like him to transmit an honored name to a numerous posterity. The Assembly re-elected Gov. Hopkins to fill the vacancy, who continued for four years successively to be chosen by the people. The most energetic measures were taken to prosecute the war. It was resolved to raise a regiment of one thousand men, and officers were appointed for it, no officer to receive his commission until he had enlisted a certain number of men.[2] The treasurer was directed to hire specie, or lawful money bills, at six per cent. interest, and to give bonds for the same, payable at the close of the next year in silver, or in old tenor bills at the rate of

CHAP. XVII. 1758. Feb. 22.

March 14.

[1] He was for two years deputy governor—in 1741-2, and for eleven years governor of the colony—in 1743, '44, '46, '48 to '55, and 1757.

[2] The officers already in the service were retained. The new ones appointed for the ten companies were as follows: Godfrey Malbone, Colonel; Henry Babcock, Lieut.-Col.; Daniel Wall, Major. Col. Malbone declined, and at the May session Lieut.-Col. Babcock was made Colonel; John Potter, jr., Lieut.-Col.; Joseph Coggeshall, commissary; John Bass, chaplain and surgeon's mate. The new company officers chosen at this (March) session were: Captains—Ebenezer Jenckes of the 5th; James Tew, jr., of the 6th; Samuel Rose of the 7th; Nathaniel Peck of the 8th; who had been lieutenants in the former campaign. 1st Lieutenants—Benjamin Eddy of the 5th; Valentine Morse, 6th; William Tripp, 7th; Joshua Allen, 8th; Edward Smith, 9th. 2d Lieutenants—Moses Palmer of the 1st; Thomas Park, 2d; Philip Baker, 3d; Samuel Stoneman, 4th; George Shearman, 5th; Abner West, 6th; Oliver Reynolds, 7th. Ensigns—Eseck Carr, 1st; Mitchel Case, 2d; Nathaniel Bowdish, 3d; Tamberlin Campbell, 4th; Richard Smith, jr., 5th; Thomas Tew, 6th; Caleb Tripp, 7th; Thomas Rose, 8th; Thomas Aylesworth, 9th. Lieut. Giles Russel was made adjutant.

CHAP. XVII. five pounds ten shillings to a dollar. If unable to negotiate a sufficient loan within twenty-five days, a new issue
1758. of lawful bills to the amount of four thousand pounds was
March to be made, redeemable within two years by taxation;
but at the next session the sum was increased to ten
thousand pounds, bearing five per cent. interest, and the
time of payment extended to five years. Ten thousand
pounds were appropriated to the work on Fort George,
15. and the garrison was increased. Orders were sent from
Gen. Abercrombie requiring an embargo to be laid on all
the colonial ports, which was forthwith done by vote of
the Assembly. The legislature of Connecticut proposed
April a convention to be held at Hartford to arrange the quotas
19. of men and supplies to be furnished by each colony, according to the plan of Pitt, but no action appears to have
May 3. been taken on the subject. The Assembly repealed the
act of the past year forbidding trade with the Spanish settlement at Hispaniola, as no such restriction existed in the
other colonies. A protest against this repeal was entered
by nine members on the ground that Monte Christo, the
port in question, was an inconsiderable place, while the
French Fort Dolphin, very near it, would conduct the ac-
8. tual traffic. As soon as the fleet had sailed, Abercrombie
wrote to remove the embargo at the end of two weeks,
15. and a few days later he ordered the Rhode Island regiment
to be sent forward to Albany. The plan of the campaign
was similar to that which, under General Shirley, had
proved abortive. To reconquer Cape Breton, to drive
the French from Lake George and Fort Du Quesne, with
an invasion of Canada as the ultimate blow, was the design of the ministry. The first measure was successful.
A fleet of thirty-seven ships of war, under Admiral Bos-
cawen, with an army of ten thousand men under Gen.
Amherst, with whom Wolfe acted as brigadier, and Montgomery and Barre, names destined to win imperishable
lustre in this war, were subalterns, laid siege to Louisburg.
June 8. Three thousand men and eleven ships of war defended the

place, but the works were out of repair, the ships were cut off in detail, and after a gallant defence of seven weeks, Louisburg surrendered. With it Cape Breton, Prince Edward, and other dependencies, passed forever from the power of France, and the Gulf of St. Lawrence became henceforth a British possession. CHAP. XVII. 1758. July 27.

The expenses of the war bore heavily on the people. Nearly two thousand British troops were quartered at Providence in March and April, before the expedition under Amherst had sailed, while the cost of sustaining the native regiment, raised for the land service, was enormous. To meet the war loans and to redeem the colonial paper, the Assembly assessed a tax of six thousand pounds in lawful money bills, thus calling in the issue of two years before, and laid a further tax of one hundred and ten thousand pounds, old tenor.[1] Newport had long been a thriving commercial town, but until now had no permanent newspaper published within it. The Newport Mercury was established at this time, and the first number was issued on the day the Assembly commenced its session. It has continued to the present time without interruption, except during the British occupation of the island,[2] and is now one of the oldest, if not the oldest existing newspaper in the country. The second object of the ministry, undertaken simultaneously with the siege of Louisburg, resulted in disaster. Abercrombie, with an army of fifteen thousand men, embarked at Fort William Henry in flatboats, to attack Ticonderoga, June 12. July 5.

[1] The tax bill of this session arranges the towns by their respective counties. The town of Newport paid one-fifth of the entire tax. Newport county paid £42,350; Providence county, £26,400; Kings (now Washington), £24,100; Kent, £11,550, and Bristol, £5,600. The lesser tax of £6,000 was apportioned in the same ratio.

[2] This interruption lasted about three years, from Dec. 2, 1776, to Jan. 5, 1780, during which time the Mercury was printed in Rehoboth, where it continued to divide with the Providence Gazette the patronage of the public printing from the Rhode Island General Assembly. Providence Gazette, March 6, 1779.

CHAP. XVII. at the outlet of Lake George. The next morning the French outposts were driven in, and in the afternoon an
1758. engagement ensued, in which the French were defeated,
July 6. but the young Lord Howe, the idol of the army, was slain.
8. On the eighth, Abercrombie, without waiting for his artillery, ordered the assault. Ticonderoga was garrisoned by only thirty-six hundred men, but the defences were strong and the brave Montcalm was the commander. The regulars led the attack, followed by the New York provincials. The Connecticut, New Jersey, and Rhode Island regiments were drawn up three hundred yards in the rear, prepared to support the assailants. The storming party were repulsed, and column after column advancing to their support, were mowed down by the terrific fire of the French. The carnage was immense. At the end of the first hour the reserve was ordered up. Col. Babcock, receiving a wound in his knee while posting his regiment within forty yards of the breastwork, was borne from the field. Three of his officers[1] were also wounded. The battle lasted four hours, when Abercrombie, having lost two thousand men in killed and wounded, ordered a retreat, and the next day, to the surprise and
9. mortification of his officers, fell back upon Fort William Henry.[2] This defeat cost him his command. He was soon afterward superseded by Gen. Amherst.[3]

Aug. 21. Desertions from the army were frequent. The Assembly requested the governor to issue a proclamation upon the subject. Deserters were required to report themselves to the war committee within ten days, to be sent back to the army, in which case they should be recommended to mercy. Rewards were offered for their detection, and

[1] Capt. John Whiting and Lieuts. Russell and Smith.

[2] A graphic account of this battle is given by Col. Babcock in his despatch to Gov. Hopkins, July 10, 1758. Unfortunately the list of killed and wounded in his regiment, accompanying the letter, is lost.

[3] Orders to this effect were issued from Whitehall September 18.—Pitt's Circular to the Colonies.

penalties imposed upon any who might conceal them. A singular clause in the act illustrates a custom of the times. The expenses of arresting a deserter were to be deducted from his wages, and in case "there is not enough due to a deserter to pay such premium, he shall be sold by one of the committee of war for payment thereof, and stand committed to gaol until he is sold." A new war loan was required, and the treasurer was authorized to hire as many of the lawful money bills of credit as possible, not exceeding in value one hundred and fifty thousand pounds, old tenor, for one year at six per cent. It was found that the light-house duty on shipping was insufficient. It was therefore increased to fifteenpence sterling on coasting vessels, and to twopence sterling per ton on all other vessels.

CHAP. XVII. 1758. Aug.

The expedition against Fort Frontenac, now Kingston, designed by Col. Bradstreet, was carried out with great success, and did much to retrieve the disaster at Ticonderoga. About three thousand provincials, with four brass twelve-pounders and two howitzers, marched for 14.
Oswego. In this army were some companies, three hundred and twelve men, of the Rhode Island regiment, under Major Wall. Embarking in open boats on Lake Ontario, Bradstreet landed on an island in sight of Fort 25.
Frontenac, and proceeded to reconnoitre. At seven o'clock in the evening, the whole force landed, unopposed, within a mile of the fort. At ten the next morning the cannonade commenced, at seven hundred yards' distance, 26.
and continued till night, when the Americans secured a breastwork nearer the fort, from which, at daybreak, they threw shells, and soon obliged the garrison to surrender. Nine armed vessels and a great quantity of military stores, 27.
valued at forty thousand pounds sterling, destined for Fort Du Quesne, were taken. The fort was destroyed, and the victors returned to Oswego the next day.[1] The 28.

[1] Letter of Major Daniel Wall to Gov. Hopkins, dated Oneida Station, 17th September, 1758.

CHAP. XVII. 1758. loss of the Americans in the action was slight, but many suffered from sickness on the homeward march, and while detained at the site of the present village of Rome, in erecting Fort Stanwix. The fall of Fort Frontenac insured the capture of Fort Du Quesne by cutting off the supplies and causing the desertion of the Indian allies. That expedition was under the command of Gen. Forbes, Sept. 12. with seven thousand men. Advanced detachments of his army had repeated conflicts with the enemy with varied Oct. 15. success. The attempt was about to be abandoned for the Nov. 12. season, when the arrest of some prisoners made known the weakness of the garrison. A portion of the army pressed forward, under the lead of Washington, and found the 25. fort deserted and the works destroyed. Hugh Mercer, with two regiments of Virginians, were left to maintain the position. The place was called Fort Pitt in honor of the energetic minister. The populous city of Pittsburg is now the noblest monument to his fame.

Oct. 25. The war loan authorized in August, seems not to have been contracted as yet, for the Assembly now instructed the treasurer to hire, in specie or bills of credit, a sum not to exceed two hundred thousand pounds, old tenor, and if the entire loan was not effected in thirty days, the deficiency was to be met by the issue of lawful money bills, redeemable in five years. The loan and the issue were to be redeemed by a tax on the colony.

The plans of Pitt for the next campaign required the same force, twenty thousand men, to be raised in the colo- Dec. 9. nies, and circulars to that effect were sent from Whitehall. 13. Gen. Amherst recommended that the provincial troops be retained in the service through the winter, to be ready 18. early in the spring. The Assembly accordingly resolved to retain all the effective troops in their pay, discharging only the higher officers, and to enlist new soldiers who were to have the same wages and billeting as the retained troops. The report of a committee upon flags of truce, made at this session, shows that ten had been granted and used within two years, besides some applications for them that were refused by the governor. The law upon this subject[1] was revised, to require that every flag of truce sailing from the colony should carry all the provisions of war then here, if the vessels were capable of doing so, at the rate of a man for every ton of measurement. The destruction of the court-house in Providence by fire, was a serious calamity at this time, involving not only the expense of a new one, but also the loss of the entire collection of what afterwards became the Providence Library Company, whose books were kept in a chamber of the building. A lottery, to raise two thousand dollars, one-half towards rebuilding the court-house, and the other for the library, was granted the next June.[2]

CHAP. XVII. 1758. Dec. 24.

Rhode Island was relied upon, not without reason, to furnish something more than her share of seamen for the royal navy whenever a deficiency in that branch of the service called for recruits. A colony in which nearly one-fifth of the adult male population were at this time engaged on board of private armed ships, while more than one-seventh of the remainder were in the land service of the King, might be expected to furnish fighting men, especially on their favorite element. The commander of the fleet had long been accustomed to maintain a correspondence with this colony. Admiral Durell wrote from Halifax for as many able-bodied seamen as could be furnished, and at a later date expressed his thanks for the force so promptly sent. Gen. Amherst wrote to order the regiment to be at Albany by the tenth of April. The Assembly voted to furnish one thousand men, as last year, in thirteen companies, to be ready to leave by the

1759. Feb. 14. Sept. 3. Feb. 16. 26.

[1] Passed February, 1747.

[2] This act was repealed in February, 1760, and new grants were made of lotteries to raise $1,200 for the library, and $1,000 for the court-house. At the same session a lottery was granted to raise £24,000, old tenor, to erect the market-house in Newport.

CHAP. XVII. 1759. Feb. 26. twenty-fifth of March.[1] Sixteen thousand pounds in lawful money bills were appropriated for this object, and a tax of eleven thousand pounds of the same currency was assessed, payable in October. The outstanding bills, known as the Crown Point money, were called in, and their redemption provided for out of the billeting money, amounting to six hundred pounds sterling, received from Gen. Amherst. Something over a hundred and twenty thousand pounds, in old tenor bills, which had been called in from time to time, were destroyed. The allowance made to innkeepers for billeting regular soldiers, was increased to twenty-five shillings a day, and a fine was imposed upon all who should refuse to entertain such soldiers when properly placed in their charge. The growth of Providence led the Assembly to pass two important acts; the first related to fires, and gave authority to blow up buildings if necessary to stop the progress of the flames, and also to elect, at annual town meetings, three "Presidents of Firewards," whose powers and duties were fully defined in the act. The second divided the town, setting off the western part, and incorporating it as the town of Johnston, so named in honor of the attorney-general of the colony.

[1] Henry Babcock, Col.; Daniel Wall, Lieut.-Col.; John Whiting, Major. Three of the companies were to be led by the field-officers. Most of the former officers remained in the service, and were now promoted, one, and a few of them, two grades. Only the names of the new ones who now appear for the first time in arms are here subjoined:—Captain, Thomas Fry, jr.; 1st Lieutenants, Tibbitts Hopkins, William Sheehan, Jonathan Spear, Thomas Jenckins; 2d Lieutenants, Joseph Stanton, jr., Benjamin Carr, Daniel Byrn, Moses Bowdish, Moses Warren, Solomon Roffey, Samuel Watson, jr., Thomas Collins, Samuel Weatherby, William Pulling; Ensigns, William Bennet, Stukely Stafford, Thomas Swineburne, jr., Arthur Fenner, jr., George Cornel, Recorde Tabor, Nathan Rice, Asa Bowdish, Asa Kimball, John Manchester, John Beverley, Nathan Bliven, Peleg Slocum.

Lieutenant Giles Russel, adjutant; Joseph Hollway, commissary; Thos. Rodman, surgeon; Benjamin Brown and Thomas Monroe, surgeon's mates. Lieutenant-Colonel Wall did not join the regiment, and was cashiered by the Assembly in August.

The last letter that the colony ever received from its CHAP. XVII.
now venerable agent, Richard Partridge, who for thirty-
four years had guarded its interests near the home govern- 1759.
ment, was written, while on his death-bed, to recommend Mar. 1.
his successor, like himself a member of the society of Friends, and whom he had named as one of his executors.

The application of Admiral Durell was acted upon by May 2.
the Assembly, and inducements were offered for seamen to enlist. Those thus entering the naval service were to be accounted part of the one thousand men ordered for the campaign, the regiment not being yet quite full. Ten thousand pounds were appropriated for Fort George, and the treasurer was directed to hire the money at six per
cent. interest. A letter from Joseph Sherwood announced 11.
the death of Partridge, and his own course, as executor, in regard to the colonial business. The accounts of Rhode Island had been sent to Partridge, and presented by Sherwood with a petition for their allowance. Pitt, whose power was supreme, obtained an appropriation of two hundred thousand pounds sterling from Parliament, to be divided among the colonies for their expenses in the last campaign. The stimulus thus given to renewed exertion, was felt in the rapid enlistments that were everywhere
made. The Rhode Island regiment still wanted a hun- June
dred and fifteen men to complete its ranks. The Assem- 11.
bly took vigorous measures to supply the deficiency, and sent forward the men to join the other troops at Albany. The Masonic society in Newport was incorporated at this time with the title of "The Master Wardens, and Society of Free and Accepted Masons." A lottery for raising twenty-four hundred dollars was granted them to erect the Mason's Hall, and the first public celebration of the Order that was ever held in Rhode Island, took place this year, with religious services at Trinity church. The Assembly had heretofore met in the three counties of Providence, Newport, and Kings. An annual adjournment to

CHAP. XVII. Kent, in turn from the other counties, was now established.

1759. June The object of the present campaign, was the conquest of Canada. Its success was complete, although not without severe losses on both sides. Admiral Saunders, with a powerful fleet conveying an army of eight thousand men
26. under Gen. Wolfe, appeared before Quebec. Gen. Amherst, with twelve thousand troops, was to take Ticonderoga and Crown Point, and thence to advance by way of Lake Champlain to co-operate with Wolfe; while a provincial army under Gen. Prideaux was to attack Niagara, and thence to enter Canada by way of Lake Ontario. The latter expedition came first in order of time. Prideaux
July 7. was killed at the opening of the siege, and Sir William Johnson, who was present with a large body of the Six Nations, assumed the command. A strong force of French and Indians, advancing from the west to the relief of
23. Niagara, was routed by Johnson, and the greater part were made prisoners. All hope of aid being thus cut off,
25. the garrison, consisting of six hundred men, surrendered.

Encumbered by his prisoners, and without the necessary transports or supplies, Johnson was unable to carry out the plan of invading Canada. The army under Amherst was composed of about equal numbers of regulars and provincials. The strong positions around Lake George were held by feeble garrisons, the main body of the enemy being drawn off for the defence of Quebec.
26. Ticonderoga was abandoned almost without a blow, and
Aug. 7. Crown Point was likewise deserted. Ample time was thus afforded to Amherst to execute the remainder of the plan, and so to secure the conquest of Canada. Although there were no vessels upon Lake Champlain to convey the army, the march upon Montreal could have been accomplished by land in less time than was wasted in repairing Ticonderoga, and in constructing useless fortifications at Crown Point. Meanwhile, Wolfe was conducting the siege of Quebec under great disadvantages. The watch-

ful eye of Montcalm was ready to detect the slightest CHAP. XVII. error of his enemy, and his fertility of resource was suggesting means of delay that might prolong the siege till 1759. winter should close the river and place the hostile fleet at his disposal. After two months of anxious suspense, daily but vainly hoping to receive aid from the side of New York, and constantly engaged in active operations with the enemy, Wolfe resolved to scale the almost inaccessible heights at a short distance above the city, and there, on the Plains of Abraham, to decide, in a pitched battle, the fortunes of an empire. The landing was effected Sept. 12. under cover of the night. Jutting rocks and tangled thickets aided the men, one by one, in their daring climb up the side of the precipitous cliff. In the morning, to the dismay of Montcalm, the whole British army were there, drawn up in battle array before the city. A brief 13. but bloody conflict ensued. The armies each numbered about five thousand men. Wolfe, wounded at the commencement of the action, and again soon after, still led the last charge of the British right wing against the columns of Montcalm, and was slain. "Now, God be praised, I die happy," were his last words, as, when borne to the rear, he was told that the French were in full retreat. Their gallant leader shared the same fate. Twice mortally wounded, he fell while rallying his beaten troops at the gate of the city, and died commending to De Ramsay, the chief of the garrison, "the honor of France." Thus fell two of the most gifted and accomplished soldiers who ever lived. Brave, generous, and loyal, history records no nobler names than those of Wolfe and Montcalm. The loss of the French was five hundred killed and one thousand taken prisoners, that of the English, six hundred in killed and wounded. Five days after the battle, Quebec 18. capitulated. A garrison of five thousand men under Gen. Murray was left to hold the place, and the fleet withdrew to winter at Halifax.

While these stirring events were in progress abroad,

CHAP. XVII. nothing of interest occurred within the colony. The old law forbidding the purchase of Indian lands, intended to 1759. protect the aboriginal proprietors in their rights, was re- Aug. 20. pealed upon petition of Thomas Ninegret, and permission was given to him and all other Indians to dispose of their real estate on equal terms with other subjects of the King.[1] A large amount of old tenor bills were burnt. Joseph Sherwood was commissioned as agent of the colony in England. William Mumford was chosen captain, and John Beard lieutenant of Fort George.

Great was the joy in America at the capture of Que- Oct. 31. bec. The Assembly appointed a day of public thanksgiving to be held the next month. This was their only act of general interest except to forbid the importation of raw hides from North Carolina, on account of a murrain among the cattle in that province.

Nov. 13. When the news reached England, a royal proclamation was issued, appointing a day of public thanksgiving throughout Great Britain, and ordering the colonies to do 22. the same. This had already been done in Rhode Island. Everywhere bonfires, illuminations, orations, and the voices of prayer and praise, had attested the general joy at this brilliant close of a great campaign. The royal approbation at the conduct of the colonies was expressed Dec. 13. through Gen. Amherst, who, in his letter to Rhode Island, complimented Col. Babcock in the warmest terms, and requested that the government would again retain the whole regiment in pay during the winter, and would also continue the pay of the officers, but the troops had already been disbanded.

To complete the reduction of Canada, and if possible

[1] This act was repealed upon petition of the tribe, August, 1763, and a committee was appointed to set off and bound the various tracts of land heretofore appropriated to the Narraganset Sachems, for the sole use of the tribe, Ninegret agreeing to execute proper deeds of the same to the tribe; but the tribe could not agree among themselves what lands should be set off, so that the committee could do nothing, and reported accordingly in June, 1764.

to drive the French from every part of the continent, was reserved for a new campaign. The usual circular to the colonies stimulated their zeal with the promise of Parliamentary bounty. The appropriation made for them in the previous year, of which the part assigned to Rhode Island was about eighty-eight hundred pounds sterling, could not be paid immediately. It was proposed to fund the whole amount in a government stock, bearing four per cent. interest, to which the provincial agents were invited to subscribe the amounts due to their respective colonies. Sherwood notified Rhode Island that he had entered her name on the subscription, as this seemed the best course, and that the stock would be paid off in a few months. Again the Assembly voted to raise a regiment of one thousand men for the next campaign.[1] To supply money to carry this act into effect, an issue of lawful money bills to the amount of sixteen thousand pounds, payable in five years, and bearing five per cent. interest, was made, to be redeemed at maturity by taxation; and to meet the payments that would be due to the soldiers at the close of the campaign, an immediate tax of fifteen thousand five hundred and forty-seven pounds, lawful money, to be collected in October, was assessed. No allowance for the war expenses of 1756 had ever been made to Rhode Island by the home government, although some of the other colonies, more fortunate in this respect, had received their indemnity. The accounts had not been forwarded to England in season, but were afterward sent out. The amount, for which Sherwood now petitioned, was forty-two hundred and twelve pounds sterling, but it was never allowed. Parliament appropriated the same amount as

CHAP. XVII. 1760. Jan. 7. 31. Feb. 25. Mar. 17. 31.

[1] The field-officers appointed were Christopher Harris, colonel; John Whiting, lieutenant-colonel; Thomas Burket, major. The company officers differed but little from those of last year. The new ones were, of the 1st Lieutenants—Jeremiah Shaw, jr.; 2d Lieutenants—William Eldred; Ensigns—James Pearse, Edward Cross, Othniel Tripp, Thomas Mitchell.

Lieutenant Stoneman was chosen adjutant, Thomas Rodman, surgeon.

CHAP. XVII. last year to the colonies for "expenses incurred by them in levying, clothing, and pay of the troops raised by 1760. April 12. them," and Sherwood advised this colony that in making up their account, care should be taken to distinguish the charges so specified in the vote. The supplies voted in March for the treasury were found to be insufficient for the despatch of the regiment. A further issue of ten thou-
May 7. sand pounds, lawful money bills, was ordered to be made on similar terms for this object, and also one thousand pounds toward the court-house in Providence.

Thus far this "lawful money" had been but sparingly issued, and provision for its redemption by taxation was always made with each new issue. The receipt of specie from England at various times, had also tended to preserve this latest style of bills of credit from the depreciation that had affected the old bank bills, now called the old tenor, and also the new tenor, and Crown Point paper. Within the past year the issues of lawful money bills had largely increased, the time for its redemption had been lengthened, and thus the colony were accumulating a debt which the stormy period soon to commence would prevent their extinguishing. Depreciation in values, and a commercial revulsion, were inevitable in the not distant future. An attempt had been made in October, to settle up the Paper Money Office, created at the time of the early bank issues, and a large amount of the uncollected bonds given for those loans were put in suit; while a yet larger amount, which already had been sued, were reported as worthless. The "bank system" had utterly failed, and given place to the later method of paper issues. We have seen how this later paper had depreciated, until the greater caution adopted with the lawful money bills arrested the fall, and had thus far preserved this newest form of paper money at its par value; but any relaxation of caution was liable to produce renewed
6. disaster. The British government stock was very soon redeemed, and the portion due to Rhode Island, which,

after deducting many charges and expenses, amounted to CHAP. XVII.
eight thousand pounds sterling, was shipped in Spanish
dollars and Portuguese gold. The value of old tenor 1760.
bills at this time, was fixed by the Assembly at six June 9.
pounds for one dollar.

A court of commissioners was holden at Newport, for July 23.
the trial of two men, who were convicted of piracy and
robbery on the high seas, and were soon afterwards exe- Aug. 21.
cuted on Easton's Beach.

Heretofore the freemen from all parts of the colony had been accustomed to deposit their votes in person at Newport on the day of election for general officers in May. The old law permitted proxy voting, but the custom had fallen into disuse. The Assembly now enacted 18.
that the freemen should deposit their proxy votes for general officers at the regular town meetings on the third Wednesday in April, and that none but members of the Assembly should be permitted to vote at the election in Newport on the first Wednesday of May. The qualification for a freeman was also prescribed. He was to own real estate to the value of forty pounds, lawful money, equal to a hundred and thirty-three and one-third dollars, or that would bring an annual rent of two pounds. The eldest son of such freeman might also vote in right of his father's freehold.

The events of the war are soon told. In April, De April.
Levi, the successor of Montcalm, with ten thousand men,
marched from Montreal to recover Quebec. Murray
rashly gave him battle at Sillery, and was defeated. De 28.
Levi then laid siege to the city, but the timely arrival of
a portion of the British fleet compelled him to abandon May 17.
the attempt. The capture of Montreal was all that remained to complete the conquest of Canada. Three British armies concentrated upon the town for this purpose. The main army under Gen. Amherst, ten thousand strong, rendezvoused at Oswego, and thence descended the Lake
Ontario and river St. Lawrence to Montreal, where Sept. 7.

CHAP. XVII. 1760. Murray, with four thousand men, ascending the river from Quebec, had already arrived. The next day Col. Haviland, with thirty-five hundred men, advancing from Crown Point by way of Lake Champlain, also appeared. An open town, in a country that for four years had been on the verge of famine could make no stand against this overwhelming force. Montreal was surrendered without a struggle, and with it all western Canada, including Michigan. There remained to France upon the western continent only a feeble colony at the mouth of the Mississippi. But there were many who foresaw in the annexation of Canada the independence of America.

Oct. 25. The sudden death of George II. was followed the next
26. day by the proclamation of his grandson as George III. A new reign had commenced, the longest and the most eventful in English annals. A new policy was shortly to be inaugurated, the most fatal to the cause of British supremacy; but for a time there was little change in the ministry, and none in colonial policy. Pitt retained his place, and Britain augmented her power.

The conquest of Canada being completed, the Assem-
29. bly voted to disband the regiment in fifteen days after it should be discharged by the commander-in-chief, and also requested the governor to proclaim a day of general
Nov. 20. thanksgiving for the result of the campaign. This was done, and the occasion was celebrated with the usual rejoicings.

Dec. The death of Thomas Ward, who for fourteen years had been secretary of the colony, occasioned a special session of the Assembly to choose a successor. His brother,
31. Henry Ward, was elected secretary, and retained the office for thirty-eight years, until his death.

1761. At this session, Gov. Hopkins offered to the members,
Jan. 1. in their private capacity, to withdraw his name from the political canvass, "for the peace of the colony," provided Mr. Ward would do the same. To this proposal Ward
2. replied the next day, stating his reasons for opposing

Hopkins, and leaving the subject in the hands of the free- CHAP.
men. XVII.

Funeral ceremonies in honor of the late King were 1761.
performed at Newport, at the close of which his Majesty Jan. 19.
George III. was proclaimed by the sheriff from the court-house.

The next day a sermon on the death of George II. was 20.
preached by the Rev. Ezra Styles, in presence of the civil
and military officers of the colony. Parliament made 31
another grant to the colonies for the past year, of the same amount as for the three previous campaigns. The
appointment of John Temple to be Surveyor-General for Feb. 12.
the northern colonies, to execute the acts of trade and navigation, was a prelude to serious disturbances. The enforcement of these acts had always been resisted in America, and was especially odious in Rhode Island. The London custom-house followed up this measure by
appointing Nicholas Lechmere to be Searcher and Land 25.
Waiter at Newport. At the same time the Board of Trade sent over their usual series of twenty questions respecting the condition of the colony. The illegal traffic carried on from the northern colonies with the French West Indies, under cover of flags of truce, gave offence to the British merchants; but it was too lucrative to be easily stopped. In vain did the crown officers, aided by some of the governors, apply to the courts for writs of assistance; warrants to search for smuggled goods and to demand aid in the work from all persons. The granting these writs was resisted by the merchants of Boston, who retained council to oppose them. It was on this question that the voice of James Otis was now first heard in defence of "the rights of the colonies." The writs were legal, and as such were granted, but were rarely used on account of the odium attaching to them. This was the first open murmur of discontent between the colonies and the mother country. In the course of the controversy,

CHAP. XVII. new ideas were developed, to which there could be but one logical result—revolution.

1761. New sources of trade were always encouraged in Rhode Island, and patent rights were readily granted to any who would introduce desirable branches of industry. James Lucena, a Portuguese subject, was naturalized by Feb. 23. the Assembly, and an exclusive right for ten years was bestowed upon him to manufacture soap, similar to that made in Castile, of which he knew the process. At the expiration of his patent, he was to reveal the secret to the Assembly. Lotteries were granted for continuing the pavement of streets in Newport, and to commence paving in Providence from Weybosset Bridge, north, south, and west. An amendment to the election law was made, allowing any freeman who should move from one town into another, to vote upon certificate of his being a freeman, provided he owned a sufficient freehold estate in his new place of residence, and also permitting the eldest son of a freeholder to become a freeman without being propounded for three months, as was required in all other cases.

Although the conquest of Canada was completed, it was deemed necessary in order to protect the newly acquired territory, to keep a large force in the field, equal to two-thirds of that heretofore employed. Designs against the French West Indies were also to be carried Mar. 30. out. The Assembly voted to raise six hundred and sixty-six men in seven companies,[1] and directed the treasurer to hire eight thousand pounds, lawful money, for nine months at the rate of seven per cent. interest per annum; failing in which, an issue to that amount in bills of credit, payable in five years and bearing five per cent. interest,

[1] John Whiting, colonel; Samuel Rose, lieutenant-colonel; Christopher Hargil, Major. The company officers whose names appear for the first time in the service, were, of 2d. lieutenants—Andrew Boid, Abraham Hawkins, Hezekiah Saunders; Ensigns—William Prior, Comfort Carpenter, Joseph Brownel, Elias Burdick.

to be redeemed by taxation, was to be made. A tax of CHAP.
sixteen thousand pounds, lawful money, was assessed, to XVII.
be collected in November. The troops were ordered by 1761.
Gen. Amherst to be sent forward to Albany. The Assem- April 26.
bly had always, until this year, met on the day before
the general election to act upon the admission of freemen.
The recent law, requiring the actual election of State
officers to be held at the town meetings, rendered this
course no longer necessary. The legislature therefore met May 6.
on election day, the first Wednesday of May. The proxies
sent from the towns were placed in charge of the clerk of
the House, and the usual business of admitting freemen
of the colony was postponed for one month, when the
minor officers were chosen, and William Read was made
captain, and Caleb Carr lieutenant of Fort George. At June
each change in the command of the fort, a full report was 8.
required of its condition and armament. At this time
there were twenty-six mounted cannon in the battery, besides fourteen cannon for the colony sloop of war, a few
old guns, and a large amount of ammunition and small
arms. An act to ascertain the value of rateable estates, 22.
fixed the tax valuation of several descriptions of property,
in old tenor money. "Servants for life between fourteen
and forty-five years of age" were "valued at five hundred
pounds; horses and mares from two to four years of age,
at forty pounds per head," above that age at eighty
pounds; oxen of four years and upwards at ninety
pounds; other cattle from forty to seventy pounds; goats
at three, sheep at five, and swine at twelve pounds each.

Gen. Amherst, determined to be in season, wrote re- 15.
questing Rhode Island to keep one company of sixty-four
men in pay the next winter.[1] The appropriation made July
by Parliament to the colonies for the year 1759, was not 3.
paid until this time, and then only one-half in cash, and

[1] The colonies rarely sent into the field quite the number of men voted by them. The deficiencies this year were larger than usual, and about in

CHAP. XVII. 1761. the balance in exchequer orders, bearing four per cent. interest. The share of Rhode Island was ninety-three hundred and thirty-eight pounds sterling, of which one-half was placed in the hands of the agent, subject to draft, and the remainder he received in stock, as had been the case with the previous appropriation.

Aug. 15. Negotiations for peace in Europe were broken off by the formation of that singular alliance between the Bourbon sovereigns, known as the "Family Compact," and the simultaneous signing of a special Convention between France and Spain. By the Compact it was agreed that the several branches of the Bourbon family should sustain each other against all foreign powers; questions of peace or war involving any one of them thus becoming the common cause of all. By this arrangement, in which Spain was the loser, the aid of her fleets was at a later period secured to the republican cause in America, when Louis XVI. embraced the popular side. By the Convention, Spain bound herself to declare war with Great Britain, unless peace should be concluded before the first of May, and both these great powers resolved to unite, if possible, all the lesser commercial states in a league against the maritime supremacy of England.[1] This course, of which Pitt was secretly advised, rendered a war with

a like proportion among the several colonies. From General Amherst's return of troops engaged in this campaign, made to the War Office, we find:

	No. Voted.	No. Raised.	Remained in Winter.
New Hampshire,	534	438	51
Massachusetts,	3,220	2,637	591
Rhode Island,	666	395	64
Connecticut,	2,300	2,000	323
New York,	1,787	1,547	173
New Jersey,	600	554	64
Virginia,	1,000	1,000	
North Carolina.	500	225	

The southern troops were mainly employed in active hostilities against the Cherokee Indians.

[1] Lord Mahon's History of England, chap. xxxvii.; Bancroft's U. S., chap. xvii. vol. iv. p. 403–5.

Spain imperative. The majority of the ministry desired peace, and refused to sanction any other policy. Pitt insisted upon war, and thus aided the intrigue that was forming among his colleagues to oust him. CHAP. XVII. 1761.

The coronation of George III. and his young queen took place while these important events were in progress, but produced no change in the temper of the ministry. A few days later Pitt resigned the seals, the ascendency of Lord Bute was complete, and the Earl of Egremont became secretary of the colonies, the place once so ably filled by the fallen premier. A pension of three thousand pounds a year for himself, and a place in the peerage for his wife, with the title of Baroness of Chatham, was the present reward of the man who, within five years, had raised England from a condition of comparative humility to be the greatest power in the world. Sept. 22. Oct. 5.

A meeting at which only private business was transacted, was followed by the regular autumnal session of the Assembly, when the sixty-four men, required for winter service, were retained to garrison Fort Stanwix. An excise upon liquors sold at retail, which had existed for many years, was continued, and the rate fixed at three shillings a gallon, currant wine, a domestic production, only excepted. Bills of exchange on England for the colony's war money were ordered to be sold at five per cent. premium, and the proceeds to be applied in redeeming lawful money bills, six shillings of which, or four and sixpence sterling, were reckoned as one dollar. The law requiring the legislature to sit in the several counties, compelled frequent adjournments. This session was begun in Newport, and adjourned to South Kingstown. The custom was fatiguing and useless. It seems to have arisen from local jealousies. Its effect was to prevent a full attendance of members, and often, from this cause, to create the heart-burnings it was intended to allay. An instance of such a result occurred at this adjournment. Sept. 7. Oct. 12. 28.

Two remarkable natural phenomena marked the year.

CHAP. XVII. The first was in the spring, when two shocks of an earthquake were felt, between two and three o'clock at 1761. night, all over New England. Mar. 12. The other was a terrible north-east storm, which occurred in the recess of the Oct. Assembly. 23–4. The spire of Trinity Church was blown down, and the tide rose to an unparalleled height, sweeping away Weybosset Bridge in Providence. Great damage was done to the shipping and wharves, and large trees were torn up by the violence of the gale. An application was 28. made to the Assembly for aid in rebuilding the bridge, and one thousand pounds were allowed for that object. Eight members of the House protested against the appropriation, on the ground that but thirty-five members were present, fourteen of whom were from Providence county; whence it appears that but thirteen deputies, besides those directly interested, participated in the vote. We have seen that lottery grants for every variety of object had become frequent. One was made at this time for building a church in Johnston, but the most singular purpose for which this ready but doubtful device was solicited, was the making a passage around Pawtucket Falls, "so that fish of almost every kind, who choose fresh water at certain seasons of the year, may pass with ease." It was represented that the country above the falls would derive much advantage by thus facilitating the access of the fish to the upper waters. A lottery to raise fifteen hundred pounds, old tenor, was granted for this purpose.[1]

The first theatrical company that ever performed in America, came to Newport this autumn from Williamsburg, recommended by the governor and council, and many leading planters in Virginia. The manager was David Douglass. Their application for a license was at

[1] Twelve years later, in August, 1773, the Assembly passed "an act making it lawful for any one to break down or blow up the rocks at Pawtucket Falls, to let fish pass up," what was done in that way in 1761 having been found to be of public utility, and "the said river" was "declared a public river."

first refused by the town, but afterward granted, and the performances were well attended. A temporary theatre was built, which was blown down in the great gale, and the comedians narrowly escaped with their lives. During the year there was an extensive emigration from New England to Nova Scotia. About one hundred persons went from the single town of Newport.[1] CHAP. XVII. 1761.

The fleet designed to operate in conjunction with Rodney against the French colonies in the West Indies, sailed from New York with an army of twelve thousand men, (Nov. 15.) partly provincial troops, under Gen. Monckton, who had just been appointed governor of that province. The war was now to be prosecuted with equal vigor at the opposite extreme of North America, and with the same result as in Canada. The circular of the Earl of Egremont required (Dec. 12.) the same number of provincials to be raised for the coming as for the past campaign. The zeal of Rhode Island, ever ready for service on the sea, was further stimulated by the allowance of four hundred pounds sterling as (23.) bounty for the seamen sent to Admiral Durell two years before. The rejected policy of Pitt was triumphantly vindicated by the course of events that soon compelled (1762.) the new ministry to adopt it by declaring war against (Jan. 4.) Spain. A new enemy was now to be engaged, renewed efforts were to be made by the colonies, and Parliament appropriated a hundred and thirty-three thousand pounds (Feb. 6.) sterling towards their war expenses. The triumph of British arms in the West Indies was decisive. Martinique, the richest of the French possessions in that quarter, surrendered, and soon the entire outer group of the Carib- (14.) bean Islands fell before the fleet of Rodney. The seas swarmed with privateers, to the utter destruction of French commerce. But a greater enterprise and a more brilliant victory were to result from the new war. The conquest of Cuba was to humble the pride of Spain, and

[1] Bull's Memoir of Rhode Island.

CHAP. XVII. to become the crowning glory of the war in America. For this object the colonies were required to furnish additional troops. 1762. Feb. 21. The quota assigned to Rhode Island, by order of Gen. Amherst, was a hundred and seventy-eight men. The regular regiment of six hundred and sixty-six 22. men, was voted by the Assembly,[1] and five thousand pounds in lawful money bills, to be redeemed at the end of five years by taxation, were emitted to cover the expenses. The additional quota of a hundred and seventy-eight men, was raised at an adjourned session, and a further issue of two thousand pounds was made on this account. Mar. 23.

A disastrous fire, in the month of February, destroyed all the stores on Long Wharf, in Newport. Some of the sufferers petitioned for and received the grant of a lottery for their benefit. Several such grants were made at the same time; one to raise a thousand dollars for putting a steeple on St. John's Church in Providence, and one for opening the communication with the sea from the great pond on Block Island which had been closed, whereby the cod and bass fishery had been spoiled, and what was once a secure harbor for fishing vessels, could no longer be entered.

Party spirit now rose very high in Rhode Island. The hostility between town and country acquired fresh stimulus from the report of a committee to ascertain the value of ratable estates which was made at the recent session. Twenty deputies recorded their protest against the adoption of the report, because, in their opinion, it laid too large a proportion of taxes upon the country towns. To quiet a strife which had so long and so bitterly distract-

[1] The regimental officers were Samuel Rose, colonel; Christopher Hargil, lieutenant-colonel; Nathaniel Peck, major. The company officers who now appear for the first time in the service were:—1st lieutenants—Samuel Thornton, Thomas Cotterill; 2d lieutenant—William Herenden; ensigns—Daniel Coggeshall, jr., Alexander Brown, Simeon Stevens, Jonathan Miller, Ishmael Wilcox, Beriah Hopkins, John Tefft.

Surgeon, Benjamin Brown; adjutant, Lieutenant Asa Kimbal.

ed the colony, Samuel Ward, following the example of Gov. Hopkins the year before, submitted to the General Assembly a series of proposals in writing, which were, that Gov. Hopkins and himself should each resign their pretensions to the office of governor; that some Newport gentleman should be chosen to that place, and suggesting the name of Gideon Wanton; that the deputy-governor should be selected from Providence, and naming Nicholas Cook or Daniel Jenckes, both of the Hopkins party, as suitable persons; and that the Assistants should be equally chosen from the two parties. This effort at conciliation was not accepted by the other side. Perhaps the fact that the governorship, by this arrangement, would be given to the Ward or opposition party, while the Magistrates were to be equally divided, was thought too great a concession to be made by the dominant interest which for four successive years had held the power.[1] The result was a renewal of the contest more fiercely than ever at the next election, and the complete triumph of the Ward party by the choice of Samuel Ward as governor, and a majority of the council, six of whom were new members, while of the other four two were from Newport, the stronghold of the victorious party.

CHAP. XVII. 1762. Feb. 26.

May 5.

For the great expedition against Cuba, shortly to sail from New York, Gen. Amherst ordered two hundred and seven men from Rhode Island to be sent on immediately, and soon after wrote for the remainder of the regiment to be forwarded to Albany. Trade with the enemy was carried on by the colonies to an extent that roused the indignation of the home government, by whose orders Amherst wrote to the northern colonies, threatening an embargo unless the exportation of provisions should in-

April 2. 11. 15.

[1] These "proposals for peace," and many other valuable papers relating to the Ward and Hopkins controversy, and to other important periods in the history of this State, were deposited a few years since in the office of the secretary by Richard R. Ward, Esq., of New York, a grandson of Gov. Samuel Ward.

CHAP. XVII. 1762. May 7. stantly cease. Soon after this, a seizure of papers belonging to French subjects in New York, disclosed a plan for obtaining supplies so extensive that Amherst at once wrote to Massachusetts, Rhode Island, and Connecticut, to lay an embargo upon all but transport vessels engaged in government employ. In little more than a month, supplies for the British forces having been received from June 13. England, it was removed. The detachment of Rhode Island troops destined for the West Indies was in command of Lieutenant-colonel Hargil. To defray the expenses of their outfit, two thousand pounds, lawful money May 5. bills, were issued by the Assembly. Col. Whiting was authorized to enlist the Rhode Island troops at Fort Stanwix, whose term was about to expire, into the regiments of regulars.

The first instance in the history of the colony, where the sentence of death was passed upon a convicted burglar, occurred at this time. The criminal petitioned for pardon, and received a reprieve of fourteen months, until his case could be presented to the King with a recommendation to mercy.[1] An addition to the fire act required June 14. six fire hooks and ladders to be kept in Newport; that each dwelling-house should be furnished with a leathern bucket, having the owner's name painted upon it, and a ladder to reach to the top of the house, or in lieu thereof, a trap door in the roof; that gunpowder should be stored in the public powder-house, excepting only twenty-five

[1] It is believed that the doctrine that the death penalty is unlawful originated in Rhode Island. It is found in that dangerous paper, submitted to the town of Providence in the winter of 1654–5, which asserts, "that it is blood guiltiness, and against the rule of the gospel, to execute judgment upon transgressors against the private or public weal," and which called forth the masterly letter of Roger Williams defining his idea of liberty of conscience. Had this been the only corollary to be deduced from that perilous document, Williams would hardly have combated it in the manner he did. Ante, chap. viii., vol. i., p. 254. In this case the pardon was refused, and the burglar was hung on Easton's beach, November 16, 1764, the last execution that has taken place in the county of Newport up to this time, except for military offences during the Revolution.

pounds, which any person might keep in a tin canister at his own residence. The mode of landing and shipping powder on board vessels in the harbor, was also regulated. CHAP. XVII. 1762.

The most brilliant achievement of British arms was the capture of Havana. A powerful fleet, under Admiral Pococke, had sailed from England in March, destined for this point. Having joined a part of Rodney's squadron, the armament, consisting of thirty-seven ships of war, a hundred and fifty transports, and an army of ten thousand men, appeared off the Moro. The Spanish garrison numbered forty-six hundred men. The siege was most difficult. Under a burning sun, in a sickly climate, against a resolute foe and an almost impregnable castle, the steadiness, valor, and endurance of the troops were tried to their utmost. Reinforcements of twenty-five hundred negroes from the other islands, at the commencement of the siege, and of colonial troops under Gen. Lyman arriving from New York some weeks later, increased the force to nearly fifteen thousand men. At length, after incredible hardships and a fearful loss of life, a breach was effected, the whole army rushed to the assault, and the strong castle of the Moro was carried by storm. The batteries were turned upon the city of Havana, which two weeks later surrendered, and "the gem of the Antilles" became the prize of British valor. The treasure captured was immense, by some estimated at three millions sterling, but the cost was dear. It is said that when the city capitulated, there were not more than twenty-five hundred men of the besieging army fit for service. Upon the continent the cessation of active operations had so impaired all interest in the war, that desertions were frequent, and recruiting was difficult. Gen. Amherst wrote to request that a company be retained, as last year, for winter service, and took occasion to reprove the colony for raising so few recruits for the regular corps. The Assembly voted to retain one company at Fort Stanwix, and gave orders to allow recruits to be enlisted in accord-

June 6. July 30. Aug. 13. 4. 23.

CHAP. XVII. 1762. ance with that letter. The accounts of the colony were thoroughly examined, and detailed reports were presented by committees appointed to examine the books of the committee of war, the general treasurer, the naval officer, and the paper-money office respectively. From the latter it appears that there were outstanding in bills of credit, of old tenor, over ninety-three thousand pounds, of Crown Point bills twenty-three hundred pounds, and of lawful money, sixty-six thousand pounds.[1] An act to suppress theatrical exhibitions was passed. Douglass had moved his company from Newport, built a theatre, and commenced playing in Providence, where large numbers of people came from Boston to attend the performances. July The citizens, considering the theatre a nuisance, voted in town meeting to petition the Assembly for its suppression, and this act, which remained in force for some years, was accordingly passed.

Sept. 18. The last important event of the war in America, was the re-capture of St. John's, which had been surprised by a French squadron under Admiral De Ternay early in the season. The garrison, numbering seven hundred and seventy men, surrendered to Lord Colville, and thus the great island of Newfoundland, the key to the St. Lawrence, once more fell into the hands of England, and completed the conquest of the French possessions east of the Mississippi.[2]

21. To supply the treasury, and to pay off the troops, whose return was shortly expected, an emission of four thousand pounds in lawful money bills, bearing five per cent. interest, to be redeemed by taxation at the end of

[1] The exact amounts were £93,687 15*s.* 2½*d.* old tenor, £2,321 17*s.* Crown Point, £66,403 4*s.* 6*d.* lawful money. For a concise account of the colonial currency of Rhode Island, the reader is referred to an able pamphlet upon this subject by Hon. Elisha R. Potter, entitled "A brief account of Emissions of Paper Money made by the colony of Rhode Island." Providence, 1837. 48 pp.

[2] General Amherst's letter of 12th October, with a copy of the capitulation of the Count de Haussonville, 18th September, 1762.

five years, was made, and a tax of eight thousand pounds, payable in November, was laid, of which Newport was assessed fifteen hundred and sixty, and Providence five hundred pounds. The apportionment of this tax gave great dissatisfaction. Several deputies entered a protest against it, and some of the towns refused to assess their portion until a new estimate was ordered. Violations of the laws regulating the admission of freemen and manner of voting, led to an amendment of the statute, providing that whoever should give or receive a deed of real estate for election purposes, should be disfranchised; that suspected voters might be challenged at the polls; that the certificates of those voting thereby should bear date within ten days of the time of election; that whoever should vote without due qualification, or should cast more than one vote for any officer, should be fined twenty pounds; and that in the admission of freemen of the colony, and in the conduct of the general elections, the Assembly should join in grand committee and not act in separate Houses. This act was closely connected with the political controversy then raging in the colony. The last clause was enacted in consequence of the conduct of the Upper House at the spring election, upon a question of the admission of freemen. The Assembly being in grand committee, certain proxy votes were thrown out as being cast by unqualified persons, whereupon the governor and assistants withdrew, claimed a negative upon the proceedings of the deputies, and received and counted the rejected votes, which were for Ward. This caused much excitement. It was considered as a high-handed proceeding on the part of the Upper House, and was used in pamphlets and political articles with disastrous effect upon Ward at the ensuing election, as we shall see.

CHAP. XVII. 1762. Sept. 21.

The third newspaper printed in Rhode Island, and the first in Providence, was now commenced by William Goddard. It was called "The Providence Gazette and Country Journal." In its columns Gov. Hopkins publish-

Oct. 20

CHAP. XVII. 1762. ed the first and only chapter of his "Account of Providence," intended to be a history of the State, but which was suspended in consequence of the difficulties that ensued, leading to the Revolution. That the old feeling of Puritan hostility to "the heretic colony," was not yet extinguished, this publication was a means of proving. While this chapter, which occupied several articles, was appearing in the Gazette, Mr. Goddard received several abusive letters from Massachusetts inquiring how much he received for it, and containing many other remarks insulting to the editor, the author, and the colony.[1]

Oct. 27. Advices of the payment of the war appropriation for 1760 having been received from the agent, the treasurer was ordered to draw upon him for the amount, eighty-eight hundred sixty-one pounds, twelve shillings, sterling, and to redeem therewith as many lawful money bills of credit as possible. A small portion of the fund due to each colony was retained by the home government until the returns of Gen. Amherst should inform them of the exact number of troops furnished by each colony. The governor was requested to write to Sir Jeffrey for a copy of his returns to the war office, that those relating to the Rhode Island regiment might be compared with the muster-roll of the colony. The Assembly ordered a public thanksgiving to be held on the eighteenth of November, for the happy result of the war.

Upon news of the capture of Havana reaching Europe, preliminaries of peace, which had been agreed upon by the other belligerents, and only resisted by Spain until
Nov. 3. the result of that siege could be known, were signed at Fontainebleau, and an armistice ensued. The colonial
23. troops returned from the West Indies broken down by disease, and more than decimated by the casualties of war. From a despatch of Gen. Amherst, we learn that

[1] This fact was communicated to the late Judge Eddy by Mr. Goddard himself, and is found under date of August 18th, 1817, the day when the information was obtained, among Judge Eddy's historical MSS.

many of the Rhode Island regiment died upon the homeward passage, and their ranks had become fearfully thinned by the disasters of the campaign. Of the two hundred and seven men under Lieutenant colonel Hargil, but one hundred and twelve survived the siege of Havana. The great war was ended. Although, pending the discussion of the preliminaries, it was expedient, in order to keep up a show of force, to recruit the regular troops in the several colonies, for which purpose Amherst allotted the forty-eighth regiment to be recruited in Rhode Island, yet the result proved this precaution to be unnecessary. The definitive treaty of peace, known from the place of its signature, as the Peace of Paris, was concluded between France and Spain on one hand, and England and Portugal on the other. France lost every foot of ground upon the North American Continent. All east of the Mississippi was ceded to England, and New Orleans, with the whole of Louisiana west of the river, was transferred to Spain as indemnity for the losses she had sustained. The free navigation of the river was guaranteed. Spain ceded Florida to England in exchange for the Havana. The most valuable of the conquered West India Islands were restored to France, with certain rights of fishery in the Gulf of St. Lawrence. In Europe each of the conflicting powers received back its own, but the existence and nationality of Prussia was established by the heroism and statesmanship of the great Frederick. India, next to America, was the theatre of the most important changes effected by the war. The French, everywhere beaten, abandoned the right to fortify their settlements in Bengal, and the foundation of that magnificent Indian empire, whose story reads like the pages of romance, was laid by the prowess of British arms.

CHAP. XVII. 1762. Dec. 8. 1763. Feb. 10.

Such were the chief results of the most wide-spread, costly, and sanguinary strife which the world had ever seen. England had attained the pinnacle of power. The possession of the Ohio valley, for which the war had been

CHAP. XVII. 1763. commenced nine years before, had led to the conquest of a continent in the West, the foundation of an empire in the East, and the undisputed supremacy of the seas over the whole earth. Territorial ambition could grasp no more. It had already seized too much; and before the colossal fabric could become fairly united under one central government, the most momentous political convulsion of modern times was to originate a new order of things, and to wrest forever from the crown of England her brightest jewel. Already had proposals to tax the colonies been made in the British Parliament. Royal governors and superseded commanders-in-chief returning from America, dissatisfied with the people, had urged the ministry to more rigid measures of colonial policy. The acts of Trade and Navigation, always unpopular, had of late become more obnoxious by the renewed vigor with which they were pressed. It was objected to the retaining of Canada in place of the West India Islands, in the treaty of peace, that it would strengthen the American colonies for revolt. Prophesies of future independence, at no remote period, were made by intelligent foreigners, and even hinted at in Parliament during the discussion of the treaty, as well as entertained by thoughtful, far-sighted statesmen at home. The controversy concerning the writs of assistance, had led to the discussion of natural rights, until the idea, if not the language, of liberty had become familiar to the popular mind. These were significant facts in which the ear of historic fancy can almost hear the distant drum-beat of the Revolution.

CHAPTER XVIII.

1763—1768.

FROM THE PEACE OF PARIS, FEBRUARY 10, 1763, TO THE CLOSE OF THE WARD AND HOPKINS CONTROVERSY, APRIL, 1768.

CHAP. XVIII. 1763. Feb. 10.

The Peace of Paris concluded a war in which, for nine years, the colonies had been learning their military strength, becoming enured to the hardships of the camp, and acquiring the customs of martial life. Their internal administrations had proceeded all the while with the same regularity as ever before. Increased taxation and an abundance of military legislation were the only new features in their domestic system. Thus the habit of self-government was daily gathering strength, while the discipline of the camp, so soon to be needed for its preservation, was steadily pursued. Many stern lessons of self-denial, of loss, and of baffled enterprise, had been learned in the course of this war. From the port of Providence alone, forty-nine vessels of all sizes, with cargoes of great value, had been captured by the enemy within the past seven years.[1]

28. The General Assembly granted a lottery to improve Church's Harbor, in Little Compton, by erecting a wharf or breakwater as a shelter for fishermen, and another to construct a draw in Weybosset bridge, for the convenience of trade and ship-building, which were carried on exten-

[1] Providence Gazette, January 21, 1765, where a list of 65 vessels, from ships to sloops, lost since the declaration of war in 1756, is given, 16 of which had been wrecked, and the remainder captured.

CHAP. XVIII. sively in what is now the cove. A large amount of soldiers' clothing belonging to the colony, in the hands of
1763. Volikert Douw, who during the whole war had been the
agent for Rhode Island at Albany, was ordered home.
Mar. 26. Although the war in Europe was ended, the colony was
advised that the House of Commons had again made an
appropriation of a hundred and thirty-three thousand
pounds for the American provinces. Along the whole
frontier the Indians were in arms under the lead of Pon-
tiac, "the king and lord of all the northwest." It was
proposed to maintain a standing army of ten thousand
men in America, for which, at present, and until the Indians could be quelled, there was need. Orders were sent
April 29. from Whitehall for all the colonies to appoint a day of
thanksgiving.

The conduct of the Ward party at the last election, art-
fully represented by their opponents, in political pamphlets, some of which are still in existence, lost them the
May 4. power. For two successive years Hopkins was re-elected,
with a majority of the assistants on his side, and so violent
was the feeling between the factions, that committees
were appointed at this session to count again the proxy
votes cast the preceding year for deputy-governor and
assistants, where there had been an opposition. To remedy
June 13. the confusion arising from so many varieties of paper
currency, the Assembly decreed that silver and gold only
should be legal tender in the discharge of contracts, unless by special agreement. The value of many English
and foreign coins in lawful money bills was established.
Debts contracted in old tenor bills were to be discharged
by paying so much of the bills as was equal in actual
value to the nominal debt, or so much of silver or gold
as the bills were worth. A scale of depreciation of old
tenor bills, adopted in this act for the guidance of the
courts, embracing a period of thirteen years, shows the
value of a Spanish dollar to have been five pounds fifteen
shillings in 1751, and to be seven pounds at the present

time. Several deputies entered their protest against various clauses of this statute. CHAP. XVIII.

Indian hostilities required that Gen. Amherst should send the regulars against them, and retain in service a portion of provincial troops to garrison the frontiers. He therefore notified the governor of Rhode Island, that the soldiers of this colony must be kept at Fort Stanwix. Captain Cornell accordingly advanced additional bounty to the men, whose terms of enlistment expired on the first of July, and wrote for orders from the government. 1763. June 17. 24.

In the distribution of the Parliamentary appropriation for 1760, Pennsylvania and Connecticut received more than their share, and thus became debtors to the other colonies. The matter was arranged between the several agents in England, that the debt should be paid in this country upon application made by the creditor colonies. Pennsylvania owed Rhode Island nineteen hundred and ten pounds sterling, and Connecticut owed six hundred and thirty-one pounds.[1] The governor was requested to send them copies of the agreement made by the agents, and to ask payment of the above amounts. A tax of twelve thousand pounds, lawful money, was assessed, three-quarters of it to redeem paper bills, and the remainder for the expenses of the government. By order of the Assembly, peace was generally proclaimed throughout the colony, and a public thanksgiving was held. Ex-Governor Richard Ward died at this time, aged seventy-four years.[2] Aug. 1. 15. 25. 21.

The vigor with which the home government pressed the Acts of Trade and Navigation is seen in the increased

[1] Pennsylvania paid her debt to Rhode Island the next year; that of Connecticut was settled between the agents of the two colonies in England.

[2] He was secretary of the colony for nineteen years, from 1714 to 1733; was elected deputy governor in 1740, and on the death of Governor Cranston in July of that year, was chosen by the Assembly to succeed him, and by the people for the two following years. He was the father of Governor Samuel, and of the late and present secretaries of the colony, Thomas and Henry Ward.

CHAP. XVIII. activity everywhere manifested in the revenue service.
A large number of new officers were appointed, and more
1763. rigid rules in the discharge of their duties were adopted.
Sept. 1. Temple, the new Surveyor-General, residing at Boston,
appointed Abraham Frances to be Searcher and Preven-
14. tive at Providence. The London custom-house sent a
commission to John Robinson at Newport to be Collector
and Surveyor for Rhode Island, in place of Thomas Clift,
removed because he was not a resident of the colony, and
Oct. 3. Temple appointed William Taylor as Comptroller of Cus-
11. toms for the port of Newport. The Board of Trade issued
a circular to the colonies, representing that the revenue
had not kept pace with their developing commerce, and
did not yield one-quarter part of the cost of its collection,
and requiring the suppression of illicit traffic with foreign
nations, and that proper protection should be given to
22. the custom-house officials. The Earl of Colville stationed
H. B. M. ship Squirrel, Captain Richard Smith, at Newport for the winter, "for the encouragement of fair trade by the prevention of smuggling."[1] That violations of the revenue laws were of constant occurrence, the legislative records prove. Memorials from the Vice-Admiralty officers, and proceedings of the colonial courts, and of the Assembly upon the same, indicate the necessity there was for greater vigilance, if even the semblance of authority was to be maintained by the home government. Had the enforcement of the Acts of Trade been the only grievance of which the colonies had to complain, the Revolution might never have occurred. When we consider that in commercial communities like this, these Acts were among the earliest causes of complaint, and that their enforcement was but the execution of laws which, although opposed, were never questioned as to their abstract right or justice, but only as to their application to

[1] Admiral Colville's letter to Governor Hopkins, Halifax Harbor, October 22, 1763.

CHAP. XVIII.

the colonies, and that the new principles introduced by the revolution still recognize those upon which these Acts were based, we can better understand why so many provincial families, connected with this branch of the home government, remained loyalists when the great struggle for independence ensued. 1763. Oct.

Of the appropriation for 1761, Rhode Island now received as her share, six thousand and eighty-two pounds, 26.
a part of which the Assembly applied to the redemption of bills of credit. The town councils were authorized to regulate monthly the assize of baker's bread in their respective towns. Upon the recall of Sir Jeffrey Amherst to England, Major-Gen. Thomas Gage, a name afterwards to become odious in America, was appointed to the Nov. 17.
chief command. Gen. Gage wrote to all the New England governments for their co-operation in the war against the Indians, and required of Rhode Island a battalion of two hundred men in four companies to be sent to Albany early in the spring. Dec. 6.

The Jews had become an important element in the population of Newport. There were now more than sixty families of the Hebrew faith in that town, many of whom were distinguished for their wealth and commercial enterprise. They had commenced, the previous year, to erect a Synagogue, which was now dedicated with great pomp 2.
and ceremony to the worship of the God of Abraham.

The famous Sugar act, or Molasses act, as it was called, passed thirty years before, and which had then given occasion to Partridge, the Rhode Island agent, to sound the key-note of revolution,[1] had just expired by limitation. Notice that, with some alterations, it would be revived 1764.
and made perpetual, having been received, an earnest remonstrance against it was made by the Rhode Island Jan. 24.
merchants to the General Assembly, and a special session was held to consider the subject. The governor was re-

[1] Ante, chap. xvi., p. 124.

CHAP. XVIII. 1764. quested to send certified copies of this paper to Sherwood, the agent, to be presented to the Board of Trade, and to direct him, in connection with agents of the other northern colonies, or any three of them, to use his influence in behalf of the objects of the memorial. The governor was also requested to write directly to the Lords of Trade on the same subject. The extent of the foreign trade of Rhode Island for the past year, and especially of that with the French sugar islands; the advantage of this latter to Great Britain, as well as to the colonies; with a strong representation that it should be left free, instead of being clogged by duties, were the subjects of this and of similar communications made during the year. From an exhibit of the custom-house books at Newport, contained in the memorial, we find that for the past year there were a hundred and eighty-four foreign clearances to Europe, Africa, and the West Indies, and three hundred and fifty-two vessels engaged in the coasting trade and fisheries, employing an aggregate of twenty-two hundred seamen.

The death of the deputy-governor, John Gardner, who for the past eight years had held that office, occurred soon
Feb. 27. after the adjournment of the Assembly. At the next session Joseph Wanton, jr., was chosen to the place. Rhode Island College, now known as Brown University, was incorporated, and was first located at Warren, but six years later was removed to Providence. The origin of this Institution is due to the Philadelphia Association of Baptist Churches, formed fifty-seven years before, which had early projected plans for the education of their ministry. The existing schools of learning in America, were so exclusively controlled by other denominations, that it was almost impossible for a Baptist clergyman to be educated in any of them without too great a sacrifice of principle and position. The credit of establishing the University in this State belongs to Rev. Morgan Edwards,
1761. who three years before had emigrated from Wales, and become pastor of the first Baptist church in Philadelphia.

It was chiefly by his exertions in raising funds and books at home and abroad, and by his efforts with the legislature, that the college was founded, and a charter obtained, in Rhode Island, more liberal than any that then existed in America.[1] James Manning, afterward the first president of the college, was deputed by the Association to become a leader in the work, and travelled as far as Halifax upon the business, stopping at Rhode Island to discuss the plan with some prominent men of the colony.[2] The charter expressly forbids the use of religious tests. The corporation is divided into two Boards—the Trustees, thirty-six in number, of whom twenty-two must be Baptists, five Quakers, five Episcopalians, and four Congregationalists, and the Fellows, twelve in number, of whom eight, including the President, must be Baptists, and the remainder of other denominations. Twelve Trustees and five Fellows form a quorum. The college estate, the students, and the members of the faculty, with their families, are exempt from taxation and from serving as jurors.

1764. 1762. 1763. 1764. Feb. 27.

It may here be stated, as illustrating the independent position of this institution with regard to the State, that the only pecuniary favor ever asked or obtained for it from the General Assembly was at the September session, 1776; and this can scarcely be called a favor, for it was merely an act of justice. The donations, amounting to more than four thousand dollars, had been made with the condition that the sums should be put at interest, and kept undiminished. They were loaned to the colony, and remained in the treasury when the Act of March, 1776, was passed, requiring all creditors to receive the amounts due to them, or to forfeit the interest after a certain time. In September the corporation petitioned to be excepted,

[1] Funeral sermon of Dr. Edwards by Rev. Dr. William Rogers, his successor as pastor of the Philadelphia church, and a graduate, in 1769, of the first class of seven men educated at Rhode Island College.

[2] Backus History of Baptists, ii. 236; Tustin's Historical Discourse, pp. 113–123.

CHAP. XVIII. 1764. for obvious reasons, from the operation of this act. The prayer was granted, and the interest annually paid as before.

The last of the old tenor bills, emitted fourteen years before, and called the ninth bank, were called in at this time. The mortgages given upon loans of that issue were to be redeemed at the rate of seven pounds for a silver dollar, and the name of "old tenor" was abolished.[1] The war money for 1762 was now paid over to the colonies. The portion due to Rhode Island, five thousand pounds sterling, was drawn for, and the proceeds were appropriated to redeem lawful money bills. Exchange on England was now at par.

For half a century there had been no legislation on the subject of beasts of prey; but of late wolves, once so destructive on the island, had so increased in the north and west parts of the colony, that a bounty of four pounds a head was offered for killing them.

The scheme of taxing the colonies, which the prime minister, Grenville, had nearly perfected, included, besides the custom-house duty, a stamp tax. All commercial or legal documents, to be valid in courts of law, were to be written on stamped paper sold at fixed prices by government officers. A stamp duty was also placed upon newspapers. Mar. 9. Upon the meeting of Parliament these measures were proposed, and without a division, or scarcely a dissent, it was voted "that Parliament had a right to tax the colonies."

April 5. The stamp act was postponed that the colonies might select some other form of import if they preferred, but the

[1] One deputy, James Barker, entered a rhyming protest against this act, as follows:

"I do beg leave for to protest
Against this bill, which doth transgress
Against our Sovereign Lord the King;
Likewise, injustice is therein;
For I can't see, upon my soul,
Why two-fifths should discharge the whole."

sugar act was passed at once. This reduced the duty upon molasses from sixpence a gallon, under the old act, which amounted to prohibition, to threepence, which was considered a revenue standard. It also placed a duty on coffee, spice, wines, and many foreign goods, and prohibited the export of lumber or iron except to England.[1] It strengthened the courts of Vice-Admiralty, and provided effectual means of collecting the revenue. 1764.

At the general election the same officers were continued, the people confirming the choice of deputy-governor made by the Assembly. The number of insolvent petitions granted at this time showed that although the efforts of the past few years to regulate the currency and encourage commerce, had been successful to a considerable extent, they were not entirely so. Yet the revulsion was not so serious as the former one had been, and is scarcely worthy of notice except for the difficulty it caused in collecting taxes. This was so great that the treasurer was ordered to issue warrants of distress against the collectors who failed to gather in promptly the taxes assigned to them to receive. May 2. June 11.

The news of the passage of the sugar act, and of the proposition for a stamp act, created great excitement in America. A special session of the Assembly was convened. A committee of correspondence was appointed[2] to confer with the other colonies upon measures for procuring a repeal of the sugar act, and the lessening of the duties recently imposed, and for preventing the passage of the stamp act, or the laying of any other tax, or impost, upon the colonies, inconsistent with their rights as British subjects. The agent was also directed "to do every thing in his power, either alone or by joining with the agents of the other governments, to effect these purposes." July 30.

[1] The restriction on lumber was removed the next year, and a bounty put upon its importation; the duty on coffee was lowered.

[2] Governor Hopkins, Daniel Jenckes, and Nicholas Brown.

CHAP. XVIII. 1764. July. The first of a series of difficulties, which every year became more exasperating, between the King's armed vessels and the inhabitants of Newport, now took place. The conduct of Lieut. Hill, commanding the schooner St. John, gave offence to the colony, and an order was given by two of the magistrates to the governor of Fort George, to fire upon the vessel, which was done. This was a bold proceeding, but no account of the cause that led to it, or of the result is preserved. The next year the matter was referred to by Capt. Leslir of the Cygnet, and the Assembly requested the governor to send home a statement of the case, and to lay a copy of it before that body; but no subsequent reference is made to the affair. Nine years later the royal commission to inquire into the destruction of the Gaspee, proposed to investigate the affair of the St. John, but were overruled by some of their number.

Sept. 10. The fees of the custom-house officers were revised by a committee, to report at the next session; the Assembly claiming to exercise the right they always had maintained in this matter, of stating for themselves the salaries of crown officers. The act was protested against by several deputies on various grounds, some that the fees were too high, others that due respect for the officers was not shown in the passage of the act. A tax of twelve thousand pounds was laid, one-sixth of it for current expenses, which might be paid in old tenor bills at twenty-three and a half for one of lawful money, and five-sixths of it in these latter bills to redeem the same. This tax, also, was protested against as being too heavy for the colony, in its present crippled condition, to pay. The Board of Trade had required a full statement of the paper money issues of the colony to be sent to them. It was accordingly prepared, approved by the Assembly, and transmitted (Oct. 31.) by the governor. It showed forty thousand pounds of bills emitted for war purposes to be still in circulation, equal in value to thirty thousand pounds sterling, which, with a few old tenor bills yet outstanding, would expire by limitation within three years. This was exclusive of a large debt due to private persons for loans contracted during the war. CHAP. XVIII. 1764.

We have already seen indications of party divisions in the colony upon questions relating to external affairs, quite distinct from the domestic struggle between the rival governors. That this was assuming a serious form, and was conducted in a secret manner, appeared from information received while this Assembly was in session, that a petition to the King to vacate the charter of the colony had been sent out. The agent was instructed to oppose the petition, and to procure a copy of it with the signatures.[1]

Another supply of money, amounting to thirty-five hundred sixty-two pounds sterling, probably a portion of the war appropriation for 1763, was received by the agent, and drafts, at two and a half per cent. premium, Nov. 27. were drawn on him, the proceeds to be applied to redeeming bills of credit. The Assembly adopted an address to the King on the subject of taxation, and appointed the committee who prepared the address, also to peruse a pamphlet by Gov. Hopkins, entitled "The rights of the colonies examined," and should they approve it, to have two copies made and sent to the agent to be printed and used as might seem to him most advantageous.[2] This address and the memorial to the Parliament, accompanying the remonstrance to the Board of Trade, were conceived in a higher strain than any that were sent out by the other colonies.[3] The justice of Parliament in applying the Acts of Trade to the colonies, was expressly denied, and in the correspondence with the other govern-

[1] The petition seems not to have been presented, as Sherwood writes, April 11, 1765.

[2] The stamp act was already passed when the copies of the pamphlet were received, so that it was too late, and the Rhode Island agent did not print it. Sherwood's letter

[3] Hutchinson, iii. 115.

CHAP. XVIII. ments, the determination of Rhode Island "to preserve
its privileges inviolate," was coupled with an invitation
1764. to devise a plan of union for the better maintenance of
the liberties of all. The suggestion of a general union for
May this object, first emanated from the town of Boston. It
is contained in the instructions to their representatives at
the general court in May, drawn by Samuel Adams, and
adopted by that body in a memorial prepared by James
June Otis to be sent to the agent in England. A circular was
at the same time sent to the other colonies, desiring their
united assistance to avert the common danger.

1765. The paper money was fast disappearing by means of
Feb. 25. heavy taxation imposed for the purpose of its redemption.
The treasurer was now directed to issue his notes, payable in two years at five per cent. interest to the holders of the bills emitted five years before, and a tax of twelve thousand four hundred and sixty-eight pounds fifteen shillings, lawful money, was laid to be paid in these notes. Efforts of this kind to preserve the credit of the colony were frequent and earnest. Since the war of the revolution there has been no taxation in this State, comparable in severity to that which the colonists thus placed upon themselves to preserve their financial credit. But yet greater efforts were in store for them, and a sterner trial was close at hand.

27. The stamp act passed the House of Commons by a
vote of five to one, notwithstanding the splendid defence
of the colonies made by Col. Barre and by Gen. Conway,
which so endeared their names to the American people.
March The House of Lords concurred without debate, but the
8. assent of the King was deferred, owing to his mental
22. malady, for two weeks, when it was signed in his behalf
by a commission. The first direct impulse was thus given to the revolution by a Parliament determined to coerce upon principle, and a monarch whose mind was wandering with insanity.

It is long since the aborigines of Rhode Island, who

formed so prominent a feature in the early history of the colony, have arrested our attention. They had become civilized, christianized, and settled as agriculturists on the fields which a century before were tracked only by their war path or lighted up by their council fires. Although time has proved their organization to be radically incapable of permanent development in the new direction that European contact had given it, yet it is pleasing to observe that their expiring thoughts evince, if not an aptitude to receive, at least a desire to know, those things which pertain to a higher life. The Society for Propagating the Gospel had, during the past year, sent Mr. Bennet as a teacher, with books, to the remnant of the Narragansets. The Sachem, Thomas Ninigret, now petitioned the society to establish a free school for the children of the tribe; and closes a truly eloquent letter with the "prayer that when time with us shall be no more, that when we, and the children over whom you have been such benefactors, shall leave the sun and stars, we shall rejoice in a far superior light."[1]

CHAP. XVIII. 1765. April 26.

At the general election the Ward party triumphed by a majority of two hundred in a vote of nearly forty-four hundred. Samuel Ward was chosen governor, Elisha Brown deputy-governor, and the entire list of assistants was changed. The Providence Gazette was discontinued for more than a year, partly from want of proper support, which the imposition of the stamp act seriously impaired.

May 1. 11.

Difficulties between British ships of war touching at Newport, and the townsmen, had commenced the past year in the case of H. B. M. schooner St. John. Another matter that caused great irritation now occurred. The Maidstone, a vessel belonging to the British navy, lay in the harbor of Newport, and for several weeks had impressed seamen from vessels arriving there, and even from wood boats and river crafts plying in the bay. The only

[1] Letters and papers—1761, 1776, p. 22, No. 2, in Mass. His. Soc.

CHAP. XVIII. sailors who escaped impressment were the natives of Newport, whom policy forbade to be thus abused. These
1765. arbitrary proceedings caused the port to be avoided.
Even the usual supplies received from coasters were withheld, and wood obtained from the Narraganset shore had
become scarce, no one daring to incur the risk of impressment. The harbor was deserted by all but the dreaded
Maidstone, or ships returning from foreign voyages, un-
conscious of the danger that awaited them. A brig that
June 4. arrived in the afternoon from Africa, was immediately
boarded by the officers of the Maidstone, and the whole
crew, after a severe scuffle, were pressed into the naval
service. At nine o'clock the same evening, about five
hundred sailors and boys, exasperated by this affair, seized
the Maidstone's boat at one of the wharves, and dragged
it through Queen street to the Common, where it was
burned amid the shouts of the excited mob. The action
was too sudden for the authorities to interfere, nor do we
find that any redress was obtained by the officers.

10. A petition for dividing Providence was granted, contrary to the protest of the deputies from that and some
other towns, and the town of North Providence was incorporated. Providence contained over four hundred
freemen, of whom those in the compact part were engaged
in commercial pursuits, and those in the north were farmers. This was the chief argument for the division. The
north burial ground, used also as a training field, was
reserved to the people of Providence for these purposes.

The Massachusetts House of Representatives proposed
a Congress of delegates to meet at New York in October,
to consult on the condition of the colonies, and to devise
means of presenting a statement thereof to the home government, asking for relief. This resolve was communicated to the other legislatures, and was a formal adoption
of the suggestion contained in the Boston instructions the
July 13. past year. A change in the ministry, although resulting
from domestic reasons alone, yet promised well for the

colonies. Grenville gave place to the Marquis of Rock- CHAP.
ingham, and Gen. Conway became secretary for the colo- XVIII.
nies and leader of the House of Commons, with the duke 1765.
of Grafton as his colleague. This change was joyfully
received in America, but before it occurred, the passage
of the stamp act was already known, and great disturbances had ensued. In the Virginia Assembly the match-
less eloquence of Patrick Henry had embodied the spirit May 30.
of resistance to arbitrary taxation in a series of resolutions
which were passed by a close vote. Massachusetts had June 6.
proposed the Congress just mentioned, and South Carolina was the first to follow her example in appointing dele- July 25.
gates to attend it.

In Providence a special town meeting was convened, Aug. 7.
at which a committee[1] was appointed to draft instructions
to their deputies in the General Assembly.[2] The following week they reported a series of resolutions very similar 13.
to those passed in Virginia, which were afterwards adopted by the Assembly with some additions, to which we
shall presently refer. No overt act of violence occurred
in Providence. In Boston a mob attacked the house of
secretary Oliver, the stamp distributor, and compelled
him to resign the office. An extra number of the Provi- 15.
dence Gazette, which had been for some time suspended,
was issued, with "VOX POPULI, VOX DEI," in large 24.
letters above the title, and "Where the Spirit of the LORD
is, there is LIBERTY. St. Paul." as a motto. In this
sheet the spirit of resistance manifested in Boston was ex-
tolled, the instructions of the Providence town meeting
to their deputies were published, with extracts from Col.
Barre's famous speech in Parliament, and from other colonial papers against the stamp act. The resignation of Augustus Johnston, the attorney-general who had been ap-

[1] Stephen Hopkins, Nicholas Cooke, Samuel Nightengale, jr., John Brown, Silas Downer, and James Angell.

[2] The instructions and resolutions are printed in full by Judge Staples in Annals of Providence, pp. 210–13.

CHAP. XVIII. pointed stamp distributor for Rhode Island, was also
announced in this extra; he refusing "to execute his
1765. Aug. office against the will of *our Sovereign Lord the People*
(to use his own words)."[1] The pulpit was urged to
denounce the stamp act, and a leading clergyman of
25. Boston, Jonathan Mayhew, preached against it. The
next day the riots were renewed. The houses of the Admiralty
and revenue officers, and even of the lieutenant-
governor, Hutchinson the historian, were plundered, and
26. although the town formally disapproved the conduct of
the mob, no punishment was inflicted on the offenders.
At Newport the demonstrations were equally violent.
Effigies of three prominent citizens,[2] who had incurred
27. the popular odium by advocating the measures of Parliament,
were drawn through the streets, hung on a gallows
in front of the court-house, and in the evening were cut
down and burnt in the presence of assembled thousands.
28. On the following day the houses of these obnoxious persons
were plundered by the mob, and they were compelled
to flee for protection on board the Cygnet, sloop-of-war,
then lying in the harbor. The revenue officers,
in fear for their lives, sought the same refuge and closed
30. the custom-house. They addressed a letter to the government,
demanding protection, and refusing to resume their
offices until security was guaranteed to them.[3] In the
absence of the governor, Gideon Wanton, jr., of the council,
31. replied, assuring the officers that all danger was passed,
and inviting them to resume their duties. This did not
quiet their fears. They demanded a guard for their pro-

[1] Providence Gazette Extraordinary, Saturday, August 24, 1765, page 4.

[2] Augustus Johnston, Attorney-General of the colony; Martin Howard, jr., an eminent lawyer; and Doctor Thomas Moffat, a Scotch physician. The two latter returned to England. Howard was appointed Chief Justice of N. Carolina the next year, and Moffat, comptroller of customs at New London.

[3] Letter signed John Robinson, collector; J. Nicoll, comptroller; and Nicholas Lechmere, searcher, dated Cygnet, Newport Harbor, August 30, 1765.

CHAP. XVIII.

1765. Sept. 1.

tection, and also the arrest of Samuel Crandall, a ringleader of the rioters, who had dictated, as the terms upon which the collector might again set his foot on shore, that the custom-house fees should be regulated according to the late act of Assembly, in defiance of an act of Parliament, and that a prize sloop with molasses, under the guns of the Cygnet, awaiting the decision of an Admiralty Court at Halifax, should be restored. A daring plan, for the capture of this prize, was made known to Capt. Leslir of the Cygnet, and by him communicated to Gov. Ward. It was intended to man a number of boats and take possession of Fort George; then, with the boats, to cut out the sloop, and in case of resistance from the Cygnet to fire upon her from the fort. Had this attempt been made, either the Cygnet would have been sunk by the guns of the fort, and the revolution have commenced, as it did a few years later in the same waters, or the town would have been destroyed. But better counsels for the time prevailed; measures were taken to secure the fort, and harmony was shortly restored. The popular feeling was assuaged by a lawful and peaceful demonstration against the stamp act, such as had been made in Providence. The deputies were instructed by a 3.
town meeting to give their "utmost attention to those important objects—the court of admiralty and the act for levying stamp duties," at the approaching session of the Assembly. They were reminded that "It is for liberty, that liberty for which our fathers fought, that liberty which is dearer to a generous mind than life itself, that we now contend. The cause is vast and important." [1]

So far were the British government or people from anticipating any resistance to the stamp act in America, that even the colonial agents, after vainly exerting their influence against it, gave a qualified assent to the measure, and thus inadvertently misrepresented the feeling of their

[1] Newport Town Records, September 3, 1765, p. 804.

CHAP. XVIII. 1765. Sept. principals and increased the confidence of the ministry. The appointment of distributor was sought by the agents for their friends, or conferred by the treasury department upon the prominent colonial as well as Crown officers. Even Franklin, specially instructed, as agent of Pennsylvania, to oppose the scheme of Parliamentary taxation, obtained the place of distributor for an intimate friend in Philadelphia. A request from the Treasury Board was
14. sent to the governor of Rhode Island to aid in distributing the stamps, by appointing under-distributors in every town, who should give proper bonds and be kept well supplied with stamps, and to report any remissness in the execution of their office.

16. One of the most important sessions ever held by the General Assembly was now convened at East Greenwich. The governor was requested to issue a proclamation for the arrest of the recent rioters at Newport, and to prevent a recurrence of such disturbances. Metcalf Bowler, and Henry Ward, the secretary, were chosen as commissioners to attend the Congress at New York. Instructions were prepared by a committee[1] for their guidance, in which the loyalty of the Assembly to the King and Parliament are declared, yet " they would assert their rights and privileges with becoming freedom and spirit," and the delegates are directed " to express these sentiments in the strongest manner " in the Representation and Address proposed to be made by the Congress to the home government.[2] A committee was also appointed[3] " to consider what is necessary to be done by this Assembly respecting the stamp act," and to report as soon as possible. They presented a series of six resolutions which, like the pre-

[1] Othniel Gorton, Daniel Jenckes, and George Haszard.

[2] For a copy of these instructions as entered upon the Colony Records, see Appendix J.

[3] Benjamin Greene, of Newport, Job Randall, of Scituate, William Hall, of N. Kingston, Moses Brown, of Providence, and Henry Ward, the secretary of the colony and delegate to the congress.

vious acts of Rhode Island, were more energetic and concise than any that had yet been adopted by the other colonies, and pointed directly to an absolution of allegiance to the British crown, unless the grievances were removed.[1] Five of these were nearly in the terms of the instructions given by the town of Providence to their deputies. The first four had already been passed in Virginia, and the fifth, which had been offered there by Patrick Henry, and passed by one vote, but was rescinded the next day, was adopted by the Providence town meeting, and unanimously passed by the Assembly, as expressing precisely the views they were determined to maintain. This denied the right of any power but the General Assembly to levy taxes upon the colony, and absolved the people from obedience to any law, designed for that purpose, originating from any other source. To these the Assembly added a sixth, directing the officers of the colony to proceed as usual in the execution of their trusts, and agreeing to save them harmless in so doing. This was bold legislation, but the temper of the times and the spirit of the colony were correctly represented therein.

CHAP. XVIII. 1765. Sept.

The discovery of another bed of iron ore on the Pawtuxet River, in Cranston, made early in the spring, was esteemed of great importance. A company was formed, and a furnace erected on the northern branch of the river, and the petitioners[2] were allowed to erect a permanent dam, provided they would construct a suitable passage for fish around it, and maintain the same from the tenth of April to the twentieth of May annually, agreeable to a law that had been in force for thirty years.

Oct. 7.

The second General Congress, or convention of delegates from all the colonies, based on the principle of that held at Albany, about twenty years before, met at New York. Nine colonies were represented, six by appoint-

[1] See Appendix K.

[2] Stephen Hopkins, Israel Wilkinson, Nicholas and Moses Brown, for themselves and their partners.

CHAP. XVIII. ment of their legislatures, and three by individual action. Virginia and North Carolina had had no session since the
1765. Massachusetts call was issued; Georgia and New Hamp-
Oct. shire also sent no delegates; but all signified their approval of the design of the Congress, and their adhesion to its acts. The colonies represented, arranged themselves in geographical order, and each was allowed one vote. After a session of nearly three weeks, in which the great principles of "liberty, privileges, and prerogative" were earnestly debated, the Congress adopted a Declaration of the Rights and Grievances of the Colonies. They denounced the idea of any representation except through their own legislatures as impracticable; thus repelling the scheme proposed in Parliament by Pownall, formerly governor of Massachusetts, for allowing them a direct representation in that body. They claimed, as the birthright of Englishmen, that they should not be taxed without their own consent, and that the trial by jury should be preserved, unobstructed by the recent extension of the powers of Courts of Admiralty, where one judge alone, whose tenure of office was the royal will, presided, deciding, without a jury, both the law and the fact, and taking commissions upon all condemnations. These ideas were embodied in an address to the King, and in memorials to each House of Parliament, which, being signed by most of the delegates whose powers permitted them to do so, were forwarded to England.[1] News of the opposition to the stamp act having reached England, the ministry, divided in their views of its justice or policy, hesitated to enforce it by an appeal to arms. The time was drawing near when it was to take effect. A
24. circular was despatched[2] to all the American governors,

[1] The resolutions adopted by the Convention, October 19, 1765, with the address to the King, the memorial to the House of Lords, and the petition to the House of Commons are printed in the Appendix to Hutchinson's Hist. of Mass., vol. iii. pp. 479–487. Lond. Edit. 1828.

[2] Conway's Circular, October 24, 1765. Letters, 1763–75, No. 35.

counselling "lenient and persuasive methods," in order to restore peace, but in case of further violent outbreaks to employ "a timely exertion of force;" for which purpose they were to call upon Gen. Gage or Lord Colville for assistance. The day following the issue of this cautious and somewhat undecided circular, the Congress at New York adjourned, and at the earliest opportunity their proceedings were reported to the several legislatures, by whom they were cordially approved. In the Assembly of Rhode Island the report of the delegates was entered upon the records, and copies of the journal and of the memorials were filed with it in the secretary's office, not to be made public before information of their presentation in England should be received. Copies of these addresses were also sent to the agent in London, with the request that he would unite with the other agents in presenting and enforcing them, and to employ counsel for that purpose. The thanks of the colony were voted to Col. Barre for his spirited defence of their rights in the House of Commons. This was in accordance with the Providence instructions to their deputies in August. A day of public thanksgiving was appointed, in which prayers for "a blessing upon the endeavors of this colony for preserving their valuable privileges," were to be offered. The day before the stamp act was to take effect, all the royal governors, with Fitch of Connecticut, took the oath to sustain it. Samuel Ward, "the governor of Rhode Island, stood alone in his patriotic refusal."[1] But the people had already settled the question. The fatal day dawned upon a nation united in their determination of resistance. Not a stamp was to be seen. Everywhere the distributors had resigned, some by force, and others of their own free-will. The wheels of every government in America were stopped at once. Commerce was crushed, law was annulled, justice was delayed, even the usages of domestic

CHAP. XVIII. 1765. Oct. 25. — 30. — 31. — Nov. 1.

[1] Bancroft's History U. S., vol. v., p. 351.

CHAP. XVIII. life were suspended by this anomalous and terrible act.
Not a ship could sail, not a statute could be enforced, not
1765. a court could sit, nor even a marriage take place, that
Nov. was not in itself illegal, so far as the British Parliament
could make it so; for every one of these acts required
the evidence of stamped paper to establish its validity.

But yet further demonstrations were necessary to bring
the people and government of Great Britain to their
senses. Non-importation agreements were at once entered
into by the leading merchants in America, following the
example of New York; and a combination for the support of American manufactures, and to increase the supply of wool, by ceasing to consume lamb or mutton, was
soon afterwards formed. Riots occurred in New York,
resulting in the surrender of the stamped paper by Lieutenant-governor Colden, with the sanction of Gen. Gage
himself, to the municipal authorities, amid shouts of
"Liberty, Property, and no Stamps." In Newport, at a
4. town meeting, over which the governor presided, a military guard was established, and a night patrol organized
5. to preserve the peace. Gunpowder-Treason-night had
always been a time of festivity, and it was feared that a
tumult might occur, but the occasion passed off quietly.

The revenue officers, feeling bound by the act of Par-
21. liament, addressed a letter to Augustus Johnston, distributor of stamps for Rhode Island, requiring him to supply
the custom-house. He replied, stating the circumstances
22. of his resignation in August, and that the stamps for this
colony were lodged for safe-keeping on board the Cygnet,
so that he could not comply with their demand. The
correspondence was submitted on the same day to Gov.
Ward, with a request for his advice what course to pursue.
28. The day appointed for thanksgiving was duly celebrated.
The triumph over an unjust and unconstitutional act, was
complete in Rhode Island where, under the sixth resolu-
Dec. tion of the September Assembly, the judicial courts held
their regular terms, unawed by the feeling which, in the

other colonies, suspended, for a time, that department of their several governments. CHAP. XVIII.

At the opening of Parliament, attention was directed to American affairs, but it was not till after the holidays, that the great debate commenced, which lasted through several weeks. Grenville, the late prime minister, and author of the stamp act, opposed with much bitterness the motion for its repeal. The now venerable Pitt, unconnected with any party, but still the most powerful man in the kingdom, was in his seat to pronounce that magnificent speech, the crowning effort of his noble mind, in which he "rejoiced that America has resisted," and declared "that England has no right to tax the colonies." In the course of the debate, Franklin was brought before the House of Commons, and sustained a long examination upon the condition and temper of America, which produced a marked effect upon the feelings of the House. It was in this debate, too, that Edmund Burke first displayed his splendid oratory in the cause of the colonies. The repeal was carried in the Commons by a majority of one hundred and eight, and later in the Lords by ninety-four votes;[1] but it was accompanied by a declaratory act, asserting the right of Parliament "to bind the colonies in all cases whatsoever," and both bills received the royal assent on the same day. 1766. Jan. 14. Feb. 13. 22. March 18.

The governor of Rhode Island had no stated salary, but sums of money were voted to him from time to time by the Assembly. Thirty pounds a year was now voted to ex-governor Hopkins for former services, and the same amount to Gov. Ward for the past year. To meet current expenses, the treasurer was empowered to hire one thousand pounds, or to issue bills of credit to that amount, redeemable in two years by taxation. Organizations under the name of "Sons of Liberty," a term first applied to the Americans by Col. Barre in his famous speech Feb. 24.

[1] Botta's History of the War of Independence, i. 88.

CHAP. XVIII. 1766. against the stamp act, had sprung up in all the colonies; but we believe that to Rhode Island was reserved the peculiar honor of initiating a similar order, composed of the gentler sex, known as "the daughters of liberty." Its origin is ascribed to Dr. Ephraim Bowen, at whose house eighteen young ladies, belonging to prominent families in March 4. Providence, assembled by invitation, and employed the time from sunrise till evening in spinning. They resolved to purchase no more British manufactures, unless the stamp act should be repealed, and adopted other resolutions, perhaps more patriotic than prudent, to accomplish this desirable end. They were handsomely entertained by the doctor at dinner, but cheerfully agreed to omit *tea* at the evening meal, to render their conduct yet more consistent. The association rapidly increased in numbers, so that their next meeting was held at the court-house. This was for the purpose of spinning a handsome piece of linen as a premium for the person who should raise the largest amount of flax during the year, in the county of Providence.[1] Thus the spirit of resistance pervaded every portion of society, and the determination to oppose the stamp act, even to "the destruction of the union" of the colonies with the mother country, was declared at a meeting in Providence held at this time. "Liberty Trees," so called from the great elm in Boston, where the opponents of the stamp act were wont to assemble, began to be set up. In Newport, Capt. William Read, a deputy from that town, gave a piece of land for the purpose of planting a tree of liberty, and the patriotic impulse was followed in other places. The circular an-
31. nouncing the repeal of the stamp act, and the passage of the declaratory act, also gave notice of a bill, then under discussion, and soon afterward passed, to revise the trade laws in favor of the colonies. This was skilfully used by Conway as a proof of the good-will and forgiveness of

[1] Boston Chronicle, April 7, 1766.

Parliament, and as an occasion for the display of grati- CHAP.
tude from the colonists. But the chief object of his ver- XVIII.
bose paper was to urge the colonies to accede quietly to 1766.
a bill, obliging their legislatures to indemnify the sufferers
by the late stamp act riots; and gratitude was bespoken
in their behalf by the Secretary, because their evidence
had been given dispassionately in favor of a repeal of the
act. About this time a paper mill was established at
Olneyville near Providence. The revision of the Acts
of Trade was soon completed, and Sherwood, the faithful May 9.
agent of Rhode Island, enclosing a copy of the resolutions, congratulates the colony "that every grievance is
now absolutely and totally removed."[1] The duty on 15.
molasses was reduced to one penny a gallon, that upon
sugar, coffee, and spice was modified, and other alterations were made, favorable to colonial commerce.

At the annual election, the same officers were con- 7.
tinued. When the news of the repeal of the stamp act 16.
reached America, unbounded joy pervaded the colonies.
The declaratory act, entitled an act "securing the depend-
ency of the colonies," which accompanied it, was considered as a merely formal matter. In Providence the
anniversary of the king's birth was selected as a day of June
public rejoicing, to attest at once the loyalty of the peo- 4.
ple, and their love of liberty. Bells, cannon, flags, martial music, a procession, and a discourse at the Presbyterian church, after which the people returned to the court-house, where his Majesty's health was drank, with a royal salute of twenty-one guns, occupied the morning. The afternoon was spent in drinking thirty-two loyal and patriotic toasts, accompanied by the discharge of cannon, the sound of drum and trumpets, and the wild huzzas of the delighted and excited multitude. In the evening there was a grand display of fireworks at the court-house, and "an elegant boiled collation," after which, at eleven

[1] Sherwood to Rhode Island, Letter 45.

CHAP. XVIII. o'clock the company retired. The next evening a grand ball was given to the "Daughters of Liberty," at which
1766. June there "was the most brilliant appearance of ladies this town ever saw."[1] In Newport, and elsewhere, similar
9. rejoicings took place. The Assembly adopted "an humble address of thanks to His Majesty" for the repeal of the stamp act, and voted their thanks to the merchants of London for their exertions in favor of America. An appropriation was made to build a new court-house in Bristol, upon the site of the old one. A public thanksgiving
26. was held throughout the colony, by proclamation of the governor at the request of the Assembly, "in acknowledgment to the Supreme Being for the repeal of the late act of Parliament imposing stamp duties."

For ten years the colony had vainly applied for its proportion of the military allowance, long since paid to the other colonies, for the campaign of 1756. A difficulty in adjusting the accounts according to the Treasury regulations, had prevented the payment at the proper time, and the enormous war expenses of subsequent years had caused it to be delayed. The indefatigable Sherwood at length obtained a favorable report from the war office, allowing, after many deductions, the sum of twenty-six hundred and seventy-three pounds sterling, to be due to
July 25. Rhode Island. But the Treasury Board still refused to pay the money, alleging to the agent, as a reason for delay, that as a requisition had been sent by the crown to the colony to indemnify the officers who had suffered in the late riots, the governor would wait to see what action was taken upon it by the Assembly. This step was fatal to the claim, for reasons that will presently appear.

Another change in the ministry, brought about chiefly by the aspect of American affairs, now took place. The venerable Pitt again became prime minister, receiving
29. from the king, at the same time, a place in the peerage

[1] Providence Gazette—revived, August 19, 1766. Staple's Annals, 215.

with the title of Earl of Chatham, for accepting which he was severely but unjustly censured. Conway gladly exchanged his difficult post as Secretary for the colonies, which was taken by the Earl of Shelburne, while he, accepting another position in the State department, became leader of the House of Commons. Charles Townshend, who as one of the Grenville ministry, had supported the stamp act, but latterly had advocated its repeal, became Chancellor of the Exchequer, with the Duke of Grafton as First Lord of the Treasury, and Camden, the eloquent defender of America in the House of Peers, was made Lord Chancellor. Lower places were assigned to Col. Barre, to Lord North, and many others. This cabinet, although denounced by Burke as "a piece of diversified mosaic," was the most liberal that England had yet seen; and could it have remained without the later modifications to which it was subjected, America might have had no further cause of complaint. But Pitt, whose failing health and advancing years had led him to seek refuge from the stormy Commons, in the quiet seclusion of the Peers, could no longer direct affairs with the energy that had once made England great and himself all-powerful. The liberal portion of his ministry soon lost ground before the more active supporters of prerogative who composed it, so that it had been better for his fame, and happier for America, at the time, had the Earl of Chatham never assumed the seals.

CHAP. XVIII. 1766.

Heretofore the official correspondence between the colonies and the home government had been conducted with the Board of Trade. An order in council now repealed the regulation under which this had been done, and required all such communications to be addressed directly to the king.

Aug. 8.

Seventy years before, Samuel Sewall of Boston, one of the original purchasers of Pettaquamscot, had given five hundred acres of land in what was now the town of Exeter, to maintain a grammar-school for the children of

CHAP. XVIII. 1766. Sept. 8. the inhabitants upon that purchase. The gift had long lain neglected, but was now revived by petition to the Assembly that proper powers might be conferred to carry out the design of the donor. Any magistrate of the county was empowered, at the call of any five freeholders residing within the old purchase, to summon a meeting of the inhabitants, who might choose proper officers and do all other acts necessary to carry out the benevolent purposes of the grantor. At the next session the town of Oct. 29. Exeter had leave to build a school-house, near the east end of the town, on the public highway, which was laid out ten rods wide. An act for the preservation of oysters was passed, forbidding them to be taken by drags, or otherwise than by tongs, under a penalty of ten pounds. Parents and masters were held liable for the violation of this law by their children or servants, and the owners of boats engaged in evading it were subject to a double fine. Barberry bushes being supposed to injure grain, a special act for their destruction in the town of Middletown was passed. Upon application of any freeholder, the person upon whose grounds they grew was required to cut them up within one month, or, in case of his neglect to do so, they might be destroyed, by warrant from a justice, at the expense of the complainant."[1]

The letter of the agent, announcing the award of money due to Rhode Island, and the reasons assigned by the Treasury Board for withholding its payment, was laid before the Assembly. They replied that no claims for redress had been made upon them, and when such were made in a proper manner, they should be duly considered; that they could not conceive why the money should be detained, for that this delay was "by no means submitting the sufferings of the persons recommended in his Majesty's instructions, to the determination of the General Assembly;" that this colony was in distress for the

[1] Six years later, in August, 1772, the Assembly extended this act over the whole colony.

CHAP. XVIII. 1766.

money, having expended largely in the late war on the faith of promises which had long since been redeemed as to the other colonies; that the mob were not encouraged by people of position, as had been asserted; and that the assurance of this Assembly, upon that point, was entitled to as much weight as were the suggestions of their enemies across the sea. Letters to this effect were sent to the agent, to the Lords of the Treasury, and to the colonial secretary. It was the spirited reply to an unmanly subterfuge on the part of the ministry, but it was fatal to the claimants on either side. As yet no petitions for indemity had been presented, and when, at an adjourned session, in Providence, the three principal sufferers by the riot appeared with their claims, Johnston and Moffat in person, and Howard by attorney, no notice whatever was taken of their complaints. The newspapers report that the petitioners "were referred to next session, that the inhabitants of the colony might direct their representatives therein," but not a word appears upon the records of this, nor of any subsequent session for more than eight months, to show that the matter was brought before them. The Assembly and the people were thoroughly aroused at the injustice of the proceedings, and preferred to sacrifice their own admitted claims rather than submit to this unusual and arbitrary mode of forcing from them an act of justice.[1]

Dec. 8.

A tax ordered at the last session was now apportioned

[1] It is from other sources than the colony records that we learn that Howard's claim amounted to £970, Moffat's to £1,310, and Johnston's to £373 1*s*. 3*d*., a total of £2,653 1*s*. 3*d*., of which £890 were charged by the two former for their trip to England. A committee reported upon Moffat's claim in December, 1772, with a list of items amounting to £179 10*s*. 6*d*. which was voted to be paid. Another committee in August, 1773, reported upon the claims of Howard and Johnston, reducing the former to £111 18*s*., and the latter to £76 10*s*., which sums were voted "to be paid when and as soon as the General Assembly shall receive information that the money due from the crown to the colony for their services in the expedition against Crown Point, in the year 1756, shall be received by the agent of this colony in Great Britain."

CHAP. XVIII. 1767. among the towns. Six thousand pounds, lawful money, and seventy-five thousand in old tenor were assessed upon the colony to be paid in these bills respectively, to redeem the treasurer's notes given for the former and the old ten per cent. bonds, yet outstanding, issued for the latter. This, like most of the recent tax acts, was protested against by many deputies, chiefly because it was apportioned without regard to the valuation made four years previously as a guide for taxation. Such a departure from a settled rule was considered to be a dangerous precedent, and an arbitrary act on the part of the administration. It lost them the power at the next election. To counterfeit any coin, or knowingly to pass any such, was made a capital offence, and to cut or divide coin, which was often done in order to make small change, was prohibited under a penalty of ten times the value. The new digest of laws, which had occupied a committee for several months, was completed in September, and a committee was then appointed to examine it. It was a work of great labor, as appears by the reports of the revising and examining committees made in October, and was far more complete than any digest before attempted. Two hundred copies were now ordered to be printed and distributed throughout the colony.

Feb. 23. Protection to the fisheries was always an object of attention with the General Assembly. An act to prevent the Pawtuxet and Pawcatuck Rivers from being obstructed by wears or seines, so as to prevent the passage of fish in the spring, was enforced by a penalty of fifty pounds. As each emission of lawful money bills of credit, most of which had five years to run, was about to mature, measures were taken to redeem them, either by immediate taxation, or by issuing treasury notes to be exchanged for them; a process which was a virtual extension of the bills. The paper now falling due, was ordered to be redeemed in this manner. The treasurer was to issue his notes at six per cent. interest, to be paid in two years by

CHAP. XVIII. 1767. Feb. 28.

a tax on the colony; and to counterfeit these notes was liable to the same punishment as for counterfeiting the bills. A new issue of two thousand pounds in bills of credit, payable in two years was made, to supply the treasury.

Mar. 18.

The anniversary of the repeal of the stamp act was celebrated with great rejoicings, similar to those that followed the reception of the news. This occasion, the first triumph of successful resistance, continued for several years to be observed as a holiday. Since the act[1] requiring the general officers to be voted for on town meeting day, instead of the first Wednesday in May, the third Wednesday in April had become the period of decisive political struggle, while "election day," as it still continues from ancient habit to be called, ceased to be any thing more than the occasion for the official promulgation of the result, and the inauguration of the new government at Newport. At this election the Hopkins party were reinstated by over four hundred majority, the largest that had been obtained on either side during the controversy. The strength of Hopkins lay in the north. In Providence not a single vote was cast at this time for his opponent, while Ward was strongest in Newport, where he polled three times as many votes as his adversary, and obtained a majority of nearly two hundred. Stephen Hopkins was again declared governor, and Joseph Wanton, jr., deputy-governor. The entire list of ten assistants was also changed. The political revolution was complete. The tax act had destroyed the Ward party, and the professions of their opponents to be "Seekers of Peace,"—a motto inscribed upon the Hopkins tickets—insured success. This profession was honorably redeemed by the victors in withdrawing, at the close of the year, for the sake of peace, from future contests. The new government committed a serious error at the outset in allowing

April 15.

May 6.

[1] Passed, August 18, 1760.

CHAP. XVIII. 1767. those towns which were in arrears for the last two taxes, to pay their proportion according to the estimate made five years before, thereby invalidating the subsequent tax acts of the Assembly, and weakening its power. A strong and numerously signed protest was entered against this proceeding. It was certainly carrying party spirit to a dangerous extent, and operated unjustly upon those towns that had already paid according to the later laws. At the same time they passed an order for a new valuation of ratable property to be made. The bill was brought in at the next session. It levied a poll tax upon all males over eighteen years of age, except settled ministers, and a property tax to be estimated as follows: The annual rent of all kinds of real estate was to be determined, and the value of improved lands to be estimated as equal to twenty years rent; of houses, wharves, mills, &c., at fifteen years rent; personal estate, slaves, waste lands, and trading stock, except ships and cargoes at sea which were put at two-thirds value, were to be taxed at their full value. Debts were to be deducted from the personal estate. Sworn lists were to be rendered by every tax-payer, or if refused, the assessors were to fix their own valuation without remedy, and the offender was to be taxed fourfold. A protest was entered against this project, chiefly on the ground that it favored the traders at the expense of the landowners. A lottery was granted to raise twenty-five hundred dollars for putting a new steeple upon Trinity Church, the old one being much decayed. The rate of interest was fixed at six per cent. and usurious contracts subjected the lender to the loss of principal and interest. When North Providence was set off from Providence, some of the compact portion of the latter town was included in the former. A petition for restoration was granted, and a new boundary established, conforming very nearly with that now existing. The right to use the north burial-ground as a cemetery and parade-ground was extended to the people of North Providence.

June 8.

29.

CHAP. XVIII. 1767.

Meanwhile measures were in progress in England to prove that the declaratory act was something more than a mere formality. Parliament, having therein asserted the abstract right to bind America, were preparing to test its reality. The opposers of the stamp act, Pitt especially, had taken a distinction, more nice than wise in its application to the colonies, between external and internal taxes. Townshend, upon whom, as Chancellor of the Exchequer, devolved the proposal of ways and means, availed himself of this distinction to raise a revenue in America by means of custom duties, which should be applied to support the civil officers in the colonies, and thus make them independent of the local assemblies. To this end he proposed a small duty on glass, lead, paints, and paper, and that the export duty of one shilling a pound on tea sent from England should be removed, and an import duty of threepence a pound placed upon it in America. This, while it really lessened the burden upon the American consumer, made the tax, greatly diminished as it was, more palpable, besides putting a stop to smuggling tea from the Dutch. He also proposed a Board of Commissioners of Customs, having the same powers with that in England, who should prevent illegal traffic, and determine disputes, now carried to England, with less cost and trouble to the parties. These were the two leading measures of the government, in introducing which their author denounced several of the colonies for acts of insubordination, and among them Rhode Island for having postponed making indemnity to the sufferers in the late riots. But these were passed over, while an example was to be made of New York for refusing entire compliance with the billeting act, requiring provision to be made for a large number of royal troops to be quartered in that city. During the late war, soldiers had been cheerfully billeted in all the colonies, for which indemnity was allowed; but an act requiring them to be supported by the colonies, in fact establishing a standing army, now that the occasion

May 13.

CHAP. XVIII. for it had passed, was deemed a grievance, and New York refused to provide for more than a limited number. To
1767. punish her for this incontumacy, Townshend moved that the legislative power of the New York Assembly be suspended until they would comply with the billeting act.
July These three measures were passed, and in the bill organizing the customs commissioners, a clause was inserted, legalizing the writs of assistance, against which the first murmur of discontent in the colonies had been raised by
Aug. 7. the merchants of Boston. Notice of the passage of these acts was given by Sherwood in a letter that contains also a censure from the ministry on the conduct of Rhode Island in prosecuting the collector Robinson. The As-
31. sembly, by order of the Treasury Board, appointed a committee to examine the complaint made by him against the Judge of the Court of Vice-Admiralty, and the Attorney General. Disagreements between the colonial and revenue officers were incessant, and mutual recriminations were constantly made to the home government, of hindrance in collecting duties and of tyranny in the mode of exacting them. To trace the manifold phases that these troubles assumed, would be both tedious and useless. They present the opposite sides of the same principle—resistance to the Acts of Trade on one hand, and the determination to enforce them at all hazards on the other—with very much of wrong-dealing upon both.[1]

The three principal sufferers by the stamp act riot had again presented their claims at the June session, and were ordered to bring in an account with items under oath.

[1] Upon this particular complaint the committee reported in October that no ground for it existed. The collector refused to attend the meeting of the committee, and the Assembly "having no knowledge of any prosecution had against that gentleman, either by the Assembly or the Magistracy," ordered the sheriff to wait upon Mr. Robinson with a copy of the agent's letter, "and request his answer, whether he has any knowledge of any such complaint being made," and if so, to require a copy thereof. A copy of this note was sent to the agent in England, and the governor was requested to write to the ministry on the subject if he thought best.

Having failed to do this, the claim was again deferred, and the first vote upon the subject that appears upon the records, now required them to fulfil the former order as soon as possible. CHAP. XVIII. 1767.

The Warren Association of Baptist Churches, the earliest of its kind in New England, had its first celebration this year at Warren. It originated with the Warren church,[1] and had for its object to secure for the denomination in the neighboring colonies those civil and religious rights hitherto enjoyed solely by the established church. The location of the College at Warren, made this town the centre of Baptist influence in this region, and a proper place for the initiation of such an enterprise. The annual meeting was appointed for the first Tuesday after commencement, as that occasion drew together many leading men of the church from all parts of the country. In a few years the Association extended over New England, and held its meetings at various places. It became an active body in the cause of civil and religious liberty, presenting many able addresses upon this subject to the government of Massachusetts and to the Continental Congress through the whole period of the revolution. Although the Association has no longer that intimate connection with the university which at first existed, and the growth of Baptist churches in New England has given rise to many other similar associations, the parent body still continues to exert a wide-spread and beneficent influence over the objects of its charge. Sept.

At this crisis, just as the fatal acts that were destined to rupture the British empire were adopted in Parliament, their gifted but erring author closed his brilliant career. 4.
Had the death of Charles Townshend occurred at the opening, instead of the close of that memorable session, how different might have been the fortunes of England!

[1] August 28, 1766, the Warren Church voted "That an association be entered into with sundry churches of the same faith and order, as it was judged a likely method to promote the peace of the churches."

CHAP. XVIII. A circular from the treasury enclosed a copy of the Board
of Revenue act. The commissioners were stationed at
1767. Boston as being alike the centre of commerce and of dis-
Oct. content. John Robinson, the collector of Newport, was
appointed one of the new Board. The Assembly took no
immediate notice of these recent acts of Parliament, but
28. on the same day that it met, a new movement was commenced by the people of Boston. Gov. Bernard had refused to call a special session of the General Court to consider the obnoxious measures. A public meeting was
therefore held to devise plans for the encouragement of
industry, economy, and manufactures. It was resolved
to discontinue the importation of British goods, and the
consumption of all unnecessary articles. Mourning apparel
was discountenanced, as being wholly of English manufacture, and means were taken to procure the adhesion of
other communities to this legal, peaceful, but effectual
Nov. mode of nullifying the duty act. The arrival of the
5. revenue commissioners at Boston caused no excitement,
20. and when the day came, upon which the act was to take
effect, there were no duties to be paid, and no orders upon
which they might accrue had been sent out. Providence
25. soon followed the example of Boston,[1] and the next day
26. Newport appointed a committee on the same subject to
report at a future meeting. A placard was put up on the
27. door of the court-house the following night, urging the
people to seize the money in the custom-house "by way
of reprisal for the money due this colony from the
crown." The riotous appeal was not regarded, and at the
Dec. adjourned meeting a reward of fifty pounds was offered for
4. the arrest of the author. The thanks of the town were
sent to the council of Boston for their "wise and whole-
some" recommendations, and resolutions similar to those
therein proposed were adopted, and sent to each town in
the colony for their concurrence. Thus the combination

[1] The Providence agreement was signed December 2d. The measure was to take effect in Rhode Island, January 1, 1768.

spread rapidly throughout the colonies, and the agreements were everywhere signed. The cause of revolution received a powerful impulse from the pen of John Dickinson of Pennsylvania, whose letters against Parliamentary taxation, over the signature of "A Farmer," were universally circulated in pamphlet form, and republished in all the newspapers.

CHAP. XVIII. 1767.

At the October session, the Assembly had required Ninigret to execute a deed of the Indian school-house lot in Charlestown to the colony, and had also appointed a committee to settle the accounts of the Sachem, by paying his debts with his personal property, so far as it would go, and selling lands to satisfy the remainder. This was considered so great a grievance by the tribe, that they resolved, by the advice of Sir William Johnson, to send Tobias Shattock to England as their agent, to seek redress from the king.[1] George Rome, who had been a resident of the colony for six years as agent for creditors in England, and had been unfortunate in his efforts to recover their claims before the courts or the Assembly, wrote a very long and severe letter, probably to Dr. Moffat, in which he unsparingly denounced the courts and government of this colony, (but making honorable exception of James Helme, Chief Justice of the Superior Court,) and the rebellious spirit of all the colonies, and urged the establishment of royal governments throughout America as the only mode of averting impending evil.[2] A copy of this letter, with others written against the colonies, was obtained in England nearly six years later by parties resolved to learn who were the enemies of America. Rome's letter was then printed, and was the first positive evidence discovered respecting the persons who, three years before this time, had been reported to the Assembly as having petitioned for a revocation of the charter.

Dec. 8.

22.

[1] Shattock's letter to the committee, December 8, read December 29, 1767. Letters, 54.

[2] Trumbull papers, vol. xxiii. No. 21.

CHAP. XVIII.

1767. Dec. 2.

1768. Jan. 1.

A vigorous effort in behalf of free schools was now made in Providence. At the adjourned meeting that adopted the resolutions in favor of industry and economy, it was proposed to establish four public schools in the town. The committee to whom the subject was referred, reported a plan which was approved, but found too costly for the existing state of the treasury.[1] The design "of a free school supported by a tax, was rejected by the poorer sort of the people, being strongly led away, not to see their own as well as the public interest therein."[2] But, notwithstanding the opposition of these objectors, one large school was voted at once, and it was shown that its cost would be more than saved by the citizens if they should all unite in the project just agreed to, for promoting economy. A brick school-house was erected during the summer, and the oversight of the public, and also of the private schools, was placed in charge of a committee of nine, of whom the town council formed a part.[3] Thus freedom and education went hand in hand with industry and economy, in the minds of the fathers of the revolution. A census of the town showed its population to be little short of three thousand.[4]

[1] Providence Gazette of January 2d and 9th, 1768.

[2] Moses Brown's memorandum appended to Governor Bowen's report, Staples' Annals, pp. 500.

[3] The proprietors, who, with the town, had erected this building, were incorporated February 26, 1770. The house was two stories high, and the upper story was occupied for a private school, the lower as a free school.

[4]

Men over 21 years of age,	530
Women do.	628
Young men from 14 to 21,	217
Do. women do. do.,	183
Boys between 5 and 14,	302
Girls do. do.	289
Children under 5 years,	470
Blacks—males,	155
Do., females,	184
Total.	2,958

Providence Gazette, January 2, 1768.

CHAP. XVIII. 1768.

The business of the colonies had become so pressing, that a third secretary was necessary upon whom the American department alone should devolve, and the Earl of Hillsborough was appointed to the place. Other changes in the cabinet occurred, and Lord North reluctantly assumed the delicate post of Chancellor of the Exchequer. The first movement of the new secretary was to notify the colonies of his appointment, and to require from Rhode Island a transcript of her laws. The General Court of Massachusetts, after maturely deliberating on the condition of the province, and adopting a petition to the king, addressed a circular to the other colonial assemblies, inviting co-operation in the assertion of their rights. The Rhode Island Assembly at once responded to this appeal by preparing "a suitable address to his Majesty, and also a letter to" the ministry, stating the grievances of the colonies.

Jan. 23. Feb. 11. 29.

A patent right for fourteen years was granted to Samuel Jackson and others, to dig coal from a mine supposed to exist in Providence; but the indications of coal in this vicinity proved to be fallacious. At the October session, Gov. Hopkins had intimated his intention of no longer being a candidate for the chief magistracy.[1] Since the death of Gov. Greene, the personal contest between Gov. Ward and himself had lasted ten years, in seven of which he had triumphed. The position of the colony required that this bitter feud should be quelled. He therefore proposed a union of the factions by the withdrawal of each of their leaders, either of whom, as might be agreed, should nominate a governor from the friends of the other, and these in turn should name a deputy-governor from the opposite side; the assistants, in like manner, to be equally apportioned between the two parties. The plan was adopted at the spring election, and the famous controversy between Ward and Hopkins ceased forever, April.

[1] G. Rome's letter of December 22, 1767.

CHAP. XVIII. 1768. in the presence of a more momentous struggle, in which the State was soon to be involved. This consolidation of political parties, that for so long a period had divided the counsels of the colony, was a movement so significant of the future, that it may well form an era, and invite a pause, in the course of our history. The most violent party strife that for a century had distracted the popular mind, was suddenly hushed in view of the portentous conflict about to commence. As the fury of contending armies has sometimes been restrained by the wilder uproar of the elements, so the hostile factions in Rhode Island were awed into peace by the threatening storm about to overwhelm the colony. That the idea of independence had become familiar to the public mind, contemporary papers fully prove, and positive legislation was soon to establish. That the present realization of this idea was contingent upon the action of the British ministry, whether to yield or to persist in the exercise of arbitrary power, is equally certain. Absolute independence was only desired as a remedy for evils which might yet be averted. But the temper of England warned the more thoughtful colonists that the disposition to alleviate their burdens could only be purchased by concessions, which, as freemen and as Englishmen, they could not offer. Unconditional submission to the authority of Parliament, taxation without representation, and the support of standing armies in time of peace, were measures so subversive of the principles of Magna Charta, that another Runnymede, with the Parliament and the people in place of the king and his barons, appeared inevitable. What King John conceded, and thereby preserved a crown, George III. refused, and lost an empire.

Union for resistance was the motive, if not the motto, of the coalition that was now perfected in Rhode Island, and ere long to extend throughout the continent. Fleets and armies were soon "to cover our shores and darken our land." Maddened at the bold and apparently defiant attitude of the colonies, Parliament and people together resolved to crush sedition before granting justice. The power that had so lately humbled France, and become mistress of mankind, scorned the idea of armed resistance from feeble provincials, and thought to crush out liberty itself by a display of force. But England forgot that the great minister, whose genius had compassed her supremacy, was the firmest friend of the principles she now hoped to subdue, and of the people she sought to conquer. His mighty mind had sunk beneath the weight of empire, and in a sad condition, almost of imbecility, he still retained the seals to be but a cipher in his cabinet. His wisdom could no longer guide the councils of the king, nor his energy direct the prosperity of the nation. England had forgotten, too, that a long series of desperate conflicts on the western continent had trained her trans-atlantic subjects to the use of arms. Nor did she understand the spirit of unanimity that could not only quell a protracted feud in her smallest colony, but which everywhere pervaded her excited provinces. From the far south, skilled in border warfare with savage tribes, from the central colonies, richest in the appliances of resistance, and from populous and determined New England, one voice had gone forth, and one pregnant symbol had been adopted. "Join or Die," was now the universal motto, soon to give place to the last colonial battle-shout of "Liberty or Death." The capture of Cape Breton and the conquest of Canada, had taught the Americans the great lesson of self-reliance, and the same

> "—drums that beat at Louisburg,
> And thundered at Quebec,"

were soon to roll the charge on Bunker Hill, and rattle the reveillè in Rhode Island.

APPENDIX J.

INSTRUCTIONS TO THE COMMISSIONERS APPOINTED SEPT. 16, 1765, TO ATTEND THE CONGRESS AT NEW YORK IN OCTOBER.

(FROM THE COLONY RECORDS, PAGE 343.)

CHAP. XVIII. APP. J.

It is Voted and Resolved, That the following be the Instructions to the Commissioners who shall be appointed by this Assembly, to meet Commissioners of the other governments at New York:

Gentlemen,

This Assembly taking into consideration the late Act of the Parliament of Great Britain for levying stamp duties upon the Colonies in North America, and extending the jurisdiction of the Courts of Admiralty, are humbly of opinion, that the said Act is oppressive and injurious, and deprives us of some of our most essential Rights and Liberties; which we have enjoyed ever since the first settlement of the colony; which have been confirmed by a Royal Charter, and have never been forfeited nor contested, but have ever been recognized by the King and Parliament of Great Britain.

The House of Representatives of the Province of the Massachusetts Bay, have proposed a meeting of committees appointed by the several British Colonies on this Continent, at New York, on the first Tuesday in October next, to consult together upon the present circumstances of the colonies, and the difficulties to which they are, and must be reduced, by the operation of the said Act of Parliament; and to consider of a general and united, dutiful, loyal, and humble Representation to his Majesty and the Parliament; and to implore Relief.

This Assembly, willing to exert themselves to the utmost for the preservation of their inestimable Rights and Liberties; and having the pleasure to be informed that the Inhabitants of the other Colonies are actuated by the same principles; that some of them have, and others are about appointing Commissioners for the aforesaid purpose; Have, and do hereby appoint you to be Commissioners in behalf of this Colony, to meet those that are or shall be appointed by the other Colonies, at the proposed Congress; And do give you the following Instructions and Directions to be observed by you in discharging your trust, viz.:

You are directed to repair to New York in such season as to be ready to proceed upon business with the other Commissioners on the first Tuesday in October next.

You are also directed, and fully empowered and authorized, to unite with the other Commissioners, or the major part of them, in preparing such an humble, dutiful, and royal Representation and Address as is above mentioned; and to sign the same in behalf of this Colony: And also to join with the other Commissioners in taking the proper measures for laying the said Representation and Address before His Majesty and the Parliament, at the first opening of the session.

This Assembly have hearts filled with the sincerest affection and loyalty to His Majesty, and have the highest sense of their subordination to that august assembly the British Parliament; Nevertheless, they would assert their Rights and Privileges with becoming freedom and spirit; And therefore you are directed to use your endeavors that the said Representation and Address express these sentiments in the strongest manner.

You are further directed to assure the other Commissioners that this General Assembly will give their Agent, in London, all necessary orders and power to enable him to co-operate with the Agents of the other Colonies, in every necessary measure for procuring relief in these important affairs.

The general decay of trade and commerce, which is so severely felt in all the Plantations upon this Continent, induces us further to direct you: That if a majority of the other Commissioners shall think it prudent to make any Representation to His Majesty and the Parliament upon that subject, you join with them in an humble, dutiful Address to procure the restrictions and burdens laid upon commerce to be alleviated.

And further, if any other measure shall be proposed and agreed upon by the majority of the Commissioners who shall meet upon this occasion, for obtaining relief, you are hereby empowered to join and unite with them in such measures, if they shall appear to you reasonable and probable to answer the desired end.

To you, gentlemen, this Assembly have committed Concerns of the last consequence to themselves, to their Constituents, and to Posterity; And we hope the just sense you entertain of the importance of the Trust we have placed in you, will induce you to exert all your capacities to discharge it in such manner as to do Honor to yourselves, and service to the Colony.

APPENDIX K.

RESOLUTIONS ASSERTING THE RIGHTS AND PRIVILEGES OF THE INHABITANTS OF THIS COLONY. PASSED SEPTEMBER 1765.

(FROM THE COLONY RECORDS, PAGE 346.)

CHAP. XVIII. APP. K.

This Assembly, taking into the most serious consideration, an Act passed by the Parliament of Great Britain, at their last session, for levying stamp duties, and other internal duties in North America; Do Resolve:

1. That the first Adventurers, Settlers of this His Majesty's Colony and Dominion of Rhode Island and Providence Plantations, brought with them and transmitted to their Posterity, and all other His Majesty's subjects since inhabiting in this His Majesty's Colony, all the privileges and immunities that have at any time been held, enjoyed, and possessed by the People of Great Britain.

2. That by a Charter granted by King Charles the Second, in the 15th year of his Reign, the Colony aforesaid is declared and entitled to all the Privileges and Immunities of natural born subjects, to all intents and purposes, as if they had been abiding and born within the Realm of England.

3. This His Majesty's liege People of this Colony have enjoyed the right of being governed by their own Assembly in the article of taxes and internal police; and that the same hath never been forfeited or any other way yielded up, but hath been constantly recognized by the King and People of Great Britain.

4. That, therefore, the General Assembly of this Colony have, in their representative capacity, the Only exclusive Right to lay taxes and imposts upon the Inhabitants of this Colony; And that every attempt to vest such power in any Person or Persons whatever, other than the General Assembly aforesaid, is unconstitutional, and hath a manifest tendency to destroy the Liberties of the People of this Colony.

5. That His Majesty's liege People, the inhabitants of this Colony, are not bound to yield obedience to any Law or Ordinance designed to impose any internal taxation whatsoever upon them, other than the laws and ordinances of the General Assembly aforesaid.

6. That all the officers in this Colony, appointed by the authority thereof, be, and they are hereby directed, to proceed in the execution of their respective offices, in the same manner as usual; And that this Assembly will indemnify and save harmless all the said officers on account of their conduct agreeable to this Resolution.

CHAPTER XIX.

1768—1772.

FROM THE UNION OF PARTIES FOR RESISTANCE TO ENGLAND, APRIL, 1768, TO THE DESTRUCTION OF HIS MAJESTY'S SCHOONER GASPEE, JUNE 10TH, 1772.

THE political amnesty concluded between the rival governors, received the popular sanction by an overwhelming vote. Josias Lyndon was chosen governor by nearly fifteen hundred majority, carrying twenty-three towns. In the other five towns small majorities were given for the late deputy-governor, whose great popularity was signally attested during the next seven years. Nicholas Cooke was elected deputy-governor, and the assistants were equally divided among the partisans of the contending interests. CHAP. XIX. 1768. April 20.

When the Massachusetts circular, addressed to the other colonial assemblies, reached England, it gave great 15.
offence to the government. Copies of it were at once enclosed in a royal circular to the other twelve colonies, 21.
denouncing it as "factious," and requiring the assemblies to treat it "with the contempt it deserves," by taking no notice of it. A clause, which does not appear in Hillsborough's circular to Rhode Island, further ordered the governors to dissolve their assemblies should they give countenance to the "seditious paper."[1] In several colo-

[1] Bancroft's History of United States, vol. vi., p. 144.

CHAP. XIX. 1768. nies this was done, and Massachusetts was still further commanded to rescind the resolutions upon which the appeal had been made, upon penalty of forfeiting its government. So exasperated had the ministry become by this open attempt at combination, that no chance of reconciliation, or of any alleviation of the grievances that had caused it remained, while this measure continued unretracted. The last Parliament but one that was ever to legislate for America, was returned at this crisis. It was imbued with the same hostile spirit of its predecessor, and took early measures to coerce the colonies, whom a little gentleness might still have retained. While such excited feelings existed in the two countries, it was natural that collisions should occur between the officers of one and the
May 3. people of the other. A fatal affray between some people at Newport, and three midshipmen of the Senegal, man-of-war, lying in the harbor, resulted in the death of Henry Sparker, who was run through the body by an officer named Thomas Careless. The coroner's inquest returned a verdict of wilful murder. Another man was severely wounded. As the Superior Court did not meet till September, the Assembly, upon petition of the prisoners,
4. granted a special court for their trial in June, when they were acquitted on the ground of self-defence. The com-
14. plaints of the Revenue Board produced another circular from the ministry, calling on the respective governments to sustain the custom-house officers in the discharge of
31. their duties. Charles Dudley was deputed by the Board to be collector and surveyor of Rhode Island in place of Robinson, who had become one of the new commissioners.
June 8. A more serious result of these complaints was a peremptory order to Gen. Gage to send a regiment to Boston, and the despatch of a naval force by the Admiralty, to sustain Bernard. This was the first direct act of hostility against the colonies, soon to be followed by resistance on one hand, leading to greater rigor on the other. At the same time an affair occurred in Boston, which increased

the hatred between the people and the officials. The CHAP. XIX.
Romney, a fifty-gun ship ordered from Halifax by the
commissioners, impressed some New England seamen, one 1768.
of whom was rescued. On the same evening, the sloop June 10.
Liberty, belonging to John Hancock, was seized upon
pretence of smuggling, and anchored under the guns of
the Romney. A riot ensued, and the commissioners took
refuge with the troops at Castle Island. No proceedings
were had against the rioters, but the people in town meeting requested the governor to procure the withdrawal of 14.
the Romney, which he had no power to do. The General Court was then in session. The council condemned
the conduct of the rioters, but the lower house took no
notice of the matter. The Rhode Island Assembly met at 13
the same time, but did not refer to these events, although
the public mind was greatly agitated by them. The
newspapers contained full accounts of all these transactions.
At a town meeting in Providence, an address to John
Dickinson was adopted, expressing a cordial concurrence 20.
in the views maintained by him in the letters of "A
Farmer," and concluding with the "hope that the conduct
of the colonies on this occasion will be peaceable, prudent,
firm, and joint; such as will shew their loyalty to the best
of Sovereigns, and that they know what they owe to
themselves, as well as to Great Britain." For this ad- July 7.
dress, Dickinson returned a letter of thanks, commending
the stand taken by the town of Providence in defence of
their rights.[1] Similar addresses were sent to him from all
parts of the country. The circular that had been sent in
behalf of the revenue officers in the several governments
two months before, was now repeated in favor of the com- 11.
missioners, upon whom the entire regulation of these subjects devolved. The spirit of resistance was gaining
ground, and popular demonstrations for freedom were
becoming frequent. A great elm in front of Olney's 25.

[1] Staples' Annals, 219–21; Providence Gazette, June 25, 1768.

CHAP. XIX. tavern in Providence was dedicated as a tree of liberty in the presence of a large assemblage, before whom an oration was pronounced by Silas Downer.[1] 1768. Aug. 14. Upon news of the affair of the sloop Liberty reaching England, two more regiments were ordered from Ireland to be sent to Boston. The circulars addressed to the colonial governors had of late been submitted by them to their legislatures, and often become the basis of offensive action. To prevent this, Sept. 2. an order was issued, forbidding any letter, or portion thereof, from the ministry, to be shown to the assemblies without express permission from the King. 12. The adjourned session of the Rhode Island Assembly was rich in correspondence. An address to the King, praying relief from the recent revenue acts, with a letter to Hillsborough on the same subject, and another in reply to his about the Massachusetts circular, wherein the sentiments of that paper were defended, and regret was expressed that it had been denounced by the ministry as "factious or disloyal," were prepared. Replies to the late government circulars, on the obstructions offered to custom- 17. house officers, were also sent, denying that such hindrances had occurred in this colony; and copies of former letters, relating to the action of the House in regard to the sufferers by the stamp act riot, and urging payment of the war money so long unjustly withheld from Rhode Island, were transmitted to the ministry.

In obedience to the royal mandate, Gov. Bernard had suppressed the Massachusetts legislature, on the first of July, upon their refusal the day previous, by a vote of ninety-two to seventeen, to rescind the resolutions upon which "the seditious circular" was based. The expected 12. arrival of troops caused a town meeting to be held in Boston, to request the governor to convene the General

[1] This discourse was printed, and a copy is preserved by the R. I. Historical Society. The words pronounced by Downer in the act of dedication are given by Judge Staples.—Annals of Providence, 222; Providence Gazette, July 30, 1768.

Court. Upon his refusal to do so, a convention of dele- CHAP.
gates from the whole province was called, to meet at XIX.
Boston in ten days. One hundred and four towns and 1768.
districts, nearly every settlement in Massachusetts, were Sept. 22.
represented in this first popular convention. Bernard
again refused to summon a general court, and denounced
the convention as treasonable. The attempt to quarter
the troops upon the town, under the new billeting act,
while the government barracks were yet unfilled, was
clearly illegal. The law was on the side of the people, in
resisting the demands of Gage and Bernard. The convention sat six days and adopted an address to the King, and
a letter to their agent, vindicating the province from the
charge of rebellion, but protesting against Parliamentary
taxation and standing armies. Scarcely had they ad- 27.
journed, when eight ships of war and several transports,
with about a thousand troops, arrived at Boston. The 28.
ships being arranged so as to command the town, the Oct.
troops were landed. Part of them encamped on the 1.
Common, and others, after some delay, were allowed a
temporary shelter in Fanueil Hall and the Town House;
but the people positively refused to provide for their support, beyond the express letter of the act of Parliament,
which required the action of the legislature, a body that
no longer existed in Massachusetts. Gen. Gage came in
person from New York to settle the difficulty, but with- 15.
out success. He was compelled to hire houses in which
to quarter his men, and to furnish them from the military
fund. At the same time further changes occurred in the
cabinet. The Earl of Shelburne, who had succeeded Gen.
Conway as one of the colonial secretaries, was removed to
give place to Rochford, a pliant tool of the Duke of Grafton, whose ascendency was now complete. Chatham
resigned the seals. The glory of England was soon to be
shorn of its lustre.

In Rhode Island the Assembly established the salary 26.
of the deputy-governor at fifteen pounds, being one-half

CHAP. XIX. that of the governor. They also incorporated the Whipple Hall Society of Providence. This was an educational
1768. movement made by the proprietors of "Whipple Hall," a building erected in the north part of Providence for a private school, which afterwards became the first district
Nov. school, and continued for sixty years.

8. At the opening of the new Parliament, the factious spirit of the colonies formed the burden of the royal ad-
10. dress. Additional forces, sent to crush this spirit, reached Boston, and soon about four thousand troops, with a formidable fleet, were present to overawe the town. But no rebellion existed, no overt act of treason had been committed, non-importation agreements were not unlawful, and the denial of a right to tax was not a forcible resistance to authority. There was nothing for the military arms to effect, unless it was to provoke rebellion. Gage, having vainly tried to induce the people to provide
24. for the troops, quartered them at the expense of the crown, and returned to New York. That the determination of King and Parliament to yield none of their pretensions, but to use their power upon the people of Boston in order to test the question of supremacy, was irrevocable, became manifest in the addresses of both Houses, in
15. reply to the King's speech. It was further displayed in Hillsborough's letter to Rhode Island, enclosing copies of these addresses, and disapproving the petitions and letters sent by the Assembly in September. Finally the
Dec. Parliament ordered that the offenders in Massachusetts should be sent to England to be tried, under a statute of
1769. 35 Henry VIII., for treason committed abroad. In vain
Jan. did Edmund Burke, Col. Barre, and the old governor Pownall, who had grown liberal with age, oppose in the Commons this rash decision. Lord North, although his own judgment and feelings were on the side of America, was the too faithful mouthpiece, as well as minister, of
26. the King. At his request the resolutions were introduced in the Commons, and carried by a large majority. But

the scheme was impracticable as well as unjust, and could never be carried out. CHAP. XIX.

In reply to the letters respecting the war money due to Rhode Island, Hillsborough wrote that they had been laid before the Lords of the Treasury, together with a communication from Dr. Moffat stating that, although he had presented a sworn estimate of his losses to the Assembly, indemnity was still denied him. 1769. Feb. 20.

At the winter session the General Assembly occupied themselves entirely with domestic affairs. Laws were passed making the real estate of a deceased person liable for his debts, exempting school and church lands from taxation, incorporating Trinity Church in Newport, the earliest instance of the incorporation of a church in this colony, and allowing the furnace company in Scituate to keep up their dam in the spring, notwithstanding the requirement of the old law for protecting fisheries.[1] The general estimate of ratable estates having been completed, was adopted by statute as the basis for future taxation. The entire valuation of the colony amounted to £2,111,295 10*s.* 7*d.*, or, $7,037,652, at the current value of lawful money, six shillings to a dollar.[2] A tax of six thousand pounds, lawful money, and of all the outstanding old tenor bills, amounting to £93,687 15*s.* 2*d.*, was assessed. Six shillings, lawful money, was now worth eight pounds, old tenor. At the general election, Joseph Wanton, the father of the late deputy-governor, Col. Wanton, was chosen governor, and Darius Sessions, deputy-governor, and continued to hold their offices by annual election, the former for seven years, and the latter for six years, until near the period of independence. The Assembly appointed a committee of inquiry, to report at the next session, 27. April. 19. May 3.

[1] The same privilege was granted, February, 1770, to the old Furnace company on the south branch of the Pawtuxet River.

[2] In this report the towns are arranged by counties. The valuation of Newport County is £705,274 14*s.* 4*d.*; of Providence, £530,908 10*s.* 4*d.*; of Kings, £540,748 14*s.*; of Bristol, £99,914 7*s.* 1*d.*; and of Kent, £234,449 4*s.* 10*d.*

CHAP. XIX. 1769. upon what proceedings had been had in reference to the sufferers by the stamp act riot, and also to answer Lord Hillsborough's letter concerning the statement of Dr. Moffat.

The hostility of the people to the revenue officers, was increased by the injustice of government, respecting this affair, and manifested itself in unlawful acts. A gross outrage was committed at Providence upon the person of Jesse Saville, a tide waiter of the custom-house. While in the discharge of his duty, he was violently assaulted and then tarred and feathered. A reward of fifty pounds sterling for the perpetrators of this act was vainly offered by the commissioners of customs.

May 18.

June 2.

3\. The interesting phenomenon of the transit of Venus, was observed with great accuracy in Providence. Joseph Brown, distinguished no less for his scientific acquirements than for his commercial enterprise, procured a complete set of the necessary instruments, a reflecting telescope, micrometer, and sextant, to be made in London. An observatory was erected on the hill, where the street since called, in commemoration of the event, Transit street, is laid out, and every pains was taken to secure a perfect observation that should determine the latitude of the place. Mr. Brown was assisted by Gov. Hopkins, Dr. Benjamin West, and other gentlemen interested in scientific subjects.[1] The result of the calculations, established the latitude of Providence to be 41° 50′41″ north. The longitude, determined by the immersions of Jupiter's satellites, compared with similar observations at Cambridge, was found to be 71° 16′ west from Greenwich.[2]

[1] These were Moses Brown, Dr. Jabez Bowen, Joseph Nash, and Capt. John Burrough. Dr. West wrote a pamphlet upon this matter, entitled "An Account of the Observation of Venus upon the Sun," 22 pp., Providence, 1769. It was dedicated to Gov. Hopkins, and is now very scarce.

[2] These results, when we consider the defective character of the instruments employed, as they would be considered at this day, approximate very closely to those obtained by the U. S. Coast Survey, by which the position

In Newport the same observations were conducted by Rev. Dr. Stiles, the instruments being furnished by the liberality of Abraham Redwood. CHAP. XIX. 1769.

May 16. In Virginia, the House of Burgesses unanimously passed a series of resolutions; that in them was vested the sole right of taxation for the colony; that the right of petition, and of obtaining the concurrence of other colonies therein, was indisputable; that the right of trial by jury within the colony was sacred, and the conveying of persons to England to be tried was a violation of justice; and that an address, setting forth these sentiments, should be transmitted to the King. The speaker was ordered to send copies to every colonial assembly, requesting their concurrence. Lord Boutetort, the governor, upon hearing of these resolves, immediately dissolved the legislature. The Rhode Island Assembly cordially approved the action of Virginia, and replied to the letter of Peyton Randolph, speaker of the House. In fact, these resolutions went hardly as far, and certainly no further, than those already adopted four years before in Rhode Island, at the suggestion of the Providence town meeting, the substance of which had previously been introduced by Patrick Henry, and a portion of them rejected by the Virginia legislature.[1] But what had then elicited a warm debate, and was passed by a close vote in Virginia, was now a unanimous act of that patriotic body. The progress of free principles is apparent in the contrast which four years presents in the conduct of the leading southern colony. The Assembly enacted that special courts of Common Pleas might be held for the prosecution of custom-house officers charged with violations of the fee list established by the colony, or with neglect of duty; the decisions of such courts to be final. June 12.

April. Meanwhile great excitement existed in England, soon

of the cupola of University Hall, Brown University, was ascertained to be lat. 41° 50′ 17″ N., long. 71° 23′ 40″.

[1] See *ante*, chap. xviii., p. 261, and App. K.

CHAP. XIX. 1769. April. to be equally aroused in America, at the arbitrary conduct of Parliament in repeatedly declaring vacant the seat of John Wilkes, member for Middlesex. This popular demagogue, whose vices and whose subsequent treachery proved him to be unworthy of the position to which talent and circumstances conspired to raise him, came, by the imprudence of his enemies, to embody the principle of free representation. For years the hostility of the King had been displayed towards Wilkes. A scandalous poem and a seditious pamphlet had presented the first opportunity, six years before, for a civil prosecution as a means of removing his obnoxious presence from the House of Commons.[1] But he had been four times returned by an enthusiastic constituency, who regarded him as a martyr to tyranny. The last time, Col. Luttrell, his opponent, was declared elected, although having but one-quarter of the votes, Wilkes being held as incompetent for a seat. This was a great stretch of prerogative and a dangerous infringement upon the British constitution. London was filled with tumult. "Wilkes and Liberty" became the rallying cry, and for once the Americans found sympathy among the people of England when their own cherished rights were assailed by an obstinate King, and an obsequious Parliament. The old party names of Whig and Tory, were now revived in England to designate the foes of prerogative, and the

[1] The poem was an Essay on Woman, a paraphrase of Pope's Essay on Man, and represented by Rev. Mr. Kidgell, who wrote an account of it, as the most blasphemous and obscene work ever printed. The name of the Bishop of Gloucester was appended to the notes, for which the author was arrested, upon complaint of the House of Lords, for breach of privilege. A very few copies of it were privately printed at Wilkes' own house, but three of which appear to have got into circulation, as was proved upon the trial; so that it could not be said to have been published, but Wilkes' opponents made great use of it against him. The pamphlet was No. 45 of the North Briton, a series of political articles written by Wilkes, of which this number was pronounced to be "a seditious libel" upon the authority of Parliament. It was ordered to be burnt by the common hangman, and its author imprisoned. These events occurred in November, 1763.

"friends of the King," and were applied in America to the opponents of Parliamentary usurpation, and to the partisans of the government. CHAP. XIX. 1769.

The disturbances in London, combined with the determined resistance of the colonies, brought the ministry to a pause in their mad career. A meeting of several colonial agents with Lord Hillsborough, communicated to July 5.
Rhode Island by Sherwood, obtained from him the assurance that all idea of raising a revenue in America had been abandoned, and that the late revenue act, except the tax on tea, would shortly be repealed. The motion to repeal Townshend's act had already been made by Pownall, and referred to the next session of Parliament. Before Hillsborough's circular, announcing this intention, reached America, more serious demonstrations occurred in Rhode Island. The British armed sloop Liberty, Capt. William Reid, cruising in Long Island Sound and Narraganset Bay, in search of contraband traders, had needlessly annoyed all the coasting craft that came in her way.
Two Connecticut vessels, a brig and a sloop, were brought 17.
into Newport on suspicion of smuggling. An altercation ensued between the captain of the brig and some of the Liberty's crew, in which the former was maltreated, and his boat fired upon from the vessel. The same evening the people obliged Reid, while on the wharf, to order 19.
all his men, except the first officer, to come on shore to answer for their conduct. A party then boarded the Liberty, sent the officer on shore, cut the cable, and grounded the sloop at the Point. There they cut away the mast and scuttled the vessel, and then carried her boats to the upper end of the town, and burnt them. This was the first overt act of violence offered to the British authorities in America. Meanwhile the two prizes got under way and escaped. Gov. Wanton, at the request of the collector and Comptroller, issued a proclamation for the arrest of the offenders, and the Revenue Board at Boston offered a reward of one hundred pounds

CHAP. XIX. sterling to any one who would inform against them, but
without effect.

1769. July New York had been the first to adopt non-importation
agreements, and was zealous to maintain them, writing to
the other colonies to renew them, in consequence of which
25. a meeting was called at the liberty tree in Providence,
but the proceedings are not preserved. The contemplated
repeal of Townshend's act did not produce the intended
effect. It was not the tax, but the principle of the bill,
that gave offence, and that principle was distinctly recognized
in the proposed repeal. "There must always be
one tax to keep up the right," said the King to Lord
North,[1] and the threepence duty upon tea was therefore
27. excepted from the general repeal. At Boston the merchants
voted that a partial repeal was insufficient, and
renewed their agreement not to import British goods, except
a few specified articles. At this juncture, Gov. Bernard,
who had recently been made a baronet, was recalled,
31. and Lieutenant-governor Hutchinson was again left
at the head of the provincial government. In Newport
the merchants, exasperated at the heavy charges made by
the custom-house officers, bound themselves to pay no
more than the regular fees prescribed by a law of the
colony, to prevent strangers from being imposed upon in
like manner, and to aid each other in prosecuting the
officers for any such violations of the legal fee list.

Aug. 4. The payment of the war money of 1756, was still withheld.
Hillsborough wrote in reply to the June letter,
that nothing could be done about it till the opinion of the
Lords of the Treasury upon the papers submitted to them
was known.

Sept. 7. Four years had elapsed since the College at Warren
was organized, and the graduating exercises of commencement
day now opened a new era, and established
the earliest State holiday in the history of Rhode Island.

[1] Bancroft's U. S., vol. vi., p. 277.

CHAP. XIX.

It was a great occasion for the people of the colony, and as each recurring anniversary of this time-honored institution of learning calls together from distant places the widely-scattered alumni of Brown University, we do but renew, on a more extended scale, the congratulations that crowned this earliest festival of Rhode Island College. The first graduating class consisted of seven members, some of whom were destined to fill conspicuous places in the approaching struggle for independence.[1] It was noticed as a significant fact that all who participated in the events of the day, from the President to the candidates, were clothed in American manufactures. 1769. Sept.

The dispute respecting the northern boundary, settled fifty years before, and subsequently revived on the complaint of Massachusetts,[2] was again brought up, after eighteen years silence, upon petition of Moses Brown, 11.
and a committee appointed to examine the subject.[3] Augustus Johnston renewed his claim for indemnity for losses by the stamp act riot, and a committee was directed to inquire into the facts.

Upon a suggestion from New York, the Providence Oct. 10.
merchants extended the non-importation agreements indefinitely, until every portion of the revenue act should

[1] The members of this class were Charles Thompson, Valedictorian, and afterwards a chaplain in the revolutionary army; Richard Stites, salutatorian; Joseph Belton, Joseph Eaton, William Williams, William Rogers, afterwards a chaplain in the revolutionary army, and James Mitchell Varnum, afterwards a Brigadier-General in the Revolution, an eloquent member of Congress from Rhode Island, and finally Judge of the North-western Territory.

[2] Ante, chap. xvii., p. 180.

[3] They reported in October, referring to the attempt to run the line in 1750, and to the joint interest of Connecticut in having it properly established, and recommended that that colony be invited to consult with the Rhode Island committee upon the measures to be taken for a proper adjustment of the line. The extent of land claimed, as appears by Mr. Brown's memorial, February, 1770, was 4 miles 56 rods in width along the whole northern line of 22 miles in length. On 23d March, 1770, Mr. Brown wrote to Gov. Trumbull, giving a history of the matter to that time, and asking the cooperation of Connecticut. Trumbull Papers, vol. iii., p. 40.

CHAP. XIX. be repealed. Boston adopted the same course. There was a division of sentiment in the country upon this ques-
1769. Oct. tion, some being disposed to accept the partial repeal as a conciliation from the ministry, and consequently to import to a certain extent, while others insisted upon no relaxation of the measures already adopted. In many places individuals delayed to sign the new agreement, and
10–24. repeated meetings were called. In Providence four were held within two weeks, before the arrangement was perfected by the adhesion of all the merchants in the import trade.

A murrain had again broken out among cattle on the island, and at the same time many cases of hydrophobia appeared among dogs. To prevent the spread of these
25. disorders, it was forbidden to export cattle from the island to any other town, and the town councils were empowered to take such action as they deemed best on the subject. A dog law was also passed, authorizing every freeman to kill dogs found running at large anywhere in the colony. These acts were to be in force for four months. The Virginia resolutions of May, which had been received and approved in June, were now formally adopted by a vote of the House, and an address to the King, as therein recommended, was prepared.

Nov. The town of Newport was now at the height of its prosperity. The population numbered more than eleven thousand. Industrial enterprises were numerous and varied, embracing extensive manufactories of oil, candles, sugar, rum, and hemp. Nearly two hundred vessels were employed in foreign commerce, among which there was a regular line of London packets, and between three and four hundred coasting craft conducted the domestic trade.[1] As yet no permanent College buildings had been erected at Warren, and the ultimate location of the institution

[1] The town contained 17 manufactories of sperm oil and candles, 5 rope walks, 3 sugar refineries, 1 brewery, and 22 rum distilleries. Bull's Memoirs of Rhode Island.

depended upon the relative subscriptions that might be CHAP.
made for it in different towns. The corporation, at a meet- XIX.
ing held in Newport, allowed six weeks for the inhab- 1769.
itants to raise their subscription and present their claim Nov.
to have it established in that county. The town entered warmly into the contest, with every prospect of success, and the Mercury contained stirring appeals to the 20
people upon the advantages to result from securing it there.[1]

A ship from London having arrived at Providence Dec.
with some goods that were in violation of the non-importation agreement, these articles were surrendered by the 9.
importers to a committee, to be stored until the repeal of
Townshend's act. The perplexities of the ministry led 1770.
the Duke of Grafton to resign his place, and Lord North Jan. 23.
became prime minister. The colonies had become the
great question in England, their proceedings were watched
with an interest never before felt, and orders were sent by Feb.
Hillsborough to require not only copies of the laws, but 17.
of the journals of each legislative meeting, to be sent to him.

A petition was presented to the Assembly, again to 26.
divide the town of Providence, and to erect the west side into a separate town to be called Westminster; but it was not granted.[2] The statute regulating the distribution of real property among the heirs of persons dying intestate, was passed at this session. Such estate, held in fee simple, was to be divided, a double portion to the eldest son, the remainder in equal shares among the other children; or if no son, then equally to all the children; and if no children, then equally among the next of kin, or their representatives, the widow's dower being in all cases reserved.

[1] Newport Mercury, Nov. 20, and Providence Gazette, Nov. 25, 1769.

[2] A census return dated January 1, 1768, states the number of houses on the west side of the river in Providence at 102, and the people at 911, of whom 189 were children from 5 to 14 years of age, fit for school. Foster Papers, Miscel., vol. xi.

CHAP. XIX. The arrogance of the royal troops, and the restiveness of the people under an open and arbitrary attempt at
1770. coercion, led to an attack upon the soldiers, and the firing
Mar. 5. upon the populace, known as the "Boston massacre," by which five of the rioters lost their lives. It was a repetition, on a larger scale, of the Sparker affair at Newport, and with nearly the same result. At the trial of the prisoners in October, they were defended by John Adams and Josiah Quincy, two of the popular leaders, and were all acquitted except two, who were convicted of manslaughter and slightly punished. On the same day with this bloodshed, Lord North moved the long-promised repeal of Townshend's act, except the duty on tea. A few
April 9. days later Pownall moved to include tea also, on grounds of expediency. This was defeated, because it would be a surrender of the right to tax the colonies, but the repeal passed.

18. On the day of the annual town meetings for casting proxies for general officers, Gov. Ward again appeared as a candidate, and carried several towns, but Wanton received a handsome majority, and the same officers as
May 2. last year were declared elected. The struggle for the location of the College was decided in a meeting of the
Feb. 7. corporation, by twenty-one to fourteen, in favor of Providence, which had proved the ablest competitor in the subscription. Newport had raised four thousand pounds, and Providence two hundred and eighty more. Warren and Greenwich had both sought to obtain it, but were surpassed by their more wealthy and populous rivals.
Mar. 27. The site was chosen, and ground broken for the foundation as soon as the season would permit, and in seven
May 14. weeks the corner-stone was laid by John Brown, in presence of many friends of the institution. Dr. Manning, resigning the charge of the church at Warren, which he held in connection with the Presidency, removed at once with the undergraduates, to Providence. The building was occupied by the students in December.

CHAP. XIX.

1770. May 31. The effect of the repeal of Townshend's act was soon felt in a relaxation of the non-importation agreement throughout the colonies. The Boston and Rhode Island merchants decided to renew the imports of British and India goods, but a few days later a town meeting in Providence resolved that this action was too hasty, and that for the present the old agreements be adhered to, until the tax on tea should be repealed.

June 6. A committee to wait on the merchants with this decision, reported that they had agreed to countermand all orders except for certain specified articles. The list was not satisfactory, and the town voted that only such goods as were included in the old agreement, and were imported by the other colonies, should be allowed.

11. The General Assembly granted a petition to divide the town of Warren, and incorporated that portion of it west of Warren River by its former name of Barrington. Thus Barrington became for the second time a distinct township, and Warren was divested of the larger portion of its territory.[1] Newport had imported goods in violation of the agreement, and great indignation against the whole colony was thereby aroused. Meetings were held in the southern and western colonies to break off all trade with Rhode Island. But opinion was everywhere much divided upon the question of continuing the restrictions upon commerce, and soon nearly all the colonies came to the decision to import any article, except tea. A few still held out, but within three months the agreements were everywhere virtually rescinded, and tea alone remained subject to prohibition. Providence had been included in the denunciations against Newport, and took measures at a town meeting to show that they were undeserved, for the merchants there had quietly submitted to the action of the people. The proofs presented were

July. Aug. 28. Sept. 5.

[1] Barrington was first incorporated by Massachusetts in 1718, and remained a separate town till the annexation to Rhode Island in 1747, when it was merged in Warren. Ante, chap. xvi., p. 162.

CHAP. XIX. 1770. satisfactory to the Boston merchants, who adopted a vote exculpating Providence from the accusations that had been made against Rhode Island.

Sept. 10. The Assembly prohibited the currency of old tenor bills after the first of January, and required that they should be exchanged for treasury notes, having one year to run, at the rate of six shillings, lawful money, for eight pounds. A tax of twelve thousand pounds was assessed, two thousand for current expenses, and the remainder to redeem treasury notes formerly given for redemption of bills of credit. The laws for restraining Indian and colored servants, and regulating the manumission of slaves, in Newport, were revised. Those found abroad after nine o'clock at night were to be confined in a cage, instead of the jail, till morning, and then to be whipped with ten stripes unless redeemed for a small sum by their masters. In cases of manumission, the owner was to give proper security that the subject should not become a public charge, and the free papers were to be recorded. Suitable penalties were imposed for violations of any part of this law, and a failure to conform thereto invalidated an act of manumission. The statute applied only to Newport, where, however, the greater portion of the slaves in the colony were held. A bill was also ordered to be prepared, to prevent the further importation of slaves into Rhode Island, but no action was had upon it at present.

8. Orders were received from England to deliver up Castle William to Gen. Gage, to be further fortified and garrisoned by regular troops. This was a direct violation of the Massachusetts charter, by which the command of the forts, as well as the militia, was vested in the governor, and this fort had been built and maintained at the expense of the colony. But Hutchinson obeyed the order, and himself took refuge in the fort for several days, through fear of the indignation which this betrayal excited.

Oct. 3. The jail in Kings county was broken open in the night,

CHAP. XIX.

by persons in disguise, and the prisoners, the greater part
of them counterfeiters, of whom one, named Casey, was
under sentence of death, were released, and made their 1770.
escape upon horses provided for them by the liberators. Oct.
The Assembly offered a reward of fifty pounds for the 29.
perpetrators of this outrage, and the same for the recovery
of Casey. Oliver Arnold, attorney-general of the colony, 9.
died at this time. He had held the office for five years,
having succeeded Johnston, who resigned after the stamp
act riot. His great reputation as a lawyer and scholar
caused his death, at the early age of thirty-four years, to
be deeply lamented. A violent storm again blew down a
part of the spire of Trinity church at Newport, and caused 19.
an immense loss of life and property along the coast.
Newport suffered very severely in this gale. A few
weeks later, two large fires also occurred there, the first Dec.
destroying several dwellings, and injuring the custom- 28.
house, and the second sweeping a large number of stores 1771. Jan.
with much valuable property from one of the wharves. 18.

A year of unusual quietness commenced. Nothing of much importance happened. There was a lull in the political storm, both in America and England, and hopes of a peaceable adjustment of pending disputes began to revive. Even Franklin wrote that if no new disturbances occurred to aggravate the government, every thing might
be settled in a satisfactory manner. Hutchinson received Mar. 14.
his commission as governor of Massachusetts, and between him and the General Court, the usual disagreements continued, but without serious result. The revenue system, that constant source of vexation, destined ultimately to precipitate the war of revolution, was everywhere disregarded. Smuggling was almost openly carried on, and occasional altercations occurred in consequence. Hillsborough, in a letter to Rhode Island, repeats the com- July 19.
plaints of the commissioners of customs, with regard to
these disputes, and refers to one in which the collector at
Newport had lately been maltreated, but no other record April.

CHAP. XIX. 1771. April of such an affair, as happening during this year, appears. Botta speaks of a tumult at Providence, in which the King's ship Wasp was burnt, but this must be an error, as no trace of such an event can be found, and no vessel of that name was at Rhode Island.[1]

17. May 1. There was no opposition to the existing officers at the spring election. The Assembly appointed Henry Marchant, the new attorney-general, who was about to visit England, to be joint agent with Sherwood in behalf of the colony, especially for the recovery of the old war debt. A petition to set off the village of Pawtuxet from Warwick and Cranston, and erect it into a distinct town, was referred with an order of notice. This project was several times attempted, but never with success. Gen. Gage had written to Gov. Wanton, requesting that quarters should be provided for the sixty-fourth regiment. The consideration of the letter was postponed, and the governor was desired, in case the troops should arrive, and supplies be asked for before the next session, to convene the Assembly. A recruiting party of the twenty-ninth regiment was already at Fort George, and the accounts for their maintenance presented by the captain of

June 10. the fort and others, were allowed, as under the old billeting act. A charter of incorporation was granted to the Second Congregational church at Newport, under the charge of Dr. Stiles. This was the third church incorporated by the Assembly.[2] Appeals to England from the decision of the Superior Court were restricted to suits involving more than three hundred pounds currency.

[1] Botta's History of the War of Independence, edit. 1826, vol. i., p. 107. This is no doubt a mistake both in name and date, for the destruction of the Gaspee, which took place the next year, and of which Botta makes no mention. The ships of war stationed at, or that put into Narraganset Bay that year, were the frigate Arethusa, 36 guns; ships Lizard, 28, Rose, 20, Mercury, 24, Swan, 20, Hind, 20, Kingfisher, 14, Viper, 12; schooners, Gaspee, 8, and Vesper, 14. Bull's Memoirs.

[2] The first was Trinity at Newport, February, 1769; the second, the Benevolent Congregational at Providence, October, 1770.

CHAP. XIX. 1771.

Marchant was directed to carry with him a statement of the northern boundary claim, in order to obtain a decree, if possible, to have the line established in accordance with the charters of Massachusetts and Rhode Island. A new and more complete insolvent law was enacted, whereby debtors were enabled to obtain a discharge, with the assent of a majority, in number and amount, of the creditors, by surrendering all their property, real and personal, to the creditors, upon oath, unless a reasonable suspicion of fraud should exist. The majority of assenting creditors, or the Judges of the Court, were to appoint three assignees to carry out the terms of the surrender, whose powers and duties were fully prescribed in the act. Certain necessary articles of furniture were allowed to be retained by the insolvent, and should the dividend upon his estate amount to seventy-five per cent. of his debts, he was permitted to reserve five per cent., or if it was only fifty per cent., then two and a half per cent. for his own support. Perjury on the part of the petitioner for the benefit of the act was punished with imprisonment, the pillory, and the loss of one ear.[1] A tax of twelve thousand pounds, equal in amount, and for the same purposes, with that of the last year, was assessed. A lottery for building the market-house in Providence was granted.[2] This mode of raising money for all purposes, civil or religious, had become so common, that scarcely a session occurred without one or more of these grants being made. Aug. 19.

Gov. Hutchinson, following an old form in the provincial charter, which gave to the governor of Massachusetts the command of the militia and forts in Rhode Island, and being instructed in his commission to conform thereto, enclosed a copy of that clause of the charter to Gov. Wanton. The firmness of Rhode Island from the outset, Sept. 2.

[1] This act was repealed the next year, in May, 1772.

[2] The corner-stone of the Market-house was laid on Tuesday, June 8th 1773, by Nicholas Brown. Providence Gazette, June 12, 1773.

CHAP. XIX. 1771. had rendered this provision nugatory. The experience of Sir William Phipps, eighty years before, of Bellemont, of Dudley, and of every royal governor since their times, might have served as a hint to Hutchinson to spare himself the futile labor of the notice. A singular proposal,
Oct. 16. from Bristol, was made through the press, by one who styled himself "A friend to Property," and was disaffected to the existing government of the colony, to overthrow its constitution. Arguing that in small States an elective legislature must always be a source of disorder and corruption, he proposed that a committee be appointed, who should either divide the colony between Massachusetts and Connecticut, or apply to the King for a royal governor to be placed over it. A spirited reply was made a
24. few days later, from the same town, denouncing the proposed change, and demolishing the pleas upon which it rested.

Roads, bridges, and public buildings, occupied the Assembly at its autumn session. The new court-houses in Providence and Greenwich were ordered to be finished, and a new prison to be built in Newport. Provision was made for repairing bridges, and erecting new ones in different parts of the colony. The highway law was revised so as to require the surveyors, upon penalty of a fine, to perform their duty, and to compel the inhabitants to work four days annually upon the roads. The year passed away, as it had begun, very quietly; but the lull in the tempest was nearly over, and the fiercer blast was soon to come.

1772. A memorable instance of the triumph of law over popular prejudice, occurred early in the year. One David Hill, of Wrentham, was detected by the committee of inspection at New York, in selling goods included in the non-importation agreements. They induced him to deposit the property with a merchant until the revenue acts should be repealed. A mob seized the goods and destroyed them. Hill brought an action in Rhode Island,

CHAP. XIX.

where he found property belonging to some of the committee, alleging that he had given up his goods upon compulsion. The case was tried before the Superior Court, upon appeal from the Common Pleas, where a verdict had already been rendered for Hill, and the ablest counsel in the colony were employed on both sides. The public feeling was strongly against the plaintiff, for his claim was adverse to the cause of liberty. The judges were subject to annual election. The jurors were returned from different towns in Providence county, and were never charged by the court. Yet the Superior Court confirmed the judgment of the Inferior, and gave the plaintiff two hundred and eighty-two pounds damages and costs. Under all the circumstances this verdict, in favor of a stranger, against their own prejudices, and in a case where patriotism itself would seem to dictate an opposite course, shows a reverence for law and a regard for justice, on the part of both bench and jury, that entitle them to the highest honor; while the subsequent re-election of the court by the Assembly, a few weeks later, enhances our respect for that popular tribunal.[1] This affair is the more honorable to the court and the colony from the fact that while it was in progress, the people were harassed by the conduct of his Majesty's schooner Gaspee, of eight guns, which, in company with the Beaver, had been stationed in Narraganset Bay, to enforce the revenue acts. Lieutenant Duddingston, the commander, had practised every annoyance upon vessels in the bay, detaining them often without a colorable pretext, stopping even market boats, and in some cases plundering the people on shore. He had violated the charter of the colony in acting without

1772. Mar. 20.

21.

[1] The court was composed of Ex-Governor Stephen Hopkins, Chief-Justice; James Helme, 2d; Benoni Hall, 3d; Metcalf Bowler, 4th; Stephen Potter, 5th. They were elected in June, 1770, again in May, 1771, and re-elected after this most unpopular but righteous decision in May, 1772. A protracted controversy upon points involved in the case was conducted in the papers after the trial. Annals of Providence, 228; Providence Gazette of March 28th, April 4th and 18th, May 2d and 9th, 1772.

CHAP. showing his commission, and had exceeded his authority
XIX. by making illegal seizures, and sending captured prop-
1772. erty to Boston for trial, contrary to an act of Parliament
that required such trials to be held in the colony where
Feb. the seizure was made. His arbitrary conduct had
20. already excited public attention, and was cautiously re-
29. ferred to in the papers of the day. Complaints were
made by the inhabitants of Providence to deputy-govern-
or Sessions, who, upon consulting Chief-justice Hopkins,
received as his opinion "that no commander of any vessel
has a right to use any authority in the body of the colony,
without previously applying to the governor, and showing his warrant for so doing, and also being sworn to a
Mar. due exercise of his office." Sessions then communicated
21. the complaints, and the judge's opinion, to Gov. Wanton,[1]
who immediately sent the high sheriff on board the
22. schooner, with a letter to the commanding officer, requiring him to produce his commission and instructions. The
23. next day Duddingston sent, by a junior officer, an arrogant reply, to which Gov. Wanton answered directly, re-
peating his demand, and assuring Duddingston of safety
in coming on shore. Duddingston enclosed the correspondence to Admiral Montagu at Boston, who took sides
April with the lieutenant, and addressed an extremely insolent
8. letter to Gov. Wanton, defending the conduct of Duddingston, ridiculing that of the governor, and threatening,
in case the rescue of any prize was attempted, "to hang
May 6. as pirates" the parties concerned. Gov. Wanton laid this
letter before the Assembly, together with his very spirited
8. reply, in which he informs Montagu, "that I do not receive instructions for the administration of my govern-

[1] Original in Foster Papers, vol. iv., printed in "Documentary History of the Destruction of the Gaspee," by Hon. William R. Staples. 56 pp. double column 8vo, Providence, 1845, where all the correspondence, depositions, and journals of the commission of inquiry are published; and to which the reader is referred as authority for the statements of the text, without making specific references to each document consulted by the author on this subject.

ment from the King's Admiral stationed in America." The Assembly directed copies of the correspondence to be sent to England, with a narrative of the proceedings referred to therein. CHAP. XIX. 1772. May

The other matters presented at this session were of less importance. A sale of one-half the right of a spring of water on the west side of the river at Providence, had been made by John Feild to certain parties, for the purpose of conveying water in pipes to that part of the town. These persons were incorporated as the Feild's Fountain Society, with ample powers for their object. This is the earliest instance of a charter of this kind being granted in the colony.[1] A spirit of opposition to law was manifested in New Shoreham by a combination of the people to resist the service of writs and executions. To remedy this evil, the inhabitants were cited to appear, at the August session in Newport, to show cause, if any existed, why some more effectual law should not be made, applicable to that town.

Gov. Wanton wrote to Lord Hillsborough, complaining of Montagu's insolence, and of the conduct of the 20.
Gaspee and Beaver. Duddingston also wrote to the Admiral, giving the details of his first interview with Wan- 22.
ton, and admitting that he had knowingly violated the law by sending a captured sloop with rum to Boston, but had expected the commissioners of customs there would sustain him, because he knew the prize could not be safely retained at Newport. He also states that the owner of the rum was Mr. Greene of Coventry, a member of the House; if so it was Nathaniel Greene, soon to become a great leader of the revolutionary armies.[2] Meanwhile

[1] The Rawson's Fountain Society in Providence was incorporated at the October session the same year. The Cooke's Fountain Society in East Greenwich was incorporated in October, 1773.

[2] In this Duddingston was mistaken, as he soon had occasion to know. The owners were Jacob Greene & Co., of Warwick. The firm consisted of Jacob, William, Elisha, Christopher, and Perry Greene, who soon afterwards, at the July term of the Common Pleas, brought suit and recovered

CHAP. XIX. 1772. the vexatious interference of the armed vessels continued, until an occasion offered for the destruction of the Gaspee. The sloop Hannah, Capt. Benjamin Lindsey, from New June 8. York, arrived at Newport, reported at the custom-house, and the next day proceeded up the river. The Gaspee, 9. as usual, gave chase, but ran aground on Namquit, since called Gaspee Point, below Pawtuxet, and the Hannah escaped, arriving safely at Providence about sunset. The situation of the enemy was soon proclaimed by beat of drum, calling upon those who desired to go and destroy the vessel, to meet that evening at the house of James Sabin.[1] Eight long-boats with five oars each, were provided by Mr. John Brown, and soon after ten o'clock the party embarked at the wharf directly opposite the house, and proceeded with muffled oars, but undisguised, upon their daring enterprise. Capt. Abraham Whipple, afterwards commodore, who three years later fired, in Narraganset Bay, the first American broadside ever discharged at any portion of his Majesty's navy, commanded the expedition. It was long past midnight when the party approached the vessel, where they were joined by another boat from Bristol. Twice the hail of the sentinel

judgment against Duddingston for the illegal seizure. Nathaniel Greene, the future general, was at that time a deputy from Coventry.

[1] This house, then unfinished, was occupied as an inn. It was soon afterwards purchased and completed by Welcome Arnold, who resided there till his death in 1798. It then became the residence of his eldest son, Samuel G. Arnold, father of the writer, and subsequently of his youngest son, Richard J. Arnold, the present owner, who has altered and enlarged it materially within a few years. It is now the winter residence of the author of this history. The house is No. 124, on the east side of South Main Street, at the north-east corner of Planet Street. This brief sketch of the history of a homestead may find an excuse in the rich revolutionary associations that surround it. The year before his death, Colonel Ephraim Bowen, the last survivor of the Gaspee expedition, wrote an account of that affair, which was engrossed by his daughter, and now hangs in the dining-room of the old mansion, the identical room in which the plot was laid. A copy of Colonel Bowen's narrative will be found in Appendix L at the close of this chapter.

was disregarded, when Duddingston himself, leaping on the gunwale, hailed, but received no answer. A second time he hailed and was answered, in terms energetic and profane, by Whipple, who, at the same time, ordered his men to spring to their oars. Shots were then fired from the vessel and returned by the boats. While Whipple was replying, a musket ball, fired by Joseph Bucklin, wounded the lieutenant in the groin, and as he fell the attacking party boarded the schooner at the bow, and after a brief struggle, drove the crew below, and became masters of the deck. The men surrendered, were bound, and put on shore. Duddingston was severely wounded in the arm and body. He was attended by Dr. John Mawney, then a student of medicine, who accompanied the expedition as surgeon. This was the first British blood shed in the war of independence. CHAP. XIX. 1772. June.

It was near daylight, when, the lieutenant's wounds 10.
being dressed, he was landed at Pawtuxet, and the captors, having set fire to the vessel, returned to Providence. In the flames of the burning Gaspee were consumed that night the last hope or wish of pardon. The forms of law were to be complied with, a few short years of increasing irritation and of earnest preparation were to ensue, but the end was already foreseen, and for this colony there alone remained to prepare, quietly but with vigor, for the inevitable war.

Midshipman Dickenson sent a report of the capture 11.
to the Admiral, who transmitted a copy of it to Gov. Wanton, with the request that he would take measures to apprehend the offenders. Deputy-governor Sessions also advised that a large reward should be offered for their
detection, and stated that such was the opinion of the 12.
principal gentlemen in the town. The governor issued his proclamation accordingly, offering one hundred pounds sterling to any person who would furnish evidence sufficient for conviction. An active correspondence ensued 15.
between the governor, the admiral, and the lieutenant, 16.

CHAP. XIX. whose wounds, though severe, proved not to be mortal, and an account of the capture was sent to Lord Hills-
1772. borough by Gov. Wanton.

July. But the excitement occasioned by this daring act, did not prevent the steady course of justice. It is one of the most striking facts connected with the affair, that at the
20. July term of the Common Pleas in Kent county, an action was brought by Jacob Greene and Company, against Duddingston, for the rum and sugars seized by him in the spring, on its passage from Greenwich to Newport, and sent to Boston for condemnation. A verdict for the plaintiffs was rendered, with two hundred ninety-five pounds damages and costs. Duddingston appealed to the Supe-
Dec. rior Court, but failing to appear, the case went by default. He afterwards petitioned the Assembly for a new trial, on the ground of unavoidable detention from the meeting of the court. The petition was granted on condition that he would deposit the amount of the judgment with the clerk of the court to await the result.

A mulatto slave, named Aaron Briggs, who was engaged in the expedition, and afterwards escaped from his master and went on board the Beaver, came near exposing the whole party, most of whom were among the leading men in Providence, with some from Bristol. Admiral Mon-
July 8. tagu forwarded his deposition to Gov. Wanton, requesting him to arrest the persons therein named, for examination; but Wanton, although eventually a loyalist, instead of
10, 11, 16. obeying the request, took depositions invalidating the testimony of Aaron, and forwarded them to Montagu, who,
22. although unconvinced, as he afterwards informed Wanton, was obliged to rest satisfied, and detained the slave. The Assembly approved the conduct and correspondence
Aug. 17. of the governor in this affair, and also appointed the deputy-governor and chief-justice to inquire, in behalf of Duddingston, concerning a sum of money belonging to him in the hands of a man who refused to surrender it, and advised Duddingston, in case these referees could not

settle it, to adopt his legal remedy. It should be remembered that suits against Duddingston for his illegal acts were threatened before the destruction of the Gaspee, and still maintained, but the case of Hill had proved that these would not prevent his receiving justice in any good cause where he might be a plaintiff. CHAP. XIX. 1772. Aug.

To present an unbroken narrative of these important events, requires that we should pass over to the next chapter the occurrences of a year following the destruction of the Gaspee, and confine our attention to that subject alone. When the news reached England, the King's
proclamation was issued, offering a reward of one thou- 26.
sand pounds each, for the arrest and conviction of the two leaders of the affair, and five hundred pounds each for any other of the offenders, with a free pardon, in addition, to any one concerned, except the two chiefs, who would
implicate the rest. A commission was issued to Joseph Sept. 2.
Wanton, governor of Rhode Island, Daniel Horsmanden, Frederick Smythe, and Peter Oliver, chief-justices of New York, New Jersey, and Massachusetts, and Robert Auchmuty, judge of vice-admiralty at Boston, or any three of them, to inquire into and report upon the facts. Instructions were given for their guidance, by the third article 4.
of which they were required to communicate to the government of Rhode Island any information they might obtain as to the persons concerned in the outrage, that they might be sent to England for trial.

Meanwhile Lieutenant Duddingston had returned to Oct. 16.
England, and was there tried by court-martial on board the Centaur, man-of-war, at Portsmouth, for the loss of the Gaspee. Upon a full inquiry he was honorably acquitted.

The commission and instructions were sent to Admiral Dec. 11.
Montagu, and by him transmitted to Gov. Wanton, who
at once notified the commissioners. The King's procla- 14.
mation was posted by the sheriffs throughout the colony, 22.
and the Admiral was informed that the court would prob- 24.
ably assemble in about a week. Upon the arrival of the 31.

CHAP. XIX. New York and New Jersey judges at Newport, Wanton
wrote to Montagu that a quorum was in attendance, and
1773. desired his presence. Montagu excused himself, but sent
Jan. 2. full powers to Capt. Keeler of the Mercury, the senior
officer on the Newport station, to act in his stead, who
4. was summoned to attend at the opening of the court.
5. The next day the commissioners met at the State House
and continued in session three weeks. Montagu's pres-
14. ence was deemed essential, and he accordingly came to
20. Newport, but returned in a few days. Duddingston had
gone to England, and it was chiefly in regard to his evidence that the Admiral was summoned. But the incle-
ment season, the engagements of the Admiral, and the
absence of Duddingston, so retarded proceedings, that at
the end of three weeks, spent in correspondence and in
25. taking a few depositions, the court adjourned for four
months.

Mar. 26. The Admiralty instructed Montagu that he might intrust to Capt. Keeler his business with the court of inquiry,
unless his presence with them should be indispensable.
May 24. He accordingly sent to Keeler two of the Gaspee's company who had been sent out from England to identify the
27. prisoners, should any be taken. Keeler notified Gov.
Wanton, as president of the commission, of their arrival,
but as he could not come on shore, on account of a writ
being out against him, he desired notice of the time of
meeting that he might send one of his officers with the
31. witnesses. The full court being assembled, proceedings
June 1. were resumed. Further testimony was taken, and the
depositions of Aaron and others having been submitted to
the Justices of the Superior Court, their presence was
7. requested by the commissioners. It was shown that
Aaron's evidence was obtained under compulsion by
Capt. Linzee, of the Beaver, and hence was entitled to no
12. weight. The commissioners declined to express an
opinion on this point, contrary to that of the justices.
Nothing was discovered upon which an arrest could be

made. It was proposed to inquire into the affair of the schooner St. John, that occurred nine years before, but the motion was overruled by a majority of the commissioners. After an abortive session of three weeks, a final report to the King was prepared, announcing the failure to make any material discovery in the matter, and the belief "that the whole was conducted suddenly and secretly." The facts in the case were briefly stated, the action of the inhabitants and of the local government thereupon was rehearsed and commended, and the conduct of Duddingston in the execution of his powers was blamed as imprudent and arbitrary. The opinion of the Justices upon the testimony of Aaron was cited and approved, and the conduct of Capt. Linzee, in obtaining that deposition by force, was censured. The court then adjourned.

CHAP. XIX. 1773. June 22.

24.

The most honorable feature in the whole transaction, is that the large rewards, amounting from six hundred to eleven hundred pounds sterling, were offered in vain. The perpetrators of the deed were well known. They were among the most prominent citizens of the colony, and some of the younger and more rash accomplices, had openly boasted of the occurrence the next day, while the smoke of the burning vessel yet darkened the sky. The court of inquiry were composed of loyalists who were honest and earnest in their examination, but no direct evidence could be obtained, except that of the slave whose testimony was successfully impeached.

Much has been said in chronicle and song, of a later achievement in the adjoining province, where a party, disguised as Indians, threw overboard a cargo of tea; while the captors of the Gaspee, until a very recent date, have remained almost "unknown, unhonored, and unsung." The Boston tea party have been lauded for performing an act of exalted patriotism and unequalled daring. But we submit that the seizure of a merchantman requires less courage than the capture of a man-of-war, while the pa-

CHAP. XIX. 1773. triotic impulse that would face, undisguised, the desperate danger of the latter enterprise, is no less worthy of historic fame. The affair of the Gaspee is still more deserving of commemoration as it was the first bold blow, in all the colonies, for freedom, and the earliest blood shed in the war of independence. It was the beginning of the end. The Revolution had commenced.

APPENDIX L.

AN ACCOUNT OF THE CAPTURE AND BURNING OF THE BRITISH SCHOONER GASPEE.

APP. L. In the year 1772, the British Government had stationed at Newport, Rhode Island, a sloop-of-war, with her tender, the schooner called the Gaspee, of eight guns, commanded by William Duddingston, a lieutenant in the British navy, for the purpose of preventing the clandestine landing of articles subject to the payment of duty. The captain of this schooner made it his practice to stop and board all vessels entering or leaving the ports of Rhode Island, or leaving Newport for Providence. On the 10th day of June, 1772, Capt. Thomas Lindsey left Newport in his packet for Providence, about noon, with the wind at north; and soon after the Gaspee was under sail in pursuit of Lindsey, and continued the chase as far as Namcut Point, which runs off from the farm in Warwick, about seven miles below Providence, and is now owned by Mr. John B. Francis, our late governor. Lindsey was standing easterly with the tide on ebb, about two hours, when he hove about at the end of Namcut Point, and stood to the westward, and Duddingston, in close chase, changed his course and ran on the point near its end and grounded. Lindsey continued in his course up the river, and arrived at Providence about sunset, when he immediately informed Mr. John Brown, one of our first and most respectable merchants, of the situation of the Gaspee. He immediately concluded that she would remain immovable until after midnight, and that now an opportunity offered of putting an end to the trouble and vexation she daily caused. Mr. Brown immediately resolved on her destruction, and he forthwith directed one of his trusty shipmasters to collect eight of the largest long-boats in the harbor, with five oars to each, to have the oars and row-locks muffled to prevent noise, and to place them at Fenner's wharf, directly opposite the dwelling of Mr. James Sabin, who kept a house of board and entertainment for gentlemen, being the same house purchased a few years after by the late Welcome Arnold, one of our enterprising merchants, and is now owned by and is the residence of Col. Richard J. Arnold, his son. About the time of the shutting of the shops, soon after sunset, a man passed along the Main street, beating a drum, and informing the inhabitants of the fact, that the Gaspee was aground on Namcut Point, and would not float off until 3 o'clock the next morning, and inviting those persons who felt a disposition to go and destroy that troublesome vessel, to repair in the evening to Mr. James Sabin's house. About 9 o'clock I took my father's gun, and my powder-horn and bullets, and went to Mr. Sabin's, and found the south-east room full of people, where I loaded my gun, and all remained there till about 10 o'clock, some casting bullets in the kitchen, and others making arrangements for departure; when orders were given to cross the street to Fenner's wharf and embark, which soon took place, and a sea-captain acted as steersman of each boat, of whom I recollect Capt. Abraham Whipple, Capt. John B. Hopkins, (with whom I embarked,) and Capt. Benjamin Dunn. A line from right to left was soon formed, with Capt. Whipple on the right, and Capt. Hopkins on the right of the left wing. The party thus proceeded till within about sixty yards of the Gaspee, when a sentinel hailed, "Who comes there?" No answer. He hailed again and no answer. In about a minute Duddingston mounted the starboard gunwale in his shirt, and hailed, "Who comes there?" No answer. He hailed again, when Capt. Whipple answered as follows: "I am the sheriff of the county of Kent, God damn you; I have got a warrant to apprehend you, God damn you, so surrender, God damn you." I took my seat on the main thwart, near the larboard row-lock, with my gun by my right side and facing forwards. As soon as Duddingston began to hail, Joseph Bucklin, who was standing on the main thwart by my right side, said to me, "Eph. reach me your gun, I can kill that fellow." I reached it to him accordingly, when, during Capt. Whipple's replying, Bucklin fired and Duddingston fell, and Bucklin exclaimed: "I have killed the rascal!" In less time than a minute after Capt. Whipple's answer, the boats were alongside of the Gaspee, and she was boarded without opposition. The men on deck retreated below, as Duddingston entered the cabin. As it was discovered that he was wounded, John Mawney, who had for two or three years been studying physic and surgery, was ordered to go into the cabin and dress Duddingston's wound, and I was directed to assist him. On examination it was found that the ball took effect

CHAP. XIX. APP. L.

about five inches directly below the navel. Duddingston called for Mr. Dickinson to produce bandages and other necessaries, for dressing the wound, and when finished orders were given to the schooner's company to collect their clothing and every thing belonging to them, and put them into their boats, as all of them were to be sent on shore. All were soon collected and put on board the boats, including one of our boats. They departed and landed Duddingston at the old still house wharf at Pawtuxet, and put the chief into the house of Joseph Rhodes. Soon after, all the party were ordered to depart, leaving one boat for the leaders of the expedition, who soon set the vessel on fire, which consumed her to the water's edge.

The names of the most conspicuous are Mr. John Brown, Capt. Abraham Whipple, John B. Hopkins, Benjamin Dunn, and five others, whose names I have forgotten, and John Mawney, Benjamin Page, Joseph Bucklin, and Turpin Smith, my youthful companions, all of whom are dead, I believe every man of the party, excepting myself; and my age is eighty-six years this twenty-ninth day of August, eighteen hundred and thirty-nine.

August 29th, 1839. EPHRAIM BOWEN.

The reader will observe two discrepancies between the above narrative and that given in the text; one as to the name of Capt. Lindsey, which was Benjamin, as given in the papers of the day, and not Thomas, as stated by Col. Bowen; the other as to the date of the affair. The Hannah arrived at Newport on the 8th of June, and the next afternoon proceeded up the bay, chased by the Gaspee. The attack was planned and executed on the night of the 9th, but not completed, by the burning of the vessel, till daylight of the 10th, so that either date, the 9th or 10th, is applicable to the event.

CHAPTER XX.

1772—1776.

FROM THE CAPTURE OF THE GASPEE, JUNE 1772, TO THE CLOSE OF THE COLONIAL PERIOD, MAY 4th, 1776.

CHAP. XX.

1772. June

WHILE the capture of the Gaspee was exciting the public mind throughout the colonies, and while the bold assertion of the supremacy of law over arbitrary power was being made in Rhode Island, by the trial of Duddingston upon a civil suit for damages, a case involving the high question of freedom in another form was agitating the courts and the people of England. For some years past the subject of negro slavery had been discussed in Massachusetts, and two years before this time an act to prohibit the further importation of Africans was moved in the Assembly of Rhode Island. The case of Somerset, a slave from Virginia, taken to England by his master, and there refusing service, for which he was about to be shipped to Jamaica for sale, came up, on a writ of habeas corpus, before the Court of King's Bench. The famous decision of Lord Mansfield declared that slavery 22.
could only exist by positive law, and that the contemplated action of the owner in this case, was directly contrary to the laws of England. He therefore decreed the discharge of Somerset, and proclaimed the doctrine that slavery could not exist on English soil. The effect of this decision upon the colonies, was to confirm the views already expressed by many writers, to stimulate legisla-

CHAP. XX. tion against the system, and to hasten the emancipation of slaves in New England.

1772. Aug. 17. The General Assembly laid another tax of twelve thousand pounds, being the third of this amount, and for similar purposes, in annual succession. The crime of horse stealing had become so frequent, that a severe statute was enacted against it. The estate of the offender was to be confiscated, he was to be three times publicly whipped with thirty-nine lashes, to be banished from the colony, and in case of his return to suffer death. A reward of six pounds was to be paid to any one who should arrest the thief, and the horse might be recovered by its owner without regard to any sale, the old legal maxim *caveat emptor*, being specially applied to the purchase of horses.[1] The small-pox having again been introduced by a vessel arriving at Newport, it was proposed in the Assembly to allow the practice of inoculation. This preventive, which humanity owes to the Turks, was violently opposed by

Oct. 26-7-8 29. many persons.[2] In Newport, town meetings were held on four successive days, to instruct their deputies on the subject. The attendance was very full, and the vote close, but only once did the advocates of inoculation secure a small majority of seven, the decision in the other three cases being adverse upon a larger, but yet closer vote. In

28 consequence of this the Assembly rejected the proposition, and the only mode of prevention that remained was that of quarantine or the hospital. The occasions for firing royal salutes from the fort were established. They were the birth-days of the King and Queen, the anniversaries of the accession and coronation of his Majesty, and election day. The accounts of the sufferers by the stamp act riot were again discussed, reductions in them proposed,

[1] This act was essentially modified at a later day, but some of its provisions remained in force until a recent period. For the last infliction of whipping in Rhode Island, which was for this cause, see chap. v. vol. i., p. 129, note.

[2] For a note upon this subject, see chap. xii. vol. i., p. 523.

and the proceedings ordered to be sent to England, with another application for the payment of the old war debt. The thanks of the colony were voted to Henry Marchant, 1772. Oct. who had returned home with encouraging reports, never to be realized, of the prospect of speedy payment. Lotteries for several churches were granted, among which was one for King's Church in Providence, now St. John's, which also was incorporated at this session.

On the day that this Assembly met, an important movement was commenced in Boston, to state the rights of the colonies, with the infringements thereon, and to communicate the same to the other towns in the province, with the request for an interchange of views on the subject. To the attempts to tax the colonies and to restrict their trade, was added a new cause of complaint—the proposal in the instructions to the Gaspee commissioners, to send the guilty parties to England for trial. The action of Boston met with a ready response from the other towns, Nov. 20. and when the report of the committee upon rights and violations was made, the movement was already well advanced, and the spirit of resistance was freely manifested throughout the province.

A short session of the General Assembly was held, at Dec. 14. which nothing of interest was done. In this first stage of the revolution, committees of correspondence were preparing the results, and performing the duties which, at a later period, devolved upon the legislatures. The affair of the Gaspee occupied all minds. Hutchinson proposed to annul the charter of Rhode Island, and a committee[1] 25. wrote to Samuel Adams for his counsel in the matter. His reply was an appeal for union, since "an attack upon 28. the liberties of one colony was an attack upon the liberties of all."[2] The year closed amid gloomy forebodings of evil. The court of inquiry upon the destruction of the

[1] This committee consisted of Deputy-Governor Sessions, Chief-Justice Hopkins, John Cole, and Moses Brown.

[2] Bancroft's History of U. S., chap. xlviii., vol. vi., p. 441.

CHAP. XX. Gaspee, opened the new year. Their failure has already
been detailed. The Assembly convened at Greenwich
1773. while the court was sitting at Newport, as if to watch
Jan. 11. their proceedings, but nothing occurred on the part of
the commissioners to call for legislative action. Gov. Wanton exhibited his instructions to arrest the offenders, and send them to England for trial. This was a severe blow to the colony, thus to be singled out as the victim of royal displeasure, and to bear the test of an unconstitutional decree. But resistance was determined upon. Chief-Justice Hopkins asked the advice of the Assembly what course he should adopt, and was told to use his own discretion when the case arose. "Then, for the purpose of transportation for trial, I will neither apprehend any person by my own order, nor suffer any executive officers in the colony to do it,"[1] was the prompt reply of this fearless champion and earliest advocate of colonial freedom. Fortunately the results of the commission did not warrant an arrest, and the inevitable crisis was yet for a time delayed.

The arrogant temper of Admiral Montagu was not
19. allayed by his visit to Rhode Island. He complained to
the Admiralty that proper respect was not shown to his flag, the fort having failed to salute upon his arrival. Lord Dartmouth, who, the preceding August, had succeeded the Earl of Hillsborough as American Secretary,
Mar. 3. rebuked the colony for this neglect, and ordered that the
broad pennant should, in all cases, receive in Rhode Island, as elsewhere, the customary honors.

The Boston movement to unite all the towns in the province, with an ultimate view to a similar union of the
4. colonies, was approved by the legislature of Virginia, and
immediately extended, by that body, over all the colonies. Resolutions, advising the appointment of intercolonial
12. committees of correspondence were unanimously passed,

[1] Letter of Dr. Stiles, of Newport, February 16, 1773, in Bancroft's History of U. S., vol. vi., p. 451.

and sent to every colony for general approval and adoption. Thus was created at once, in effect, an American Confederacy, to complete which but one more step was needed—that these several committees should convene and form an American Congress. It was reserved for Rhode Island, ere long, to propose this final measure for the formation of the American Union. CHAP. XX. 1773. March

The suits against Duddingston were not the only evidence given by the people of this colony of their determination to make the military subordinate to the civil power. To maintain their chartered rights was ever the object nearest to their hearts, and this could only be secured by firmness of conduct in every case that infringed upon their liberties. The naval officers, unused to a freedom that dared to hold them personally accountable for their acts, were overbearing in their mode of fulfilling their commissions. The loss of one vessel, and the harassing suits against her commander, had not sufficed to convince the officers of the spirit of the people, or to subject them to the control of the civil laws. Since these events, Capt. Keeler, of the Mercury, the senior officer on the station, had arrested, in September last, the master and mate of the brig Spywood, at Newport, from the West Indies, and had seized a portion of the cargo legally entered at the custom-house. Two actions of trespass were brought against him by the officers, and one of trover by the owner of the brig, which were tried at this term of the 19.
Superior Court, and verdicts found for the plaintiffs in each case. It has already been mentioned, that at the adjourned meeting of the court of inquiry in May, Keeler May
was unable to attend on account of writs being out against him which prevented his coming on shore.

Although the May session of the Assembly was always short, and usually confined to the election of 5.
officers, the one now held was extremely important, on account of the action of the deputies in response to the house of burgesses in Virginia. They unanimously

CHAP. XX. 1773. May adopted the proposals made by that body, and in conformity therewith, were the first to follow the example of Virginia in electing a committee of correspondence, whose duties were "to obtain the most early and authentic intelligence of all such acts and resolutions of the British Parliament, and measures of the ministry, as may relate to, or affect, the British colonies in America; and to maintain a correspondence and communication with the other colonies, respecting these important considerations."[1] They were directed to obtain from the governor a copy of the commission and proceedings of the Gaspee court of inquiry; to report the further action of said court from time to time, and to transmit copies of the same to Virginia and to all the other legislatures. The committee
15. immediately sent out its circulars to the other colonies, extolling the patriotism of the Virginia resolutions, and urging a prompt compliance with the proposals. Warlike precautions were also taken at this time. The platforms for the battery at Fort George were repaired, and new carriages were made for the guns formerly used on the colony war-sloop. The people of New Shoreham renewed their petition for a harbor at Block Island, to be made by opening the passage from the salt pond, which had been closed for many years, and a committee was appointed to examine the locality, who reported favorably as to the feasibility of the plan.

The embarrassed condition of the East India company, led to further legislation in Parliament on their behalf. The drawback upon teas exported to America, which had lately been reduced to three-fifths of the duty, was now
10. revived as to the whole. The act went into effect at this time, and arrangements were made for sending large

[1] This committee consisted of Metcalf Bowler, a deputy from Portsmouth, Associate Justice of the Superior Court and Speaker of the House; Ex-Governor Stephen Hopkins, a deputy from Providence, and Chief-Justice of the colony; Moses Brown, Wm. Bradford, a deputy from Bristol; Henry Marchant, Attorney-General; Henry Ward, Secretary; and John Cole.

quantities of tea to America. It was proposed also to CHAP.
remove the import duty of threepence a pound, but to XX.
this the ministry would not consent. The determination 1773.
to tax America upon principle was irrevocable, and another trial on a larger scale was soon to be made.

The death of Joseph Sherwood deprived the colony of June 1.
the services of one who for fourteen years had been its agent in London. But the time was at hand when colonial agents would no longer be required at the British capital.

The exposure of the letters of Gov. Hutchinson, and 2.
other enemies of freedom in America, which Franklin had obtained in England and sent over to Massachusetts, caused great excitement. They were published in the papers with indignant comments. Among them was the letter of George Rome, written six years before, denouncing the government and courts of Rhode Island, and now first brought to light.[1] This letter was printed in the newspapers, and on broadside, and circulated throughout the colony as the incendiary missive of a secret foe. Aug. 16.
It was read in the General Assembly by the Speaker, a debate ensued, and its further consideration was postponed till the original, which alone could furnish the basis of legal action, could be obtained from Massachusetts. Its author was denounced at town meetings in Providence,
Johnston, and Coventry, and their deputies were instruct- 31.
ed to inquire into the truth of the charges therein contained, and, if found to be false, then to endeavor to bring the writer to justice as a public defamer.

An act was pending in Parliament to regulate the fisheries in the Gulf of St. Lawrence, the terms of which alarmed those engaged in that pursuit. A petition on
the subject was presented to the Assembly, in consequence 16.
of which a letter to Lord Dartmouth was prepared, praying that the freedom of the fisheries might not be restrict-

[1] This letter was written December 22, 1767, and is referred to under that date in chap. xviii.

CHAP. XX. 1773. ed. The debts of Thomas Ninigret, late sachem of the Narragansets, having been discharged by the sale of lands belonging to the tribe, the remaining lands were secured to them, beyond the contingency of debt, and the bounds were ordered to be surveyed. A tax of four thousand pounds was assessed, one-half to pay certain claims on the colony, and one-half for current expenses. The annual expenses of government at this period, did not vary much from two thousand pounds, lawful money, or about six thousand six hundred sixty-seven dollars.

Oct. 16. When the news of shipments of tea to four of the principal American ports was received, Philadelphia was the first to oppose the attempt, in a public meeting, by the adoption of a series of eight resolutions, wherein the consignees were requested to resign, and whoever should aid in receiving the cargoes, was pronounced as "an enemy to his country."[1] No teas were shipped to Rhode Island,
27. so that the Assembly took no action on the subject.
29. George Rome was brought to the bar of the house of deputies, upon a warrant, to answer for his libellous letter. Refusing to reply directly to the questions put to him at the examination, he was committed to jail at South Kingstown, for contempt, till the close of the session.

Nov. 5. The Philadelphia resolutions were adopted in Boston, and a vain effort was made to induce the consignees to resign. Several meetings were held through the month for this purpose, but with a like result. At length the first cargo of the "pernicious weed," so long expected, arrived
28. at Boston. People flocked in from the neighboring towns
29. to attend a great meeting, at which it was determined to send the ships back to England without discharging their teas. A permanent volunteer guard, varying from twenty-four to thirty-four men, was placed around the wharf. The consignees took refuge in the castle, but refused to
30. return the teas. The governor sent the sheriff to disperse

[1] The resolutions were printed in the Providence Gazette of October 30, 1773.

the meeting which had assembled to receive the reply of CHAP. XX.
the consignees. He was received with hisses and a refusal to dissolve. The owners of the ship, however, agreed 1773.
that the tea should not be landed. The arrival of another Dec. 3.
tea ship increased the excitement. She was moored by
the side of the first, that the same guard might watch
both. The committee of correspondence wrote to Provi- 5.
dence, Bristol, and Newport, and to other places, for advice and co-operation. A third tea ship soon followed, and 10.
was placed at the same wharf with the others. Meetings
were held daily in Boston and other towns. The twenty
days, when it would be lawful for the custom-house to
seize the first ship and land the teas, had nearly elapsed.
The crisis had arrived. A vast assemblage, estimated at
seven thousand men, gathered in Boston to take the deci- 16.
sive step. It was evening when the owner of the ship
appeared, and announced that the governor had refused a
permit for the vessel, without which she could not pass
the guns of the castle. Samuel Adams dissolved the
meeting, and at the same instant the war-whoop sounded,
and a body of forty or fifty men, disguised as Indians,
passed down to the wharf, stationed guards to prevent in-
trusion, and taking possession of the three ships, in about
two hours threw overboard all the tea, amounting to
three hundred forty-two chests. Another vessel with tea 1774.
was wrecked on Cape Cod, and a portion of the damaged Jan. 1.
cargo was landed at Castle William. The ships destined
for other ports, warned by the fate of those at Boston,
and finding no consignees upon their arrival, either returned at once to England, or had their cargoes seized for
the duties, and stored in the custom-house.

The people of Newport, anticipating an attempt on the
part of the East India Company to introduce their tea at
that place, called the first meeting held in Rhode Island 12.
on this subject. They adopted resolutions similar to those
in Philadelphia, and also agreed to sustain the other colonies in their measures. Copies of the proceedings were

CHAP. XX. 1774. Jan. 19. sent to all the towns, with a request that they would pursue the same course. Providence followed the example the next week, and in a short time most of the other towns in the colony held meetings for the same purpose. Some of these confined their attention to the duty on tea, while others entered more at large into the grievances of the colonies.[1]

27. When the news of the Boston tea party reached England, the feeling against America became intense. Franklin had already presented the petition of Massachusetts for the removal of Governor Hutchinson and of Chief-
29. Justice Oliver. At the hearing before the Privy Council, he was treated with great indignity, the petition was rejected, and his office of deputy-postmaster for America, in the execution of which he had organized, upon a remunerative basis, the postal system of the colonies, was taken from him. The Lords of the Council triumphed that day over the venerable patriot, but confessed, a few years later, that it was a costly victory. A series of meetings in the several towns of Rhode Island were held during the
Feb. 2. next two months, commencing with Westerly, the home of Gov. Samuel Ward, whose patriotic spirit prepared and supported a set of resolutions that covered the whole ground of colonial complaint. The idea of a general congress, to which he was destined to be one of the first appointed delegates, was already familiar to many minds, and was broached by the various committees of corre-

[1] Warren held the next meeting, Westerly met on February 2d, Little Compton on the 3d, Middletown on the 9th, South Kingstown, Jamestown, and Hopkinton followed, Bristol and Richmond on 28th, New Shoreham on March 2d, Cumberland 18th, Barrington 21st. The Middletown resolutions on 9th February were the most concise. "Mr. John Clarke, moderator. The town came into the following resolves:—1. Resolved, That we will have nothing to do with the East India Company's irksome tea, nor any other subject to the like duty. 2. Resolved, That we will heartily unite with our American Brethren in supporting the inhabitants of this continent in all their just rights and privileges; and we do disown any right in the Parliament of Great Britain to tax America. Voted and passed. Witness, John Barker, town clerk."

spondence. At a public meeting in Boston, John Hancock, another future delegate, proposed it in direct terms.[1] The movement was hastened by the conduct of the British ministry in preparing a series of acts to punish the town of Boston. The proposal of Lord North to this effect, was so favorably received by the House of Commons, that he at once introduced the famous act known as the Boston Port Bill, closing that harbor against all commerce. After a short debate it passed without a division, and in the House of Lords was carried almost unanimously.

CHAP. XX. 1774. Mar. 14. 18. 25. 29.

The removal of Franklin from his lucrative position of superintendent of the American post-office, was not so disastrous to the colonies as it might have been, had they not already taken the subject in hand, and prepared to organize a postal system independent of Great Britain. William Goddard, formerly printer of the Providence Gazette, and of late engaged in the same business at Philadelphia and Baltimore, undertook the arduous task of re-organizing the system throughout the colonies. He prepared a plan, and visiting every colony, submitted it to the consideration of the people, by whom it was cordially approved. The existing system was opposed as being "unconstitutional, and a usurpation of the British Parliament no longer to be borne." The act by which it was established, was denounced as being "a revenue act, formidable and dangerous to the liberties of America, as the officers have it in their power to intercept our communications, to extort what they please, and to employ them to divide us and then to enslave us."[2]

Immediately following the Boston Port Bill, came the appointment of General Gage to be governor of Massachusetts, in place of Hutchinson, who, it was rumored, was about to return to England. Thus were united the powers of commander-in-chief of the armies in America,

April 2.

[1] On 5th March.

[2] Letter of William Cooper, clerk of the committee of correspondence in Boston, to the committee of correspondence in Newport.—Boston, March 29, 1774.

CHAP. XX. to those of civil governor over a rebellious province. Four regiments of troops were ordered to accompany
1774. April Gage to his destination. The new governor was instructed to send home the chiefs of the insurrection, especially Samuel Adams, Hancock, and Warren, for trial.

Yet one more effort was made in the British Parliament for reconciliation. It was proposed to repeal the
19. duty on tea. In the debate that ensued, Edmund Burke delivered that splendid oration, the first in the series of his published works, which might have saved an empire had its eloquence and arguments availed aught against the foregone conclusion of the Commons and the ministry.

28. The next act against Massachusetts was a virtual abrogation of the charter, vesting all power in the governor, and abolishing town meetings, except for the election of local officers. This was followed by a third penal bill, transferring for trial to Nova Scotia, or England, any servants of the crown who might be charged with murder committed, in support of government, in any of the colonies. A singular and permanent result of this measure to the British people, was the abolishment of secret debates in Parliament. A fourth bill, revising the old billeting act, provided for quartering troops in Boston. The fifth and last act in this legislative drama, called the Quebec act, designed to prevent the union of Canada with the other colonies, guaranteed the church property to the French Roman Catholics, restored the civil law, and extended the boundaries of the province to the Mississippi on the west and the Ohio on the south. All of these bills, introduced in rapid succession, were passed by very large majorities. But the tragedy of Lord North was rehearsed in Parliament with greater success than attended its reception by the American people.

May 4. At the meeting for election, the Assembly ordered a census of the colony to be taken, and appointed one man in each town for that purpose. The result showed the entire population to be 59,678, of whom 54,435 were

whites, 3,761 blacks, and 1,482 Indians.[1] Renewed at- CHAP.
tention to military matters began to be shown. Arming XX.
and drilling were undertaken at private expense. A de- 1774.
termined spirit was aroused, which contemplated further May
and united resistance to British aggression. The House of Deputies of Rhode Island had sent a circular to all the colonies, urging immediate union for the common safety. Favorable replies had already been received from the greater number. Important events now succeeded each
other in rapid succession. The news of the Boston Port 10.
Bill hastened the crisis. A conference of committees from the neighboring towns was called at Boston, and on
the day that it met, Metcalf Bowler,[2] Speaker of the 12.
Rhode Island Assembly, brought to them the joyful news that every government had acceded to the proposals of the circular, and the preliminaries for a union were complete. The next day Gen. Gage arrived, and landed at 13.
Castle William, where Hutchinson had some time before
taken refuge. After a delay of four days at the castle, he 17.
made his public entry into Boston, amid salutes and appropriate civic tokens of respect.

On the same day the people of Providence, assembled in town meeting, formally proposed the last remaining act necessary to a union of the colonies—the Continental Congress. The idea had become familiar to the popular mind; it had been proposed in the addresses of public

[1] Newport contained 9,209 inhabitants, and Providence 4,321. The number of families in Providence was 655, and of dwelling-houses, 421. In this census, only those actually at home at the time were counted. Seamen, and other temporary absentees, were omitted. The returns were made at the June session. The population by counties was: Newport, 15,929; Providence, 19,206; Kings, 13,866; Kent, 7,888; Bristol, 2,789.

[2] Hon. Metcalf Bowler died at Providence, September 19, 1789, at an advanced age. He was an eminent merchant in Newport prior to the French war and down to the Revolution, at which time he was among the most active friends of liberty. For several years he was a Judge of the Superior Court, and Speaker of the House of Deputies. He lost his ample fortune during the war, and at the return of peace removed to Providence, where he kept a boarding-house until his death.

CHAP. XX. 1774. May 17.

speakers, and suggested by committees of correspondence; but the formal proposition had never yet been made by any responsible and authorized body. The movement had not received the sanction of any legally constituted authority, until made at this meeting of the freemen of Providence. We therefore claim for Rhode Island the distinguished honor of making the first explicit movement, for a general congress,[1] and a few weeks later her legislature was also the very first to elect delegates to that Congress. After resolving "that this town will heartily join" with the other colonies in defence of their rights, the second resolution proposes: "That the deputies of this town be requested to use their influence at the approaching session of the General Assembly of this colony, for promoting a CONGRESS as soon as may be, of the Representatives of the General Assemblies of the several colonies and provinces of North America, for establishing the firmest Union, and adopting such measures as to them shall appear the most effectual to answer that important purpose; and to agree upon proper methods for executing the same." The next expresses sympathy with the oppressed people of Boston, and recommends "a universal stoppage of all trade with Great Britain, Ireland, Africa,

[1] Mr. Bancroft, History U. S., vol. vii., p. 40, gives this honor to New York, because the old committee of correspondence of the Sons of Liberty in that city, when about to resign their duties to a new and larger committee, on the 16th of May, the day before the Providence meeting, "proposed —and they were the first to propose—'a general congress.'" Many of the legislative and municipal committees of correspondence in Massachusetts, Rhode Island, Virginia, and elsewhere, had, before this time, suggested the idea of a congress. John Hancock had proposed it in a public meeting on the 5th of March at Boston. But none of these suggestions were, so to speak, official. They were the natural emanations of patriotic spirits, entitled to speak for themselves alone. It would be difficult to say where the honor really belongs if we are to award it to the originator of the idea of a congress at this crisis; whether it came from some individual thinker, or was first developed by some committee of correspondence. In either case, the earliest action on the subject that carried with it the weight of established authority, was that recorded in the text.

and the West Indies, until such time as the port of Boston CHAP.
shall be reinstated in its former privileges." XX.

Another subject of historical interest was acted upon 1774.
by this meeting. A man dying intestate and without May 17.
heirs, his property, which included six negroes, fell to the town. The meeting voted that "it is unbecoming the character of freemen to enslave the said negroes," renounced their claim, and took them under their protection. Carrying out the same idea to its logical result, they resolved, "as personal liberty is an essential part of the natural rights of mankind," to petition the Assembly to prohibit the further importation of slaves, and to declare that all negroes born in the colony should be free after a certain age.

A letter sympathizing with the people of Boston, was 19.
sent from Westerly, and a public meeting, held at New- 20.
port, made common cause with that town, and united in the non-importation project.

The legislature of Virginia was dissolved by the gov- 26.
ernor for its adhesion to the cause of liberty. The members met immediately, and advised a Continental Congress, which was communicated to Rhode Island, the 28.
news of whose action on that subject had not reached Williamsburg, and to the other colonies, by their committee of correspondence. Thus spontaneously did the idea of a congress shape itself, almost at the same moment, and without mutual consultation, in communities remote from each other.

The day on which the Boston Port Bill took effect, June 1.
which Virginia had set apart as a day of fasting and prayer, and almost every other colony observed as a day of mourning, Gov. Hutchinson sailed for England. The
next day news of the passage of two of the other penal 2.
bills was received in Boston. The non-importation league
was prepared, and sent to every town in Massachusetts, 5.
agreeing to suspend all trade with Great Britain, and all consumption of her fabrics after the month of August.

CHAP. XX. 1774. June 13. 15.

While the General Court of Massachusetts, to whom, by common consent, had been assigned the honor of fixing a time and place for the meeting of Congress, were arranging this important business at Salem, the General Assembly of Rhode Island met at Newport, and elected Stephen Hopkins and Samuel Ward as delegates to the Congress. At the same time they passed a series of six resolutions, counselling union, and an immediate meeting of Congress to petition for redress, and to devise measures to secure their rights, and also recommending annual sessions of the Congress. The Speaker was ordered to send copies of these resolves to all the other colonies. Thus Rhode Island, as she had been the first, through the means of town meetings, to propose a Continental Congress, was also the earliest to appoint delegates to attend it. It is significant of the unanimity of the people in this matter, that the two delegates selected, were the ex-governors whose rival parties had for so many years divided the councils of the colony.

Military matters, naturally enough, were next considered. The stores at Fort George were examined. The charter of the Providence county Artillery, granted thirty years before, was amended by a change of name to the "Cadet Company," the corps was officered on a regimental basis, and the right of the line assigned to it in express terms, to avoid any future "dispute and altercation." The Light Infantry Company of Providence, to consist of one hundred men, was then chartered, and its station appointed to be "in front of the left wing of the regiment." The Assembly appointed a day of fasting and prayer, in view of the troubles threatening the country, and with especial reference to the distresses of Massachusetts. A vote of commiseration for the poor of Boston, with a promise of future assistance, was passed.

The subject of slavery, which four years before had received attention, was again considered, in consequence of the action of the town of Providence. "As those who are desirous of enjoying all the advantages of liberty themselves, should be willing to extend personal liberty to others," reads the preamble, and then proceeds to enact "that for the future no negro or mulatto slave shall be brought into this colony," or if any were brought in they should thereby become free, except the servants of passing travellers, or of British colonists, residing here for a term of years, who on their departure should take their slaves with them, or negroes brought from Africa by way of the West Indies, whose owners should give bonds to export them within one year. To prevent slaves being brought here for the purpose of receiving their freedom, and so becoming a charge upon the public, a fine was prescribed, which was also attached to the harboring any slave thus introduced. In this decided action, Rhode Island again took the lead of all her sister colonies. The earliest law against slavery to be found in the pages of American history, save only an imperfect statute of Massachusetts, somewhat earlier, but much less explicit, was enacted by Rhode Island in 1652.[1] The sentiments of the people, adverse to the system, were afterwards expressed from time to time in various statutes relating to the subject, but of late years attention had been drawn to it more directly by the free discussion that for some time had been going on in the papers and pamphlets of the day. This discussion had led, four years before, to a proposal in the Assembly, of the measure now enacted, and of which the immediate cause appears to have been that which moved the people of Providence in their action, and is recited in the preamble.

CHAP. XX. 1774. June

This Assembly granted a lottery of two thousand pounds for erecting the new church of the First Baptist Society in Providence, which was completed and occupied the following May. They also incorporated the First Congregational Church at Newport, being the sixth

[1] See chap. viii., vol. i., p. 240.

CHAP. XX. 1774. June charter of the kind granted in the colony. Rev. Samuel Hopkins was pastor of this church. His views on certain doctrinal points were peculiar, and were enforced with the energy of conviction, and the ability of a solid intellect, giving rise to a religious party called from his name, Hopkinsians. His writings upon all questions display remarkable power, and his tracts on slavery doubtless aided to effect the abolition of the system in this colony, as above recorded. The distinctive doctrine in the Hopkinsian theology, was the addition to the five points of Calvinism of a milder element of charity, making piety to consist in pure benevolence, and ranking selfishness among the greatest, as it is the most common of sins.

30. The fast day appointed by the Assembly, was observed with great solemnity throughout the colony. Ships of
July 1. war with more troops began to arrive at Boston. The town assumed the appearance of a vast camp, business was suspended, and much distress prevailed among the poorer classes. From every part of the country contributions of money and provisions were made for their relief.
Aug. 12. A town meeting in Providence instructed their deputies
19. to procure a grant of money from the colony, to be made in behalf of Boston. A similar meeting was held at New-
22. port. The General Assembly met at Greenwich, but nothing of importance was done, except to incorporate the Congregational Church in that town, which had recently
29. been formed. Subscriptions were raised in Greenwich to
30. purchase provisions for Boston, and the next day at Newport the town appointed a committee to receive donations for the same object. In Jamestown, Westerly, and other towns, liberal sums were given for this purpose. Many citizens left the beleaguered town in search of work, and others, friendly to the British government, sought refuge abroad from popular odium. Among these latter, one Jonathan Simpson, a hardware dealer, came to Providence. His Tory views were disliked by the people, who
20. one Saturday night covered his doors and windows with

tar and feathers. On Monday he prudently returned to CHAP.
Boston. In the same week, one De Shazro, a tinman, XX.
came from Boston intending to settle at Providence, but 1774.
the inhabitants, knowing him to be a Tory, warned him Aug. 25.
away, and he went back the next day. A meeting was
soon after held to protest against the town being made a 30.
resort for the enemies of the country, and to request the
council legally to remove any such persons, in order to
prevent further breaches of the peace. That night some
riotous demonstrations occurred, in consequence of which
another meeting was held to protest against such proceed- 31.
ings, and to insist upon the supremacy of the laws.

The seizure by Gage of a large quantity of powder Sept.
and some cannon belonging to the province, caused great 1.
excitement. All over Massachusetts and a portion of
Connecticut, under Gen. Putnam, the people arose in
threatening attitude, and began to march towards Boston.
The counsellors whom Gage had selected, were compelled
to resign their seats, and while these tumults were in progress, Gage suggested to the ministry the employment of
Indians to fight against America—a scheme which stirred
the indignant eloquence of Chatham and Burke to utter,
although in vain, those great master-pieces of British
oratory against this climax of cruelty. A siege was now
impending from the land side of the town, and to preserve
his position, Gage commenced to fortify Boston Neck. 5.
The same day the Continental Congress met at Philadelphia.

Twelve colonies, Georgia alone being unrepresented, sent fifty-three delegates to that body. It was agreed to vote by colonies, and that each should have one vote. The destinies of America hung upon the deliberations of that noble band. They adopted a Declaration of Rights, and recommended an "American Association" to sustain them, the chief articles of which were, non-intercourse with Great Britain, till their grievances should be redressed, abolition of the slave trade, encouragement of

CHAP. XX. 1774. Sept. home industry, and the appointment of committees of inspection in every town and district, to see that its terms were kept inviolate. They also adopted a petition to the King, letters to the other British colonies, addresses to the Canadians, and to the people of Great Britain, and votes of thanks to the friends of America in Parliament. Independence was not yet thought of, but hopes of reconciliation were still entertained.

12. A serious riot occurred at Providence, the first that we have noticed arising from the license question. One McCam had been informed against for keeping an unlicensed dram-shop. He and his friends made search at night for the informer. Joseph Nightengale, with a few other gentlemen attempted to dissüade them. The mob afterward surrounded the house of Col. Nightengale, and McCam attacked him with a cutlass, inflicting several wounds. The citizens soon dispersed the mob, arresting several of them, who were committed to jail for trial. A
13. more serious affair took place at East Greenwich, requiring military aid from Providence to restore peace. Stephen Arnold, of Warwick, a Judge of Common Pleas, unjustly charged with Tory principles, had been hung in effigy at Greenwich. A mob of several hundred people from Warwick, threatened to destroy the village in revenge for the insult put upon their townsman. Deputy-Governor Sessions ordered the Cadets and Light Infantry to Greenwich, to support the sheriff. A parley ensued, which resulted in Judge Arnold's making a written acknowledgment of his wrong in countenancing a riot, while he maintained his right to freely express his views, and declared himself opposed to the scheme for taxing America. This declaration being publicly read by him, both of the excited crowds dispersed peaceably, and the soldiers returned home.

26. The town of Scituate chose a committee of correspondence, and collected donations for the relief of Boston. Bristol, Warren, North and South Kingstown, Gloucester,

North Providence, Coventry, Smithfield, Johnston, Tiverton, and East Greenwich were active in the same cause, and sent large droves of sheep to the distressed Bostonians.[1] Great activity prevailed in organizing the militia. At Pawtuxet, Warren, East Greenwich, and other towns, companies were formed, and those in Providence were increased by a grenadier, an artillery, and a cavalry corps.

CHAP. XX. 1774.

Oct. 5. 7. 11. Massachusetts, where, Gage having refused to qualify the General Court at Salem, a provincial convention was formed, which met at Concord and assumed the government, subject to the action of the General Congress, was in a complete state of revolution.

19. An order in council was issued at this time, to prohibit the exportation of arms and ammunition from Great Britain. Dartmouth notified the colonies to seize any military stores that might be there imported, contrary to this decree. The action taken upon it in Rhode Island, as soon as it became known, was characteristic, decisive, and as the event proved, contagious.

26. The day on which Congress dissolved, the General Assembly met at Providence. A tax of four thousand pounds, as last year, was laid upon the colony. Military

[1] In the Mass. Hist. Society archives the correspondence of the Boston committee with the contributors to the relief of the poor in that town in 1774–5, is preserved. MS. copies of all these letters that related to Rhode Island are now in the hands of the writer. Since these were made, the greater part have been published in iv. Mass. Hist. Cols., vol. 4. The dates of the action of the towns above enumerated, and of others on the same subject, mentioned in these pages, with the amount and kind of donations sent by each are specified in the correspondence, but the enumeration of each of these particulars would require more space than our limits afford. We give them in a note, arranged in the order in which, from the dates of the correspondence, it appears the donations were sent:—Scituate 120 sheep, Gloucester 95, Smithfield 150, Johnston 57, East Greenwich 25 sheep and 4 oxen, Tiverton 72 sheep, S. Kingstown, 135, Providence 136 and £51 in cash, Newport $1000 or £300, Cranston 4 oxen, N. Kingstown 70 sheep, Bristol £48, Warwick 5 oxen, N. Providence £18.—Total, 860 sheep, 13 oxen, £417 in money, Little Compton sent £30, which does not appear in the correspondence; and there were several large subscriptions by private persons besides.

CHAP. XX. 1774. Oct. business occupied the session, which lasted but four days. The Newport Light Infantry, Providence Grenadiers, Kentish Guards, Pawtuxet Rangers, and Gloucester Light Infantry were chartered. Among the applicants for these charters, were Jonathan Arnold for the Grenadiers, and James M. Varnum, Christopher and Nathaniel Greene, and Archibald Crary for the Kentish Guards—names soon to become illustrious upon broader fields of civic and martial emprise. The Providence county militia were divided into three regiments, each to be a battalion, and the whole to form one brigade. The Light Infantry
29. held their first dress parade at the close of the session, concluding with a dinner to the company.

Nov. 5. The Rose, frigate, Capt. Wallace, was stationed at Newport for the winter, and repeated the annoyances of the Gaspee. Subscriptions for the relief of Boston con-
21. tinued. Providence sent a hundred and twenty-five pounds; Little Compton soon after voted thirty pounds, and Cranston sent some fat cattle. The advice of Congress in regard to the preservation of sheep, was com-
24. mended to the people of Providence by the committee of correspondence; and shipments of these animals to the West Indies were stopped. Newport was the first town in the colony to adopt the recommendations of Congress,
25. by appointing a temporary committee of inspection to act till after the meeting of the Assembly.

A new Parliament, the last that was ever to legislate for revolted America, had just been elected. At its open-
30. ing, the King presented the condition of the colonies, and the rebellion in Massachusetts as the absorbing topic. The venerable Chatham made one more effort, in connection with Franklin, to effect a reconciliation. But George III., who possessed a love of prerogative like that of Elizabeth, without her ability to sustain it, would listen
Dec. 1. to no accommodation. The next day was the time set by Congress for the renewal of the non-importation scheme; that relating to non-exportation was deferred till nine

months later. A special session of the General Assembly was called, to hear the reports of the delegates to act upon the proceedings of Congress. These were received and approved, and the same delegates were elected to attend the next Congress in May. The letter of the Earl of Dartmouth respecting military stores, was laid before the Assembly, and immediately all the cannon and ammunition at Fort George, except three guns, were ordered to be removed to Providence by Col. Nightengale, with two assistants, there to be kept in his charge. This was done the next day, more than forty cannon, with a large amount of powder and shot, being thus conveyed to a place of safety. In reply to a demand from Wallace for an explanation of this act, Gov. Wanton distinctly told him it was done to prevent him from seizing the guns, and that they would be used against any enemy of the colony.[1] A copy of Dartmouth's circular was sent at once to the Provincial Congress in Massachusetts. The colony fire arms at Newport were ordered to be distributed to the several counties in proportion to their tax rate. Four new companies, the Scituate Hunters, Providence Artillery, and Fusileers, and North Providence Rangers, were chartered, and four brass four-pounders were purchased and loaned to the Providence Artillery. The office of Major-General was created, subject to annual election, and Simeon Potter, of Bristol, was chosen thereto.[2] The militia law was revised in detail, providing "in what manner the forces within this colony shall march to the assistance of any of our sister colonies when invaded or attacked." The Assembly adjourned after a busy session of six days.

1774. Dec. 5

10.

[1] This removal of the cannon and stores, when referred to at all by historians, has generally been represented as a movement of the populace, like that in New Hampshire, which resulted from it; but it will be seen above that it was a deliberate act of the Assembly, and was officially defended, in terms not to be mistaken, by the governor.

[2] During Philip's war, in 1676, the office of Major of the colony was created, whose duties were those of a Major-General, but this latter military rank was not adopted till the present time.

CHAP. XX. The action of Rhode Island in dismantling Fort George was communicated to the people of Portsmouth,
1774. New Hampshire, who at once took forcible possession of
Dec. 14. the castle in that harbor, carried away a hundred barrels of powder, and the next day, returning in greater force, seized all the cannon and other stores.[1] On the same night a slight riot occurred at Newport, the mob doing damage to the houses of some of the officers of customs. The leaders were arrested and punished. The temporary
16. committee of inspection at Newport was made permanent,
17. and similar committees were appointed in Providence, and the other towns. These committees held monthly meetings, and their recommendations carried with them the force of law. The manufacture of fire-arms began to be extensively carried on in Rhode Island, and several of the chartered or independent companies, as they were called, were already furnished with home made muskets, while the casting of sixty heavy cannon, besides field
1775. pieces, at the iron works, superseded for a time the forg-
Jan. 4. ing of cables and anchors. Lord Dartmouth issued a circular to the governors, to prevent, if possible, the appointment of delegates to attend the Congress. But the revolution was fairly begun, and the first regular battle, the first blood shed since the capture of the Gaspee, was soon to take place.

Heretofore we have noticed to some extent, the progress of events in England and in the other colonies, leading to the final struggle; but after this time events crowd so rapidly, that our limits, as well as the design of this work, require that we confine ourselves more exclusively to the affairs of this colony. Enlistments everywhere proceeded rapidly, and orders for arms from
Feb. Providence were incessant. One hundred and forty guns
16. were called for by North Kingstown. As the time ap-

[1] Letter of Gov. Wentworth to Gov. Gage, Portsmouth, December 14, 1774, where the cause of the rising is stated as above. Belknap's New Hampshire, App. No. 27, vol. iii., p. 444.

proached when, by agreement of Congress, the use of tea CHAP.
was to be suspended, the committee of inspection at Prov- XX.
idence issued an address to remind the people of it, and to 1775.
urge conformity. Other towns followed the same course. Feb. 25.
The day came. Tea was everywhere proscribed. The March
next afternoon some three hundred pounds of the forbid- 1.
den luxury were publicly burnt in market square, with 2.
copies of ministerial documents and other obnoxious
papers. At the same time the word "tea" was obliter-
ated from the shop signs with brush and lampblack, by
some ardent son of liberty.

A general muster of the militia of the colony was held. April 3.
In the county of Providence, two thousand men, besides
a troop of horse, were under arms, and in Kent county
nearly fifteen hundred. This was exclusive of the chartered companies. Returns from the other counties are not
on record. The next day the independent companies 4.
were reviewed. Military enthusiasm was universal. The
Provincial Congress of Massachusetts resolved to raise an 8.
army, and requested the other New England colonies to
furnish their quotas for the common defence. The critical
moment was at hand. Gage secretly sent a force at midnight to capture some military stores at Concord. Reaching the village of Lexington towards sunrise, they came 19.
upon a body of minute-men at drill. A fight ensued, the
provincials were dispersed, and the British advanced to
Concord, where they destroyed the stores. But the alarm
had spread, and minute-men poured in from every side,
repulsed the enemy, and drove them back to Charlestown.
The war had begun in earnest.

News of the battle of Lexington reached Providence
the same night. Expresses were sent off to the other
towns and to Connecticut. The military assembled, and 20.
the next day a thousand men were on their march from
Providence for the scene of strife, but were countermanded by expresses from Lexington. The Assembly convened 21.
immediately at Providence. Ammunition was distributed 22.

CHAP. XX. 1775. among all the towns. The Providence Artillery and Fusileer companies were united under one charter, and are now known as the Providence United Train of Artillery. A day of fasting and prayer was appointed. Nathaniel Greene and William Bradford were sent to Connecticut to consult with the Assembly of that colony for the common defence. An "army of observation," to consist of fifteen hundred men, was voted to be raised at once. The governor, deputy-governor, and two assistants, protested against this levy as an act of war, and a violation of their oaths of allegiance. As the presence of the enemy rendered Newport an unsafe place for future deliberations, it was decided to hold the ensuing election at Providence.

April 22. On the same day that these important measures were adopted in Rhode Island, the Massachusetts Congress voted to raise an army of thirteen thousand six hundred men, and to call on the other New England colonies to make up the force to thirty thousand. The King's ships continued to annoy the commerce in the bay. Two vessels loaded with flour belonging to John Brown, who was on board of one of them coming from Newport, were
26. seized. Mr. Brown was sent in one of the prizes, with the greater part of the flour to Boston, but was soon released by Gen. Gage, and allowed to return home.

Feb. 7. Parliament, in a joint address to the throne, had taken strong ground against the colonies. This was followed by a resolution of the House of Commons, passed at the instigation of Lord North, conciliatory in its tone, but intend-
Mar. 3. ed simply to divide the colonies. Dartmouth enclosed this resolution in a long and carefully framed circular to the colonies, urging their acceptance of the conditions of peace therein proposed. These papers were sent to the
May 2. Assembly by Gov. Wanton, whose presence was prevented by illness, with a letter deprecating their action at the recent session, and asking their calm consideration of the condition of the colony—in other words, opposing any

further resistance. The next day the Assembly met, and proceeded as usual to the choice of officers. At the general election, which took place on the day of the battle of Lexington, the same general officers had been chosen, but several now declined to serve, and others were chosen in their stead. Among these was deputy-governor Sessions, in whose place Nicholas Cooke was elected. Four new assistants were also chosen in grand committee to fill vacancies. A committee of safety, composed of two from Providence and one from each other county, was appointed, who were to furnish and pay the troops, and with the two highest military officers, were to direct the movements of the army of observation, if required to march beyond the colony. They were also to send to Congress an account of the expenses of raising this army.[1] The offices of State were removed to Providence.

CHAP. XX. 1775. May 3–7.

The boldest act of legislation recorded in any of the colonies, up to this time, was now performed by this Assembly, in suspending Joseph Wanton from the office of governor, to which he had just been elected for the seventh time. He had protested against the act for raising the army of observation; he had neglected to issue his proclamation for the fast-day appointed by the Assembly; he had failed to be present to take the oath of office at this session; and he now refused to sign the commission for the officers of the new army; "by all which he hath manifested his intentions to defeat the good people of these colonies in their present glorious struggle to transmit inviolate to posterity those sacred rights they have received from their ancestors." The magistrates were therefore forbidden to administer to him the official oath, unless in open Assembly, "according to the unvaried

May 3.

[1] The committee of safety were William Richmond for Newport, John Smith and Daniel Tillinghast for Providence, John Northup for Kings, William Bradford for Bristol, and Jacob Greene for Kent. Captain Joseph Stanton, jr., for King's county, was afterwards, June 28, added to this committee. In "Men and Times of the Revolution, or Memoirs of Elkanah Watson," on pp. 20–23, is an account of Mr. Brown's capture, and of the expedition sent out from Plymouth to rescue him.

CHAP. XX. 1775. practice," and with the consent of the Assembly, and until the oath was thus taken he was disqualified from acting as governor. Henry Ward, Secretary, was empowered to sign all commissions, civil or military, and the deputy-governor was authorized to convene the Assembly at his discretion.

The army was formed into one brigade of three regiments, composed of eight companies each, with a train of artillery; the whole under command of Brigadier-General Nathaniel Greene. Each regiment was to occupy the flanks and centre in rotation, to preserve their equality of rank, and the same rule was to be observed among the field officers.[1] Bills of credit to the amount of twenty

[1] One regiment was raised in the counties of Newport and Bristol under Colonel Thomas Church, one in Providence under Colonel Daniel Hitchcock, and one in Kent and Kings under Colonel James M. Varnum. The officers were, of Colonel Church's regiment, Lieutenant-Colonel, William Turner Miller; Major, John Forrester; Captains-Lieutenant, William Ladd, Matthew Allen, John Topham; Captains, Sion Martindale, Thomas Tew, Jonathan Brownell, Benjamin Seabury, and of the artillery, John Crane; Lieutenants, Nathaniel Church, James Smith, George Tennant, Benjamin Diamon, Jonathan Simmons, Sylvanus Shaw, Gilbert Manchester, and of the artillery, Joseph Balch, Captain-Lieut.; Ensigns, Cornelius Briggs, James Brown, jr., Stephen Tripp, James Child, 2d, Christopher Bennet, Godfrey Brown, Israel Church. Of Colonel Hitchcock's regiment, Lieutenant-Colonel, Ezekiel Cornell; Major, Israel Angel; Captain-Lieutenants, Simeon Thayer, Stephen Kimball, John Field; Captains, Andrew Waterman, John Angell, Christopher Olney, Jeremiah Olney, Nathaniel Blackmar; Lieutenants, John Spurr, Jonathan Smith, David Richmond, William Aldrich, Coggeshall Olney, Ephraim Bowen, jr., Levi Tower, Samuel Thornton; Ensigns, William Potter, George Dorrance, jr., Samuel Black, David Dexter, jr., Stephen Olney, Cyprian Sterry, Nathaniel Field, Abraham Tourtellot. Of Colonel Varnum's regiment, Lieutenant-Colonel, James Babcock; Major, Christopher Greene; Captain-Lieutenants, Archibald Crary, John Hoxsie, Edmund Johnson; Captains, Thomas Holden, Samuel Ward, jr., James Gardiner, Christopher Gardiner, jr., John Randall; Lieutenants, John S. Dexter, Jonathan Bates, jr., John Reynolds, Joseph Barton, Elijah Lewis, Thomas Phillips, Nathaniel Hawkins, Oliver Clark; Ensigns, Joseph Holloway, John Holden, Joseph Arnold, Joshua Collins, Samuel Bissell, William Potter (son of Ichabod), and Stephen Wells. Peter Phillips was made commissary of the army. The field-officers each had command of a company, and their immediate subor-

thousand pounds were issued, bearing two and-a-half per cent. interest, and redeemable by taxation at the end of two and five years. Provisions were forbidden to be exported from the colony. Copies of these proceedings were sent to Connecticut and New York. The Assembly adjourned on Sunday, after a laborious and most important session. CHAP. XX. 1775. May 7.

10. On the day that Congress met at Philadelphia, Ticonderoga and Crown Point, the two strong fortresses that had given so much trouble during the French war, were captured by surprise, one by Ethan Allen, the other by Seth Warner. Congress still aimed at conciliation. New England alone was resolved on independence, but the time was rapidly approaching when but one opinion would prevail. An American army of some sixteen thousand men was encamped on Jamaica Plains, and daily receiving accessions. About one thousand men of the Rhode Island "army of observation," with the United Train of Artillery, having their four field-pieces, and a siege battery of twelve eighteen and twenty-four-pounders, had marched to the scene of action before the first of June.

June 3. Collisions between the royal forces and the people were frequent; such an affair occurred at Newport at this time, but without serious result. The committee of inspection were active in enforcing the terms of the American Association. In Providence they visited the stores 12.
to see that no goods were sold at enhanced prices, and a little later the sale of mutton was forbidden for a time. July 17.
The people who would submit to such restrictions rather than pay a small duty on tea, showed a devotion to principle that was worthy of freedom.

dinates were known as Captain-Lieutenants.* At the adjourned session, June 12, William Blodgett was appointed secretary to the army, and at the extra session, June 28, John Martin was made brigade surgeon, and Charles Bowler was appointed baker to the army of observation near Boston.

* This title was abolished, March, 1776, and those who held it were ranked as captains.

CHAP. XX. 1775. June 12. The Assembly met by adjournment at Greenwich. Gov. Wanton appeared, and demanded to have the oath of office administered; but failing to give satisfaction, they refused his request, and continued the suspension act.
13. The next day he addressed them a letter, explaining and defending his conduct in regard to the four points objected against him, but without effect. William Potter, one of the two assistants who had joined in the protest against the act for raising an army, presented a memorial, assigning his reasons for having done so, expressing regret for his conduct, and committing himself fully to the cause of liberty; in consideration of which he was "reinstated in the favor of" the Assembly. The articles of war for the government of the army, in fifty-three sections, with a patriotic preamble, were adopted,[1] and an act to prevent desertion was passed. The deputy-governor was requested
14. to write to Capt. Wallace of the Rose frigate, to inquire why he annoyed the commerce of the colony, and to demand the restoration of a packet detained by him. This he did at once in a spirited letter, to which Wallace re-
15. plied, without delay, asking who Cooke was, and if the colony was not in a state of rebellion? The Assembly ordered both letters to be printed in the papers. A few hours afterwards, the detained packet, whose delivery had been demanded by Cooke, and which was armed and employed as a tender to the Rose, was chased on to Conanicut shore, and captured by an armed sloop in the colony's service, after a sharp firing on both sides. This was the beginning of a glorious national era in the naval enterprise of Rhode Island. To Capt. Abraham Whipple, who commanded the war-sloop, is thus due the honor of discharging the first gun upon the ocean, at any part of his Majesty's navy in the American Revolution.[2] Two

[1] The rules for the government of the army, afterwards established by Congress, were adopted by the Assembly, Jan. 17, 1776, and these articles were repealed.

[2] The correspondence between Whipple and Captain Sir James Wallace,

armed vessels were at once ordered to be equipped for the defence of the colony; the largest to carry ten four-pounders, and fourteen swivel guns, with eighty men; the smallest to carry thirty men. They were called the Washington and the Katy. Both were placed under the command of Abraham Whipple, the hero of the Gaspee, with the rank of Commodore.[1] Such was the commencement of the American navy.

CHAP. XX. 1775.

A further issue of ten thousand pounds in bills of credit was made. The postal system in Rhode Island was fully organized at this session, by the establishment

of the Rose frigate, which took place at this time should be preserved. Wallace had learned who it was that led the attack on the Gaspee, and wrote as follows: "You, Abraham Whipple, on the 10th June, 1772, burned his Majesty's vessel, the Gaspee, and I will hang you at the yard-arm. JAMES WALLACE." To which note, more curt than courteous, Whipple replied with equal brevity, "To Sir James Wallace, *Sir*, Always catch a man before you hang him. ABRAHAM WHIPPLE."

The capture of the Margaretta, by the people of Machias, on the 11th May, was a private affair, precisely similar to that of the Gaspee, and, like that event, reflects great credit on the courage and spirit of the actors. The capture of the Gaspee was, in effect, the commencement of the Revolution, and Abraham Whipple led the attack. It was the first popular rising directed against a British armed vessel. The affair of the 15th June, 1775, was between two regular armed vessels, one in the colonial service of Rhode Island, the other in that of the King, and was the first proper naval action in the Revolution. In either case, the honor that has always been claimed for Whipple, of firing the first gun of the Revolution upon the water, appears to be his due. The real "Lexington of the Seas" was the affair of June 10, 1772, and not that of May 11, 1775, as commemorated by Mr. Cooper, (Naval History, vol. 1 p. 65); while, to continue the parallel, that of June 15, 1775, was the Bunker Hill, although with a more fortunate result, for it settled the question of the ability of Provincial cruisers to cope with those of the Crown.

[1] The officers of this embryo squadron were as follows:—of the large vessel, "Abraham Whipple, Commander, with the rank and power of Commodore of both vessels," John Grimes, 1st Lieutenant, Benjamin Seabury, 2nd Lieutenant, William Bradford, (of Providence) Master, Ebenezer Flagg, Quartermaster;—of the small vessel, Christopher Whipple, Commander, William Rhodes, Lieutenant. Ch. Whipple refused, and John Grimes was made commander. The Committee of Safety was empowered to fill vacancies.

CHAP. XX. 1775. of routes, officers, and rates of postage, and the appointment of post-riders. William Goddard had completed his plan, and laid it before Congress, but this colony anticipated, by nearly six weeks, the action of that body on the subject.[1] Congress having recommended the twentieth of July to be observed as a day of fasting and prayer throughout the colonies, the Assembly requested the deputy-governor to issue his proclamation accordingly.
June 17. This important session closed with the week, and upon an eventful day. The Rose, frigate, Swan, sloop-of-war, and a tender, came up the river in pursuit of prizes, and while absent from Newport, five vessels which they had previously taken were boarded and carried off by the people of that town.

Congress, while yet seeking a peaceful adjustment of grievances, by again petitioning the King, and appealing to the British nation, as it had before done, resolved to establish an army, to be enlisted as were those of the several colonies, till the close of the year. At the suggestion of New England, George Washington was chosen com-
15. mander-in-chief. Four major-generals and an adjutant were also appointed,[2] and the following week eight briga-
22. diers, among whom was Nathaniel Greene, were chosen.[3]

During this interval, a great battle was fought. The British army now numbered ten thousand men, and Gage

[1] On the 26th July, Congress adopted Goddard's plan of a Continental post office, and Franklin was appointed Postmaster General.

[2] These were Artemas Ward, of Massachusetts, then captain-general of the army before Boston, Charles Lee, a British soldier of fortune, lately settled in Virginia, Philip Schuyler, of New York, and Israel Putnam, of Connecticut, then serving under Ward as a brigadier. Horatio Gates, a retired English officer, and like Lee, settled in Virginia, was made adjutant-general, with the rank of brigadier.

[3] They were Pomeroy, Heath, and Thomas, of Massachusetts, Wooster and Spencer of Connecticut, and Greene of Rhode Island, all general officers with Colonial commissions, Sullivan of New Hampshire, a member of Congress, and Montgomery, of New York. Pomeroy declined. The colonels and subalterns in the army before Boston were also commissioned by Congress. Joseph Trumbull was made commissary-general.

proclaimed martial law. A detachment of twelve hun- CHAP.
dred Americans under Col. Prescott, in order to invest XX.
Boston more closely, was sent to occupy Bunker's Hill, 1775.
but by some mistake they advanced to Breed's Hill, still June
nearer the town. All that night they worked at throwing 16.
up a redoubt, and, undisturbed by a heavy cannonade
which, in the morning, was opened upon them by the 17.
astonished enemy, they continued their labor until noon, extending a line of breastwork down the hill. Before three o'clock, about three thousand British troops under Howe, having set fire to Charlestown, commenced the attack. The result we know. The victory, like that of Pyrrhus, was more costly than defeat. The loss on either side was more than one-third of the number engaged, and among them was the gallant Warren. Gage was superseded in his command. The ability of raw provincials, unsupported, and unrefreshed, after nearly twenty-four hours of incessant toil, to withstand the charge of veteran troops, was tested on that memorable day, to the satisfaction of America, and the dismay of her enemies.

The battle of Bunker Hill, like that of Lexington, occasioned an extra session of the Assembly, which was 28.
called by warrant of deputy-governor Cooke. Committees were ordered to visit every house in the colony, to take an account of arms and ammunition to be transmitted to Congress. All the saltpetre and brimstone were ordered to be collected and forwarded to New York, where, as in Virginia and Pennsylvania, powder-mills were in operation. The garrison at Fort George was discharged, the few remaining guns were brought off, and the fort abandoned. A signal was established at Tower Hill, to give warning of the approach of a fleet, and a beacon was set up at Providence to spread the alarm. Every man in the colony capable of bearing arms was required to equip himself for service. One-fourth part of the militia were enlisted as minute-men, to drill for half a day in every fortnight, in which body the independent companies were

CHAP. XX. 1775. June 28. included. The Rhode Island forces, now incorporated with the grand army before Boston, were placed under the direction of Washington, and six additional companies of sixty men each were ordered to be raised and sent forward, two to each regiment, to join the brigade, which with this accession numbered about seventeen hundred men.[1] As if to cut off all further connection with Great Britain, the act allowing judicial appeals to be taken to England was repealed. Another issue of ten thousand pounds in bills of credit was made, to meet these new
23. war expenses.[2] Five days before this, Congress had adopted the system of paper currency, by voting to issue two millions of dollars in Continental bills, to which another million was shortly added.

July 2. Washington soon afterwards arrived at the camp, and established his head-quarters at Cambridge. The national
20. fast day was observed with great solemnity throughout the colonies. It was a day of alarm to Newport. Wallace threatened to bombard the town, on account of the desertion of some of his men supposed to be detained there. Five boats were prepared, and the ships took position, but
22. after two days of terror, Wallace sailed on a cruise.

At Providence the entrance to the harbor was fortified between Field and Sasafras Points, and a battery of six eighteen-pounders was erected on Fox Point. The beacon on Prospect Hill, where the first one had been erected more than a century before, was fired in order to test its
Aug. 17. fitness as a signal. The flames were observed over an

[1] The officers chosen for these six companies were as follows: Captains, Ebenezer Flagg, Thomas Gray, Levi Tower, Israel Gorton, Ethan Clarke, and Christopher Smith; Lieutenants, Joseph Perry, Lemuel Bailey, Silas Talbot, James Williams, Thomas Cole, and Thomas Sweet; Ensigns, Noel Allen, William Southworth, Reuben Sprague, Joseph Harris, John Woodmansie, and Oliver Tefft.

[2] This made £40,000 issued in May and June, 1775, bearing interest. The whole of these bills were called in, and new ones for the same amount, but without interest, were emitted in January, 1776.

area of country extending from Cambridge to New London and Norwich, and from Newport to Pomfret.[1] CHAP. XX.

Another important session of the Assembly was now held. All the sheep and other live stock were ordered to be brought off from Block Island, and two hundred and fifty minute-men were drafted for the purpose, as it was a perilous undertaking. The islands in the bay, except Rhode Island, were also cleared of most of their stock to prevent its falling into the hands of the enemy, and arrangements were made to sell it to the army.[2] A bounty of three shillings a pound was offered for the manufacture of saltpetre in the colony, and the same price was affixed to its sale.[3] Eight field-pieces were ordered to be cast at the two iron furnaces. It was forbidden, under heavy penalties, to pilot any of the King's ships within the waters of Rhode Island. In addition to the two war-sloops already in service, two "row galleys," or gun-boats, of thirty oars, each to carry sixty men, afterwards reduced to fifty, and one eighteen-pounder, besides swivel guns, were ordered. These were named the Washington and the Spitfire. The Rhode Island delegates in Congress were instructed "to use their whole influence for building, at the Continental expense, a fleet of sufficient force for the protection of these colonies, and for employing them in such manner and places as will most effectually annoy our enemies, and contribute to the common defence of these colonies." Here was another point in which Rhode Island was the first to suggest, and the foremost to act, in behalf of a system of national defence; and a little later

1775. Aug. 21–26.

[1] A similar beacon was afterwards erected on Tonomy Hill, and fired on 20th June, 1776.

[2] By a report made at the October session, it appears that the stock removed from Block Island amounted to 1,908 sheep, valued at £534 9s.; from Conanicut, 82 cattle, 444 sheep, at £850 9s.; and from Prudence, 56 cattle, and 384 sheep, at £530, which sums were paid to the owners from the treasury.

[3] This act was repealed in January, 1776, and saltpetre works were ordered to be set up in every town in the colony, and one powder-mill to be established in the State.

CHAP. XX. it was appointed chiefly to her to carry out the idea of
an American navy. The Continental currency was
1775. adopted as lawful tender, and whoever should refuse either
Aug. colonial or general bills of credit, was declared to be an
enemy to his country. A large committee was appointed
to act during the recess of the Assembly, with power to
direct the naval force of the colony.

22. The British ships threatened an attack on Providence,
but advanced no further than Conimicut Point. The
batteries and redoubts in the harbor were manned, and
the military were under arms to repulse them when the
enemy withdrew, having captured a brig from the West
Indies off Warwick Neck, and pillaged the island and
adjacent shores of much live stock. A permanent garrison of seven men to each gun, with Esek Hopkins as
commander, Samuel Warner, lieutenant, and Christopher
29. Sheldon, gunner, was placed at the Fox Point battery.
The first Rhode Island officer who fell in the war, Adjutant Augustus Mumford, was killed at this time in the
siege of Boston by a cannon shot from the enemy.

Sept. 5. When Congress re-assembled at Philadelphia after a
recess of five weeks, the Georgia delegates took their
seats, and "The Thirteen United Colonies" were com-
6. plete. The College Commencement was held in a strictly
private manner, in deference to the condition of the
country. A town meeting at Providence was held, to
7. prevent the shipment of a quantity of flax-seed about to
be sent to Europe. Although three days remained before
the non-exportation agreement, entered into by the former
10. Congress, was to take effect, it was thought best to adopt
this course to allay jealousy in the other colonies.

Oct. 3. The delegates laid before Congress their instructions in
regard to a Continental navy. The plan was favorably
received, although not matured till some weeks later.
There was instant occasion both at home and abroad, to
employ the embryo squadron already afloat in Rhode
Island. Congress desired to intercept two ships bound

to Canada with military stores, and resolved to request CHAP. XX.
Gov. Cooke to despatch one or both of the colony's war-
sloops on that service, and to use every precaution to keep 1775.
secret the object of the expedition. But a more pressing Oct.
necessity existed at home. The British fleet at Newport,
being reinforced by four more vessels in search of supplies,
Capt. Wallace made a threatening demand upon the
islands of Rhode-island and Conanicut for live stock. A
force of six hundred men, comprising five companies from
Providence, with a part of the Tiverton and Little Compton militia, under Esek Hopkins as chief, and William
West as second in command, commissioned by the Recess 4.
Committee for special service, marched at once to New- 5.
port to secure the stock, repel the invaders, and arrest
George Rome for aiding the enemy, and send him, with
any British officers or men whom they might find on
shore, to Providence, "to be dealt with according to their
demerits."[1]

At the same time Gov. Cooke and Secretary Ward
went to Cambridge to assist in a committee of Congress
for establishing the army. The greatest alarm pervaded
the doomed inhabitants of Newport. The town had become a camp, and every moment it was expected that the
formidable fleet moored in front would reduce it to ashes.
A violent storm prevailed for two days, during which the 5–6.
exposure and suffering of the fleeing population was great.
Many families removed with their property. For four 7–8.
days the streets were almost blocked with carts and carriages of every sort, seeking a place of safety. A shock
was given to the prosperity of the ancient capital, from
which it has never recovered. But the place was too important as a rendezvous to be wantonly destroyed, and
Wallace attempted to soothe the people by promising
immunity to their market boats in return for supplies of
beer and fresh provisions. On Saturday he withdrew his 7.

[1] Commission signed by Nichs. Cooke. D. Gov., Oct. 4, 1775, in Hopkins' MS. papers, vol. 2, in R. I. Hist. Soc.

CHAP. XX. fleet, and in the evening, with fifteen sail, anchored in line in the harbor of Bristol.

1775. Oct. Sending his barge to the wharf, he demanded that four of the magistrates should come off to the fleet, which was refused; but an offer to treat with any persons who might be sent on or near to the shore was made, with a guarantee for their personal safety. A heavy cannonade was then opened upon the town. The night was dark and rainy. A severe epidemic was then raging in Bristol. More than sixty persons were carried out upon their sick beds, and with the women and children, hurried off in carriages to seek refuge from the general ruin. The bombardment continued above an hour, and more than a hundred and twenty cannon were discharged. Much damage was done to public and private buildings, but fortunately no one was killed by the shot, although some of the sick died from exposure. Wallace required a hundred sheep and fifty cattle, but reduced his demand to forty sheep, which the town wisely furnished, and the next afternoon the
8. fleet departed, after plundering the neighboring farms.

A still worse fate befell the town of Falmouth, in
18. Maine, now Portland, which was nearly destroyed by a bombardment. All the seaport towns of America were threatened with the same calamity. At Providence, further defences were prepared. A floating battery was constructed, fire ships were made, and a boom and chain, to be stretched across the channel, was furnished, when the
31. Assembly convened, and the colony assumed the completion of these works. Esek Hopkins and Joseph Brown were appointed to go through the colony to decide what places should be fortified, and in what manner. Batteries were erected at Pawtuxet and other places, and the troops on Conanicut and Block Islands were reinforced. The manufacture of saltpetre was undertaken by the colony.

Nov. 1. On the second day of the session, the emancipation act was brought in. The abolition of the slave-trade had been accomplished more than a year before. It was now proposed to terminate the system of chattel slavery in Rhode Island, by declaring free "all negroes, as well as other persons, hereafter born within this colony," and to provide for the liberation of existing slaves, at the will of the owners, by proper regulations. Suitable provisions were made in the bill to prevent such liberated slaves from becoming a charge upon the public. The act was referred to a future session, meanwhile to be printed and laid before the town meetings for instruction to the deputies thereupon.

Another regiment of five hundred men in eight companies was enlisted for one year, "for the defence of the united colonies in general, and of this colony in particular."[1] Two new independent companies, the Kingston Reds, and the Captain General's Cavaliers, a troop of horse in Providence county, were chartered. Several memorials and declarations from persons whose language or conduct had excited suspicion, or who had incurred the displeasure of the Assembly, were presented; among them was one from the late deputy-governor Sessions, in regard to his protest against the army act, all of which were favorably received. Some of these persons were under arrest for their connection with what was known as Brigadier Ruggles' Association, whose members were enlisted in the royal cause under Col. Gilbert, then on board

[1] The officers chosen for this regiment were: Colonel William Richmond; Lieutenant-Colonel Gideon Hoxsie; Major Benjamin Tallman, (who resigned Jan. 25, to build a Continental frigate;) Adjutant Benjamin Stelle; Captains Caleb Gardiner, Billings Throop, Job Pearce, Thomas Wells, 2d; Christopher Manchester, William Barton, James Wallace, Charles Dyer; Lieutenants Benjamin Fry, Caleb Carr, Malachi Hammet, Augustus Stanton, Walter Palmer, Charles Lippit, John Rogers, Zorobabel Westcott; Ensigns Jonathan Wallen, Peleg Heath, Benjamin Burlingame, Peleg Berry, Jonathan Duval, Squire Fisk, William Davis, Royal Smith. Other officers chosen at this time were, Nathan Miller, commissary to General Hopkins' troops, Benjamin Page, captain of 1st row-galley, Joshua Babcock, major-general of militia.

CHAP. XX. 1775. Nov.

a British tender in the bay.[1] Decrees of forfeiture were passed upon the estates of many persons who upheld the ministerial party, and were known as Tories.[2] An act was passed denouncing death, and the forfeiture of property, against any who should furnish supplies to, or hold correspondence with the enemy.

Great distress prevailed among the poor, especially on the exposed islands in the bay. At Newport, meetings had been held to memorialize Congress, and to petition the Assembly on the subject. Two hundred pounds were now appropriated for the removal of such as could leave the town, and the support of those who remained, and a tariff of prices for such removals was made. Newport was allowed to furnish supplies to the British ships, to ensure the safety as well as the support of the inhabitants.[3]

[1] Timothy Ruggles was a brigadier-general in the French war, and a delegate from Massachusetts to the Congress of 1765, at New York, where he was made president of that body, from whose proceedings he dissented, became a Tory, and was one of Gage's mandamus councillors in Massachusetts, in 1774. While acting in this latter capacity, near the close of the year, he drew up a paper, known as Brigadier Ruggles' Association, consisting of a preamble and six articles, which was sent for signature among the troops, binding them to sustain each other against any revolutionary movement, and disowning the authority of Congress, or of the Committees of Correspondence, which they agreed to resist by force. Under this Association, Colonel Thomas Gilbert, who had served with Ruggles in the French war, at the request of Gage, raised a body of 300 Loyalists, to preserve order in Bristol County, Massachusetts. In March, 1775, he wrote to Captain Wallace at Newport for aid to preserve his position. The letter was intercepted, and Gilbert took refuge on board of a British tender in the bay, where he had communication with some of the Tories in this colony, as above mentioned.

[2] Among these sequestered estates were those of the late Governor Hutchinson, of Massachusetts, Samuel Sewall, Gilbert Deblois, John and Jonathan Simpson—all of Boston, but holding property in Rhode Island;—and of Dr. Thomas Moffat, Ralph Inman, George Rome, Jahleel and Benjamin Brenton, late residents of Newport. The last-named gentleman was reinstated in the favor of the Assembly, and his estates were restored in January, he having proved that the charges against him were ill-founded, and that he was a friend to the liberties of his country.

[3] At the next session, in January, 1776, this permission was continued. The amount of supplies was 2,000 lbs. of beef per week, and a certain quan-

CHAP. XX. 1775. Nov.

The people of Nantucket were permitted, under adequate guarantees, to purchase provisions in this colony. The statute of limitations was repealed to prevent ultimate loss to creditors, who, on account of the general distress, forebore to bring suits for the recovery of debts. All the public records were removed from Newport to a place of safety.

The suspension act against Gov. Wanton had been continued at each session since its passage in May. Having failed to give satisfaction to the Assembly, and continuing to manifest Tory sympathies, he was now formally deposed, and the office of governor was declared vacant. 7.
The deputy-governor, Nicholas Cooke, was elected in his place, and William Bradford, of Bristol, was chosen deputy-governor. When we consider how firm Gov. Wanton had been in sustaining the rights of the colony for years against the assumptions of British naval officers, his great personal popularity, consequent thereupon, and that his first shrinking from the progressive action of the patriotic party was on the act for raising an army, which he truly enough construed to be an act of rebellion, we can better understand the feeling that pervaded the colony, once the most loyal, and now the foremost to strike for independence. Yet in both positions the colonists were consistent, because acting in both upon the determination to maintain their chartered rights, first against the assaults of their neighbors, and now against the power that had resolved to destroy them. It was a bold act, a fitting supplement to the affairs of the Gaspee and the levying an army, and an appropriate precedent to the final act, abjuring allegiance to the British crown, which was speedily to follow.

The colonial debt accumulated rapidly at this period. Another emission of bills of credit to the amount of twenty thousand pounds was made, payable by taxation

tity of beer, and £200 additional were appropriated for the removal of the poor.

CHAP. XX. 1775. Nov.

in five years, without interest. But these war expenses were in the common cause of all the colonies, and it was but right that Congress should assume them, as it did. The liability for the three millions of Continental bills, was distributed pro rata among the colonies. A committee was appointed to receive the money due to Rhode Island, who, with the delegates in Congress, were empowered to adjust the account with the United Colonies, which was drawn up and presented at this session, amounting to nearly forty-five thousand pounds. One hundred and twenty thousand dollars of this account, was soon afterwards paid. At the close of this important session, the
10. Assembly appointed the twenty-third instant as a day of public thanksgiving.

9. The day before the adjournment, another naval action took place in Narraganset Bay, between two privateer sloops from Providence, and a British schooner, three tenders, and a bomb-ketch that came out from Newport to attack them, but were repulsed after a conflict of some hours.

Congress, acting upon the suggestion of the Rhode Island delegates, appointed a marine committee, and resolved to fit out four armed vessels, for which Esek Hop-
5. kins was selected as commodore. Two expeditions against Canada were meanwhile in progress. One under
3. Montgomery, after a siege of several weeks, captured St. Johns, on the Sorel River, and thence marched to Mon-
9. treal, which at once surrendered. The other, under Arnold, consisting of eleven hundred men, of whom two hundred and fifty were Rhode Island troops,[1] after a

[1] See Rhode Island Memorial to Congress, Jan., 1776, State Records, pp. 321–3. The troops in this expedition were divided in two battalions. The first led by Lieutenant-Colonel Christopher Greene, comprised seven companies, three of which, commanded by Captains John Topham, of Church's regiment, Simeon Thayer, of Hitchcock's, and Samuel Ward, of Varnum's, with, perhaps, one more, were from Rhode Island. These officers were taken prisoners in the attack of Dec. 31. A journal kept by Captain Thayer was first published in "The Spirit of '76, in Rhode Island, by

severe march of six weeks through Maine, encamped opposite Quebec. Many obstacles prevented an immediate assault, and it was not till the close of the year, when Carleton had had time to complete his defences, that the unsuccessful attack was made, which resulted in the death of the gallant Montgomery, the wounding of Arnold, and the repulse of the besiegers. CHAP. XX. 1775. Dec. 31.

The proposal of Wallace to spare Newport on condition of being furnished with provisions, was referred by the town council to Gen. Hopkins, who, under the late act of Assembly, permitted it to be accepted; the supplies, in stated quantities, to be furnished by one person. To this restriction Wallace assented, and agreed not to suffer his men to land "unless the rebels enter." Hopkins was encamped in Middletown with a considerable force. The correspondence between the parties was printed by order of the Recess Committee. While this matter was pending, Charles Dudley, the collector of customs, fled for refuge on board the Rose. The Recess Committee allowed Brigadier-General Hopkins to accept command of the continental fleet, and sent the Katy, under Whipple, to Philadelphia, with over a hundred men shipped for that service. They also took into their charge the personal effects of Dudley and of George Rome, some of which were stored in Providence, and others sold at auction. By their order several Tories were arrested, an artillery company was established as a part of the new regiment, and officers were appointed for the row-galley Washington.[1] Nov. 14. 15. 16. 15. 28. 29.

Benjamin Cowell, 352 pp., 8vo, Boston, 1850," which, with the author's remarks upon the expedition, App. A., pp. 283–94 of that important work, will be found deeply interesting. Major Henry Sherburne, of Rhode Island, was attached to Montgomery's expedition that went by way of the Lakes.

[1] Benjamin Page was appointed captain by the Assembly. The committee filled the list with John Tillinghast and Jacob Westcott as lieutenants, and David Arnold, master. Page resigned in Jan., and Oliver Gardner was made captain; D. Arnold, 1st lieutenant; and Ebenezer Hill, master. Of the 2d galley, John Grimes was made captain in January, with the

CHAP. XX.

1775. Dec.

11. Congress ordered that the Katy should be sent to cruise on the southern coast. A committee of one from each colony, Stephen Hopkins being the one from Rhode Island, was appointed to organize and equip a navy.
22. They confirmed Esek Hopkins as commander of the fleet, and Abraham Whipple as captain of the frigate Columbus.

A British force landed on Conanicut, at the east ferry,
10. and crossing the island, burned all the dwellings near the road, twelve in number, besides barns, plundering the inhabitants, and carrying off a quantity of live stock. The Recess Committee ordered barracks to be built on
18. Wonumetonomy[1] Hill, and a laboratory for making artillery stores to be established in Providence.[2] The brutal attack on Jamestown greatly alarmed the colony. The town council of Newport accepted the offer made by Providence county to receive and provide for four hundred of the poor of that town, and took measures for their removal. Thus the hospitality which, a hundred years before, had been extended by the people of Aquedneck to the scattered inhabitants of Providence during Philip's war, was reciprocated in this hour of peril, by their descendants. Gov. Cooke applied to Gen. Washington for a regiment of the line to defend Rhode Island, and that Gen. Lee might be sent at once to command the forces.
19. All the minute-men of the colony were sent to the defence of the island, and formed into one regiment under Col.

command of both galleys; Samuel Westcott, 1st lieutenant; Samuel Vial of Rehoboth, 2d lieutenant; Francis Bradfield, master. Each was to carry 50 men.

[1] This hill, just north of Newport, bore the name of the last Sachem of the Aquednecks, who was conquered by the Narragansets before the arrival of the English. It is often erroneously called Miantinomi hill, after the great Sachem of that name, and by a common corruption, Tammany hill, from the abbreviation, Tonomy hill, which was generally used.

[2] A year later, another laboratory was established in Providence. The first of these works was set up in the brick school-house in Meeting street, where it continued from December, 1776, to August, 1784. The other was in Whipple Hall from February, 1777, to February, 1781.

William West, and Lieutenant-Colonel Christopher Lip- CHAP.
pitt. West was appointed to succeed Hopkins in the XX.
command of the island. Forty eighteen-pound cannon 1775.
and twenty twelve-pounders were ordered to be cast. Dec.

Gen. Lee proceeded to Providence, and was at once 21.
made commander-in-chief of all the forces on the island. 22.
The Cadets and a body of riflemen accompanied him to 23.
the island. With a force of eight hundred men, he
marched into Newport, summoned the Tories, and admin- 25.
istered to them a remarkable oath, which was taken by
all but Col. Wanton and two custom-house officers, who,
on their refusal, were sent as prisoners to Providence,
where Rome and other Tories were already confined.
Lee's services could not be spared from the camp, and
after giving directions for fortifying the island, he came 27.
up to Providence. The minute-men were dismissed, and
the committee voted "that one of the best beds, with the 28.
furniture taken from Charles Dudley, be presented to
Gen. Lee." Two days later he returned to Cambridge, 30.
and reported to Washington, who, in a letter to Hancock, 31.
President of Congress, approved of his method of "making
friends of those that were our enemies," and enclosed a
copy of the oath as "a specimen of his abilities in that
way." [1]

[1] It reads as follows: "I, John Bours, here, in the presence of Almighty God, as I hope for ease, honor, and comfort in this world, and happiness in the world to come, most earnestly, devoutly, and religiously swear neither directly nor indirectly to assist the wicked instruments of ministerial tyranny and villainy, commonly called the King's troops and navy, by furnishing them with provisions or refreshments of any kind, unless authorized by the Continental Congress, or the Legislature as at present established in this particular colony of Rhode Island. I do also swear by the same tremendous and Almighty God that I will neither directly nor indirectly convey any intelligence nor give any advice to the aforesaid enemies so described, and that I pledge myself, if I should, by any accident, get the knowledge of such treason, to inform immediately the Committee of Safety. And, as it is justly allowed, that when the sacred rights and liberties of a nation are invaded, neutrality is not less base and criminal than open and avowed hostility, I do further swear and pledge myself, as I hope for eternal salvation,

CHAP. XX. When the Recess Committee, under the act drafting
one-quarter of the militia as minute-men, ordered the
1775. levies to the defence of Rhode Island, a riot occurred at
Dec. 23. West Greenwich to prevent the enlistment, and was re-
26. peated by the same parties three days later. Some of the
1776. leaders were imprisoned at Providence, and the Assem-
Jan. 8–17. bly ordered the arrest of others. During the session, the
British fleet of twelve sail came up to Prudence Island,
12. and landed two hundred and fifty troops. A company of
minute-men were driven off, seven dwellings were burnt,
13. and a hundred sheep taken. The next day reinforcements were sent from Warren and Bristol, an action that
lasted three hours ensued, when the British were driven
to their ships with a loss of fourteen killed and many
wounded. The Americans had four wounded and one
14. taken prisoner. The next night two houses were burnt on
Patience Island, and after cutting wood on Hope Island,
15. the ships returned to Newport. The Assembly stationed
a company of artillery and minute-men at Warwick Neck,
and fortified that point. They also despatched the troops
at Prudence to the defence of Bristol. A night patrol
was set, and artillery companies, with two field-pieces
and fourteen men each, were formed in all the seaboard
towns, seventeen in number, requiring a force of two hundred and thirty-eight men and thirty-four guns. The regiment of five hundred men raised at the last session, was increased to seven hundred and fifty, besides an artillery force of one hundred and five men to be attached to it,[1] and another regiment of seven hundred and fifty men

that I will, whenever called upon by the voice of the Continental Congress, or that of the Legislature of this particular colony, under their authority, take arms and subject myself to military discipline, in defence of the common rights and liberties of America. So help me God.

"Sworn at Newport, Dec. 25, 1775. John Bourse."

[1] For the four new companies the officers were: Captains Josiah Gibbs, Jr., Cornelius Briggs, Benjamin Diamond, Samuel Phillips; Lieutenants John Holden, Lemuel Bailey, James Smith, Paul Herrington; Ensigns Philip Arnold, Benjamin Church, Isaac Eastlick, Benjamin West; Quarter-

was raised, the two to form one brigade.[1] No military officer under pay, except of the militia, could be a member of the Assembly. A memorial was adopted, and forwarded to Congress by Gov. Cooke, setting forth the exposed condition of the colony, with a hundred and thirty miles of coast line, besides two navigable rivers, and a hostile fleet in its waters constantly plundering the islands and shores, and enumerating the efforts already made in the common cause as well as for local defence, and asking continental aid in its behalf.[2] The thanks of the Assembly were voted to the towns of Rehoboth and Swanzey for the zeal with which they rallied to the aid of this colony upon every occasion of alarm.

master John Handy. The artillery officers were: Edward Spalding, captain; William Bull, captain-lieutenant; Joshua Sayer, 1st lieut.; Ebenezer Sherman, 2d lieut.; Timothy Brown, lieutenant Fire-worker.

[1] The officers of the new regiment were: Colonel Henry Babcock; Lieutenant-colonel Christopher Lippitt; Major Adam Comstock; Captains Job Olney, Jonathan Brownell, James Tew, Asa Kimball, Andrew Waterman, Loring Peck, David Dexter, jr., William Potter, (son of John,) Benjamin Peirce, Augustus Stanton, John Carr, Thomas Gorton; Lieutenants William Drowne, William Jones, Joseph Belcher, jr., Benjamin Hoppin, Nehemiah Randall, Arthur Fenner, (son of Edward,) Peleg Slocum, Christopher Dyer, Simeon Martin, Joshua Bliven, Alexander Thomas, Thomas Arnold; Ensigns Jacob Williams, Gilbert Richmond, Bryant Millman, Anan Winsor, Wilson Rawson, Stephen Paine, David Sayles, William Potter, (son of Ichabod,) William Belcher, Thomas Noyes, Stephen Borden, Michael Spencer; Adjutant William Tyler; Quartermaster, Benjamin Bourne.

Officers for the brigade—Christopher Olney, major; John Bartlet, surgeon; Joseph Rhodes, Ebenezer Richmond, and John Chace, surgeon's mates. The changes in this large number of officers were so frequent, from resignation and promotion, that to enumerate them would be tedious and useless—every session of Assembly made some changes. These will not be noticed in future, until the reorganization of the service, in the autumn of 1776, when the Rhode Island forces were all embodied in the Continental army and marched abroad. The same remark applies to the naval service of the colony. The officers often changed from one service to the other.

[2] A copy of this memorial was given to General Washington, who confirmed its statements, and warmly urged its object in a letter to John Hancock, president of Congress, New York, April 30, 1776. John Hancock's manuscript letter-books, No. 5, p. 17, in Massachusetts Historical Society. For this course, Washington received the thanks of the Assembly in June.

CHAP. XX. 1776. Feb. 4. A descent of the British fleet upon Point Judith, whence a number of sheep and cattle were taken, caused much excitement, owing to the alleged connivance of some prominent persons suspected of being Tories. These were arrested and examined by the committee of safety, who were constantly employed in investigations of this sort.
10. South Kingston applied to Gov. Cooke for an additional force to guard the coast of that township. The fleet paid
15. another visit to Prudence Island, and burnt a few more houses and a windmill. The inhabitants had already evacuated the island, taking off their grain and live stock.

The first American squadron that ever got to sea,
17. sailed at this time from Delaware Bay under Commodore Hopkins. We shall soon have occasion to notice its progress.[1]

23. The people of Newport in town meeting adopted a memorial to the Assembly, complaining of the severity with which Gen. West, commanding the troops on the island, enforced the act against communicating with the British fleet, and of his seizing suspected persons and detaining them for examination. They prayed the Assembly to forbid the troops from entering the town, and to leave the control of the supplies to the council, without the supervision of the General. West denounced this meeting as a Tory movement; but the position of Newport at the time was most critical, for it was placed, as it were, between two fires, and liable to destruction at any moment from either. A dispute in regard to rank arose between Colonels Babcock and Richmond, of West's brigade, which ultimately resulted in the resignation of the former, although his claim to precedence was allowed, and he was for awhile placed in command of the brigade by
26. the Assembly. Gen. West complained to that body that

[1] It comprised 8 vessels—the ships Alfred, of 24 guns, Dudley Saltonstall, captain, and the Columbus, 20, Abraham Whipple; the brigs Andrew Doria, 14, N. Biddle; Cabot, 14, John B. Hopkins, (son of Com. H.;) the sloops Providence, 12; Hornet, 10; Wasp, 8; Fly, tender.

the Tories, arrested by him and sent to Providence, were allowed to return, thus impairing his influence as a commander, and tendered his resignation, which was accepted. Although these men, among whom was Col. Wanton, were discharged by the Assembly, a vote was passed justifying West for their arrest. CHAP. XX. 1776. Feb. 26.

Hard money being required for carrying on the war in Canada, Congress applied to all the colonies to furnish as much as possible, and a large committee was now appointed to collect what they could in Rhode Island.[1] The minute-men were all dismissed, and their places supplied by enlisted troops, of whom seventy were sent to Jamestown to defend that exposed position. 27. A census of men and arms was taken this month in Providence. The population was 4,355, of whom just one-sixth were effective men, with about five hundred stand of arms.

The fleet under Com. Hopkins was ordered to rendezvous at Abaco for fifteen days, after which he made a descent on New Providence, captured the two forts, with a large amount of military stores and over a hundred cannon, which were put on board the ships, and taking the governor, lieutenant-governor, and one of the council as prisoners, sailed for home. Mar. 3.

The evacuation of Boston, which was immediately occupied by Washington, relieved Massachusetts from the presence of the enemy, who sailed for Halifax. 17. It was supposed that their destination was New York, and that they would touch at Newport. The Assembly was at once convened, and a memorial was sent to Gen. Washington, asking that the army, on its march to New York, might pass through this colony. 18. An application for forty heavy cannon was also made. A volunteer patrol com-

[1] Hancock wrote to Gov. Cooke on this subject, April 30. The collections proceeded slowly, for the colony was almost drained of specie before this requisition. $1,173, all that could be got, were sent from Rhode Island, as appears from a letter from Gov. Schuyler to Gov. Cooke. Fort George, May 23, 1776.

CHAP. XX. 1776. Mar. pany, which had existed for some time at Newport, was organized, and placed under the brigadier of the island-forces. Two thousand muskets were ordered for the colony. Fortifications were raised at Howland's and Bristol ferries. Privateering was legalized in conformity with an act of Congress, and a prize court established, of which John Foster was appointed judge. Many persons having removed from the more exposed towns, the Assembly permitted them to retain their former legal residence, and to vote in those towns by returning for that purpose upon election days. Another emission of twenty thousand pounds in bills of credit was made.

25. The death of Hon. Samuel Ward, delegate in Congress, was a severe and unexpected blow. His eminent services to the country, as well as to the colony, were appreciated by his associates, and a public funeral was ordered by Congress, to which the other public bodies in Philadelphia were invited.[1]

31. An alarm, which for the time proved false, that the
April 1. British fleet were entering the bay, caused Gov. Cooke to write an urgent letter for aid to Gen Washington, who at once hastened the march of Generals Greene and Sullivan towards Providence. Both brigades, the former of five and the latter of six regiments, reached Providence in a
5. day or two, followed by Washington himself, with Gates

[1] His death took place on the night of the 25th March, 1776, of small-pox. The proceedings upon it are thus recorded in the journals of Congress:—

"In Congress, Tuesday, March 26, 1776.

"The Congress being informed that Mr. Ward, one of the delegates of Rhode Island, died yesterday; Resolved—that this Congress will in a body attend the funeral of Mr. Ward, to-morrow, with a crape round the arm, and will continue in mourning for the space of one month.

"Resolved—that Mr. Hopkins, Mr. S. Adams, and Mr. Wolcott be a committee to superintend the funeral, and that they be directed to apply to the Rev. Mr. Stillman, and request him to preach a funeral sermon on the occasion; that the said committee be directed to invite the Assembly and Committee of Safety of Pennsylvania, and the other public bodies in Philadelphia, to attend the funeral."

and other general officers. Spencer's brigade, of five regiments, arrived the next day, and in the evening a grand entertainment was given to the commander-in-chief, 1776.
who, on the day following, left for New York, whither April. 7.
the army, there being no cause of detention in Rhode Island, had preceded him.

This was a stirring week both in the military and naval annals of the colony. As Washington left Providence, Com. Hopkins, with his victorious fleet, arrived at New London, having added fresh laurels to his conquest of Nassau, by a series of engagements off the coast within
the past three days. On Thursday he captured the 4
schooner Hawke, of six guns, Capt. Wallace, son of Com.
Wallace, and on Friday the bomb brig Bolton, of eight 5.
guns. On Saturday, before daylight, he engaged the 6.
frigate Glasgow, of twenty-four guns, and her tender, and after an action of three hours, compelled her to run for Newport. His own fleet was too much scattered when the Glasgow was discovered, to come properly into action, and too heavily laden to pursue the chase. The tender
was taken, and all arrived safely the next day at New 7.
London.[1] When the Glasgow reached Newport, the
British squadron went out in pursuit of Hopkins. That 6.
night a battery was planted on Brenton's Point, which compelled the frigate to retreat farther up the bay, and
the next day to put to sea. Soon afterward the Scarboro', 7
of twenty guns, and another vessel of sixteen guns, with
two prizes, anchored in Newport harbor, and the same 11.
night were attacked by the two row galleys from Providence, the prizes retaken, and the ships of war compelled by the galleys and a battery at Newport to seek refuge under Conanicut Island, where another battery was
shortly placed, which obliged the two ships to put to sea, 14.
leaving the bay, for the first time in many months, entirely free from British cruisers.

[1] A detailed account of these engagements, which our limits do not permit, will be found in Cooper's Naval History, i. 77–80.

CHAP. XX. Congress sent on the requisite papers for letters of marque, and appointed Daniel Tillinghast prize agent for 1776. this colony. The cannon taken at Nassau were dis- April tributed, by order of Congress, to various places. Thirteen of them were mounted upon a new fort at the Point in Newport. Old Fort George was reconstructed, and another work erected on Brenton's Point. These defended the harbor.

But difficulties were rife in the military service. Col. Babcock was placed under arrest for some misconduct towards his officers. He was dismissed in May, on the ground of insanity, and Lieut.-Col. Lippitt was promoted to the place. Hopkins applied to Washington for the loan of two hundred men from the army, to supply the losses 26. occasioned by sickness, and with these he brought the fleet from New London to Providence, where he landed over one hundred sick, chiefly with small-pox. Capt. Whipple 30 of the Columbus, having been blamed for not closing with the Glasgow in the late action, demanded a court-martial, May 6. which was held on board the Alfred, at Providence, and resulted in his acquittal. It was shown that the want of wind, and his position to leeward, prevented a nearer approach. Capt. Hazard of the Providence was cashiered for disobedience of orders. Other troubles, of a like nature, were in prospect, as will presently appear.

1. The last colonial Assembly of Rhode Island met at Providence. The same general officers were chosen, the people having confirmed the election of Deputy-Governor Bradford, made by the Assembly in November. The Smithfield and Cumberland Rangers were incorporated. It was resolved to erect a marble monument over the grave of the late Samuel Ward, "in testimony of the respect due to his memory, and in grateful remembrance of his public services." William Ellery was appointed in his place as a delegate to Congress, with Stephen Hopkins, for one year.

The last important act in the colonial history of

Rhode Island, is now to be recorded. It was the Act abjuring allegiance to the British crown; in effect, a Declaration of Independence. It closes the colonial period of our history, for it established Rhode Island as an independent State two months before the general Declaration of the United Colonies. CHAP. XX. 1776. May 4.

However reluctant other portions of the continent may have been to entertain the idea of a final separation from the Mother Country, in this colony the desire for absolute independence was early conceived and steadily followed. Of the two parties that elsewhere existed in America, the Loyalists or Tories, and the Whigs, the former sustained the ministry, the latter, while it opposed the oppressive measures of the King, hoped and labored for conciliation. A few leading minds in many of the colonies, no doubt foresaw the inevitable result, and secretly urged it forward. In Rhode Island the Loyalists, considerable both in number and influence, occupied a position not very different from that of the less active Whigs in other colonies. Wanton, while governor of the colony, was as firm in the spirit of resistance as any Whig, up to the overt act of treason in levying war, and he fairly represents the Tory faction here, with a few exceptional cases from among the Revenue and other Crown officers. The Whigs, on the other hand, aimed from the beginning at independence. Every act since the close of the Ward and Hopkins controversy in 1768, seems directed to that one object. The democratic charter of Rhode Island enabled the legislature to represent fairly and fully the will of the people, and their will was, at all hazards, to preserve that charter, albeit at the expense of their former loyalty. The stamp act produced the fusion of rival factions three years later. The destruction of the Gaspee, the commencement of the Revolution, was a result of that fusion; and its logical and premeditated conclusion was

"An act, repealing an act entitled 'An act for the more effectually securing to His Majesty the allegiance of his subjects, in this his colo-

CHAP. XX. 1776. May 4.

ny and dominion of Rhode Island and Providence Plantations,' and altering the forms of commissions, of all writs and processes in the Courts, and of the oaths prescribed by law.

"Whereas, in all States, existing by compact, protection and allegiance are reciprocal, the latter being only due in consequence of the former; and whereas, George the Third, King of Great Britain, forgetting his dignity, regardless of the compact most solemnly entered into, ratified and confirmed to the inhabitants of this colony, by his illustrious ancestors, and, till of late, fully recognized by him,—and entirely departing from the duties and character of a good King, instead of protecting, is endeavoring to destroy the good people of this Colony, and of all the United Colonies, by sending fleets and armies to America, to confiscate our property, and spread fire, sword, and desolation throughout our country, in order to compel us to submit to the most debasing and detestable tyranny; whereby we are obliged by necessity, and it becomes our highest duty, to use every means with which God and nature have furnished us, in support of our invaluable rights and privileges, to oppose that power which is exerted only for our destruction.

"Be it therefore enacted by this General Assembly, and by the authority thereof it is enacted, that an act entitled 'An act for the more effectually securing to his Majesty the allegiance of his subjects, in this his colony and dominion of Rhode Island and Providence Plantations,' be, and the same is hereby repealed.

"And be it further enacted by this General Assembly, and by the authority thereof it is enacted, That in all commissions for offices, civil and military, and in all writs and processes in law, whether original, judicial, or executory, civil or criminal, wherever the name and authority of the said King is made use of, the same shall be omitted, and in the room thereof, the name and authority of the Governor and Company of this colony shall be substituted, in the following words, to wit: 'The Governor and Company of the English Colony of Rhode Island and Providence Plantations.' That all such commissions, writs, and processes, shall be otherwise of the same form and tenure as they heretofore were; that the Courts of Law be no longer entitled nor considered as the King's Courts; and that no instrument in writing, of any nature or kind, whether public or private, shall, in the date thereof, mention the year of the said King's reign; Provided, nevertheless, that nothing in this act contained, shall render void or vitiate any commission, writ, process, or instrument heretofore made or executed, on account of the name and authority of the said King being therein inserted."

Then follow the forms of oaths prescribed under the new order of things.[1]

CHAP. XX. 1776. May 4.

[1] The original draft of the above Act or Declaration is said to be in the handwriting of Dr. Jonathan Arnold, a deputy from Providence, and afterwards a member of the Continental Congress. History should preserve the names of the actors in this closing scene of our Colonial drama. May, 1776.

MEMBERS OF THE GENERAL ASSEMBLY, AND GENERAL OFFICERS.

Nicholas Cooke, governor. William Bradford, deputy-governor.
Henry Ward, secretary. Henry Marchant, attorney-general.
Joseph Clarke, general Treasurer.

ASSISTANTS.

John Collins, Simeon Potter, Ambrose Page, John Sayles, John Jepson, James Arnold, Jonathan Randall, Peter Phillips, William Potter, Thomas Church.

DEPUTIES.

Newport.
John Wanton, S. of G.,
Samuel Fowler,
George Sears,
Gideon Wanton,
Thomas Freebody,
Joseph Belcher.

Providence.
Jonathan Arnold,
John Brown,
John Smith,
Amos Atwell.

Portsmouth.
Metcalf Bowler,
John Coddington,
John Thurston.

Warwick.
William Greene,
Jacob Greene,
Charles Holden, jr.,
John Waterman.

Westerly.
Joshua Babcock,
Joseph Noyes.

North Kingstown.
John Northup,
Sylvester Gardner.

South Kingstown.
Samuel Seager,
Samuel Babcock.

East Greenwich.
Job Comstock.
Thomas Shippee.

Jamestown.
Samuel Carr,
Benjamin Underwood.

Smithfield.
Daniel Mowry, jr.,
Andrew Waterman.

Scituate.
William West,
Christopher Potter.

Gloucester.
Richard Steere,
Chad Brown.

Charlestown.
Joseph Stanton, jr.,
Jonathan Haszard.

West Greenwich.
Thomas Tillinghast,
Judiah Aylesworth.

Coventry.
Ephraim Westcott,
Jeremiah Fenner.

Exeter.
George Peirce.

Middletown.
Joshua Barker,
Nicholas Easton.

Bristol.
Shearjashub Bourne,
Nathaniel Pearce.

Tiverton.
Gideon Almy,
John Cooke.

Little Compton.
Thomas Brownell,
Daniel Wilbur.

Warren.
Cromwell Child,
Sylvester Child.

Cumberland.
John Dexter,
Elisha Waterman.

Richmond.
Samuel Teft,
Richard Bailey.

Cranston.
Andrew Harris,
Zuriel Waterman,

Johnston.
John Fenner,
Peleg Williams,

North Providence.
Thomas Olney,
Jonathan Jenckes, jr.

Barrington.
Edward Bosworth,
Thomas Allen.

Hopkinton,
John Larkin,
Thomas Wells.

Metcalf Bowler, speaker, and Josias Lyndon, clerk of the Lower House.

CHAP. XX. 1776. May 4. The records of the Assembly had always closed with the loyal motto, "God save the King." At the close of this session, the words were changed, and "God save the United Colonies," appears, for the first time, on the archives of the ancient Plantations.[1]

Rhode Island had become in form, as well as in spirit, an independent State.

[1] But few references to authorities have been made in this chapter, and a few preceding it, nor will many be given in the remainder of the work. They are very numerous, and for the most part are in manuscripts not very accessible to the general reader. They are principally the Hopkins and Foster papers in the Rhode Island Historical Society; the Hutchinson, Trumbull and Hancock papers and letter books in the Massachusetts Historical Society, the journals of the Recess Committee, extracts from the journals of Congress, the records of the Assembly, and many volumes of original letters, filed and bound in the Secretary's office of this State, besides the papers of some private families, kindly loaned to the writer—all in manuscript. The Providence Gazette, of which a complete set, from its commencement in 1762, is preserved in the Rhode Island Historical Society, and the collections of the several State historical societies, with many other histories, local, State, and general, are the printed authorities relied upon in this work.

CHAPTER XXI.

1776—1778.

FROM THE ACT OF INDEPENDENCE, MAY 4TH, 1776, TO THE BATTLE ON RHODE ISLAND, AUGUST 29TH, 1778.

AT the next issue of the Providence Gazette, after CHAP.
the passage of the act of independence, the arms of Great XXI.
Britain, which had always appeared at the head of the 1776.
paper, were dropped. John Paul Jones, late first lieu- May
tenant of the Alfred, was sent by Com. Hopkins, in charge 10.
of the sloop Providence, to carry the borrowed soldiers to
New York, and there to enlist a crew, after which he returned to the station. One of the armed schooners taken
in the late cruise, was purchased by Congress for the
Continental service, and named the Hopkins.[1] On the
urgent recommendation of Gen. Washington, Congress
took into continental pay the two regiments lately raised 11.
in Rhode Island. Of the thirteen frigates ordered by
Congress in December, two were built in this colony, the
Warren of thirty-two and the Providence of twenty-eight
guns. Benjamin Tallman superintended the construction
of one, if not both of them. They were launched at Provi- 15&18
dence within the same week.

The surrender of the Cedars, an advanced fort near 19.
Montreal, and the capture of a detachment, comprising a 20.

[1] Letter of Hancock to Com. H.—Hopkins Papers, vol. ii.; R. I. Hist. Soc.

CHAP. XXI. part of the Rhode Island regiment, sent by Gen. Arnold
from Montreal, under Major Henry Sherburne, to rein-
1776. force that garrison, were fatal to the cause in Canada.
June The army were soon after obliged to retreat, and the conquest of Canada was abandoned. The question of inde-
7. pendence was moved in Congress by Lee of Virginia, and
gave rise to protracted debate, in which there appeared at
first but seven States in favor of, to six against the measure.
But the war was prosecuted with unabated vigor. Large
bodies of troops were raised, and the ships were manned.
8. John B. Hopkins and Samuel Tompkins were appointed
to command the two frigates built at Providence, the former to the Warren, the latter to the Providence, in which
he was superseded by Whipple a few months later. The
10. Assembly resumed its sessions at Newport, which of late
had been held elsewhere, owing to the presence of the
enemy. It was resolved to establish a hospital in each
county for inoculation for the small-pox.[1] A few members protested against the act. The delegates were instructed to propose to Congress a general system of inoculation in the army and navy, where the small-pox, especially in Canada, was raging to a fearful extent. By the advice of Congress a census of the colony was ordered to be taken. A test oath, to be administered to all suspected persons, was adopted. Quakers were exempted from the operation of this act, out of respect to their views on the subject of oaths. Five persons in Newport, who refused to subscribe the test, were removed to Gloucester, there to remain at large upon parole. James Honeyman voluntarily resigned his royal commission as advocate-general of the Court of Vice-Admiralty for this colony. The revival of trade was promoted by an act permitting
commerce with all parts of the world, except Great Britain
17. or her dependencies, and appointing two Intendants, one

[1] This was done at Providence, in August, and a list of over 400 persons inoculated at the Small-pox Hospital in Providence, in September and October, is preserved in the Foster Papers, vol. x.

at Newport, and one at Providence, to supervise the CHAP.
same.[1] The Assembly then adjourned till August. XXI.

Three days afterward Admiral Lord Howe arrived off 1776.
the coast of Massachusetts, whence he sent a circular to June. 20.
all the colonial governors announcing that he and his
brother, the General, were empowered to grant pardon to
all who would submit and aid in restoring peace; but his
"Declaration" had no effect. A few days later a British
fleet under Sir Peter Parker was repulsed in the attack on 28.
Fort Moultrie, before Charleston. Two days afterwards,
Gen. Howe with about eight thousand troops, including
the late Boston garrison, arrived at Sandy Hook, and dis- 30.
embarked at Staten Island, where he was soon joined by July 2.
the Admiral.

The instructions to Com. Hopkins had been referred May 8.
to a special committee of seven members. The Marine June 13.
Committee reported that complaints were made against
him, and Capts. Saltonstall and Whipple, for breach of
orders. They were accordingly summoned to Philadel- 14.
phia by Hancock, and the Marine Committee were or- July 2.
dered to enquire into the subject. They acquitted the
two captains, and sent them back to their commands. 11.
The next day the special committee on Hopkins was discharged, and his instructions, with the complaints against 12.
him, were referred to the Marine Committee. The commodore waited upon Congress, and obtained a copy of the Aug. 5.
charges against him. These originated with the Anti-
New England feeling, pervading members from other
States, and their chief point was that he had made the
successful descent upon Nassau instead of cruising along
the southern seaboard, as it was claimed that his instructions required. The following week he was heard in re- 12.
ply. After a debate in which he was ably defended by
John Adams, Congress disapproved his conduct in not 15.
proceeding direct to the Carolinas, and the next day 16.

[1] At the August Session, Henry Ward was chosen Intendant of Trade for Providence, and Solomon Southwick for Newport.

CHAP. XXI. passed a resolution of censure. It was attempted to
cashier him on the spot, which was prevented for a time
1776. by the exertions of Adams, and Hopkins was directed to
Aug. 22. resume the command of the fleet, and cruise against the
British fishery at Newfoundland; but the efforts of his enemies ultimately prevailed, and in the following March he was suspended from the service, and on the second of January, 1778, was dismissed. No commander-in-chief has since been appointed for the navy.[1]

June 28. Another debate ensued on the question of independence, when a draft of the Declaration was reported to
July 1. Congress. Nine colonies voted for it in Committee of the
4. Whole, and on the final action, the measure was adopted
by all but New York, whose delegates, being without instructions, declined to vote. The Provincial Congress of
9. that State, however, gave it their sanction a few days
later, and the act thus became unanimous. Attention was at once given to the northern army, and the president
5. was ordered to write to Gov. Cooke to send fifty ship-car-
penters from Rhode Island to Gen. Schuyler, to build vessels for the defence of the lakes.

The declaration of independence at once altered the position of the loyalists, and compelled the wavering to decide which party they would espouse. In Newport Col. Lippitt took measures to ascertain the feelings of those whose position was doubtful, by tendering the test oath before Judge Bowler, to about eighty persons, all but three of whom refused it and were disarmed. The As-
18. sembly, convened at Newport to take formal action upon
the resolution of the fourth in Congress, voted that they "do approve the said resolution, and do most solemnly engage that we will support the said General Congress with our lives and fortunes." Measures were taken to proclaim it with military honors, and the national salute
20. of thirteen guns, at Newport. The event was celebrated

[1] Journals of Congress. Cooper's Naval History, I.—80. Autobiography of John Adams.

with great rejoicings, and the burning of the King's arms at Providence. The legal title of the government was altered by the Assembly to "The State of Rhode Island and Providence Plantations." The two row-galleys were sent to New York to be placed under the orders of Gen. Washington. A fine of a hundred pounds was decreed against any one convicted of acknowledging, in any manner, even in preaching or praying, the supremacy of the King of Great Britain, and whoever should refuse to sign the test act was disfranchised, and rendered incapable of suing in the courts, or of petitioning the Assembly for relief from judgment.[1] A fine of fifty pounds was established against any who should attempt to depreciate the Continental or State bills of credit, and a further issue of ten thousand pounds in these bills, having six years to run, was made. Eleven of the prominent Tories of Newport, were sent into different towns to remain on parole. The records of this Assembly close with the words "God save the United States." The August session was the last that was held at Newport for four years. Officers were appointed for the brigade taken into continental pay. The field-officers were recommended to Congress, the subalterns were elected in grand committee.[2]

1776. July

Aug. 19.

[1] At the September session, all officers, civil or military, and all attorneys-at-law, were required to subscribe the test-oath, except Quakers; and members of the Assembly from towns where all the electors had not taken the oath were forbidden to take their seats, and new elections were ordered to be held in those towns.

[2] The officers recommended to Congress were—of the 1st regiment, Colonel William Richmond; Lieutenant-colonel Caleb Gardiner; Major Benjamin Tallman; of the 2d regiment, Colonel Christopher Lippitt; Lieutenant-colonel Adam Comstock; Major James Tew. These were confirmed by Congress, September 7.

The officers chosen for Richmond's regiment were as follows:—

Captains—Thomas Wells, 3d, Christopher Manchester, James Wallace, Josiah Gibbs, Jr., Benjamin Diamond, Samuel Phillips, Jr., Caleb Carr, Abimeleck Riggs, Malachi Hammett, Royal Smith, Lemuel Bailey, and Jonathan Wallen.

Lieutenants—Peleg Berry, Walter Palmer, Jonathan Duval, Jr., Philip

CHAP. XXI. 1776. Aug.

A deed of chivalrous daring, the first of many exploits in the war that were to illustrate the cool courage and heroic self-devotion of Capt. Silas Talbot, was performed by him during this month, on the Hudson River. An old sloop, rigged into a bomb-boat, was placed under his command, and prepared as a fire-ship, with which he sought to strike a blow that should inspire terror in the enemy, and give confidence to his countrymen in the approaching conflict. Ascending the river to Fort Washington, he arranged his plans to attack the Asia, a sixty-four gun-ship, at anchor, with two other British men-of-war, a few miles below. When all was ready, the little vessel got under-way in the dead of night, and drifting slowly down with the tide, was almost afoul of the Asia before being discovered. Scarcely had one broadside from the doomed ship awakened the slumbering echoes of the highlands, before the grappling irons were fastened to her

Arnold, Philip Traftan, Benjamin West, Samuel Stevens, Squire Fisk, Stephen Hopkins, Ebenezer Macomber, Benjamin Church, and Edward Arrowsmith.

Ensigns—John Pearce, Peleg Simmons, Jr., Benjamin Burroughs, Elisha Parker, Benjamin Stelle, John Handy, Samuel Hicks, Henry Alexander, Zephaniah Brown, Joseph Springer, Philip Palmer, and Moses Watson.

Adjutant, Benjamin Stelle; Quartermaster, John Handy; Surgeon, John Bartlett.

The officers chosen for the 2d, or Lippitt's regiment, were;

Captains—Nathaniel Blackmar, Jonathan Brownell, David Dexter, Loring Peck, John Carr, Thomas Gorton, Arthur Fenner, Benjamin Hoppin, Simeon Martin, Christopher Dyer, Thomas Arnold.

Lieutenants—Wilson Rawson, William Jones, David Searle, Gilbert Grant, Alexander Thomas, Ichabod Prentice, Jacob Williams, Abraham Tourtellot, William Belcher, Peleg Hoxsie, Thomas Noyes, and Reuben Hewit.

Ensigns—Joseph Bowen, Gilbert Richmond, Samuel Dexter, Joseph Read, Brenton Bliss, Caleb Mathews, William Pullen, John Cowen, Philip Martin, John Holden, Benjamin Bourne, and David Melvil.

Adjutant, John Holden; Quartermaster, Benjamin Bourne; Surgeon, Isaac Ross Bliven; Major of Brigade, William Barton.

The officers of artillery were: Robert Elliott, captain; William Bull, captain-lieutenant; Joshua Sayer, 1st lieutenant; Nathaniel Gladding, 2d lieutenant; Rhodes Packard, lieutenant fireworker.

CHAP. XXI. 1776. Aug.

side, and a column of fire that shed the brightness of noonday across the surrounding gloom flashed up from the blazing bomb-boat. The man who ignited the train, immediately jumped overboard, according to orders, while Talbot remained for a few moments to ensure the success of his plan. He was badly scorched, owing to this delay, but otherwise escaped unharmed, amid a storm of shot that was hurled at the retreating boats. One officer, Ensign John Thomas, of the Rhode Island line, was drowned upon this expedition. The Asia was saved from total destruction only through the desperate efforts of her crew and those of the other two ships. So alarmed were the enemy at this gallant assault, that they slipped their cables and gained a more secure position below the city. In the following year,[1] Congress promoted Capt. Talbot to the rank of major, on account of this "spirited attempt," and recommended him to Washington for employment.

The arrival of nine thousand German troops, chiefly 12.
Hessians, at New York, increased the British force in America to twenty-two thousand men, under Gen. Howe, and twenty-five ships-of-war under Admiral Howe, besides which a third division of Hessians, five thousand strong, was daily expected. The effective force under Washington was less than twenty thousand. Gen Howe began to 22.
remove his army from Staten Island to Long Island, where Greene, now appointed a major-general, commanded, with 26.
about nine thousand men, but was obliged by severe illness to relinquish the command to Putnam. Some hard fight- 27.
ing ensued, in which Generals Sullivan and Stirling were taken prisoners, and Capt. Benijah Carpenter, of the Rhode Island line was slain. The next day the British attacked the American lines at Brooklyn, but were re- 28.
pulsed. Washington, finding the position untenable, resolved to abandon the island, and on the following night, 29.

[1] Oct. 10, 1777.

CHAP. XXI. in person conducted the retreat, and under cover of a dense fog, landed the whole army safely at New York.

1776. Sept. 2. Before this retreat was known in Rhode Island, the Assembly ordered the entire brigade to the relief of Long Island. Col. Lippitt's regiment, with a detachment of artillery were to march at once. A committee[1] was sent to New York, with a letter from Gov. Cooke, to inform Washington of the condition of the colony, and obtain his views upon the best method to adopt for its defence. Ten flats, to carry seventy men each, were constructed for service in the bay. The people of New Shoreham, being completely in the power of the enemy, were forbidden all communication with the continent, in order to prevent intelligence from reaching the British. Block Island became a convenient place for the exchange of seamen and other prisoners during the war. More money was required for the treasury, and in the new issue of £20,001 in bills of credit that was voted, the continental denomination of dollars was for the first time adopted, and $66,670, being that amount at the rate of six shillings to a dollar, were emitted.

The Assembly had anticipated the action of Congress,
3. who, the next day, wrote to them to send aid to New York, and called on Massachusetts to send a regiment of her militia to Rhode Island, to supply the place of the continental troops thus withdrawn.

14. The departure of the troops for New York, left the
17. State defenceless. Another regiment was enlisted at once, by order of the Recess Committee, to serve for three months, under Col. John Cooke, and stationed upon the island. They were soon reinforced by a body of Massachusetts militia under Col. Cushing.

13. The committee from Rhode Island waited upon Gen. Washington, and remained in camp four days, during which most important events occurred. The Americans

[1] Joshua Babcock, John Collins, and Joseph Stanton.

evacuated New York, and the British entered it under a heavy fire from their fleet. The next day a battle was fought near Harlaem, in which Varnum's and Hitchcock's regiments distinguished themselves, and Lieutenant Noel Allen, of the Rhode Island line, was killed.[1] Congress resolved to enlist for three years, or during the war, an army of eighty-eight battalions, of seven hundred and fifty men each, two of which were to be raised in this State. The term battalions was used for regiments, to obviate a difficulty in the exchange of prisoners. CHAP. XXI. 1776. Aug. 14, 15, 16.

17. Washington replied to the Rhode Island letter, thanking the Assembly for their promptness in ordering the two battalions to his relief, and discussing at length the subjects presented to him by the committee.[2] Congress, in notifying the State of the new army arrangement, in which the troops already in service were to form a part, desired that it should be ascertained what number of the officers and men would engage to serve during the war. They increased the pay of the army, and wrote another letter, urging that means be adopted to prevent its disbanding. 24. Oct. 9.

Capt. Whipple, having just returned from a successful cruise in the Columbus, in which he had taken some valuable prizes, was promoted to the new frigate Providence. New regulations were adopted for the navy, conferring upon the officers assimilated rank with those of the army, and encouraging enlistments by an increase of prize money. The defeat of the flotilla under Gen. Arnold, on Lake Champlain, after a bloody action against a greatly superior force, opened the road to Crown Point, which had been abandoned by the Americans, and was now occupied by the enemy. 10. 12. 20.

The new army arrangement, reducing the three Rhode Island regiments now in the field to two, required a re-

[1] Major-General Greene to Governor Cooke, 17th September, 1776. No. 62.

[2] This letter, of six closely written foolscap pages, dated 17th September, is No. 60 of the Rhode Island State Collection for 1776.

CHAP. XXI. 1776. Oct. modelling of the list of officers, and a reduction of their number. Gen. Greene prepared a list to be recommended to the State for appointment, which was sent on by Washington. It was important to know who would agree to serve through the war before making the selections. Col.
15. Lippitt sent on the names of several of his officers who volunteered, but many declined to hand in their names for fear of being dropped. The march of Col. Richmond's regiment, whose term of enlistment was nearly expired,
17. had been countermanded by Gov. Cooke with the approval of Washington.

Privateering was conducted on a large scale, and with great success from all the seaports of the continent. We have the names of no less than sixteen vessels, many of them heavily armed and well manned, that were thus engaged at this time from Rhode Island alone, and doubtless there were many more. The service that these, as well as the continental cruisers, rendered to the country, by obtaining supplies of many articles which the colonial policy of England had prevented being produced in America, was incalculable. "Without the succors that were procured in this manner, the Revolution must have been checked at the outset."[1] Rhode Island was a rendezvous both for national and private cruisers, and the papers of the day are filled with the proceedings of admiralty courts held at Providence, and with the reports of their maritime exploits.

28. On the same day with the indecisive battle of White Plains, the Assembly met at South Kingstown, and elected the officers recommended by Washington for the new battalions.[2] Joseph Clarke was appointed for this State

[1] Cooper's Naval History, I., 223, where an anecdote is given in the note, confirming the statements of the text.

[2] For the 1st battalion, J. M. Varnum, colonel (he declined); Adam Comstock, lieutenant-colonel; Henry Sherburne, major; Captains—Ebenezer Flagg, Silas Talbot, Thomas Cole, John S. Dexter, Simeon Martin, Jonathan Wallen; Paymaster, Jonathan Hazzard; 1st Lieutenants—Joseph Arnold,

a commissioner of the Loan office, lately established by Congress in all the States, and the penalty of death was decreed against any one who should counterfeit the bills issued by any of these Loan offices. CHAP. XXI. 1776.

The health of the venerable Hopkins preventing his constant attendance upon Congress, Deputy-Governor Bradford was chosen as a delegate to that body. The thanks of the Assembly were tendered to Mr. Hopkins for his services, and he was requested to continue them as soon as he was able. The two paymasters were sent on to Gen. Washington, with a letter from the Assembly and the new commissions for the officers. The last Thursday in November was appointed as a day of Thanksgiving. Those towns whose local officers had neglected to subscribe the test, were required to hold new elections. Under this law the last recorded town meeting held at Newport for three years, was holden to fill the vacancies Nov.
thus occasioned. 14.

The capture of Fort Washington, and the occupation 16.
of the west side of the Hudson River by the British, compelled the evacuation of Fort Lee, then in command of 20.
Gen. Greene. Cornwallis entered the Jerseys, and occupied Newark. Then commenced that memorable re- 24.

William Belcher, Timothy Lock, Samuel Bissell, Wilson Rawson, William Potter, John Handy, Thomas Noyes; 2d Lieutenants—Ichabod Prentice, John Chapman, John Remington; Ensign, Zephaniah Brown; Quartermaster, Clarke Brown. For the 2d battalion—Daniel Hitchcock, colonel; Israel Angell, lieutenant-colonel; Christopher Smith, major; Captains—Jeremiah Olney, William Tew, Coggeshall Olney, Ephraim Bowen, William Bradford, Jr., John Carr, Abimalech Riggs; 1st Lieutenants—Stephen Olney, William Allen, William Littlefield, Gilbert Grant, Joseph Whitmarsh, Daniel Pearce, Amos Crandall, Micah Moulton; 2d Lieutenants—Thomas Hughes, Duty Jerrald; Ensigns—Ebenezer West, Holliman Potter, Thomas Waterman, Oliver Jenckes, Richard Hunniwell; Quartermaster, Cyprian Sterry: Paymaster, Charles Holden.

It will be seen that many vacancies are left among the company officers, especially of the lower grades. These were to be filled by the officers at their discretion. Both battalions were much changed by death and promotion during the winter.

CHAP. XXI. treat which, for the ensuing month, placed the American cause in utmost peril.

1776. Nov. 16. Congress proposed a convention of the New England States to be held at Providence in December, to consider the subject of currency, and how to sustain the continental credit.

Col. Richmond's regiment being disbanded, another
21. was raised by the Assembly, for three months' service, to include six in every one hundred men above eighteen years of age in the State. John Sayles, jr., was appointed colonel.[1] The inducements to privateering so impeded enlistments for the army, that the Assembly proposed to the other States to lay a general embargo until the quotas required by Congress were filled. This measure was also
27. suggested by Gen. Lee in a letter to Gov. Cooke a few days later. Cols. Varnum and Hitchcock, and the com-
28–30. mittee who had taken on the commissions, all sent home lists of officers who declined to serve, and of others recommended to fill the vacancies, a duty which Washington entrusted to them, who were afterwards confirmed by the Assembly.

A gloomy period in the affairs of Rhode Island was about to commence; one which was to task to the utmost the military energies of the State by making it, for nearly three years, the theatre of war. Seven ships of the line,
Dec. 2. and four frigates, under Sir Peter Parker, appeared off Block Island, and the next day went up the sound to join the fleet of seventy transports, having on board about six thousand troops destined for Newport. All the militia of the State were immediately under arms, and expresses were sent as far as New Hampshire to summon aid. The

[1] Benjamin Tallman was appointed lieutenant-colonel, and Thomas Potter, jr., major of this regiment. The company officers of this and of Colonel Cooke's command were chiefly taken from the recently disbanded forces, and as they were enlisted but for three months, before which time an entirely new military organization was made on a more permanent basis, their names are not given. Stephen Wigneron was appointed surgeon to this brigade, which was stationed upon the island.

Recess Committee advised Com. Hopkins to put to sea, but this he was unable to do for want of men. They ordered another regiment to be drafted, of which Joseph Stanton was made colonel, and John Reynolds lieutenant-colonel, and appointed Gen. West as brigadier of the troops on the island. One full regiment of Providence county militia volunteered for service on the island, without awaiting the draft, and was placed in command of Col. Chad Brown. An embargo was laid on all privateers and merchantmen, to facilitate the manning of the navy. The women and children in the seaboard towns, especially Newport, Providence, Bristol, and East Greenwich, were advised to move, with their furniture, to the interior. Prisoners of war were placed on board Com. Hopkins' ships, or sent into the country for security. The stock on Rhode-Island and Conanicut was driven off. Warwick Neck was defended by Col. John Waterman's Kent county regiment, Pawtuxet by Col. Samuel Aborn, and Tower Hill by Col. Joseph Noyes. There were about seven hundred troops on the island when the enemy, having throughout the week made several feints at landing in Connecticut, entered the bay, and rounding the north end of Conanicut, anchored off Stoddard's shore in Middletown.

CHAP. XXI. 1776. Dec. 5. 6. 7.

On the following day the army disembarked, one regiment at Long wharf, the main body at Greensdale,[1] in Middletown, and after a night of pillage, the next morning marched into Newport.[2] A large portion of them were quartered at the farm houses on the island during the winter. Besides English infantry and a corps of light

8.

[1] Now the residence of the Hon. Nathaniel Greene, grandson of Maj. Gen. Greene, and lately for many years State Senator from Middletown.

[2] Here occurs a large gap, and the only one, in the records of the town of Portsmouth, the most complete, best preserved records in the State. The last meeting before the British occupation was held on the 2d Dec., to enlist the 16 men apportioned to be raised by that town, and for other business. The meeting then adjourned to 10th Dec. Then follows this memorandum: "Rhode Island, &c. On Sunday, 8th day of Dec., 1776,

CHAP. XXI. 1776. Dec. horse, there were several Hessian regiments, the whole under command of Gen. Clinton.[1] Earl Percy, and Major-General Prescot, were also in the expedition. The American troops left the island. Col. Cook encamped at Tiverton, and Gen. West at Bristol. Assistance was poured in from the neighboring States. From Massachusetts, the Bristol and Plymouth county brigades, under Godfrey and Cushing, with three regiments and a train of artillery from Worcester and Boston, were despatched by the legislature; and from Connecticut three regiments and five companies with a small body of cavalry, were sent by Gov. Trumbull. These were quartered at all the defensible points on each side of the bay. The State and the island were two great and hostile camps. Providence was given up to military occupation. Many of the inhabitants moved away, the college exercises were suspended, and the building was occupied as barracks, and afterwards for a military hospital.

The Assembly convened at Greenwich, but for greater safety, adjourned to Providence. A council of war, composed of ten members, was appointed, to exercise the
10. power heretofore held by the Recess Committee, and re-
12. quests were sent to the other New England colonies to send committees to Providence to devise means for raising an army, and thus to relieve the militia now in the field. A brigade of three regiments, two of infantry, each of seven hundred and fifty men in eight companies, and one of artillery, of three hundred men in five companies, was

about 8000 of British troops landed and took possession of this island, and remained until Monday, the 25th day of October, A. D. 1779, for which time the Inhabitance was greatly opresed." The next recorded meeting was held Nov. 27, 1779.

[1] The British regiments were the 22d, Col. Campbell; 43d, Col. Marsh; 54th, Col. Bruce; 63d, Col. Sell, of infantry; and Col. Ennis's regiment of artillery. The Hessian regiments were Haynau's, Beno's, Dedford Landscraft Socier's, and Anspiker's. The last was composed of men all six feet in height.

ordered to be enlisted for fifteen months' service.[1] Gen. Varnum was appointed to this brigade, having resigned his colonelcy in the army at New York, and Gen. Malmedy, a French officer recommended to the State by Gen. Lee, was appointed "Chief Engineer, and Director of the works of defence in this State," with the rank of brigadier. Jonathan Clarke was appointed Linguist to Gen. Malmedy, with the rank of major. 1776. Dec.

The proposal for a convention at Providence was at 16.
once adopted by Massachusetts. Connecticut was equally 18.
prompt, and New Hampshire also elected a committee on 19.

[1] The officers of this brigade were: Of Infantry—Cols. Benjamin Tallman, Joseph Stanton; Lieut. Cols. Christopher Smith, Archibald Crary; Majors Wm. Bradford, Jr., Wm. Barton; and Cyprian Sterry, Brigade Major.

Officers of Tallman's Regiment.—Captains—Abimelech Riggs, Caleb Carr, Reuben Ballou, James Williams, James Parker, Thomas Allen, Christopher Manchester, Benjamin Church. 1st Lieuts.—David Bacon, Ebenezer Macomber, Wm. Sayles, Jacob Belknap, Rufus Barton, Wm. Lawless, Walter Palmer, Henry Alexander. 2d do.—Wm. Allen, Walter Channing, Benj. S. Wallcott, Zadock Williams, Jonathan Maxson, Thomas Swan, Robert Rogers, Daniel Green. Ensigns—Abm. Andrews, Daniel Fiske, Samuel Whipple, Daniel Sheldon, Barber Peckham, Thomas Pearce, Joshua Babcock 2d, Joseph Hopkins (S. of S.) Adjutant—Benjamin Stelle. Quartermaster—John Handy.

Of Stanton's Regiment.—Captains—Thomas Thompson, Royal Smith, Malachi Hammett, James Albro, Peleg Slocum, Josiah Gibbs, Benjamin West, Nathaniel Hawkins. 1st Lieuts.—Peleg Berry, Wm. Coon, Micah Whitmarsh, John Cole, Gabriel Allen, Philip Traftan, Joseph Springer, John Pearce. 2d Lieuts.—Matthew Randall, Edward Crandall, Job Greene, Francis W. Gardner, David Bently, Isaac Johnston, Charles Dyre, Edward Coleman. Ensigns—Daniel Stafford, James Cotterell, Wm. Whipple, Joseph Manchester, Nathan Westcott, George Briggs, Asa Kenna, Joseph Rhodes. Adjutant—Jonathan Duval, Jr. Quartermaster—Solomon Townsend, Jr.

Of the Artillery Regiment.—Col.—Robert Elliot. Lt. Col.—Wm. Wall. Major—Job Pearce. Captains—Joshua Sayer, Jabez Westcott, Samuel Sweet, Gideon Westcott, Ebenezer Adams. Capt. Lieuts.—Nathaniel Gladding, Philip Morse, John Warner, Samuel Angell, John Garzia. 1st Lieuts.—Rhodes Packard, Thomas Carlile, Wm. Comstock, Amos Jillson, Joseph Crandall. 2d Lieuts.—Wm. Ham, Ezekiel Burket, Elijah Babbitt, Uriah Westcott, John Proud. Lieut. Fireworkers—Edward Price, Cyrus Manchester, Wm. Page, Benjamin Bickford, Wm. Fiske. Adjutant—Wm. Dennison. Quartermaster—George Richards.

CHAP. XXI. the first day that her legislature met. Major-General Lincoln arrived at Providence with orders to take the
1776. chief command. It was reported that the enemy intend-
Dec. ed to march to Boston by way of Providence. Martial
20. law was proclaimed by the council of war. The Assem-
23. bly met at Providence, and two days later the New England convention, composed of three members from each
25. State,[1] also assembled. Hon. Stephen Hopkins was chosen president. The two bodies consulted together through
26. the session. The convention advised that an army of about six thousand men should be concentrated in this State, and assigned the quotas to be furnished by each
29. State—to Massachusetts, nineteen hundred, to Connecticut, eleven hundred, to New Hampshire, three hundred, and to Rhode Island eighteen hundred, besides a thousand continental troops.

The question of currency was also discussed, and it
27. was recommended that no more paper money be issued, unless in extreme cases, but that taxation, and borrowing at five per cent. be resorted to for the supply of the treasuries. The Assembly approved of this resolve, and ordered a loan of forty thousand pounds to be raised upon State notes, to be redeemed in two years by a tax. The convention also agreed upon an act to prevent monopolies, regulating the prices of labor, of food, clothing, and the essentials of life, which the Assembly adopted, with some additions, and affixed penalties to its violation.

Two fire-ships were ordered to be placed in charge of Capt. Silas Talbot. The two regiments whose short terms of enlistment had nearly expired, were disbanded, in order that the men might enter the new brigade. The whole effective force of the State was drafted for service, in three divisions, each to serve one month. An army hospital was established under the direction of Dr. Jona-

[1] The R. I. members were Hon. Stephen Hopkins, Hon. Wm. Bradford, and Henry Ward, Esq.

than Arnold. The Assembly now fixed the pay of its CHAP.
members at nine shillings a day, but the act gave so much XXI.
dissatisfaction, that it was repealed the following April. 1776.
While these two bodies were sitting at Providence, events Dec.
of great importance took place at the seat of war. Congress had adjourned to Baltimore, as it was feared that 20.
Philadelphia would be captured, and did not return till
the following March. To check the progress of the
enemy, Washington recrossed the Delaware in the night, 25.
with less than twenty-three hundred men, and forming his
army in two divisions under Generals Greene and Sullivan, attacked the Hessian advanced post at Trenton early 26.
the next morning. The two divisions assaulted the town
from opposite sides at the same time, and in a few minutes,
with a charge of bayonets, routed the surprised and bewildered enemy. The desperate condition of the army,
of which a large portion was about disbanding, their term
of service closing with the year, led Congress to confer 27.
upon Washington almost dictatorial powers, for six
months, that he might reorganize it upon a better basis.

The last night of the year was a turning point in the 31.
Revolution. The remnants of the army were assembled
at Crosswicks; the time of the New England regiments
had expired, except Lippitt's, which had but eighteen
days more to serve, and as yet there were none but raw
militia to take their place. The whole army did not
number four thousand men, and Cornwallis, with ten
thousand men, was said to be marching from Princeton
to attack them. In the brigade commanded by Col.
Hitchcock, as the oldest colonel, were the three Rhode
Island regiments, Varnum's, Hitchcock's and Lippitt's,
with two from Massachusetts. Lippitt's regiment comprised more than one third the number of men. Gen.
Mifflin, at the request of Washington, harangued the bri- 1777.
gade to persuade them to volunteer for another month. Jan. 1.
"He did it well," says an eye-witness, and every man
poised his firelock as the signal of assent. Within two

CHAP. XXI. 1777. Jan. 2. hours the army was on a night march for Trenton, which it had left two days before, and where it arrived the next morning. Scarcely had the soldiers entered the houses, so lately vacated by the Hessians, when the drums beat to arms. Cornwallis was approaching the town. Some troops were sent out to check his advance, and Hitchcock's brigade was ordered to cross the bridge, over a small creek that empties into the Delaware near that place, to cover their retreat. Near the close of the day the British entered the town, driving before them the American detachment. The brigade opened ranks to let the fugitives pass through, and then closing in solid column, left in front, commenced a retreat to the bridge, exposed to a flanking fire at all the cross streets. The enemy attempted, by an oblique movement, to cut them off from the bridge, but were prevented. The brigade passed in safety, and re-formed on the other side of the creek, while the artillery, planted upon and at the right and left of the bridge, checked the advance of the British until the brigade returned to the edge of the stream and repulsed them.

All honor to the gallant men who, there, by the side of Washington, defended the pass at Trenton bridge! Upon their bravery, for one short but pregnant hour, hung the destiny of America; for had Cornwallis crossed the bridge, the whole army must have surrendered. Yet history has scarcely noticed the deeds of that eventful day, without which the victory at Trenton would have been in vain, and the battle of Princeton would never have been fought.

At midnight Washington silently withdrew his army, and by a circuitous route advanced on Princeton, where, at sunrise, a victory was obtained over three British regi-
3. ments, two of them already on their way to join Cornwallis. Gen. Mercer, of Virginia, was killed in this action. After the battle, Washington, taking Col. Hitchcock by the hand, expressed high admiration of his con-

duct and of that of his troops, and desired him to convey CHAP. XXI.
his thanks to the brigade. A third night's march brought
them, near midnight, to Somerset Court House, where 1777.
the exhausted troops laid down on the frozen ground Jan.
without food or shelter. The next day they went into 4.
winter quarters at Morristown. New Jersey had been recovered by the masterly achievements of the past few days. Soon after the encampment at Morristown, Col. Hitchcock died, the brigade was broken up, and the regiments were stationed at different places until their term of voluntary enlistment expired, when they were sent off in small parties for home, unpaid, half clothed, and penniless,

"——— to beg their bread
Through realms their valor saved." [1]

For six months no decisive action occurred, but skirmishes, in which the Americans generally prevailed, were frequent along the opposing lines.

The New England convention closed their proceedings 1.
by recommending the last Wednesday of the month to
be kept as a solemn fast, and adjourned the next day. 2.
The Assembly appointed the fast day, passed a vote approving the acts of the convention, and adjourned at the same time.

The British frigate Cerberus, laying at Fogland Ferry, 10.
in the East passage, was driven from her moorings by the troops at Little Compton who brought two pieces of artillery to bear upon her, damaged the hull, killed six of the crew, and wounded many others. The Americans had one man wounded.

Gen. Arnold, sent by Washington to assist in the defence of Rhode Island, arrived at Providence. He was 12.
made a major-general by Congress, and Col. Varnum was appointed a brigadier. The arrival of the Marquis de

[1] For a more full account of the affair at Trenton bridge, and of the sufferings of the army at this time, see Cowell's "Spirit of '76," pp. 307–10.

CHAP. XXI. Lafayette, to enter the service, at this time, was a great help to the American cause.

1777. Jan. 14. Four days after the repulse of the Cerberus, the British landed upon Prudence Island, and burned the last remaining buildings, thus completing the desolation begun by Wallace. Gen. Clinton returned to England, leaving Lord Percy in command.

Washington disapproved of raising the brigade lately ordered in Rhode Island, lest it should interfere with the enlistment of the two battalions assigned to this State.
20. He wrote an earnest letter on the subject, followed by
24. another of similar purport. But when the real state of
Feb. 9. affairs was made known to him by Gov. Cooke,[1] he approved the plan, and thanked the State for its exertions.

Mar. 3. The British erected batteries on the heights at the east side of the island, near Fogland Ferry, and also at the north, on Butt's Hill. The proceedings of the New England
Jan. 28. land convention, forwarded to Congress, were discussed
Feb. 15. at intervals for several weeks, and finally approved, except the proposals that the bills on which loans were to be procured should bear interest, and similar measures were recommended to the other States. Congress also
Jan. 31. advised the States to enter upon their public records a copy of the Declaration of Independence, with the signatures, which was done here at the March session.

Feb. 3. The Assembly elected a portion of the officers for the two continental battalions[2] that were being raised, and

[1] This correspondence, preserved in the State's collection of 1777, is printed in the "Spirit of '76," pp. 127–33.

[2] Many of the officers in the two regiments recently disbanded in New Jersey, retained their commissions in the two new battalions. The command of the 1st was reserved for Col. Christopher Greene, who had not yet been exchanged since his capture at Quebec. The officers now chosen were: Of the 1st Battalion:—Major—Samuel Ward; Capts.—John Topham, Elisha Lewis, Oliver Clarke; Lieuts.—Joseph Whitmarsh, Peleg Hoxsie, Elias Hull, James Webb, Ichabod Prentice, Edward Slocum, William Davis, Jr., Samuel Hicks; Ensigns—Elias Blanchard, Elias Thompson, Samuel Northup, Richmond Springer, Wm. Gardner, Henry Tew, Jr., Jonathan

allowed soldiers of the State brigade, the fifteen months' men, as they were called, to enlist in the new regiments; but recruiting, for some reason, proceeded very slowly. The old act for the relief of tender consciences, which had so long protected the Quakers from military service, and at each approach of war had been revived, was again enacted. Henry Marchant was chosen a delegate to Congress, making three representatives from this State now in that body. William Greene was elected chief-justice. A new loan of fifty thousand pounds, upon notes payable in five years, with four per cent. interest, was ordered. CHAP. XXI. 1777. Feb.

The Marine Committee sent orders to Com. Hopkins, to despatch four vessels under Capt. Paul Jones of the Alfred, upon an expedition; but that portion of the navy blocked up at Providence, could neither be manned or got to sea. A British schooner of eight guns having run aground between Prudence and Patience Islands, the sloop Providence went down to capture her, but the crew set fire to and blew her up before the Providence could reach the spot. A week later the row-galley Spitfire, now schooner-rigged, in covering the landing of a party to bring off hay from Rhode Island, had an action, which lasted for several hours, with a battery on the shore, in which the Americans lost one man killed and several wounded.[1] 5. 14. 21.

Davis, Daniel Tillinghast; Adjutant—John Holden, Jr. Of the 2d Battalion: —Col.—Israel Angell; Lt. Col.—Jeremiah Olney; Major—Simeon Thayer; Capts.—David Dexter, Stephen Olney, Wm. Allen, Wm. Potter, James Williams; Lieuts.—Thomas Hughes, Dutee Jerauld, Ebenezer West, Thomas Waterman, Sylvanus Shaw, Wm. Humphrey, Oliver Jenckes, Benedict Tew, Barber Peckham, Samuel Bissell, Job Clapp; Ensigns—John Harris, Thomas Waterman, Jabez Arnold, Mathew Coggeshall, John Finch, Benjamin L. Peckham, Robert Helme, Christopher Phillips.

In May, Col. Greene was chosen to command the 1st battalion; Simon Smith, Luke Greene, Asa Miner and Israel Stoddard were chosen Ensigns of the same; John Cooke, Quartermaster; Peter Turner, Surgeon; Charles Thompson, Chaplain. In Col. Angell's battalion, Sylvanus Shaw was made a Captain; Nathan Olney, Lieut.; Elijah Hawkins and Joseph Cornell, Ensigns; and Ebenezer David, Chaplain.

[1] The officers of the Spitfire were, Isaac Tyler, Capt.; Josiah Simmons and Abel Weathers, Lieuts.; chosen in Dec., 1776.

CHAP. XXI. 1777. March 5. A valuation of the property in the State was presented to the Assembly, and a tax of sixteen thousand pounds was voted. A deputation of six Oneida chiefs arrived at Providence, and appeared before the Assembly, by whom some valuable presents were made to them. Their business was to pledge the neutrality of their tribe in the war, if not their active aid against the English. An expedition to attack Rhode Island the coming week was planned, the militia were called out to serve till the twentieth, and volunteers in the neighboring towns of Massachusetts were called upon, to meet at Tiverton on the twelfth of the month. Large rewards were offered for prisoners taken from the enemy. But the States were deficient in the quotas assigned to them by the recent convention. New Hampshire had sent none, only a portion of the others had yet appeared, and the one thousand continental troops could not be had, the forces having been sent off to the defence of Ticonderoga.[1] The attempt was, therefore, re-
24. luctantly deferred. At the adjourned session, Generals Varnum, West, and Malmedy, were discharged, their services being superseded by the continental officers already sent by Washington. A census of all males above sixteen years of age was ordered, that the effective force of the State might be accurately known. Places were designated where freemen of the four towns in possession of the enemy[2] might meet, if as many as seven in number, and vote for State and town officers at the ensuing election. Delegates in Congress, hitherto appointed by the Assembly, were hereafter to be elected by the people at the same time with State officers. In addition to the Loan Office, Congress had established lotteries to raise funds, and thus to sustain the credit of the continental bills. Agents to sell tickets were sent to all the States, and this Assembly denounced the penalty of death against

[1] Letter of the Assembly to Gov. Trumbull, March, 1777.—Trumbull Papers, Vol. vi., No. 57.

[2] Newport, Middletown, Portsmouth and Jamestown.

any one who should counterfeit these tickets. Congress CHAP.
also resolved that State bills of credit might be exchanged XXI.
for Loan Office certificates, such amounts to go towards 1777.
paying the continental debt due to the States. Mar.

A serious misunderstanding had arisen in the navy, concerning the distribution of prize money, which had not yet been divided. The Assembly had written to the Marine Committee, and had also conferred on the subject with Com. Hopkins, between whom and the prize agents and officers much correspondence had passed. A decision
adverse to the views of the commodore was rendered by 25.
the committee, before whom charges and complaints against him were presented by several officers. The next
day he was suspended from his command by Congress, 26.
and formal notice of their action was sent to him by the 29.
President in a brief letter.[1]

The row-galley Washington blew up near Bristol, de- April 2.
stroying eight men. The Marine Committee ordered the 5.
two new frigates at Providence to be sent to sea, and if not yet manned, to go round to Boston for a crew. Congress recommended to the State to make another attempt 16.
to dislodge the enemy from Rhode Island, but some months passed before the effort could be renewed. On the general voting day the soldiers at the several posts were allowed by the council of war to cast their proxies for State and town officers, which were sent to their respective towns.

The Assembly granted a charter to the Newtown 17.
Rangers, a company doing duty at Updike's Newtown, now Wickford. They also took measures to enlist five hundred men for the two continental battalions, to be ready on the tenth of May, by apportioning that number among the towns to be raised by draft, and required those who, under "the act for the relief of tender consciences," were personally exempt from military service, to be

[1] Hancock's Letter Books, No. vi., p. 170.

CHAP. XXI. equally with other citizens, subject to the draft, and if drawn, to hire substitutes. The attack on Danbury, in

1777. April 26. repelling which Gen. Wooster was slain, gave a stimulus to the recruiting service in New England.

The doctrine of popular sovereignty in its broadest application, has nowhere been more clearly defined, or more

28. signally illustrated, than in the instructions given at this time by the town of Scituate to their deputies. In this paper is found the earliest protest against the inequalities of representation fastened upon the State by the royal charter, and the most republican ideas of the origin of that instrument, as being primarily derived from the people. The townsmen of Scituate held that, upon the Declaration of Independence, the charter became void, and hence that no legal government existed in the State, "as it appears," say they, "that at the time our ancestors petitioned the King of Great Britain to take them under his protection, the power of government was vested in the people, and by them legally vested in the King, by which he was clothed with authority to grant said charter; and upon the Declaration aforesaid, the power again vested in the people, where, we are convinced, it still remains, as we do not find the people have, since that time, either by any person legally authorized by them, or themselves, fixed any settled form of government." They complain especially that the charter allows but two representatives to any but the four original towns, and instruct their deputies to procure an act, establishing a form of government, to be submitted to the people for adoption or amendment, in which the representation shall be adjusted on a basis of population and property.[1]

May 5. The return of Lord Percy to England, left Gen. Prescott in command at Newport. The British army established a newspaper at that place, called the Newport

[1] The Committee who drafted these instructions were Ezekiel Cornell, Wm. West and Rufus Hopkins.—Foster Papers, Vol. xi.

Gazette. The people at the late election chose the same general officers as last year, except that William Channing was made attorney-general in place of Henry Marchant, who was elected a delegate to Congress with Hopkins and Ellery. The Assembly empowered Capt. Hopkins, of the frigate Warren, to impress seamen for his crew, and soon after gave the same power to Capt. Whipple of the Providence. The enlistments proceeded so slowly, that additional bounties were offered, and one thousand men to be raised for the State brigade, were apportioned among the towns. In Exeter there was so much disaffection, that Gen. Spencer was requested to march some troops into that town, to seize the turbulent leaders, and protect the well-disposed inhabitants. The scarcity of small money led to the emission of bills to the amount of forty-five hundred pounds in fractional parts of a dollar. A premium of sixty pounds was offered for every ton of steel, similar to the German, that should be manufactured in the State. The monopoly act, regulating the prices of indispensable articles, was revised at great length, and a treason act, denouncing death against any who should be found guilty of making war, or aiding in the same, against this State or the United States, was passed.

CHAP. XXI. 1777. May 7. 19.

The lines of a fort on College Hill in Providence, were laid by Gen. Spencer, to be completed by the inhabitants. 13.
Much activity was observed among the enemy at Newport. A large fleet sailed for New York with reinforcements for Gen. Howe, promising a more active campaign for the latter half of the year. The stars and stripes were adopted by Congress for the national banner, but the order was not promulgated till September. The Assembly adopted the United States' navy regulations for the vessels in the service of this State, and ordered the council of war to procure five vessels for the State, two to be armed as cruisers, and three to be employed in importing goods required in the public service. The embargo upon

20. June 14. 16.

CHAP. XXI. 1777. June shipping was repealed, and the corps of officers for the State brigade was revised, and new appointments made.[1] The row-galley Washington was repaired and rigged as a schooner, and placed in command of Joseph Mauran.

22. A movement to dislodge the enemy from New Brunswick was made, under command of Gen. Greene. Two divisions advanced from Middlebrook, one composed of two brigades, by the east side of the Raritan River, the other, of Varnum's brigade, by the west. Howe retreated towards Amboy, losing about three hundred men in a skirmish with Morgan's riflemen.

July 6 The evacuation of Ticonderoga by Gen. St. Clair surprised every one. Burgoyne, who with an army of eight thousand men had just arrived before it, was inspired with a rash confidence by the event.

7. The Assembly appointed three delegates[2] to attend a convention at Springfield, to consider the subject of currency, and the defence of Rhode Island. They also voted a sword to Major Simeon Thayer for his services in the second continental battalion for this State.

A daring act, which more than atoned for the capture of Lee, seven months before, was skilfully planned and gallantly executed by Lieutenant-Colonel William Barton. This was the seizure of Gen. Prescott, the British commander on Rhode Island. He was quartered with an

[1] The regimental officers now chosen were: Of the 1st Regiment—William Barton, Lieut.-Col.; Nathaniel Hawkins, Major. Of the 2d Regiment—Archibald Crary, Col.; John Topham, Lieut.-Col.; James Williams, Major. The artillery regiment remained as in December. The long list of company officers given on p. 391 was much altered at this time. Indeed, the changes were so constant from resignation, casualty, and exchanges from one to the other service, State and Continental, that it would be tedious and useless to enumerate them. The brigade was first enlisted in Dec., 1776, for 15 months ending 16th March, 1778; then re-enlisted for one year, and again for another year ending 16th March, 1780, when it was disbanded, after 3 years and 3 months' service. The pay-roll of the brigade, giving the names of all the officers and privates at that time, is printed in Cowell's Spirit of '76, pp. 65–117.

[2] Hon. Stephen Hopkins, Dep. Gov. Wm. Bradford, and Paul Mumford.

aide-de-camp, at a house in Portsmouth on the west road, about five miles from Newport. Barton was stationed at Tiverton. Selecting six trusty officers and thirty-four men, the party rowed to Bristol, in five whaleboats, on the fourth of July, and thence, on the night of the sixth, to Warwick Neck, where a storm detained them for two days. On the third night afterward he embarked. In perfect silence the boats were pulled between Prudence and Patience Islands, so near to the enemy's ships as to hear the cry, "All's well," of the sentinel on board, and landing on the Portsmouth shore, about a mile from their destination, the party marched in five divisions to the house. The sentinel on guard was secured by stratagem, one division watched the road, while three others entered at the different doors. Prescott was taken in bed, his aide-de-camp leaped from a window but was arrested, and the whole party silently returned to the boats. They passed the ships before any alarm was given, and at daylight reached Warwick Neck. The whole affair occupied six and a half hours. Prescott and his aide were carried in a coach to Providence, and four days later, for greater safety, were sent, on parole, to Connecticut to be placed in charge of Gov. Trumbull. Gen. Pigot was ordered from New York to take command of the British army on Rhode Island. Congress voted a sword to Col. Barton for this gallant act. A few months later he was appointed aide-de-camp to Gen. Greene, and then made a colonel by Congress, who specially recommended him to Gen. Washington.[1]

CHAP. XXI. 1777. July 4. 6. 9. 10. 14. 25. Dec. 5. 24.

[1] An account of this affair, with depositions of parties concerned, and a list of their names, is given in "Spirit of '76 in Rhode Island," pp. 47–50. A complete narrative by Colonel Barton himself, in manuscript, is preserved in the Foster papers, Miscel., volume 1. A copy of Prescott's parole from Trumbull papers, vol. vi., No. 179, is here given:

"State of Rhode Island and Providence Plantations.

I Richard Prescott, Esq., major-general in the service of his Brittanick Majesty, being made a prisoner of war by the army of the United States of America, do promise upon my word and honor, and upon the faith and credit of a gentlemen, to depart from here to the First Society in the town

CHAP. XXI. The New England convention, in which New York was also represented by one delegate, met at Springfield.
1777. Hon. Stephen Hopkins was president. They remained in
July 30. session one week. To remedy the evils arising from an
Aug. inflated paper currency, they recommended that all State
2. bills be redeemed by taxation, that no more be issued except for small change, and that taxes be assessed quarterly to defray war expenses. They also advised that the
4. monopoly act, having failed of its purpose, be repealed, but that soldiers and their families be supplied by the State, to the extent of their wages, at the prices stated in that act, and that laws against engrossers be passed; that restrictions upon trade between the States should be re-
6. moved, and that for the defence of Rhode Island an army of about four thousand men be maintained by the New England States.[1] These proceedings were afterwards approved by Congress, and made the basis of important action.

Many slight affairs with the enemy occurred in the bay. The Renown, a fifty-gun ship, was driven from her
2. moorings off Dutch Island, by the fire of Col. Elliot's artillery. The same night a party landed on the island and secured some stock, after which, proceeding to Conanicut, in emulation of Barton, they brought off two prisoners.
5. Three days later a foraging party of two hundred British

of Lebanon, in the State of Connecticut, being the place of my destination and residence, and there to remain until otherwise disposed of by Governor Trumbull (who is desired by General Spencer to take the particular charge of me) until the Commander-in-chief of the United States shall manifest his pleasure with regard to my disposal, or until I shall be duly exchanged or discharged; and that I will not directly or indirectly give intelligence of any kind, or say or do anything to the prejudice of the United States of America, during the time of my restraint.

Given under my hand, at Providence, this 14th day of July, A. D. 1777. RD. PRESCOTT."

Major William Barrington, the aide-de-camp, signed a similar parole, July 12th.

[1] These proceedings are filed in the Secretary's office. The important portions are printed in "Spirit of '76," pp. 136–40.

landed in Narraganset, and were repulsed by the militia with some loss on both sides. On the same day Capt. Dyer, with a company of sixty men, crossed from Tiverton to the island, attacked a body of seventy of the enemy who had fired on some fishing boats, and drove them to their fort. Dyer was wounded in this affair. The battle of Bennington checked the contemplated advance of Burgoyne into New England, where he proposed a junction, at Springfield, with Pigot's forces from Rhode Island. 1777. Aug. 16.

The Assembly passed the necessary laws to carry out the views of the Springfield convention, and also prohibited the distillation of grain, on account of the scarcity of provisions. They voted eleven hundred and twenty dollars to Col. Barton and his party for the capture of Prescott and his aide, and assessed a tax of thirty-two thousand pounds upon the State. Vigorous measures were also taken to supply the troops with rations and clothing, in which they were so deficient that the State brigade petitioned for relief. 18.

At the suggestion of Marchant, Congress resolved to purchase six large vessels at Providence to be used as fire ships against the British fleet in the bay, and offered large rewards for the successful employment of them. This enterprise required the concurrence of the eastern navy board with the council of war in Rhode Island, for which purpose the board were directed to repair to Providence. 21.

The distressed condition of the Rhode Island troops in the continental service, for want of proper clothing, exceeded that of the State brigade, and threatened serious results. Gen. Varnum, with Col. Angell's battalion, was stationed at Peekskill. Col. Greene's battalion was at Fort Montgomery. Col. Angell described his soldiers as being without shoes, and otherwise so poorly clad, that half of them were unfit for any duty, and the regiment had become an object of derision wherever it appeared. This was a strong contrast to the Rhode Island "army of observation," near Boston two years before, which was rep- 27.

CHAP. XXI. resented as the only perfectly appointed force in that
motley field. A mutiny broke out in Col. Greene's battal-
1777. ion, of whom Gen. Varnum, who was called on to suppress it, writes: "the naked situation of the troops when
observed parading for duty is sufficient to extort the tears
of compassion from every human being. There are not
two in five who have a shoe, stocking, or so much as
breeches to render them decent." Clothing had been
repeatedly promised but did not arrive. The troops became furious, but were quieted by Gen. Varnum, and soon
received the relief provided at the recent session of the
Assembly.

A new privateer of twenty guns, from Providence,
attempting to get to sea, was chased ashore at Seaconnet,
and burnt by the enemy. The fame of Barton, and the
large rewards offered for prisoners, led to frequent attempts
Sept. to surprise the enemy. Col. Cornell concealed a party on
3. Prudence Island in the night, and early the next morning
4. captured an officer and fifteen men who had landed from
a frigate to procure water. Three of the enemy were
killed in the skirmish, and on that night an officer and
two men were taken on Rhode Island by a party from
Seaconnet.

11. The battle of Brandywine, in which Gen. Greene com-
25. manded the reserve and covered the retreat, was followed
by the loss of Philadelphia, upon which Congress removed
to York, and again conferred extraordinary military
powers upon Washington for four months. It being reported that the British troops had left Rhode Island, Con-
14. gress requested that the State brigade should march immediately to Peekskill; but the rumor was false, and they
19. could not be spared from home. The battle on Behmus
Heights, near Stillwater, resulting in the defeat of Burgoyne, almost retrieved the ruin wrought at the fatal field
of Brandywine.

17. To follow up this success another expedition was
already planned to drive the enemy from Rhode Island.

Massachusetts had resolved to send three thousand troops CHAP. XXI.
and some artillery in addition to her two regiments now
in Rhode Island, and the Assembly ordered half the 1777.
militia of the State to be drafted for one month's service Sept. 22.
from the first of October, to be formed into a brigade of six regiments, of which Col. Cornell was made brigadier; the whole to be under command of Gen. Spencer.[1]
The enemy's force on the island was reported by Gen. 23.
Spencer to be nearly four thousand men. There were four Hessian and three British regiments, two of each on Windmill Hill, a corps of grenadiers and light infantry at Fogland Ferry, one regiment on Butts Hill, and two
near Newport. Connecticut resolved to send fifteen hun- 26.
dred men to aid in the attempt to dislodge them.

A varied fortune now attended the American arms.
The battle of Germantown, in which Sullivan and Greene Oct. 4.
led the attacking columns, and for awhile carried every thing before them, resulted in defeat, and on the same day an expedition from New York captured the forts on the Hudson River. But this success was of no avail to the enemy at the northward. Recruits poured in to the army of Gen. Gates, while that of Burgoyne, cut off from supplies, was forced to offer battle at a point six miles from Saratoga. Gen. Arnold assumed the lead, Gates not appear- 7.
ing in the field. The victory was decisive. The next 8.
day was spent in skirmishes, and Burgoyne was obliged to fall back upon Saratoga. Cut off from all communication with New York, and surrounded by a greatly superior and daily increasing force, he finally surrendered 17.
with his whole army as prisoners of war. An official return of the conquered army shows the exact number of prisoners to be five thousand eight hundred and sixty-three.

[1] This Assembly also, in conformity with a resolve of Congress against betting at horse-races, passed an Act, forbidding any bet to be made upon a horse-race, under a penalty of one hundred pounds, and forfeiture of the horse.

CHAP. XXI. The forces gathered for the attack on Rhode-island,
amounted to about nine thousand men. A large number
1777. of boats were collected at Tiverton under charge of Major
Oct. 16. Nathan Munro, but on the night fixed for the attack,
some preparations remained incomplete. A storm delayed
the attempt for three days, when it was renewed, but the
19. wind proving unfavorable and some of the boats being
seen and fired upon by the enemy, the attempt was again
postponed four days, and the place of attack was changed
to a point farther north, above Fogland Ferry. Again
23. the weather proved unfavorable. These delays disaffected
the troops, and many withdrew. Scarcely five thousand
26. could be mustered on the last night assigned for the embarcation.
A council of officers decided that it was inexpedient
to make the attempt, and the expedition was
abandoned. Great dissatisfaction was felt at this futile
result of so much preparation, and bitter complaints were
made of the inefficiency of Spencer.

22. But while this affair was in progress, a brilliant action
was fought at Redbank, a fort on the Jersey side of the
Delaware River, whither the two Rhode Island regiments
8. had been ordered after the battle of Germantown. Late
22. in the afternoon, Count Donop, with a body of twelve
hundred Hessians, summoned the fort to surrender. Col.
Greene, who had concealed all but about fifty of his men
when the officer brought the summons, replied: "with
these brave fellows this fort shall be my tomb." The
garrison being too small to defend the entire works, half
of the fort was abandoned, which aided the deception and
gave confidence to the enemy. The assault instantly
commenced, and the undefended portion of the fort was
at once occupied by the enemy. But a terrible fire was
poured upon them from the inner lines. Count Donop
fell mortally wounded, and within forty minutes the Hessians
were driven back with the loss of one-fourth of their
number. Capt. Sylvanus Shaw, of Angell's battalion,
was killed in this action. At the same time the British

ships opened a furious cannonade upon Fort Mifflin on CHAP.
Mud Island, which was gallantly defended by Col. Smith XXI.
of Maryland. Hazlewood, in command of the Pennsyl- 1777.
vania Flotilla, and some Continental ships, rendered great Oct.
service, and the next morning drove the enemy's fleet
down the river, with the loss of a sixty-four gun ship and 23.
a frigate that were blown up. For this gallant defence,
swords were voted by Congress to the three commanders, Nov. 4.
at the same time that a gold medal was voted to Gates
for the surrender of Burgoyne.

The Assembly appointed a committee to inquire into Oct. 27.
the cause of the failure of the late expedition against
Rhode-island. Gen. Cornell presented a statement of the
affair, and Gen. Spencer proposed that a joint committee 31.
from the several States be called to inquire into the facts,
and to provide for future operations. A court of inquiry
was accordingly held at Providence, and at its close made Nov. 15.
a report, exonerating Spencer, and attributing the failure
to a delay on the part of Palmer's brigade in not having
their boats in readiness on the night first assigned for the
attack, and to the unfavorable weather afterwards.

The British ship Syren, of twenty-eight guns, ran 6.
ashore at Point Judith, and was captured by the artillery
at that station. Her crew of a hundred and sixty-six
officers and men were taken prisoners and carried to
Providence.

The two forts on the Delaware, Mercer at Redbank,
and Mifflin on Mud Island, which had been so nobly defended,
were at length abandoned to the enemy, who
being reinforced from New York, fortified Province
Island, a low bank like Mud Island and almost contiguous
to it, whence they opened an incessant fire upon Fort 10.
Mifflin. Col. Smith was wounded the next day, and left 11.
the fort in command of Lieut.-Col. Russell of Varnum's
brigade. Major Simeon Thayer volunteered to relieve
Russell, and led a detachment into the fort. Three hun- 12.
dred men now composed the garrison under Major

CHAP. XXI. 1777. Nov. 15. Thayer. The enemy's ships also took position to rake the fort. The cannonade continued day and night. New batteries were opened and more ships were brought into action, some so near that hand grenades were thrown from the round tops into the fort. Another such cannonade has never been known in America. The works were utterly destroyed, the cannon dismounted, and the men exposed to cross fires in all directions from the hostile ships and batteries. Nothing remained but to leave the fort, which was done that evening, and Major Thayer with the remnant of his heroic band, crossed over at midnight to Fort Mercer. Cornwallis crossed the Delaware, with the design to attack Redbank, but as that post was
17. no longer tenable, it was evacuated, and three days after-
20. wards the enemy took possession.[1]

Congress adopted the plan of taxation, as suggested by the Springfield Convention, and recommended the
22. States to raise five millions of dollars by that means, of which the sum assigned for Rhode Island to raise was one

[1] There has been a misunderstanding as to the sword voted to Colonel Smith for the defence of Fort Mifflin. That was for the action of October 22–23, when Smith was in command, and was voted by Congress, November 4th, a week before Smith, wounded at the second attack, resigned the post, and Major Thayer took the command. The three swords then voted were made in France, and nine years elapsed before they were received. The splendor of Thayer's defence, from the 12th to the 16th November, had justly eclipsed that of Smith in the former battle; and when the swords came it was thought that Thayer should have received the Mifflin sword, and not Smith. In justice, Congress should afterwards have voted a sword to Thayer also, for his more brilliant defence in November, but Smith was entitled to and received his sword at the same time with Greene and Hazlewood, (or their representatives,) for the action in October, in accordance with the vote of November 4th, passed a week before the second battle. Much feeling was excited at the time by this apparent oversight of Thayer by Congress, and the inaccuracy of later chroniclers has caused the impression that the sword was voted for a defence made by Thayer, and through an error of Congress was given to Smith. A careful attention to the dates above given will show the exact truth of the matter. The letters of General Varnum and Colonel Angell, with some further statements on this subject, and the vote of Congress of November 4th, are given in "Spirit of '76," pp. 295–304.

hundred thousand dollars. They also advised the confis- CHAP.
cation and sale of Tory estates, and ordered an inquiry XXI.
into the causes of the failure of the expedition against 1777.
Rhode-island, which resulted very much as the inquiry Dec. 11.
at Providence had already done.[1]

The Assembly, in accordance with a resolution of Con- 1.
gress, appointed the eighteenth of December as a day of
Thanksgiving. They also levied a tax of forty-eight
thousand pounds upon the State. Washington went into
winter quarters at Valley Forge, where Howe attempted 5.
to attack him, but after some skirmishing withdrew.
The presence of the enemy on the island, and the large
force kept in the field on that account, caused a great
scarcity of provisions in this State, so that persons were 10.
sent into Connecticut to purchase them. The articles of
confederation prepared by Congress having been received,
together with a recommendation to the northern States to
hold a convention at New Haven to regulate prices, the
council of war advised that the Assembly be convened to
consider these important subjects. Before it met, the
arrival of the British fleet from the Delaware to winter at
Newport caused great alarm. An attack on Providence
was expected, many people left the place, and the council
of war, which sat daily in the recess of the Assembly, got
ready the beacon and notified the surrounding country to 18.
prepare for defence.

The Assembly sat at Providence four days. William 19–22.
Greene and Jabez Bowen were appointed commissioners to meet with those of the other States at New Haven according to the recommendation of Congress. The term of enlistment for the State brigade was to expire in March, the recruiting service proceeded but slowly, and the ranks were by no means full. The Assembly resolved to raise a brigade of fifteen hundred men, the quota assigned by the Springfield Convention, to serve for a year from the

[1] See Journals of Congress, iii. 571. General Spencer resigned on 21st December, and his resignation was accepted 13th January, 1778.

CHAP. XXI. 1777. coming March. This was in fact a re-enlistment of so many of the existing force as chose to serve, over whom Gen. Cornell was made brigadier, with but few changes in the field officers.[1]

1778. The British had also organized a corps of Tories upon the island, known as the Loyal Newport Associators. What was the number of this force, or of how many companies it consisted, we do not know. The officers of one
Jan. 1. company, appointed by Major-General Pigot, are all whose names we have been able to ascertain.[2] It was
2. proposed by Gen. Varnum to Washington, that the two Rhode Island battalions in camp at Valley Forge should be united, and that the officers of one, Col. Greene, Lieut.-Col. Olney, and Major Ward, with their subalterns, be sent to Rhode Island to enlist a battalion of negroes for the continental service. The plan was approved and the officers were sent home for that purpose. So great were the sufferings of the refugees from Newport, that an ap-
8. peal on their behalf was made to the country through the press. There were two hundred and fifty of these persons then in Providence with no means of support. The same liberality which three years before had been shown to the poor of Boston was extended to their relief.

13. Congress earnestly recommended the New England States to keep up the force in Rhode Island agreed upon

[1] Of the 1st battalion, the officers now chosen were Col. Archibald Crary, Lieutenant-colonel John Topham, Major James Williams; of the 2d, Colonel William Barton, Lieutenant-colonel Nathaniel Hawkins; Major of Brigade, John Handy; of artillery, Colonel Robert Elliot, Major Josiah Flagg. Upon Colonel Barton's receiving a commission as colonel in the Continental service, Colonel John Topham was appointed to the 2d battalion, Major Williams was promoted to be lieutenant-colonel, and Christopher Manchester was made major; Samuel Phillips was made major of Colonel Topham's regiment.

[2] Sabine's History of American Loyalists refers to this subject, page 63, and says there were possibly three companies. The officers of one company, who were appointed by Pigot, January 1, 1778, were Joseph Durfee, captain, vice Simeon Pease deceased, Giles Stanton, 1st lieutenant, John Thurston, jr., 2d lieutenant.

CHAP. XXI. 1778. Jan.

at the Springfield Convention, and advised the temporary appointment of the necessary general officers for that purpose.[1] They also accepted the resignation of Gen. Spencer, to take effect on the arrival of his successor. The convention of delegates from the eight northern States met at New Haven, and agreed upon a scale of prices for labor and produce, to be enacted by the legislatures, to take effect in March. This was the third effort of the kind which failed of its object. Massachusetts refused to pass the act, and Congress ultimately abandoned the unwise and fruitless scheme. 15.

Feb. Early in February, New Providence became again the scene of a daring enterprise in which Rhode Island took a leading part. The U. S. sloop Providence, of twelve guns, Capt. John Rathbone, landed a party of thirty men under Lieut. John Trevett of Newport, who with fifteen men scaled the walls at night, and took the fort. The remainder of the force, with some prisoners who joined them, seized a small island opposite the town. They held possession for three days, captured six vessels in the harbor, drove off a British sloop-of-war that attempted to

[1] Under this recommendation, Solomon Southwick was appointed by the Assembly in February to be deputy commissary-general of issues. Major-general N. Greene, at the earnest solicitation of Washington, took the responsible position of quartermaster-general of the Continental army, in March, and under him, Thomas Greene was made deputy quartermaster-general, in this State, and was succeeded in the autumn of this year by Ephraim Bowen, jr. John Reynolds was agent clothier for Rhode Island—a delicate and difficult post in the embarrassed state of the service, and Nathaniel Mumford was State clothier for the troops. Asa Waterman, of Norwich, Connecticut, was deputy commissary-general of purchases for Rhode Island, appointed in May. Nathaniel Norton was forage master, appointed by General Sullivan in September. The accounts of all these officers in the Staff department of the army, not directly appointed by Congress, were examined by a committee of the General Assembly, in September, 1779, in accordance with a resolve of Congress. The proceedings of this committee, which met September 29, 1779, and adjourned from time to time, are preserved in Foster Papers, volume ii.

Caleb Harris was director of the powder mill in this State. Benjamin Stelle was made assistant paymaster, in March, 1778.

CHAP. XXI. enter the port, and having spiked the guns, brought away a quantity of military stores without the loss of a man.

1778. Feb. Gen. Greene applied to Washington for the appointment at Rhode Island, to succeed Spencer, but his services could not be spared from the camp. He then suggested that the Rhode Island troops be sent home to defend their State, a measure which was also urged by Gen. Varnum, and which was conceded somewhat later.

An all-important event now occurred in Europe. The negotiations at Paris terminated in the signing of the
6. treaty of alliance between France and the United States. The independence of America was thus acknowledged by the great rival of Britain, and substantial aid to the cause of liberty was soon to be rendered by the French monarch.

9. The Assembly, acting upon the suggestion of Varnum, approved by Washington, resolved to raise a regiment of slaves, who were to be freed upon their enlistment, and their owners to be paid by the State according to the valuation of a committee. One hundred and twenty pounds was the limit of value allowed by the act. Six deputies protested against this act on the ground that there were not enough slaves to make an effective regiment, that the measure would be disapproved abroad, that the expense would be greater, and the owners be dissatisfied with the indemnity offered by the State. The articles of Confederation were accepted. The delegates in Congress were instructed to obtain certain modifications if possible, but in any event to sign the articles. The proposed amendments related to the number of representatives, that one might suffice in certain cases; to the mode of taxation, that an estimate be made every five years; and to the public lands, that they should be proportionably distributed among the States. A tax of thirty-two thousand pounds was assessed, and a bill establishing an oath of allegiance to the State was referred to the people in their town meetings for instructions to their deputies thereupon. This measure was so strenuously opposed,

on account of the position in which it might involve the Quakers, that the bill never was reported.[1] CHAP. XXI.

The frigate Warren, Capt. John B. Hopkins, having long waited a favorable opportunity to elude the enemy and get to sea, at length effected this object during a snow storm, sailing through the blockading fleet and firing broadsides as she passed, but receiving no damage from the enemy's fire. 1778. Feb. 16.

The supposed discovery of a silver mine in Cumberland promised an unexpected relief from the burdens of taxation caused by the war. A petition to the Assembly for certain facilities in working the mine was referred to a committee to examine the premises, but the hopes thus raised proved fallacious. Mar. 9.

The frigate Columbus, Capt. Hoysted Hacker, less
fortunate than the Warren, in attempting to get to sea, 27.
was chased on shore at Point Judith, and the next day 28.
was burnt by the enemy. Gen. Burgoyne, having obtained leave of Congress to proceed to England, embarked April
at Newport. His army, which since the surrender had 15.
been quartered at Cambridge, was sent into Vermont.
Gen. Sullivan, appointed by Washington to succeed Spencer, arrived at Providence, and was at once invested by 17.
the council of war with the supreme command in Rhode
Island. The arrival at Boston of the treaty of Paris, was 19.
the occasion of great rejoicings. When the news reached
Providence, national salutes were fired from the battery 21.
at Fox Point, and from the frigate Providence, which
were repeated at sunset with a military display. The
next day was a public fast throughout the country, re- 22.
commended by Congress in March, but wherever this
news had reached, it became an occasion of thanksgiving.

The sufferings of the army at Valley Forge, have too often been depicted to require more than a simple refer-

[1] The sentiments of the freemen of Providence upon the proposed bill are contained in an ably-written paper, presented at their town meeting, on 9th March, 1778, preserved in Foster Papers, vol. ii.

CHAP. XXI. ence in this place. So great was the want of clothing,
that the march of the army to their quarters in Decem-
1778. April ber, was literally tracked with blood upon the snow drifts.
Sickness was a natural result. The Rhode Island troops
suffered more than any others from this cause, owing to
their deficiency of clothing, which, although it was supplied as fast as possible from home, often came too late.
20 Lieut. John Waterman, commissary of the brigade, died
at this time, and Lieutenant William Jennings a month
later, both of small-pox. The treatment of prisoners by
the British, was such as to call forth the strongest remon-
strances from Washington. The prison-ships at Newport
were full of these unhappy victims. The council of war
24. appointed Col. Barton to convey to them supplies, and to
inquire into their condition and numbers. The next day
25. he proceeded in a cartel vessel upon his errand of mercy,
to visit the ships, jail, and hospital.

The French alliance at once changed the tone of the British cabinet. Measures of conciliation were proposed, which were indignantly rejected in America. Two bills, hastily drawn and but once read in the House of Commons, were sent over to the British commanders, and commissioners were despatched to negotiate with Congress to close the war—but upon a basis of dependence. It is not our province to follow this subject farther than to notice the reception of these bills in Rhode Island. Gen. Pigot enclosed a draught of them to Gen. Sullivan in a letter, wherein he stated "that the terms offered the rebels were more generous than they could, or had reason to expect from the hands of his most merciful master." The measures were ill-timed and the letter was insulting. The exasperated populace ordered the bills to be burnt by
28. the hands of the common hangman, which was immediate-
ly done.[1] The frigate Providence, Capt. Whipple, dur-
30. ing a dark and stormy night, forced her way through the

[1] Pennsylvania Gazette, of May 23, 1778. Letters and Papers, 1777–1780, p. 26, No. 2, in Massachusetts Historical Society.

hostile fleet in the same daring manner that the Warren had done, pouring broadsides into the British ships, and sinking one of their tenders.[1] Capt. Whipple was bound to France with important despatches relating to the new treaty, and after a successful voyage returned in safety to Boston. CHAP. XXI. 1778.

May 6. Gov. Cooke, wearied by the cares of his responsible position, now retired from office. William Greene, son of the late Gov. Greene, was chosen to the place, and continued to occupy it for eight successive years. Jabez Bowen was elected deputy-governor. It illustrates the simple manners, as well as the physical vigor of the men of revolutionary times, that Gov. Greene, although possessed of an ample fortune, was accustomed two or three times a week, during the sessions of Assembly at Providence, to walk up from Warwick, or we might say from Greenwich, as he resided on the dividing line of the two towns, and home again in the afternoon. Four delegates, Hopkins, Ellery, Marchant, and John Collins, were chosen to represent the State in Congress. The object of this was, that as the articles of confederation required each State to have at least two delegates in that body, the ill ness or absence of one or more members might not leave the State without a vote in the national councils.

11. Gen. Howe resigned the command of the British army to Sir Henry Clinton, and returned to England. Gen. Pigot, anticipating another attempt upon the island, sent

25. up the river about six hundred men, under Lieut.-Col. Campbell, to destroy a number of boats then collected in Kickemuit River, east of Warren. Landing at daylight a little below the town, they entered Warren, and marching across to Kickemuit, burnt seventy flat-boats, the galley Washington, and a grist mill. Returning to Warren they set fire to the town, destroying the Baptist church,

[1] Jonathan Pitcher, of Rhode Island, was 1st lieutenant of the Providence, and William Jones, afterwards Governor of Rhode Island, was captain of marines. Benjamin Page was also a lieutenant.

CHAP. with several other buildings, blew up the magazine, pil-
XXI. laged the houses, and carrying away many prisoners, pro-
1778. ceeded to Bristol, where the work of destruction was re-
May 25. sumed.[1] A portion of Col. Crary's regiment, quartered
in the town, retreated. Had they made a stand at the
bridge, Bristol would have been saved, for Campbell had
orders, in case of resistance, not to force an entrance. The
Episcopal church and eighteen dwellings were burnt, the
people were plundered, and some forty persons, including
a picket guard of nine men under Capt. Westcott at Pap-
poosquash Point, were taken. The whole town would
have been destroyed had not the troops rallied and attacked the enemy. An express had been sent off to Gen.
Sullivan at Providence for aid. Col. Barton, with about
twenty horsemen, hastened on in advance to harass the
retreating foe, and if possible to detain them till the main
body could arrive. Collecting some two hundred volunteers on the way, he attacked the enemy near Bristol
Ferry, and was severely wounded in the leg. The British
reached their boats at the ferry, and embarked before a
sufficient force arrived to prevent their retreat. The British loss in this skirmish was never ascertained, but from
the marks of blood along the road was supposed to be
considerable. The Americans had four men wounded.
The undefended condition of the State at this moment,
26. had favored the expedition. Gen. Sullivan writes that he
had not five hundred men at his command, and that there
were less than two hundred from the other New England
States. A special session of the Assembly was held in
28. consequence of this alarming event. To fill the ranks of
the State brigade, eight hundred and thirty-nine men
were ordered to be raised, and one-sixth part of the militia and chartered force of the State was called out for fifteen days. The circulation of State bills of credit was

[1] An amusing story of the capture of a drummer who had lagged in the rear, by a party of the heroic women of Warren, is told in Fessenden's History of Warren, p. 94, note.

prohibited after July first. The amount outstanding was CHAP.
to be exchanged for Loan office certificates as far as possi- XXI.
ble, and the balance to be redeemed by notes of the State 1778.
treasurer. May

The enemy soon made an attempt upon Fall River. 31.
A party of one hundred and fifty men landed at daybreak and burnt a mill and house by the shore, but were
prevented from proceeding further by the resolute conduct of Col. Joseph Durfee, who, with twenty-five men,
taking a strong position near the bridge, and being reinforced by some militia, drove them back after a sharp
action of an hour and a half. The British left two men
on the field. Two of the enemy's vessels, a galley and a
sloop, in attempting to cover their retreat, were driven on
to the Rhode-island shore and abandoned.

A severe correspondence now ensued between Generals June
Sullivan and Pigot, respecting the prisoners taken at 4.
Bristol. Sullivan represented the conduct of the enemy
in that affair, and in their treatment of prisoners generally, in its true light, as an outrage upon the Christian
name, and as provocative of that retaliation from which
the Americans had hitherto refrained. He wished to
know upon what terms the captives could be released.
Pigot replied, offering an exchange upon the usual terms, 10.
and saying that if it was not effected at once, they would
be sent to New York.

The commissioners appointed by Parliament to con-
ciliate America, addressed a letter to Congress, enclosing
the bills so hastily passed for that purpose. Congress
replied very briefly, returning the papers, and refusing to 17.
treat upon any other terms than those of absolute independence. The next day the British army evacuated 18.
Philadelphia, and Gen. Arnold, with a division from
Valley Forge, entered it on the following day. Congress, 19.
acting upon advices from Gen. Sullivan and Gov. Greene,
directed Washington to send home the Rhode Island 25.
troops, if they could be spared, and empowered the Navy

CHAP. XXI. 1778. Board to provide three galleys for the defence of Providence, Warren, and Taunton Rivers. The whole army had already moved from Valley Forge to attack the British in their retreat across New Jersey. Coming up with
June 28. the rear guard near Monmouth, a battle ensued, which, notwithstanding the disobedience of Lee, who commanded the American advance, in ordering a retreat, resulted, after several hours of hard fighting, in a decisive, although not brilliant victory. In this action Gen. Greene commanded the right wing, and the Rhode Island regiments, which suffered the loss of Lieutenant Nathan Wickes, and several men, were in Lee's division. Lee was placed under arrest by Washington. Two months afterwards he was tried by court-martial and suspended for one year, and soon after the expiration of this sentence, he was dismissed from the service by Congress. On the same day with the battle of Monmouth, Louis XVI. issued orders for the seizure of British vessels, whence we may date the commencement of the war in Europe.

29. In pursuance of a resolve of Congress, the Assembly laid an embargo upon provisions, to prevent their exportation. They also levied a tax of thirty-two thousand pounds, which included seventy-five hundred pounds, or one-fourth of the State's portion of the Continental tax recommended by Congress to be raised in quarterly instalments for the war service of the present year.

July 10. The arrival of the French fleets off the Capes of Delaware, was heralded throughout the country as "glorious
12. news." On the following Sunday "the most interesting interview that ever took place in America,[1] or perhaps in the world," was had between Monsieur Gerard, the French Plenipotentiary, and the American Congress. At the same time, British reinforcements began to arrive at New-
15. port. A fleet of transports brought three thousand men and sailed again to New York for four thousand more.

[1] Letter of H. Marchant, member of Congress, to Governor Greene, 14th July, 1778. Foster Correspondence, volume i.

An attack on Providence was daily expected. The enemy CHAP.
now had seven thousand men on the island, while to op- XXI.
pose them, Sullivan writes that but sixteen hundred 1778.
troops were in the field, and the other New England July 22.
States still neglected to send their quotas. The council
of war called out one-half of the effective force of the 29.
State to serve for twenty days from the first of August,
and ordered the remainder to be ready to take the field at
a moment's warning. On the same day, Count D'Estaing,
with twelve ships-of-the-line and four frigates[1] arrived off
Newport, and blockaded the enemy. The next morning,
two French ships-of-the-line sailed up to the north end of 30.
Conanicut. The British garrison on that island withdrew
to Newport, and their ships sought refuge in the harbor.
Three British vessels, the Kingfisher of sixteeen guns, and
two galleys, were blown up in the east passage, or Seaconnet River, on the approach of two other French ships.
Major-General Greene arrived at home from the army,
and was followed by Brig.-Gen. Glover, both of whom 31.
volunteered for the approaching expedition. The marquis Aug.
de Lafayette soon offered his services in the same cause. 2.
Two Continental brigades, Varnum's and Glover's, with
two companies of artillery from the army at White Plains, 3.
arrived the next day. Four British frigates and a corvette
were run ashore on Rhode-island and burnt, upon the ap- 5.
pearance of a portion of the French fleet in the middle

[1] These were ships-of-the-line, Languedoc, Tonnant, Cesar, Zelé, Hector, Guerrier, Marseillois, Protecteur, Vaillant, Provence, Fantasque, Sagittaire; frigates, Chimére, Engageante, Aimable, Alcmene. The venerable Thomas Coggeshall, who died in Newport in 1851, February 2d, in his 92d year, was a lad working on his father's farm at the time of the landing of the British. He, with many others, was forced to work for the enemy nearly three years in driving a team. At this time, all the teams were employed in carting stores from "the point" to Brinley's rope-walk on the hill. "One day (29th July, 1778) the officers came down from the hill, and by their actions it was evident that something important was in their knowledge, and when we got to the top of the hill with our loads, we saw far off the fleet of Count d'Estaing—*darsn't laugh—not then*," said Mr. C., in narrating to the writer, some ten years since, the events of this important day.

CHAP. XXI. 1778. passage.[1] Several other vessels were at the same time burnt by the enemy in and near Newport harbor, to avoid capture, and others were sunk to obstruct the passage.
Aug. 6. Volunteers began to pour in from the neighboring States,
7. and Gen. Sullivan proceeded to the camp at Tiverton to take command. D'Estaing, with twelve ships-of-the-line, under a heavy cannonade from the British batteries, en-
8. tered the harbor of Newport to co-operate with the American army. The British then destroyed their two
9. remaining ships.[2] The next morning Gen. Sullivan, with about ten thousand troops, began to cross from Tiverton to the north end of Rhode-island, and the French troops destined for his support were disembarked upon Conanicut. On the same evening, Lord Howe, with thirty-six sail, of which thirteen were ships-of-the-line and seven frigates, appeared off Point Judith. It had been agreed that D'Estaing should land four thousand men on the west side of Rhode-island to co-operate with Sullivan, but this event deranged the entire plan. That night the
10. French troops were embarked, and the next morning D'Estaing, eager for battle, put to sea. Sullivan took possession of the forts at the north part of the island, which were abandoned by the enemy. The British retired within their lines about three-fourths of a mile from Newport, burning all the houses for a mile or more to the north and east of the "two mile corner." A strong detachment, composed of light troops, independent companies, and a corps of fifty men from each brigade, under Col. Livingston, advanced within a mile and a half of the
11. hostile lines, and orders were given for the whole army to push forward the next morning. The right wing was

[1] These were the Lark, Orpheus, and Juno, 32s; Cerberus, 28, and Falcon, 16.

[2] These were, the Grand Duke, transport, of 40 guns, burnt; and the frigate Flora, 32, sunk. The prize money awarded by the French Government for the destruction of all the British vessels was 600 livres per gun, and the number of guns thus taken was 212. A livre was worth at that time two-thirds of a dollar

commanded by Maj.-Gen. Greene, the left by Gen. Lafayette, the second line of Massachusetts militia by Maj.-Gen. Hancock, late President of Congress, and the reserve by Col. West. A terrible storm, one of the most violent gales upon record, arose that night and lasted for two days. The opposing squadrons, having spent one day in manœuvring for the weather gage, were about coming to action when this gale dispersed them. Some attempted to fight in the midst of the hurricane, but the damage by storm was greater than that of battle. The ships were scattered. The Languedoc, the Admiral's flag-ship, and the Tonnant were dismasted, and all were more or less disabled. On shore the fury of the tempest was no less dreadful. The tents were prostrated, and the army, exposed on the wet ground to a cold and drenching rain, suffered severely. Some of the men died from exposure, and a great number of horses perished. The ammunition was much damaged, some of it entirely spoiled, but the injury from this cause proved to be less than was at first feared.

CHAP. XXI. 1778. Aug. 12–13.

When the storm had abated, the French fleet captured two of the British cruisers,[1] and repelled the attacks of the Renown and the Preston, fifty-gun ships, upon the two dismasted vessels, but nothing was heard from either squadron for several days. In the early morning, Sullivan advanced with his whole army, and at two o'clock encamped within two miles of the enemy's lines, which extended from Tonomy Hill to Easton's Pond, near the beach. The same night a detachment occupied Honeyman's Hill, on the enemy's right, within half a mile of their front line of works on Bliss's Hill, which it commands. Entrenchments were thrown up during the night, and for five days, in the course of which several other batteries were erected at different points, a heavy cannonade was kept up along the lines, and the enemy were compelled to

15.

16–20.

[1] The Senegal, sloop of war, and the Carcass, bombketch.

CHAP. XXI. evacuate one of the outworks upon their left near the bay.

1778. Aug. 17. Meanwhile the council of war called out the remaining half of the effective force of the State to supply the loss of the French auxiliaries, and the deficiency in the quota of troops expected from the neighboring States. By a letter
18. from Gen. Sullivan, it appears that at this moment there were of rank and file under his command, but about sixteen hundred men from this State, and fourteen hundred from Massachusetts, while three thousand had been expected from each, and but four hundred from Connecticut, out of fifteen hundred that were promised; but the "spirited resolves" of the council of war, as he terms
19. them in his next letter, restored the general's confidence in the success of his plans. An embargo, which continued for one week, was laid upon all vessels, in order that their crews might serve in the expedition.

20. The return of the French fleet, although in a dilapidated condition, gave a momentary joy to the besieging army, who now felt certain of capturing the whole British force within forty-eight hours. Sullivan sent Greene and Lafayette to persuade D'Estaing to co-operate in the reduction of Newport. Great was the consternation, when,
21. the next day, the Admiral announced his intention to proceed immediately to Boston to refit, and actually sailed at nightfall. The American officers drew up a protest against his departure at such a crisis. Lafayette refused
22. to sign the paper. A fast vessel was despatched to overtake the fleet and deliver the protest to D'Estaing. Congress submitted the papers relating to the affair to Gerard, with a request to know his opinion upon it. In the position which the United States then held towards France, this proceeding was as politic as it was singular, for although every effort was made to suppress the protest, it could not fail to come to the knowledge of the Minister.[1]

[1] In the secret despatch of Gerard to the Comte de Vergennes, in which this Protest is severely handled, while the conduct of Congress, in promptly

So great was the scarcity of provisions at this time, CHAP.
that there were hundreds of people in Providence without XXI.
bread or the means of obtaining it, and corn was sold at 1778.
eight dollars a bushel. Nor could vessels be sent to bring Aug.
flour on account of the embargo, until the pressing wants
of the population required it to be repealed. Great dis- 25.
satisfaction now pervaded the camp, and desertions became frequent. Half of the New Hampshire volunteers,
writes one of their officers, had already gone, and the rest 26.
could not be induced to remain. The siege had meanwhile been pressed with vigor, and the enemy had abandoned all their outworks except one. It was Sullivan's 27.
intention to storm the works, but the army, by the withdrawal of the volunteers, was found to be reduced to only
fifty-four hundred men. It was therefore determined in 28.
council, to fall back upon the fortified hills at the north, and there await the return of the French fleet, to hasten which, Lafayette proceeded to Boston. Nearly three thousand volunteers, supposing that nothing would be done till the return of the French, had left within twenty-four hours, and others were still leaving. The retreat commenced in the evening, and by two o'clock that night, the army encamped on Butts Hill, the right wing on the west road, and the left on the east road, with covering parties on each flank. Col. Livingston's light corps was stationed on the east road, and another under Col. Laurens, Col. Fleury, and Major Talbot, on the west road, each three miles in front of the camp, and in their rear was the picquet of the army under Col. Wade.

Early the next morning the British forces marched out 29.
in two columns by the two roads, and at seven o'clock the attack commenced. The American light corps were supported by the picquet. A series of severe skirmishes ensued, and a regiment was sent to reinforce each of the

furnishing him with all the papers pertaining to it, is highly applauded, the Minister closes the subject with the sententious remark—"Malheureusement, ce pays est peuplé de têtes exaltées."

CHAP. XXI. 1778. Aug. 29.

two corps, with orders for them to retire upon the main body, which they did in excellent order. One account attributes to Major Talbot the commencement of the action, on the west road. Another, more circumstantial, states that the first desperate stand was made at a cross road connecting the two main roads, near the Gibbs place, about five and a half miles from Newport, where a middle road, parallel to the two and very near the east road, extends northward from the cross road. A broad field, enclosed by stone walls, occupies the space between the east and middle roads, and is bounded on the south by the cross road. Here the twenty-second British regiment, Col. Campbell, which had advanced by the east road, divided, and one half of it turned to the left into the cross road. A portion of the American picket was concealed in this field, and the divided twenty-second fell into the ambuscade. A scene of fearful slaughter ensued. Short, sharp, and deadly was the struggle. The Americans, leaping from behind the walls, poured a storm of bullets into the very face of the astonished foe, and before their bewildered enemy could recover from the shock, they had reloaded, and with another sheet of fire, completed the work of death. Nearly one-fourth part of the ill-fated twenty-second were cut down by this murderous assault. Two Hessian regiments came up to their support, but the Americans had already retreated, according to orders. An attack was now made upon the American left wing, but the enemy were repulsed by Gen. Glover, and retreated to their works on Quaker Hill.

The Hessian columns were formed upon a chain of highland, extending northward from this hill. The American army was drawn up in three lines; the first in front of their works on Butt's Hill, the second in rear of the hill, and the reserve near a creek about half a mile in the rear of the first line. The distance between Butt's and Quaker Hill is about one mile, with marshy meadow and woodland between.

About nine o'clock a heavy cannonade commenced, and continued throughout the day. For the next hour there was constant skirmishing among the advanced parties, until two British ships of war and some light armed vessels, coming up the bay, opened a fire upon the right flank of the Americans, under cover of which the enemy made a desperate effort to turn the flank and storm an advanced redoubt on the American right. The action now became general along that portion of the line. For nearly seven hours the battle raged with but little intermission, but for the first hour after the British ships began to fire, while the attempt to turn the American flank was made, the conflict was at its height. The carnage was frightful. Down the slope of Anthony's Hill, a western continuation of Quaker Hill, the Hessian columns and British infantry twice rushed to the assault and were repulsed in the valley with great slaughter. Sixty were found dead in one spot. At another, thirty Hessians were buried in one grave. Major-Gen. Greene commanded on the right. Of the four brigades under his immediate command, Varnum's, Glover's, Cornell's, and Greene's, all suffered severely, but Gen. Varnum's perhaps the most. A third time the enemy, with desperate courage and increased strength, attempted to assail the redoubt, and would have carried it but for the timely aid of two continental battalions despatched by Sullivan to support his almost exhausted troops. It was in repelling these furious onsets, that the newly raised black regiment, under Col. Greene, distinguished itself by deeds of desperate valor. Posted behind a thicket in the valley, they three times drove back the Hessians who charged repeatedly down the hill to dislodge them; and so determined were the enemy in these successive charges, that the day after the battle the Hessian colonel, upon whom this duty had devolved, applied to exchange his command and go to New York, because he dared not lead his regiment again

CHAP. XXI. 1778. Aug. 29.

CHAP. XXI. to battle, lest his men should shoot him for having caused them so much loss.

1778. Aug. 29. While this furious conflict was in progress on the British left, Gen. Lovell's brigade of Massachusetts militia, was ordered to engage their right and rear, which was done with complete success. The ships of war also were driven off by the well-served guns of two heavy batteries that were brought to bear upon them. The desperate courage of the enemy availed them nothing against the equally resolute valor of the Americans. They at last gave way, and retreated to their fortified camp on Quaker Hill, closely followed by the victors who captured Brady's battery upon the hill. Sullivan desired to attack them in their works; but the army had now been for thirty-six hours without rest or food, and continually on the march, at labor, or in battle. The assault was therefore abandoned, and both armies occupied their camps in the afternoon, although the cannonade was continued until night. A return of the killed, wounded, and missing, shows the whole loss of the Americans in the action to be two hundred and eleven. That of the British was at first supposed to be about seven hundred, but was afterwards found to amount to one thousand and twenty-three, including those taken prisoners.

When we consider that of the five thousand Americans engaged in this battle, only about fifteen hundred had ever before been in action, and that they were opposed by veteran troops superior both in numbers and discipline, with a degree of obstinacy rarely equalled in the annals of warfare, we can understand the remark said to have been made by Lafayette in speaking of the battle on Rhode-island that "it was the best fought action of the war."[1]

[1] In addition to the authorities enumerated in the note at the close of chapter xx., there are some new ones consulted in the present chapter which should be mentioned. These are chiefly the Journals of the Council of War in Rhode Island, in four manuscript volumes, and documents ob-

tained in the French Archives at Paris by the writer in 1847. These are despatches from M. Gerard to the Comte de Vergennes; the journal of an officer on board Le Languedoc, the flag-ship of the Count d'Estaing; the Admiral's report to his Government, made December 5, 1779; and copious extracts from papers relating to prizes taken, and to the expenses and operations of the fleet. All these are to be found in "Le Ministere de la Marine et des Colonies; Archives Personnel, E. Estaing (Le Comte de)." The liberality of the French Government, under all regimes, in allowing to historical students, when properly presented, free access to its archives, has often been remarked, and the author can bear testimony to its truth, and to the courteous alacrity of gentlemen connected with the various public offices in aiding his researches. Some details, relating to the French fleet, gathered from these researches, which are not mentioned in the text, may here be noted. Nine prizes were taken by D'Estaing, and sold in Providence. The net proceeds of these sales, in Continental currency, was $437,955. Besides the hospital at Bristol Ferry, there was one also for a short time at Kingston. The expenses of these establishments, including the transportation of the sick to Boston in 1778, were $57,573. The pilots who brought the fleet from New York to Newport, in July, received 300 livres each. The larger vessels had two pilots. French money was reckoned in livres tournois, soldi, and derniers. 12 Derniers = 1 soldo, and 20 soldi = 1 livre tournois, valued in October, 1778, at 10½*d.*, sterling, when sterling exchange was at £4, New England currency, for £1 sterling. The loss of the French squadron in the campaign of 1778 was 53 killed, of whom were 3 officers and 23 soldiers; and 99 wounded, of whom were 3 officers and 47 soldiers, besides the crew of a prize brig lost at sea.

The writer also received much valuable information from several aged men—all of whom were witnesses, and some were actors in the scenes herein described; from John Howland, late president of the Rhode Island Historical Society; from Thomas Hornsby and Thomas Coggeshall, of Newport; Asa Freeborn, and Seth Anthony, of Portsmouth; with whom (in company with the late Dr. John W. Richmond, who for many years resided at Portsmouth, and was intimate with these and other participators and witnesses of the campaign of 1778) the writer conversed, he obtained much that was interesting respecting this period. The notes of these conversations, chiefly had in 1849, he has carefully preserved. The author desires to make this acknowledgment as a tribute to the memory of these venerable men, all of whom have since been gathered to the grave.

CHAPTER XXII.

1778—1781.

FROM THE RETREAT FROM RHODE-ISLAND BY GENERAL SULLIVAN, AUGUST 30th, 1778, TO THE SURRENDER OF LORD CORNWALLIS AT YORKTOWN, OCTOBER 19th, 1781.

CHAP. XXII. 1778. Aug. 30.

THE morning after the battle, Sullivan received advices from Gen. Washington, that Lord Howe was approaching with five thousand troops for the relief of Newport, and also a letter from Boston that D'Estaing could not return as soon as he expected. It was therefore resolved, in a council of officers, to leave the island. The heavy baggage and stores were sent off through the day, while tents were pitched in sight of the enemy, and the troops were employed in fortifying the camp as if for permanent occupation. All day a ceaseless cannonade was kept up on both sides. At dark the tents were struck, the light baggage and the troops passed down, and before midnight the main army had crossed the ferry to Tiverton. The Providence regiment, as being the best boatmen, were employed in rowing them over. Lafayette returned that night, and was greatly mortified at having failed to be present at the battle. He had made great efforts to arrive in season, having ridden from Boston, a distance of nearly seventy miles, in six and a half hours. Under his supervision the pickets and covering parties were now brought off without the loss of the smallest article of baggage, although exposed to the constant fire of the

enemy, from which Sullivan's Life Guards, who brought CHAP.
up the rear, suffered rather severely. The retreat was XXII.
not only skilfully conducted, but admirably timed, for 1778.
early the next morning the British fleet, with the army of Aug.
Sir Henry Clinton, was seen off Newport, from Tiverton 31.
Heights.

The great dissatisfaction expressed by the American
officers at the departure of the Count D'Estaing, gave
much uneasiness to Washington and was highly displeas-
ing to Lafayette. To soothe the feelings of the latter,
Washington addressed him a kind letter from the camp Sept. 1.
at White Plains, and also wrote to Generals Sullivan and
Greene to use their influence in allaying the excitement.[1]
The General Assembly, which met three days after the 2.
retreat, took no notice of this affair, nor indeed of the
battle. Sullivan's army was now reduced to twelve hundred continental and two thousand State troops, besides
some militia whose term of service was about to expire,
while that of the enemy, just reinforced, numbered nearly
eleven thousand. In this situation he wrote to Gov.
Trumbull for further aid, as an attack on Providence was 4.
expected. But the enemy employed their force in a
different direction. A fleet of forty ships and transports
sailed for New Bedford, and landing four thousand troops,
burnt that town and part of Fairhaven, with a great 5.
amount of shipping at the wharves.

The thanks of Congress were voted to Gen. Sullivan 9.
and his army for their gallantry in the late battle, and
their conduct in the retreat, and Major Morris, the aide-
de-camp who carried Sullivan's despatch to Philadelphia,
was made a lieutenant-colonel. The body guard of Gen.
Sullivan, selected from the State brigade, received promo- 10.
tion from him for their behavior in covering the retreat.[2]

[1] These letters are printed in "Spirit of '76," pp. 333–6.

[2] Aaron Mann, who commanded them on that occasion was made captain, Levi Hoppin 1st lieutenant, George Potter 2d lieutenant, and John Westcott ensign, in General Orders, issued September 10, 1778. They

CHAP. XXII. 1778. The thanks of Gen. Washington to the officers and men engaged in the battle were also communicated in general orders.

Sept. 17. The arrival of Admiral Byron at Newport, with a part of the new squadron destined to operate against America, produced several changes. Soon afterwards Lord Howe returned to England, and Sir Robert Pigot, leaving the command of the army on Rhode-island once more in the hands of Gen. Prescott, also went home.

Oct. 25. A daring enterprise, attempted by Major Silas Talbot, added to the fame already acquired by this amphibious officer. By land or sea he was ever ready to serve his country, and by his brilliant deeds upon both elements, proved himself to be equally at home on either. The east passage was blockaded by the Pigot galley, a stout vessel of two hundred tons, armed with eight twelve-pounders, defended by strong boarding-nettings, and having a crew of forty-five men. Talbot determined to take her. In a small sloop called the Hawk, equipped with two three-pounders and a corps of sixty men, under Lieutenant Baker, selected from the troops then quartered in Providence, he embarked on his perilous expedition. A
26. headwind detained him the first night in the river, but the next day he passed in safety the British battery at Bristol Ferry, and anchored in Mount Hope Bay to await
27. a favorable wind. The following day he proceeded alone to Little Compton to reconnoitre, and finding the Pigot armed at all points, he obtained fifteen more men under Lieutenant William Helme of Topham's reigiment. The
28. next night being very dark, and the wind favorable, they made sail until near the fort at Fogland Ferry, where they lowered sail and silently drifted with the tide, under bare poles, past the battery. It was so dark that they

were commissioned by resolve of the Council of War, December 7, to bear date from October 23. The corps was known as Sullivan's Life Guards, and was selected by Lafayette to cover the rearguard in the retreat, on the night of August 30, 1778.

had to send out a boat with muffled oars to find the galley. This done they crowded sail and bore down upon the enemy. A volley of musketry greeted their approach, and was answered by a discharge of small arms from the Hawk; but before the Pigot could bring her cannon to bear, the jibboom of the Hawk tore through the nettings and caught in the foreshrouds. Lieutenant Helme, followed by his command, ran along the bowsprit, and boarded the enemy. Her crew were driven below, the commander alone fighting gallantly on deck. The galley was taken without the loss of a man on either side, and the Hawk with her prize bore away for Stonington. For this gallant act, Congress made Talbot a lieutenant-colonel.

CHAP. XXII. 1778. Oct. 29. Nov. 14.

The Assembly, then in session, passed a vote of thanks to the officers and men of the expedition.[1] A tax of thirty thousand pounds was assessed, and a new estimate of taxable property in the State was ordered to be made. Another act for the relief of the poor in Newport was passed, providing for their settlement and support in the different towns. The scarcity of provisions, owing to the protracted military operations in the State, had become so distressing, that Gov. Greene, by vote of the Assembly, wrote to Connecticut requesting that the embargo there existing upon all articles of food, might be so far removed, as to allow of their exportation to Rhode Island. The conduct of "engrossers and forestallers," as they were termed, or speculators, as they styled themselves, in buying up necessary articles of every kind, especially food and clothing, for private gain, induced Congress to issue a circular to all the States, calling for legislative action upon the subject.

Oct. 26–31. 31. Nov. 11.

The arrival of Admiral Byron with twelve ships-of-the- 13.

[1] A few weeks later, the Pigot was purchased by Government, at the suggestion of General Sullivan, to be used as a guard ship in Providence river, where she arrived December 1. Captain Jeremiah Clarke was appointed to the command; Benjamin Cozzens and Joseph Gardner, lieutenants.

CHAP. XXII. line at Newport, after an unsuccessful cruise for the French
fleet off Boston, caused some alarm. They remained for
1778. one month to refit, and then sailed for the South, whither
Dec. 14. the war was now transferred.

Another terrible storm, more severe than that which
12. had disabled the contending squadrons in August, caused
great disaster on sea and shore. The depth of the snow, and
the intensity of the cold, was unparalleled in this vicinity.
Sentinels were frozen at their posts, or stifled by the
whirling snow, and so many Hessians perished from cold
and exposure on that dreadful night in Newport, that this
gale was long known as "the Hessian storm."

Another exploit, although not comparable to that of
Talbot, was performed in the east passage by Lieut.
17. Chapin, of Col. Sherburne's regiment. With six men in a
whale boat, he captured a brig bound to New York,
having first driven the crew into the rigging. The prisoners,
among whom was the wife of Sir Guy Johnston, were
landed at Seaconnet.

28. The Assembly voted swords to Lieut.-Col. Talbot, and
to Lieut. Helme for their gallant capture of the Pigot.
30. A day of thanksgiving was held at the close of the year,
by recommendation of Congress. An act for supplying
the army with forage, fuel, horses, and other necessaries,
enabling the military officers, through the medium of the
civil power, to seize upon any such articles, was imme-
1779. diately found to be so impolitic in its purpose, and so
Jan. 19. difficult of execution, that Gen. Cornell and other officers
urged the governor to convene a special session for its repeal.
This was done, and at the same time an appropriation of five hundred pounds was made for the relief of the
poor at Newport. The deplorable condition of the State
21. was represented in a touching letter from Gov. Greene to
the Assembly of Connecticut. "The most obdurate
heart," he writes, "would relent to see old age and child-
hood, from comfortable circumstances reduced to the
necessity of begging for a morsel of bread." Two thou-

sand persons driven from Rhode-island were scattered about, homeless and penniless through the State, but chiefly in Providence, dependent upon public or private charity. Deputy-Governor Bowen, and President Manning were sent to represent the case to the Assembly of Connecticut, and obtain leave to purchase grain in their behalf, while others were to solicit donations. A memorial to Congress for an abatement of a portion of the continental tax assigned to Rhode Island was also prepared, and noble was the response to both of these appeals. The Connecticut legislature allowed seven thousand bushels of grain to be exported to Rhode Island, and recommended a prompt and liberal contribution to be made throughout their State for the relief of the sufferers. Within two months, donations amounting to five hundred bushels of grain, and four thousand three hundred pounds in money were collected in that State. This noble liberality was imitated by the far South through the action of Congress. A resolution was passed, requesting the States of Connecticut and New York to repeal their embargo upon bread stuffs for the benefit of Rhode Island, and a few weeks later the State was relieved from fifty thousand dollars, being one-sixth of her allotted quota of the continental tax, which was generously assumed by the State of South Carolina, with the consent of her delegates. This release was virtually an admission by Congress, of the self-evident truth that Rhode Island had done more than her part, and suffered more than her share in the common cause; but the assumption by South Carolina was no less an act of generous patriotism on her part, worthy of the land of the Rutledges, of Moultrie, and of Marion.

CHAP. XXII. 1779. Jan. 23. Feb 8. Mar 2.

Although no formidable invasion was again attempted by the enemy in Rhode Island, yet predatory incursions by detached parties became more frequent and annoying than ever, and continued so till the island was evacuated. In one of these a small party landed in North Kingstown by night, and carried off a great quantity of sheep, cattle,

Feb. 1.

CHAP. XXII. 1779. and corn. The Assembly therefore advised Gen. Sullivan to purchase another vessel, in addition to the Pigot, for the defence of the bay. They passed a vote of thanks
Feb. 22. to him for his conduct since taking command of the army in this State. They also assessed two very heavy taxes, one of ninety thousand pounds for Continental use, and another of sixty thousand pounds for State purposes, and took measures to sustain for another year, the brigade of fifteen hundred men whose term of enlistment was about to expire.[1] Complaints of unequal representation, first embodied in the Scituate instructions,[2] had become so frequent, that the Assembly debated a plan to remedy the evil, and reduce the number of deputies so as not to exceed two from each town, but the measure failed by a non-con-
28. currence of the two houses.[3]

Mar. A second newspaper, styled the "American Journal
4. and General Advertiser," was commenced in Providence by Southwick and Wheeler. It was printed every Thursday and continued about five years.

9. To enlist the new brigade, money was needed, but the treasury was empty. William Rhodes, sheriff of Providence, was sent to Connecticut to obtain a loan of twelve thousand pounds for this purpose. The money was hired for one month. The Springfield compact was not kept by the other New England States. There were now but two thousand Continental troops in Rhode Island, while the
11. British force was upwards of six thousand. Letters were

[1] The officers were the same as now commanded the brigade, with some transpositions since the former organization. Brigadier General Cornell commanded the brigade. The officers of the artillery regiment were Colonel Robert Elliot; Josiah Flagg, lieutenant-colonel. Of the 1st battalion of infantry, Colonel Archibald Crary; Lieutenant-colonel Nathaniel Hawkins; Christopher Manchester, major; Samuel Montgomery, surgeon. Of the 2d battalion, Colonel John Topham; Lieutenant-colonel James Williams; Major Samuel Philips. Stephen Wigneron, surgeon.

[2] *Ante*, chap. xxi., p. 400.

[3] The Act, having failed to pass, is not entered upon the Records, but the proceedings of the two Houses are preserved in Foster Papers, vol. ii.

sent to Connecticut and New Hampshire, urging them to CHAP.
send on their quota of troops, for the State was never XXII.
more exposed than at this time. 1779.

Brigadier-General Varnum now resigned his commis- Mar. 18.
sion in the army, and Major-General Sullivan was called
away to conduct an expedition against the Indians in New
York. A meeting was held in Providence to express the 19.
feeling of respect entertained for this favorite general,
and addresses were also presented to him from the officers 22.
in this State, military, medical, and staff, and from the
order of Freemasons. A voluntary escort attended his
departure as far as Johnston, where a public dinner was 29.
given him by his late companions in arms. Gen. Glover
succeeded to the command for a few days, till the arrival April.
of Major-General Gates who was received with great en- 3.
thusiasm. The council of war placed him in command of 5.
all the Rhode Island troops, and an elegant entertainment 6.
was given to him.

The predatory excursions of the enemy were extended 2.
in all directions. Another attempt was made against
New Bedford, but finding the people prepared to repulse
them, they sailed away. Soon afterwards seven hundred
men landed on Conanicut Island, including a portion of 14.
Fanning's Tory regiment, and the next day about the
same number were embarked in flatboats at Newport. 15.
Great alarm prevailed, and preparations were made at
every post along the bay to repel the invaders; but this
expedition was also destined to the eastward, and visiting
Nantucket, brought away a dozen vessels, chiefly loaded
with oil. A party also landed at Swanzey, burnt one 19.
house, and took six prisoners.

The movements of the enemy were generally known in advance, through the ingenuity and daring of Isaac Barker of Middletown. Pretending to be a Tory, he remained on his farm upon the east side of the island, in plain sight of the Seaconnet shore. A British colonel was quartered at his house, from whom Barker often

CHAP. XXII. 1779. April learned the designs of the enemy. A system of signals was arranged between him and Lieutenant Chapin of Sherburne's regiment, stationed on the opposite shore, by means of bars and a stake in a stone wall which could be easily seen from Seaconnet with a spy-glass. The farm was near North Point, which extends some distance into the bay, and towards the end of the point is a ledge of rocks wherein was a crevice used by Barker as a post office. In this crevice he would deposit a letter at night when anything of importance was to be communicated, and the next day would arrange the signal at the bars. Chapin would then come over in a boat on the first favorable opportunity by night and get the letter. This method of communication required great courage and address, but was successfully practised by Barker for fourteen months, from August, 1778, till the British left the island, although at the constant risk of his life. Several times he narrowly escaped being discovered.[1]

16. The arrival of the U. S. ships Warren, Capt. John B. Hopkins, Queen of France, Capt. Joseph Olney, and Ranger, Capt. Simpson, at Boston, from a short and most successful cruise, gave great joy. These ships had sailed under Capt. Hopkins as senior officer but a short time before, and off Cape Henry captured a fleet of seven British vessels, one twenty-gun ship and six transports, with very valuable stores, and twenty-four British officers bound to Georgia. One of the officers admitted that the loss of this fleet would more than counterbalance all the British success in the South. The value of the captured stores was estimated at eighty thousand pounds sterling.[2]

22. Brigadier-General John Stark arrived at Providence, and took the command vacated by the resignation of Gen.

[1] A more detailed account of this affair is given in "Spirit of '76," pp. 181–4.

[2] Cooper's Naval History i. 150, states that Hopkins sailed from Boston on 18th April, upon this cruise, but the papers of the day mention his arrival home on the 16th April, with the prizes.

Varnum. A uniform system of tactics, prepared by CHAP.
Baron Steuben was now introduced into the militia as XXII.
well as the regular service, and copies of it were sent to 1779.
this State. Gen. Glover's brigade was called to the west- April
ward, leaving Rhode Island yet more exposed to the
enemy. Gates urged Connecticut to send her quota, and 28.
Gov. Greene wrote to New Hampshire to forward hers. 29.
Not a man from either State was now in Rhode Island.
Gov. Trumbull replied that Connecticut was not bound May 1.
by the terms of the Springfield convention, unless the other
States that were less exposed, also sent their quotas.
Congress again recommended that the terms of that agree- 7.
ment should be kept by the several parties to it, and Gen.
Starke again represented the defenceless condition of 10.
Rhode Island to his native State.

The Assembly formed the militia of the several coun- 5.
ties into brigades, and chose Gen. Varnum to be major-
general.[1] They also recommended to Congress certain
officers to fill vacancies in the first continental battalion
from this State.[2] Col. Crary of the first regiment of State
infantry, in Cornell's brigade, resigned his commission 7.
on account of the depreciation of paper money which
disabled him from supporting his family. A solemn fast
was observed throughout the country by recommendation 6.
of Congress. Another descent was made upon Point
Judith by a body of Tories from Rhode Island, and a 8.

[1] The brigadiers elected were, William West, for Providence; Joseph Stanton, for Kings; Nathan Miller, for Newport and Bristol Counties. General Varnum had lately resigned his Continental commission, as brigadier, and could therefore accept the post of major-general of the State.

[2] The officers of the 1st Rhode Island battalion in the campaign of 1779, taken from a list prepared by Lieutenant-colonel Ward at this time, were as follows: Colonel Christopher Greene; Lieutenant-colonel Samuel Ward; Major Ebenezer Flagg; Captains Elijah Lewis, Thomas Cole, John S. Dexter, Thomas Arnold, John Holden, Edward Slocum, Joseph Arnold; Lieutenants Daniel Peirce, Zephaniah Brown, Robert Rogers, David Johnson, Elias Thompson, Enoch Stanton, Charles Peirce, John Cooke, Daniel Dexter. Chandler Burlingame was recommended in June as a lieutenant in this battalion.

CHAP. XXII. large number of sheep and cattle were carried off. At
this time a British fleet was devastating Virginia, while
1779. an army under Prevost was laying waste the fairest por-
May tions of South Carolina.

But upon the sea the American arms were more successful. The U. S. sloop Providence, Capt. Hacker, ar-
11. rived at Providence with two prizes, one a valuable ship
loaded with rice, the other the British cruiser Diligent, of
twelve guns, which was captured after a bloody action, in
which the enemy lost twenty-eight men, and the Providence twelve, among whom were the sailing-master,
James Rogers, of Newport, and Lieutenant Chilton of
the marines. A sloop was also taken off Newport by
13. three armed boats of the State flotilla.

A party of a hundred and fifty men from a British
21. fleet of nine sail, then ravaging the coast, landed in South
Kingstown, burnt one house, plundered two others, and
made prisoners of a sergeant's guard and some of the inhabitants, fifteen in all, but were finally driven off by
some troops who captured one of their sloops with five
prisoners.

To arrest the rapid and alarming depreciation of continental money, Congress resorted to increased taxation.
Forty-five millions of dollars were assessed upon the
States, of which the part assigned for Rhode Island to
raise was seven hundred fifty thousand dollars, a crush-
ing burden in the exhausted condition of this State, subject as it was to constant incursions of the enemy, and
June obliged to keep a large force in the field. Even now an
3. expedition from New York, up the Hudson, threatening
an attack on Fishkill, Gen. Gates ordered the militia to
be ready to march to that point. There was more than
they could do at home. A foraging party again landed
6. at Point Judith, and carried off eight prisoners, besides a
number of sheep and cattle. They were repulsed by Col.
Jackson's light corps, with some loss of wounded on each
side. Next morning they landed at another point in

South Kingstown, and burnt two houses. Yet the Assembly boldly met the demands made upon them, and levied two taxes, one of two hundred twenty-five thousand pounds, to meet the action of Congress, and another of sixty thousand pounds for State purposes. A protest against the mode in which these taxes were apportioned among the towns was made, by those which had so lately been plundered by the enemy, but no resistance was offered to their collection. The two infantry regiments in the State brigade were consolidated under Col. Topham. The resignation of Col. Crary, with many of his officers, and the deserted ranks of the brigade, of which the two infantry regiments were now reduced to two hundred thirty-three men, and those destitute of clothing and in arrears for pay, as appears by a return made by Gen. Cornell, rendered this course necessary. By the advice of Gen. Gates, a corps of light infantry was raised for special service under Lieutenant-Colonel Barton, consisting of four companies of fifty-four men each, besides officers, whose appointment was left to the commander.[1]

CHAP. XXII. 1779. June 14. 15.

Gen. Gates had sent Lieut.-Col. Talbot to sea in a small sloop of a hundred tons, called the Argo, armed with ten guns and a crew of sixty men, to guard the coast. He captured the Lively,[2] a ten gun privateer, with three prizes, which now arrived at Providence, and soon afterwards returned to port with two large vessels of twelve and eighteen guns taken off Sandy Hook, after a desperate engagement of four and a half hours. This success was followed up by Capt. Whipple, who, during the same month, in the frigate Providence, as senior officer, with two other U. S. ships, attacked a large fleet of English merchantmen under convoy of a ship-of-the-line and some

July 7.

[1] The four captains were Henry Dayton, John Garzia, Charles Handy, and Stephen Babcock.

[2] The Lively was at once fitted out as a privateer, in command of Esek Hopkins, jr., and was very successful.

CHAP. XXII. 1779. July smaller cruisers,[1] and sent eight of them safely into Boston. The value of these prizes was over a million of dollars. These triumphs were somewhat impaired in August, by the misfortune of the Penobscot expedition, under Gen. Lovell and Capt. Salstonstall, in which the frigate Warren, sloop Providence, and her late prize the Diligent, were burnt to prevent their capture.

Upon the departure of Glover's brigade, Jackson's and
4. Angell's regiments were ordered from the south part of the State to Providence, which left the Narraganset country much exposed. Sir George Collier, and Gov. Tryon were ravaging the Connecticut shore. New Haven was
5. plundered. Fairfield was burnt, and on the same night a
7. party of Tories landed at Fall River, robbed some houses, and carried off thirteen prisoners, leaving behind them copies of a royal proclamation, offering pardon to repent-
9. ant rebels. Norwalk was also burnt. But these outrages were soon checked by the storming of Stony Point on
16. Hudson River by Gen. Wayne, an act of heroism that inspired the enemy, for a time, with greater caution.

Many of the forays from Newport were conducted by Tory refugees, whose cruelty had become proverbial. One was attempted near the close of July, against Seaconnet, for the purpose of seizing Major William Taggart and his two sons, who were very obnoxious to the enemy. Major Taggart commanded the flotilla of gun-boats, under Gen. Sullivan for more than a year, and his son William, jr., served under him as a captain. This service had lately been suspended, and the two officers retired to their farm in Little Compton. A party of Tories landed on the Point, and seized the sentinels on the shore, but the alarm being given, they only captured five prisoners, two of whom were Capt. Taggart and his brother. The latter was brutally murdered in attempting to escape. The

[1] These ships sailed from Boston 17th June, and arrived back again on 21st August, after the most successful cruise of the war as to pecuniary results; they brought also 135 prisoners.

others were taken to the jail in Newport.[1] Col. Barton's CHAP. XXII.
corps of infantry were raised for the special purpose of
protecting the seaboard from these forays. They were 1779.
furnished with whaleboats built expressly for that service, July
and were despatched by Gates with instructions to recon- 24.
noitre the island, take prisoners, and gain information respecting the enemy. These expeditions were conducted in great silence, with muffled oars, and were limited to the waters of the bay.

The Argo having been refitted with twelve guns, Tal- Aug.
bot again sailed by order of Gates, to cruise against the 2.
enemy. He soon captured the Tory privateer King 7.
George, of ten guns, belonging in Newport, Stanton Hazard commander, which he carried by boarding, without the loss of a man. This vessel had been a great annoyance to the whole coast, and her capture was hailed as a signal triumph. Col. Jackson's Massachusetts regiment
was now ordered to Boston to reinforce the ill-fated Pe- 10.
nobscot expedition. Col. Godfrey's Bristol County regiment, with three hundred other Massachusetts militia, were sent into Rhode Island to supply their place.

In consequence of an earnest address to the States, made by Congress in May, respecting the financial condition of the country, which address had been read from all the pulpits in Rhode Island by request of the General Assembly, a convention was held in East Greenwich, at which Gov. Greene presided. To arrest the rapid depreciation of the currency, to supply the Continental treasury, so as to prevent further emissions, and to establish a scale of prices, were the objects of this and of similar conventions held in the several States. A maximum scale of prices for many staple articles of consumption was adopted, while that for manufactures, with the rates of labor and board, were referred to the separate towns, which

[1] An interesting account of this affair, and the escape of Captain Taggart and Captain Benjamin Borden, of Fall River, from the jail in Newport, is given in "Spirit of '76," pp. 324–6.

CHAP. XXII. 1779. Aug. were desired to hold meetings immediately for this purpose. Trading in gold and silver was discountenanced, and the Assembly were recommended to raise one-third of a million of dollars, being the Rhode Island proportion of twenty millions proposed by Congress to be loaned by the States to the general government. Provision was made for another meeting of the convention to revise the tariff at present adopted, and an address to the people of
12. the State was published.

23. The Assembly recommended the people to open subscriptions for the continental loan. They also directed the sheriff to detain certain slaves, who, it was found, had been purchased to be carried South, in violation of the manumission act, and instructed a committee[1] to prepare a bill to prevent slaves from being purchased and carried out of the State against their consent. A bill to confiscate the estates of Tories was also ordered.

25. Baron Steuben, Inspector-General of the army, arrived at Providence on a tour of official duty. The State pow-
28. der-mill in North Providence was accidently blown up, and two men were killed. The troops had hitherto been quartered in public or private buildings, having no regu
Sept. 6. lar barracks. Congress now ordered barracks to be erected in Rhode Island at government expense, their location and dimensions to be determined by Gen. Gates.

13. The subscriptions to the public loan not being filled, the Assembly apportioned the amount, one hundred thousand pounds, among the towns, and required the assessors to collect it from those who were best able to contribute. Although this assessment was not a tax in form, it was one in reality, and was enforced with the same process and penalties. An examination of the accounts of all the officers in the Staff Department had been urged by Congress in their May address. A bill prescribing the mode of conducting the enquiry and appointing an examining

[1] Rouse J. Helme, David Howell, and Welcome Arnold.

board was passed. The investigation was commenced soon CHAP. XXII.
after the rising of the Assembly.[1]

The Argo returned to Providence after a very success- 1779.
ful cruise, having taken four valuable prizes since the Sept. 16.
King George. An account of this cruise was sent to John
Jay, which was published by order of Congress, and Talbot received a commission as captain in the navy. As 17.
the limited number of ships did not admit of his having a
more suitable command, he continued his exploits in the
Argo. Meetings had been held in all the towns to act
upon the proceedings of the Greenwich convention. As
the points left to be settled by the separate towns could
better be arranged by a general consultation, a new convention of committees was held at the same place. The 27.
prices of labor, and of articles not settled by the former
convention, were fixed, to be in force at the expiration of
two weeks. Massachusetts proposed another convention 28.
of the five Eastern States to be held at Hartford, to pro
duce greater uniformity in the action of the States on
these subjects. The council of war laid an embargo on 30.
the exportation by water, of all kinds of provisions, to continue for three months, and forbade the carrying of live Oct. 2.
stock or groceries into Connecticut, as engrossers from
that State were buying up these articles here. They also
appointed Hon. Stephen Hopkins and Charles Holden
commissioners to attend the Hartford convention, and prepared instructions for their guidance.

The war at the South was unsatisfactory. Gen. Lincoln held Charleston, but Savannah was in the hands of
Prevost. D'Estaing, after some success in the West
Indies, united with Lincoln to besiege Savannah. After
several weeks' delay, an attempt was made to carry the 9.
town by assault. The allies were repulsed with great
slaughter, and among the killed was the brave Polish
Count Pulaski. D'Estaing himself was wounded, and im-

[1] See chap. xxi., p. 413, Note.

CHAP. XXII. mediately reimbarked his forces to return to the West Indies. Sir Henry Clinton resolved to concentrate his
1779. forces at the South, which had become the seat of war.

Oct. 11. A fleet of fifty-two transports arrived at Newport from New York to embark the garrison, seven thousand men, with the military stores and such of the Tories, with their effects, as chose to follow the waning fortunes of the crown. It was evident that the island was to be evacuated.
16. Gov. Greene issued a proclamation, forbidding any person to land on Rhode-island or Conanicut to molest the inhabitants after the enemy had withdrawn. The embarcation commenced immediately. The transports were successively brought to the wharves and laden with the heavy ordnance and stores of the army, and the movable property of the royalists, forty-six of whom, with their families and a large number of liberated slaves, embarked in the fleet. As fast as the ships were loaded, they were hauled out to their moorings off Brenton's Point. The barracks at that point and the light-house at Beaver Tail were burnt. The north battery was levelled, but the old fort on Goat Island was spared. When all was ready, the inhabitants were warned to keep within doors during the
25. day of embarcation, on pain of death. All day the troops were marching from the town to Brenton's Point, where, as fast as they arrived, they were conveyed in boats on board the ships. At sunset the fleet sailed, and Rhode Island was relieved from the presence of an enemy, who for three years had spread desolation and terror over the whole State. The forests that once covered the island had been cut down, till scarcely a tree remained. Houses without number had been destroyed, gardens laid waste, farms broken up, and on all the hills frowning bastions and lines of circumvallation, many of which remain to this day, looked down upon deserted fields and blood-stained meadows more desolate than when, a century before, they had been the battle-ground of a savage but less ruthless foe. Newport never recovered from the cruel

CHAP. XXII. 1779. Oct.

blow. More than half the population had forsaken the island, and the commerce that once filled the crowded wharves was either annihilated, or had sought less hazardous resorts, never to return.[1] The Jews, whose enterprise had done so much for their adopted State, had all left the town. Aaron and Moses Lopez, who at one time owned twenty-seven square-rigged vessels, several of which were whaleships, besides many smaller craft, nearly all of which were lost during the war, moved to Providence and afterwards to Leicester. Moses Hays, another eminent merchant, had removed to Boston shortly before the war, and was followed by the Riveiras and others of the Hebrew faith.[2] Isaac Touro, the priest, with his two sons, fled to Jamaica when the British came to Newport, and neither of them ever returned to reside there; although the munificence of Abraham, one of the sons, still keeps in repair the deserted temple of the God of Jacob, and guards with filial reverence the cemetery in which repose the ashes of his fathers.[3] Aaron Lopez intended to return after the war, but was drowned in Scot's Pond, near Providence.[4] His son Joseph was almost the only one of all this interesting and indomitable race who resumed business in the nearly ruined town of Newport.

The remnant of the great Jewish families who returned, gradually declined. Not one of their descendants now remains in Newport. Moses Lopez, nephew of Aaron, was

[1] More than 500 houses were destroyed; and the damage committed by the British during their occupation was estimated at nearly £125,000—as reported by a Committee of the Legislature at June session, 1782—in the town of Newport alone.

[2] Jacob Rodriguez Riveira, who introduced the manufacture of spermaceti, of which Newport before the war enjoyed the monopoly, returned to Newport, and died there, February 19, 1789, in the 72d year of his age, but we do not find that he resumed his former enterprise after the peace.

[3] Abraham Touro died in Boston in 1822. He left a fund of $10,000 for the support of the synagogue and cemetery in Newport, and $5,000 to keep in repair the street on which they front, and which is now called from his name—Touro street.

[4] 28th May, 1782.

CHAP. XXII. 1779. Oct. the last who left the place. He removed to New York a few years before his death. His body was brought to Newport for interment in the Jewish cemetery.

The enemy left behind them a number of horses belonging to the cavalry regiment, and also the contents of the forage yard uninjured; but they carried with them the records of the town from its settlement. The vessel containing these precious papers was sunk at Hurl Gate. Three years afterwards the half-obliterated fragments were returned to the town, and a copy was made of such portions as were still legible. The morning after the evacu-
26. ation, the troops quartered at Tiverton, under Gen. Stark, crossed over to the island and occupied Newport, and Col. Barton was sent on with orders to prevent any boat from landing there without a permit.

20. The convention at Hartford proposed a new scale of prices, on a basis of twenty for one, and advised a general convention to be held at Philadelphia in January, to adopt the scheme. This action obviated the necessity of another meeting of the Rhode Island committees at Green-
25. wich as had been intended. The Assembly, which met on the day of the evacuation, had much additional business to do on account of that event. The militia coast guard, which had been kept up at great expense for three years, were dismissed. The ferries from Newport to South Kingstown were re-established and repaired. The four island towns which had so long been held by the enemy, were empowered to resume their corporate functions, by calling meetings to elect local officers and deputies; but all Tories were prohibited from taking part in these proceedings. The non-intercourse act, by which New Shoreham had so long been cut off from the State, was repealed. A general embargo was laid upon every article, nothing was to be exported by sea or land while the neighboring States persisted in a similar policy. This act was designed as one of retaliation, and had become necessary for self-preservation. The militia system was

regulated anew, all previous laws being now digested into one compendious act. The acts confiscating the estates of Tories, and prohibiting the involuntary sale of slaves out of the State, which had been moved in August, were now reported and passed. The former provided that complaints should be entered by the attorney-general, with a full statement of the offence, and a description of the estate, to be tried by the Superior Court of the county where the property lay. A special term of the court was appointed to be held at Providence to receive the complaints, which were to be continued one term for trial, notice being given to the parties proceeded against. The slave act provided that in case of an attempt to sell a slave to be carried out of the State against his will, the owner should forfeit all claim to the slave, and the latter should receive his freedom. To prevent any undue influence in obtaining the consent of a slave to be sold, a certificate of two Justices was required, setting forth that the slave had twice appeared before them, alone, with an interval of three days between the interviews, and stated his consent to be sold, naming the person and residence of the desired purchaser. A fine was attached to any violation of this act, but a slave of notoriously bad character might be sold, upon judgment of court, anywhere within the United States.

CHAP. XXII. 1779. Oct.

During the session, the surgeons of the line[1] presented a memorial to the Assembly, complaining that the medical staff had been overlooked in the action of Congress providing for other officers in the army, and asking such redress as other States had afforded, in the shape of some guarantee that equal provision would be made for them as for other officers at the close of the war. The memorial was supported by the certificates of the field officers 30.

[1] The memorial was signed by Samuel Tenny and Peter Turner, surgeons, and Elias Cornelius, and John Parish, mates. They were attached to Colonels Greene and Angell's battalions of the line.

CHAP. XXII. of both regiments to the justice of the appeal, and to the merits and services of the petitioners.

1779. Nov. 8. As the presence of the enemy no longer required the attention of Gates, he was called hence to join the grand army, leaving Brig.-Gen. Cornell in command. On his departure, a suitable address was presented to him by the
11. people of Providence. The council of war ordered the estates of the Tories who had left in the fleet, to be taken possession of by the sheriff of Newport. The officers of the Staff Department were reduced in number by the dismissal of most of the assistants, and the buildings and other property left by the British were sold for the benefit
17. of the State. Gen. Cornell was requested to repair the College, to permit no more sick soldiers to be placed there, and to provide a proper place for a general hospital, as the officers of the College desired to occupy it again as soon as possible for the instruction of youth; but this was
Dec. 3. not yet to be. When the northern army went into winter quarters, Angell's regiment was stationed at Danbury; Greene's remained in Rhode Island; Sherburne's was probably with the main army near Morristown.[1]

9. A general thanksgiving was held by recommendation
13. of Congress. The Assembly levied another tax of one

[1] All three of these Continental battalions, besides the three regiments of State troops, were in this State during 1779. Colonel Sherburne's regiment did not wholly belong to Rhode Island, and less is known of it than of the others. The rolls are imperfect. Such names as can now be ascertained as connected with it are given by Mr. Cowell, on page 196 of "Spirit of '76 in Rhode Island." The partial list of officers is as follows: Colonel Henry Sherburne, Major William Bradford, Captain James Webb, Lieutenants Seth Chapin, Benjamin Sherburne, Ensign Henry Sherman; besides whom, there were 35 non-commissioned officers and privates from Rhode Island, whose names are found on a war office list for 1779. By the same return, and by a letter from General Washington, 20th February, 1780, there appear also a number of Rhode Island men in other regiments, viz., Colonel Crane's—James Gardner, adjutant; Joseph Perry, 1st lieutenant, and 2 non-commissioned officers; in Colonel Hazen's—Samuel Stanford, ensign, and one private; in Colonel Livingston's—Ezekiel Cook, ensign; in Colonel Jackson's—1 sergeant and 17 privates; and in Major Gibbe's Guard—5 privates. See Letters, 1779–80, No. 75, and 1780, No. 62.

hundred twenty thousand pounds to meet the State's proportion, four hundred thousand dollars, of the continental tax. At the same time they passed the act upon which the Revolutionary debt of Rhode Island, which has never yet been discharged, is based. By this act the State pledged itself to its soldiers, "for their proved fidelity, firmness, and intrepidity, in service," that at the close of the war it would "make good to them or their legal representatives the wages of the Establishment of Congress whereon they engaged." These balances of a depreciated and ruined currency, if not adjusted by Congress, were to "be paid them as soon as the circumstances of the State will admit." Upon the faith of this pledge, and as a part of the same act, those of the three continental regiments then in the Rhode Island line, whose terms of service were about to expire, were re-enlisted for the war. How their part of the contract was kept, these pages will record. How the State has fulfilled its pledge, the handful of hoary veterans who yet survive in lingering hope of tardy and oft-rejected justice, can testify. That other States have ignored the like claim upon them is no excuse for us.

1779. Dec. 13.

William Ellery was appointed a delegate to the convention at Philadelphia, and John Collins was requested not to resume his seat in Congress for the present, as one representative was deemed sufficient until the articles of Confederation should be adopted. The Argo was commissioned for a three months' cruise in the West Indies, under Capt. Talbot, but before he could get to sea, the owners re-claimed the sloop, and Congress ordered it to be restored to them.[1] Great distress prevailed among the

[1] The Argo was purchased from her New York owner by a company of Providence merchants, and again equipped as a privateer. Captain Talbot, there being no Continental ship unofficered, took command of the General Washington privateer, and was soon after captured by the enemy, thrust into the Jersey prison-ship, and finally sent to England, and confined in the Dartmoor prison, till he was exchanged in December, 1781, and reached home the following Spring, after nearly two years' absence, and having

CHAP. XXII. poor, owing to the unusual severity of the winter. Donations of wood were made by the State to the towns of
1779. Newport and Bristol. The garrison at Newport was re-
Dec. 15. duced to five hundred men, and a month later to one hundred and eighty, on account of the difficulty of obtaining fuel. The remainder of the troops were quartered in the barracks at Tiverton. Those of the New Hampshire and Massachusetts troops who could be spared, were sent home. The suffering for want of fuel is represented in piteous terms by Gen. Cornell. So intense was the cold during this winter, that the entire bay was frozen over for six weeks, and the ice extended out to sea as far as the eye could reach. Wood sold for twenty dollars a cord. A famine threatened the State. Corn was worth four silver dollars a bushel, and potatoes two dollars, prices which in those days were unparalleled, except during some brief seasons of great scarcity.

Another descent upon South Carolina was undertaken. Near the close of the year Sir Henry Clinton and Lord Cornwallis, with a powerful squadron under Admiral Ar-
26. buthnot, sailed from New York with the design to attack
1780. Jan. 2. Charleston. A violent storm soon afterwards scattered the fleet and delayed for a time the intended attack. This storm was very destructive along the whole coast, and seemed to presage the disaster and distress that were to make this the gloomiest year of the whole war. The cruel treatment received by American prisoners at the
5. hands of the enemy, at length roused Congress to pass an act of retaliation, and decree the same allowances and treatment in all respects to British prisoners that were meted to ours.

suffered an imprisonment of unparalleled severity. He resided in Providence till 1786, when he removed to Philadelphia, where he married for his second wife a granddaughter of General Mifflin, and settled in Western New York. He soon was sent to Congress, but his naval tastes led him again on the sea. He superintended the construction of the frigate Constitution, and afterwards commanded her in the *quasi* French war. When the navy was reduced, in 1801, he retired, and died in New York in 1813.

CHAP. XXII.

The Newport Mercury, which had been suspended, or rather removed to Rehoboth for three years, was now revived by Henry Barber. The convention of Northern States at Philadelphia met, and adjourned till April; but meanwhile, so rapid was the depreciation of the currency, that no effectual effort could be made to regulate prices. Congress established the army for the present year at thirty-five thousand men, and assigned the Rhode Island quota at eight hundred and ten. To complete this number, the Assembly at once took the necessary steps, and also laid a tax of one hundred eighty thousand pounds, the State's quota of a continental tax of forty-five millions of dollars, which was to be paid in three monthly instalments.

1780. Feb. 7. 15. 28.

Congress adopted a new plan to arrest the depreciation of the currency, now sunk to forty for one, by cancelling the old bills as fast as they were returned by a monthly State taxation of fifteen millions, and issuing new bills to one-twentieth of the amount; these new bills to be based on the credit of the separate States in fair proportion, to draw interest at five per cent., and to be redeemed by the States in six years. One dollar of these new State bills was equal to forty of old continental money, of which the amount now in circulation was two hundred millions. The proportion of continental money required from Rhode Island by this act, was twenty-six hundred thousand dollars, all of which was promptly paid. Massachusetts and Delaware were the only other States that met these heavy demands without delay.[1] Congress advised the repeal of the laws making the old bills legal tender. They also desired that the several legislatures might be called to-

Mar. 18. 20.

[1] In Letters 1779–80, No. 78, is an abstract of the accounts of all the States, in reference to the requisition of 18th March, 1780; and in Letters 1781–2, No. 97, is an account made up at the Treasury to May 3, 1782—showing that this State had paid up in full, and the account balanced. Delaware had overpaid a small amount, and Massachusetts was still owing a trifling sum on this account. All the other States were very much in arrears. Some had paid nothing at all.

CHAP. XXII. 1780. Mar. 23. gether, to consider the proposed scheme of finance; but before the news reached Rhode Island, the Assembly had already been specially convened to devise means for procuring supplies for the army, and had adjourned; nor was it thought best to call another session.

The enemy were constantly making incursions from April their headquarters at Staten Island into New Jersey, where the American army was stationed, at and near 16. Morristown. In one of these a party attacked Parasmus, where Col. Sherburne's regiment was quartered, set fire to a house in which they had taken refuge, and took fifty-two prisoners, including several officers, among whom was Lieut. Sherman who was wounded. The annual fast-26. day, recommended by Congress, was duly observed. After a short visit to France, Gen. Lafayette returned to 28. the United States in the frigate Hermione, the first of a powerful fleet that was soon to gladden the heart of America.

Civil honors now tempted some of the best military officers in Rhode Island to leave the service. Gen. Cor-May 1. nell, Col. Topham, and Col. Elliott all resigned their commissions. The two latter were chosen deputies from Newport. The former was elected by the Assembly a mem-3. ber of Congress in place of Stephen Hopkins, there having been three candidates for first representative, and no election by the people. Gen. Varnum and Daniel Mowry had been elected by the people, at the annual voting day, in place of Marchant and Ellery. John Collins was the only one of the old members now returned. Gen. William West was chosen deputy-governor in place of Jabez Bowen. The act making paper bills legal tender for contracts prior to the Revolution was repealed, and the new financial scheme proposed by Congress was accepted. To meet this fresh burden, and the heavy war expenses of the State, two taxes of one hundred eighty thousand pounds each were levied, one for three months' proportion of the continental monthly tax of fifteen millions of dollars, the

other for State purposes. This State had already loaned CHAP.
to the continent more money than all the States south of XXII.
Pennsylvania combined, and her delegates in Congress 1780.
foresaw in this fact what was afterwards experienced, "a May
great difficulty in liquidating the loan office certificates."[1]

The surrender of Charleston was a terrible blow to the 12.
American cause. Nearly twenty-six hundred prisoners, being almost one-fourth of the actual force in the field, and four frigates, among which was the Providence, fell into the hands of the enemy. The whole southern country was conquered.

It was proposed by the council of war to break up the 13.
hospital at Providence, that the college might be restored
to its legitimate purpose; but Col. Greene protested 18.
against abandoning so essential an element of military efficiency. Events were soon to justify the colonel's views.

A phenomenon, known as "the dark day," occurred 19.
at this time, which occasioned much comment among the intelligent, and greatly alarmed the ignorant. For several days the air had been filled with a dry smoky vapor, so that the sun could be looked upon with the naked eye, and the moon appeared as in a total eclipse. On the morning of the nineteenth, this darkness increased. There was a slight thunder shower, after which the gloom thickened at about ten o'clock, and continued for more than five hours, so that candles were required at noonday, and all business was suspended. There was but little wind. In the afternoon the sky resumed the appearance of a cloudy day. The darkness extended from the western part of Connecticut as far east as New Hampshire, perhaps farther, but was not observed on the Hudson River. The phenomenon presented somewhat varied aspects, as to changes and duration, in different localities.

It is not strange that so remarkable an appearance was associated by the uninformed with the dreary political

[1] Letter of General Ezekiel Cornell, member of Congress, to Governor Greene, 18th June, 1780. Letters 1780, No. 47.

CHAP XXII. 1780. May prospects that then shrouded the whole country in gloom. Never, except for a few weeks preceding the battle of Trenton, had the hope of independence seemed so desperate. Nor was the conquest of the entire southern country by the enemy the worst feature of the case. Sumpter, and Marion, and Clark, with their gallant followers still lurked in the swamps of Carolina, and many bold and hopeful hearts beat with them, waiting only for a skilful general to reunite the scattered array of southern war. The northern army was dispirited and almost disbanded. Meat they had long been deprived of, and but two days' provisions of any sort remained in camp. The currency had so depreciated, that a continental paper dollar would only pass for twopence, and even at that the troops were five months in arrears for pay. Forage could not be obtained for the horses, or clothing for the men. The largest and wealthiest States were deficient in their taxes. A complete paralysis seemed to prevail among the people, while the triumphant enemy, flushed with victory at the South, were preparing to crush out the last remnant of resistance in the despairing and now disaffected army in the North. The troubles and anxieties that beset the commander-in-chief at this critical period, no pen can describe. He daily expected the complete dismemberment of the army by its own act, or its utter destruction by the enemy. Two battalions of the Connecticut line actually marched
22. out from the camp, refusing longer to fight for a country so regardless of the sufferings endured in its defence. Washington feared that the whole camp would follow the dangerous example. A committee of Congress hastened
25. to Morristown, and there put forth a very lengthy circular, an earnest and last appeal to the several States, representing the dreadful condition of affairs, and the certainty that all former efforts would be lost by a speedy submission to the British arms, without still greater sacrifices were instantly made. The appeal was successful, the confidence of the army was restored, and the country appear-

ed, although slowly, to waken from its lethargy. The CHAP. XXII.
success of Tarleton at Waxhawes, completed for a time
the subjugation of Carolina, but that State was consider- 1780.
ed as already lost by the fall of Charleston. Sir Henry May
Clinton, leaving Cornwallis in command, returned to New York to co-operate with Kniphausen who was then ravaging New Jersey.

The expected arrival of the French fleet caused increased activity in Rhode Island. Dr. Craick was sent 25.
to Providence to provide hospitals for their use. The June.
public boats were ordered to be repaired, and the credit
of the State was loaned for the purpose, as the continental 1.
credit was so low that the work could not be done upon that alone. The Congressional committee at Morristown
followed up their appeal with large demands upon the 2.
Northern States for supplies and for men. The French fleet were known to be close at hand, and Washington desired to strike a blow before their arrival, or at least to have the army in a fit condition to co-operate promptly with the allies. A militia force was therefore called out to serve for three months. The quota of Rhode Island was one regiment of six hundred thirty men, to be ready to take the field in six weeks. The supplies required to be furnished by Rhode Island, were seventy-one thousand six hundred seventy-five pounds of beef, thirty hogsheads of rum, and twenty-two hundred eighty-five bushels of forage grain. These large amounts were to be supplied monthly in advance, commencing with the first of July. Two hundred draft horses were also required.

The Hermione, after landing Lafayette at Boston, proceeded on a cruise, and having engaged a British frigate
with some advantage, put in to Newport. The labor of 8.
raising the British vessels, sunk in the harbor two years before, now commenced. Congress settled a scale of depreciation for loan office certificates by which those issued prior to September 1777 were equal to specie, and subsequent emissions decreased in value in geometrical pro-

CHAP. XXII. 1780. June 12. portion so rapidly, that the last issue of this kind of paper made in the past March was at forty for one.[1] Upon this basis the Assembly raised all fees and fines forty for one upon the rates established before the war. The dangerous system of State bills of credit, which had been abandoned for nearly four years, was now revived. Twenty thousand pounds in bills bearing interest at the rate of six per cent. were emitted, to be redeemed in specie the following January. To ensure their redemption, a tax of five thousand pounds was voted, and provision made for selling four of the recently confiscated farms, containing about twenty-eight hundred acres, the proceeds to be devoted to this purpose. These bills were made a legal tender, as silver or gold, in all contracts, and the old Tendry act was suspended. Measures were taken to enlist six hundred and ten men to fill up the two continental battalions, and certain officers, recommended by Washington, were appointed in Col. Angell's command.[2] Hospitals for the French forces were established. The barracks at Tiverton, and a farm near Bristol, were designated for that purpose. An act also passed confirming to the French the rights and privileges stipulated in the treaty of Paris. Rhode Island was the first State to legislate in favor of the allies on this important subject.

16. Major-General Heath arrived to take command of this
23. department. A small but bloody action was fought at Springfield, New Jersey, where, as at Trenton, it devolved upon the Rhode Island line to defend the pass of a narrow bridge against fearful odds. The coincidence between these two affairs is striking, as to the locality of the battles, the critical condition of the army and the country on each occasion, and that the brunt of the fight in both cases was borne by the Rhode Island troops. Kniphausen occupied Elizabethtown where, being reinforced by Sir

[1] Letters 1779–80, No. 136.

[2] Lieutenants John Hubbard, Joseph Wheaton; Ensigns John M. Greene, John Rogers, William Pratt, Joseph Mashury, Jeremiah Greenman.

Henry Clinton, the whole army, seven thousand strong, CHAP. XXII.
advanced on Springfield, then guarded by Gen. Greene
with less than a thousand men. Greene posted his troops 1780. June
on a hill in rear of the town, detaching two parties to
oppose the enemy at different approaches. One of these
was a portion of Col. Angell's regiment, only a hundred
and seventy men, sent to check a division of fifteen hundred of the enemy at an entrance of the village which was
by a bridge across the Rahway. For forty minutes this
gallant band sustained the whole shock of the overwhelming force opposed to them, when they were obliged to
give way, and the British entered and burnt the town.
The desperate defence of the bridge, satisfied the enemy
not to advance farther, and Clinton returned the same
night to Staten Island. The American loss was seventy-
two in killed and wounded, more than one half of whom
were in Col. Angell's regiment. Among the wounded
were Capt. Stephen Olney, and Ensigns Rogers, Greene,
and Greenman. Washington highly complimented this 26.
regiment in general orders, and in a letter to Gov. Greene
he writes: "The gallant behavior of Col. Angell's, on 29.
the 23d instant at Springfield, reflects the highest honor
upon the officers and men. They disputed an important
pass with so obstinate a bravery that they lost upwards
of forty in killed, wounded, and missing, before they gave
up their ground to a vast superiority of force." He adds
in conclusion, "The ready and ample manner in which
your State has complied with the requisitions of the Committee of co-operation, both as to men and supplies, entitle her to the thanks of the public, and affords the
highest satisfaction to Your Excellency's most obedient
servant George Washington."

Commissary-General De Corny, in behalf of the French 24.
government, applied for the college to be used as a hospital by their troops. It had been specially designated by
Dr. Franklin, and embodied in De Corny's instructions,
to obtain this building. As every effort was to be made 25.

CHAP. XXII. 1780. July 3. to please the allies, this request was granted, and the college was given up to him the next day by order of the council of war. An embargo was also laid upon all vessels in order to facilitate enlistments in the line. This was removed by the Assembly the following week from merchant ships, but continued in force as to privateers. Col. Barton's corps of light infantry were disbanded, and enlisted into the continental line. A decree of banishment was passed against all Tories, thirty-six of whom were named in the act, but deserters from the continental regiments were pardoned, with the assent of Washington, on condition of an immediate return to duty.

10. The arrival of Admiral De Terney with a fleet of forty-four sail, and six thousand troops under Count De Rochambeau, was hailed with joy throughout the country.
11. The next day the army landed and were put in possession of the forts, and on the following night the town was illuminated in honor of the guests.[1]

17. Gov. Greene convened the Assembly, upon whom an unusual amount of business now devolved. Addresses of welcome to the French General and Admiral were prepared, and arrangements made for a public dinner, to be given at a future day to all the French officers. A burial ground was assigned to them on Papoosquash Point. A court of admiralty was established in the State. The monthly supplies for the army were apportioned among the towns, and William Bradford was appointed to attend a convention of New England States at Boston, to adopt some uniform mode of furnishing such supplies. To meet the balances due to the continental troops for depreciation of pay, the confiscated lands and the proceeds of the sale of

[1] The French army were led by Lieutenant-general le Comte de Rochambeau; Major-generals Baron de Viomesnel, le Chevalier de Chatellux, and Comte de Viomesnel; Brigadier-generals Comte de Choisy; Duc de Lauzun; Comte de Custine, and M. de Beville. The regiments were, the Bourbonnois, Royal Deux Ponts, Soissonnois, Saintonge, and Lauzun's Legion, with a battalion of artillery, a corps of sappers and miners, and of the Royal Guides. The fleet comprised 12 ships of war and 32 transports.

wrecks were appropriated, but some of the men declined to receive the land in settlement of their claim. The regiment of six hundred and thirty militia, to serve for three months, under Washington, in co-operating with the French army, were ordered to be raised. A new estimate of taxable property, which had been nearly two years in preparation, was reported, and made the basis of the most severe taxation that had ever yet been sustained by a patriotic but impoverished people. First, a tax of four hundred thousand pounds in continental money was laid, payable in four monthly instalments from the first of September; second, a tax of five thousand pounds in silver, or the new State bills, to be paid at the same time. Both of these were for the use of the State. The tax of five thousand pounds voted in June was also apportioned, to be collected with the other two taxes. Third, and to complete in one desperate effort the burden imposed by the act of Congress of March eighteenth, to sink the remaining portion of the State's quota of old continental bills, a tax of four hundred twenty thousand pounds was made, payable in those bills, in six monthly instalments from October first. To supply a circulating medium, in accordance with the scheme of Congress, State bills of credit to the amount of thirty-nine thousand pounds, being one-twentieth of the amount of continental money already sunk, were issued, bearing five per cent. interest, to be redeemed in six years by an annual tax, in specie or its equivalent, of eighty-six hundred and fifty pounds.[1] Of this fund, according to the scheme referred to, three-fifths went to the United States to be credited in account with Rhode Island, and two-fifths were reserved for the State.

CHAP. XXII. 1780. July

The addresses to the French commanders were pre- 21
sented by a committee of the Assembly, and replied to by Rochambeau in pleasing terms. The Admiral de-

[1] The amount of all these taxes voted at this session, and all but the last mentioned, payable within six months, reduced to a specie standard, is $126,369 50.

CHAP. XXII. ferred his reply till a later occasion. On the same day a
British fleet of sixteen ships of war appeared off Newport.
1780. All was now a scene of excitement. Gen. Heath wrote
July 26. to Gov. Trumbull for assistance, and desired that one
thousand Connecticut militia should assemble at Greenwich. The council of war called out all the militia of this State under Gen. Varnum. The Massachusetts militia came to the rescue, and a determined spirit was everywhere manifested. But suddenly the hostile squadron
30. left the anchorage at Block Island and sailed away. The
militia were dismissed to their homes by the advice of Rochambeau, but only to be called back immediately on
31. the reappearance of the enemy. Another week of excite-
ment ensued, to end like the first in the withdrawal of the
Aug. 7. English and the dismissal of the troops so hastily gathered
to repel them. But from the secure position of Gardiner's Island, the British fleet continued to watch the movements, and virtually to blockade the ships and army of the French. Thus for the third time, twice at Newport and once at Savannah, had the co-operation of the allies proved inefficient.

16. The defeat of Gates by Cornwallis at the battle of
18. Camden, followed by the utter route of Sumpter's corps
by Tarleton, appeared to seal the doom of the South. The brave Baron de Kalb fell in this action, and a large number of prisoners were taken, but most of these were rescued by the gallantry of Col. Marion, while on their march to Charleston. This misfortune dimmed the lustre of Saratoga, where Gates had received the honor really due to the desperate valor of Arnold. A court of inquiry was
Oct. 5. ordered by Congress to examine the causes of the disaster
at Camden, and Washington, being called upon to name a successor to Gates, appointed Greene. Major-Gen. Greene, after more than two years' service in the arduous and thankless office of quartermaster-general, had resigned
Aug. 15. that place, upon a re-organization of the department, and
received from Washington a testimonial of his ability and

integrity in the discharge of its multifarious duties. Col. CHAP.
Pickering was appointed by Congress as his successor. XXII.

A deputation of nineteen Oneida warriors visited New- 1780.
port, where they were entertained by the French com- Aug. 20.
manders and Gen. Heath, and received many presents.
A grand review of the French army was held, which gave 24.
great satisfaction to a vast concourse of spectators, and
the next day, being the anniversary of the birth of Louis 25.
XVI., was observed by the firing of salutes and decorat-
ing the ships of the fleet.

Congress called for another sum of three millions from 26.
the States, but Rhode Island was in no condition to meet
further demands at present. The Assembly convened at Sept. 11.
Newport for the first time in four years, and met at the
Redwood Library. The State House had been used by
the British as a hospital, and was much dilapidated.
Every church in the town, except Trinity, had been occupied for barracks, and was in a ruinous condition. Rev.
Gardiner Thurston of the Second Baptist Church, the
only clergyman who remained in town, held public worship in Trinity Church until his own could be repaired.
The alarm of a British invasion had suspended in several
towns the collection of one of the taxes ordered in July,
for which further time was allowed, and no new burden
could as yet be laid upon the exhausted people.

A military execution was a rare event in the American
army, although several had occurred in the British camp
during the occupation of Newport. One now took 19.
place in Col. Greene's regiment quartered on the island;
a soldier was shot for desertion. The saddest event in
this year of misfortunes now transpired. The treason of
Major-General Arnold, which had for some months been
in progress, was discovered by the arrest of Major Andre, 23.
revealing the plot to surrender West Point to the enemy.
Gen. Greene, then in command of the army during the
temporary absence of Washington, communicated to the 26.
troops, in general orders, the disheartening news. The

CHAP. XXII. 1780. Sept. baseness of the most brilliant officer in the American
service, presents a mournful contrast to the stern integrity
and incorruptible patriotism of the three obscure militia-
men,[1] who resisted the tempting bribes offered them by
Andre for his release. Fortunately for America, the
type of national character in the revolutionary struggle is
to be found in the humble captors of Andre, and not in
the dashing general whose plans of treason they defeated.
Greene was president of the court-martial held for the trial
29. of Andre; Lafayette and Steuben were members. His
own confessions condemned him as a spy; and as such,
Oct. 1. Washington, although with much reluctance, signed the
death-warrant that doomed him to the gallows.

3. Congress took early measures to arrange the army for
the coming year. Only one regiment, to consist of five hundred and eighty rank and file, was required from Rhode
9. Island. Massachusetts proposed another convention, to
be held at Hartford in November, further to consider
the subject of supplies, discussed at Boston in August, and
also the best methods of recruiting the army. The Duke
11. de Lauzun came to Providence to obtain quarters for a
part of his legion during the winter. The council of war
15. billeted two hundred and fifty of the men, provided
stables for their horses, and magazines for their stores and
forage, and directed the town authorities to furnish suitable rooms for the officers. A part of the legion wintered
at Lebanon, Connecticut. Detachments of French troops
were also stationed at Bristol and Warren, the head-
quarters being at Newport.

23. The Assembly voted to enlist two hundred and twenty
men to complete the quota assigned to this State for the
next campaign, and appointed William Bradford to attend
Nov. 8. the convention at Hartford. This convention, of which
Bradford was president, sat for two weeks. They advised
that the recruits be enlisted for the war, as desired by

[1] John Paulding, David Williams, and Isaac Van Wart.

Congress, instead of limiting the term, as had hitherto been done, to the great detriment of the service. The general condition of the country was considered, and a series of ten resolutions, embodying their views, was adopted, and sent in a circular to the several States. Orders were sent by Washington for Col. Greene to march to West Point, where the two Rhode Island regiments were to be consolidated. Rochambeau suggested that a guard should be stationed at Point Judith, to prevent communication with the enemy. The forts at Butt's Hill and elsewhere on the island were garrisoned by the French.

CHAP. XXII. 1780. Nov. 22. 27.

The Assembly again levied heavy taxes; one of six thousand pounds in specie, to pay one-fourth of the balance of depreciation due to the troops, the other three-fourths to be paid in confiscated lands; one of ten thousand pounds, also in specie, for the regiment to be raised for the next campaign; and one of one million pounds, in old continental bills, two-fifths of which was to go to the State treasury, and the remainder to the United States. By the apportionment of the two specie taxes, it appears that South Kingstown was now by far the wealthiest town in the State, paying double the sum assigned to Newport, and one-third more than the proportion of Providence. A scale of monthly depreciation of continental money, from January, 1777, to the past April, was adopted, to be a guide in all questions of contract, and the act making these bills a legal tender, which had been suspended for some time, was finally repealed. At this time these old bills stood at seventy-two for one. William Bradford was appointed the commissioner on the part of Rhode Island, to act with the other Northern States represented in the late convention at Hartford, for contracting to supply the French forces.

The national thanksgiving was observed as usual. Dec. 7.
Admiral de Terney died suddenly at Newport. He was 15.
buried with great pomp in Trinity churchyard, where, five years later, a monument, with a full inscription of his

CHAP. XXII. rank and services, was erected by order of the King of France. The disasters of the year began to be retrieved
1780. towards its close, by the success of partisan warfare at
Nov. 20. the South. Gen. Sumpter defeated Tarleton's cavalry and a body of British infantry at Black Forks after a severe
Dec. 16. action. This was followed by a second defeat of the famous English partisan, in an attempt to surprise Colonels Clarke and Marion at Ninety-six. Tarleton having received several wounds in this engagement, and lost many of his men, returned to Charleston. Other less important affairs occurred soon after in the same quarter, so that hopes of recovering that section of country began to revive.

1781. The most fortunate year of the war opened with the strongest contrast between the political and the military prospects of the country. As to the former, affairs were in favorable progress. In October, Connecticut had resolved to cede her western territory to the Confederation,
Jan. 2. and Virginia now gave up her immense possessions in the same region to the common union. Every thing promised a speedy adoption of the articles of confederation. But in the army a dangerous mutiny broke out. The Pennsylvania line claimed their discharge, affirming that they had enlisted "for three years *or* the war," while the officers claimed that the enlistment was "for three years *and* the war." The new recruits received large bounties. This dissatisfied the older ones, besides which they were without food or clothing, and there was no money with which to pay them. The whole line revolted, attacked their officers, and marched out of the camp towards Princeton. Committees from Congress and from the Pennsylvania Assembly, succeeded in calming the discontent, and two British emissaries whom Clinton had sent
10. to tamper with them, but in vain, were given up and hung as spies. Most of the revolters received their discharge. A part of the New Jersey line then revolted, but were put down by troops sent from West Point, and two of the

ringleaders were shot by sentence of a court-martial. CHAP. XXII.
Washington recommended that bounties be given to the troops that had been long in service, and sent Gen. Knox 1781. Jan.
into New England to represent the alarming condition of the camp, and to obtain money and supplies. Arnold, with a fleet at his command, was in the Chesapeake, ravaging Virginia.

But affairs were about to take a favorable turn. The active co-operation of Spain against England, had been secured by the "Family Compact," made in 1761. Holland, whose neutrality had been violated by Great Britain in the case of some prizes carried there by Paul Jones, which the Dutch refused to deliver up on demand, and for which refusal the English minister had threatened war, now declared war against England. 12.
A battle was fought at Cowpens, where Gen. Morgan defeated a su- 17.
perior force under Tarleton.

The Assembly repealed the act, passed when the British came to Newport, whereby the poor of the island who removed into other towns were supported by the State. Feb. 3–7.
Congress applied to the States for power to lay an import duty of five per cent. upon all foreign goods and prizes. Three French ships were despatched by D'Estouches, the successor of De Terney, to attack Arnold's fleet in the Chesapeake. He escaped with most of his vessels to Portsmouth, but the frigate Romulus and some smaller prizes were taken, and the expedition returned in safety 27.
to Newport. Washington sent a force of twelve hundred New England and New Jersey troops under Lafayette, to aid in the expulsion of Arnold.

To supply the place of the French army, which was soon to be withdrawn, the Assembly called out twelve 26.
hundred militia to serve for one month under Brig.-Gen. Nathan Miller. They also promoted certain officers of the line,[1] and elected Jabez Bowen chief-justice, in place of Shearjashub Bourne, deceased.

[1] Lieutenants Z. Brown, D. S. Dexter, to be captains in Colonel Greene's

CHAP. XXII. 1781. Mar. At noon of the first of March, the confederation of the thirteen States was completed in Congress, and celebrated with bells and cannon and every demonstration of joy by
6. the citizens of Philadelphia. Washington arrived at Newport to arrange with Rochambeau for an active campaign. His reception was most brilliant; the whole French army were drawn up to salute him, in the evening the town was illuminated, and the next night a splendid
7. ball was given him by the citizens. The Admiral imme-
8. diately sailed with the entire fleet, and a portion of the army, to co-operate with Lafayette in Virginia. The
10. British squadron at Gardiner's Island sailed in pursuit,
16. and off the Chesapeake, an engagement ensued with no important advantage to either side. Arbuthnot withdrew
26. into the bay, and D'Estouches returned to Newport to refit. On the departure of the British fleet, Gen. Lincoln ordered all the Rhode Island militia, except three hundred,
12. to be dismissed, which was done by Gen. Miller. Washington remained but a few days in Newport, whence,
13. passing through Bristol and Warren, he came to Providence, where a joyful welcome greeted him. Military
14. honors, an illumination, a public dinner, and a grand ball, with suitable addresses, occupied the two days of his visit.

For several weeks Gen. Greene and Earl Cornwallis had manœuvred in North Carolina, advancing and retreating as occasion required, until at length the two armies
15. encountered in a pitched battle at Guilford Court-House. Although Greene was obliged to retreat with the loss of his artillery, yet the advantage remained with him, so much had the enemy suffered. Cornwallis was compelled to fall back for supplies, and Greene determined to carry the war into South Carolina, where Lord Rawdon, with a small force, held possession.

19. The Assembly appointed delegates to the convention

regiment. Lieutenant D. Jerauld to be captain; (the title was captain-lieutenant, but the rank was that of captain.) Ensigns J. M. Greene, J. Masury, and H. Shearman to be lieutenants in Colonel Angell's regiment.

of Eastern States to be held at Providence in April, to consult upon a plan by which Congress would be enabled to raise a permanent fund for carrying on the war. Metcalf Bowler, and Nicholas Brown were appointed to meet a commissioner of the Treasury Board, who was coming to adjust the account of Rhode Island with the United States. Congress made a requisition upon the States for six millions of dollars, to be paid in specie, or its equivalent, in quarterly instalments. These money contributions were independent of the heavy drafts for supplies of every kind that were constantly made, and which were more promptly met by the smaller States than by the larger ones. Col. Pickering, the new quarter-master-general, required the State to furnish for its continental battalion, a hundred and sixty tents, six hundred eighty-three knapsacks, and the same number of haversacks to complete their equipment. Although four delegates were annually elected to Congress, the State, from motives of economy, had for some time kept but one, Gen. Varnum, in his seat. Gen. Cornell being upon the Board of War, was frequently absent with the army. The terms of the confederation required, that at least two should be present from each State, without whom its vote would be lost. The President therefore wrote to Gov. Greene to send on another delegate to complete the representation; but this was deferred till the new election, now close at hand.

CHAP. XXII. 1781. Mar. 23. April 17. 20.

The second battle of Camden, although not so disastrous as that lost by Gates eight months before, resulted in the repulse of Greene by Lord Rawdon. But, as at Guilford, although the enemy kept the field, the fruits of victory remained with the Americans. Rawdon was obliged to evacuate Camden, and the capture of a chain of posts by Sumpter, Marion, and Lee, immediately after, recovered the greater part of South Carolina, and enabled Greene to despatch Col. Lee against Augusta. West Florida was at the same time recovered by the Spaniards. A Spanish army from New Orleans, with a squadron from

25. May 10.

CHAP. XXII. Havana, besieged Pensacola, which surrendered to Gov. Galvez of Louisiana.

1781. May 2. At the general election, Deputy-Governor William West was dropped, and Jabez Bowen was again elected to that office, which he retained for five years. William Ellery was restored to his seat in Congress in place of John Collins. The other three members of Congress, with the remaining State officers, were unchanged. The object of electing four delegates in Congress, was, that two might be present at all times, relieving each other semi-annually. Varnum and Mowry were requested to take their seats for the first six months, to be succeeded by Ellery and Cornell. A small State cruiser, to be armed with three guns, was ordered to be equipped for the defence of the coast. The annual fast day, by resolution of Congress,
3. was held at this time.

6. Admiral de Barras arrived from France to take com-
14. mand of the fleet. A sad event now occurred to deprive the State of some of its gallant soldiers, and the country of two of its bravest and most distinguished officers. The American army were stationed near Fishkill. Col. Greene's regiment were encamped at "Rhode Island Village," part of them occupying an advanced post some ten miles distant, at Points Bridge, on the Croton River, where Col. Christopher Greene and Major Ebenezer Flagg were quartered. Before daybreak, a body of two hundred and sixty of the enemy's light horse forded the river above, and surprised them in the rear. Major Flagg was murdered in his bed. Col. Greene, first wounded, was taken into the woods and cut to pieces. Both of these officers had won great distinction, especially at Red Bank, where Greene commanded, and their loss was severely felt. About forty of the Rhode Island regiment were killed or taken prisoners in this tragic affair. Lieutenant-Col. Jeremiah Olney succeeded to the command, and retained it through the war.

17. The project of a national bank was now submitted to

Congress by Robert Morris, and adopted. To relieve the CHAP.
French army at Newport, about to march for the seat of XXII.
war, Washington required that five hundred militia should 1781.
take the field. Rochambeau communicated this order to May 27.
Gov. Greene. The Assembly at once called them out to 28.
serve for one month under Col. Crary. Two taxes were levied, one for twenty thousand pounds in specie, to meet current expenses, and one of six thousand pounds in the new continental currency issued by the State, to redeem one-sixth part of that emission. They also established an additional scale of depreciation for old continental money, from the time the first scale was adopted. Within the year these bills had sunk from forty for one to a hundred and sixty for one.

The surrender of Augusta to Col. Lee still further June
weakened the British hold at the South. Cornwallis now 5.
bent his whole energy against Virginia, whither reinforcements from New York were sent to him. Rochambeau,
with the advanced guard of the French army, left New- 9.
port. A siege battery of eight heavy guns was forwarded by this State, at the request of Washington, to meet them at Hartford. They were destined soon to thunder at Yorktown. The army marched in four divisions, by way of Providence and Hartford, to join the American forces on the Hudson. A small garrison was left at Newport under Brigadier-General de Choisy. Great efforts were made to keep up the supplies. Gen. Heath was intrusted with this duty by Washington, and earnest appeals were successfully made to the eastern States on this subject. Rhode Island alone furnished daily two thousand rations of fresh beef, or sixty thousand pounds a month, besides rum and other stores. A convention of delegates from New England and New York, which was to have met in
April, assembled at Providence to arrange this difficult 26.
matter, and apportioned the supply among the States. Deputy-Governor Bowen appeared for this State. The
quota to be furnished by Rhode Island was continued as July 3.

CHAP. XXII. 1781. above. Rum, salt, and clothing were also to be supplied. The Assembly apportioned their supplies among the towns on the basis of the tax estimates.

June 19. The repulse of Gen. Greene at Ninety-Six, was but a temporary check. Rawdon, compelled to contract his lines, abandoned the post. In Virginia, where Lafayette
26. had been reinforced by Gen. Wayne, Cornwallis received
July 6. a check near Williamsburg, and another more severe, by a body of Wayne's troops, near Jamestown. As De Choisy was in command at Newport, the services of Col. Crary were dispensed with, and Lieutenant-Col. Kimball was made commandant of the militia, of whom but three
10. hundred and fifteen were on duty. He sent an expedition to Block Island in pursuit of a party of Tories recently landed there, but the refugees, as they were commonly
Aug. 14. termed, escaped. Another militia regiment, under Lieut.-Col. Tillinghast, was sent to Newport. By his report it numbered two hundred fifty-five men.

Eleven years had elapsed since any alteration had been made in the townships of the State. A petition to divide Scituate, which had been pending for some months, was
20. granted by the Assembly, and the western half of the town was set off and incorporated as the town of Foster.
23. A corps of French troops were sent to guard the maga-
25. zines at Providence. The departure of the French fleet to join the powerful squadron of the Count de Grasse, from the West Indies, at the Chesapeake, obliged the Assembly to provide further for the defence of the State. The militia in service were relieved by another levy, and additional batteries were mounted at Easton's and Brenton's Points. The redoubts at Pawtuxet, at Kettle, and at Field's Points, were also strengthened. The officers of the Rhode Island battalion of the line were confirmed in their new rank.[1]

[1] Lieutenant-colonel Jeremiah Olney was made lieutenant-colonel commandant; Captain Coggeshall Olney, 1st major; John S. Dexter, 2d major; Lieutenants Daniel S. Dexter, and Dutee Jerauld, captains; Ensigns J.

The State had a narrow escape from invasion at this time. Sir Henry Clinton was accurately informed of the plans and movements of the French, and of the condition of the forts and forces at Rhode Island. He formed a plan to attack Providence, to seize the French stores and magazines there deposited, and to capture the French fleet at Newport, in conjunction with Admiral Graves. The expedition was arranged for the sixteenth, but was accidentally delayed till the twenty-eighth, when, as it was on the point of leaving New York, news reached Charleston that De Barras had sailed from Newport, and thus "was lost an opportunity of making the most important attempt that had offered the whole war."[1]

CHAP. XXII. 1781.

The expedition of Arnold against his native State, caused great alarm in New England. After Cornwallis entered Virginia, Arnold returned to New York, and was sent by Sir Henry Clinton with a fleet and seventeen hundred troops to ravage the coast of Connecticut. Landing his forces in two divisions at the mouth of the Thames, with one he pillaged and burnt New London, while the other attacked Fort Griswold, which, after a gallant defence by Col. Ledyard, was carried by assault, and the whole garrison put to the sword. A strong force of militia from the neighboring country coming to the rescue, the enemy hastily withdrew. Gov. Trumbull called on
the militia of Rhode Island to march to the aid of Con-

Sept. 6.

7.

Greenman, and William Pratt, lieutenants; and Reuben Johnson, ensign. Upon the consolidation of the two battalions, Colonel Angell, Lieutenant-colonel Ward, Major Thayer, Captains Tew and Lewis, Surgeons P. Turner and J. Parrish had retired from the service. The captains who remained were, Allen, Brown, Cole, Dexter, Holden, Humphrey, Hughes, C. Olney, and S. Olney. A complete muster-roll of this regiment is printed in "Spirit of '76," p. 217–23.

John Welsh and Robert Hunter were afterwards made ensigns in February, 1782, and Ensign John Rogers was made a lieutenant, *vice* Oliver Jenckes, deceased.

[1] Narrative of Lieutenant-general Sir Henry Clinton, K. B., relative to his conduct during part of his command of the King's troops in North America; 8vo, London, 1783.

CHAP. XXII. necticut, but the retreat of the invaders rendered it unnecessary. At the same time Gen. Greene surprised and
1781. defeated a body of the enemy at Eutaw Springs after a
Sept. 8. sharp action. The combined French fleet under De Barras and Count de Grasse, engaged a powerful English squadron under Admiral Graves off the Chesapeake. The British suffered most, but neither party desired to come to close action. The French succeeded in landing their troops, and the British, foiled in their attempt to succor Cornwallis, returned to New York. In consequence of the alarm occasioned by the attack on New London, the militia and independent companies throughout this State
20. were called to arms, and a grand review was held. The
21. United Train of Artillery appeared the next day with the four brass field-pieces lately granted them by the General Assembly.[1]

Washington, having manœuvred some time near New York to deceive Clinton with the idea of an attack on that city, had suddenly marched with the allied army to the head of Elk River, where a fleet of transports was prepared to carry them to the scene of action. The Rhode Island regiment formed a part of this force. The French army, reinforced by three thousand men from the fleet of Count de Grasse, numbered seven thousand men, the continental troops fifty-five hundred, besides thirty-five hundred Virginia militia, making sixteen thousand men assembled for the siege of Yorktown. Cornwallis, with about half that number, was strongly intrenched within the town, which was fortified by redoubts thrown up
30. before it. At the close of the month, the allies commenced their approaches, and at the end of a week, hav-
Oct. 6. ing completed their first parallel, opened a fire upon the enemy. The British were very active in repairing their

[1] Two of these guns were afterwards taken back by the United States. The remaining two continued in the custody of the Providence Artillery, until about eighteen years ago, when they were loaned by the State to the Warren Artillery Company, where they now remain.

works as fast as they were damaged by the ceaseless storm of shell and shot which for the next nine days was hurled upon them, night and day, with scarcely an intermission. Their own lines were defended by one hundred pieces of cannon, which dismounted many of the guns of the besiegers, and rendered an assault essential, in order to silence two of their most effective batteries. These were two very strong redoubts, in advance of their principal line, from which the British fire was most galling, and which it was important for the allies to include within their second parallel, now nearly ready. Orders were given by Washington, to storm these positions. That on the right was assigned to the Americans under Lafayette and Col. Hamilton, the other to the French under the Baron Viomesnil. Soon after daylight, Washington made a short address to the troops detailed for this perilous service. Both bodies then advanced to the assault. The American forlorn hope was led by the French colonel Gimatt. A detachment of the Rhode Island regiment, under Capt. Stephen Olney, headed the storming column. They marched in perfect silence and with unloaded guns, determined to carry the works at the point of the bayonet. The distance was but about four hundred yards. When half way there, the column halted to make the final disposition for attack. One man from each company was detailed for the forlorn hope. Six or eight pioneers now led the way, as many of the forlorn hope came next, then Col. Gimatt, with half a dozen volunteers, preceded the column, which was led by Capt. Olney.

CHAP. XXII. 1781. Oct. 14. 15.

The dreadful silence was broken by a heavy discharge of the enemy's musketry as the assailants reached the abatis. One wild huzza burst from their lines, as, sword in hand, the leaders broke through the first obstructions, and the column, with fixed bayonets, entered at the breach. While the pioneers were attempting to cut away the abatis, some of the eager assailants climbing through it, entered the ditch. Among these was Olney, who, as

CHAP. XXII. 1781. Oct. soon as a few of his men collected, forced his way between the palisades, and leaping on to the parapet, called out in a voice that rose above the din of battle, "Captain Olney's company—form here!" A gun-shot wound in the arm, a bayonet thrust in the thigh, and another in the abdomen, from which the caul protruded, so that he was obliged to press in the intestines with one hand, while he parried the bayonets with the other, answered this first defiant shout that proclaimed the fall of Yorktown. Olney was borne from the field, but not until the regiment had mostly entered the redoubt, and he had directed them to "form in order."[1] In ten minutes after the first fire of the enemy, the fort was taken. The French column met with greater resistance, but in half an hour both of these strong positions had surrendered. The besiegers at once included the captured redoubts in their second
16. parallel, which was completed the next day, bringing the opposing batteries within musket range of each other. The walls of Yorktown crumbled before the terrible fire of the besiegers. The artillery, under command of Gen. Knox, was served with such precision as to excite the admiration of the French engineers, and the astonishment, as they afterward declared, of the English themselves. The British fire slackened, their ammunition was nearly exhausted, and their artillery broken and dismounted. A sally was made during the night, and some of the cannon in the second parallel were spiked. It was a fierce but fruitless effort of despairing valor. Cornwallis then attempted to pass the river to the opposite post of Glocester. A party of the army had already crossed, when a sudden tempest drove the boats down the stream. A lull in the storm enabled the scattered forces to regain the

[1] Biography of Revolutionary Heroes, by Mrs. Williams, 12mo, 312 pp., Providence, 1839. Life of Captain Stephen Olney, p. 278. In this work Mrs. Williams has performed a patriotic service, in rescuing from oblivion many anecdotes and adventures in the lives of these "departed champions of American independence," General William Barton, and Captain Olney.

bank, and those who had reached Glocester were brought back. At daybreak a tremendous fire was opened along the whole line upon the now ruined town. Further resistance being hopeless, Cornwallis proposed to capitulate, and asked twenty-four hours in which to arrange the terms. Washington granted but two. The articles were signed the same day, and on the next the allied armies entered Yorktown. On the following morning, Lord Cornwallis, with the whole British army, marched out of the town, and formally surrendered. The loss of the allies in the siege, was stated at four hundred and fifty; that of the enemy, at one hundred more. Two British frigates, several smaller ships of war, and many transports, with fifteen hundred seamen included in the surrender, were given up to the French. The whole number of prisoners, exclusive of seamen, was seven thousand two hundred forty seven.

CHAP. XXII. 1781. Oct. 17. 18. 19.

This decisive victory was a virtual termination of the war. The gallantry of Olney was lauded by Lafayette in general orders, and more handsomely recognized in a private correspondence; but History has hitherto failed to record the fact that the first sword that flashed in triumph above the captured heights of Yorktown, was a Rhode Island sword.

CHAPTER XXIII.

1781—1786.

FROM THE SURRENDER OF CORNWALLIS, OCTOBER 19TH, 1781, TO THE RISE OF THE PAPER MONEY PARTY IN RHODE ISLAND, MAY 1786.

CHAP. XXIII. THE news of the surrender of Cornwallis was everywhere received with the wildest demonstrations of joy.
1781. Oct. The firing of cannon, the display of French and American flags with the British beneath them, the ringing of bells, and every possible token of extravagant delight, hailed
25. the welcome news when it reached Providence. The next
26. night a splendid ball was given by a gentleman of Virginia to the citizens of Providence, and a grand display
29. of fireworks took place. The General Assembly altered the name of King's County, in order "to obliterate, as far as may be, every trace and idea of that government which threatened our destruction," and decreed "that in perpetual and grateful remembrance of the eminent and most distinguished services, and heroic actions of the illustrious commander-in-chief of the forces of the United States of America, the said county shall forever hereafter be known and called by the name and stile of Washington." As it was deemed best that a small force should still be kept ready for defence, a company of one hundred men, under Capt. Henry Dayton, was raised to serve till the first of April. Col. Robert Elliott, late of the artillery

regiment in the State brigade, and who, since his retire- CHAP. XXIII.
ment had been Intendant of Trade for Newport, died during the session, and William Taggart was appointed In- 1781.
tendant. Oct. 31.

The new town of Foster having failed to organize in Nov.
season to be represented in the legislature, the first town
meeting for that purpose was now held by their order. 19.
Col. Turner's regiment of Massachusetts militia was dis- 24.
missed from service in this State by order of the council
of war, as all danger of invasion had passed. Congress
had called upon the States for eight millions of dollars
for the coming year, of which the Rhode Island quota
was two hundred and sixteen thousand dollars. The
State was exhausted and could not meet the demand in
silver. The Assembly therefore instructed the delegates Dec. 10.
to confer with Robert Morris about receiving such army
supplies as this State produced, in payment of a portion of
that amount, and that the remainder might be expended
within the State to preserve a circulating medium. The
damage done by the enemy during the war was ordered to
be estimated by the justices of the several towns, and a
return to be made to the Assembly.

Soon after the battle of Yorktown, a portion of the
army was sent into Carolina, to reinforce Greene, and the
remainder were returned in the transports to the head of
the Chesapeake. Among the latter was the Rhode Island
regiment, now thinned by the casualties of war, and the
diseases of the camp. A tedious passage of twenty-one
days brought them to the Elk River, whence by easy
marches they reached Philadelphia. The small-pox had 12.
broken out on the passage, and a virulent fever, unknown
and uncontrollable in its character, added to the horrors
of the journey. Capt. Allen reported fifteen deaths from
these disorders on the route to Philadelphia, and made a
list of one hundred and six men, among whom was Lieut.
Oliver Jenckes, who died in battle or by disease from the
commencement of the siege to the middle of the ensuing

CHAP. XXIII. March.[1] During the year more than one-third of this
gallant corps had fallen in the service.[2] The return of the
1781. shattered regiment to their homes the following spring,
Dec. after this glorious but deadly campaign, was not unlike
that which we have recorded on a previous page, when
the remnant of Col. Hargil's broken band returned from
the fatal siege of Havana. A day of thanksgiving and
13. prayer was observed throughout the country by order of
Congress, in grateful commemoration of the crowning
victory of the war.

The national bank, which had met with the approval
31. of Congress in May, was incorporated by the name of the
1782. Bank of North America, to continue for ten years. It
Jan. 7. went into operation the following week with a capital of
four hundred thousand dollars, afterwards increased to
two millions. This monument of the genius of Robert
Morris became the model upon which the great banking
interest of America is based—a fact of peculiar interest to
this State, where banking has since been so successfully
conducted, and especially to the city of Providence, now
the fourth city in the Union in the amount of its capital
thus employed, and the second in the number of its
banks.[3] The appeal of the delegates from Rhode Island
14. was answered by Morris in a letter, setting forth conclusive reasons why the proportion of the continental tax
assigned to this State could not be reduced, and why no
part of it should be received in produce. The army must

[1] Captain William Allen to Theodore Foster, Philadelphia, December 15, 1781. Foster Corresp., vol. i. Same to same March 18, 1782. Foster Papers, vol. x.

[2] Deputy Gov. Jabez Bowen to Gov. Trumbull, February 12, 1782. Trumbull Papers, vol. xvi. No. 35.

[3] The Bankers' Magazine for February, 1859, gives a list of all the places in the country having more than one million of dollars in bank capital. New York has 50 banks, Providence 38, Boston 36. The capital of the New York banks is $66,600,000; of Boston, $31,960,000; of New Orleans, with 12 banks, $16,557,000; and of Providence, $14,544,000; next come Philadelphia, Baltimore, and Charleston, with 18, 15, and 9 banks respectively, and a little short of $11,000,000 capital each.

be kept up, and the quota of troops from this State was CHAP.
fixed by Washington at six hundred eighty-one, to be in XXIII.
the field by the first of March. The deficiency to be 1782.
made up in order to complete this number, was two hun- Jan.
dred fifty-nine, so great had been the loss sustained by the
regiment at the close of the campaign which they had entered upon with full ranks.

The Assembly passed an act, punishing with death 28.
any one who should counterfeit the bills of the Bank of
North America, the first paper money in the country that
was made redeemable in specie on presentation. A census
of the State was ordered to be made,[1] and a new estimate
of taxable property was reported, which amounted to
nearly three millions of pounds, lawful money. A tax of
eighteen thousand pounds in silver was laid, two-thirds
of it for the State, and the remainder, with an equal
amount in addition to be paid in produce, for the United
States. But as Morris declined receiving any portion of
the tax in this form, at the next session a further tax of Feb.
six thousand pounds in silver, was levied for the general 25.
government. The number of troops required to complete
the regiment was apportioned among the towns, to be
enlisted for nine months; besides which a company of
fifty-five men was raised to serve on the island for the
same period, under Lieutenant James Miller.

But measures were in progress in England, which March
rendered these preparations useless. A resolution passed 4.
the Commons, declaring all who should advise the continuance of the war in America, to be enemies to the King
and country. Lord North retired from the ministry, and 20.
was succeeded by the Duke of Grafton as Privy Seal. 27.
The Marquis of Rockingham, who seventeen years before
had superseded Grenville, and become the leader of a
short-lived, liberal cabinet, became first lord of the
Treasury. A bill was at once introduced, to enable the 28.

[1] The population of the State was ascertained by this census to be 51,869; Newport had 5,531; and Providence, 4,310.

CHAP. XXIII. 1782. May 8. King "to conclude a peace and truce with the revolted colonies in North America." Sir Guy Carleton being sent over to bring the truce, and to succeed Sir Henry Clinton as commander-in-chief, arrived at New York in May. But the proposals contained nothing in regard to independence, and sought to establish peace without the concurrence of France; two defects, either of which would have been fatal to the purpose sought. Congress de-
31. clined to consider the proposition, and required that the negotiation should be conducted at Paris.

April 12. The brilliant victory of Admiral Rodney over Count de Grasse in the West Indies, almost annihilated the French maritime power in the American seas, and had it occurred at an earlier period, must have prolonged the war. The British force comprised thirty-seven ships-of-the-line, and ten frigates; that of the French, thirty-three ships. The battle lasted nearly twelve hours, and resulted in the loss or capture of one-third of the French squadron. Holland having formed an alliance with France, now ac-
19. knowledged the independence of the United States, and received John Adams as minister. The annual fast, which during the war had been appointed by Congress
25. every spring, was again observed.

May 1. At the spring election, John Collins, Ezekiel Cornell, Jonathan Arnold, and David Howell were chosen delegates to Congress—all new members except Gen. Cornell. Howell was sent on to take the place of Ellery, as the colleague of Cornell. The Assembly ordered new quarters to be found for the French hospital, that the college might be repaired and restored to the corporation, and the grounds cleared of the temporary buildings erected by the French.

Discontent prevailed in the army. Some of the officers seeing no prospect of obtaining their pay from a bankrupt treasury, attributed the evil to a defect in the form of government, and sought to substitute a monarchy for a republic. With this object, overtures were made to Washington to assume the sceptre of America. The indignant rebuke with which the great patriot crushed the plot, history has recorded. The British still held Savannah. A strong detachment of their force having marched out of the city, was defeated by Gen. Wayne in a night attack, at a point about four miles from town on the Ogeechie Road, and driven in with great loss. This was the last important action of the war, although skirmishes with the Indians afterwards occurred, and in Carolina a partisan warfare was still sustained. CHAP. XXIII. 1782. May 24.

Another tax of twelve thousand pounds, in silver, for continental use, was levied by the Assembly. June 10.

The evacuation of Savannah, which was immediately occupied by Gen. Wayne, left but two important posts, New York and Charleston, in the hands of the enemy. A discussion was at this time going on in Congress, which plainly foretold the position that Rhode Island was to occupy in the important political movements soon to take place. The necessity of granting to Congress the power to levy an import duty of five per cent., was strongly urged by Morris. Nearly all the States had consented. Georgia had not yet given a reply, but this delay was attributed to her having so recently emerged from the war. Rhode Island steadily refused to assent to the measure, for reasons given by Howell to a committee appointed by Congress to ascertain why these two States had not concurred with the other eleven. An account of this interview with the committee was transmitted by him 30.
to Gov. Greene. It was contended that the exposed condition of Rhode Island required all the resources of her trade for purposes of defence, and that this was guaranteed by the articles of confederation; that this duty bore unequally upon Rhode Island as a maritime State, which required her trade to protect her from the inland duties that her neighbors might legally impose; that it infringed upon the sovereignty of the State, which could better collect its own revenues than could be done by an external power; that Congress were not accountable for July 11.

CHAP. XXIII. 1782. the moneys thus to be placed in their hands; that it would create an army of office-holders, whose influence would tend to corrupt the public morals; and last, but not least, that Congress had as yet come to no decision in regard to the public lands, of which Rhode Island claimed her proportionate share as having been won by the common blood and treasure of all the States. She would never yield the right to levy duties within her borders, until the equal right of the thirteen States to the public domain was established by Congress. Howell suggested that each State should have the appointment of collectors in its own territory, and be credited with the amount of revenue collected therein, this sum to be deducted from the State's proportion of continental taxes. This was the beginning of a contest, in which Howell was to be persecuted by his peers for the perverseness of Rhode Island in maintaining the ground thus taken. Here were laid down distinctly and broadly the doctrines of free trade as a measure of protection, of State sovereignty, and of the equal right
Aug. of all the States in the national domain. Morris request-
2. ed a copy of these objections, to which he prepared a reply, but avoided any reference to the last, which was destined to be the most difficult one to surmount. The assenting States had granted the power with many restrictions, and encouraged by the firmness of Rhode Island on this question, some of them began to re-consider the subject. Maryland was inclined to withdraw her assent. That of Massachusetts having been given by act of the
19. legislature, was negatived by Gov. Hancock, as being adverse to the liberties of the people.

Tory privateers continued to infest the coast, and two
2. vessels were cut out of the harbor of Newport at night
19. by one of these marauders. The Assembly endeavored to enlist two hundred recruits for the army, and forty for service at Newport, and also postponed the time for collecting the last tax. Enlistments and taxation both proceeded slowly, for the former were unnecessary, and the

latter too frequent for a State that had so long been drained of men and money. The pay of delegates in Congress was fixed at four dollars a day while on duty. CHAP. XXIII. 1782. Sept.

The affairs of the college were now revived. Four students who had pursued their studies to the end were graduated in course, and three others, who were in the junior class when the institution was broken up, also received their degrees. The building was repaired, and again occupied for its legitimate purposes.

Gov. Cooke, who was in office at the commencement of the revolution, died at this time, just too soon to wit- 14.
ness the triumph of the great cause to which he had devoted the last years of his life. The royal commission to Richard Oswald to conclude a treaty of peace with the United States, was signed at Westminster, and certified copies of the instrument were given at Paris by Oswald, 21.
to be sent to all the States.

Gen. Cornell was appointed inspector of contracts for Oct. 1.
the army, an office which obliged him to be absent from his seat in Congress, and Dr. Arnold was sent on to supply his place. This change was very agreeable to Howell, with whose views on the question of impost Arnold entirely agreed, while Cornell inclined to those of the majority. The delegation had therefore been divided on the most important subject before the country, but now became united. Their appeals to the State to resist the impost act until the question of the public lands should be decided, were frequent and earnest, and as the event proved, successful. The settlement of the accounts of the several States with the general government, had received the attention of Congress in February. Under the act then passed, Edward Chinn, of New York, was now ap- 21.
pointed commissioner to settle with Rhode Island. In no instance was a citizen of any State made commissioner for the State to which he belonged, and all were instructed to arrange the accounts in as liberal a manner as possible for the States.

CHAP. XXIII. The French army being on their march to the eastward, Rochambeau applied to the governor to furnish
1782. quarters in Providence for their officers. The Assembly
Oct. 28. requested the town council to provide them, and sent a committee to meet the French in Coventry, to inform them of the arrangements. The next week Rochambeau
Nov. 8–10. reached Providence, followed two days later by the army.
25. At an adjourned session, the General Assembly ordered an address to be prepared, expressing to the Count De Rochambeau their sense of the services rendered by himself and the army to the cause of America. This was
27. presented by a committee, and appropriately answered by the French general the next day. Both addresses were entered upon the State records. The Treasurer was ordered to give his notes for the balance due to the Rhode Island continental regiment upon their depreciation account, the notes to carry compound interest at six per cent., payable in four years. An act was also passed to consolidate the paper money of the State. The outstanding bills of credit were to be carried to the treasurer, who was to calculate their value by the scale of depreciation formerly adopted, and issue his notes at six per cent., for the value so ascertained.

28. The annual thanksgiving was held by recommendation
30. of Congress. Provisional articles of peace were arranged between Great Britain and the United States, to be embodied in a treaty when peace should be made between France and England. The main body of the French army,
Dec. after encamping for a month in North Providence, marched to Boston early in December, whence they embarked in the spring for France. The second division only, remained in their quarters on the east side of the Pawtucket turnpike, just north of the city line. The
14. evacuation of Charleston by the enemy, left South Carolina free to organize a settled government. Only one important post now remained to the British troops.

Oct. 10. Congress, determined to press the impost act to a

conclusion, called upon the States of Rhode Island and CHAP. XXIII.
Georgia for an immediate decision. The lower House of
Assembly, fifty-three deputies present, voted unanimously 1782.
to reject it, and wrote to the President of Congress, giving Nov. 30.
some of their reasons for this course; that the operation
of the act would be unequal; that it conflicted with State
sovereignty; and that it made Congress independent of
the States. Mr. Collins went on to relieve Howell, whose
term of service was nearly expired, and carried the
Speaker's letter. Before the answer was received, Congress appointed a committee of three to go to Rhode Island Dec. 6.
and represent the real nature and objects of the bill. An
attempt was at the same time made to injure Howell with
his constituents, on account of the publication of extracts
from his letters in the Boston papers, containing foreign
news, which, although it was publicly known in Philadelphia, Congress wished, if possible, to suppress, and a committee was appointed to ascertain the author of these letters. The object of this movement was apparent from
the previous one made the same day. It was a plot to
break down Howell, who was considered as the chief
obstacle in the way of the adoption of the impost act.
Upon the reception of the letter announcing its rejection, 12.
Howell moved a repeal of the act appointing a deputation
to visit Rhode Island, but was defeated. On the same
day the committee of inquiry reported that the newspaper
articles misrepresented the contents of the foreign letters
to which they referred, and instructed the secretary of
foreign affairs to write to the governor of Rhode Island,
and ascertain who was the author of these articles. Mr.
Howell having avowed himself to be the author of the
letters from which extracts had appeared in the papers,
Congress discharged the secretary from that duty in a 18.
resolution reflecting upon Howell. An exciting debate
then ensued. Howell entered a declaration and protest
against the attempt of Congress to infringe upon the
liberty of its members, and the rights of the States. Many

CHAP. XXIII. motions were made on each side. Howell was voted
down upon every point, and a copy of the foreign letters,
1782. which related chiefly to loans contracted in Europe,
Dec. together with the proceedings of Congress during this
20. debate, were ordered to be sent to the governor of Rhode
Island. Through this trying ordeal, Howell was warmly
sustained by his colleague, Dr. Arnold, and the attempt
to injure him at home proved as futile as did the purpose
for which the plot was laid. Howell was returned by his
constituents, and the State stood firm in resistance to the
1783. Jan. impost. Mr. Howell, after having been detained for some
6. weeks in defending himself, left for home. Arnold and
Collins remained.[1] The acts of Congress relating to the
affair, duly certified, were soon afterward forwarded to
16. the governor.

Preliminaries of peace between France, Spain, and
20. Great Britain were signed at Versailles. It was well for
America, as for the world, that this protracted struggle
was about to close, for to raise money, even for the cause
of independence, seemed almost impossible. So exhausted
had every portion of the country become, that of the eight
millions of dollars required for the expenses of the past
31. year, an account made up at this time shows that less
than half a million had been collected. Four of the States
had paid nothing, and the remaining nine had done but
little.[2] Privateering continued to be pursued on both
sides. A "refugee" armed boat from New York came
Feb. 16. into Narraganset Bay with a crew of eight men, who encamped on Hope Island for several days, and on their

[1] The letters of Dr. Arnold and Mr. Howell, with a copy of the journals of Congress during this debate, giving all the details of this singular affair, are preserved in letters 1782–3, Nos. 22, 23, 33, 44, 45.

[2] Delaware, North and South Carolina and Georgia had paid nothing. Of the $216,600 required from this State, only $37,785 had been paid, and the other States were still more deficient, and but $422,162 had been paid by all. The payment made by this State was over one-fifth part more of its quota than was paid by any other State on the requisition for 1782. Prov. Gazette, 30 August, 1783.

departure captured a packet sloop from Newport bound to Providence. They were chased by a sloop from Newport, the prize was retaken, and the boat's crew were all made prisoners. CHAP. XXIII. 1783.

An alarming combination was formed in the southern towns of Massachusetts to resist the collection of taxes. Armed bands entered Rhode Island, and rescued several persons who had been arrested for obstructing the collectors. The infection spread until twelve or fourteen towns, chiefly in Massachusetts, met in convention with the avowed purpose of paying no more taxes, and of overthrowing the government. Jan. A meeting was held in Killingly to disseminate similar views in Connecticut. Deputy-Governor Bowen wrote to Gov. Trumbull to advise him of this movement, 31. and also to Gov. Hancock, recommending some joint action of the three States to put a stop to the dangerous conspiracy.[1] In Gloucester the rioters had proceeded to great lengths, not only seizing cattle which had been distrained for taxes, but rescuing prisoners while on trial for that offence. Deputy-Governor Bowen acted with energy in this crisis, and caused Feb. 24. the arrest of the ringleaders. The Assembly took vigorous measures to crush the insurrection, and ordered the Attorney-General, assisted by Gen. Varnum, to prosecute them to the extent of the law. They also informed the governors of Massachusetts and Connecticut of the affair, that united measures might be taken to suppress it. Thirteen of the rioters acknowledged their crime, and petitioned for pardon, but only two of them were received as State's evidence.

The attempt in Congress to injure Howell at home, for his firm opposition to the impost act, drew from the Assembly a letter, vindicating the course of their representative, and a series of resolutions, approving his conduct and that of Dr. Arnold in the whole affair; that the

[1] Dep. Gov. Jabez Bowen to Gov. Trumbull, Providence, 31 Jan., 1783. Trumbull Papers, Vol. xviii., No. 18.

CHAP. XXIII. 1783. Feb. 4. declaration and protest of the eighteenth of December were "highly approved;" that the extracts of letters sent by Congress, confirmed the representations of Howell in the printed articles which had been made the ostensible cause of the proceedings against him; that the opposition to the impost act was "a meritorious service rendered to this State, and to the cause of freedom in general;" and that the governor enclose a copy of the resolutions in his answer to the letter from the President of Congress. Instructions were also given to the delegates to oppose the recent action of Congress against Vermont, and to advocate the independence of that State. Arrangements were made by which the creditors of the confiscated estates of absentees should be paid. A tariff act "for raising a revenue for the support of the government" of the State was passed. It levied specific duties upon all imported articles, and provided for entering goods in bond for exportation. It placed a duty upon all domestic liquors, carriages, dogs, and billiard tables, and established "collectors of excise" to enforce the act in each county. Silas Talbot was appointed collector for Providence. The appointment of Edward Chinn to settle the accounts of this State with the United States was approved, and Ebenezer Thompson was made commissioner on the part of Rhode Island, to prepare the accounts and to assist Chinn. A proposal to divide the town of South Kingston was made and submitted to the inhabitants for their consideration.

But the most important act of this session, not in a practical point of view, but for the interest it has excited as a matter of history, was that short statute extending to Roman Catholic citizens the same rights with Protestants, and repealing, in effect, the disabling clause, "[Roman Catholics excepted]," which had crept in, no one knows how or when, in the act which defined the requisites for citizenship.[1] The "Act declaring the rights and privileges

[1] This statute reads as follows: "Be it enacted, &c., That all the rights and privileges of the Protestant citizens of this State, as declared in and

of his Majesty's subjects within this colony," concludes with the words, "and that all men [professing Christianity] and of competent estates, and of civil conversation, who acknowledge and are obedient to the civil magistrate, though of different judgment in religious affairs, [Roman Catholics excepted,] shall be admitted freemen, and shall have liberty to choose and be chosen officers in the colony, both military and civil." In some of the printed digests, the word "only" is inserted after "Catholics," and the parenthetical marks around the words "professing Christianity" are omitted. Such is the case with the earliest printed copy of the laws,[1] while others are printed as above. Three questions arise respecting the phrases thus parenthesized. When and how they came upon the statute book, and what was their effect? The two former of these questions may be discussed together.

CHAP. XXIII. 1783. Feb. 24.

That a law excluding Roman Catholics as such, would be a violation of the spirit of the charter, if not of its letter also, all who read that instrument will admit. That such a law could not have been passed at the time alleged in the repealing act is obvious, not only from this fact, but from the position of English politics at the time. Charles II., himself apparently a Romanist from choice, was seeking to obtain that toleration for his own church which, by the Declaration of Breda, he had promised to all. The feeble colony depending solely upon his protection against their more powerful neighbors, could not, in their very first legislation under the charter, have adopted a measure so certain to offend the King. Yet the repealing act refers the law to that date. This difficulty, however,

by an act made and passed the first day of March, A. D., 1663, be, and the same are hereby fully extended to Roman Catholic citizens; and that they being of competent estates, and of civil conversation, and acknowledging and paying obedience to the civil magistrates, shall be admitted freemen, and shall have liberty to choose and be chosen civil or military officers within this State, any exception in the said act to the contrary, notwithstanding.' State Records, Feb., 1783, p. 412.

[1] Digests were printed in 1719, 1730, 1744, 1752, and 1767.

CHAP. XXIII. 1783. Feb. is easily explained. In the several digests all the statutes relating to any one subject were collected into one, which bore the date of the earliest law upon that subject, and as an act declaring the rights of the people, was necessarily 1663. passed by the first legislature under the royal charter, all later acts and alterations on that subject were classed as one law under that date.

1680. The report of Gov. Sandford seventeen years later, shows that in his time there were no Roman Catholics in the colony, and that if there had been they would have enjoyed the same protection in their religious rights as 1684. any other people,[1] and four years later a similar guaranty was expressly given by the Assembly to certain Jewish petitioners.[2] We must look later than 1684 for the insertion of these clauses. They exist in a manuscript copy of the laws made in 1705. Between these two dates, therefore, we may expect to find that the interpolations occurred, and that they grew out of the exigencies of English politics we consider certain. The same cause that rendered their existence impossible under the Stuarts, rendered it equally impossible that some such restrictions should not exist upon the accession of William of Orange. After the battle of Boyne had crushed the hopes of the Jacobite leaders, treachery assumed the place of manly opposition in the councils of the Papal party. Early in 1696, a plot to assassinate William III. was discovered. 1696. Stringent measures were immediately adopted against the Roman Catholics. Associations of loyalty, as they were termed, were formed throughout England, in which the subscribers swore to support the King and to defend his person with their lives. A form "proper to be entered into" for this purpose was sent to America, and these associations were organized in all the colonies except Rhode Island. No traces of any action of the kind by individuals can be found in this State. All the other

[1] See Chap. xi., App. F. Vol. 1, p. 490. [2] Vol. 1, p. 478–9.

colonies had laws against Romanism, infidelity, and every sort of heterodox opinion. Rhode Island had none, nor did the colony ever pass any such by any formal vote. Four years later the Earl of Bellemont, after many efforts, procured a manuscript copy of the laws of Rhode Island and sent it to England. Unfortunately, the only manuscript copy now in the British state paper office, is mutilated. Two pages, being the first leaf, are missing. This is probably the Bellemont copy, and if so, we think the missing leaf, if ever recovered, will be found to contain the phrases parenthesized as above, and which were inserted at that time by the collecting committee to meet the exigency which we have mentioned.

CHAP. XXIII. 1783. 1700.

In the instructions given by Queen Anne to Gov. Dudley, in 1702, occur these words: "You are to permit a liberty of conscience to all persons, (except Papists,) so they be contented with a quiet and peaceful enjoyment of the same, not giving offence or scandal to the government." Dudley was commissioned as governor of Massachusetts and commander of the forces in Rhode Island and Kings Province. Here are positive orders from the crown to the governor, who was vested with extensive powers in Rhode Island, although that power was never recognized in this colony, that he should refuse toleration to Papists. The letter and spirit of this command cannot be mistaken. The causes that produced it we have stated. The same causes compelled the revising committee to insert in the Body of Laws the parenthetical clauses so adverse to the letter of the charter and the spirit of the colony, in order that their privileges, then threatened by the powerful influence of Bellemont, might not be taken from them. For these reasons we should assign the year 1699 as the date of the interpolations, and the measures pursued by the English government in consequence of Jacobite excesses as the cause.

1702.

What was the effect of these clauses? Nothing. Not only was the Roman Catholic clause repealed as soon as

CHAP. XXIII. 1783. the exclusion that it worked could have a practical effect upon any considerable number of persons of that faith, but long anterior to the Revolution, both Roman Catholics and Jews were not only allowed in Rhode Island, as they were nowhere else in New England, the quiet enjoyment of their religious faith and forms of worship, but were on several occasions, upon petition to the Assembly, naturalized as citizens of the colony. These were mostly Roman Catholics, among whom we have noticed Stephen Decatur, a Genoese, the father of the celebrated commodore, after seven years service as an officer of a privateer
1753. out of Newport, was naturalized in 1753. For many years prior to that time there was scarcely a session of the Assembly when one or more cases of the kind did not occur in which the names and nationalities of the parties show them to be either Roman Catholics or Jews. Soon
1755. after the great earthquake at Lisbon, a large number of persons of the Hebrew faith established themselves at Newport, and introduced many branches of industry to which that place owed much of its commercial prosperity. Some of these were naturalized and others were not.
1761. Lucena, the Portuguese, was naturalized in 1761 by the
1762. Assembly, and the next year the petitions of Aaron Lopez and Isaac Elizar for the same favor were rejected by the Superior Court upon grounds that were not only a violation of the spirit of the charter, but a direct disregard of an act of Parliament.[1]

[1] The records of the court read as follows: "The petition of Messrs. Aaron Lopez and Isaac Elizar, persons professing the Jewish religion, praying that they may be naturalized on an act of Parliament, made in the 13th year of his late Majesty's reign, George II., having been duly considered, and also the act of Parliament therein referred to; this Court are unanimously of opinion that the said act of Parliament was wisely designed for increasing the number of the inhabitants in the plantations, but this colony, being already so full of people that many of His Majesty's good subjects, born within the same have removed and settled in Nova Scotia and other places, cannot come within the intention of said act. Further, by the charter granted to this colony, its appears that the free and quiet enjoyment of the

It will be observed that the petitioners ask to be naturalized under an act of Parliament. The court construed the act to suit their purpose, going behind the record to pronounce upon the probable or possible intention of the act, which was an assumption of extra-judicial power, and then rejected the petition as if it had asked for freemanship, which it did not. The admission of freemen of the towns was an act of the councils, and freemen of the colony were admitted by the Assembly to whom the application for that purpose should properly have been made by these petitioners if freemanship was what they sought. Naturalization was granted properly by the courts, but usually by the Assembly, who exercised judicial prerogatives in this matter as in many others. The decision in the case of Lopez appears to be irregular in every respect. It subverts an act of Parliament, violates the spirit of the charter, enunciates principles never acted upon in the colony, and finally dismisses the case on a false issue. We know of but one cause that can explain all this, in a single word—party spirit. The strife between Ward, then chief-justice, and Hopkins, then governor, was at its height, resulting in the defeat of Hopkins at the ensuing election. Some of the details of that contest, herein recorded, exhibit as gross violations of right and of usage as does this decision, but none so utterly absurd.

CHAP. XXIII. 1783.

Here we may remark that the charter of Rhode Island guaranteed, and the action of the colony uniformly secured, to all people perfect religious freedom. It did not confer civil privileges, as a part of that right, upon any one, and

Christian religion and a desire of propagating the same were the principal views with which this colony was settled, and by a law made and passed in the year 1663, no person who does not profess the Christian religion can be admitted free of this colony. This court, therefore, unanimously dismiss this petition as wholly inconsistent with the first principles upon which the colony was founded and a law of the same now in force." Superior Court, March Term, 1762.

CHAP. XXIII. 1783. such only were entitled to these whom the freemen saw fit to admit. The colony was a close corporation and has ever remained so. At the adoption of the constitution, the proportion of freemen to the inhabitants of the State was as one to eleven. At the very time that the Superior Court rejected the petition of these Jews, a synagogue, the only one in all America, had been commenced, and was dedicated the following year. The Hebrew faith was here protected to the fullest extent, when everywhere else it was denounced. The right to be admitted a freeman, or even to be naturalized, was purely a civil one depending upon the view that the town councils, the General Assembly, or the courts, might take of the merits of each individual case. The right to reject was absolute, the reasons assigned for the rejection in the decree above given were false, violating both the policy and the practice of the colony, as well as the spirit of the charter, and the acts of Parliament.

It is worthy of notice, too, that in this Roman Catholic enabling act, the other parenthetical phrase [professing Christianity] is not included, so that to this day, or at least down to the adoption of the State constitution in 1843, if these words were ever considered as law, no one, not a Christian, could ever have been admitted a freeman, nor, under the construction of the court in the case of Lopez, even have been naturalized. That it never was in reality a law, or presumed to have any binding force at all, is evident from the repeated cases of Jewish naturalization by the Assembly, as well as from the fact that no repealing statute, as in the case of Roman Catholics, was ever passed. That both of these clauses were interpolated by the revising committee for the same purpose and at the same time, appears to us to be certain. That they were passed upon by the Assembly in the several revisions that were made in the eighteenth century, when the digests were received and ordered to be printed, is probably true. In that sense they may be considered as having been enacted by the Assembly. But that they never had the force of statutes, that the most important one was repealed by a specific act as soon as it came, by reason of French Catholic settlers in the State, to have a practical bearing, and that the other was never viewed as of any importance whatever, not even being worthy of repeal, we think that any one who carefully studies both the spirit and the letter of Rhode Island history will be convinced. CHAP. XXIII. 1783.

Great discontent prevailed in the army with respect to the half pay for life which had been promised, and which it was proposed to commute to full pay for five years. Either of these plans were acceptable, but a graver question grew out of the poverty of the treasury, as to how the army was to be paid at all. Some advocated a funding of the public debt, and payment in continental certificates; others, that the States separately should provide for their own debts and for the payment of the army. While this question was under discussion, an anonymous appeal to the passions of the officers appeared from the camp at Newburgh, and a call for a meeting of all the officers to consider measures of redress was issued. Washington denounced this secret proceeding in general orders, and summoned a council of officers to hear the report of their committee then in waiting upon Congress. At this meeting he exerted all his influence to calm the excitement, and so successfully, that when he withdrew, the officers passed resolutions of confidence in the justice of Congress, and of disapproval of the anonymous appeals. The plan of five years' full pay was adopted by Congress, to be paid in money or in six per cent. stock. This action was disapproved in many of the States, and some of the legislatures, opposed to any extra pay, passed resolutions against it. The delegates from this State had been instructed to oppose it. Feb. Mar. 10. 11. 15. 22.

The news of the preliminaries of peace reached Philadelphia in a vessel sent by Count D'Estaing to recall the 23.

CHAP. XXIII. French cruisers and privateers. Congress immediately issued orders to "recall all armed vessels cruising under
1783. commissions from the United States." A few days later, upon receiving official confirmation of this happy event,
April 11. the cessation of hostilities was proclaimed by Congress.
18. It was communciated by Washington in general orders to the army, and the next day the proclamation was read at
19. the head of every regiment, just eight years from the day of the battle of Lexington.

It was not in vain that Rhode Island had for two years firmly opposed the impost act. Essential as it was to the stability of government that some powers should be granted to Congress beyond what the articles of confederation conferred, there were points to be settled, apart from the question of the western lands, which time and full discussion could alone determine. The qualified assent which had been given to the act by most of the other States, yielding to the pressure of Congress, was less satisfactory than a consent obtained after deliberate examination of the scheme and the perfecting its details. This was the result of the refusal of Rhode Island to grant the power when first requested. Portions of the old act were in violation of the articles of confederation, and in the opinion of the people of this State, there would be no limit to the usurpation of power by Congress if the barrier of State sovereignty was once overstepped. We shall see that this feeling was soon to be carried to too great an extent upon the more vital question with which this history will close; but in the present instance at least, it accomplished an important object in obtaining from Con-
18. gress a new impost bill, more carefully prepared, in which many objections were removed, and a provision was inserted for altering the eighth article of confederation, which secured to the States the sole power of taxation. The new act was limited to twenty-five years, and gave the appointment of collectors to the States. Arnold and
23. Collins forwarded the bill and resolution to Gov. Greene,

approving them in the main, but suggesting a few alterations as still further guards to the rights of the States. But this act was destined to the same fate as its predecessor. The plan of impost was not agreed to by all the States till the adoption of the constitution. 1783. April

The cessation of hostilities was published at Providence, and the proclamation forwarded to each town in the State. 22. The event was celebrated with great demonstrations of joy. 25. Firing of cannon and ringing of bells ushered in the day. A procession, a sermon by Rev. Enos Hitchcock in the First Baptist Church, followed by an oration from Asher Robbins, occupied the morning. At noon the proclamation was read from the balcony of the State House, and in two other public places, amid acclamations and military salutes. A public dinner at the State House succeeded. The frigate Alliance, lately returned from a cruise in the West Indies, fired salutes, and all the shipping was decorated with flags. In the evening there was an illumination and a display of fireworks. On the same day similar rejoicings took place at Newport, with the addition of hanging the effigy of Benedict Arnold the traitor.

At the spring election, Collins and Cornell gave place May 7. to Henry Marchant and William Ellery, who were again chosen delegates to Congress. Arnold and Howell were re-elected. Howell and Ellery were sent on to represent the State. Intercourse with New Shoreham was renewed, and the rights of the inhabitants were restored. Commerce with Great Britain was revived, and the acts against illicit trade with the enemy were repealed. Public papers, that during the war had been removed from Newport, were now returned, and several persons imprisoned for holding communication with the enemy, were released. Legislation was directed to the new aspect of affairs, the return of peace.

The Revolutionary war had ended in the independence of the American colonies. Great Britain had lost the

CHAP. XXIII. 1783. May finest portion of her empire, and during the past seven years had doubled her national debt, which now amounted to two hundred and forty millions of pounds. The debt of the United States was about seventy millions of dollars, of which forty-five millions pertained to the federal government, and the remainder to the several States. The war debt of Rhode Island alone amounted to over seven hundred thousand dollars. This was a grievous burden to an impoverished country.

13. The Society of the Cincinnati was formed by the officers of the army encamped on Hudson River.[1] As the final treaty was still delayed, the army could not be
26. disbanded. Congress resolved to instruct Washington to
June. 2. grant furloughs to most of the soldiers. This he did in general orders, which caused great dissatisfaction, as the officers looked upon it as a mode of quietly dispensing with their services, and leaving them unpaid. Three months' pay had been promised to the whole army, and this was delayed for want of funds. Washington now ad-
18. dressed a farewell letter to the governors of all the States, a long, earnest, and patriotic communication, reviewing the past, speaking hopefully of the future, and under four distinct heads presenting the points most essential to secure the prosperity of the republic.[2] These were, "an indissoluble union of the States under one Federal head, a sacred regard to public justice, the adoption of a proper peace establishment, and the prevalence of that pacific and friendly disposition among the people of the United States," which should disregard local prejudices and lead to mutual concessions. Three days afterward, Greene took leave of the Southern army in an address, wherein he
21. compliments their patience and their bravery.

[1] The officers of the R. I. Cincinnati, appointed in December following, were, Maj. Gen. Greene, President; Maj. Gen. Varnum, Vice President; Col. Henry Sherburne, Secretary; Lt. Col. Com. J. Olney and Major John Dexter, Treasurers.

[2] This address fills twenty large folio pages, and is in letters 1782 & '3, No. 85.

The delay in preparing the notes in which the three CHAP. XXIII.
months' pay was to be given to the army, caused a meeting of a portion of the Pennsylvania line, who marched 1783.
from Lancaster to Philadelphia without their officers, and June
surrounding the State House, demanded instant payment.
Washington sent a superior force to Philadelphia, who
suppressed the revolt, but Congress, disgusted at the
feeble conduct of the local authorities, adjourned to 26.
Princeton.

The insular and remote position of New Shoreham, we
have observed from the first settlement of Block Island,
required legislation quite different from that of the other
towns. The difficulty of having deputies always present
at the sessions of the General Assembly, led the people of
that town to elect Ray Sands, a resident of South Kingstown, but a freeholder of New Shoreham, to represent the
town. The Assembly passed a special act, permitting 23.
the town to send non-resident deputies who should be
freeholders, but such deputies were thereby disabled during their term of office, from acting as freemen of the
town where they resided, nor was this act to be held as a
precedent for any other town. A tax of twenty thousand
pounds in specie was assessed. The tariff or "excise" act
was repealed, and a new one adopted, levying a duty of
two per cent. ad valorem upon all imports, to meet the
interest on the State debt.

The frigate Alliance, Capt. John Barry, sailed from July 1.
Providence for Virginia, and thence to Europe. Soon
after this last cruise, she was sold by the government, and
became an Indiaman. The trade with China was commenced at this time by the merchants of Boston, who
fitted out the first ship that ever sailed from the United Aug.
States to that remote country. This example, we shall
see, soon stimulated the enterprise of Providence to embark in the same trade.[1]

[1] The honor of being the first ship from the United States engaged in the

CHAP. XXIII. While at Princeton, Congress resolved to erect an equestrian statue of Washington at the place that should 1783. be agreed upon as the capital of the country. At their Aug. 26. request he waited upon them, and received the thanks of united America for his eminent services, expressed in an address by the president.

Sept. 3. The definitive treaty of peace was signed at Paris early in September, and as soon as it was ratified by Congress, Oct. 18. a proclamation was issued to disband the army on the third of November. Commercial agents of France were established throughout the country. Philip Joseph de L'Etombe was appointed consul for the New England States, and Joseph M. S. Toscan vice consul for the same. Their exequaturs for Rhode Island were given them by 27. act of the Assembly. Four months later, De Marbois was received as consul general for the United States.[1] The Second Baptist Society at Newport, under Rev. Gardiner Thurston, was incorporated as the Six Principles Baptist Society. A decree of banishment was passed against a Tory, who had assisted the enemy in several plundering excursions within this State during the war, and had returned without leave. Death was denounced against him in case he should again return.

Nov. 2. The day previous to the disbanding of the army, Washington issued his farewell orders, taking leave of his old companions in arms. A small force was retained in 15. service, but the greater portion of these were discharged

China trade, was claimed for the ship Empress of China, of 360 tons, which sailed from New York 22d Feb., 1784: arrived at Canton 20th August, sailed 27th Dec. for New York, where she arrived 11th May, 1785. This voyage was mentioned by Congress as "the first effort of the citizens of America to establish a direct trade with China." The ship mentioned in the text was certainly prior to the Empress of China, in fitting for the voyage, and her outward cargo was reported as worth $150,000; but at what time she sailed from Boston the writer cannot say.

[1] Afterwards Consular agents were appointed by Toscan, in the principal ports. Thomas Lloyd Halsey, residing at Providence, was made the French agent for the State of Rhode Island.

two weeks later. The remnant of the British forces, most CHAP.
of which had already sailed for England, evacuated New XXIII.
York, and went on to Staten Island to await their embar- 1783.
cation. Gen. Knox, with a body of troops, marched into Nov. 25.
the city with Gov. Clinton and Gen. Washington, the
latter of whom, on the same day, took leave of the officers
of the army. On the same day, too, Major-General Nathaniel Greene arrived at his residence in Newport. A
committee of the town waited upon him with an address 26.
of welcome, to which he returned an appropriate reply. 29.
The whole progress of Gen. Greene, from the scene of his
triumphs, was a continued ovation. Everywhere he was
received with enthusiasm as the saviour of the South, and
the second only to the commander-in-chief in the council
or the field. At Charleston the thanks of the Assembly Aug. 12.
were conveyed to him by the governor of South Carolina.
At Baltimore a public reception was given to him. Con- Sept. 30.
gress voted that two brass field-pieces, captured by him Oct. 28.
in Carolina, be engraved with a suitable inscription, and
presented to him. And now that he had once more returned to his home, there only remained for him to receive the joyous welcome of his fellow-citizens, and the
merited acknowledgments of the legislature of his native
State.

The definitive treaty of peace, the first article of which Dec.
recognizes the independence of the thirteen States, was
received by a vessel at Providence from London, and im- 2.
mediately printed in an extra of the Gazette. A national
thanksgiving was held by appointment of Congress. The 11.
Assembly that was to meet that week, was prorogued by
the governor till the fourth Monday of the month. The 22.
Quakers presented a petition, respecting the abolition of
slavery; an act was framed for that object, referred to the
next session, and ordered to be printed. A copyright act,
securing to authors in this State the benefit of their works
for twenty-one years, was passed—"there being no property more peculiarly a man's own than that which is pro-

CHAP. XXIII. 1783. Dec. duced by the labor of his mind." The benefit of the act was restricted to authors who were citizens of this State, or of those States who should pass similar laws, and a penalty of three thousand pounds, lawful money, was affixed to its violation.[1]

Congress had passed a resolution,[2] that twelve hundred thousand dollars should be raised by the States to meet the interest due upon loan office certificates, of which sum twenty-eight thousand eight hundred dollars were assigned to Rhode Island. The Assembly required the keeper of the loan office in this State, to consolidate all such certificates held by Rhode Island citizens, to endorse the present value upon the same, and to pay one year's interest thereon out of the proceeds of the late tax, and to issue new certificates for the unpaid balance. The colonial government having passed away forever, a revision of the laws became necessary, and a committee for that purpose was appointed. An address of congratulation to Gen. Greene upon his
26. return to this his native State was adopted, and together with the General's reply, was entered upon the records. Several towns also sent their addresses, and a warm reception was given him at Providence a few weeks later.

While these events were taking place in Rhode Island, the closing scene of the Revolutionary war occurred at Annapolis, where Congress was then in session. Wash-
23. ington resigned his commission to the legislative body from whom he had received it, and took what he hoped

[1] In connection with this early copyright law of Rhode Island, it may be mentioned as an interesting fact, that the first known copyright granted under the United States law upon this subject was to a Rhode Islander, on the 9th of May, 1795. The book was entitled "*Christianity the True Theology*, an answer to *The Age of Reason*. By Wm. Patten. A. M., Minister of the Second Congregational Church in Newport." Printed at Warren, Rhode Island, by A. Phillips. Mr. Patten was ordained pastor of the church at Newport, 24th May, 1786, as successor to Rev. Ezra Stiles, D. D., who, although he had been President of Yale College since June 1778, had retained his pastorate at Newport, and preached occasionally until this time.

[2] 4th September, 1782.

and believed was a final "leave of all the employments of public life."

1784.

At the return of peace, all minds were occupied with the important questions relating to a reorganization of government. Parties began to be formed, and although no material differences of opinion were manifested in the elections for the next two years, yet the causes from which an entire change in State officers then occurred, were already in operation, and we may therefore date the formation of new political parties, and the revival of old ones existing prior to the Revolution, from this period. Of the two great parties that divided the country, one favored the confederation, and feared the establishment of a central government; it was the exclusive advocate of State sovereignty. The other felt the weakness of the articles of confederation, and desired a closer union of the States under a general head. The State Rights party were largely in the majority in Rhode Island. The mercantile classes favored the Union. The agricultural interests clung to the confederation. Thus the seaports were placed in opposition to the country towns, which then held the political control of the State. A revival of the former feud between town and country, existing previous to the war, was the result. Another element was added to embitter the hostility of the rival parties. A heavy debt rested upon the State, to pay which, taxation was the only resource. This debt was chiefly in the hands of the commercial class. The farmers owed the traders. Paper money was the ready and often tried expedient for paying an old debt, by contracting a new one. Hence the strife between paper and specie parties was now revived. Thus two of the old colonial questions were again brought out, to mingle with the new dispute that was to bring the State to the very verge of civil war. The ratification of the definitive treaty of peace by Congress was simultaneous with the gathering of these opposing forces for the conflict, that was to continue almost as long, and to become

Jan. 14.

CHAP. XXIII. scarcely less bitter, than that which was thus formally closed.

1784. A new weekly paper, called the United States' Cronicle, was commenced in Providence by Bennett Wheeler, in place of the American Journal, which had ceased to exist. It advocated the views of the federal party. The act for the gradual abolition of slavery, that had been
Feb. 23. framed at the previous session and presented to the people through the public press, was passed by the Assembly. All children born of slave mothers after the first of March, were to be free, the cost of their rearing was to be paid by the towns where they were born; and to defray these charges, the council might bind out to service the males, till the age of twenty-one, and the females till eighteen; their education was also provided for. The next year the clause requiring them to be reared at the expense of the towns was repealed, and that charge was laid upon the owner of the mother. In case of slaves, liberated by their owners, becoming a public charge, they were to be supported like other paupers, and not by their claimants, as was required by the old manumission act passed ten years before. This provision was afterwards limited to slaves who were under thirty years of age at the time of their emancipation. The clause in that act permitting slaves brought from the West Indies to be exported within one year was repealed, and the introduction of slaves for sale, upon any pretext whatever, was forbidden. The test oath prescribed early in the Revolution, was abolished, and a new oath or affirmation of allegiance to the State, to be administered upon the admission of freemen, was adopted. The standards of the Rhode Island line
28. were presented to the State by Lieut.-Col. Olney, and placed in custody of "the governor for the time being, to be by him carefully preserved, to perpetuate the noble exploits of that brave corps." The delegates in Congress were instructed to request that body to convene in Rhode
May 26. Island at their next session. Mr. Ellery accordingly

moved that Congress adjourn to meet at Newport in October, but after some debate, Trenton was substituted.

1784. Mar.

To obtain the cession of the great western domain from the States that claimed it, now occupied the attention of Congress. After long delay and many alterations in the scheme, as first proposed, the territory north-west of the Ohio River, ceded by Virginia, was accepted. As the other claimant States were expected soon to follow the example of Virginia, a committee, composed of Thomas Jefferson, Chase of Maryland, and Howell of Rhode Island, proposed "a plan for the temporary government of the western territory." This plan divided the territory into ten new States, and contained a provision excluding slavery from every portion thereof after the year 1800. The anti-slavery clause required the assent of nine States, failing in which it was struck out, and the report was then adopted. Howell moved for a committee to consider what measures could be taken by Congress to obtain further cessions of western lands, and what disposition could best be made of the country that it was expected would be obtained from the Indians by treaty; also for regulations for opening a land office. Five commissioners, of whom Gen. Greene was one, were appointed to conclude a treaty of peace with the Indians, and great reliance was placed upon Greene to obtain large cessions of territory, which was peculiarly important to the States, like Rhode Island, having defined boundaries and no claim to western lands.

A movement was made to establish a bank at Providence, upon the plan of that already in successful operation in Philadelphia, and a meeting for that purpose was 8.
called; but the project failed for the present, and was not consummated till after the lapse of seven years, when the Providence Bank, the oldest in the State, went into operation.

To supply the wants of the treasury, beyond what the States had furnished, Morris had drawn drafts on Holland,

CHAP. XXIII. 1784. a portion of which were paid from the proceeds of loans obtained in that country upon the credit of the confederation. But this resource soon failed, and many of the drafts were sent back protested. The amount necessary to be raised immediately, in order to preserve the public credit by taking up the protested drafts, was six hundred thirty-six thousand dollars. This sum was apportioned
April 1. among the States, and a circular was sent to each one, calling earnestly for its quota. That of Rhode Island was thirteen thousand seven hundred and three dollars. Seven
12. States had already complied with the terms of the new impost act, but in a manner so qualified, that it was thought that when the necessary number of nine States should agree to it, some of these would withdraw their assent. For these reasons, and from the evident necessity of some general rules for the conduct of foreign commerce,
21. Congress asked from the States a limited power to regulate trade with other countries for fifteen years, and commissioners were soon afterwards sent to Europe, to negotiate treaties on the basis of reciprocity.

May 5. At the general election, John Brown was chosen a delegate to Congress, in place of Jonathan Arnold, who had removed to Vermont. Henry Marchant resigned his seat in Congress, and no one was chosen to fill the vacancy, so that the delegation now consisted of Ellery, Howell, and Brown. All the other officers remained unchanged. Intendants of Trade were appointed for Bristol and East Greenwich, as well as for Newport and Providence. John Handy was chosen State Auditor, the first regular appointment of such an officer, whose duties had heretofore been performed by committees. The appointment was only temporary, the Assembly changing its Auditor at almost every session. The office of the General Treasurer was removed from Providence to Newport, where it had always been kept before the war. This called forth a strong protest from eighteen deputies of the northern towns. The most important act of the session was the incorporation of the City of Newport. The city was divided into four wards, and organized with a Mayor, four Aldermen, six Councilmen, and a Clerk. At the first meeting held under this charter, George Hazard was chosen Mayor of the city. The municipal government was fully organized at the next meeting, and went into immediate operation. CHAP. XXIII. 1784. June 1. 4.

The articles of confederation provided, that during the recess of Congress, government should be administered by a committee of one from each State. This committee met at Philadelphia, but soon broke up, leaving national affairs without a head. The sessions of Congress were afterwards continued through the year, although often impeded for want of a quorum. The General Assembly established the term of their delegates at one year from the first Monday of November succeeding their election, and required that the Secretary should furnish them with commissions, signed by the governor, under seal of the State. A tax of twenty thousand pounds was levied, a part to meet the requisition for the protested drafts, partly to redeem bills of credit funded upon real estate, and the remainder for current expenses. The State duty on foreign goods was raised from two to two and a half per cent. The impost act of five per cent. proposed by Con gress, was discussed, and after a long debate was rejected by a majority of forty in the House of Deputies. 28. July 1.

The British frigate Mercury arrived at Newport from Halifax, and while in the harbor, one of the crew, being an American seaman, was discharged upon demand of the mayor of the city. It would seem that the arrogant claims of a later day, which produced the second war with Great Britain, were not then enforced. 19.

At the adjourned session, upon petition of the Sabbatarians, they were allowed to pursue their usual avocations on Sunday, so conducting themselves as not to interfere with the devotions of their neighbors on that day, and not opening their stores, or following mechanical, or other Aug. 23.

CHAP. XXIII. 1784. noisy business, in compact places, to the disturbance of others. The value of gold coin in common circulation, was fixed by statute, and the size of casks and modes of packing meats and fish were regulated.

Sept. 1. The usual commencement exercises at college were omitted this year, as none of the under-graduates had completed their course of study, owing to the interruptions of the war. The most interesting movement in the cause of education that occurred at this time, was the establishment of the Friends' school at Portsmouth, under the auspices of the "New England Yearly Meeting." Isaac Lawton was the Principal. It was discontinued after four years' trial, for want of support, but was revived in 1814, through the munificence of wealthy members of the Society, and established on a permanent basis in Providence, where it remains a flourishing institution to this day.

22. A French squadron of seven ships from the West
Indies touched at Newport, and received a cordial wel-
Oct. 4. come. A grand ball was given to the officers. General
23. Lafayette also visited Providence. The bells were rung,
and national salutes fired in honor of his arrival. The
24. next day he went to Newport as the guest of Gen. Greene,
and upon his return was present in the evening at a meet-
25. ing of the Cincinnati, where Gen. Varnum, in behalf of
the officers of the Rhode Island line, made him an address.
26. On the following day a public dinner was given him, and
an address from the Assembly, then in session, was presented, in reply to which he thanked the State for the particular favors which the French army had always received here. At the conclusion of these ceremonies, another national salute was fired, and the general left for Boston. The State address and reply were entered upon the records.[1]

[1] Among the minor matters of local interest at this time, may be mentioned the placing a spectators' gallery around the deputies' room in the State House at Newport, and enclosing the Court House parade in Providence

CHAP. XXIII.

1784.

For some years past, twenty-one deputies, and five assistants had made a quorum of the General Assembly. This act was now repealed, and a majority of the lower house, which was composed of seventy deputies, and seven members of the council, was required in order to transact business. The Church at Bristol was incorporated by the name of the Catholic Congregational Society. Cannons were mounted, and ordnance stores provided for the fort on Goat Island, which had been dismantled. It was named Fort Washington, after bearing the names of the successive sovereigns of England since the reign of Anne. Deputy-Governor Bowen renewed the debate upon the United States impost scheme, by submitting a bill drafted in conformity with that act, which was read, but no action taken upon it.[1]

Nov. 1. Dec. 23. 1785. Jan. 11.

After a recess of five months, Congress resumed its session at Trenton. Ellery and Howell were the delegates from this State. In less than two months it adjourned to meet at New York, where all the subsequent sessions were held. But little of interest, either State or national, occurred during the year. The elements of strife, slowly gathering strength in the past year, were first manifested at the opening of the Assembly, in a petition, numerously signed from many towns, praying that a new bank of paper money might be made. A large majority deeming the measure to be injurious, rejected the petition. This was the signal for organizing the opposition to bear upon the election, but another year elapsed before their efforts were successful. In addition to the duty of two and a

Feb. 28.

" with posts and rails, so as to prevent teams from passing thereon," both of which were ordered at the August session, and the arrival from London on 4th October, of " a large and elegant clock, also a bell weighing 25 cwt.," for the First Baptist Church in Providence. The duties upon these latter articles, and also upon some books and apparatus imported for Providence and Dartmouth Colleges, were remitted by order of the Assembly at this, the October session. This bell proving defective, was recast at the Hope Furnace, and was hung October 20, 1787. Its new weight was 2387 lbs.

[1] The bill is in letters 1783–5, No. 47.

CHAP. XXIII. 1785. half per cent. on foreign goods, an impost duty of five per cent., ad valorem, and an annual impost of one silver dollar on every one hundred acres of land, on every male poll of twenty-one years of age, and on horses, was laid. This act was to be in force twenty-five years, and from the revenue thus derived, eight thousand dollars were subjected to the order of Congress for payment of interest on this State's proportion of the foreign debt. The remainder was appropriated for paying the interest of the domestic debt of the United States due within this State. But the law was not to take effect till the other States had adopted similar imposts, and upon the same terms another act was passed, impowering Congress to regulate the foreign trade of the United States, to which was added, in October, the power to regulate domestic trade. The United Congregational Society in Tiverton was incorporated, and at the May session the Amicable Congregational Church, in the same town, was also chartered. Provision was made for the support of soldiers in the black regiment, who might become dependent upon charity.

Mar. 16. In Congress, John Brown was appointed one of the commissioners for erecting the federal buildings, which it was then proposed to locate on the banks of the Delaware.
18. Congress limited the time for bringing in claims against the United States. A circular to this effect, sent to all the States, was printed, and distributed among the people. Information was received that both Georgia and New York had refused to enact impost bills, so that the act of Rhode Island on this subject became void; and indeed it was not till the first session of Congress under the consti-
May 2. tution, that the measure became general. In consequence of the failure of this law, the Assembly added to the two and a half per cent. impost act, a duty of seven and a half per cent. upon all foreign goods imported in British vessels. This was to meet the interest on the State debt. The changes made at the spring election affected only the

delegates in Congress. Brown was returned, but Marchant, Ellery, and Howell, gave place to George Champlin, Paul Mumford, who for some time had been chief-justice of the State, and was now succeeded by Ellery, and Peter Phillips, also a judge of the Superior Court. Theodore Foster was made judge of the Court of Admiralty. The statute of limitations, which had been repealed at the commencement of the Revolution, was now revived. CHAP. XXIII. 1785. May

A dispute arose at this time with regard to the fishery in Pawcatuck River. Violence was resorted to by the contending parties, and a Connecticut captain was chased into Stonington by a party of Rhode Island fishermen, and mobbed. Complaints were made to the authorities of Connecticut, and the legislature of that State appointed a committee of three to meet at Stonington, in September, with a committee from Rhode Island, to adjust the difficulty. Gov. Griswold informed Gov. Greene of this affair, and requested corresponding action on the part of Rhode Island.[1] The Assembly accordingly appointed a committee of three to meet with those of Connecticut, to quiet the disturbance and regulate the fishery. An additional tariff act was passed, levying specific duties upon all kinds of tools, and an ad valorem duty of from five to twenty per cent. upon hats, articles of leather, furs, paper, and many other matters, expressly "for encouraging the manufacture thereof within this State and the United States." While the previous impost acts, to which this was not an amendment but an addition, were designed for revenue, this was avowedly a measure of protection as declared in the title. 12. June 25. 27.

Massachusetts now made a movement which resulted in the formation of the Constitution of the United States, by proposing that Congress should call a convention of July 1.

[1] Gov. Matthew Griswold to Gov. William Greene, 25 June, 1785. Letters 1783–5, No. 67.

CHAP. XXIII. the States to revise the scheme of confederation, so that greater powers might be given to the national legislature.

1785. July 13. The death of the venerable patriot, Stephen Hopkins, in the seventy-ninth year of his age, took place at Providence. For nearly the whole period of his manhood, he had been engaged in public life. Chosen town clerk of Scituate, his native town, in 1731, for nearly forty-five years he was engaged in some kind of official duty connected with the town, the legislature, the judicial, or the executive departments of the State, or the national Congress. During the second Spanish war, we have seen[1] that he was appointed with William Ellery, to consult with commissioners from other colonies upon the defence of the country, and before the "old French war" had commenced, he was chosen governor of the colony. No man in the eighteenth century filled so large a space in the history of this State, and very few, of any State, exerted so wide an influence upon the destinies of the country. Franklin was perhaps the only person who equalled him in this respect. He was probably the first man in America, certainly the first in high official position, to deny the right of the British Parliament to control the colonies. Long before the voice of James Otis roused the men of Massachusetts to the assertion of their rights, or the eloquence of Patrick Henry thrilled the Virginia burgesses with the utterance of prospective treason; more than twenty years before he and his life-long colleague affixed their names, in behalf of Rhode Island, to the Declaration of Independence; Stephen Hopkins, then uniting in himself the offices of governor and chief-justice of the colony, made use of this remarkable expression: "What have the King and Parliament to do with making a law or laws to govern us by, any more than the Mohawks have? And if the Mohawks should make a law or laws to govern us, we are as much obliged to obey

[1] Ante chap. xvi., p. 152.

them as any law or laws the King and Parliament could CHAP.
make;" and "That as our forefathers came from Leyden, XXIII.
and were no charge to England, the States of Holland 1785.
had as good a right to claim us as England had."[1] These
sentiments were a direct corollary from the spirit of the
free charter of Rhode Island, and were sustained by their
author, in all his public and private acts, to the close of his
eventful life.

The Assembly incorporated the Benevolent Baptist Aug.
Society of Warren, and laid a tax of twenty thousand 22.
pounds to be collected before the close of the year. The Sept.
Pawcatuck River committees met at Stonington upon the 14.
appointed day, and having collected evidence and exam- 15.
ined the premises, agreed upon a mode of settlement that 16.
should prevent a recurrence of the disorders, which had
arisen chiefly from a contested right to a weir across the
river owned by parties in both States. They agreed that
all suits arising out of the affair should be withdrawn,
and acts of amnesty passed in favor of all concerned, and
prepared a bill regulating the mode of conducting the
fishery, to be passed by both legislatures, and held as a
compact between them, which was enacted at their succeeding sessions.

Congress made a requisition for three millions of dol- 27.
lars to meet the interest of the present year upon the national debt. The proportion for Rhode Island to pay,
was $64,636. The balances due from this State to the
general government upon the several requisitions of the
past few years, including this last, as presented in the Oct. 1.
treasurer's account, amounted to $126,067, of which about
$56,000 was to be paid in specie, and the balance in loan
office certificates and other paper.

[1] These expressions are contained in the deposition of Job Almy, of Tiverton, in the famous libel suit of Hopkins *vs.* Ward, tried in Worcester county, Mass., June, 1757, and were uttered in conversation with Almy upon a case in which he was plaintiff, and recovered, before the Superior Court at Newport in March, 1756. A report of the libel suit is given in the Monthly Law Reporter for October, 1859, Vol. 22, pp. 327–39. On page 338, Almy's deposition is cited in full.

CHAP. XXIII. 1785. Oct. 14. News that Algiers had declared war against the United States was communicated by John Jay, minister of foreign affairs, to the several States. The intelligence had reached France in July, and been sent by Paul Jones to warn American commerce in the Mediterranean. Although no formal declaration of war had been proclaimed, seizures of American vessels were made by that piratical power, and in the month of August several were taken, the news of which had not yet reached America. The object was plunder, and to place the United States under contribution to Algiers, as the maritime States in that vicinity had already permitted themselves to be abused in this way.

The State of Georgia having presented to Gen. Greene a valuable estate, in token of his eminent services, he left Newport, where he had resided since the peace, and sailed for Savannah with his family. The Treasury Board ap-
29. pointed Joseph Clarke, the State Treasurer, to be commissioner of the Loan office for Rhode Island; he declined, or was soon succeeded by chief-justice Ellery. At the October session, the Assembly incorporated the Benefi-
31. cent Congregational Society of Providence, being the fourth Church charter granted this year, and the thirteenth of the kind in the history of the State. The whole of the recent tax was appropriated to the use of the general government, and ordered to be paid into the Loan office, two-thirds of it in interest certificates, and the remainder in specie and certificates for teaming services during the war. An act to regulate trade was passed, prohibiting all commerce in British vessels, except those built in this State on English account, which might take their first outward cargoes upon the same terms as American ships. The operation of this act was suspended at the next session until Connecticut should pass a similar law. Since the close of the war, Congress had failed to appoint the annual thanksgiving, and the observance of it, although
Dec. 1. continued in the adjoining States, was suspended in

Rhode Island until this year, when the custom was revived, and the day observed by appointment of the Assembly.

The deplorable condition of trade, both foreign and domestic, indicated the necessity of some action on the part of the States to adopt "a uniform system in their commercial regulations." For this purpose Virginia, which had been the first to move in so many important matters, called for a convention of the States to meet at Annapolis in September, appointed commissoners on her part to attend it, and requested Rhode Island and the other States to do the same. The baleful influence of paper money issues was soon to crush the prosperity of this State, but slowly recovering, at best, from the exhaustion of the war. Foreseeing the repetition of the petitions for a paper bank, the people of Providence prepared a memorial to the Assembly in opposition to the movement. A paper currency that should remain at par would be a poor substitute for specie, and could effect no good, while one that should depreciate was abhorrent to justice, as it would furnish the means of nominally paying a large debt with a really small value. This argument was fully presented in the remonstrance, which was signed by about three hundred persons.[1] The Assembly rejected the petition for a bank by a vote of nearly two to one. The State being without a representation in Congress, Rev. James Manning, and Gen. Nathan Miller were appointed delegates. A petition from the inhabitants of Potowomut to be annexed to East Greenwich was laid over, with an order of notice to the town of Warwick, to appear at the next session in answer thereto. Col. Olney reported a list of all the officers in the Rhode Island line, thirteen in number, killed during the war, and of the invalids entitled to pensions under a late act of Congress. The impost act, for the benefit of the United

Jan. 21.

Feb. 19.

27.

[1] This remonstrance is given in full in Staples' Annals of Providence, pp. 297–303.

CHAP. XXIII. States, passed the preceding February, was repealed, and
a new one enacted, placing specific duties upon certain
1786. groceries, and a five per cent. ad valorem duty on all other goods. The collectors were to be appointed by the Assembly and made accountable to Congress. The act, like the former one, was to be in force for twenty-five years, but not to take effect till the other States had passed similar laws. The act intended to give Congress power to regulate foreign trade, not being in conformity with
March 3. their views, a resolution upon this subject passed that
body, and the legislature was "earnestly solicited to re-
4. consider their act," in a letter from the secretary enclosing
the resolve. In consequence of this, at an adjourned ses-
13. sion a new act was passed, impowering Congress to prohibit trade in this State with the vessels of nations having no treaties with the United States, and to forbid such nations to import goods not of their own production, and also to regulate trade between the States. To encourage home manufactures, a bounty of a penny a pound upon hemp and flax, and of a shilling a head for all sheep raised in the State, was offered. To relieve the distress, which was now so great that farms sold at a quarter of their value, a law, known as the Tender Act, was passed to enable the transfer of real estate, and certain personal effects, at an appraised value, in settlement of debts, the property to be redeemable on payment of the money and interest within one year. An excise act was adopted to secure a fund "for the payment of the public debts" and current expenses of government. This law placed an excise upon spirits, sugar, tea, &c., and a tax on carriages, dogs, horses, and billiard tables.

The Rt. Rev. Samuel Seabury, bishop of Connecticut,
the first American prelate who had received Episcopal
15. ordination in England, officiated for the first time in this
State, at Trinity Church in Newport, in the ceremony of
admitting a candidate, John Basset, a young Scotchman,
19. to the priesthood. On the following Sunday he preached

in Providence, where, on his return from a visit to Boston, he administered the rite of confirmation to seventy persons at St. John's Church. 1786. April 3.

There was great difficulty in obtaining a full representation of the States in Congress. Six months of the session had already passed, and but seven States were present. Rhode Island had sent no delegates, until now that Manning took his seat, but without his colleague, so May 2. that the State could as yet have no vote, and more than two months were still to elapse before the presence of Miller removed the disability. In the absence of Dr. Manning, Perez Fobes officiated as president of the College.

The rising party, which for two years had been gathering strength, prevailed at almost every point in the spring elections. A new system was about to be inaugurated, more destructive in its effect upon the peace and prosperity of the State than any which had yet been attempted, and whose baleful influence was to extend far beyond the period when its name and objects passed away.

CHAPTER XXIV.

1786—1790.

FROM THE ACCESSION OF THE PAPER MONEY PARTY, MAY 3D, 1786, TO THE ADOPTION OF THE CONSTITUTION OF THE UNITED STATES, MAY 29TH, 1790.

CHAP. XXIV. 1786. May 3. THE triumph of the paper money party at the general election was complete. One half of the assistants and thirty-eight out of the seventy deputies were changed. John Collins was chosen governor, and Daniel Owen deputy-governor, over Greene and Bowen, and held their offices for four years. Gen. Varnum, Gen. Miller, George Champlin, and Peleg Arnold were elected delegates to Congress. The collection of the last tax, and the recent excise act, were suspended for the present, and after a warm debate a paper money bank of one hundred thousand pounds was made. The sum of a hundred and sixty thousand was first proposed, but this was amended in the upper house. Newport, Westerly, Bristol, and Providence stoutly opposed the scheme, but in vain, and the deputies from the latter town entered their protest against the act. The bills were to be loaned to the people according to the apportionment of the last tax, upon a pledge of real estate of double their value, and to be paid into the treasury at the end of fourteen years. The Assembly ad-
6. journed on the fourth day of the session, having accomplished the worst business that for many years had stained the records of the State.

Caleb Harris, who had been appointed by Congress as surveyor of the western territory on the part of Rhode Island, having resigned, that body elected Ebenezer Sproat to fill the vacancy. 1786. May 22.

Gen. Nathaniel Greene died at his estate in Georgia, from inflammation of the brain, caused by exposure to the sun. He was interred in Savannah with every mark of respect. Thus at the early age of forty-four years, this gallant soldier, the saviour of the South, whose fame stands second only to that of Washington, in all the qualities that form a general or a statesman, passed away. America has known but one patriot more renowned. Rhode Island owns no greater name. June 19. 20.

The depreciation of the new paper bills commenced with their issue. To sustain them if possible, the Assembly, by a kind of forcing act, subjected any person who should refuse to receive the bills on the same terms as specie, or in any way discourage their circulation, to a penalty of one hundred pounds, and the loss of the rights of a freeman. The Tender Act was repealed. The former tax, which had been suspended, was ordered to be collected, and another tax of the same amount was laid, payable in the new bills. Jabez Bowen and Samuel Ward were appointed to attend the commercial convention proposed by Virginia. 26.

The result of the forcing act was a complete stagnation of business. Merchants discontinued their dealings, and traders closed their shops. The farmers, who had pledged their lands for the paper bills, to retaliate upon the traders, refused to bring their produce to market. The distress occasioned by their withholding the necessaries of life was so great, that a town meeting was held in Providence, to devise means of obtaining supplies. It was recommended that no farmer be molested in bringing his produce to market and selling it upon such terms as might be agreed on between buyer and seller, that the shops be opened to supply any such persons, and that the imme- July 24.

CHAP. XXIV. 1786. July diate relief of those in want of bread, five hundred dollars should be borrowed and sent abroad to buy corn, to be sold or substituted by the town council. A riot took place at Newport, where a mob attempted to force the grain dealers to sell their corn for paper money. At
31. South Kingstown a meeting was held, to advise non-intercourse with the merchants and traders, and to call a State convention to further this design.

Aug. 2. The requisition of Congress to meet the obligations of the current year, amounted to $3,777,000, of which the Rhode Island quota was $81,377. Of this sum $46,764 was to be paid in specie, and the balance in "indents," or loan office certificates of overdue interest on the domestic debt of the general government. The coinage of
8. the United States was regulated by the adoption of the decimal system, but the mint was not established till two months later; nor was it put in operation till the following year, and then nothing was coined but a few tons of cents.[1] On the same day Congress voted a monument, with a suitable inscription, to the memory of Major-General Greene, to be erected at the seat of the Federal Government. This, like most of the resolves of that body, was never carried into effect, and the only monument to the great chieftain that now exists, is the one erected by the gratitude of the State of Georgia in the city of Savannah.

In consequence of the meeting at Providence, a con-
10. vention of the country towns of the county was held at Scituate to devise measures for enforcing the recent bank act. They adjourned to meet with the State convention
22. in East Greenwich, at which sixteen towns were represent-

[1] The die for the first United States' cent was established by Congress July 6, 1787. The earliest federal coinage were the cents of that year, having on one side 13 circles linked together, a small circle in the middle with "United States" around it, "we are one" in the centre: on the reverse, a dial and sun, the date, 1787, and "Fugio," with the words, "mind your business" below the dial.

1786. Aug. 22.

ed. This convention voted "to support the acts of the General Assembly," and adopted a report, recommending that body to enforce the penal laws in favor of paper money, with further amendments if such were needed, and advising the farmers to withhold their produce from the opponents of the bank. Providence was represented by five of its strongest men,[1] who, with two or three others, attempted in vain to rescue the credit of the State by offering conciliatory propositions; but no compromise would be entertained by the excited and triumphant partisans of a worthless currency. The proceedings were sent immediately to the General Assembly, specially convened on the same day at Newport for the purpose of passing an additional forcing act in favor of the paper money. This act suspended the usual forms of justice in regard to offenders against the bank law, by requiring an immediate trial, within three days after complaint entered, without a jury, and before a court of which three judges should form a quorum, whose decision should be final, and whose judgment should be instantly complied with on penalty of imprisonment. The complaint must be made within ten days after the offence was committed, and the act was to be in force until all complaints that should be made within ten days after the rising of the Assembly had been tried. The fine for the first offence was fixed at from six to thirty pounds, in the discretion of the court, and for the second from ten to fifty pounds. This monstrous act of injustice was carried through the legislature by a large majority, and the solemn protest against it as a violation of every principle of moral and civil right, of the charter, of the articles of confederation, of treaty obligations, and of every idea of honor or honesty entertained among men, that was presented by the deputies from Providence, Newport, New Shoreham, Bristol, and Warren was rejected, and not allowed to appear upon

[1] David Howell, Welcome Arnold, William Rhodes, Jabez Bowen and Joseph Nightingale.

CHAP. XXIV. the records. As if to add one more proof of folly and of
partisan infatuation to this reckless legislation, it was re-
1786. solved that the arrears of continental taxes might be paid
in the new paper currency. The popular passion which
in Massachusetts had already begun to be displayed in
armed resistance to the process of law, in Rhode Island
assumed the forms of law to do equal violence to private
rights. A convention of all the towns in Providence coun-
Sept. 13. ty met at Smithfield to consult upon further measures of
hostility towards the merchants, whom they accused of
exporting specie, and thus causing the distresses of the
State. A plan of "State Trade" was proposed, to be
submitted to the General Assembly, and the governor was
requested to call a special session for the purpose. The
plan was for the State to provide vessels and import goods
on its own account, under direction of a committee of the
legislature; that produce, lumber, and labor, as well as
money, should be received in payment of taxes, and thus
furnish the cargoes in return for which specie and goods
could be obtained. Interest certificates were no longer to
be received in payment of duties, but the private importers were to be compelled to pay them in money. The
act making notes of hand negotiable was to be repealed,
and the statute of limitations shortened to two years.
Such were some of the recommendations of the Smithfield
convention. It is needless to say that Gov. Collins did
not call a special session to consider this absurd and agra-
rian scheme.

While the impracticable idea of a State trade was
being discussed in the interior of Providence county, the
11. national trade convention assembled at Annapolis. Nine
States had appointed delegates to this meeting, but those
from five only were in attendance. Jabez Bowen was on
his way, but did not arrive in time to represent Rhode
Island. The delegates took no definite action, but made
14. a report advising a general convention to be held at Philadelphia in May, to discuss a plan for enlarging the powers

of Congress as well as for regulating the commerce of the country.

The forcing acts speedily provoked litigation to test their validity and constitutionality. John Trevett, of Newport, entered a complaint before Paul Mumford, chief-justice of the Superior Court, against John Weeden, a butcher, of the same place, for refusing to receive paper money at par in payment for meat. The excitement throughout the State was intense, and a great concourse of spectators were present at the trial, which took place before a full bench. Gen. Varnum and Henry Marchant appeared for the defendant. Varnum opened the pleadings. In a long and very able argument, of nearly three hours, he showed the unconstitutional character of the bill, and the dangerous precedent sought to be established thereby. Henry Goodwin, who, the next year, succeeded William Channing as attorney-general, was counsel for the complainant. He argued in favor of the acts, and contended that no bill of rights existed in this State which they could violate. Marchant closed the case with a brief tribute to the exhaustive eloquence of his colleague, affirming that he could add no more to what had already been said. Two of the judges also spoke against the acts; the other three were of the same mind; and when the next morning Judge Howell delivered the opinion of the court, declaring the acts to be unconstitutional and void, and dismissing the complaint against Weeden as a matter not within their jurisdiction, one universal shout of approbation rang through the crowded court-house.

1786. Sept. 18. 25. 26.

Just at this time Manning and Miller wrote from New York, where a paper bank had also been made, that Congress would not receive any State bills in payment of their requisitions, and that the acts of Rhode Island in this respect had brought great discredit upon the State. The discontent in Massachusetts extended to New Hampshire, where an armed mob at Exeter demanded from the

28.

CHAP. XXIV. 1786. legislature a remission of taxes, and also what was virtually the same thing, an immediate issue of paper money.

But the Assembly of Rhode Island, whose political omnipotence was no idle boast, as we have occasionally seen in these pages, when private persons had given them offence, could not brook this interference of the highest judicial tribunal with what they deemed their vested prerogative of control over all the interests and concerns of

Oct. 2. the State. A special session was immediately convened at Newport. Their first business was to summon the judges before them "to assign the reasons and grounds" of the late decision.[1] Three of the judges obeyed the summons, but the other two being detained by sickness, the hearing was postponed till the next session. Another act "to stimulate and give efficacy to the paper bills," and known as the Test Act, was prepared and sent to every town to obtain the sense of the people thereupon, before making it a law. This indicated a little caution, learned from the decision of the court; although the new bill was so full of disgraceful reflections upon the opponents of paper money, and the oath prescribed therein as a test of party allegiance, was so stringent that but three towns, one in Washington and two in Providence counties, were found so benighted as to give it their assent. An

[1] No language can convey so correct an idea of the arrogance of this summons as the resolution itself. It reads thus: "Whereas it appears that the Honorable, the Justices of the Superior Court of Judicature, Court of Assize, &c., at the last September term of the said Court, in the county of Newport, have by a judgment of the said Court, declared and adjudged an Act of the Supreme Legislature of this State to be unconstitutional, and so absolutely void. And whereas it is suggested that the aforesaid judgment is unprecedented in this State, and may tend to abolish the Legislative Authority thereof, it is therefore voted and resolved, That all the Justices of the said Court be forthwith cited by the Sheriffs of the respective counties in which they live, or may be found, to give their immediate attendance on this Assembly, to assign the reasons and grounds of the aforesaid judgment; and that the clerk of the said Court be directed to attend this Assembly at the same time, with the Records of the said Court which relate to the said judgment."

effort at conciliation was made in the lower house by the CHAP.
appointment of a "committee of ways and means to give XXIV.
credit to the paper money," in which the opposition were 1786.
fairly represented; but their report was rejected, and the Oct. 7.
Assembly adjourned.

Meetings were held in all the towns to discuss the "Test Act," which was only another forcing act in a most odious form, subjecting private property to the will of the Assembly, and punishing with disfranchisement whoever should refuse to take the oath to receive the
paper bills at the same rate as silver or gold. In Provi- 17.
dence a committee, appointed to draft instructions for 18.
their deputies, reported the next day, showing at great length wherein the proposed measure was unlawful, unjust, and impolitic.[1] The citizens of Bristol also instructed 21.
their deputies to oppose it. Newport did the same, and so in fact did nearly every town in the State.

To garrison the frontier posts, a standing force of seven hundred men had been kept up since the peace. The Indians on the north-western border were at war, and
Congress voted to add thirteen hundred and forty men to 20.
the army, of whom Rhode Island was to furnish one hundred and twenty. The expense of this force, estimated at
$530,000, was apportioned among the States. The amount 21.
to be raised by this State was $11,390. The Assembly Nov.
enlisted the men to serve for three years.[2] Every town in 1.
the State, except North Kingstown, Scituate, and Foster, having rejected the test act, it was voted down by the lower house almost unanimously. The session lasted but one week, only four days of which were occupied with business, a storm having delayed the arrival of a quorum until the third day. The same reason probably prevented the attendance of Judge Gilbert Devol, and the chief-jus-

[1] See Staples' Annals, pp. 306–311.

[2] The officers of this corps were Major William Allen, Capts. John Holden, David Sayles, Lieuts. Henry Sherman, Benjamin Sherburne, Ensign George Tillinghast.

CHAP. XXIV. 1786. Nov. tice, whose illness at the previous session had caused the postponement of the inquiry into the conduct of the court. The other three judges answered the summons. Their examination was the chief business of the session. Judge Howell defended the opinion of the Bench in an able argument upon the unconstitutionality of the bill, and asserted the independence of the court; contending that the Supreme Judiciary of the State were not accountable to the General Assembly or to any other power on earth, for their judgments. His associates, Joseph Hazard and Thomas Tillinghast, concurred in these views. The Assembly "Resolved, that no satisfactory reasons had been rendered by them for their judgment," but as there was
4. no ground for impeachment, discharged them from further attendance on this business.

Although the scarcity of money was so great that land rents were paid in corn, and barter became almost the only mode of trade, industrial pursuits were not neglected, and domestic manufactures were encouraged by acts of legislation. The infancy of American cotton spinning, dates from this period. Attempts at producing
16. machinery suitable for the purpose were aided by the legislature of Massachusetts. A company was soon formed in Providence to prosecute the business.[1] The first spinning jenny constructed in the United States, was made by them. It had twenty-eight spindles, made by Daniel Jackson, an ingenious coppersmith in Providence. A carder, and spinning frame were also procured, and the machinery was set to work, the following year, in the chamber of the market-house, upon the manufacture of jeans, a fabric having linen warp and cotton filling.[2]

[1] Daniel Anthony, Andrew Dexter and Lewis Peck, were the copartners in this first enterprise in that department to which the State now owes so much of its prosperity and importance.

[2] A more detailed account of the origin and rise of the manufacturing interest in Rhode Island than the limits of this work will permit, is contained in a series of "Letters from the Pawtuxet," recently published in the Providence Journal, from the pen of Mr. Henry Rousemaniere, of Warwick, which deserves to be embodied in a more permanent form.

No thanksgiving was appointed in Rhode Island this year, but the people of Bristol kept the festival on the day observed in Massachusetts. The insurrection led by Daniel Shays, had now reached an alarming height. He occupied Worcester with more than a thousand men, preventing the sitting of the court in that town, and also at Springfield. Gov. Bowdoin called out four thousand militia under Gen. Lincoln to suppress the revolt. The difficulties continued through the winter, and many border towns of the adjoining States sympathized with the insurgents in their hostility to courts of law. CHAP. XXIV. 1786. Dec. 5.

The Assembly adopted some of the recommendations of the Smithfield convention, by shortening the statute of limitations to two years, and requiring actions on notes of hand to be brought in the name of the original promisee. They also re-enacted the excise law, and raised the import duty to five per cent. The petition of Deputy-Governor Owen and others, praying for "the exclusive privilege of a coinage for this State, for the period of twelve years," was granted. The forcing acts, pronounced void by the court, were formally repealed, and the penalty of death was denounced against counterfeiters of the paper money. Gen. Varnum and Peleg Arnold were requested to take their seats as delegates in Congress. The treasurer was ordered to pay off one-fourth part of the State debt, certain described paper, called four per cent. notes, excepted, in the bills received for taxes, and to endorse the payment on the notes. 25. to 1787. Jan. 6.

This act was nothing less than a fraud upon the creditors of the State. However honest the original intentions of the paper money party may have been—and that many of its supporters really imagined that this currency would relieve the public burdens for a time, until returning prosperity should enable the State and the people fully to discharge their contracts, there can be no doubt—this, and subsequent acts of a like nature on the part of the Assembly, and the advantage that was taken by individuals to

CHAP. XXIV. effect a nominal payment of debts with these greatly depreciated bills, indicate too clearly the ultimate design
1787. Jan. entertained by the dominant party. The paper had already depreciated to six paper dollars for one of silver. The newspapers were filled by the Judges of Common Pleas with notices of deposits of lawful money bills made with them by certain persons, who had "in all respects complied with the law respecting the paper currency," for the full payment of their debts. The madness of party spirit displayed upon this question was equalled only by that which, a few months later, upon a still more important matter, brought the State to the very verge of civil war. The insurrection of Shays was at this moment proving that "no desperately indebted people can long endure a regular, sober government," and we can scarcely be surprised at the sympathy with this reckless outlaw, which we shall soon see was manifested by the Assembly.

Owing to the depreciation of the bills, the town of Cranston, finding it impossible to support their poor according to the laws of the State, directed their auditors
20. to settle the accounts "upon principles of equity, having due regard to the value of paper money at the time when such accounts are exhibited," and drew up a petition to the Assembly against the "bank" laws.

Feb. A new question was about to arise yet more difficult in its solution, and more important in its results. Con-
21. gress passed a resolution approving of the convention that was to meet at Philadelphia in May, to revise the constitution, and recommending the States to appoint delegates to attend it. Henceforth these two elements of strife were so completely mingled, that it is often difficult to distinguish between them, and the more so as the prominent men of the paper money party, and the States' Rights party were nearly the same, while their opponents in the hard money party were mostly those who favored the constitution, and who were known somewhat later as the Federal party. Yet the principles involved in the

two questions were entirely distinct. There was no necessary connection between repudiation and State Rights, or between a specie basis for contracts and a Federal constitution. 1787. One set of these opposing principles was local, or State, the other national in its application; but for the present, the struggle was mainly between the two money parties. A new journal, called the Newport Mar. 1. Herald, was established in Newport by Peter Edes, to oppose the measures of the paper money party. The March term of the Superior Court was adjourned for 7. three weeks by the chief justice. The reason assigned, was the embarrassment in the administration of justice, on account of the continued depreciation of the paper currency, and that the Assembly might have an opportunity of remedying the evil.

The proceedings of this Assembly were remarkable. 12. Jacob Richardson, postmaster of Newport, was summoned before them on account of an alleged insult to Gov. Collins in taking from him two official letters, and refusing to deliver them without first having the postage paid. Richardson was dismissed upon agreeing to sign a paper, asking pardon of the governor and the Assembly for his conduct. The repeal of the city charter of Newport, was another act of despotic authority. A petition for this purpose had been presented in October, signed by one hundred and four persons, representing only about one-seventeenth part of the city tax, and was opposed by the remonstrance of more than four hundred citizens of that place. The lower house had passed a resolution, granting the petition, but the upper house or Senate referred the subject to the present session, when a hearing was had before them, the resolution of the deputies was concurred in, and the charter of Newport taken away. It is said that the real cause of the repeal was a controversy between the city and Nicholas Easton, with respect to the right of taking gravel from Easton's beach. Referees of high character in Connecticut, had decided in favor of the city,

CHAP. XXIV. 1787. March

and Mr. Easton, whose influence with the Assembly was very great, adopted this mode of expressing his dissatisfaction.[1] Yet more singular was the course adopted in regard to official communications, from Congress and the State of Massachusetts, that were submitted by the governor. The former letter, with two others from Virginia and North Carolina, presented at the same time, related to the constitutional convention soon to be held in Philadelphia. It was moved to appoint delegates to that convention. In the debate that ensued, the majority expressed a great regard for the articles of confederation, and declared their unwillingness to interfere with the present system. The motion was defeated by a majority of twenty-three votes. To test the sincerity of this profession, one of the minority then moved the passage of an act to assess this State's proportion of the continental tax as required by Congress under the said articles; but the act was not adopted, and the subject of the requisition was postponed. The Massachusetts letter contained a request for assistance in arresting the leaders of the late insurrection, some of whom had fled to Rhode Island. A motion that the governor issue his proclamation for their apprehension, was lost by a majority of twenty-two. The sympathies of the dominant party were made apparent by these votes.

But a greater act of wrong and injustice was yet to be performed. A committee appointed in October to inquire into the origin and condition of the State debt, and the remedies to be applied thereto, made a report that there was due in notes of the treasurer, bearing six per cent. interest, the sum of £106,976 12*s.* 3*d.*, and in notes at four per cent. interest, £46,071 4*s.* 6*d.*, making £153,047 15*s* 9*d.*;[2] that the six per cent. notes were given for money loaned, for soldiers' wages and depreciation of wages, and for debts due from the confiscated estates; but

[1] Bull's Memoirs of Rhode Island.

[2] Equal to $510,159,30.

that some of these notes were also given for continental CHAP.
money, which was paid out of the treasury to individuals, XXIV.
on whose hands it had greatly depreciated, and for this 1787.
reason all of the six per cent. notes should in equity be Mar.
subject to a deduction. To this it was replied, that the State had received specie from many of the holders, and that as the notes had been consolidated, the whole of them expressed the real value of what had been received by the public. This was admitted, and no deduction was made from the principal sum. The committee further reported that the four per cent. notes were issued in payment of debts due from government in 1777, and passed as money, and in this state suffered depreciation. They recommended that the scale be applied to them, and they be redeemed at the rate of forty dollars of the notes for
one dollar of paper money. A bill for this purpose passed 16.
the House, but was lost in the Senate. A resolution was
then adopted to ascertain the value that was given for 17.
them by the present holders, to form the basis of a settlement, and the whole report, thus amended, was referred to the next session, with an order that a copy of it should be sent to every town, that the deputies might be instructed by their constituents on the subject. The report being thus disposed of, an amendment of the act of December was passed, having in view what was a virtual repudiation of nearly the whole debt. The four per cent. notes, which had before been excepted, were now included in an act for paying off in paper money, one-fourth part of the State debt. All holders of State securities were required to present them to the treasurer within six weeks, and receive five shillings in the pound thereupon, or to forfeit that amount, and interest was to cease immediately upon the rising of the Assembly. The paper was now passing at the rate of six dollars for one of silver. To meet in some measure the difficulties that had caused the Superior Court to adjourn, a bill was proposed by the minority, making it legal tender at the rate of four for one. It was

CHAP. XXIV. thought that this measure would, to some extent, restore credit to the currency, and harmony to the State, but it
1787. Mar. was rejected in the House by a majority of seventeen. A proposition to refer it to the people was also lost. Many persons out of the State had attempted to avail themselves of the provisions of the act for emitting paper money, by depositing the bills with the Justices of Common Pleas in payment of their debts to citizens of Rhode Island, precisely as the inhabitants had done. But this was not allowed, and the justices were required to return to the debtors the sums thus received.

A tax of twenty thousand pounds was assessed. An act to alter and reduce the representation, so that each town should send but two deputies, was referred to the people for a decision, and ultimately defeated. A statute to prevent bribery at elections was passed, prescribing a form of oath or affirmation to be taken by all freemen. At the close of the session, about two o'clock on Sunday
18. morning, a bill was brought in to the lower house to prevent attorneys-at-law from being eligible as members of the Assembly. This was an attempt to revive an old statute, passed nearly sixty years before, and repealed almost immediately. In the present case, it did not proceed so far, but was withdrawn by the mover. The Assembly then adjourned after a brief but stormy and most disastrous session. The rival parties, more than ever exasperated against each other, a natural result of the violent measures carried by the majority over the superior ability and skill in parliamentary debate, of a compact and resolute minority, now separated, to prepare for another bitter struggle in the spring elections.

27. The people of Newport returned to the old form of town government, which continued for sixty-six years.[1]
26. The Superior Court at Newport, four judges present, declined to try any case in which a large sum was involved.

[1] The City of Newport was incorporated the second time at the May session, 1853, and the charter was adopted on the 20th May.

The next week, at the term for Washington county, a full CHAP.
court was present for the first time since the decision XXIV.
against the validity of the penal law. More than twenty 1787.
bills in equity for the redemption of mortgaged estates April
were on file. The suitors came prepared with paper
money, in handkerchiefs and pillow cases, to redeem their
lands. One bag filled with more than fourteen thousand
dollars, was brought to redeem a single estate. It was
moved that the court cause the bills to be counted, and
the tender to be recorded by the clerk. In the argument
upon this motion, the court held that they had nothing to
do with the money before rendition of judgment, nor was
it for them to be instrumental in proving a tender. The
parties then had the bills counted by private persons out
of court, hoping thus to avail themselves of the act by
proving a tender. But the court refused to try any cause
of the kind, and referred them all over to the next term.
Thus the important question, whether paper money should
be received at par in redemption of mortgages, and payment of contracts, devolved upon the new court to be
elected by the next Assembly.

A violent article from the Newport Herald, upon the
proceedings of the General Assembly at their late session,
was copied into a newspaper in New York, with a caption 6.
and comments insulting to the State. The Rhode Island
delegates in Congress appealed to Gov. Clinton to rebuke 7.
Francis Childs, the printer, for the publication of a libel.
Their letter was laid before the legislature of New York.
Childs defended himself in a subsequent article, more 9.
bitter than the first. The delegates had adopted the
wrong course to vindicate the State, for a libel was a
matter for the courts, not for an Assembly to recognize,
and the State had given too serious an occasion for all
that the articles contained. But this external assault produced the effect that abuse, whether merited or not,
usually exerts, especially when coming from those who 18.

CHAP. XXIV. have no concern in the matter; it strengthened the paper money party at the town elections.

1787. April The rebellion in Massachusetts being quelled, the new levies, ordered by Congress ostensibly to act against the Indians, but really to sustain the government in that
24. State, were dismissed. A committee appointed in Providence to consider the two bills referred to the people by
30. the Assembly in March, presented an elaborate report against any alteration of the representation,[1] and another upon the State debt, vindicating the validity of the whole outstanding claims, but declining to instruct the deputies upon the details of the subject, leaving it to their candor to decide upon it with impartial justice.[2]

May 2 The triumphant party in the General Assembly, proceeded to procure the judicial sanction for their acts, by removing four of the judges of the Superior Court. Chief Justice Mumford was the only one retained. Before the revolution, the naval officers were appointed by the governor. Since that time the Intendants of Trade were annually chosen by the Assembly. This power was now restored to the governor, who was made sole arbiter of trade and commerce, with the power to appoint deputies at all the ports to discharge the duties of Intendants of Trade, for whose conduct in office he was to be responsible.

Congress now proceeded in earnest to settle the accounts
7. of the States with the general government, and directed the Treasury Board to appoint five commissioners for that purpose. In July, Royal Flint was appointed for the four eastern States.

25. The convention at Philadelphia organized with dele-

[1] See Staples' Annals, pp. 312–319.

[2] In conclusion the committee say, "When the State shall find itself in a condition to perform some of its promises, it will be time enough to criticise and higgle about their exact value; for, in the opinion of your committee, there is much good sense in the Italian proverb, that '*an acre of performance is worth the whole land of promise.*'" Prov. Gazette, 19 May, 1787.

CHAP. XXIV. 1787.

gates from seven States. Four other States soon appeared. The members from New Hampshire had not yet been appointed, and did not take their seats until July, after which time Rhode Island alone was without a representation in that body. The absence of these two States in the earlier stages of the convention was fortunate, for in the preliminary discussions, two parties appeared. Six States desired a national government, while five favored a State rights policy. The interest of the smaller States, inclined them to take the latter view, so that had these two States been present, the party that sought merely to amend the existing articles of confederation, would have had a majority, and the great difficulty that was found in removing the objections of the smaller States, might have proved insurmountable. A letter from the merchants of Providence was read in the convention, approving of its object, and pledging their efforts to secure the adoption of the constitution by the State of Rhode Island.

June 11.

At the adjourned session of the Assembly, a motion to appoint delegates to the federal convention passed the Senate, but was defeated in the lower house by a majority of seventeen votes. The federal party was now distinctly organized, keeping steadily in view the national relations of the State, and finally succeeding, after three years of conflict, in bringing Rhode Island into the Union. A bill to repeal all acts repugnant to the treaty with Great Britain, recommended by Congress as a pre-requisite for the evacuation of the frontier posts, which were still held by England as a guarantee for the fulfilment of the treaty by the United States, also passed the Senate, and was defeated in the House by a majority of ten. Rouse J. Helme and John Jenckes were appointed to complete the accounts of the State against the General Government, preparatory to the visit of the treasury commissioners. By a report made at this session, it appears that about twenty-seven thousand pounds of the State debt had been discharged under the late act, with about thirteen thou-

CHAP. XXIV. 1787. sand pounds of paper money, and that some of the creditors, having refused to receive it, had forfeited their claims. Another quarter part of the six per cent. notes was ordered to be paid in the same way, whether the parties had received their bills for the first quarter or not. By this process it was expected to liquidate the indebtedness of the State within two years. The paper had still further depreciated, and now passed at the rate of eight for one. Thirty thousand pounds of the paper currency had been placed in the treasury in March, to pay about four times that amount. Under the operation of these acts, it seemed probable that the whole debt would be sunk, and the larger portion of the money appropriated to redeem it, would still remain in the treasury. The immorality of this proceeding was so glaring, that many churches of different denominations, excommunicated their members for tendering paper money.[1]

July 4. But all parties could unite in the celebration of national independence. This festival was especially observed by the Cincinnati, whose proceedings usually formed the principal feature of the day. A military parade, an oration, and a public dinner with thirteen patriotic toasts, had become a regular part of the ceremony on fourth of July. There is one point, however, in which these celebrations differed from those of a later day, and which strikes us as singular. For many years after the peace, the Declaration of Independence was not read upon these occasions. It was considered as being a declaration of war with Great Britain, and therefore inappropriate in time of peace.

Business of the greatest importance required a full Congress, yet but seven States were present. The Rhode Island members had gone home, and were earnestly
7. solicited by the Secretary to return. No notice was taken of this request, and for more than a year Rhode Island was

[1] Bull's Memoirs of Rhode Island.

unrepresented in the national councils. For although the Assembly in September passed a resolution directing them to resume their seats at the opening of the new Congress on the first of November, before that time political affairs had so changed, that the order was not obeyed, if indeed it was seriously intended. Dane introduced the famous ordinance for the government of the north-western territory, which excluded slavery from that region, and was passed unanimously by the eight States then present, four of which were Southern.

1787. July 11. 13.

The Assembly had adjourned to meet at Bristol in August. For some reason the upper house did not attend, and after waiting two days for their appearance, the deputies separated. The governor called a special session at Newport, at which the chief business was to assess a tax of thirty thousand pounds, and to prepare a letter to the President of Congress, assigning the reasons why Rhode Island was not represented in the Philadelphia convention. This letter called forth the spirit of the opposing parties. It was a State rights document, so full of misrepresentations, in the opinion of the minority, that the deputies from Newport and Providence protested against it. One hour only was allowed to them to draw up their protest, and it may be considered as a particular act of favor that when, at the expiration of the time, the paper was read to the Assembly, it was allowed to be entered upon the records. The letter represented that the Assembly had not power to appoint delegates, as this right could only belong to the people at large. It set forth the doctrine of popular sovereignty, and of the entire subserviency of the legislature to the public will, in singular contrast with the despotic authority which its authors had exercised within the past few months. The protest pointed out the inconsistency between the professions of the letter and the practice of the Assembly, and deplored the spirit that would defend an error with ill-founded reasons, rather than acknowledge a mistake.

Aug. 20. 22. Sept. 10.

CHAP. XXIV. After nearly four months of incessant labor, the constitution received the signature of a majority of its framers, and was submitted by Washington, President of the Convention, to the consideration of Congress. That body, in which every State but Rhode Island was now represented, sent a copy of it to the several legislatures, to be submitted for ratification to a convention of delegates, chosen by the people in each State. As soon as the assent of nine States had been made known to Congress, an order was to issue for the election of President of the United States, and the constitution was to go into operation.

1787. Sept. 17.

28.

Oct. 29. The question came before the General Assembly upon a motion for printing and distributing to the towns, copies of the report of the convention, and recommending the appointment of delegates, as therein provided. This was voted down by a large majority, but a vote to print and circulate a thousand copies was afterwards passed. A memorial from the Quakers, asking for an act against the slave trade, which had been for some months before the Assembly, was acted upon. A law prohibiting the African slave trade was enacted, with penalties of one hundred pounds for each person imported or transported from Africa, and one thousand pounds for the vessel thus engaged. The act requiring the second quarter of the six per cent. notes to be paid, was enforced by a decree of forfeiture against all creditors who should fail to apply to the treasurer for payment, within two months.

Nov. 8. The account forwarded from the United States' Treasury Board, showed a balance due from Rhode Island, upon the requisitions of Congress, of $153,185 in indents, and $90,816 in specie. The aggregate of the specie arrears at this time, was $3,668,208, so that the universal complaint now made against this State for its reckless financiering and its disregard of federal relations, however well founded in view of its domestic policy, would

appear to come with an ill grace from many of the con- CHAP.
federated States. XXIV.

The East India trade, which was destined to develop 1787.
the enterprise of the State to a remarkable degree, and to
become for the next half century the source of so much
wealth to the merchants of Providence, commenced at this
time. The ship General Washington now cleared at Dec.
Providence for that remote region, and was the first ves- 19.
sel from Rhode Island engaged in the trade.[1]

The two smallest States in the Union were the first
and the last to adopt the constitution. Delaware led the 7.
list that Rhode Island was to close. Pennsylvania came 12.
next, and New Jersey speedily followed. The new year 18.
opened with the accession of Georgia. Connecticut soon 1788. Jan. 2.
came in. Within about one month, the larger portion of 9.
the requisite number of States had adopted the new
system, but then, for another month, the subject was in
suspense, awaiting the doubtful action of Massachusetts.
The struggle in that State was severe, for several of its
leading patriots, as well as the great mass of the people,
were at first opposed to the constitution. After a long
debate, the convention accepted it by a small majority, Feb.
suggesting, however, nine amendments to be proposed in 7.
Congress. The federal party in Rhode Island, watched
with eager interest for this result, and some of them attended the debates, but at the meeting of the Assembly, 25.
the subject was kept back till nearly the last day of the
session.

A great number of persons who had forfeited half of their State notes under the recent laws, were permitted by special acts to receive their pay from the treasurer. For several sessions petitions of this kind continued to be acted upon. The Quakers, ever solicitous that justice

[1] The last East Indiaman that entered at the port of Providence was the ship Lion, from Canton, arrived January 30, 1841. The last clearance for the East Indies was the ship Panther, for Batavia, December 23, 1841; both ships belonging to Edward Carrington.

CHAP. XXIV. should be done among men, and oppression be banished from the earth, having succeeded in their effort against 1788. the slave trade, again appeared, by petition, asking for Feb. 27. the repeal of the act making paper money a legal tender at par value, and also that the statute of limitations be restored to its former terms. The memorial was ordered to be printed, that the deputies might be instructed by their constituents upon these points. In the lower house, 29. a long debate ensued upon a motion to call a State convention to consider the constitution, in the manner proposed in the report of its framers. The State rights party desired to refer the subject directly to the people in their town meetings, and it was so decided by a vote of fifteen to forty-two. The national party opposed a reference that was certain to defeat the constitution. The only mode by which it could be hoped to secure the ratification, was that pursued in Massachusetts, by offering amendments, and this could not be done except by a State convention. Thus it was certain that many of its friends would vote against it, or would refrain from voting, as the event proved. "Better have no action at all," said they, "than one that is not recognized in the instrument itself, and which by depriving the people of the power to suggest alterations, must result in defeat." An Mar. 1. appropriate conclusion of the session was made by passing an act, requiring the creditors of the State to present their notes to the treasurer, and receive the third payment of one quarter part thereof, with interest, before the tenth of May, on penalty of forfeiting so much of their claims.

The national party, hopeless of success, and disapproving of the action of the Assembly, resolved not to 24. vote upon the constitution. In Bristol and Little Compton alone was there any thing like a contest, and there the Federalists succeeded by small majorities.[1] The State contained more than six thousand freemen, less than

[1] In Bristol the vote was 26 for and 23 against the constitution. In Little Compton 63 to 57.

half of whom voted upon the question.[1] In Providence, where the friends of the constitution were in the majority, the meeting, which was very full, refused to vote by ayes and nays, and a committee was appointed to draft a petition to the General Assembly. Only one vote upon the question was deposited, and that was in the negative. Another was offered in the affirmative in order to tie the first, but the voter was induced to withdraw it.[2] In Newport, only eleven votes were cast, ten against and one in favor of the constitution. In Warwick and East Greenwich, the minority protested against the whole proceeding as illegal, but in most of the towns the question was carried in the negative by acclamation. The Providence memorial, adopted two days later, pointed out the objections to the mode of decision prescribed by the Assembly; that it prevented the country and seaport towns from mutually hearing and discussing each other's views; that the information essential to a just decision could not easily be conveyed to all the freemen; that many persons would be excluded from voting at all who might desire to offer amendments, which could not be done if the question was taken in town meeting; that Congress required a convention to be held, and would receive propositions for amendments only through that source; and that such a convention must ultimately be called, as the State could not exist out of the Union; they therefore prayed that some action might be taken by the Assembly to accomplish this object. Similar petitions were presented from Newport and other towns.

1788. Mar. 24.

26.

The Assembly at first refused to receive them, but finally did so. No reply was made to the arguments offered in their behalf. The majority refused to discuss

31.

[1] The whole number of votes cast was 2,940, of which 2,708 were nays and 232 ayes.

[2] The negative voter was Samuel Sampson, an attorney-at-law in Providence. James Field was the person who offered to tie this vote. Staples' Annals, p. 321.

CHAP. XXIV. 1788. the subject, and the petitions were dismissed. The object of the session was simply to count the votes on the constitution, a report of which was forwarded to Congress. The Quaker memorial against the Tender Act produced no effect upon the Assembly, but their petition with regard to the statute of limitations was taken up, the existing act was repealed, and the old one, extending the time for bringing suits of law in personal actions to six years, was revived. Both of these subjects had been referred to the people, and the votes of the Assembly accorded with the weight of instructions upon them.

April 12. If we may judge from the tone of some private letters that passed between prominent men of the State just before the spring election, the arrangement of the constitutional ticket was not satisfactory to the national party, the unpopularity of whose candidates contributed not a little to their total defeat.[1] Peleg Arnold, Jonathan J.
16. Hazard, Thomas Holden, and John Gardner, were chosen delegates to Congress, and the two former soon took their
May 7. seats. The new Assembly differed somewhat in persons, but nothing in politics, from its predecessor. No business, except the usual election of officers, was done until the adjourned session.

April 28. Maryland had just accepted the constitution, and South Carolina soon followed the example, making the eighth
May 24. State. The New Hampshire convention had adjourned to obtain further instructions from the people. Every eye was turned with intense anxiety to watch the fate of the Union while it hung upon the decision of that State.
June 9. Such was the position of affairs when the General Assembly again convened at Newport. But the all-important question was still held in abeyance. Nothing was done but to assess a tax of thirty thousand pounds, and to extinguish another portion of the State debt. The time for receiving payment for the third quarter of the six per

[1] See letter of William Channing to Theodore Foster, 12 April, 1788. Foster Correspondence, Vol. I.

cent. notes, was extended one month to those who had already acknowledged the validity of the forcing acts, by receiving payment on either of the other two quarters, and the fourth quarter, making the whole amount of those notes, was declared to be forfeited by all who, having failed to demand payment upon the other three quarters, should neglect to present their notes to the treasurer within the month. It appears that on the second instalment of the debt, about £10,500 had been paid, and the balance forfeited under the act. CHAP. XXIV. 1788. June

At length the convention of New Hampshire, having reassembled, ratified the constitution, proposing the same amendments that Massachusetts had done. The provisions of the new system were complete. The American Union could now be formed! Long and loud were the demonstrations of joy when this news reached Providence. All day the church bells rang, and cannon roared from Federal Hill. Schools and college had a holiday. The students formed a procession on the college grounds, which they named "Federal Parade." There could be no mistaking the national sentiments of the citizens of Providence. A town meeting was called to arrange a joint celebration of the anniversary of independence, and of the completion of the national Union. On the same day Virginia, where the constitution had been warmly opposed, adopted it, suggesting several alterations in its terms, and also the addition of a bill of rights. 21. 24. 27.

The federal proclivities of Providence, gave great offence to the people of the country towns, who assembled in arms to prevent the proposed celebration. The public in town and country had been invited to the festival, through the newspapers, and special invitations were sent to the governor and council, the general officers and the Superior Court, nearly all of whom were of the opposite party. This the State rights party chose to view as an indignity offered to themselves, and an insult to the State, in which, as they asserted, four-fifths of the people were July 3.

CHAP. XXIV. 1788. July 3. inimical to the constitution. An ox, roasted whole, formed a part of the entertainment. This was prepared during the preceding night, on the plain north of the cove, now known as Smith's Hill. The country was greatly excited by false rumors respecting the objects and character of the celebration. In the evening armed bands collected in the adjoining woods, threatening an attack upon the town. At about eleven o'clock, a committee went out to ascertain their demands. It was agreed that early the next morning, the town committee should meet with the leaders of the rioters, among whom were two members of the Assembly, and a Judge of the Superior Court, to endeavor to arrange the matter to their mutual satisfaction.
4 Accordingly at seven o'clock in the morning of the fourth, the two committees met, and after a conference that lasted about an hour, agreed upon terms satisfactory to both parties. The rioters dispersed, and some of them, leaving their arms behind, came into town and took part in the celebration. The number collected during the night was variously estimated from three hundred to a thousand men, and as the morning approached, the force rapidly increased, until it assumed alarming proportions. The leaders of the country party expected that by noon three thousand men would rally to their support. The affair was happily arranged by an assurance on the part of the town committee, that the festival was mainly in commemoration of the Declaration of Independence, was gotten up at private expense, and would include nothing that could offend the prejudices of the country. The thirteenth regular toast was altered from "the nine States" to "the day," a concession that gave satisfaction to the other side. In all other respects, the celebration proceeded as originally arranged. The usual national salutes were fired, an oration occupied the morning, and at two o'clock the procession marched to the hill, where a table more than a thousand feet long was spread under a canvass canopy. Between five and six thousand people partook of the din-

ner. The ox, roasted whole, was the principal attraction CHAP.
of the feast, although other materials were amply pro- XXIV.
vided. At six o'clock the procession returned to the 1788.
court-house parade, and there separated with thirteen July.
cheers. A statement of the disgraceful affair that had marred the opening of the day, and threatened to change the joyous festival to a scene of fraternal strife, was published in the papers by a leader of the movement, expressed in boastful terms to convey the idea that the townsmen had been compelled to yield unmanly concessions to the mob. This called forth a counter statement from the town's committee, presenting their view of the case. The whole exhibits a melancholy picture of the violence of party politics, that could give occasion for such a demonstration.[1]

That the national party were not intimidated by this
hostile attitude of their opponents, appeared the next after- 5
noon, when the news reached Providence that Virginia had accepted the constitution. Ten cannon were fired by the artillery company, and answered by ten discharges from the continental guns on Federal Hill. The bells were rung, and a procession was formed which paraded the streets, with joyous shouts, until evening. New York, where the contest had been as close as in Virginia, soon
afterwards adopted the constitution, on similar terms, and 25.
issued a circular to the States, requesting their co-operation 26.
in favor of the proposed amendments. When the news
reached Providence, another rejoicing, like that over Vir- 29.
ginia, was had, with some additions of peculiar significance. The standard of the Rhode Island revolutionary regiment was displayed on Federal Hill. On the south side of Weybosset Bridge, eleven flag-staffs were erected, from each of which the national ensign was unfurled, bearing the name of a State, the majority by which it had adopted the constitution, and the date of that event.

[1] Providence Gazette, 12 July, 1788. Staples' Annals, p. 329–335.

CHAP. XXIV. These were arranged in historical order, beginning with Delaware and ending with New York. On the north
1788. side of the bridge were two flag-staffs, one inclining about
July 29. thirty degrees, with a small flag bearing the name of North Carolina, the date upon which the convention was to meet, and the motto "It will rise." The other was a bare pole inclining in the opposite direction from North Carolina, at an angle of forty-five degrees, with a paper label affixed, bearing the words "Rhode Island in hopes." The banner of France floated from the parade. At eleven o'clock, eleven cannon were fired from Federal Hill in honor of the eleven ratifying States. This was repeated from the bridge in the afternoon, with eleven cheers, and
Aug. 7. again at sunset from the hill. A few days later, North Carolina conditionally accepted the constitution, dependent upon the adoption, by the other States, of certain specified amendments. As eleven States had ratified it without reserve, confident of the adoption of their proposed amendments by the constitutional number of two-thirds of the States, the qualified action of the twelfth State presented no greater obstacle to the completion of the Union, than did the perverseness of Rhode Island.

Congress had already extended the time for adjusting the accounts of the several States, and in order to prevent
Sept. 9. dissatisfaction, now appointed three commissioners to examine those claims for which no vouchers could be found. These were very numerous in all the States, owing to the confusion that prevailed in every department of the pub-
13. lic service during the war. They also appointed a time and place for the constitution to go into operation. On the first Wednesday of January presidential electors were to be chosen, who were to meet in four weeks from that day to choose a president and vice-president, and at the end of four more weeks, on the fourth of March, the government was to be organized at New York. In view of
Oct. 20. these facts, Peleg Arnold, one of the delegates in Congress, wrote home an urgent letter, recommending that the

State should at once take up the subject of the constitu- CHAP.
tion, and propose such amendments as would reconcile XXIV.
the people to a federal union. 1788.
The Assembly, convened at Providence, showed no Oct. 27.
disposition to enter upon the great discussion. Arnold Nov.
returned home to present to them the importance of im- 1.
mediate action, but in vain. The proposal to call a convention was voted down by a decided majority, and a motion to repeal the paper money act shared the same fate. The New York circular, suggesting a convention of the States to consider certain proposed amendments to the constitution, was ordered to be printed and circulated in all the towns that the people might instruct their deputies whether they wished delegates to be appointed to such a convention or not. A payment of one fourth part of the notes given for the old four per cent. notes was ordered, the claim to be forfeited if not presented within two months. The same time was allowed for the payment of the residue of the six per cent. notes. A report upon the accounts of Rhode Island with the United States, showed the claims for which the government commissioner had already received vouchers to amount to £568,290, exclusive of the sums due to the soldiers for depreciation of pay, amounting to £64,000, which were rejected by the commissioner. George Olney was added to the committee to collect the equitable claims against the general government for which no vouchers existed. J. J. Hazard and John Gardner were directed to proceed to New York and take their seats in Congress.

Thanksgiving day was duly observed in the State. 27.
The people of Providence instructed their deputies to Dec.
move, at the approaching session of the Assembly, for a 6.
convention to adopt the constitution, and to propose amendments. The town of Portsmouth, although opposed
to the constitution, approved of the suggestions in Gov. 20.
Clinton's letter, and desired that Rhode Island should join in a convention of States so to amend it that this State

CHAP. XXIV. could accept its provisions and enter the Union. Other towns in which the State rights party predominated, took
1788. Dec. a similar action upon the New York circular, but there were not enough to accomplish the object.

29. The Assembly again refused to call a State convention. Two military companies were chartered, the North Kingstown Rangers, and the Washington Independent Company, of Exeter. Nothing further of a public nature was
1789. Jan. 3. done. The Assembly adjourned at the close of the week, as was the usual custom. It rarely occurred that a session extended beyond one week.

The return of commercial prosperity was slow indeed. Two causes contributed to the utter prostration of the State. One was the destruction of the great mercantile interest during the war, and the immense exertions, vastly disproportioned to the numbers or the ability of the people, which this State had made in the struggle for independence. The other was the poverty of the General Government, in whose behalf, as in a common cause, these efforts had been made, which prevented any thing like an equitable adjustment of the claims of the several States, and from whom Rhode Island, in the final settlement, received the least of all. Deficient as she had been for the last four years in meeting her quota of the federal requisitions, she had been scarcely more backward in that respect than most of her sister States, and at the period of which we are writing, not only in "equitable claims," as those were termed for which no vouchers could be produced, but in legal and certified claims acknowledged by the United States commissioner to be justly due, she was to an enormous amount a creditor State; and so remains to this day, after the compromise adjustment that was subsequently made. The one dark stain upon her history, which we have not attempted to excuse, and do not now propose to justify, was the result of a poverty from which there was no apparent escape. Scorn and reproach for the error into which distress had driven her,

1789. Jan.

and for the obstinacy with which she now held out for better terms from the confederated States, were the reward of a valor that had not been surpassed, and of a self-devotion in the common cause, which few, if any, of her compeers had equalled. We have seen that at this moment the recorded debt of the confederation due to Rhode Island, amounted to nearly two millions of dollars, and with the depreciation upon soldiers' wages, which although not allowed by government was justly chargeable to it, exceeded that sum. This statement does not include the equitable claims of which no account had yet been rendered.[1] But a tithe of this debt has ever been paid by the general government, and there are now States in the Union, some of whom were among the loudest in their denunciations of Rhode Island, that have never made up the arrears of their revolutionary requisitions. Could only a small part of what was due to the State have been paid into her exhausted treasury, the distresses that gave rise to the paper money party, and secured its baleful predominance for four disastrous years, would have been somewhat relieved, the credit of the State would have been preserved, and history would have recorded the story of her trials and her triumphs for two centuries of time, without a blot; nor would the mistaken policy that for another year was to rule her councils, and keep her out of the Union, have prevailed.

Among the indications of awakening enterprise, we find the establishment of a rolling and slitting mill near Providence, for preparing iron to be made into nails, a branch of industry that under the British rule was for-

[1] This account of equitable claims was rendered by the committee, John Jenckes and George Olney, to the General Assembly on 26 October, 1789, and amounted to £277,988 11s. 1½d., or $725,900; no part of which was ever received from the general government. A supplemental account reported at the January session, 1790, added the sum of £60,212 16s. 1½d., or $200,508 to this sum. A further report of £6,643 8s. 1d. due on this account was made by Mr. Olney at the May session.

CHAP. XXIV. 1789. Jan. bidden to the colonies. Upon a humbler scale, but one that gave more conclusive evidence of that recuperative power which was to restore the wasted energies of the State, may be mentioned the frequent meetings of women, in all ranks of life, to spin flax. A great deal of linen yarn was made in this way, and no lady considered it beneath her dignity to devote a portion of her time to this effectual method of redeeming the fortunes of her country. The encouragement given to domestic industry, was universal. Men of property and influence appeared in homespun garments, and American woollen cloths were worn in preference to foreign fabrics. A people animated by such sentiments, could not long remain depressed.

Gen. James M. Varnum, who had lately emigrated to
10. Ohio, died at Marietta. His eminent services as a soldier have been recorded in these pages. His ability as a lawyer was recognized by all. He was also an accomplished scholar, and a brilliant orator.

The first step in the organization of the federal government, was the choice of presidential electors, which
7. took place on the appointed day in all the States of the Union, except New York, where a disagreement in the legislature as to the mode of proceeding, prevented an election. Members of the federal Congress had already
Feb. been chosen. Four weeks later the electoral colleges met
4. in their respective States, and unanimously elected George Washington President of the United States. For Vice-President, John Adams received a plurality of the votes cast for several candidates, and was therefore chosen.
Mar. The old Continental Congress expired by its own limita-
3. tion. Quietly, and almost unnoticed, after a career that has no parallel in history, it went out. The great purpose of its creation having been accomplished, it gave place to a more vigorous organization. But one of its chief defects, the delay of members in taking their seats,
4. was transmitted to its successor. No quorum of the first federal Congress was present to put the new government

in operation, and for nearly a month this disability con- CHAP.
tinued. The day was celebrated by the federalists in XXIV.
Providence with the firing of eleven guns at sunrise, noon, 1789.
and sunset. Gardner, the only delegate from Rhode March
Island who was present at the closing scene of the Continental Congress, returned home. A notice of his anoma- 6.
lous position, concludes with the remark, "on the first
Wednesday of March, he found himself the only living
member of a departed body, and returned here a delegate
to a power that is no longer known;" and it might have
been added, 'from a State that is no longer recognized.'

The General Assembly met at East Greenwich, and 9.
proceeded to extinguish the remainder of the State debt
by requiring all outstanding notes, not already forfeited,
to be presented to the treasurer before the eighth day of
May, to be redeemed in paper money. The bills were
now passing at the rate of twelve dollars in paper for one
of silver. Thus had the paper money party at length
attained the object of its organization. Had a general
act of insolvency, relieving all debtors from their liabilities, and the State from its legal obligations been passed
in the first instance, the same end would have been more
speedily accomplished, and the means would not have
differed very widely from those that were actually employed. The Tender law of May, 1786, in its operation
upon private contracts, was in fact an insolvent act, and
in its relation to the public debt, by compelling a compo-
sition with the creditors of the State in which they could
receive but a trifling portion of their claims, it fell but
little short of repudiation.[1] A protest against this final
outrage, was made by the people of Providence in the
instructions sent to their deputies while the Assembly 10.
was in session. The neighboring States had retaliated
upon Rhode Island, by prohibiting their courts to try any

[1] Mr. Hildreth presents this subject in its true light, and shows a generous appreciation of the position of Rhode Island at this time. History of U. S., Vol. IV., pp. 34, 35.

CHAP. XXIV. suit for debt brought by a citizen of this State; but no representation of the injustice, or the impolicy of their
1789. Mar. course, could move the majority to repeal the odious statute. Another object of the instructions, was to secure
13. a State convention. This also was voted down by a large majority. A tax of twenty thousand pounds was laid. The only good thing done at this time, was the incorporation of the "Providence Association of Mechanics and Manufacturers," an institution that served to organize the efforts then making to develop the resources of the State, and whose beneficent influence has steadily increased to the present hour.

The new Congress comprised fifty-nine representatives,
30. a quorum of whom having at length assembled, the House was organized. A week later, the majority of the Sena-
April 6. tors having arrived, the votes for President and Vice-President were counted, and messengers were sent to Mount Vernon and Massachusetts to summon the elected officers.
21. Vice-President Adams was inaugurated immediately upon his arrival at New York. Washington, whose progress through the country which had been the scene of his severest trial, and his most brilliant success, was "one
23. long triumphal march," reached the city two days later. The ceremony of the inauguration was delayed for one
30. week, to allow time to complete the new Federal Hall. The first business before the House was to provide a revenue by placing a duty on imports. In framing this bill, North Carolina and Rhode Island were necessarily treated as foreign States, and subjected to pay a duty upon all goods, not of their own production, which they should import into the Union. In view of so fatal an isolation, a petition from many freemen of Newport and
May 6. Providence was presented to the General Assembly, praying them to call a State convention. The new Assembly, although of the same political character as the old, treated this petition with greater respect than former ones had received, but referred it to the next session. There was

1789.

no change in general officers, except that David Howell was chosen attorney-general in place of Goodwin, who was very ill and soon afterwards died. Some symptoms of yielding to the exigencies of the times were shown in the passage of a new impost act adopting all the federal imposts and duties, and authorizing their collection in the same moneys as in the Federal ports. Yet this act could have no other effect than to double the tax upon Rhode Island importers, since most of the foreign goods brought in here were sold in other States. Hence it was ruinous to the commerce of the State.

At the adjourned session, an embargo, to continue for four months, was laid upon all kinds of grain; but still the necessity that produced this legislation was not enough to break down the majority. The standing motions to call a State convention, and to repeal the Tender law, were again defeated, the first by a majority of eleven, and the second by seven votes. Another military company, the Coventry Rangers, was chartered. There were at this time one hundred and one vessels, exclusive of river craft, owned in Providence, amounting to nearly ten thousand tons, more than three quarters of which were employed in foreign trade and on whaling voyages. All this was liable to ruin if the existing policy of the State should long be maintained. The ship General Washington returned from China after an absence of nineteen months. July 5.
This was the first arrival at Providence direct from Canton.

Although the deputies had always been chosen semi-annually, the political complexion of the Assembly was usually determined by the spring elections, when the general officers, including the assistants, were chosen. The latter body, formerly called the council, was now with the two executive officers, termed the upper house, and afterwards received the name of Senate. On this occasion, the election of deputies in several towns showed some changes that inspired the federal party with hope that the day of deliverance was at hand. This hope was

Aug. 25.

CHAP. XXIV. 1789. Aug. 27.

expressed in a petition to Congress, representing the distressed condition of the State, and praying that Rhode Island commerce might be exempted from foreign duties in the ports of the Union. President Manning and Benjamin Bourne, were deputed to present the petition to Congress. Newport and Bristol sent similar petitions by the hands of Henry Marchant.

Sept. 15.

The governor called a special meeting of the Assembly at Newport. For the first time for more than three years, the unbroken phalanx of the paper money and State rights parties wavered. The first measures of the Assembly were to repeal the embargo on corn, and to order town meetings to be held in October, to instruct the deputies on the subject of calling a convention to consider the constitution. The details of the impost act were framed in accordance with the bill enacted by Congress. The State was divided into two districts. Providence and Newport were made ports of entry and delivery. The other seaboard towns were made ports of delivery only, and the requisite officers were appointed. A drawback upon rum, sugar, and chocolate, manufactured in the State for exportation, was allowed. The operation of the Tender law was suspended. Here appeared a gleam of returning justice. But yet more significant of approaching change was a letter prepared by the Assembly to the President and Congress of the eleven States. This address assigned the reasons that had influenced the majority to oppose the constitution. It set forth the attachment of the people to their democratic charter, and the fear that this would in some degree be limited by the new federal system; that for this cause they had waited to observe its operation, and to see if the proposed amendments would be adopted, before yielding their assent to the new government. The paper presented the State rights view with a degree of candor creditable to its authors, and appealed to the memories of the past with a skill that reminds us of the earlier examples of Rhode

Island diplomacy recorded in the previous volume of this history.[1] CHAP. XXIV.

The effect of the petitions from the seaports was most favorable. Congress exempted, for a limited time, the vessels of Rhode Island and of North Carolina from paying the foreign tonnage or impost duties, thus placing them on the same footing with ships belonging to the Union. Soon after the adjournment of Congress, Washington made a tour through the Eastern States, but avoided entering Rhode Island. 1789. Sept. 19.

At an adjourned session of the Assembly, held at Greenwich, the amendments to the constitution, recently adopted by Congress, were ordered to be printed for the use of the freemen at their approaching town meetings. Owing to the depreciation of paper money, the statute of limitations was repealed, as it had been during the war, and the time allowed for the redemption of mortgaged estates was extended from five years to twelve years. So much of the act for emitting paper money as made the bills a tender at par was repealed, and debtors were authorized to substitute property, at an appraised value, for money, in discharge of their liabilities. By the same act, the depreciation of paper bills was settled at fifteen for one. Oct. 12.

The result of the appeal to the freemen on the question of the constitution, was more consonant with the views of the anti-federal party, as they were now called, than with the interests of the State. The weight of instructions was against calling a convention. The House therefore rejected the proposition by a vote of seventeen to thirty-nine. A fortnight later, the new convention held in North Carolina, ratified the constitution. 19. 29. Nov. 13.

Rhode Island stood ALONE.

The day of annual thanksgiving and prayer, appointed by the Assembly, was held with unusual solemnity. 26.

[1] The address is printed in full, in Staples' Annals, pp. 342–5, and a portion of it in Hildreth, IV., 147–9.

CHAP. XXIV. 1790. "Health and plentiful harvests" had been vouchsafed to the people of the State, but there were many who prayed for a political blessing, which, in the madness of party strife, had been denied.

Jan. 11. The General Assembly convened at Providence. The River Machine Company was incorporated to keep the harbor of Providence free from obstructions, and was empowered to collect two cents a ton, for that purpose, from all vessels above sixty tons burthen. This company soon afterwards prepared the commercial statistics of Providence. By their report there were then owned in that port, one hundred and ten sail, of ten thousand five hundred and ninety tons, exclusive of river craft; and in a petition subsequently made to Congress for a continuance of the right to assess harbor dues, they stated that "there is a greater number of vessels belonging to this port, than to New York," and that "it is a place of more navigation than any of its size in the Union." The population of Providence at this time, was 6,380, and of the State 68,-
15. 825. On the day that the act of Congress in favor of Rhode Island vessels expired by limitation, a bill was introduced into the lower house of Assembly by Benjamin Bourn of Providence, to call a convention, to meet on the twenty-second of February, to decide upon the constitution. After a long debate it was carried by a majority of five, thirty-four in favor, to twenty-nine against the
16. measure. The next day the Senate non-concurred. There were eight assistants present, who were equally divided on the question, and the vote of deputy-Governor Owen was cast in the negative. By the same vote the Senate passed a bill, to call town meetings for the purpose of instructing the deputies whether to call a convention or not. This was equivalent to a defeat of the whole subject. The bill was sent down to the House, where, after a long debate it was voted, late in the evening, by a majority of fourteen, to non-concur. Both branches then
17. adjourned till the next morning, which was Sunday, when

Henry Marchant of Newport, offered a substitute for Mr. CHAP.
Bourn's bill, altering the time for holding the convention XXIV.
to the first of March, and directing that a copy of the act 1790.
be sent to Congress. This passed by a majority of twenty- Jan. 17.
one, thirty-two yeas to eleven nays. A bill then came
down from the Senate similar to the one that passed that
body the day before, with the addition of a preamble.
This was rejected in the House by nearly the same vote,
and Marchant's bill was sent up for concurrence. Meanwhile, one of the anti-federal assistants, who was a minister, having become impressed with the impropriety of
Sabbath legislation, and the necessity of attention to his
parochial duties, had left town. This made a tie in the
Senate, and threw the casting vote upon Gov. Collins,
who, after a speech in which he assigned the distresses of
the State resulting from disconnection with the Union as
the reason for his vote, decided for concurrence, and the
bill passed. The excitement in the town was intense.
The churches were almost deserted. A dense crowd had
gathered in and around the State-House, and when the
result was announced, long and loud were the shouts of
joy that went up from the vast assemblage. The Assembly then adjourned, after voting that a copy of the act
should be forwarded to Congress, with a request that the
indulgence granted to Rhode Island commerce might be
continued. This was conceded, and the act extended to
the first of April.

Town meetings were held throughout the State on the Feb.
day appointed to choose delegates to the convention. 8.
Each town was to send the same number as it had of
deputies in the Assembly. When the important day ar- Mar.
rived, every member was present at South Kingstown. 1.
Deputy-Governor Owen was chosen president, and Daniel
Updike secretary. It soon appeared that a majority were
opposed to the constitution. On the second day, rules 2.
were adopted to govern the proceedings, the constitution
was read, and a discussion arose which continued through 3-4.

CHAP. XXIV. the two following days, when a committee of two from each county was appointed to prepare amendments. The
1790. Mar. 5. next day they reported a Bill of Rights in sixteen articles, resembling that proposed by New York, and eighteen amendments to the constitution. The debate on these points continued the greater part of two days, when Mar-
6. chant moved in form that the constitution be ratified. A motion to adjourn was made, in order to prevent the vote. Upon this a debate arose, on a point of order, involving the power of the convention to adjourn without deciding the question which they were appointed to determine. An adjournment to the fourth Monday in May, then to meet at Newport, was carried by forty-one to twenty-eight, a majority of thirteen.

Active preparations were made for the approaching election. The vote of Gov. Collins for calling the convention, had made him unpopular with his party The anti-federal members of the convention on the day of the adjournment, offered the office of governor to Deputy-Governor Owen, who declined to serve. A movement was
22. made in Providence, to form a coalition party. The New-
24. port committee united with them in proposing to Arthur Fenner, an anti-federalist, then clerk of Common Pleas in Providence, to head a ticket upon which there should be a federalist deputy-governor, and a nearly equal number of assistants from each party. Fenner, in a modest letter to the
29. committee, referred the subject to the freemen. Two days
31. later the committee called a nominating convention, which
April 6. met at East Greenwich, and formed a "coalition or federal prox."[1] An anti-federal proxy was also published, with

[1] The term "Prox," used for ticket in political parlance, is a purely Rhode Island word, originating as early as 1647, when upon the first departure from a democratical form of government, the representative system was introduced, and voting by proxy was permitted. As early as 1640 there are indications of this practice, which was revived with greater force in 1664. All the freemen of the colony were originally required to vote in person at Newport, for the annual election of general officers. The inconvenience of this course led in 1664 to the revival of proxy voting, which had fallen into

the name of Daniel Updike for attorney-general in place of David Howell, and with six assistants, different from those on the federal ticket. The other general officers were the same on both proxies. At the election, the anti-federal party triumphed. The seven candidates upon that ticket alone, were chosen after a sharp contest. The others were elected by general consent.

CHAP. XXIV. 1790. April 21.

The new General Assembly met at Newport, and declared Arthur Fenner governor, and Samuel J. Potter deputy-governor.[1] A charter was granted to the Cranston Blues, a military company. May 5.

The feeling in Congress was imbittered against Rhode Island by the repeated delays in adopting the constitution. The extension of privilege to vessels of this State had already expired. A bill was brought into the Senate to prohibit all commercial intercourse with Rhode Island, 18. and to require payment of twenty-seven thousand dollars in specie, due upon the old continental requisitions. Still more decisive measures were taken by the Federal party within the State, to compel a prompt and favorable decision of the question. On the day appointed for the convention to reassemble at Newport, a large meeting of the 24. freemen of Providence instructed their delegates, in case of the rejection of the constitution, or further postponement of the question, "to enter a solemn and spirited protest against such rejection or adjournment," and resolved, in that event, to unite with Newport and such other towns as might join them, in an application to Congress for protection, and to be received into the Union. Fortunately

disuse; and nearly a century later, in 1760, it was again revived in a special statute requiring the freemen to vote for general officers at their town meetings. It thus became general, and the paper on which the names of the candidates voted for were written, was called a prox. In time this came to be applied to the list of candidates put forward by the different parties. The word is better than "ticket," because more distinctive and precise in its meaning. It continued in use in this State until within a very few years.

[1] Gov. Fenner continued in office till 1805, and Dep. Gov. Potter till 1799, by annual election.

CHAP. XXIV. there was no occasion for the exercise of the doubtful power herein assumed.

1790. May 26. No business was done in the convention, until Wednesday, when the instructions from the several towns were read. A motion to adopt the Federal constitution, with the Bill of Rights and amendments before reported, the latter to be recommendatory, was made. A test question was presented by a motion to adjourn, which the president, upon appeal, decided to be in order. A warm debate arose, and it was defeated by a majority of nine votes. The motion to adopt the constitution was then taken up, and the instrument was read. The State House could not contain the crowd of people assembled to witness the momentous proceedings. For more ample accommodation,
27. the convention removed to the Second Baptist Church, where for three days the great debate continued. Many of the delegates were bound by instructions to vote against the adoption, and there was no time to obtain from their constituents a revision of those instructions, as had been done in the case of New Hampshire. Had it been so, it was thought the majority would have been greater. At
29. five o'clock on Saturday afternoon, the final vote was taken. Thirty-four members voted to adopt the constitution, and thirty-two voted in the negative. A majority of two votes saved the people of Rhode Island from anarchy and the State from dismemberment.

The news reached Providence before midnight, and was announced by ringing of bells and the booming of
30. cannon. The next day the returning delegates were received with a national salute of thirteen guns. "Patriotism again encroached on piety, as when the vote for calling the convention passed in the preceding January, and the stillness of the Sabbath morning was broken by the joyful roar of artillery." [1]

June 1, 2. In all the seaport towns, and many others, the event

[1] Staples' Annals, p. 349.

was celebrated, the following Tuesday and Wednesday, CHAP.
with every token of joy. The news was forwarded by XXIV.
the President of the convention to the President of the 1790.
United States in a letter of which Col. William Barton June
was the bearer, and was communicated in a special mes- 1.
sage to both houses of Congress. The further consideration of the bill to prevent commercial intercourse with Rhode Island, was dismissed, and bills for extending the laws of the United States over the new State were introduced.

Governor Fenner convened a special session of the 7.
General Assembly, at which all the members of the government took the oath or affirmation of fealty to the constitution. The mode of electing members of Congress was prescribed. Joseph Stanton of Charlestown, and Theodore Foster of Providence, were chosen United States
Senators, and at the subsequent election by the people, Aug.
Benjamin Bourn was chosen to be the Representative in Congress. Soon after the adjournment of that body, President Washington visited Rhode Island, and was received with great enthusiasm throughout the State.

Thus Rhode Island came into the American Union, cautiously but firmly taking upon herself the obligations of the constitution. For more than a century and a half, the State had enjoyed a freedom unknown to any of her compeers, and through more than half of that period, her people had been involved with rival colonies in a struggle for political existence, and for the maintenance of those principles of civil and religious freedom which are now everywhere received in America. Well might the people of Rhode Island hesitate to surrender ever so small a portion of that liberty which to other States was yet but an experiment, when to them it had long been an established fact. A jealousy of more powerful States had with too good reason been deeply implanted in the Rhode Island mind. The memory of former sufferings could not be at once effaced, although the glorious epoch of the Revolu-

CHAP. XXIV. 1790. tion divided the past from the present. The first State to strike a blow for freedom was the last to recognize a system by which that freedom could best be preserved. Since that memorable day, the experience of seventy years has taught Rhode Island the value of the Union. May her sons forever guard the sacred trust, and the emblematic anchor of the State hold fast upon the Constitution.

APPENDIX M.

A LIST OF THE CHIEF MAGISTRATES OF RHODE ISLAND.

APP. M. At *Providence* there was no Chief Magistrate until the organization of the colony under the Parliamentary Patent in 1647. The government was a pure democracy from the settlement in 1636, until 1640, when a committee of five men, called "disposers," were invested with a partial control of local affairs. At *Warwick* a similar system prevailed.

Portsmouth, (first called Pocasset.)

Judges.

1638, March 7,	William Coddington,	to April 30, 1639.
1639, April 30,	William Hutchinson,	" March 12, 1640,

when Portsmouth and Newport were united.

Newport.—Judge.

1639, April 30, William Coddington, to March 12, 1640.

After the union of Portsmouth and Newport, the title of *Governor* was given to the Chief Magistrate, and William Coddington held the office till the organization of the colony, May 19, 1647.

PRESIDENTS UNDER THE PARLIAMENTARY PATENT.

1647, May,	John Coggeshall,	to May, 1648.
1648, do.	William Coddington,	" do. 1649.
1649, do.	John Smith,	" do. 1650.
1650, do.	Nicholas Easton,	" Aug., 1651.

The return of Coddington from England, in August, 1651, with a commission for life as Governor of Rhode-island and Conanicut, caused a separation of the mainland towns from the islands, which continued till the repeal of his commission arrived, in February, 1652-3, after which, a conflict between the two General Assemblies, each claiming to represent the chartered colony, prolonged the separation. The mainland towns continued to elect

Presidents of Providence and Warwick.

1652, May,	John Smith,	to May, 1653.
1653, do.	Gregory Dexter,	" do. 1654,

and the island towns upon the suspension of Coddington, elected

President of Aquedneck.

1653, May, John Sandford, senior, to May, 1654,

when the union was re-established. We resume the list for the whole colony.

1654, May,	Nicholas Easton,	to Sept. 12, 1654.
1654, Sept.	Roger Williams,	" May, 1657.
1657, May,	Benedict Arnold,	" do. 1660.
1660, do.	William Brenton,	" do. 1662.
1662, do.	Benedict Arnold,	" Nov. 25, 1663.

GOVERNORS UNDER THE ROYAL CHARTER.

1663, Nov.	Benedict Arnold,	to May, 1666.
1666, May,	William Brenton,	" do. 1669.
1669, do.	Benedict Arnold,	" do. 1672.
1672, do.	Nicholas Easton,	" do. 1674.
1674, do.	William Coddington,	" do. 1676.
1676, do.	Walter Clarke,	" do. 1677.
1677, do.	Benedict Arnold,	" June 20, 1678, died.
1678, Aug. 28,	William Coddington,	" Nov. 1, 1678, died.
1678, Nov. 8,	John Cranston,	" Mar. 12, 1680, died.
1680, March 16,	Peleg Sandford,	" May, 1683.
1683, May,	William Coddington, jr.,	" do. 1685.
1685, do.	Henry Bull,	" do. 1686.
1686, do.	Walter Clarke,	" June 29, 1686,

when the charter was suspended by Sir Edmund Andros. It was resumed May 1, 1689, but Gov. Clarke, declining to act, Deputy-Governor Coggeshall conducted affairs till

1690, Feb. 27,	Henry Bull,	to May, 1690.
1690, May,	John Easton,	" do. 1695.
1695, do.	Caleb Carr,	" Dec. 17, 1695, died.
1696, Jan.,	Walter Clarke,	" March, 1698.

CHAP. XXIV. APP. M.

1698, March,	Samuel Cranston,	to April 26, 1727, died.
1727, May,	Joseph Jenckes,	" May, 1732.
1732, do.	William Wanton,	" Dec., 1733, died.
1734, do.	John Wanton,	" July 5, 1740, died.
1740, July 15,	Richard Ward,	" May, 1743.
1743, May,	William Greene,	" do. 1745.
1745, do.	Gideon Wanton,	" do. 1746.
1746, do.	William Greene,	" do. 1747.
1747, do.	Gideon Wanton,	" do. 1748.
1748, do.	William Greene,	" do. 1755.
1755, do.	Stephen Hopkins,	" do. 1757.
1757, do.	William Greene,	" Feb. 22, 1758, died.
1758, March 14,	Stephen Hopkins,	" May, 1762.
1762, May,	Samuel Ward,	" do. 1763.
1763, do.	Stephen Hopkins,	" do. 1765.
1765, do.	Samuel Ward,	" do. 1767.
1767, do.	Stephen Hopkins,	" do. 1768.
1768, do.	Josias Lyndon,	" do. 1769.
1769, do.	Joseph Wanton,	" Nov. 7, 1775, deposed.
1775, Nov.,	Nicholas Cooke,	" May, 1778.
1778, May,	William Greene, jr.,	" do. 1786.
1786, do.	John Collins,	" do. 1790.
1790, do.	Arthur Fenner.	

APPENDIX N.

N.

LIST OF THE DEPUTY-GOVERNORS OF RHODE ISLAND.

Of *Aquedneck*, William Brenton, from March 12, 1640, to May, 19, 1647. The office did not exist under the Parliamentary Patent.

Deputy-Governors under the Royal Charter.

1663, Nov.,	William Brenton,	to May, 1666.
1666, May,	Nicholas Easton,	" do. 1669.
1669, do.	John Clarke,	" do. 1670.
1670, do.	Nicholas Easton,	" do. 1671.
1671, do.	John Clarke,	" do. 1672.
1672, do.	John Cranston,	" do. 1673.
1673, do.	William Coddington,	" do. 1674.
1674, do.	John Easton,	" April, 1676.[1]

[1] Walter Clarke, First Assistant, was acting deputy-governor after the adjourned session of the Assembly, April 11, 1676, as appears by his letter

1676, May,	John Cranston,	to Nov. 8, 1678.
1678, Nov.,	James Barker,	" May, 1679.
1679, May,	Walter Clarke,	" do. 1686.
1686, do.	John Coggeshall,	" June, 1686.

Charter suspended, June 29, 1686, by Sir E. Andros, resumed

1689, May 1,	John Coggeshall,	to May, 1690.
1690, do.	John Greene,	" do. 1700.
1700, do.	Walter Clarke,	" do. 22, 1714, died.
1714, June 15,	Henry Tew,	" do. 1715.
1715, May,	Joseph Jenckes,	" do. 1721.
1721, do.	John Wanton,	" do. 1722.
1722, do.	Joseph Jenckes,	" do. 1727.
1727, do.	Jonathan Nichols,	" Aug. 2, 1727, died.
1727, August,	Thomas Fry,	" May, 1729.
1729, May,	John Wanton,	" do. 1734.
1734, do.	George Hassard,	" June, 1738, died.
1738, July 5,	Daniel Abbott,	" May, 1740.
1740, May,	Richard Ward,	" July, 1740.
1740, July 15,	William Greene,	" May, 1743.
1743, May,	Joseph Whipple,	" do. 1745.
1745, do.	William Robinson,	" do. 1746.
1746, do.	Joseph Whipple,	" do. 1747.
1747, do.	William Robinson,	" do. 1748.
1748, do.	William Ellery,	" do. 1750.
1750, do.	Robert Hazard,	" do. 1751.
1751, do.	Joseph Whipple,	" Nov. 2, 1753.
1753, Nov. 2,	Jonathan Nichols, jr.,	" May, 1754.
1754, May,	John Gardner,	" do. 1755.
1755, do.	Jonathan Nichols, jr.,	" Sept. 8, 1756, died.
1756, Sept.	Jonathan Gardner,	" Jan. 1764, died.
1764, Feb. 27,	Joseph Wanton, jr.,	" May, 1765.
1765, May,	Elisha Brown,	" do. 1767.
1767, do.	Joseph Wanton, jr.,	" do. 1768.
1768, do.	Nicholas Cooke,	" do. 1769.
1769, do.	Darius Sessions,	" do. 1775.
1775, do.	Nicholas Cooke,	" Nov. 7, 1775.
1775, Nov.	William Bradford,	" May, 1778.
1778, May,	Jabez Bowen,	" do. 1780,
1780, do.	William West,	" do. 1781.
1781, do.	Jabez Bowen,	" do. 1786.
1786, do.	Daniel Owen,	" do. 1790.
1790, do.	Samuel J. Potter.	

of 12 April, to the people of Providence, and was chosen governor at the ensuing election, May 3, 1676.

CHAP. XXIV.
APP. O.

APPENDIX O.

WILLIAM BLACKSTONE.

To the researches of my friend Mr. Sylvanus Chace Newman, the genealogist, whose untiring zeal in decyphering tombstones, as well as ancient manuscripts, has earned for him the name of the "Old Mortality" of Rhode Island, I am indebted for the subjoined facts, explaining the mystery that has long shrouded the life of the first settler of the State, and proving the existence at this day of lineal descendants from him. The family of William Blackstone has until lately been supposed to be extinct, and in correction of that statement, made in the note at the bottom of page 99, vol. i. of this work, Mr. Newman has kindly sent me the following letter:

PAWTUCKET, R. I., December 3, 1859.

To Hon. Samuel Greene Arnold, Author of "History of Rhode Island."

DEAR SIR:—In Vol. I. page 99, of your History of this State, you repeat the *long supposed fact*, that the family of William Blackstone, whom you correctly designate as the first settler of the territory now known as the State of Rhode Island, "is now extinct." Such was truly the long supposed fact among earlier historians; but Time is the great revealer of facts. After a very careful collation of all the records relating to this matter now known to be in existence, I have no doubt that the following summary is substantially correct. William Blackstone [our Pilgrim, then spelled Blaxton] was descended from a family of some distinction who had long inhabited the vicinity of Salisbury in the west of England; he was born in 1595, entered Emanuel College, Cambridge, England, and in 1617, took the degree of A. B.; in 1621, received the degree of A. M., and entered into Episcopal orders; in 1623 came to America with the expedition of Robert Gorges, whose objects were to establish an Episcopal Colony, but they being dissatisfied with the general aspect of the country, and prospects before them, soon abandoned their enterprise, and returned to England, leaving Blackstone, who chose to stay and pitch his tent at Shawmut [now Boston] as its sole inhabitant, where he remained till the spring of 1635, when he left and established his home at Study Hill, where after forty years' residence, he died at the age of eighty, and was buried on the 28th of May, 1675, old style, equivalent to June 8, new style, being 184 years ago last June, [1859.] Mr. Blackstone, in 1659, married a Boston widow, [Stevenson,] and at his death left one child, a minor, [John,] who, on Sept. 10, 1692, sold the estate his father left, to David Whipple, and removed into the then village of Providence, where he became a shoemaker. The old Book of Records in the Archives of Providence, shows him to be there in 1699. No birth of a child is recorded to him, but as many pages are missing, there might once have been such a fact recorded; and I establish the fact through the following facts: A child named John Blackstone was born that year, who after various voyagings about the world, finally became a man of character and property, and settled at Branford, Ct., where he died, and the following is a copy from his tombstone. "In memory of John Blackstone, who departed this life Jan. 3, 1785, aged 85 years, eleven months, and 15 days." This tombstone, and the change in style, establishes his birth to be in 1699; and in a document still in existence, he states that he "was born in Providence, New England, in 1699." Now as there was then no other of that name in any of the New England colonies, I regard it as conclusive that this John, whose memorial is above copied, was the son of John Blackstone the shoemaker, and his wife Catherine [Gorham] of Providence; and grandson to the Pilgrim, many of whose nobler qualities he seemed to have inherited, instead of adopting the indolence of his father. His descendants (one of whom, Hon. James Blackstone, now [1859] resides on his original homestead in Branford, Ct.) have been few and sparse, but highly respectable in each generation; and about a dozen very worthy families, mostly in the 7th generation from this forefather of Rhode Island, are now living in the two States of Connecticut and New York.

The above is but one of the many instances where, by the historic mistake of some early writer, later generations have lost sight of their origin, and where it has fallen to the lot of Genealogy to restore.

The life and character of the illustrious first settler of Rhode Island, possess ample claims to an honorable memory; but as that is more particularly the work of the Biographer, and well knowing the value of your time and space, I have endeavored to condense the above facts into as brief a compass, as the scattered and entangled material would seem to admit of; and you are at liberty to make such use of

CHAP. XXIV. APP. O.

all or any part of this synoptical sheet as you may think conducive to the interests of posterity.

Respectfully your Obt. Servant,
S. C. NEWMAN,
Genealogist.

The same gentleman has solved the question in regard to the non-appearance of the name of John Smith, the miller, in the deed of Roger Williams to the original settlers of Providence, mentioned on page 101 of vol. i. It is known there were at that early day, four John Smiths in the colony, two of whom, father and son, were millers. The father was the companion of Williams, and was already dead when the deed made in 1666, and ante-dated Oct. 8, 1638, was executed. This correction will be made in the text, should this work ever reach a second edition.

GENERAL INDEX TO VOLUME SECOND.

G.

H

I

J

M

N

O

P

Q

R

T

U

V

W

END OF VOLUME SECOND.

www.ingramcontent.com/pod-product-compliance
Lightning Source LLC
LaVergne TN
LVHW021222110826
845150LV00002B/219

* 9 7 8 1 4 2 5 5 6 4 7 3 5 *